新曲綫 New Curves | 用心雕刻每一本......

http://site.douban.com/110283/

http://weibo.com/nccpub

用心字里行间　雕刻名著经典

Marketing

10/e

Roger A. Kerin
Southern Methodist University

Steven W. Hartley
University of Denver

William Rudelius
University of Minnesota

市场营销

第 10 版

双语教学通用版

罗杰·凯林
〔美〕 史蒂文·哈特利 著
威廉·鲁迪里尔斯

王成慧 林 静 译注

人民邮电出版社
北 京

图书在版编目（CIP）数据

市场营销：第10版：双语教学通用版 /（美）凯林等 著；王成慧，林静 译.
—北京：人民邮电出版社，2016.4（2018.4重印）
ISBN 978-7-115-41519-6

I. ①市… II. ①凯… ②王… ③林… III. ①市场营销学－双语教学－教材 IV. ① F713.50

中国版本图书馆CIP数据核字（2016）第022436号

Roger A. Kerin, Steven W. Hartley, William Rudelius
Marketing, 10th Edition
ISBN 0-07-352993-1

北京市版权局著作权合同登记号：01-2012-3549

市场营销（第10版，双语教学通用版）

◆ 著　　［美］罗杰·凯林　史蒂文·哈特利　威廉·鲁迪里尔斯
译　注　王成慧　林　静
策　划　刘　力　陆　瑜
责任编辑　徐向娟　李　丹
装帧设计　陶建胜

◆ 人民邮电出版社出版发行　北京市丰台区成寿寺路11号
邮编　100164　电子邮件　315@ptpress.com.cn
网址　http://www.ptpress.com.cn
电话（编辑部）010-84937150　（市场部）010-84937152
三河市少明印务有限公司印刷
新华书店经销

◆ 开本：850×1092　1/16
印张：26.5
字数：570千字　2016年4月第1版　2018年4月第2次印刷
著作权合同登记号　图字：01-2012-3549
ISBN 978-7-115-41519-6

定价：68.00元

本书如有印装质量问题，请与本社联系　电话：(010) 84937153

内容提要

罗杰·凯林、史蒂文·哈特利和威廉·鲁迪里尔斯教授的 *Marketing* 一书几十年来一直是美国高校本科市场营销课程教科书中的领导品牌，而本书是在三位作者通力合作所成最新版的基础上开发的双语教学通用教材。

本书运用独特、创新和有效的教学方法，全面综合地展现了当代以顾客关系管理和顾客价值创造为核心的营销理念，分析了最新的虚拟营销、互动营销和多渠道营销等主题。同时，在严密的逻辑构架下，引入大量描述企业、营销专家和企业家的生动案例，便于读者更深入地理解和掌握市场营销。

全书共 15 章，内容包括：通过营销建立客户关系与创造顾客价值；制定成功的营销与公司战略；了解消费者行为；了解客户组织；营销调研；市场细分、确定目标市场与定位；开发新产品和服务；成功的产品与品牌管理；服务营销；管理营销渠道与批发等。

本书适合作为高等院校市场营销课程的双语教材，也适合市场营销专业及其他对营销感兴趣的读者。

A MESSAGE FROM THE AUTHORS 作者简介

Who could have anticipated the incredible changes the past several years have brought to business and marketing? Every aspect of our business lives—from the economy, to government's role, to consumers' attitudes and lifestyles—have changed recently. While many of the changes have been disruptive, they create a unique challenge and opportunity for our discipline.

Marketing, more than any other discipline, is a field that embraces the changes and facilitates the development of new products, services, and ideas to respond to the new environment and improve our marketplace. You've certainly noticed the new focus on issues such as global economic growth, regulation, consumer spending, and employment. The future promises to bring many additional issues to our attention and to be an extraordinarily exciting time for marketing students. Welcome to what will surely be viewed as one of our most dramatic periods of business history. We are excited to be part of the educational journey you are undertaking!

You'll soon discover that your past experiences as a consumer provide you with a rich source of important information that will become part of your business perspective. As a student of marketing you will learn how the dynamic changes taking place change business practices. In the future, as a marketing manager, you will use your experiences and knowledge to become a true business professional. This text is our effort to help you begin the transition. We appreciate the opportunity to share our own managerial and educational expertise with you. From our perspective, your career starts here.

This edition of *Marketing* represents a milestone for us for several reasons. First, it is the 10th edition—a symbolic achievement, but more importantly it is an indication of the need for keeping up with the changes in business and marketing. Second, it is the result of more than 25 years of writing—we began writing in 1983! Finally, this edition represents our most advanced offering as an educational resource. We are committed to (1) building on our past experiences as authors, (2) continuing our leadership role in bringing new topics and perspectives to the classroom, and (3) focusing on pedagogical innovation that truly responds to new teaching and learning styles. We believe our efforts have created the most comprehensive, up-to-date, engaging, and technically advanced textbook available today. We hope you'll agree.

As you begin reading *Marketing* you will find that it uses an active-learning approach to bring marketing theories and concepts to life. Each chapter offers a balance of traditional and contemporary perspectives presented in an easy-to-read style using familiar examples of companies, products and services, and business strategies. This approach has been a "perfect match" for today's practical, visual, connected learners. The response from students and instructors has been extraordinary. *Marketing*, and its translations into 11 other languages, is now the No. 1 marketing text in the world! Our 10th edition strives to continue the tradition of past success.

Thank you for the opportunity to share our passion for marketing with you. We hope we succeed in making your studies fun and interesting and that they will become the foundation of an enlightened and productive career!

Roger A. Kerin
Steven W. Hartley
William Rudelius

Acknowledgments 致谢

To ensure continuous improvement of our textbook and supplements we have utilized an extensive review and development process for each of our past editions. Building on that history, the *Marketing,* 10th edition development process included several phases of evaluation and a variety of stakeholder audiences (e.g., students, instructors, etc.).

Reviewers who were vital in the changes that were made to this edition include:

Wendi Achey
Northampton University

Chris Anicich
California State University—Fullerton

Corinne Asher
Henry Ford Community College

Tim Aurand
Northern Illinois University

Christopher Blocker
Baylor University

Koren Borges
University of North Florida

Glen Brodowsky
California State University—San Marcos

Carmina Cavazos
University of St. Thomas

Debbie Coleman
Miami University—Ohio

Mary Conran
Temple University

Lawrence Duke
Drexel University

Karen Flaherty
Oklahoma State University

Darrell Goudge
University of Central Oklahoma

Santhi Harvey
Central State University

Ron Hasty
University of North Texas

Nathan Himelstein
Essex County College

Donald Hoffer
Miami University—Ohio

Fred Honerkamp
Northwood University

Keith Jones
North Carolina A&T State University

Philip Kearney
Niagara County Community College—SUNY

Kathleen Krentler
San Diego State University

Michelle Kunz
Morehead State University

Christine Lai
Buffalo State University

Donald Larson
Ohio State University

Harold Lucius
Rowan University

Theodore Mitchell
University of Nevada, Reno

Rex Moody
University of Colorado

James Munch
Wright State University

Brian Murray
Jefferson Community College—SUNY

Eric Newman
Cal State San Bernardino

Carmen Powers
Monroe Community College

Philip Shum
William Patterson University

David Smith
Bemidji State University

Cheryl Stansfield
North Hennepin Community College

Gary Tucker
Oklahoma City Community College

Kim Wong
Central New Mexico Community College

Jim Zemanek
East Carolina University

The preceding section demonstrates the amount of feedback and developmental input that went into this project, and we are deeply grateful to the numerous people who have shared their ideas with us. Reviewing a book or supplement takes an incredible amount of energy and attention. We are glad so many of our colleagues took the time to do it. Their comments have inspired us to do our best.

Reviewers who contributed to the first nine editions of this book include:

Nadia J. Abgrab
Kerri Acheson
Roy Adler
Christie Amato
Linda Anglin
Ismet Anitsal
William D. Ash
Gerard Athaide
Andy Aylesworth
Patricia Baconride
Siva Balasubramanian
A. Diane Barlar
James H. Barnes
Karen Becker-Olsen
Frederick J. Beier
Thom J. Belich
Joseph Belonax
Thomas M. Bertsch
Parimal Bhagat
Carol Bienstock
Kevin W. Bittle
Jeff Blodgett
Nancy Bloom
Charles Bodkin

Larry Borgen
Nancy Boykin
Thomas Brashear
Martin Bressler
Bruce Brown
William Brown
William G. Browne
Judy Bulin
David J. Burns
Alan Bush
Stephen Calcich
William J. Carner
Larry Carter
Gerald O. Cavallo
S. Tamer Cavusgil
Bruce Chadbourne
S. Choi Chan
Sang Choe
Kay Chomic
Melissa Clark
Mark Collins
Howard Combs
Clare Comm
Clark Compton
Cristanna Cook
Sherry Cook
John Coppett
John Cox
Scott Cragin
Ken Crocker
Joe Cronin
James Cross
Lowell E. Crow
Brent Cunningham
John H. Cunningham
Bill Curtis
Bob Dahlstrom
Dan Darrow
Neel Das
Hugh Daubek
Martin Decatur
Francis DeFea
Joseph Defilippe
Linda M. Delene
Tino DeMarco
Jobie Devinney-Walsh
Irene Dickey
Paul Dion
William B. Dodds
James H. Donnelly
Michael Drafke
Bob Dwyer
Eddie V. Easley
Eric Ecklund
Roger W. Egerton
Steven Engel
Barbara Evans
Ken Fairweather
Larry Feick
Lori Feldman
Kevin Feldt
Theresa Flaherty
Elizabeth R. Flynn
Charles Ford
Renee Foster
Judy Foxman
Donald Fuller
Stan Garfunkel
Stephen Garrott
Glen Gelderloos
David Gerth
James Ginther
Susan Godar
Dan Goebel
Marc Goldberg
Leslie A. Goldgehn
Kenneth Goodenday
Darrell Goudge
James Gould
Kimberly Grantham
Nancy Grassilli
Barnett Greenberg
James L. Grimm
Pamela Grimm
Pola B. Gupta
Richard Hansen
Donald V. Harper
Dotty Harpool
Lynn Harris
Robert C. Harris
Ernan Haruvy
James A. Henley, Jr.
Ken Herbst
Jonathan Hibbard
Richard M. Hill
Al Holden
Kristine Hovsepian
Jarrett Hudnal
Mike Hyman
Rajesh Iyer
Donald R. Jackson
Kenneth Jameson
David Jamison
Deb Jansky
James C. Johnson
Wesley Johnston
Robert Jones
Mary Joyce
Jacqueline Karen
Janice Karlen
Sudhir Karunakaran
Rajiv Kashyap
Herbert Katzenstein
George Kelley
Katie Kemp
Ram Kesaran
Roy Klages
Douglas Kornemann
Terry Kroeten
Anand Kumar
Nanda Kumar
Ann Kuzma
John Kuzma
Priscilla LaBarbera
Duncan G. LaBay
Jay Lambe
Tim Landry
Jane Lang
Irene Lange
Richard Lapidus
Ron Larson
Ed Laube
J. Ford Laumer
Debra Laverie
Marilyn Lavin
Gary Law
Robert Lawson
Wilton Lelund
Karen LeMasters
Richard C. Leventhal
Leonard Lindenmuth
Ann Little
Eldon L. Little
Yunchuan Liu
James Lollar
Paul Londrigan
Lynn Loudenback
Ann Lucht
Mike Luckett
Robert Luke
Michael R. Luthy
Richard J. Lutz
Marton L. Macchiete
Rhonda Mack
Patricia Manninen
Kenneth Maricle
Tom Marshall
Elena Martinez
Carolyn Massiah
Tamara Masters
Charla Mathwick
Michael Mayo
James McAlexander
Peter J. McClure
Phyllis McGinnis

Jim McHugh
Gary F. McKinnon
Ed McLaughlin
Jo Ann McManamy
Kristy McManus
Bob McMillen
Samuel E. McNeely
Lee Meadow
James Meszaros
George Miaoulis
Soon Hong Min
Ronald Michaels
Herbert A. Miller
Stephen W. Miller
William G. Mitchell
Steven Moff
Kim Montney
Melissa Moore
Linda Morable
Fred Morgan
Gordon Mosley
William Motz
Donald F. Mulvihill
James A. Muncy
Jeanne Munger
Linda Munilla
Bill Murphy
Janet Murray
Keith Murray
Joseph Myslivec
Sunder Narayanan
Bob Newberry
Donald G. Norris
Carl Obermiller
Dave Olson
James Olver
Ben Oumlil
Notis Pagiavlas
Allan Palmer
Dennis Pappas
June E. Parr
Philip Parron
David Terry Paul
Richard Penn
John Penrose
William Pertula
Michael Peters
Susan Peterson
Renee Pfeifer-Luckett
William S. Piper
Stephen Pirog
Gary Poorman
Vonda Powell
Joe Puzi
Edna Ragins
Priyali Rajagopal
Daniel Rajaratnam
James P. Rakowski
Rosemary Ramsey
Barbara Ribbens
Cathie Rich-Duval
Joe Ricks
Heikki Rinne
Linda Rochford
William Rodgers
Jean Romeo
Teri Root
Tom Rossi
Vicki Rostedt
Heidi Rottier
Larry Rottmeyer
Robert W. Ruekert
Maria Sanella
Charles Schewe
Starr F. Schlobohm
Roberta Schultz
Lisa M. Sciulli
Stan Scott
Eberhard Seheuling
Harold S. Sekiguchi
Doris M. Shaw
Eric Shaw
Ken Shaw
Dan Sherrel
Susan Sieloff
Bob E. Smiley
Allen Smith
Kimberly D. Smith
Ruth Ann Smith
Sandra Smith
Norman Smothers
James V. Spiers
Craig Stacey
Miriam B. Stamps
Joe Stasio
Tom Stevenson
Kathleen Stuenkel
Scott Swan
Rick Sweeney
Michael Swenson
Robert Swerdlow
Vincent P. Taiani
Clint Tankersley
Ruth Taylor
Andrew Thacker
Tom Thompson
Dan Toy
Fred Trawick
Thomas L. Trittipo
Sue Umashankar
Bronis J. Verhage
Ottilia Voegtli
Jeff von Freymann
Gerald Waddle
Randall E. Wade
Blaise Waguespack, Jr.
Harlan Wallingford
Mark Weber
Don Weinrauch
Robert S. Welsh
Ron Weston
Michelle Wetherbee
Sheila Wexler
Max White
James Wilkins
Erin Wilkinson
Janice Williams
Kaylene Williams
Robert Williams
Jerry W. Wilson
Joseph Wisenblit
Robert Witherspoon
Van R. Wood
Wendy Wood
Lauren Wright
William R. Wynd
Poh-Lin Yeoh
Mark Young
Sandra Young
Gail M. Zank
Leon Zurawicki

Thanks are also due to many faculty members who contributed to the text chapters and cases. They include: Linda Rochford of the University of Minnesota-Duluth; Kevin Upton of the University of Minnesota-Twin Cities; Nancy Nentl of Metropolitan State University; David Brennan of the University of St. Thomas; and Leigh McAlister of the University of Texas at Austin. Michael Vessey provided cases, research assistance, many special images, and led our efforts on the Instructor's Manual, In-Class Activities, and Instructor's Survival Kit. Kathryn Schifferle of California State University, Steven Rudelius, and Thomas Rudelius assisted with the Instructor

Newsletter. Rick Armstrong of Armstrong Photography, Nick Kaufman and Michelle Morgan of NKP Media, Bruce McLean of World Class Communication Technologies, Paul Fagan of Fagan Productions, Dan Hundley and George Heck of Token Media, Martin Walter of White Room Digital, Scott Bolin of Bolin Marketing, and Dan Stephenson of the Philadelphia Phillies produced the videos. Erica Michaels was responsible for the revision of the test bank.

Many businesspeople also provided substantial assistance by making available information that appears in the text, videos, and supplements—much of it for the first time in college materials. Thanks are due to David Ford and Don Rylander of Ford Consulting Group; Mark Rehborg of Tony's Pizza; Ann Hand and Kathy Seegebrecht of BP; Kimberly Mosford and Ryan Schroeder of Business Incentives; Vivian Callaway, Sandy Proctor, and Anna Stoesz of General Mills; David Windorski of 3M; Nicholas Skally, Linda Glassel, and Tyler Herring of Prince Sports; David Montgomery, David Buck, and Bonnie Clark of the Philadelphia Phillies; Todd Schaeffer, Amber Arnseth, and Chris Deets of Activeion Cleaning Solutions; Ian Wolfman of imc^2; Brian Niccol of Pizza Hut; Stan Jacot of ConAgra Snack Foods; Sandra Smith of Smith Communications; Erin Patton of the MasterMind Group, LLC; Kim Nagele of JCPenney, Inc.; Charles Besio of the Sewell Automotive Group, Inc.; Kate Hodebeck of Cadbury Schweppes America's Beverages, Inc.; Beverly Roberts of U.S. Census Bureau; Jennifer Gebert of Ghirardelli Chocolate Company; Michael Kuhl of 3M Sports and Leisure; Barbara Davis of Ken Davis Products, Inc.; Kerry Barnett of Valassis Communications; and Leslie Herman and Jeff Gerst of Bolin Marketing working with Carma Laboratories (Carmex). We also acknowledge the special help of a team that worked with us on the Fallon Worldwide video case: Fred Senn, Bruce Blister, Kevin Flat, Ginny Grossman, Kim Knutson, Julie Smith, Erin Taut, and Rob White.

Staff support from the Southern Methodist University, the University of Denver, and the University of Minnesota was essential. We gratefully acknowledge the help of Wanda Hanson, Jeanne Milazzo, and Gloria Valdez for their many contributions.

Checking countless details related to layout, graphics, clear writing, and last-minute changes to ensure timely examples is essential for a sound and accurate textbook. This also involves coordinating activities of authors, designers, editors, compositors, and production specialists. Christine Vaughan of McGraw-Hill/Irwin's production staff and editorial consultant, Gina Huck Siegert of Imaginative Solutions, Inc., provided the necessary oversight and hand-holding for us, while retaining a refreshing sense of humor, often under tight deadlines. Thank you again.

Finally, we acknowledge the professional efforts of the McGraw-Hill/Irwin staff. Completion of our book and its many supplements required the attention and commitment of many editorial, production, marketing, and research personnel. Our Burr Ridge-based team included Paul Ducham, Doug Hughes, Sean Pankuch, Melissa Hernandez, Carol Bielski, Matthew Baldwin, Jeremy Cheshareck, Sue Lombardi, Katie Mergen, and many others. In addition we relied on Michael Hruby for constant attention regarding photo elements of the text. Handling the countless details of our text, supplement, and support technologies has become an incredibly complex challenge. We thank all these people for their efforts!

Roger A. Kerin
Steven W. Hartley
William Rudelius

BRIEF CONTENTS 简要目录

1 Creating Customer Relationships and Value through Marketing *2*
通过营销建立客户关系，创造顾客价值

2 Developing Successful Marketing and Organizational Strategies *24*
制定成功的营销与公司战略

3 Understanding Consumer Behavior *50*
了解消费者行为

4 Understanding Organizations as Customers *78*
了解客户组织

5 Marketing Research: From Customer Insights to Actions *100*
营销调研：将消费者信息变成行动

6 Market Segmentation, Targeting, and Positioning *128*
市场细分、确定目标市场与定位

7 Developing New Products and Services *152*
开发新产品和服务

8 Managing Successful Products and Brands *176*
成功的产品和品牌管理

9 Services Marketing *204*
服务营销

10 Managing Marketing Channels and Wholesaling *226*
管理营销渠道与批发

11 Customer-Driven Supply Chain and Logistics Management *252*
消费者驱动的供应链与物流管理

12 Retailing *276*
零　售

13 Integrated Marketing Communications and Direct Marketing *304*
整合营销传播与直接营销

14 Advertising, Sales Promotion, and Public Relations *332*
广告、销售促进和公共关系

15 Pulling It All Together: The Strategic Marketing Process *366*
整合战略营销过程

DETAILED CONTENTS 详细目录

1 CREATING CUSTOMER RELATIONSHIPS AND VALUE THROUGH MARKETING 2 通过营销建立客户关系，创造顾客价值

Innovation and Marketing at 3M: How Discovering Student Study Habits Launched a New Product 3 3M 公司的创新和营销：如何发现学生的学习习惯并推出一款新产品

What Is Marketing? 4 什么是营销

Marketing and Your Career 4 营销与你的职业生涯

Marketing Matters: Payoff for the Joys (!) and Sleepless Nights (?) of Starting Your Own Small Business: YouTube!!!! 5

Marketing: Delivering Benefits to the Organization, Its Stakeholders, and Society 6 营销：向组织、组织的利益相关者和社会传递价值

The Diverse Factors Influencing Marketing Activities 6 影响营销活动的多种因素

What Is Needed for Marketing to Occur 7 营销产生的前提

How Marketing Discovers and Satisfies Consumer Needs 8 营销如何了解并满足消费者需要

Discovering Consumer Needs 9 了解消费者需求

The Challenge: Meeting Consumer Needs with New Products 9 用新产品满足消费者需求的挑战

Satisfying Consumer Needs 11 满足消费者需求

The Marketing Program: How Customer Relationships Are Built 12 营销方案：如何建立顾客关系

Customer Value and Customer Relationships 12 顾客价值与顾客关系

Relationship Marketing 13 关系营销

The Marketing Program 13 营销方案

3M's Strategy and Marketing Program to Help Students Study 14 3M 公司帮助学生学习的策略和营销方案

How Marketing Became So Important 16 营销如何变得如此重要

Evolution of the Market Orientation 16 市场导向的演进

Ethics and Social Responsibility: Balancing the Interests of Different Groups 17 道德与社会责任：平衡不同群体的利益

Making Responsible Decisions: Social Entrepreneurship Using Marketing to Help People 18

The Breadth and Depth of Marketing 18 营销的宽度与深度

Learning Objectives Review 20

Focusing on Key Terms 20

Applying Marketing Knowledge 21

Building Your Marketing Plan 21

Video Case 1: 3M's Post-it® Flag Highlighter: Extending the Concept! 21

2 DEVELOPING SUCCESSFUL MARKETING AND ORGANIZATIONAL STRATEGIES 24 制定成功的营销与公司战略

Where an "A" in a Correspondence Course in Ice Cream Making Can Lead! 25 在冰淇淋函授课程中得"A"的人将何去何从

Today's Organizations 26 当今的组织

Kinds of Organizations 26 组织类型

Making Responsible Decisions: The Global Dilemma: How to Achieve Sustainable Development 27

What Is Strategy? 27 什么是战略

Structure of Today's Organizations 27 当代组织的结构

Strategy in Visionary Organizations 28 有远见的组织战略

Organizational Foundation: Why Does It Exist? 29 组织基础：它为什么存在

Organizational Direction: What Will It Do? 30 组织方向：它将做什么

Marketing Matters: The Netflix Launch and Its Continually . . . Continually . . . Continually . . . Changing Business Model! 31

Organizational Strategies: How Will It Do It? 32 组织战略：如何做到

Tracking Strategic Performance with Marketing Dashboards 32 通过市场仪表盘跟踪战略绩效

Using Marketing Dashboards: How Well Is Ben & Jerry's Doing? 34

Setting Strategic Directions 34 确定战略方向

A Look Around: Where Are We Now? 34 环顾四周：我们现在何处

Growth Strategies: Where Do We Want to Go? 35 成长战略：我们欲往何方

The Strategic Marketing Process 39 战略营销过程

The Planning Phase of the Strategic Marketing Process 40 战略营销过程的规划阶段

The Implementation Phase of the Strategic Marketing Process 43 战略营销过程的实施阶段

The Evaluation Phase of the Strategic Marketing Process 44 战略营销过程的评价阶段

Learning Objectives Review 45

Focusing on Key Terms 46

Applying Marketing Knowledge 47

Building Your Marketing Plan 47

Video Case 2: BP: Transforming Its Strategy "Beyond Petroleum" 47

3 UNDERSTANDING CONSUMER BEHAVIOR 50 了解消费者行为

Enlightened Carmakers Know What Custom(h)ers Value 51 受启发的汽车制造商知道客户重视什么

Consumer Purchase Decision Process and Experience 52 消费者购买决策过程和购买体验

Problem Recognition: Perceiving a Need 52 认识问题：感知需要

Information Search: Seeking Value 52 搜集信息：寻求价值

Alternative Evaluation: Assessing Value 53 评估方案：价值评估
Purchase Decision: Buying Value 54 购买决策：购买价值
Postpurchase Behavior: Value in Consumption or Use 54 购后行为：消费或使用价值

Marketing Matters: The Value of a Satisfied Customer to the Company 55

Consumer Involvement and Problem-Solving Variations 55 参与度与决策类型
Situational Influences 57 环境影响

Psychological Influences on Consumer Behavior 58 消费者行为的心理影响
Motivation and Personality 58 动机与个性

Making Responsible Decisions: The Ethics of Subliminal Messages 60

Perception 60 感 知
Learning 62 学 习
Values, Beliefs, and Attitudes 63 价值观、信念与态度

Going Online: Are You an Experiencer? An Achiever?: Identifying Your VALS Profile 64

Consumer Lifestyle 64 消费者生活方式

Sociocultural Influences on Consumer Behavior 66 消费者行为的社会文化影响
Personal Influence 66 个人影响

Marketing Matters: BzzAgent—The Buzz Experience 67

Reference Groups 68 参照群体
Family Influence 68 家庭影响
Social Class 70 社会阶层
Culture and Subculture 71 文化与亚文化

Learning Objectives Review 73
Focusing on Key Terms 74
Applying Marketing Knowledge 74
Building Your Marketing Plan 75

Video Case 3: Best Buy: Using Customer Centricity to Connect with Consumers 75

4 UNDERSTANDING ORGANIZATIONS AS CUSTOMERS 78 **了解客户组织**

Buying Is Marketing, Too! Purchasing Publication Paper at JCPenney 79 采购也是市场营销！彭尼公司采购纸张

The Nature and Size of Organizational Markets 80 组织市场的性质与规模
Industrial Markets 80 产业市场
Reseller Markets 80 中间商市场
Government Markets 81 政府市场

Global Organizational Markets 81 全球组织市场

Measuring Domestic and Global Industrial, Reseller, and Government Markets 81 衡量国内市场、全球产业市场、中间商市场和政府市场

Characteristics of Organizational Buying 83 组织采购的特点

Demand Characteristics 83 需求特点

Size of the Order or Purchase 84 订单量或采购数量

Number of Potential Buyers 84 潜在购买者数量

Organizational Buying Objectives 84 组织采购目标

Going Online: Supplier Diversity Is a Fundamental Business Strategy at Procter & Gamble 85

Organizational Buying Criteria 85 组织采购标准

Marketing Matters: Harley-Davidson's Supplier Collaboration Creates Customer Value . . . and a Great Ride 86

Buyer–Seller Relationships and Supply Partnerships 86 买卖关系与供应伙伴关系

Making Responsible Decisions: Sustainable Procurement for Sustainable Growth 87

The Buying Center: A Cross-Functional Group 87 采购中心：一个跨职能团体

Charting the Organizational Buying Process 90 制定组织采购流程

Stages in the Organizational Buying Process 90 组织购买流程的步骤

Buying a Machine Vision System 90 购买机器视觉系统

Online Buying in Organizational Markets 93 组织市场中的网上采购

Prominence of Online Buying in Organizational Markets 93 组织市场的网上采购发展迅猛

E-Marketplaces: Virtual Organizational Markets 93 电子市场：虚拟的组织市场

Marketing Matters: eBay Means Business for Entrepreneurs 94

Online Auctions in Organizational Markets 95 组织市场的网上竞拍

Learning Objectives Review 96

Focusing on Key Terms 96

Applying Marketing Knowledge 97

Building Your Marketing Plan 97

Video Case 4: Lands' End: Where Buyers Rule 97

5 MARKETING RESEARCH: FROM CUSTOMER INSIGHTS TO ACTIONS 100 **营销调研：将消费者信息变成行动**

Test Screenings and Tracking Studies: How Listening to Consumers Reduces Movie Risks 101 试映和跟踪调研：怎样倾听消费者去降低电影风险

The Role of Marketing Research 103 营销调研的角色

What Is Marketing Research? 103 什么是营销调研

The Challenges in Doing Good Marketing Research 103 做好营销调研的挑战

Five-Step Marketing Research Approach 103 五步营销调研法
Step 1: Define the Problem 103 第一步：确定问题
Set the Research Objectives 104 设定调研目标
Identify Possible Marketing Actions 104 明确可行的营销行动
Step 2: Develop the Research Plan 105 第二步：制订调研计划
Specify Constraints 105 列出约束条件
Identify Data Needed for Marketing Actions 105 确定营销行动所需资料
Determine How to Collect Data 106 决定如何收集资料
Step 3: Collect Relevant Information 107 第三步：收集相关信息
Secondary Data: Internal 107 二手资料：内部的
Secondary Data: External 107 二手资料：外部的
Advantages and Disadvantages of Secondary Data 108 二手资料的优缺点

Going Online: Online Databases and Internet Resources Useful to Marketers 109

Primary Data: Watching People 109 原始资料：观察人们
Primary Data: Asking People 111 原始数据：询问人们

Marketing Matters: Buy•ology: How "Neuromarketing" Is Trying to Understand Consumers 112

Primary Data: Other Sources 116 原始数据：其他资源
Advantages and Disadvantages of Primary Data 119 原始数据的优点和缺点
Step 4: Develop Findings 119 第四步：提交结论
Analyze the Data 119 分析数据
Present the Findings 120 展示结果
Step 5: Take Marketing Actions 121 第五步：采取营销行动
Make Action Recommendations 121 提出行动建议
Implement the Action Recommendations 121 实施行动建议
Evaluate the Results 122 评估结果
Sales Forecasting Techniques 122 销售预测技术
Judgments of the Decision Maker 122 决策者的判断
Surveys of Knowledgeable Groups 123 调查懂行的团体
Statistical Methods 123 统计学方法

Learning Objectives Review 124
Focusing on Key Terms 124
Applying Marketing Knowledge 125
Building Your Marketing Plan 125

Video Case 5: Ford Consulting Group, Inc.: From Data to Actions 125

6 MARKET SEGMENTATION, TARGETING, AND POSITIONING 128 市场细分、确定目标市场与定位

Zappos.com: Delivering "Wow" through Market Segmentation and Service 129 Zappos.com：通过市场细分和提供客户服务获得成功

Why Segment Markets? 130 为何要细分市场

What Market Segmentation Means 130 市场细分意味着什么

When and How to Segment Markets 131 何时及如何细分市场

Steps In Segmenting and Targeting Markets 133 市场细分与确定目标市场的步骤

Step 1: Group Potential Buyers into Segments 134 步骤1：对潜在购买者进行细分

Going Online: What "Flock" Do You Belong to? 136

Step 2: Group Products to Be Sold into Categories 139 步骤2：将待售产品进行分类

Step 3: Develop a Market-Product Grid and Estimate the Size of Markets 141 步骤3：开发市场—产品方格图并估计市场规模

Step 4: Select Target Markets 141 步骤4：选择目标市场

Step 5: Take Marketing Actions to Reach Target Markets 142 步骤5：实施营销行动到达目标市场

Market-Product Synergies: A Balancing Act 144 市场—产品协同增效：一种权衡

Marketing Matters: Apple's Segmentation Strategy—Camp Runamok No Longer 145

Positioning the Product 146 产品定位

Two Approaches to Product Positioning 146 产品定位的两种途径

Product Positioning Using Perceptual Maps 146 利用感知图进行产品定位

A Perceptual Map to Reposition Chocolate Milk for Adults 147 再定位巧克力牛奶（给成人）的感知图

Learning Objectives Review 148

Focusing on Key Terms 149

Applying Marketing Knowledge 149

Building Your Marketing Plan 149

Video Case 6: Prince Sports, Inc.: Tennis Racquets for Every Segment 149

7 DEVELOPING NEW PRODUCTS AND SERVICES 152 开发新产品和服务

Apple's New–Product Innovation Machine 153 苹果公司的新产品创新机器

What Are Products and Services? 154 什么是产品和服务

A Look at Goods, Services, and Ideas 154 观察商品、服务和理念

Classifying Products 154 产品分类

Product Items, Product Lines, and Product Mixes 156 产品项目、产品线和产品组合

Using Marketing Dashboards: Which States Are Underperforming? 157

How Marketing Dashboards Can Improve New-Product Performance 157 营销信息板如何提高新产品的性能

New Products and Why They Succeed or Fail 158 新产品及其成败原因
What Is a New Product? 158 何谓新产品
Marketing Matters: Feature Bloat: Geek Squad to the Rescue! 160
Why Products Succeed or Fail 160 产品成败原因
Marketing Matters: From Idea to Launch: Stage-Gate® Processes in New-Product Development 163
The New–Product Process 164 新产品开发过程
Stage 1: New-Product Strategy Development 164 第一阶段：新产品战略开发
Stage 2: Idea Generation 165 第二阶段：创意产生
Going Online: IDEO—the Innovation Lab Superstar in Designing New Products 166
Stage 3: Screening and Evaluation 167 第三阶段：筛选与评估
Stage 4: Business Analysis 168 第四阶段：商业分析
Stage 5: Development 168 第五阶段：开发
Marketing Matters: Marissa Mayer: The Talent Behind Google's Familiar ***White*** *Home Page 169*
Stage 6: Market Testing 169 第六阶段：市场测试
Stage 7: Commercialization 170 第七阶段：商业化
Learning Objectives Review 172
Focusing on Key Terms 172
Applying Marketing Knowledge 173
Building Your Marketing Plan 173
Video Case 7: Activeion Cleaning Solutions: Marketing a High-Tech Cleaning Gadget 173

8 MANAGING SUCCESSFUL PRODUCTS AND BRANDS 176 **成功的产品和品牌管理**

Gatorade: Quenching the Active Thirst within You 177 佳得乐公司：满足难以抑制的渴望
Charting the Product Life Cycle 178 制定产品生命周期
Introduction Stage 178 导入期
Growth Stage 180 成长期
Maturity Stage 181 成熟期
Marketing Matters: Will E-mail Spell Extinction for Fax Machines? 182
Decline Stage 182 衰退期
Four Aspects of the Product Life Cycle 183 产品生命周期的四个方面
Managing the Product Life Cycle 186 产品生命周期管理

Role of a Product Manager 186 产品经理的角色
Modifying the Product 186 调整产品
Modifying the Market 186 调整市场

Using Marketing Dashboards: Knowing Your CDI and BDI 187

Repositioning the Product 188 产品重新定位

Making Responsible Decisions: Consumer Economics of Downsizing—Get Less, Pay More 189

Branding and Brand Management 190 品牌化和品牌管理
Brand Personality and Brand Equity 191 品牌个性与品牌资产

Going Online: Have an Idea for a Brand or Trade Name? Check It Out 193

Picking a Good Brand Name 193 选择一个好品牌名称
Branding Strategies 194 品牌战略
Packaging and Labeling Products 196 产品包装与标签
Creating Customer Value and Competitive Advantage through Packaging and Labeling 196 运用包装与标签创造顾客价值和竞争优势

Marketing Matters: Creating Customer Value through Packaging—Pez Heads Dispense More Than Candy 197

Packaging and Labeling Challenges and Responses 199 包装与标签的挑战和应对
Product Warranty 200 产品担保

Learning Objectives Review 200
Focusing on Key Terms 201
Applying Marketing Knowledge 201
Building Your Marketing Plan 201

Video Case 8: BMW: "Newness" and the Product Life Cycle 202

9 SERVICES MARKETING 204 **服务营销**

Services Get Real! 205 获得真正的服务
The Uniqueness of Services 206 服务的独特性
The Four I's of Services 207 服务 4I
The Service Continuum 209 服务连续体
Classifying Services 210 服务分类

Marketing Matters: Marketing Is a Must for 1.5 Million Nonprofits! 212

How Consumers Purchase Services 213 消费者如何购买服务
The Purchase Process 213 购买过程

Assessing Service Quality 214 评估服务质量
Customer Contact and Relationship Marketing 214 顾客接触与关系营销

Going Online: How Can You Monitor Service Failure? Blog Watching! 215

Managing the Marketing of Services 216 服务营销管理
Product (Service) 216 产品（服务）
Price 217 价 格
Place (Distribution) 217 地点（分销）
Promotion 218 促 销
People 219 人
Physical Environment 219 自然环境
Process 219 过 程
Productivity 220 生产率
Services in the Future 220 未来的服务

Using Marketing Dashboards: Are JetBlue's Flights Profitably Loaded? 221

Learning Objectives Review 222
Focusing on Key Terms 222
Applying Marketing Knowledge 223
Building Your Marketing Plan 223

Video Case 9: Philadelphia Phillies, Inc.: Sports Marketing 101 223

10 MANAGING MARKETING CHANNELS AND WHOLESALING 226 **管理营销渠道与批发**

Callaway Golf: Designing and Delivering the Goods for Great Golf 227 卡拉威高尔夫：设计和提供优质的高尔夫商品
Nature and Importance of Marketing Channels 228 营销渠道的特性和重要性
What Is a Marketing Channel of Distribution? 228 什么是分销渠道
Value Is Created by Intermediaries 228 中间商创造的价值
Channel Structure and Organization 230 渠道结构与组织
Marketing Channels for Consumer Goods and Services 230 消费品与服务的营销渠道
Marketing Channels for Business Goods and Services 231 工业品与服务的营销渠道
Electronic Marketing Channels 232 电子营销渠道
Direct and Multichannel Marketing 233 直接营销与多渠道营销
Dual Distribution and Strategic Channel Alliances 234 双重分销与战略渠道联盟
A Closer Look at Channel Intermediaries 234 渠道中间商近览

Marketing Matters: Nestlé and General Mills—Cereal Partners Worldwide 235

Vertical Marketing Systems and Channel Partnerships 237 垂直营销体系与渠道伙伴关系

Channel Choice and Management 240 渠道选择与管理
Factors Affecting Channel Choice and Management 240 渠道选择与管理的影响因素
Marketing Matters: Avon Is Calling Again in China 241
Channel Choice Considerations 241 渠道选择需考虑的问题
Going Online: Visit an Apple Store to See What All the Excitement Is About 243
Global Dimensions of Marketing Channels 243 营销渠道的全球因素
Using Marketing Dashboards: Channel Sales and Profit at Charlesburg Furniture 244
Channel Relationships: Conflict, Cooperation, and Law 245 渠道关系：冲突、合作与法律
Making Responsible Decisions: Pay to Play: The Ethics of Slotting Allowances 247
Learning Objectives Review 248
Focusing on Key Terms 249
Applying Marketing Knowledge 249
Building Your Marketing Plan 249
Video Case 10: Act II Microwave Popcorn: The Surprising Channel 249

11 CUSTOMER–DRIVEN SUPPLY CHAIN AND LOGISTICS MANAGEMENT 252 **消费者驱动的供应链与物流管理**

Apple Inc.: Supplying the iPhone 3G to the World 253 苹果公司：向全世界供应 IPHONE（3G）
Significance of Supply Chain and Logistics Management 254 供应链和物流管理的重要性
Relating Marketing Channels, Logistics, and Supply Chain Management 254 把营销渠道、物流与供应链管理联系起来
Supply Chains versus Marketing Channels 254 供应链与营销渠道
Global Suppliers and Supply Chains 255 全球供应商和供应链
Sourcing, Assembling, and Delivering a New Car: The Automotive Supply Chain 256 采购、装配并运送一辆新轿车：汽车的供应链
Supply Chain Management and Marketing Strategy 256 供应链管理与营销战略
Going Online: Build Your Own Jetta with a Mouse 257
Aligning a Supply Chain with Marketing Strategy 257 联合供应链与营销战略
Dell: A Responsive Supply Chain 257 戴尔：反应性的供应链
Marketing Matters: IBM's Integrated Supply Chain—Delivering a Total Solution for Its Customers 258
Walmart: An Efficient Supply Chain 258 沃尔玛：高效的供应链
Objective of Information and Logistics Management in a Customer–Driven Supply Chain 259 顾客驱动的供应链中信息和物流管理的目标

Information's Role in Supply Chain Responsiveness and Efficiency 259 信息对供应链的反应速度与效率的影响

Total Logistics Cost Concept 260 总物流成本概念

Customer Service Concept 261 顾客服务概念

Marketing Matters: For Fashion and Food Merchandising, Haste Is as Important as Taste 263

Customer Service Standards 263 顾客服务标准

Using Marketing Dashboards: Diagnosing Out-of-Stocks and On-Time Delivery for Organic Produce 264

Key Logistics Functions in a Supply Chain 265 供应链中物流的关键职能

Transportation 266 运　输

Warehousing and Materials Handling 267 仓储和物料搬运

Order Processing 268 订单处理

Inventory Management 269 库存管理

Making Responsible Decisions: Reverse Logistics and Green Marketing Go Together at Hewlett-Packard: Recycling e-Waste 271

Closing the Loop: Reverse Logistics 271 闭环分析：逆向物流

Learning Objectives Review 272

Focusing on Key Terms 273

Applying Marketing Knowledge 273

Building Your Marketing Plan 273

Video Case 11: Amazon: Delivering the Goods . . . Millions of Times a Day 273

12 RETAILING 276 **零　售**

84 Million Consumers Were Shopping Online on Cyber Monday. Were You One of Them? 277 星期一有 8400 万消费者会在网上购物，你是其中一个吗

The Value of Retailing 278 零售的价值

Consumer Utilities Offered by Retailing 278 零售提供的消费者效用

The Global Economic Impact of Retailing 279 零售对全球经济的影响

Classifying Retail Outlets 280 零售业态分类

Form of Ownership 280 所有权形式

Making Responsible Decisions: Environmentally Friendly Retailing Takes Off! 281

Level of Service 282 服务水平

Type of Merchandise Line 283 商品线类型

Nonstore Retailing 285 无店铺零售

Automatic Vending 285 自动售货

Direct Mail and Catalogs 286 直邮与目录
Television Home Shopping 287 电视家庭购物
Online Retailing 287 网上零售

Going Online: For Some Consumers, Shopping Is a Game! 288

Telemarketing 289 电话营销
Direct Selling 289 直接销售
Retailing Strategy 290 零售战略
Positioning a Retail Store 290 零售商店的定位
Retailing Mix 291 零售组合

Using Marketing Dashboards: Why Apple Stores May Be the Best in the United States! 295

The Changing Nature of Retailing 296 零售的渠道性质
The Wheel of Retailing 296 零售轮
The Retail Life Cycle 297 零售生命周期
Future Changes in Retailing 298 零售未来的变化
Multichannel Retailing 298 多渠道零售

Marketing Matters: The Multichannel Marketing Multiplier 299

Managing the Customer Experience 299 顾客体验管理
Learning Objectives Review 300
Focusing on Key Terms 300
Applying Marketing Knowledge 300
Building Your Marketing Plan 301

Video Case 12: Mall of America: Shopping and a Whole Lot More 301

13 INTEGRATED MARKETING COMMUNICATIONS AND DIRECT MARKETING 304 **整合营销传播与直接营销**

Integrated Marketing Communications Ushers in the ‘Age of Engage’ 305 整合营销传播恰逢其时
The Communication Process 306 传播过程
Encoding and Decoding 307 编码和解码
Feedback 308 反 馈
Noise 308 噪 音
The Promotional Elements 308 促销要素
Advertising 308 广 告
Personal Selling 309 人员推销
Public Relations 310 公共关系
Sales Promotion 311 销售促进

Direct Marketing 311 直接营销

Integrated Marketing Communications—Developing the Promotional Mix 312 整合营销传播——开发促销组合

The Target Audience 312 目标受众

Marketing Matters: Mobile Marketing Reaches Generation Y, 32/7! 313

The Product Life Cycle 313 产品生命周期

Product Characteristics 314 产品属性

Stages of the Buying Decision 315 购买决策阶段

Channel Strategies 316 渠道战略

Developing an IMC Program 317 制定营销整合传播方案

Identifying the Target Audience 318 确定目标受众

Specifying Promotion Objectives 318 明确促销目标

Setting the Promotion Budget 319 建立促销预算

Using Marketing Dashboards: How Much Should You Spend on IMC? 320

Selecting the Right Promotional Tools 321 选择正确的促销工具

Designing the Promotion 321 促销设计

Scheduling the Promotion 321 确定促销进度

Executing and Assessing the Promotion Program 322 执行和评估促销方案

Direct Marketing 323 直接营销

The Growth of Direct Marketing 323 直接营销的增长

The Value of Direct Marketing 324 直接营销的价值

Technological, Global, and Ethical Issues in Direct Marketing 325 直接营销中的技术、全球化以及道德问题

Making Responsible Decisions: Can Direct Marketing "Go Green"? 326

Learning Objectives Review 326

Focusing on Key Terms 327

Applying Marketing Knowledge 327

Building Your Marketing Plan 328

Video Case 13: Under Armour: Using IMC to Create a Brand for this Generation's Athletes 328

14 ADVERTISING, SALES PROMOTION, AND PUBLIC RELATIONS 332 **广告、销售促进和公共关系**

Advertising Moves to a New Dimension: The Third Dimension 333 广告走向一个新的维度：第三维度

Types of Advertisements 334 广告的类型

Product Advertisements 334 产品广告

Institutional Advertisements 335 机构广告

Developing the Advertising Program 336 制定广告方案

Identifying the Target Audience 336 确定目标受众

Specifying Advertising Objectives 337 明确广告目标

Setting the Advertising Budget 337 建立广告预算

Going Online: See Your Favorite Super Bowl Ads Again, and Again! 338

Designing the Advertisement 338 广告设计

Selecting the Right Media 341 选择合适的媒体

Using Marketing Dashboards: What Is the Best Way to Reach 1,000 Customers? 343

Different Media Alternatives 343 不同媒体选择

Making Responsible Decisions: Who Is Responsible for Click Fraud? 349

Scheduling the Advertising 350 确定广告进度

Executing the Advertising Program 351 执行广告方案

Pretesting the Advertising 351 预先测试广告

Carrying Out the Advertising Program 351 执行广告方案

Assessing the Advertising Program 352 评估广告方案

Posttesting the Advertising 352 事后测试广告

Making Needed Changes 353 做必要的调整

Sales Promotion 353 销售促进

Consumer-Oriented Sales Promotions 353 消费者导向销售促进

Trade-Oriented Sales Promotions 358 贸易导向销售促进

Public Relations 360 公共关系

Publicity Tools 360 公共宣传工具

Increasing the Value of Promotion 360 增加促销价值

Building Long-Term Relationships with Promotion 361 在促销中建立长期关系

Self-Regulation 361 自我调节

Learning Objectives Review 362

Focusing on Key Terms 362

Applying Marketing Knowledge 362

Building Your Marketing Plan 363

Video Case 14: Google, Inc.: The Right Ads at the Right Time 363

15 PULLING IT ALL TOGETHER: THE STRATEGIC MARKETING PROCESS 366 **整合战略营销过程**

"Breaking the Rules" at General Mills to Reach Today's On-the-Go Consumer 367 通用磨坊公司打破规则，抢夺今天的消费者

Marketing Basics: Doing What Works and Allocating Resources 368 营销基础：做有用之事并配置资源

Finding and Using What Really Works 369 发现并利用真正起作用的东西

Allocating Marketing Resources Using Sales Response Functions 370 根据销售反应函数配置营销资源

The Planning Phase of the Strategic Marketing Process 373 战略营销过程的计划阶段

The Vital Importance of Metrics in Marketing Planning 373 营销计划中衡量指标的重要意义

The Variety of Marketing Plans 374 营销计划的多样性

Marketing Planning Frameworks: The Search for Growth 374 营销计划框架：寻求增长

Marketing Matters: A Test of Your Skills: Where Are the Synergies? 377

Some Marketing Planning and Strategy Lessons 378 一些营销计划和战略教训

The Implementation Phase of the Strategic Marketing Process 380 战略营销过程的执行阶段

Is Planning or Implementation the Problem? 380 是计划还是执行出了问题

Increasing Emphasis on Marketing Implementation 381 日益重视营销计划的执行

Improving Implementation of Marketing Programs 381 改进营销方案的执行

Marketing Matters: Implementation Lessons from IBM: Converting Tough Global Problems into Results 383

Organizing for Marketing 385 营销组织

The Evaluation Phase of the Strategic Marketing Process 386 战略营销过程的评估阶段

The Marketing Evaluation Process 386 营销评估过程

Evaluation Involves Marketing ROI, Metrics, and Dashboards 387 评估包括营销投资回报率、测量指标和仪表盘

Evaluation Using Marketing Metrics and Marketing Dashboards at General Mills 388 通用磨坊公司利用营销测量指标和营销仪表盘进行评估

Learning Objectives Review 390

Focusing on Key Terms 391

Applying Marketing Knowledge 391

Building Your Marketing Plan 391

Video Case 15: General Mills Warm Delights™: Indulgent, Delicious, and Gooey! 392

MARKETING

Post-it
Post-it
Post-it
3M
EXAM ON WEDNESDAY - CH. 3,4,5
I. Selecting a speech topic & purpose
°Choosing a topic
- I know a lot about
- I want to know more about it
- Searching for topics
°personal experience, interests, skills,
Choosing a Topic
87
When you look for a speech topic, keep in mind special expertise you may have or sports, hobbies, travel, and other personal experiences that would make for an interesting presentation.

1

通过营销建立客户关系，创造顾客价值

Creating Customer Relationships and Value through Marketing

LEARNING OBJECTIVES

After reading this chapter you should be able to:

LO1 Define marketing and identify the diverse factors influencing marketing activities.

LO2 Explain how marketing discovers and satisfies consumer needs.

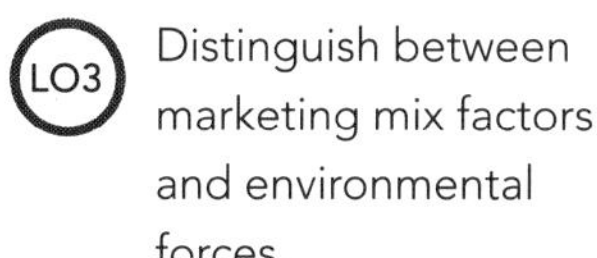
LO3 Distinguish between marketing mix factors and environmental forces.

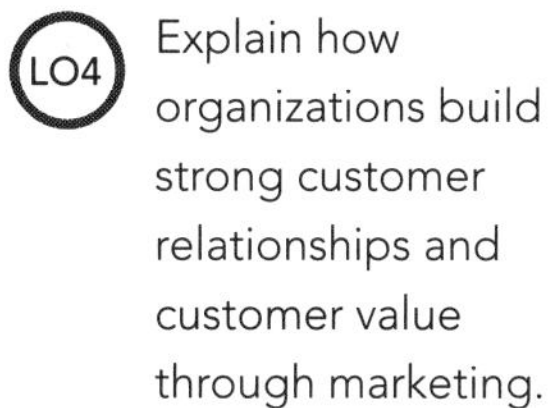
LO4 Explain how organizations build strong customer relationships and customer value through marketing.

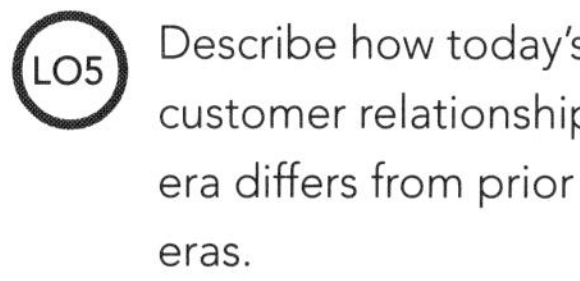
LO5 Describe how today's customer relationship era differs from prior eras.

3M 公司的创新和营销：如何发现学生的学习习惯并推出一款新产品

INNOVATION AND MARKETING AT 3M: HOW DISCOVERING STUDENT STUDY HABITS LAUNCHED A NEW PRODUCT

David Windorski, a 3M inventor, faced a curious challenge—understanding how college students study!

Specifically, how do they read their textbooks, take class notes, and prepare for exams? After finding the answers, he needed to convert this knowledge into a product that actually helps students improve their studying. Finally, Windorski and 3M had to manufacture and market this product using 3M's world-class adhesive technology.

Sound simple? Perhaps. But David Windorski invested several years of his life conducting marketing research on students' study behavior, developing product ideas, and then creating an actual product students could use. This process of discovering and satisfying consumer needs is the essence of how organizations such as 3M create genuine customer value through effective marketing. In designing a product that satisfies consumer needs, David Windorski's invention got a personal testimonial from host Oprah Winfrey on her 2008 TV show. More on this later.

Discovering Student Study Needs

As an inventor of Post-it® brand products, David Windorski's main job is to design new products. He gets creative "thinking time" under 3M's "15% Rule," in which inventors can use up to 15 percent of their time to do initially unfunded research that might lead to marketable 3M products. Working with a team of four college students, Windorski and the team observed and questioned dozens of students about how they used their textbooks, took notes, wrote term papers, and reviewed for exams.

Windorski describes what college students told him: "It's natural behavior to highlight a passage and then mark the page with a Post-it® Note or Post-it® Flag of some kind. So it's reasonable to put Post-it® products together with a highlighter to have two functions in one."

Satisfying Student Study Needs

Designing a marketable product for students was not done overnight. It took Windorski a few years of creativity, hard work, and attention to countless details. Windorski went back to his drawing board—or more literally to wood blocks and modeling clay—to mock up a number of nonworking models. These nonworking models showed Windorski how the product would feel.

---

curious 稀奇古怪的，不寻常的，难以理解的；initially 开始，最初；describe 描述，描写，形容，叙述。

3M's Post-it® Notes or Post-it® Flags

+

Felt Tip Highlighters

=

What will the product be ???

3M product that will combine Post-it® Notes or Post-it® Flags and Highlighters

For the creative way a student project helped lead to a new product for college students using 3M's technology, see the text.

His search for the 2-in-1 highlighter plus Post-it® Flags produced working models that students could actually use to give him feedback. Windorski had taken some giant steps in trying not only to discover students' needs for his product but also to satisfy those needs with a practical, useful product. Later in the chapter we'll see what products resulted from his innovative thinking and 3M's initial marketing plan that launched his products.

什么是营销 WHAT IS MARKETING?

To see how three 20-somethings launched YouTube, see the text and Marketing Matters box.

The good news is that you are already a marketing expert! You perform many marketing activities and make marketing-related decisions every day. For example, would you sell more Panasonic Viera 50-inch plasma high-definition TVs at $2,499 or $999 each? You answered $999, right? So your experience in shopping gives you some expertise in marketing. As a consumer, you've been involved in thousands of marketing decisions, but mostly on the buying and not the selling side. But to test your expertise, answer the "marketing expert" questions posed in Figure 1–1. You'll find the answers within the next several pages.

The bad news is, good marketing isn't always easy. That's why every year thousands of new products fail in the marketplace and then quietly slide into oblivion. Examples of new products that vary from spectacular successes to dismal failures appear in the next few pages.

营销与你的职业生涯 Marketing and Your Career

Marketing affects all individuals, all organizations, all industries, and all countries. This book seeks to teach you marketing concepts, often by having you actually

FIGURE 1–1
The see-if-you're-really-a-marketing-expert test

Answer the questions below. The correct answers are given later in the chapter.

1. True or false. You can now buy a satellite TV receiver for your minivan or sport utility vehicle (SUV) so that backseat passengers can watch high-definition television (HDTV) programs.
2. True or false. The 60-year lifetime value of a loyal Kleenex customer is $994.
3. To be socially responsible, 3M puts what recycled material into its very successful ScotchBrite® Never Rust™ soap pads? (*a*) aluminum cans, (*b*) steel-belted tires, (*c*) plastic bottles, (*d*) computer screens.

actually 的确，真实地，事实上；expert 行家，专家；oblivion 被遗忘的状态，湮没。

Marketing Matters > > > > > entrepreneurship

Payoff for the Joys (!) and Sleepless Nights (?) of Starting Your Own Small Business: YouTube!!!!

What happens when you drop Mentos into a bottle of Diet Coke?

Don't know the answer?

Then you're not a serious YouTube viewer! If you need an answer, ask the student sitting next to you in class. But don't try it in your room.

In one 12-month period, a single Web site—YouTube.com—revolutionized the Internet's world of videos and was named *Time* magazine's Invention of the Year for 2006. YouTube's numbers are astounding: In January 2008, 79 million viewers watched more than 3 billion user-posted videos, according to comScore.

The minds behind YouTube are three 20-somethings: Steve Chen, Chad Hurley, and Jawed Karim. Even the three entrepreneurs are astounded at their success. *Time* says the reason for YouTube's success is its rare combination of being both "edgy and easy" for users.

The three men met at PayPal, now the Internet's leading online payment service. Then they left PayPal and worked together on a new concept—a Web site where anyone could upload content that others could view. That was radical because until then only those who owned the Web site would provide the content.

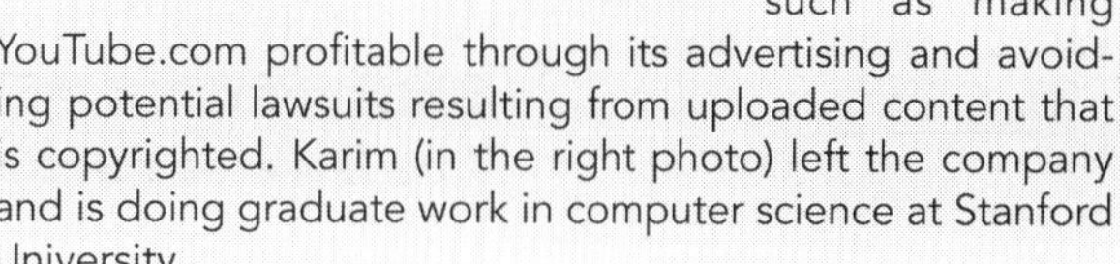

Google bought YouTube in October 2006 for $1.65 billion, only 21 months after its founding. Hurley (standing) and Chen (sitting) in the left photo are now Google employees. They now face issues such as making YouTube.com profitable through its advertising and avoiding potential lawsuits resulting from uploaded content that is copyrighted. Karim (in the right photo) left the company and is doing graduate work in computer science at Stanford University.

Where will this end? Go to YouTube.com and see for yourself!

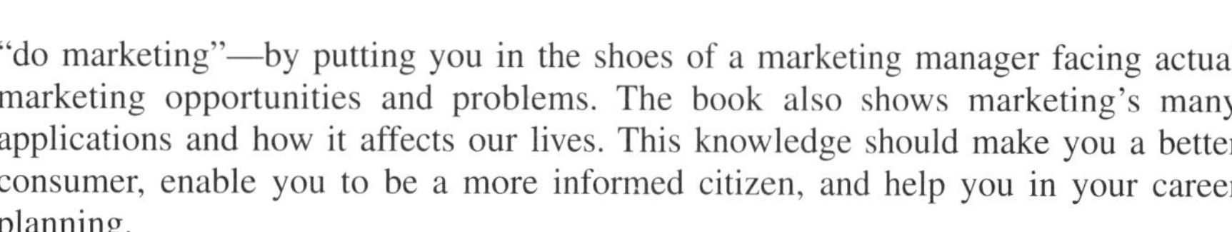

"do marketing"—by putting you in the shoes of a marketing manager facing actual marketing opportunities and problems. The book also shows marketing's many applications and how it affects our lives. This knowledge should make you a better consumer, enable you to be a more informed citizen, and help you in your career planning.

Perhaps your future may involve doing sales and marketing for a large organization. Working for a well-known company—Apple, General Electric, Target, or eBay—can be personally satisfying and financially rewarding, and you may gain special respect from your friends.

Small businesses also offer marketing careers. Small businesses are the source of the majority of new U.S. jobs. So you might become your own boss by being an entrepreneur and starting your own business. The Marketing Matters box describes the revolutionary impact three entrepreneurs in their 20s have had on the Internet—and perhaps on how you spend some of your free time. The three entrepreneurs—Steve Chen, Chad Hurley, and Jawed Karim—founded YouTube, which has achieved tremendous Internet success and is now part of Google. Not every Internet start-up reaches the 100 million viewers per month YouTube achieved in late 2008. In fact, more than half of new businesses fail within five years of their launch.

Do you or your friends have a great idea for a start-up business? But you've got no financing? Maybe Jawed Karim can help. He believes that college students have many innovative ideas but don't have the money or know how to get started. In 2008

application 应用，运用；entrepreneur 企业家；revolutionary 革命性的，突破性的，发生重大变革的。

Karim and two friends launched Youniversity Ventures, which provides venture financing to Internet software start-ups of *college students* and first-time entrepreneurs! To help the start-up team get off the ground Youniversity Ventures will invest $50,000 to $300,000 per company. If you're serious about your idea, e-mail Karim at jawed@youniversityventures.com.

结合它在2004年和2007年对营销的定义，我们认为，"**营销**是创造、沟通、传递和交换待售物，从而使组织、组织利益相关者和整个社会获益的活动。"

LO1

营销：向组织、组织的利益相关者和社会传递价值

Marketing: Delivering Benefits to the Organization, Its Stakeholders, and Society

The American Marketing Association represents marketing professionals. Combining its 2004 and 2007 definitions, "**marketing** is the activity for creating, communicating, delivering, and exchanging offerings that benefit the organization, its stakeholders and society at large." This definition shows marketing to be a far broader activity than simply advertising or personal selling. It stresses the importance of delivering genuine benefits in the offerings of goods, services, and ideas marketed to customers. Also, note that the organization doing the marketing, the stakeholders affected (such as customers, employees, suppliers, and shareholders), and society should all benefit.

为了向买卖双方提供服务，营销需要做的是：(1) 发觉潜在顾客的需要和欲望；(2) 满足这些需要和欲望。这些潜在顾客包括为自己和家庭进行购买的个人，以及为自己使用（如制造商）或转售（如批发商和零售商）而进行购买的组织。成功实现这两个目标的关键是**交换**，即买卖双方彼此交易有价值的东西，交易之后每一方状况都得到改善。

To serve both buyers and sellers, marketing seeks (1) to discover the needs and wants of prospective customers and (2) to satisfy them. These prospective customers include both individuals, buying for themselves and their households, and organizations that buy for their own use (such as manufacturers) or for resale (such as wholesalers and retailers). The key to achieving these two objectives is the idea of **exchange**, which is the trade of things of value between buyer and seller so that each is better off after the trade.

影响营销活动的多种因素

The Diverse Factors Influencing Marketing Activities

Although an organization's marketing activity focuses on assessing and satisfying consumer needs, countless other people, groups, and forces interact to shape the nature of its activities (see Figure 1–2). Foremost is the organization itself, whose

FIGURE 1–2
A marketing department relates to many people, organizations, and forces. Note that the marketing department both *shapes* and *is shaped by* its relationship with these internal and external groups.

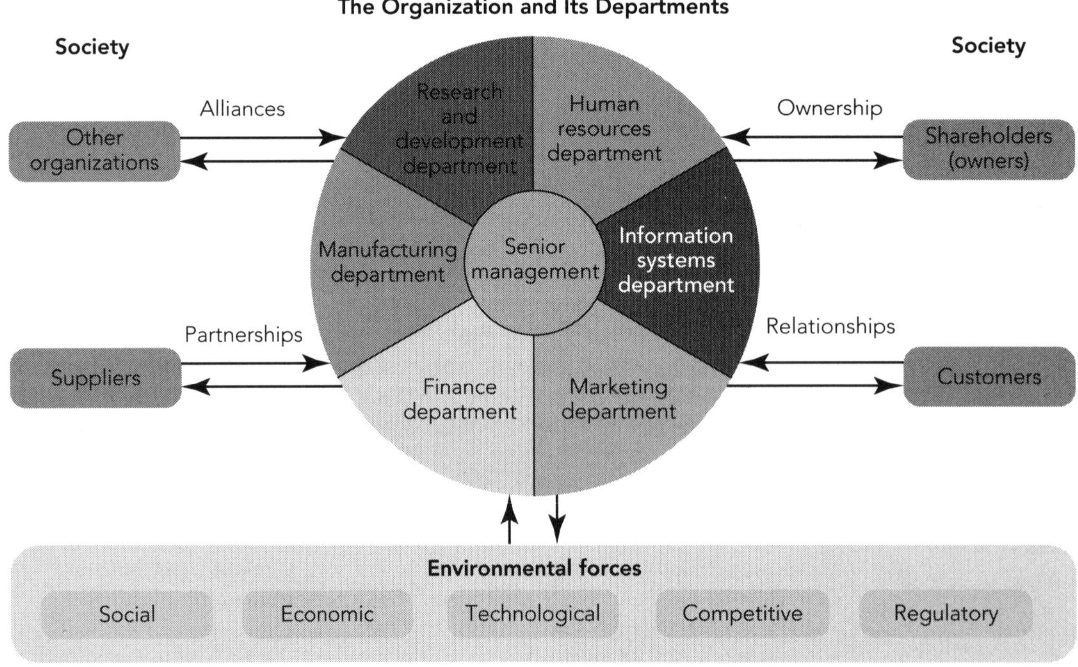

definition 清晰，分明，明确；genuine 真正的，非伪造的，名副其实的；stakeholder 利益相关者。

mission and objectives determine what business it is in and what goals it seeks. Within the organization, management is responsible for establishing these goals. The marketing department works closely with a network of other departments and employees to help provide the customer-satisfying products required for the organization to survive and prosper.

Figure 1–2 also shows the key people, groups, and forces outside the organization that influence its marketing activities. The marketing department is responsible for facilitating relationships, partnerships, and alliances with the organization's customers, its shareholders (or often representatives of groups served by a nonprofit organization), its suppliers, and other organizations. Environmental forces involving social, economic, technological, competitive, and regulatory considerations also shape an organization's marketing activities. Finally, an organization's marketing decisions are affected by and, in turn, often have an important impact on society as a whole.

The organization must strike a balance among the sometimes differing interests of these individuals and groups. For example, it is not possible to simultaneously provide the lowest-priced and highest-quality products to customers and pay the highest prices to suppliers, highest wages to employees, and maximum dividends to shareholders.

营销产生的前提
What Is Needed for Marketing to Occur

营销产生至少需要 4 个条件：(1) 两个或两个以上需要未被满足的群体（个人或组织）;(2) 每一方有满足需要的意愿和能力;(3) 有彼此沟通的途径;(4) 有用以交换的东西。

For marketing to occur, at least four factors are required: (1) two or more parties (individuals or organizations) with unsatisfied needs, (2) a desire and ability on their part to be satisfied, (3) a way for the parties to communicate, and (4) something to exchange.

Two or More Parties with Unsatisfied Needs Suppose you've developed an unmet need—a desire for information about how computer and telecommunications are interacting to reshape the workplace—but you didn't yet know that *Wired* magazine existed. Also unknown to you was that several copies of *Wired* were sitting on the magazine rack at your nearest bookstore, waiting to be purchased. This is an example of two parties with unmet needs: you, desiring technology-related information, and your bookstore owner, needing someone to buy a copy of *Wired* magazine.

Marketing doesn't happen in a vacuum. The text describes the four factors needed, say, to buy a *Wired* magazine.

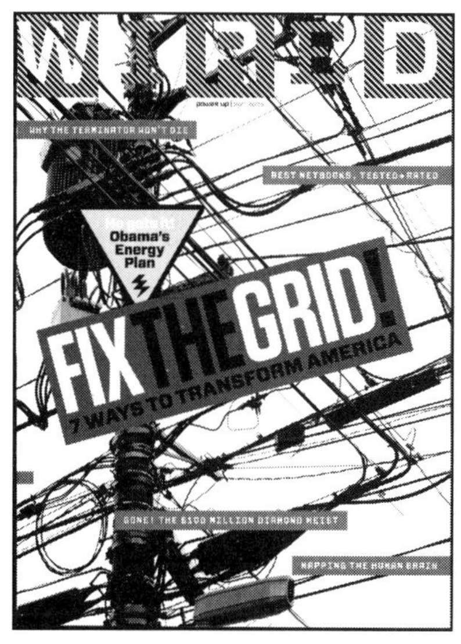

Desire and Ability to Satisfy These Needs Both you and the bookstore owner want to satisfy these unmet needs. Furthermore, you have the money to buy the item and the time to get to the bookstore. The store's owner has not only the desire to sell *Wired* but also the ability to do so since it's stocked on the shelves.

A Way for the Parties to Communicate The marketing transaction of buying a copy of *Wired* will never occur unless you know the product exists and its location. Similarly, the store owner won't stock the magazine unless there's a market of potential buyers nearby. When you receive a free sample in the mail or see the magazine on display in the bookstore, this communications barrier between you (the buyer) and your bookstore (the seller) is overcome.

Something to Exchange Marketing occurs when the transaction takes place and both the buyer and seller exchange something of value. In this case, you exchange your money for the bookstore's magazine. Both you and the bookstore have gained something and also given up something, but you are both better off because you have each satisfied your unmet needs. You have the opportunity to read *Wired*, but you gave up some money; the store

determine 决定，确定，判定；prosper 兴旺，繁荣，昌盛，成功；potential 潜在的，可能的。

gave up the magazine but received money, which enables it to remain in business. This exchange process and, of course, the ethical and legal foundations of exchange are central to marketing.

learning review

1. What is marketing?
2. Marketing focuses on ________ and ________ consumer needs.
3. What four factors are needed for marketing to occur?

营销如何了解并满足消费者需要
HOW MARKETING DISCOVERS AND SATISFIES CONSUMER NEEDS

LO2

The importance of discovering and satisfying consumer needs is so critical to understanding marketing that we look at each of these two steps in detail next.

For these four products, identify (1) what benefits the product provides buyers and (2) what "showstoppers" might kill the product in the marketplace. Answers are discussed in the text.

Vanilla-mint-flavored toothpaste in an aerosol container

Meat and cheese microwavable sandwiches

TV service in backseats of cars, minivans, and SUVs

A diet cola with ginseng and extra caffeine

---

ethical 道德的，伦理的；foundation 基础，根基；critical 极重要的，关键的。

了解消费者需求
Discovering Consumer Needs

当苹果公司推出其第二代苹果（Apple Ⅱ）个人计算机并开创一个新产业的时候，消费者其实并不真正了解其利益是什么。因此，为了学会使用个人计算机，他们不得不接受教育。

The first objective in marketing is discovering the needs of prospective customers. But these prospective customers may not always know or be able to describe what they need and want. When Apple built its first Apple II personal computer and started a new industry, consumers didn't really know what the benefits would be. So they had to be educated about how to use personal computers. Also, Bell, a U.S. bicycle helmet maker, listened to its customers, collected hundreds of their ideas, and put several into its new products. This is where effective marketing research, the topic of Chapter 5, can help.

用新产品满足消费者需求的挑战
The Challenge: Meeting Consumer Needs with New Products

罗伯特·麦克马思（Robert M. McMath）研究了 100 000 项以上的新产品开发，他提出两点关键性建议：(1) 一定要将目标集中在消费者的利益上；(2) 从过去的实践中吸取关键教训。

New-product experts generally estimate that up to 94 percent of the more than 33,000 new consumable products (food, beverage, health, beauty, and other household and pet products) introduced in the United States annually "don't succeed in the long run." Robert M. McMath, who has studied more than 100,000 of these new-product launches, has two key suggestions: (1) focus on what the customer benefit is, and (2) learn from the past.

The solution to preventing such product failures seems embarrassingly obvious. First, find out what consumers need and want. Second, produce what they need and want, and don't produce what they don't need and want. The four products shown on the next page illustrate just how difficult it is to achieve new-product success, a topic covered in more detail in Chapter 7.

Without reading further, think about the potential benefits to customers and possible "showstoppers"—factors that might doom the product—for each of the four products pictured. Some of the products may come out of your past, and others may be on your horizon. Here's a quick analysis of the four products, some with comments adapted from McMath:

- *Dr. Care Toothpaste.* After extensive research, Dr. Care family toothpaste in its aerosol container was introduced more than two decades ago. The vanilla-mint-flavored product's benefits were advertised as being easy to use and sanitary. Pretend for a minute that you are five years old and left alone in the bathroom to brush your teeth using your Dr. Care toothpaste. Hmm! Apparently, surprised parents were not enthusiastic about the bathroom wall paintings sprayed by their future Rembrandts—a showstopper that doomed this creative product.
- *Hot Pockets.* Introduced in 1983, these convenient meat and cheese microwavable sandwiches are a favorite brand among students. More than 80 varieties have been introduced, from Hot Pockets Pizza Snacks to Hot Pockets Subs and now Hot Pockets Paninis. A none-too-serious potential showstopper: Excessive ice crystals can form on the product due to variations in freezer temperatures; if this happens and the sandwich is thawed and refrozen before being microwaved, it may not taste as good.
- *AT&T CruiseCast.* In early 2009, AT&T and RaySat Broadcasting launched the AT&T CruiseCast service that enables families and commuters in the backseat of cars, minivans, and SUVs to watch over 20 channels (Disney Channel, CNBC, Nickelodeon, etc.) of satellite high-definition TV anywhere in the United States (question 1, Figure 1–1). The antenna/receiver is mounted on the roof of the vehicle and incorporates technology that overcomes line-of-sight obstacles, such as overpasses, tunnels, and so on. Potential showstopper: The initial cost of $1,299 for the antenna and $28 per month for the somewhat limited programming.
- *Pepsi Max.* In early 2009, Pepsi launched Pepsi Max. "This is the first diet cola for men" 25 and older who haven't liked the taste of other diet colas, according to the humorous "I'm Good" ad that ran during Super Bowl XLIII (2009).

---

prospective 未来的，可能成为的；helmet 头盔，防护帽；extensive 巨大的，大量的。

Pepsi Max is rebranded Diet Pepsi Max, a reformulated soft drink from Britain that was introduced to the U.S. in 2007 as the "Invigorating Zero-Calorie Cola." Pepsi Max has ginseng and extra caffeine to differentiate it from Diet Pepsi. One potential showstopper: women may not consume a soft drink specifically targeted at men.

Firms spend billions of dollars annually on marketing and technical research that significantly reduces, but doesn't eliminate, new-product failure. So meeting the changing needs of consumers is a continuing challenge for firms around the world.

Consumer Needs and Consumer Wants Should marketing try to satisfy consumer needs or consumer wants? Marketing tries to do both. Heated debates rage over this question, fueled by the definitions of needs and wants and the amount of freedom given to prospective customers to make their own buying decisions.

当一个人感觉缺乏食物、衣服和住所等基本生活用品时，需要就产生了。欲望则是基于某人的知识、文化与个性而产生的一种具体需要。假如你感到饥饿，就会有一种想吃东西的基本需要和意愿。于是你就产生了想吃苹果或者棒棒糖的欲望，因为根据以往经验及你的个性，你知道这些东西都能满足你饥饿的需要。通过在合适的场合创造出对好产品的知晓，有效的营销能够明确地塑造一个人的欲望。

A *need* occurs when a person feels deprived of basic necessities such as food, clothing, and shelter. A *want* is a need that is shaped by a person's knowledge, culture, and personality. So if you feel hungry, you have developed a basic need and desire to eat something. Let's say you then want to eat an apple or a candy bar because, based on your past experience, you know these will satisfy your hunger need. Effective marketing, in the form of creating an awareness of good products at convenient locations, can clearly shape a person's wants.

Certainly, marketing tries to influence what we buy. A question then arises: At what point do we want government and society to step in to protect consumers? Most consumers would say they want government to protect us from harmful drugs and unsafe cars but not from candy bars and soft drinks. To protect college students, should government restrict their use of credit cards? Such questions have no clear-cut answers, which is why legal and social issues are central to marketing. Because even psychologists and economists still debate the exact meanings of *need* and *want*, we shall use the terms interchangeably throughout the book.

As shown in the left side of Figure 1–3, discovering needs involves looking carefully at prospective customers, whether they are children buying M&Ms candy, college students buying highlighters, or firms buying Xerox photocopying machines. A principal activity of a firm's marketing department is to scrutinize its consumers to understand what they need and want and the forces that shape them.

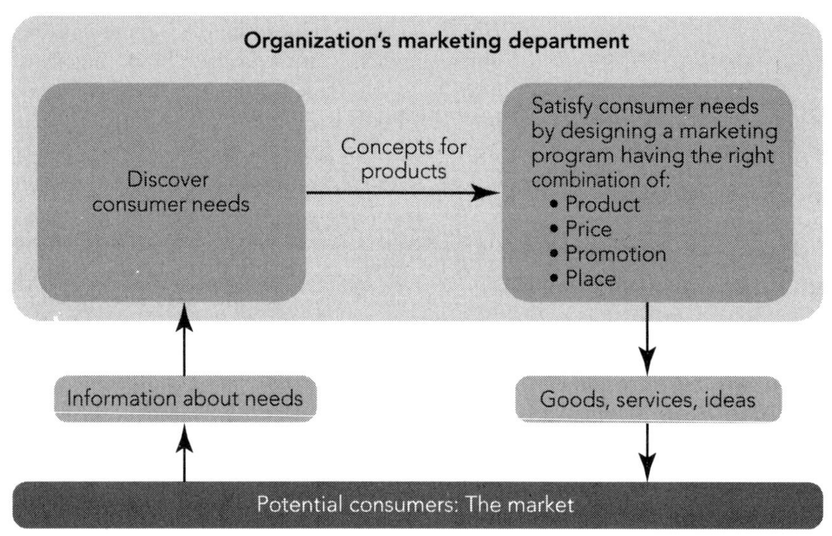

FIGURE 1–3
Marketing seeks first to discover consumer needs through extensive research. It then seeks to satisfy those needs by successfully implementing a marketing program possessing the right combination of the marketing mix—the four Ps.

---

significantly 重要的，有意义的；eliminate 消除，剔除，根除（尤指不需要之物）；restrict 约束，限制（活动或行为）；principal 首要的，最主要的，最重要的。

什么是市场 市场由潜在消费者，即那些有意愿并且有能力购买某一具体产品的人所组成。所有的市场最终都反映在人上。甚至当我们谈到一个企业购买了一台施乐复印机时，我们指的其实是企业中某个人或某些人决定购买它。当人们意识到自己存在尚未满足的需要时，就会产生购买某种产品的意愿，但仅有意愿是不够的。人们还必须具有购买能力，比如权力、时间和金钱。人们甚至可以“购买”一个想法，比如要每年检查自己的血压，或者调低温度调节器以节约能源。

What a Market Is Potential consumers make up a **market**, which is people with both the desire and the ability to buy a specific offering. All markets ultimately are people. Even when we say a firm bought a Xerox copier, we mean one or several people in the firm decided to buy it. People who are aware of their unmet needs may have the desire to buy the product, but that alone isn't sufficient. People must also have the ability to buy, such as the authority, time, and money. People may even "buy" an idea that results in an action, such as having their blood pressure checked annually or turning down their thermostat to save energy.

满足消费者需求
Satisfying Consumer Needs

Marketing doesn't stop with the discovery of consumer needs. Because the organization obviously can't satisfy all consumer needs, it must concentrate its efforts on certain needs of a specific group of potential consumers. This is the **target market**—one or more specific groups of potential consumers toward which an organization directs its marketing program.

LO3

The Four Ps: Controllable Marketing Mix Factors Having selected its target market consumers, the firm must take steps to satisfy their needs, as shown in the right side of Figure 1–3. Someone in the organization's marketing department, often the marketing manager, must develop a complete marketing program to reach consumers by using a combination of four tools, often called "the four Ps"—a useful shorthand reference to them first published by Professor E. Jerome McCarthy:

- 产品。满足消费者需要的一种物品、一项服务或一个创意。
- 价格。用以交换产品的东西。
- 促销。买卖双方之间的沟通方式。
- 分销。产品到达消费者手中的方式。

- *Product.* A good, service, or idea to satisfy the consumer's needs.
- *Price.* What is exchanged for the product.
- *Promotion.* A means of communication between the seller and buyer.
- *Place.* A means of getting the product to the consumer.

We'll define each of the four Ps more carefully later in the book, but for now it's important to remember that they are the elements of the **marketing mix**, the marketing manager's controllable factors—product, price, promotion, and place—that can be used to solve a marketing problem. For example, when a company puts a product on sale, it is changing one element of the marketing mix—namely, the price. The marketing mix elements are called controllable factors because they are under the control of the marketing department in an organization.

The Uncontrollable, Environmental Forces While marketers can control their marketing mix factors, there are forces that are mostly beyond their control (see Figure 1–2). These are the **environmental forces** in a marketing decision, those involving social, economic, technological, competitive, and regulatory forces. Examples are what consumers themselves want and need, changing technology, the state of the economy in terms of whether it is expanding or contracting, actions that competitors take, and government restrictions. These five forces may serve as accelerators or brakes on marketing, sometimes expanding an organization's marketing opportunities while at other times restricting them.

Traditionally, many marketing executives have treated these environmental forces as rigid, absolute constraints that are entirely outside their influence. However, recent studies and marketing successes have shown that a forward-looking, action-oriented firm can often affect some environmental forces, for example, by achieving technological or competitive breakthroughs.

---

sufficient 足够的，充足的；thermostat 温度自动调节器，恒温器；concentrate 集中；restriction 限制，约束，规定；entirely 完全地，完整地，全部地。

营销方案：如何建立顾客关系
THE MARKETING PROGRAM: HOW CUSTOMER RELATIONSHIPS ARE BUILT

An organization's marketing program connects it with its customers. To clarify this link, we shall first discuss the critically important concepts of customer value, customer relationships, and relationship marketing, and then illustrate these concepts with 3M's marketing program for its new Post-it® products for students.

顾客价值与顾客关系
Customer Value and Customer Relationships

Intense competition in today's fast-paced domestic and global markets has caused massive restructuring of many American industries and businesses. American managers are seeking ways to achieve success in this new, more intense level of global competition.

This has prompted many successful U.S. firms to focus on "customer value." That firms gain loyal customers by providing unique value is the essence of successful marketing. What is new, however, is a more careful attempt at understanding how a firm's customers perceive value and then actually creating and delivering that value. For our purposes, **customer value** is the unique combination of benefits received by targeted buyers that includes quality, convenience, on-time delivery, and both before-sale and after-sale service at a specific price. Loyal, satisfied customers are likely to repurchase more over time. Firms now actually try to place a dollar value on the purchases of loyal, satisfied customers during their lifetimes. For example, loyal Kleenex customers average 6.7 boxes a year, about $994 over 60 years in today's dollars (question 2, Figure 1–1).

所谓**顾客价值**，就是目标购买者所获得的包括质量、价格、便利、及时送货以及售前售后服务在内的一系列特定利益的组合。

Research suggests that firms cannot succeed by being all things to all people. Instead, firms must find ways to build long-term customer relationships to provide unique value that they alone can deliver to targeted markets. Many successful firms have chosen to deliver outstanding customer value with one of three value strategies: best price, best product, or best service.

Companies such as Wal-Mart, Southwest Airlines, and Costco have all been successful offering consumers the best price. Other companies such as Starbucks, Nike, and Johnson & Johnson claim to provide the best products on the market. Finally, companies such as Marriott, Lands' End, and Home Depot deliver value by providing exceptional service.

Southwest Airlines, Starbucks, and Home Depot provide customer value using three very different approaches. For their strategies, see the text.

clarify 阐明，阐释，说明；illustrate 表明，说明，证明；industry 工业；unique 唯一的，独一无二的。

But changing tastes can devastate once-successful marketing strategies. Lands' End, now part of Sears, must focus on strategies to defeat new groups of competitors: boutique specialty stores, catalog retailers, and Internet sellers (see Chapter 2).

关系营销
Relationship Marketing

企业可以通过实施具体的营销组合行动，建立起与其顾客的密切联系，进而实现有价值的顾客关系。

Meaningful customer relationships are achieved by a firm identifying creative ways to connect closely to its customers through specific marketing mix actions implemented in its marketing program.

建立并维持有效顾客关系的标志是**关系营销**，即为了共同的长远利益，将组织与其顾客、员工、供应商以及其他合作伙伴紧密联系起来。

Relationship Marketing: Easy to Understand The hallmark of developing and maintaining effective customer relationships is today called **relationship marketing**, linking the organization to its individual customers, employees, suppliers, and other partners for their mutual long-term benefits. Note that these mutual long-term benefits between the organization and its customers require links to other vital stakeholders, including suppliers, employees, and "partners" such as wholesalers or retailers in a manufacturer's channel of distribution. In many settings, relationship marketing is more effective when there is personal ongoing communication between individuals—both in the selling and buying organizations.

Relationship Marketing: Hard to Do Huge manufacturers find the rigorous standards of relationship marketing difficult to achieve. But today's information technology, along with cutting-edge manufacturing and marketing processes, have led to tailoring goods or services to the tastes of individual customers in high volumes at a relatively low cost. Thus, you can place an Internet order for all the components of an Apple computer and have it delivered in four or five days—in a configuration tailored to your unique wants.

But other forces are working against these kinds of personal relationships between company and customer. Researchers Fournier, Dobscha, and Mick observe that "the number of one-on-one relationships that companies ask consumers to maintain is untenable," as evidenced by the dozens of credit card and financing offers a typical consumer gets in a year. A decade ago you might have gone to a small store to buy a book or music record, being helped in your buying decision by a salesclerk or the store owner. With today's Internet purchases, you will probably have difficulty achieving the same personal, tender-loving-care connection that you once had with your own favorite book or music store.

营销方案
The Marketing Program

有效的关系营销战略有助于营销经理发现潜在顾客的需要是什么。为了满足顾客需要，他们必须将这些信息转换成企业可能开发的产品概念（图 1-3），进而将概念转换成切实可行的**营销方案**，即为了向潜在购买者提供某种商品、服务或创意而制定的一个整合营销组合计划。

Effective relationship marketing strategies help marketing managers discover what prospective customers need. They must translate this information into some concepts for products the firm might develop (see Figure 1–3). These concepts must then be converted into a tangible **marketing program**—a plan that integrates the marketing mix to provide a good, service, or idea to prospective buyers. These prospects then react to the offering favorably (by buying) or unfavorably (by not buying), and the process is repeated. As shown in Figure 1–3, in an effective organization this process is continuous: Consumer needs trigger product concepts that are translated into actual products that stimulate further discovery of consumer needs.

learning review

4. An organization can't satisfy the needs of all consumers, so it must focus on one or more subgroups, which are its ________________.
5. What are the four marketing mix elements that make up the organization's marketing program?
6. What are environmental forces?

devastate 毁坏，破坏，摧毁，蹂躏；achieve（经努力）完成，达到，获得；maintain 维持，保持；trigger 引起，发动，促使；stimulate 刺激，激励，促使，促起。

3M 公司帮助学生学习的策略和营销方案
3M's Strategy and Marketing Program to Help Students Study

3M's product line of Post-it® Flag Highlighters and Post-it® Flag pens includes variations in color and line widths.

To see some specifics of an actual marketing program, let's return to our earlier example of 3M inventor David Windorski and his search for a way to combine felt-tip highlighters and 3M's Post-it® Notes or Post-it® Flags to help college students in their studying. We will look at how Windorski worked with 3M: (1) to move his invention from ideas and mock-ups to a commercial highlighter product, (2) to add a new product that extends the product line, and (3) to undertake an actual marketing program to introduce the resulting products.

Moving from Ideas to a Marketable Highlighter Product After working on 15 or 20 wood and clay models, Windorski concluded he had to build a highlighter product that would dispense Post-it® Flags because the Post-it® Notes were simply too large to put inside the barrel of a highlighter.

Hundreds of the initial highlighter prototypes with Post-it® Flags inside were produced and given to students—and also office workers—to get their reactions. Two suggestions from users quickly emerged:

- Because of the abuse the product will take in students' pockets and backpacks, the product must protect the Post-it® Flags so they release easily when needed.
- Package the highlighter two ways—as a single yellow highlighter and as a three-pack in the favorite student colors of yellow, pink, and blue.

This customer feedback, while very useful, also caused special technical challenges for Windorski. For example, he soon discovered that to make the highlighter rugged enough for students, he had to design a rotating cover that would enclose the Post-it® Flags but not pinch them when rotated. Also, Windorski's design required that each injection-molded component of the highlighter meet tolerances less than the thickness of a piece of paper. And he worked closely with the final assembly team to ensure the highlighter achieved 3M's tight quality standards.

Adding the Post-it® Flag Pen Most of David Windorski's initial design energies under 3M's 15% Rule had gone into his Post-it® Flag Highlighter research and development. But Windorski also considered other related products. Many people in offices need immediate access to Post-it® Flags while writing with pens. Students are a potential market for this product, too, but probably a smaller market segment than office workers.

Marketing research among North American office workers refined the design and showed the existence of a sizable market for a Post-it® Flag Pen. Even here, however, Windorski encountered surprises: Consumers in one country may prefer blue ink while those in the country next door prefer black ink. The same is true of the width of line the pen produces.

A Marketing Program for the Post-it® Flag Highlighter and Pen After several years of research, development, and production engineering, 3M introduced its new products. Figure 1–4 outlines the strategies for each of the four marketing mix elements in 3M's program to market its Post-it® Flag Highlighters and Post-it® Flag Pens. We can compare the marketing program for each of the two products:

- *Post-it® Flag Highlighter.* The target market is mainly college students, so 3M's initial challenge was to build student awareness of a product that they didn't know existed. The company used a mix of print ads in college newspapers and a TV ad, and then relied on word-of-mouth advertising—students telling their friends how great the product is. Gaining distribution in college bookstores and having attractive packaging was also critical. Plus, 3M charged a price to

combine（使）结合，（使）组合，（使）综合；introduce 引进，首次引入，推行；tolerance 偏差。

MARKETING MIX ELEMENT	MARKETING PROGRAM ACTIVITY TO REACH: COLLEGE STUDENT SEGMENT	OFFICE WORKER SEGMENT	RATIONALE FOR MARKETING PROGRAM ACTIVITY
Product strategy	Offer Post-it® Flag Highlighter to help college students in their studying	Offer Post-it® Flag Pen to help office workers in their day-to-day work activities	Listen carefully to the needs and wants of potential customer segments to use 3M technology to introduce a useful, innovative product
Price strategy	Seek retail price of about \$3.99 to \$4.99 for a single Post-it® Flag Highlighter or \$5.99 to \$7.99 for a three-pack	Seek retail price of about \$3.99 to \$4.99 for a single Post-it® Flag Pen; wholesale prices are less	Set prices that provide genuine value to the customer segment that is targeted
Promotion strategy	Run limited promotion with a TV ad and some ads in college newspapers and then rely on student word-of-mouth messages	Run limited promotion among distributors to get them to stock the product	Increase awareness of potential users who have never heard of this new, innovative 3M product
Place strategy	Distribute Post-it® Flag Highlighters through college bookstores, office supply stores, and mass merchandisers	Distribute Post-it® Flag Pens through office wholesalers and retailers and mass merchandisers	Make it easy for prospective buyers to buy at convenient retail outlets (both products) or to get at work (Post-it® Flag Pens only)

FIGURE 1–4

Marketing programs for the launch of two Post-it® brand products targeted at two customer market segments.

distributors that it hoped would give a reasonable bookstore price to students and an acceptable profit to distributors and 3M.

- *Post-it® Flag Pen.* The primary target market is people working in offices. But some students are potential customers, so 3M gained distribution in some college bookstores of Post-it® Flag Pens, too. But the Post-it® Flag Pens are mainly business products—bought by the purchasing department in an organization and stocked as office supplies for employees to use. So the marketing program in Figure 1–4 reflects the different distribution or "place" strategies for the two products.

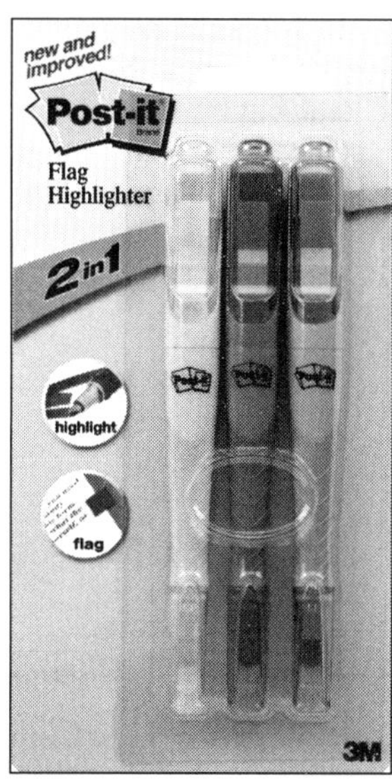

The second generation of Post-it® Flag Highlighters

How did these new products do for 3M in the marketplace? They have done so well that 3M bestowed a prestigious award on David Windorski and his team. Their success has also led Windorski to design a second generation of Post-it® Flag Highlighters and Pens *without* the rotating cover that makes it easier to insert replacement flags.

The new tapered design is also easier for students to hold and use. The packaging of the new, second-generation Post-it® Flag Highlighters prominently displays the "2-in-1" benefit.

In what must be the answer to almost every inventor's dream, Oprah Winfrey flew David Windorski to Chicago to appear on her TV show and thank him in person. She told Windorski and her audience that the Post-it® Flag Highlighter is changing the way she does things at home and at work—especially in going through potential books she might recommend for her book club. "David, I know you never thought this would happen when you were in your 3M lab . . . but I want you to take a bow before America for the invention of this . . . (highlighter). It's the most incredible invention," she said.

distributor 经销商，分销商；purchase 购买，采购；bestow 赠给，授予；incredible 不可思议的，难以置信的。

营销如何变得如此重要
HOW MARKETING BECAME SO IMPORTANT

为了理解营销何以成为现代全球经济中的一种驱动力量，我们接下来讨论：(1) 市场导向的演进；(2) 营销中的道德与社会责任；(3) 营销活动的广度与深度。

To understand why marketing is a driving force in the modern global economy, let us look at the (1) evolution of the market orientation, (2) ethics and social responsibility in marketing, and (3) breadth and depth of marketing activities.

市场导向的演进
Evolution of the Market Orientation

Many American manufacturers have experienced four distinct stages in the lives of their firms. The first stage, the *production era*, covers the early years of the United States up until the 1920s. Goods were scarce and buyers were willing to accept virtually any goods that were available and make do with them. In the *sales era* from the 1920s to the 1960s, manufacturers found they could produce more goods than buyers could consume. Competition grew. Firms hired more salespeople to find new buyers. This sales era continued into the 1960s for many American firms.

Starting in the late 1950s, marketing became the motivating force among many American firms and the *marketing concept era* dawned. The **marketing concept** is the idea that an organization should (1) strive to satisfy the needs of consumers (2) while also trying to achieve the organization's goals. General Electric probably launched the marketing concept and its focus on consumers when its 1952 annual report stated: "The concept introduces . . . marketing . . . at the beginning rather than the end of the production cycle and integrates marketing into each phase of the business."

Firms such as General Electric, Marriott, and Toyota have achieved great success by putting huge effort into implementing the marketing concept, giving their firms what has been called a *market orientation*. An organization that has a **market orientation** focuses its efforts on (1) continuously collecting information about customers' needs, (2) sharing this information across departments, and (3) using it to create customer value. The result shown in Figure 1–5 is today's *customer relationship era* that started in the 1980s, in which firms seek continuously to satisfy the high expectations of customers.

Toyota's world-class reputation among car manufacturers stems from its market orientation and understanding customer needs.

An important outgrowth of this focus on the customer is the recent attention placed on **customer relationship management (CRM)**, the process of identifying prospective buyers, understanding them intimately, and developing favorable long-term perceptions of the organization and its offerings so that buyers will choose them in the marketplace. This process requires the involvement and commitment of managers and employees throughout the organization and a growing application of information, communication, and Internet technology, as will be described

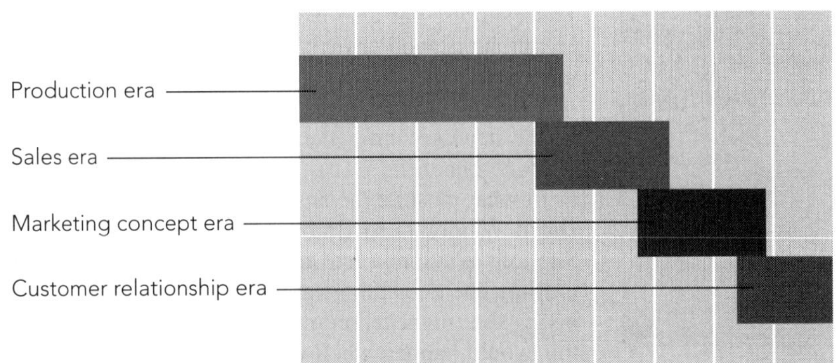

FIGURE 1–5
Four different orientations in the history of American business. Today's customer relationship era focuses on satisfying the high expectations of customers.

force 力量，影响力；integrates（使）加入，（使）融入；orientation 导向，定位。

throughout this book. Unfortunately, many expensive CRM computer systems have not provided the expected benefits because they failed to identify exactly which customer segments the company wanted to reach.

The foundation of customer relationship management is really **customer experience**, which is the internal response that customers have to all aspects of an organization and its offering. This internal response includes both the direct and indirect contacts of the customer with the company. Direct contacts include the customer's contacts with the seller through buying, using, and obtaining service. Indirect contacts most often involve unplanned "touches" with the company through word-of-mouth comments from other customers, reviewers, and news reports.

The disconnect between what companies *think they are providing* versus what customers *say they are receiving* shows how important customer experience is. A recent survey of 362 companies showed only 8 percent of them described the experience they received as customers as "superior," but 80 percent actually believed their own companies were supplying "superior" customer experience.

道德与社会责任：平衡不同群体的利益
Ethics and Social Responsibility: Balancing the Interests of Different Groups

As organizations have changed their orientation, society's expectations of marketers have also changed. Today, the standards of marketing practice have shifted from an emphasis on producers' interests to consumers' interests. In addition, organizations are increasingly encouraged to consider the social and environmental consequences of their actions for all parties. Guidelines for ethical and socially responsible behavior can help managers balance consumer, organizational, and societal interests.

道德　现有的法律与法规并不能明确处理许多营销问题。

Ethics Many marketing issues are not specifically addressed by existing laws and regulations. Should information about a firm's customers be sold to other organizations? Should advertising by professional service providers, such as accountants and attorneys, be restricted? Should consumers be on their own to assess the safety of a product? These questions raise difficult ethical issues. Many companies, industries, and professional associations have developed codes of ethics to assist managers.

Social Responsibility While many ethical issues involve only the buyer and seller, others involve society as a whole. For example, suppose you change the oil in your old Chevy yourself and dump the used oil in a corner of your backyard. Is this just a transaction between you and the oil manufacturer? Not quite! The used oil will contaminate the soil, so society will bear a portion of the cost of your behavior. This example illustrates the issue of social responsibility, the idea that organizations are accountable to a larger society.

在营销决策中，组织必须考虑到更广泛的社会福利。这其实就是一些营销专家所强调的**社会营销观念**，即组织应该在发觉并满足消费者需要的同时增加社会福利。

The well-being of society at large should also be recognized in an organization's marketing decisions. In fact, some marketing experts stress the **societal marketing concept**, the view that organizations should satisfy the needs of consumers in a way that provides for society's well-being. For example, ScotchBrite® Never Rust™ soap pads from 3M—which are made from recycled plastic bottles—are more expensive than competitors' (SOS and Brillo) but superior because they don't rust or scratch (question 3, Figure 1–1). The Making Responsible Decisions box on the next page describes how social entrepreneurship innovates to help solve the practical needs of society.

The societal marketing concept is directly related to *macromarketing*, which is the study of the aggregate flow of a nation's goods and services to benefit society. Macromarketing addresses broad issues such as whether marketing costs too much, whether advertising is wasteful, and what resource scarcities and pollution side effects result from the marketing system. While macromarketing issues are addressed briefly in this book, the book's main focus is on how an individual organization

identify 发现，察觉；exactly 精确地，确切地，正好；emphasis 重点，强调；macromarketing 宏观市场营销

Making Responsible Decisions >> social responsibility

Social Entrepreneurship Using Marketing to Help People

Fran Heitzman, founder of Bridging, Inc., loves to tell "The Story." It goes something like this: One day, Heitzman was helping a single mom stock her kitchen. When he handed her daughter some silverware, she said, "Just think Mom, now we won't have to share spoons when we eat!" Heitzman then went home and "stole five sets of silverware from our kitchen drawer" to give to those in need. "My wife didn't realize they were missing for a year and a half!"

The moral to Heitzman's story: Everyone's got too much stuff so they should give it away. That's where Bridging comes in. The not-for-profit organization matches people's surpluses of things such as dishes and furniture with other people's needs, an example of what is now called "social entrepreneurship." For example, the men in the photo are retired school teachers whose volunteer work as Bridging truck drivers gives them the personal satisfaction of helping others.

In a nutshell, social entrepreneurship applies innovative approaches to solve the practical needs of society, particularly of those members who lack the financial or political means to solve their own problems. A social entrepreneur is someone who uses inspiration, passion, creativity, and in many cases, capitalistic methods (marketing strategy and tactics, money, technology, etc.) to generate customer value for a significant segment of society through transformational change—much like a business entrepreneur. Social entrepreneurs can organize as either a for- or not-for-profit entity.

Social entrepreneurship occurs globally. For example, Hand in Hand International uses a technique called microfinance to provide small loans (about $125) to women in India who want to start and operate a small business. A Hand in Hand self-help group reaches out to the poorest, least educated, would-be businesswomen and teaches them first the basics (reading, writing, and arithmetic) and then the skills needed to operate a business. Percy Barnevik, the founder of Hand in Hand, says he wanted to "gift" his knowledge, abilities, and passion as a retired CEO to improve society's quality of life.

---

directs its marketing activities and allocates its resources to benefit its customers, or *micromarketing*. Because of the importance of ethical and social responsibility issues in marketing today, but they are touched on throughout the book.

营销的宽度与深度

The Breadth and Depth of Marketing

如今营销对每个人和每个组织都会产生影响。为了理解这一点，我们下面分析：(1) 谁在营销？(2) 营销什么？(3) 谁在购买，由谁使用？(4) 谁从营销活动中获益？(5) 怎样获益？

Marketing today affects every person and organization. To understand this, let's analyze (1) who markets, (2) what is marketed, (3) who buys and uses what is marketed, (4) who benefits from these marketing activities, and (5) how they benefit.

Who Markets? Every organization markets. It's obvious that business firms involved in manufacturing (Heinz), retailing (Target), and providing services (Marriott) market their offerings. And nonprofit organizations such as your local hospital, your college, places (cities, states, countries), and even special causes (Race for the Cure) also engage in marketing. Finally, individuals such as political candidates often use marketing to gain voter attention and preference.

营销什么　可营销的对象包括商品、服务甚至创意。商品是指能够满足顾客需要的有形物品，如牙膏、照相机或计算机。服务是指无形的东西，比如航空旅行、财务咨询或艺术博物馆。创意是指关于某个行动或某个事情的一种无形的想法。

What Is Marketed? Goods, services, and ideas are marketed. *Goods* are physical objects, such as toothpaste, cameras, or computers, that satisfy consumer needs. *Services* are intangible items such as airline trips, financial advice, or art museums. *Ideas* are thoughts about concepts, actions, or causes.

Financial pressures have caused art museums to innovate to market their unique services—the viewing of artworks by visitors—to increase revenues. This often involves levels of rare creativity unthinkable several decades ago. For example, the

---

engage 适应，（与……）建立密切关系；political 政治的，政治上的。

search for new revenues spurred the Dallas Museum of Art to stay open for 100 consecutive hours to celebrate its centennial.

France's Louvre, home to the Mona Lisa painting and Winged Victory of Samothrace statue, has now launched exotic fund-raising dinners and partnerships with museums around the world. To reach potential future visitors Russia's 1,000-room State Hermitage Museum partnered with IBM to let you take a "virtual tour" of its exhibits. To be a "virtual tourist," go to www.hermitagemuseum.org, and click on the "Virtual Visit" link.

Ideas are most often marketed by nonprofit organizations or the government. For example, your local library may market the idea of developing improved reading skills, and the Nature Conservancy markets the cause of protecting the environment. Charities market the idea that it's worthwhile for you to donate your time or money, and orchestras market fine music. States such as Arizona market themselves as attractive places for tourists to visit.

France's Louvre and Russia's State Hermitage Museum use creative marketing efforts to generate new revenues and attract first-time visitors.

Who Buys and Uses What Is Marketed? Both individuals and organizations buy and use goods and services that are marketed. **Ultimate consumers** are the people—whether 80 years or eight months old—who use the goods and services purchased for a household. In contrast, **organizational buyers** are those manufacturers, wholesalers, retailers, and government agencies that buy goods and services for their own use or for resale. Although the terms *consumers, buyers,* and *customers* are sometimes used for both ultimate consumers and organizations, there is no consistency on this. In this book you will be able to tell from the example whether the buyers are ultimate consumers, organizations, or both.

Who Benefits? In our free-enterprise society there are three specific groups that benefit from effective marketing: consumers who buy, organizations that sell, and society as a whole. True competition between products and services in the marketplace ensures that consumers can find value from the best products, the lowest prices, or exceptional service. Providing choices leads to the consumer satisfaction and quality of life that we have come to expect from our economic system.

Organizations that provide need-satisfying products with effective marketing programs—for example, Target, IBM, and Avon—have blossomed. But competition creates problems for ineffective competitors, such as eToys and hundreds of other dot-com businesses that failed a decade ago.

Finally, effective marketing benefits society. It enhances competition, which both improves the quality of products and services and lowers their prices. This makes countries more competitive in world markets and provides jobs and a higher standard of living for their citizens.

消费者怎样获益 营销创造**效用**，即产品使用者所获的利益或顾客价值。这种效用来自于营销交换过程。有 4 种不同的效用：形态效用、空间效用、时间效用与占有效用。

How Do Consumers Benefit? Marketing creates **utility**, the benefits or customer value received by users of the product. This utility is the result of the marketing exchange process and the way society benefits from marketing. There are four different utilities: form, place, time, and possession. The production of the good or service constitutes *form utility. Place utility* means having the offering available where consumers need it, whereas *time utility* means having it available when needed. *Possession utility* is the value of making an item easy to purchase through the provision of credit cards or financial arrangements. Marketing creates its utilities by bridging space (place utility) and hours (time utility) to provide products (form utility) for consumers to own and use (possession utility).

---

consecutive 连续的，不间断的；museum 博物馆，博物院；blossomed 变得成功。

learning review

7. What are the two key characteristics of the marketing concept?
8. What is the difference between ultimate consumers and organizational buyers?

LEARNING OBJECTIVES REVIEW

LO1 *Define marketing and identify the diverse factors influencing marketing activities.*
Marketing is an organizational function and a set of processes for creating, communicating, and delivering value to customers and for managing customer relationships in ways that benefit the organization and its stakeholders. This definition relates to two primary goals of marketing: (*a*) discovering the needs of prospective customers and (*b*) satisfying them. Achieving these two goals also involves the four marketing mix factors largely controlled by the organization and the five environmental forces that are generally outside its control.

LO2 *Explain how marketing discovers and satisfies consumer needs.*
The first objective in marketing is discovering the needs and wants of consumers who are prospective buyers and customers. This is not easy because consumers may not always know or be able to describe what they need and want. A need occurs when a person feels deprived of basic necessities such as food, clothing, and shelter. A want is a need that is shaped by a person's knowledge, culture, and personality. Effective marketing can clearly shape a person's wants and tries to influence what we buy. The second objective in marketing is satisfying the needs of targeted consumers. Because an organization obviously can't satisfy all consumer needs, it must concentrate its efforts on certain needs of a specific group of potential consumers or target market—one or more specific groups of potential consumers toward which an organization directs its marketing program. Having selected its target market consumers, the organization then takes action to satisfy their needs by developing a unique marketing program to reach them.

LO3 *Distinguish between marketing mix factors and environmental forces.*
Four elements in a marketing program designed to satisfy customer needs are product, price, promotion, and place. These elements are called the marketing mix, the four Ps, or the controllable variables because they are under the general control of the marketing department. Environmental forces, also called uncontrollable variables, are largely beyond the organization's control. These include social, economic, technological, competitive, and regulatory forces.

LO4 *Explain how organizations build strong customer relationships and customer value through marketing.*
The essence of successful marketing is to provide sufficient value to gain loyal, long-term customers. Customer value is the unique combination of benefits received by targeted buyers that usually includes quality, price, convenience, on-time delivery, and both before-sale and after-sale service. Marketers do this by using one of three value strategies: best price, best product, or best service.

LO5 *Describe how today's customer relationship era differs from prior eras.*
U.S. business history is divided into four overlapping periods: the production era, the sales era, the marketing concept era, and the current customer relationship era. The production era covers the period to the 1920s when buyers were willing to accept virtually any goods that were available. The central notion was that products would sell themselves. The sales era lasted from the 1920s to the 1960s. Manufacturers found they could produce more goods than buyers could consume, and competition grew, so the solution was to hire more salespeople to find new buyers. In the late 1950s, the marketing concept era dawned when organizations adopted a strong market orientation and integrated marketing into each phase of their business. In today's customer relationship era that started in the 1980s, organizations seek continuously to satisfy the high expectations of customers—an aggressive extension of the marketing concept era.

FOCUSING ON KEY TERMS

customer experience
customer relationship management (CRM)
customer value
environmental forces
exchange
market
market orientation
marketing
marketing concept
marketing mix
marketing program
organizational buyers
relationship marketing
societal marketing concept
target market
ultimate consumers
utility

APPLYING MARKETING KNOWLEDGE

1 What consumer wants (or benefits) are met by the following products or services? (*a*) Carnation Instant Breakfast, (*b*) Adidas running shoes, (*c*) Hertz Rent-A-Car, and (*d*) television home shopping programs.

2 Each of the four products, services, or programs in question 1 has substitutes. Respective examples are (*a*) a ham and egg breakfast, (*b*) regular tennis shoes, (*c*) taking a bus, and (*d*) a department store. What consumer benefits might these substitutes have in each case that some consumers might value more highly than those mentioned in question 1?

3 What are the characteristics (e.g., age, income, education) of the target market customers for the following products or services? (*a*) *National Geographic* magazine, (*b*) *Wired* magazine, (*c*) New York Giants football team, and (*d*) the U.S. Open tennis tournament.

4 A college in a metropolitan area wishes to increase its evening-school offerings of business-related courses such as marketing, accounting, finance, and management. Who are the target market customers (students) for these courses?

5 What actions involving the four marketing mix elements might be used to reach the target market in question 4?

6 What environmental forces (uncontrollable variables) must the college in question 4 consider in designing its marketing program?

7 Does a firm have the right to "create" wants and try to persuade consumers to buy goods and services they didn't know about earlier? What are examples of "good" and "bad" want creation? Who should decide what is good and bad?

building your marketing plan

If your instructor assigns a marketing plan for your class, don't make a face and complain about the work—for two special reasons. First, you will get insights into trying to actually "do marketing" that often go beyond what you can get by simply reading the textbook. Second, thousands of graduating students every year get their first job by showing prospective employers a "portfolio" of samples of their written work from college—often a marketing plan if they have one. This can work for you.

This "Building Your Marketing Plan" section at the end of each chapter suggests ways to improve and focus your marketing plan.

The first step in writing a good marketing plan is to have a business or product that enthuses you and for which you can get detailed information, so you can avoid glittering generalities. We offer these additional bits of advice in selecting a topic:

- *Do* pick a topic that has personal interest for you—a family business, a business or product you or a friend might want to launch, or a student organization needing marketing help.
- *Do not* pick a topic that is so large it can't be covered adequately or so abstract it will lack specifics.

1 To get started on your marketing plan, list four or five possible topics and compare these with the criteria your instructor suggests and those shown above. Think hard, because your decision will be with you all term and may influence the quality of the resulting marketing plan you show to a prospective employer.

2 When you have selected your marketing plan topic, whether the plan is for an actual business, a possible business, or a student organization, write the "company description" in your plan.

video case 1 3M's Post-it® Flag Highlighter: Extending the Concept!

"I didn't go out to students and ask, 'What are your needs, or what are your wants?' " 3M inventor David Windorski explains to a class of college students. "And even if I did ask, they probably wouldn't say, 'Put flags inside a highlighter.'"

So Windorski turned the classic textbook approach to marketing on its head.

That classic approach—as you saw earlier in Chapter 1—says to start with needs and wants of potential customers and then develop the product. But sometimes new-product development runs in the opposite direction: Start with a new product idea—such as personal computers—and then see if there is a market. This is really what Windorski did, using a lot of marketing research along the way after he developed the concept of the Post-it® Flag Highlighter.

EARLY MARKETING RESEARCH

During this new-product development process, Windorski and 3M did a lot of marketing research on students. Some was unconventional, while other research was quite traditional. For example, students were asked to dump the contents of their backpacks on the table and to explain what they carried around and then to react to some early highlighter models. Also, several times six or seven students were interviewed together and observed by 3M researchers from behind a one-way mirror—the focus group technique discussed in Chapter 5. Other students were interviewed individually. Windorski's first models were nonworking clay ones like he is holding in the photo below. These nonworking models told him how the innovative highlighters would feel to students eventually using the real ones. When early working models of the Post-it® Flag Highlighter finally existed, several hundred were produced and given to students to use for a month. Their reactions were captured on a questionnaire.

THE NEW-PRODUCT LAUNCH

After the initial marketing research and dozens of technical tests in 3M laboratories, David Windorski's new 3M highlighter product was ready to be manufactured and marketed.

Here's a snapshot of the prelaunch issues that were solved before the product could be introduced:

- *Technical issues.* Can we generate a computer-aided database for injection molded parts? What tolerances do we need? The 3M highlighter is really a technological marvel. For the parts on the highlighter to work, tolerances must be several thousandths of an inch—less than the thickness of a piece of paper.
- *Manufacturing issues.* Where should the product be manufactured? Because 3M chose a company outside the United States, precise translations of critical technical specifications were needed. Windorski spent time in the factory working with engineers and manufacturing specialists there to ensure that 3M's precise production standards would be achieved.
- *Product issues.* What should the brand name be for the new highlighter product? Marketing research and many meetings gave the answer: "The Post-it® Flag Highlighter." How many to a package? What color(s)? What should the packaging look like that can (1) display the product well at retail and (2) communicate its points of difference effectively?
- *Price issues.* With many competing highlighters, what should the price be for 3M's premium highlighter that will provide 3M adequate profit? Should the suggested retail price be the same in college bookstores, mass merchandisers (Wal-Mart, Target), and office supply stores (Office Max, Office Depot)?
- *Promotion issues.* How can 3M tell students the product exists? Might office workers want it and use it? Should there be print ads, TV ads, and point-of-sale displays explaining the product?
- *Place (distribution) issues.* With the limited shelf space in college bookstores and other outlets, how can 3M persuade retailers to stock its new product?

The original designs and packaging of the Post-it® Flag Highlighters and Pens at their new-product launch appear in the photo of the Post-it® product line on the opposite page.

THE MARKETING PROGRAM TODAY AND TOMORROW

The highlighter turned out to be more popular than 3M expected. The company often hears from end users how much they like the product.

So what can 3M do for an encore to build on the initial success? This involves taking great care to introduce product extensions to attract new customers while still retaining its solid foundation of loyal existing customers. Also, 3M's products have to appeal not only to the ultimate consumers but also to retailers who want new items to display in high-traffic areas.

Product and packaging decisions for the Post-it® Flag Highlighter reflect this innovative focus. In terms of product extensions, David Windorski designed new Post-it® Flag Highlighters and Pens that are easier to hold and that have the flags permanently accessible without twisting (see photo on page 15). As to packaging, it's critical that it (1) communicate the 2-products-in-1 idea, (2) be attractive, and (3) achieve both goals with the fewest words.

At 3M, promotion budgets are limited because it relies heavily on its technology for a competitive advantage. This also applies to the Post-it® Flag Highlighter. So you probably have never seen a print or TV ad for it. Yet potential student buyers, the product's main target market, must be made aware that it exists. So 3M searches continually for simple, effective promotions to alert students about this product.

Great technology is meaningless unless the product is available where potential buyers can purchase it. Unlike college bookstores that exist largely to serve students, mass merchandisers and office supply stores track, measure, and seek to maximize the profit of every square foot of selling space. So 3M must convince these retail chains that selling space devoted to its highlighter line will be more profitable than for stocking competing products. The challenge for 3M: Finding ways to make the Post-it® Flag Highlighter prominent on shelves of college bookstores and retail chains.

If the Post-it® Flag Highlighter is doing well in the United States, why not try to sell it around the world? But even here 3M faces critical questions: Which countries will be the best markets? What highlighter colors and packaging works best in each country? How do we physically get the product to these markets in a timely and cost-efficient basis?

Questions

1 *(a)* How did 3M's David Windorski get ideas from college students to help him in designing the final commercial version of the Post-it® Flag Highlighter? *(b)* How were these ideas important to the success of the product?

2 What *(a)* special advantages and *(b)* potential problems did 3M have in introducing a new highlighter-with-flags product for college students?

3 Visit your college bookstore before you answer. *(a)* Where would you display the Post-it® Flag Highlighter in a college bookstore, and *(b)* how can the display increase student awareness of the product?

4 In what ways might 3M try to promote its Post-it® Flag Highlighter and make students more aware of the product?

5 What are *(a)* the special opportunities and *(b)* potential challenges for 3M in taking its Post-it® Flag Highlighter into international markets? *(c)* On which countries should 3M focus its marketing efforts?

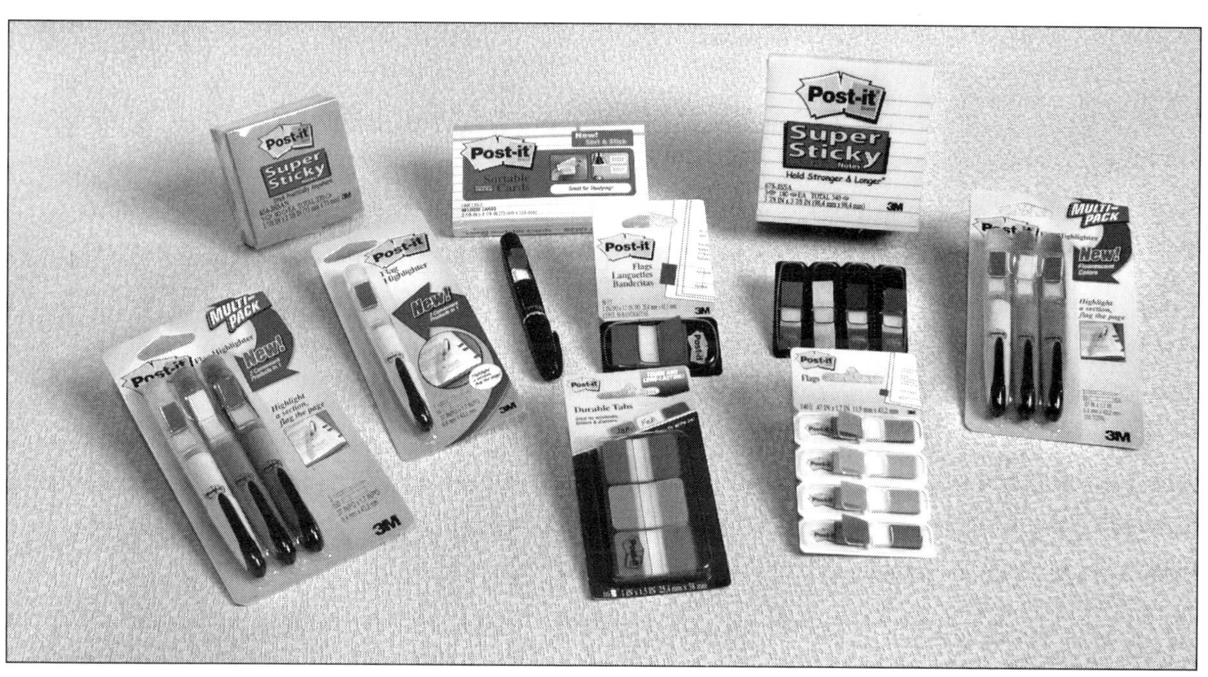

Ben & Jerry's Mission

Ben & Jerry's is founded on & dedicated to a sustainable corporate concept of linked prosperity. Our mission consists of 3 interrelated parts:

SOCIAL mission

To operate the Company in a way that actively recognizes the central role that business plays in society by initiating innovative ways to improve the quality of life locally, nationally and internationally.

PRODUCT mission

To make, distribute and sell the finest quality all natural ice cream and euphoric concoctions with a continued commitment to incorporating wholesome, natural ingredients and promoting business practices that respect the Earth and the Environment.

ECONOMIC mission

To operate the Company on a sustainable financial basis of profitable growth, increasing value for our stakeholders and expanding opportunities for development and career growth for our employees.

Underlying the Mission is the determination to seek new & creative ways of addressing all 3 parts, while holding a deep respect for individuals inside & outside the company, & for the communities of which they are a part.

2

制定成功的营销与公司战略
Developing Successful Marketing and Organizational Strategies

在冰淇淋函授课程中得“A”的人将何去何从
WHERE AN "A" IN A CORRESPONDENCE COURSE IN ICE CREAM MAKING CAN LEAD!

LEARNING OBJECTIVES
After reading this chapter you should be able to:

LO1 Describe two kinds of organizations and the three levels of strategy in them.

LO2 Describe how core values, mission, organizational culture, business, and goals are important to organizations.

LO3 Explain why managers use marketing dashboards and metrics.

LO4 Discuss how an organization assesses where it is now and seeks to be.

LO5 Explain the three steps of the planning phase of the strategic marketing process.

LO6 Describe the elements of the implementation and evaluation phases of the strategic marketing process.

Here's what the two founding entrepreneurs who aced their $5 college correspondence course in ice cream making are doing in their organization today:

- They buy their milk and cream from one dairy cooperative whose members guarantee the supplies are bovine growth-hormone free.
- Their PartnerShop, Scoopers Making Change, and Cones 2 Career programs help nonprofit organizations give jobs to at-risk youth.
- The summer 2009 limited edition "Goodbye Yellow Brickle Road" (opposite page) ice cream is a partnership with Sir Elton John to help his worldwide AIDS Foundation. The name is a play on one of his most popular song titles. The flavor is "an outrageous symphony of decadent chocolate ice cream, peanut butter cookie dough, butterbrickle and white chocolate chunks." Will it reappear in 2010?
- They are developing a "Cleaner Greener Freezer" for Ben & Jerry's U.S. retail locations, an innovative freezer that uses an eco-friendly refrigerant to save the ozone layer and reduce greenhouse gases.

This creative, funky business is Ben & Jerry's Homemade Holdings, Inc., which links its mission statement to social causes designed to improve humanity, as shown on the opposite page.

Their business started in 1978 when longtime friends Ben Cohen and Jerry Greenfield headed north to Vermont to start an ice cream parlor in a renovated gas station. Buoyed with enthusiasm, $12,000 in borrowed and saved money, and ideas from a $5 Penn State correspondence course in ice cream making, Ben and Jerry were off and scooping. Today, Ben & Jerry's is owned by Unilever, which is the market leader in the global ice cream industry—one that is expected to reach $43 billion by 2013. While customers love Cherry Garcia and the company's other rich premium ice cream flavors, many buy its products to support Ben & Jerry's social mission (opposite page).

Chapter 2 describes how organizations such as Ben & Jerry's, Medtronic, and Kodak set goals to give an overall direction that is linked to their organizational and marketing strategies. The marketing department of an organization converts these strategies into plans that must be implemented. The results are then evaluated to assess the degree to which they accomplish the organization's goals, consistent with its core values and mission.

---

correspondence course 函授课程；cooperative 合作社，合作机构；innovative 革新的，新颖的；implement 履行，实施。

当今的组织
TODAY'S ORGANIZATIONS

In studying today's visionary organizations, it is important to recognize (1) the kinds of organizations that exist, (2) what strategy is, and (3) how this strategy relates to the three levels found in many large organizations.

组织类型
Kinds of Organizations

LO1

An *organization* is a legal entity of people who share a common mission. This motivates them to develop *offerings* (products, services, or ideas) that create value for both the organization and its customers by satisfying customer needs and wants. Today's organizations can be divided into business firms and nonprofit organizations.

A *business firm* is a privately owned organization such as Amazon or Nike that serves its customers to earn a profit so that it can survive. **Profit** is the money left after a business firm's total expenses are subtracted from its total revenues and is the reward for the risk it undertakes in marketing its offerings.

In contrast, a *nonprofit organization* is a nongovernmental organization that serves its customers but does not have profit as an organizational goal. Instead, its goals may be operational efficiency or client satisfaction. Regardless, it also must receive sufficient funds above its expenses to continue operations. Charities and farm cooperatives affiliated with Ben & Jerry's are examples of this kind of organization. Both business firms and nonprofit organizations increasingly seek to achieve sustainable development, as described in the Making Responsible Decisions box. For simplicity in the rest of the book, the terms *firm, company, corporation,* and *organization* are used interchangeably to cover both business and nonprofit operations.

Organizations that develop similar offerings create an *industry*, such as the computer industry or the automobile industry. As a result, organizations make strategic decisions that reflect the dynamics of the industry to create a compelling and sustainable advantage for their offerings relative to those of competitors to achieve a superior level of performance. The foundation of much of an organization's marketing strategy is having a clear understanding of the industry within which it competes.

Both business firms such as Google and nonprofit organizations like Nature Conservancy use strategies and organizational structures to achieve their goals.

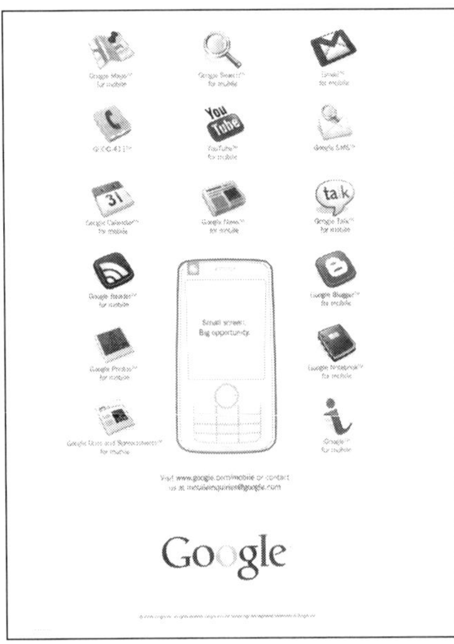

visionary 有远见的，愿景的；interchangeably 可交换地，可交替地。

Making Responsible Decisions sustainability

The Global Dilemma: How to Achieve Sustainable Development

Corporate executives and world leaders are increasingly asked to address the issue of "sustainable development." This term was formally defined in a 1987 United Nations report as meeting present needs "without compromising the ability of future generations to meet their own needs."

With more than half of the households in many developing nations below the poverty level, should the immediate goal be a cleaner environment or more food, clothing, housing, and consumer goods for its citizens? What should the heads of these governments do? What should business firms and nonprofit organizations trying to enter these developing nations do? What will be the impact on future generations?

The 3M Company developed an innovative program called Pollution Prevention Pays (3P) to reduce harmful environmental impacts, while making a profit doing so. The company estimates that the 3P program in the last quarter century has cut its pollution by 1.6 billion pounds while saving almost $900 million in raw materials and avoiding fines. The company's 2010 environmental goal is to improve energy efficiency per pound of product by 20 percent while reducing waste generated from its operations by 20 percent.

Should the environment or economic growth come first? What are the societal trade-offs?

什么是战略
What Is Strategy?

就我们而言，**战略**是组织的长期行动路线，它在传递顾客体验的同时，实现组织目标。

An organization has limited human, financial, technological, and other resources available to produce and market its offerings—it can't be all things to all people! Every organization must develop strategies to help focus and direct its efforts to accomplish its goals. However, the definition of strategy has been the subject of debate among management and marketing theorists. For our purpose, **strategy** is an organization's long-term course of action designed to deliver a unique customer experience while achieving its goals. Whether explicit or implicit, all organizations set a strategic direction. And marketing helps not only to set this direction but also to move the organization there.

当代组织的结构
Structure of Today's Organizations

Large organizations such as Medtronic and Kodak are extremely complex. They usually consist of three organizational levels whose strategies are linked to marketing, as shown in Figure 2–1.

FIGURE 2–1
The board of directors oversees the three levels of strategy in organizations: corporate, business unit, and functional.

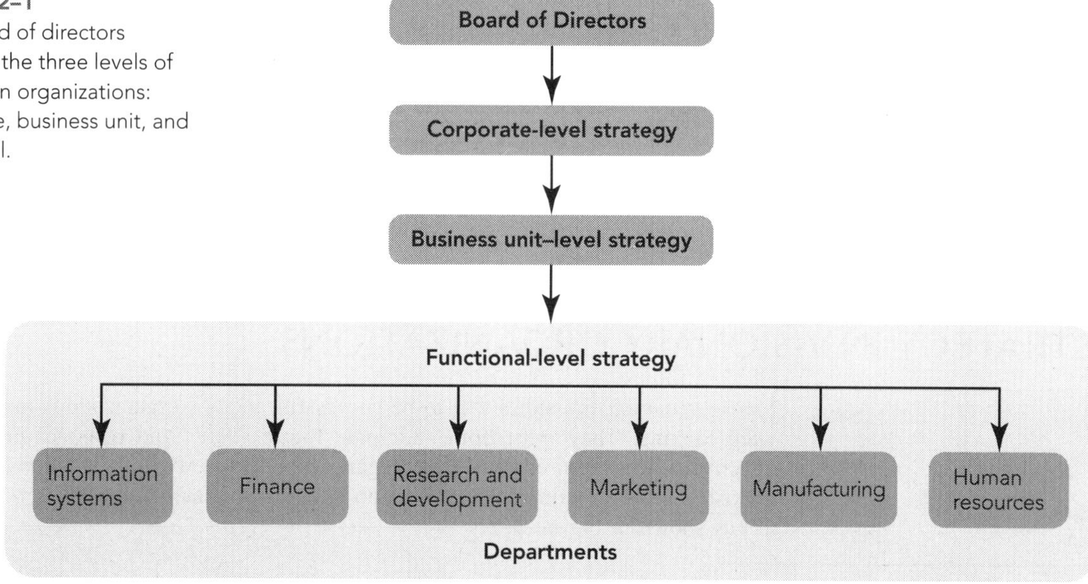

accomplish 完成，达成；explicit 明确的，清晰的，毫不隐讳的；implicit 不言明的，含蓄的。

Corporate Level The **corporate level** is where top management directs overall strategy for the entire organization. "Top management" usually means the board of directors and senior management officers with a variety of skills and experiences that are invaluable in establishing overall strategy.

The president or chief executive officer (CEO) is the highest ranking officer in the organization and is usually a member of its board of directors. This person must possess leadership skills and expertise ranging from overseeing the organization's daily operations to spearheading strategy planning efforts that may determine its very survival.

In recent years many large firms have changed the title of the head of marketing from vice president of marketing to chief marketing officer (CMO). These CMOs have an increasingly important role in top management because of their ability to think strategically. Most bring multi-industry backgrounds, cross-functional management expertise, analytical skills, and intuitive marketing insights to their job, which enables them to create and deliver value to the organization and its customers.

Strategic Business Unit Level Some multimarket, multiproduct firms, such as General Electric or Johnson & Johnson, manage a portfolio or group of businesses. Each group is a **strategic business unit (SBU),** which is a subsidiary, division, or unit of an organization that markets a set of related offerings to a clearly defined group of customers. At the *strategic business unit level*, managers set a more specific strategic direction for their businesses to exploit value-creating opportunities. For less complex firms with a single business focus, such as Ben & Jerry's, the corporate and business unit levels may merge.

Functional Level Each strategic business unit has a **functional level**, where groups of specialists actually create value for the organization. The term *department* generally refers to these specialized functions such as marketing and finance (see Figure 2–1). At the functional level, the organization's strategic direction becomes its most specific and focused. Just as there is a hierarchy of levels within an organization, there is a hierarchy of strategic directions set by managers at each level.

A key role of the marketing department is to look outward, keeping the organization focused on creating value both for it and for customers. This is accomplished by listening to customers, developing and producing offerings, and implementing marketing program activities.

When developing marketing programs for new offerings or for improving existing ones, an organization's senior management may form **cross-functional teams**. These consist of a small number of people from different departments who are mutually accountable to accomplish a task or a common set of performance goals. Sometimes these teams will have representatives from outside the organization, such as suppliers or customers, to assist them.

learning review

1. What is the difference between a business firm and a nonprofit organization?
2. What are examples of a functional level in an organization?

有远见的组织战略
STRATEGY IN VISIONARY ORGANIZATIONS

LO2

Management experts stress that to be successful, today's organizations must be forward looking. They must both anticipate future events and respond quickly and effectively. This requires a visionary organization to specify its foundation (why does it exist?), set a direction (what will it do?), and formulate strategies (how will it do it?) as shown in Figure 2–2.

---

executive 高管，管理者，经理；multimarket 多种经营的；representative 代表，代理人；accountable 有责任的；anticipate 预期，预料，预计。

Organizational foundation (why)		Organizational direction (what)		Organizational strategies (how)
• Core values • Mission (vision) • Organizational culture	+	• Business • Goals (objectives) ○ Long-term ○ Short-term	=	• By level: ○ Corporate ○ SBU ○ Functional • By offering: ○ Product ○ Service ○ Idea

FIGURE 2–2
Today's visionary organization uses key elements to (1) establish a foundation and (2) set a direction using (3) its strategies that enable it to develop and market its offerings successfully.

组织基础：它为什么存在
Organizational Foundation: Why Does It Exist?

An organization's foundation is its philosophical reason for being—why it exists—and rarely changes. Successful visionary organizations use this foundation to guide and inspire their employees through three elements: core values, mission, and organizational culture.

Core Values An organization's **core values** are the fundamental, passionate, and enduring principles that guide its conduct over time. A firm's founders or senior management develop these core values, which are consistent with their essential beliefs and character. They capture the firm's heart and soul and serve to inspire and motivate its *stakeholders*—employees, shareholders, board of directors, suppliers, distributors, creditors, unions, government, local communities, and customers. Core values also are timeless and should not change due to short-term financial, operational, or marketing concerns. Finally, core values guide the organization's conduct. To be effective, an organization's core values must be communicated to and supported by its top management and employees; if not, they are just hollow words.

Mission By understanding its core values, an organization can take steps to define its **mission**, a statement of the organization's function in society, often identifying its customers, markets, products, and technologies. Often used interchangeably with *vision*, a *mission statement* should be clear, concise, meaningful, inspirational, and long-term.

Medtronic is the world leader in producing heart pacemakers and other medical devices. Earl Bakken, its founder, wrote this mission statement for Medtronic when it was launched a half century ago, which has remained virtually unchanged:

> "To contribute to human welfare by application of biomedical engineering in the research, design, manufacture, and sale of instruments or appliances that alleviate pain, restore health, and extend life."

People see this "rising figure" mural in the headquarters of a world-class corporation. What does it signify? What does it say to employees? To others? For some insights and why it is important, see the text.

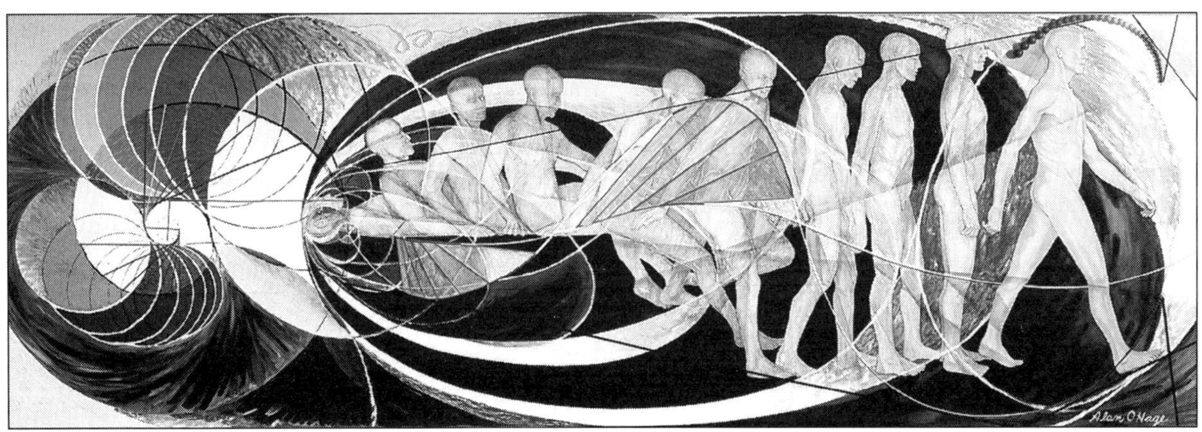

philosophical 理念的；passionate 热情的，狂热的；interchangeably 可交换的，可互换的，可交替的。

This inspiration and focus appear in the mission statements of both business firms and nonprofit organizations:

- Southwest Airlines: To be dedicated "to the highest quality of Customer Service delivered with a sense of warmth, friendliness, individual pride, and Company Spirit."
- American Red Cross: "To provide relief to victims of disaster and help prevent, prepare for, and respond to emergencies."

In the first half of the 20th century, what "business" did railroads believe they were in? The text reveals their disastrous error.

Each statement exhibits the qualities of a good mission: a clear, challenging, and compelling picture of an envisioned future.

Recently, many organizations have added a social element to their mission statements to reflect an ideal that is morally right and worthwhile. This is what Ben & Jerry's social mission statement is all about, as shown in the chapter opening. Stakeholders, particularly customers, employees, and now society, are asking organizations to be exceptional citizens by providing long-term value while solving society's problems.

Organizational Culture An organization must connect with all of its stakeholders. Thus, an important corporate-level marketing function is communicating its core values and mission to them. Medtronic has a "rising figure" wall mural at its headquarters. The firm also presents every new employee with a medallion depicting this "rising figure" on one side and the company's mission statement on the other. And each December, several patients describe to a large employee holiday celebration how Medtronic devices have changed their lives. These activities send clear messages to employees and other stakeholders about Medtronic's **organizational culture**, the set of values, ideas, attitudes, and norms of behavior that is learned and shared among the members of an organization.

组织方向：它将做什么
Organizational Direction: What Will It Do?

As shown in Figure 2–1, the organization's foundation enables it to set a direction in terms of (1) the "business" it is in and (2) its specific goals.

Business A **business** describes the clear, broad, underlying industry or market sector of an organization's offering. To help define its business, an organization looks at the set of organizations that sell similar offerings—those that are in direct competition with each other—such as "the ice cream business." The organization can then begin to answer the questions, "What do we do?" or "What business are we in?"

In his famous "Marketing Myopia" article, Theodore Levitt argues that senior managers of 20th century American railroads defined their business too narrowly, proclaiming, "We are in the railroad business!" This myopic focus caused these firms to lose sight of who their customers were and what they needed. Thus, railroads only saw other railroads as direct competitors and failed to develop strategies to compete with airlines, barges, pipelines, and trucks—firms whose offerings carry both goods and people. As a result, many railroads merged or went bankrupt. Railroads would have fared better if they had realized they were in "the transportation business."

For the reasons Netflix is altering its "business model" to respond to changing consumer demand and technologies, see the text and Marketing Matters box.

With today's increased global competition and worldwide financial crises, many organizations are rethinking their *business model*, the strategies an organization develops to provide value to the customers it serves. Technological innovation is often the trigger for this business model change. American newspapers are looking for a new business model as former subscribers get their news online and buy cars

inspiration 灵感，启示，启发；envision 想像，展望。

Marketing Matters > > > > > entrepreneurship

The Netflix Launch and Its Continually . . . Continually . . . Continually . . . Changing Business Model!

If in 1997 a customer had been charged a late fee of $40 for a VHS tape of *Apollo 13*, what might she or he have done? Maybe just grumble and pay it?

In the case of Reed Hastings, he was embarrassed, apparently paid the $40 late fee, and—this is where he's different—got to thinking that there's a big market out there. "So I started to investigate the idea of how to create a movie-rental business by mail," he told a *Fortune* magazine interviewer.

The Original Business Model

"Early on, the first concept we launched was rental by mail, but it wasn't subscription based so it worked more like Blockbuster," says Hastings, the founder and chief executive officer of Netflix. It wasn't very popular. So in 1999, he relaunched his idea with a new business model—as a subscription service, pretty much the mail business you see today with 8 million subscribers. "We named the company Netflix, not DVDs by Mail because we knew that eventually we would deliver movies directly over the Internet," Hastings says.

Netflix's Changing Business Model

The Netflix DVDs-by-mail model can deliver any one of 100,000 movies on DVD to you for a fixed monthly fee—$9 for one movie, $14 for two. But look where its business model changed over eight months in 2008: from "Watch Now," enabling regular subscribers to watch any of 1,000 streaming movies on a PC, to using a tiny $100 TV-connect box to let viewers rather awkwardly watch a streaming movie on their TV rather than a PC, to partnering with TiVo, Xbox, and others to enable their systems to let you see one of about 12,000 movies on your TV.

With Netflix breaking a series of technology barriers, its "any movie, any time" business model is literally just around the corner.

---

from Craigslist Inc. rather than using newspaper want ads. Microsoft is rethinking its business model in the new era of $200 laptops. The Marketing Matters box describes how Netflix founder and Chief Executive Officer Reed Hastings got the idea for his start-up and how his business model is changing continuously to reflect the way Internet breakthoughs are able to deliver movies more conveniently to a consumer's TV set.

Goals **Goals** or **objectives** (terms used interchangeably in the textbook) are statements of an accomplishment of a task to be achieved, often by a specific time. For example, Netflix may have the goal of being the top provider of online movies by 2011. Goals convert an organization's mission and business into long- and short-term performance targets to measure how well it is doing (see Figure 2–2).

Business firms can pursue several different types of goals:

- *Profit.* Most firms seek to maximize profits—to get as high a financial return on their investments (ROI) as possible.
- *Sales* (dollars or units). If profits are acceptable, a firm may elect to maintain or increase its sales even though profits may not be maximized.
- *Market share.* **Market share** is the ratio of sales revenue of the firm to the total sales revenue of all firms in the industry, including the firm itself. A firm may choose to maintain or increase its market share, sometimes at the expense of greater profits if industry status or prestige is at stake.
- *Quality.* A firm may offer the highest quality, as Medtronic does with its implantable medical devices.

- 销售额：如果利润可以接受，即便达不到利润最大化，一个企业可能选择维持或提高销售水平。
- 质量：一个企业可能以最高产品质量为目标，如美敦力公司在其移植医疗设备方面就是如此。

accomplishment 成就，成绩；investment 投资。

- 顾客满意度：顾客是组织存在的原因，他们的感知和行为是最为重要的。
- 雇员福利：一个企业认识到员工的重要性，所以在目标中承诺给员工好的就业机会与工作环境。

- *Customer satisfaction.* Customers are the reason the organization exists, so their perceptions and actions are of vital importance. Satisfaction can be measured with surveys or by the number of customer complaints it receives.
- *Employee welfare.* A firm may recognize the critical importance of its employees by stating its goal of providing them with good employment opportunities and working conditions.
- *Social responsibility.* Firms may seek to balance the conflicting goals of stakeholders to promote their overall welfare, even at the expense of profits.

Nonprofit organizations (such as museums and hospitals) also have goals, such as to serve consumers as efficiently as possible. Similarly, government agencies set goals that seek to serve the public good.

组织战略：如何做到
Organizational Strategies: How Will It Do It?

As shown in Figure 2–2, the organizational foundation sets the "why" of organizations and organizational direction sets the "what." To convert these into actual results, the organizational strategies are concerned with the "how." These organizational strategies vary in at least two ways, partly depending on the level in the organization and the offerings it provides customers:

Variation by Level Moving from the corporate to the strategic business unit to the functional level involves creating increasingly detailed strategies and plans. For example, at the corporate level, top managers may struggle with writing a meaningful mission statement, while at the functional level the issue may involve whether Joan or Adam makes the sales call tomorrow.

Variation by Offering Organizational strategies also vary by the organization's offering. The strategy will be far different when marketing a very tangible physical product (a Medtronic heart pacemaker), a service (Southwest Airlines flight), or an idea (donate to the American Red Cross).

The remainder of Chapter 2 covers many aspects of developing these organizational strategies.

learning review

3. What is the meaning of an organization's mission?
4. What is the difference between an organization's business and its goals?

通过市场仪表盘跟踪战略绩效
Tracking Strategic Performance with Marketing Dashboards

LO3

Although marketing managers can set strategic directions for their organizations, how do they know if they are making progress in getting there? One answer is to measure performance by using marketing dashboards.

Car Dashboards and Marketing Dashboards A **marketing dashboard** is the visual computer display of the essential information related to achieving a marketing objective. Often, it is an Internet-based display with real-time information and active hyperlinks to provide further detail. An example is when a chief marketing officer (CMO) wants to see daily what the effect of a new TV advertising campaign is on a product's sales. This also increases the CMO's accountability in using marketing resources effectively.

The idea of a marketing dashboard really comes from that of a car's dashboard. On a car's dashboard we glance at the fuel gauge and take action when our gas is getting low. With a marketing dashboard, a marketing manager glances at a

perception 感知（能力）; condition（某事完成或发生的）环境，条件；dashboard 仪表板，仪表盘。

FIGURE 2–3
An effective marketing dashboard, like this one from Oracle, helps managers assess a business situation at a glance.

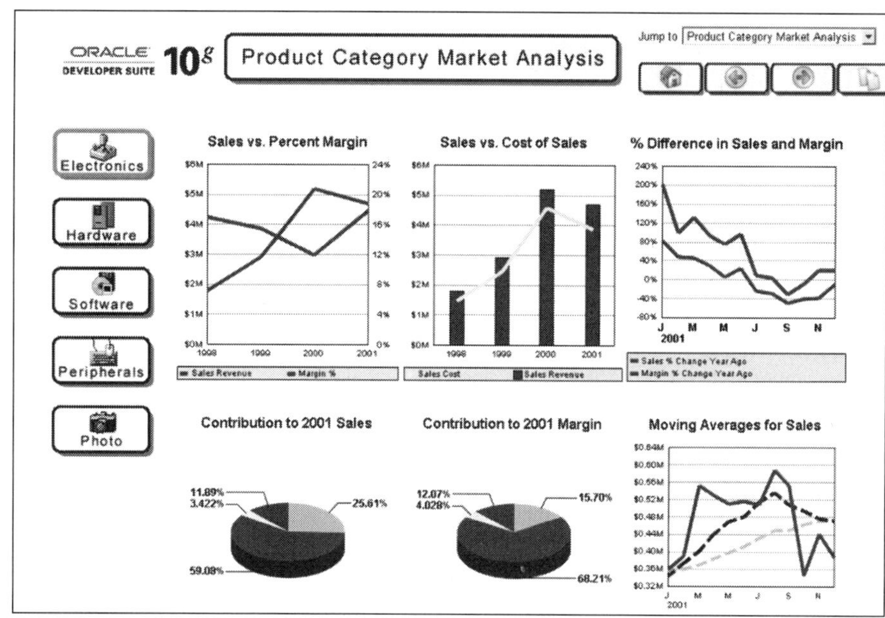

graph or table and makes a decision whether to take action or to analyze the problem further.

Dashboards, Metrics, and Plans The marketing dashboard of Oracle, a large software firm, appears in Figure 2–3. It shows graphic displays of key performance measures of a product category such as sales versus cost of sales. Each variable in a marketing dashboard is a **marketing metric**, which is a measure of the quantitative value or trend of a marketing activity or result. The choice of which marketing metrics to display is critical for a busy marketing manager, who can be overwhelmed with too much or with inappropriate information.

Dashboard designers take great care to show graphs and tables in easy-to-understand formats to enable clear interpretation at a glance. The Oracle marketing dashboard, in Figure 2–3 presents several marketing metrics on the computer screen. The three-step "challenge-findings-action" format in the Using Marketing Dashboards box for Ben & Jerry's on the next page is the one used throughout the textbook. This format stresses the importance of using marketing dashboards and the metrics contained within them to produce effective marketing strategy and program actions. The Ben & Jerry's dashboard shows that both its dollar sales and dollar market share grew from 2008 to 2009.

Most organizations tie the marketing metrics they track in their marketing dashboards to the quantitative objectives established in their **marketing plan**, which is a road map for the marketing activities of an organization for a specified future time period, such as one year or five years. The planning phase of the strategic marketing process (discussed later in this chapter) usually results in a marketing plan that sets the direction for the marketing activities of an organization.

---

graphic 图表；interpretation 解释，说明，阐明；guideline 指导方针，指导原则。

Using Marketing Dashboards

How Well Is Ben & Jerry's Doing?

As the marketing manager for Ben & Jerry's, you have been asked to provide a snapshot of the firm's total super-premium ice cream product line performance for the United States. You choose the following marketing metrics: dollar sales and dollar market share.

Your Challenge Information Resources, Inc. (IRI), provides scanner data from grocery stores and other retailers. It has just sent you a report showing that the total ice cream sales for 2009 were $25 billion. Of that total, 5 percent or $1.25 billion (0.05 × $25 billion) comprises the super-premium category—the segment of the market that Ben & Jerry's competes in. Internal company data show you that Ben & Jerry's sold 50 million units at an average price of $5.00 per unit in 2009.

Your Findings Each of the metrics you chose (dollar sales and dollar market share) are goals that firms such as Ben & Jerry's use to measure performance. They can be calculated for 2009 using simple formulas and displayed on the Ben & Jerry's marketing dashboard as follows:

Dollar sales ($) = Average price × Quantity sold
= $5.00 × 50 million units
= $250 million

$$\text{Dollar market share (\%)} = \frac{\text{Ben \& Jerry's sales (\$)}}{\text{Total industry sales (\$)}} = \frac{\$250 \text{ million}}{\$1.25 \text{ billion}} = 0.20 \text{ or } 20\%$$

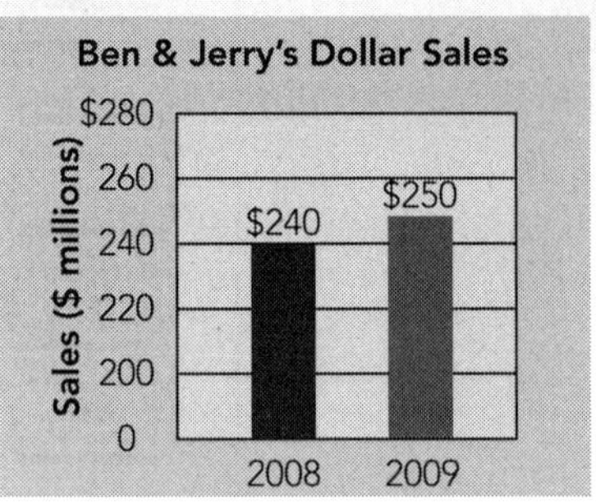

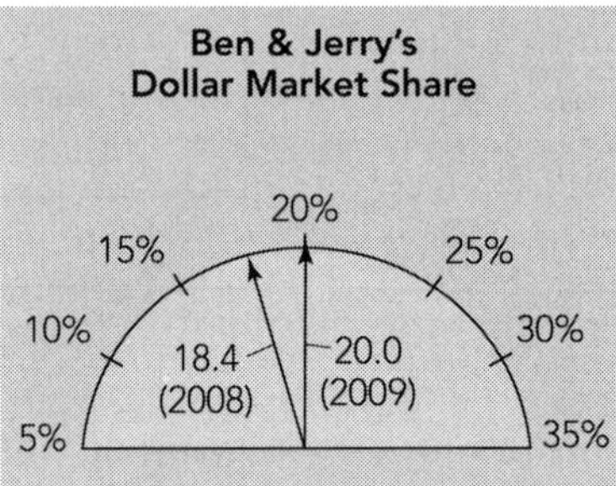

Your dashboard displays show that from 2008 to 2009 dollar sales increased from $240 million to $250 million and that dollar market share grew from 18.4 to 20.0 percent.

Your Action The results need to be compared with the goals established for these metrics. In addition, they should be compared with previous years' results to see if the trends are increasing, flat, or decreasing. NOTE: Marketers also find it useful to calculate market share based on the number of units sold, if data are available.

确定战略方向
SETTING STRATEGIC DIRECTIONS

To set a strategic direction, an organization needs to answer two difficult questions: (1) Where are we now? (2) Where do we want to go?

环顾四周：我们现在何处
A Look Around: Where Are We Now?

Asking an organization where it is at the present time involves identifying its competencies, customers, and competitors.

Competencies Senior managers must ask the question: What do we do best? The answer involves an assessment of the organization's core *competencies*, which are its special capabilities—the skills, technologies, and resources—that distinguish

distinguish 区分，辨别，分清。

Lands' End's unconditional guarantee for its products highlights its focus on customers.

it from other organizations and provide customer value. Exploiting these competencies can lead to success. Medtronic's competencies include world-class technology, training, and service that respond to life-threatening medical needs. *BusinessWeek* magazine calls Medtronic "the standard setter for quality." Competencies should be distinctive enough to provide a **competitive advantage**, a unique strength relative to competitors that provides superior returns, often based on quality, time, cost, or innovation.

Customers Ben & Jerry's customers are ice cream and frozen yogurt eaters who have different preferences (form, flavor, health, and convenience). Medtronic's customers are cardiologists and heart surgeons who serve patients. Lands' End communicates a remarkable commitment about its customer experience and product quality with these unconditional words:

Guaranteed. Period.®

The Lands' End Web site points out that this guarantee has always been an unconditional one. It reads: "If you're not satisfied with any item, simply return it to us at any time for an exchange or refund of its purchase price." But to get the message across more clearly to its customers, it created the two-word guarantee. The point is that Lands' End's strategy must provide genuine value to customers to ensure that they have a satisfying experience.

竞争对手　在当今激烈的全球竞争环境中，竞争部门之间的界限变得日渐模糊。

Competitors In today's global competition, the distinctions among competitors are increasingly blurred. Lands' End started as a catalog retailer. But today, Lands' End competes with not only other clothing catalog retailers but also traditional department stores, mass merchandisers, and specialty shops. Even well-known clothing brands such as Liz Claiborne now have their own chain stores. Although only some of the clothing in any of these stores directly competes with Lands' End offerings, all these retailers have Web sites to sell their offerings over the Internet. This means there's a lot of competition out there.

成长战略：我们欲往何方
Growth Strategies: Where Do We Want to Go?

Knowing where the organization is at the present time enables managers to set a direction for the firm and allocate resources to move in that direction. Two techniques

Kodak today must make a series of difficult marketing decisions. From what you know about cameras and photos, assess Kodak's sales opportunities for the four products shown here. For some possible answers and a way to show these opportunities graphically, see the text and Figure 2–4.

Kodak digital cameras

Kodak digital picture frames

Kodak ink-jet printers and cartridges to print photos at home

Kodak film

exploiting 充分运用，发挥；competencies 能力；guarantee 保证；retailer 零售商。

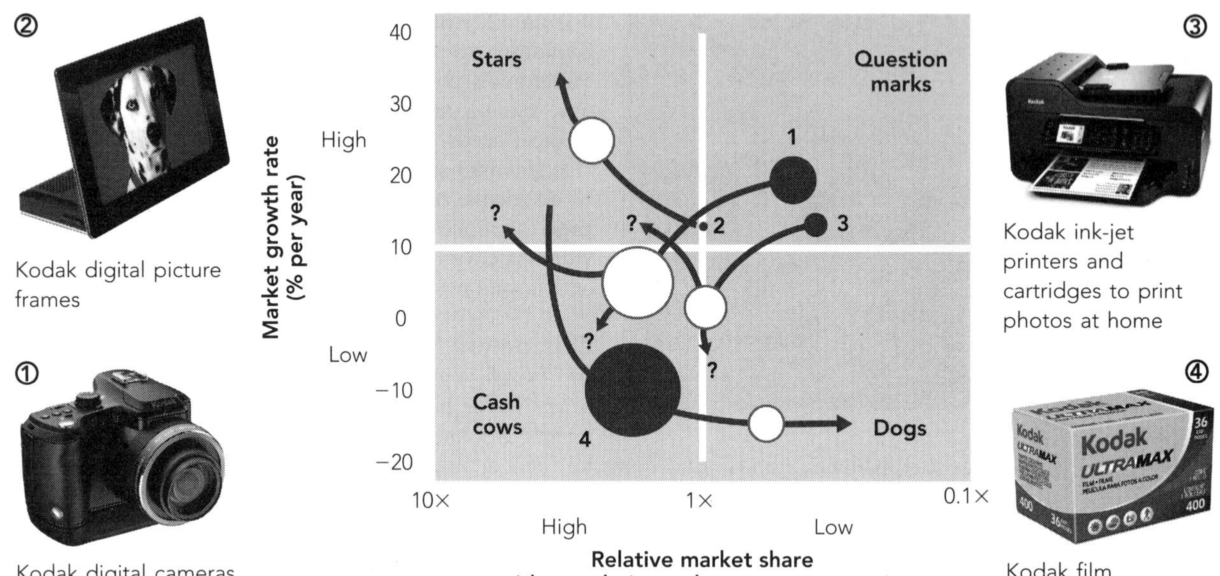

FIGURE 2–4
Boston Consulting Group business portfolio analysis for Kodak's consumer-related SBUs as they appeared in 2003 (solid red circle) and might appear in 2010 (white circle).

to aid managers with these decisions are (1) business portfolio analysis and (2) diversification analysis strategies.

Business Portfolio Analysis The Boston Consulting Group (BCG), a nationally known management consulting firm, uses **business portfolio analysis** to quantify performance measures and growth targets to analyze its clients' strategic business units (SBUs) as though they were a collection of separate investments. The purpose of the tool is to determine the appeal of each SBU or offering and then determine the amount of cash, if any, each should receive. The BCG analysis can also be applied at the offering, product, or brand level. More than 75 percent of the largest U.S. firms have used this analytical tool.

The BCG business portfolio analysis requires an organization to locate the position of each of its SBUs on a growth-share matrix (see Figure 2–4). The vertical axis is the *market growth rate*, which is the annual rate of growth of the SBU's industry. The horizontal axis is the *relative market share*, defined as the sales of the SBU divided by the sales of the largest firm in the industry. A relative market share of 10× (at the left end of the scale) means that the SBU has 10 times the share of its largest competitor, whereas a share of 0.1× (at the right end of the scale) means it has only 10 percent of the share of its largest competitor.

The BCG has given specific names and descriptions to the four resulting quadrants in its growth-share matrix based on the amount of cash they generate for or require from the organization:

- *Cash cows* are SBUs that generate large amounts of cash, far more than they can invest profitably in themselves. They have dominant shares of slow-growth markets and provide cash to cover the organization's overhead and to invest in other SBUs.
- *Stars* are SBUs with a high share of high-growth markets that may need extra cash to finance their own rapid future growth. When their growth slows, they are likely to become cash cows.

- 现金牛类是指那些通常能够产生远超过其本身产品线投资额的大量现金收入的战略业务单位。它们在缓慢成长的市场中占绝对优势份额，可以产生大量现金，以支付公司高额管理费用，并为其他战略业务单位的发展提供资金。
- 明星类是指在某个高速成长市场中占有较高市场份额的战略业务单位，为了将来的快速成长，它们需要额外的现金投入支持。当其成长速度减慢后，很可能转变为金牛类。

portfolio（业务）组合；profitably 盈利的，有利润的，赚钱的。

- 问题类是指在某个高速成长市场中占有较低市场份额的战略业务单位。它们需要大量现金投入以维持其现有市场份额，但很难实现增长。对问题类战略业务单位需要在管理上做出选择：正确的予以投资，其余的予以淘汰。
- 瘦狗类是指在某个低速成长市场中占有较低市场份额的战略业务单位。它们也许能产生足够的现金以维持自身生存，但对企业发展却无足轻重。因此，在一般情况下必须放弃瘦狗类战略业务单位，除非其关乎其他战略业务单位的发展，或出于竞争考虑，或与潜在战略联盟有一定关系。

- *Question marks* are SBUs with a low share of high-growth markets. They require large injections of cash just to maintain their market share, much less increase it. The name implies management's dilemma for these SBUs: choosing the right ones to invest in and phasing out the rest.
- *Dogs* are SBUs with low shares of slow-growth markets. Although they may generate enough cash to sustain themselves, they do not hold the promise of ever becoming real winners for the organization. Dropping SBUs that are dogs may be required, except when relationships with other SBUs, competitive considerations, or potential strategic alliances exist.

An organization's SBUs often start as question marks and go counterclockwise around Figure 2–4 to become stars, then cash cows, and finally dogs. Because an organization has limited influence on the market growth rate, its main alternative is to try to change its relative market share. To accomplish this, management decides what role each SBU should have in the future and either injects or removes cash from it.

Kodak provides an example of how new technology and changing consumer tastes force a company to convert a crisis into potential long-run opportunities. Until 2000, Kodak relied on its film for the bulk of its revenues and profits because of the billions of photos taken every year. The company made money on repeat business from traditional film sales and *not* on camera purchases. The appearance of digital cameras radically changed Kodak's business forever as film sales began to evaporate.

Four Kodak SBUs (see the solid red circles in Figure 2–4) are shown as they may have appeared in 2003 and can serve as an example of BCG analysis. The area of each solid red circle in Figure 2–4 is roughly proportional to the SBU's 2003 sales revenue. In a more complete analysis, Kodak's other SBUs would be included. This example also shows the agonizing strategic decisions that executives must make in an industry facing profound change—the situation Kodak confronted due to the arrival of digital technology.

The success of Kodak's new digital strategy and its product lines shown in Figure 2–4 depends on how millions of consumers (1) take photos and convert them into printed or online images in the coming years and (2) continue to be affected by the global economic recession. Here is a snapshot of where sales revenues were for four Kodak consumer product lines in 2003 (the solid red circles) and where they now appear headed in 2010 (the white circles).

1. *Kodak digital cameras.* In 2008, about 80 percent of U.S. consumers owned a digital camera because it is now easier to use than a film camera, is cheaper, and allows images to be uploaded and shared online. But Kodak's digital camera sales may flatten due to high household penetration, the economic downturn, and increased competition. Kodak remains No. 3 in market share behind Canon and Sony. Today more women are buying digital cameras because they are small and light. Bottom line: Kodak expects this SBU to continue to be a *cash cow*, with its new digital camera models generating mainly replacement sales.
2. *Kodak digital picture frames.* In 2007, Kodak introduced a line of digital picture frames that allowed consumers to upload, store, and view digital images. In 2008, Kodak expanded its line with more than 10 items ranging in price from $60 to $230. And in 2009, it introduced the $999 OLED (organic light-emitting diode) digital picture frame that features a high-resolution flat-panel display to present extremely sharp photo images. Global demand has exploded, and today Kodak is the market leader—clearly a *star*. By 2012, sales could approach 50 million units.
3. *Kodak ink-jet printers and cartridges to print digital photos at home.* In 2008, the ink-jet printer market dramatically changed as consumers shifted from single-purpose to multi-function machines designed to print photos, make

dilemma（进退两难的）窘境，困境；proportional 与……成比例的；strategic 战略（性）的，策略（上）的。

copies, scan images, and send faxes. Today Kodak now offers only multi-function models. Moreover, Kodak's high-quality ink cartridges make photos at half the cost of Hewlett-Packard's (HP) printers. The result: In two short years, Kodak has sold over 1 million printers. Consumers buy an average of eight ink cartridges a year. Because HP is the entrenched 300-pound gorilla in this market, the future of this *question mark* could evolve into a *star* if Kodak is able to double or triple unit sales. Or this SBU may turn into a *dog* because online printing and sharing have taken off and may soon reach $1 billion.

4. *Kodak film.* An $8 billion *cash cow* in 2003, Kodak film sales were the company's biggest single source of revenue. Now in a free fall because of digital cameras, Kodak film sales dropped to $3 billion in 2008, moving it from being a *cash cow* to a potential *dog*. Kodak stopped producing its Kodachrome slides in late 2009. Experts believe film sales will evaporate by 2012.

How can Ben & Jerry's develop new products and social responsibility programs that contribute to its mission? The text describes how the strategic marketing process and its SWOT analysis can help.

The primary strength of business portfolio analysis lies in forcing a firm to place each of its SBUs in the growth-share matrix, which in turn suggests which SBUs will be cash producers and cash users in the future. Weaknesses of this analysis arise from the difficulty in (1) getting the needed information and (2) incorporating competitive data into business portfolio analysis.

Diversification Analysis **Diversification analysis** is a tool that helps a firm search for growth opportunities from among current and new markets as well as current and new products. For any market, there is both a current product (what the firm now sells) and a new product (what the firm might sell in the future). And for any product there is both a current market (the firm's existing customers) and a new market (the firm's potential customers). As Ben & Jerry's attempts to increase sales revenues, it must consider all four of the market-product strategies shown in Figure 2–5:

- *Market penetration* is a marketing strategy to increase sales of current products in current markets, such as Ben & Jerry's current ice cream products to U.S. consumers. There is no change in either the basic product line or the markets served. Increased sales are generated by selling either more ice cream (through better promotion or distribution) *or* the same amount of ice cream at a higher price to its current customers.
- *Market development* is a marketing strategy to sell current products to new markets. For Ben & Jerry's, Brazil is an attractive new market. There is good news and bad news for this strategy: As household incomes of Brazilians increase, consumers can buy more ice cream; however, the Ben & Jerry's brand may be unknown to Brazilian consumers.

FIGURE 2–5
Four market-product strategies: alternative ways to expand sales revenues for Ben & Jerry's using diversification analysis.

Markets	PRODUCTS	
	Current	New
Current	**Market penetration** Selling more Ben & Jerry's super-premium ice cream to Americans	**Product development** Selling a new product such as children's clothing under the Ben & Jerry's brand to Americans
New	**Market development** Selling Ben & Jerry's super-premium ice cream to Brazilians for the first time	**Diversification** Selling a new product such as children's clothing under the Ben & Jerry's brand to Brazilians for the first time

cartridges 胶片盒，暗盒，墨盒；attractive 吸引人的，值得拥有（或做）的。

1. 如何将我们的资源配置到将要发展的目标业务中？
2. 如何将计划转化为行动？
3. 如何将结果与计划进行比较？如果出现偏差，是否需要新的计划？

- *Product development* is a marketing strategy of selling new products to current markets. Ben & Jerry's could leverage its brand by selling children's clothing in the United States. This strategy is risky because Americans may not see a clear connection between the company's expertise in ice cream and children's clothing.
- *Diversification* is a marketing strategy of developing new products and selling them in new markets. This is a potentially high-risk strategy for Ben & Jerry's because the firm has neither previous production nor marketing experience on which to draw to market the offerings to Brazilian consumers.

learning review

5. What is the difference between a marketing dashboard and a marketing metric?
6. What is business portfolio analysis?
7. Explain the four market-product strategies in diversification analysis.

战略营销过程
THE STRATEGIC MARKETING PROCESS

After an organization assesses where it is and where it wants to go, other questions emerge, such as:

1. How do we allocate our resources to get where we want to go?
2. How do we convert our plans into actions?
3. How do results compare with our plans, and do deviations require new plans?

To answer these questions, an organization uses the **strategic marketing process**, whereby an organization allocates its marketing mix resources to reach its target markets. This process is divided into three phases: planning, implementation, and evaluation, as shown in Figure 2–6.

FIGURE 2–6
The strategic marketing process has three vital phases: planning, implementation, and evaluation. The figure also shows where these phases are discussed in the text.

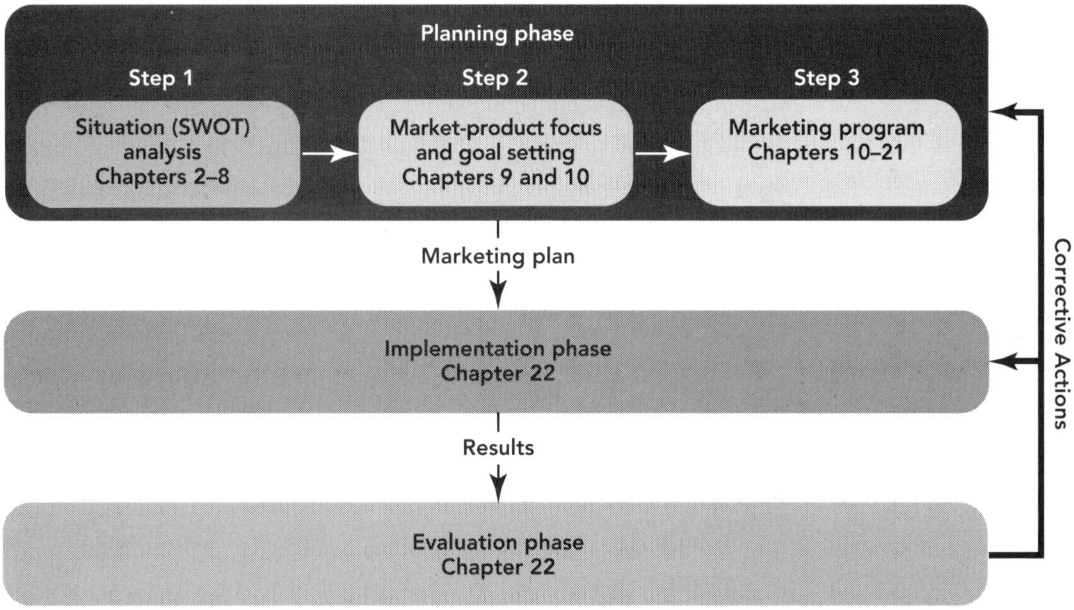

Planning phase
Step 1 — Situation (SWOT) analysis, Chapters 2–8
Step 2 — Market-product focus and goal setting, Chapters 9 and 10
Step 3 — Marketing program, Chapters 10–21

Marketing plan

Implementation phase
Chapter 22

Results

Evaluation phase
Chapter 22

Corrective Actions

leverage 利用；deviation 偏差。

战略营销过程的规划阶段
The Planning Phase of the Strategic Marketing Process

LO5

Figure 2–6 shows the three steps in the planning phase of the strategic marketing process: (1) situation (SWOT) analysis, (2) market-product focus and goal setting, and (3) the marketing program.

第一步：环境分析 **环境分析**的实质是掌握有关企业或产品近期及现在的发展状况、计划发展方向，以及影响该方向的外部因素与趋势的信息。

Step 1: Situation (SWOT) Analysis The essence of **situation analysis** is taking stock of where the firm or product has been recently, where it is now, and where it is headed in terms of the organization's marketing plans and the external forces and trends affecting it. The situation (SWOT) analysis box in Figure 2–6 is the first of the three steps in the planning phase. An effective summary of a situation analysis is a **SWOT analysis**, an acronym describing an organization's appraisal of its internal **S**trengths and **W**eaknesses and its external **O**pportunities and **T**hreats.

The SWOT analysis is based on an exhaustive study of four areas that form the foundation upon which the firm builds its marketing program:

- 识别企业所在行业的发展趋势。
- 分析企业的竞争对手。
- 评估企业本身。
- 研究企业现有与潜在顾客。

- Identify trends in the organization's industry.
- Analyze the organization's competitors.
- Assess the organization itself.
- Research the organization's present and prospective customers.

Assume you are responsible for doing the SWOT analysis for Unilever, Ben & Jerry's parent company shown in Figure 2–7. Note that the SWOT table has four cells formed by the combination of internal versus external factors (the rows) and favorable versus unfavorable factors (the columns) that identify Ben & Jerry's strengths, weaknesses, opportunities, and threats.

The task is not simply to conduct a SWOT analysis but to translate its results into specific actions to help the firm grow and succeed. The ultimate goal is to identify the *critical* strategy-related factors that impact the firm and then build on vital strengths, correct glaring weaknesses, exploit significant opportunities, and avoid disaster-laden threats.

The Ben and Jerry's SWOT analysis in Figure 2–7 can be the basis for these kinds of specific actions. An action in each of the four cells might be:

FIGURE 2–7
Ben & Jerry's: a SWOT analysis to keep it growing. The picture painted in this SWOT analysis is the basis for management actions.

Location of Factor	TYPE OF FACTOR	
	Favorable	Unfavorable
Internal	**Strengths** • Prestigious, well-known brand name among U.S. consumers • Complements Unilever's other ice cream brands • Recognized for its social mission, values, and actions	**Weaknesses** • B&J's social responsibility actions could reduce focus • Experienced managers needed to help growth • Modest sales growth and profits in recent years
External	**Opportunities** • Growing demand for quality ice cream in overseas markets • Increasing U.S. demand for 100-calorie novelties such as cones and bars • Many U.S. firms successfully use product and brand extensions	**Threats** • B&J customers read nutritional labels and are concerned with sugary and fatty desserts • Competes with General Mills and Nestlé brands • Increasing competition in international markets

assume 假定，以为，假设；specific 明确的，确切的，具体的。

- 确立优势。找出联合利华公司现有冰淇淋品牌的特定分销效率。
- 修正劣势。从其他消费品生产企业中招聘有经验的经理以促进增长。
- 挖掘机会。开发新的低脂酸奶产品线，以满足顾客对健康消费的要求。
- 避免灾难性威胁。把重点放在风险较少的国际市场上，如加拿大和墨西哥。

- *Build on a strength.* Find specific efficiencies in distribution with Unilever's existing ice cream brands.
- *Correct a weakness.* Recruit experienced managers from other consumer product firms to help stimulate growth.
- *Exploit an opportunity.* Develop new product lines of low-fat, low-carb frozen yogurts and sorbets as well as 100-calorie novelty items to respond to consumer health concerns.
- *Avoid a disaster-laden threat.* Focus on less risky international markets, such as Canada and Mexico.

Step 2: Market-Product Focus and Goal Setting Determining which products will be directed toward which customers (step 2 of the planning phase in Figure 2–6) is essential for developing an effective marketing program (step 3). This decision is often based on **market segmentation**, which involves aggregating prospective buyers into groups, or segments, that (1) have common needs and (2) will respond similarly to a marketing action. This enables an organization to identify the segments on which it will focus its efforts—its target market segments—and develop specific marketing programs to reach them.

As always, understanding the customer is essential. In the case of Medtronic, executives researched a potential new market in Asia by talking extensively with doctors in India and China. They learned that these doctors saw some of the current state-of-the-art features of heart pacemakers as less essential and too expensive. Instead, they wanted an affordable pacemaker that was reliable and easy to implant. This information led Medtronic to develop and market a new product, the Champion heart pacemaker, directed at the needs of these Asian market segments.

Goal setting involves setting measurable marketing objectives to be achieved. For a specific market, the goal may be to introduce a new product, such as Medtronic's Champion pacemaker in Asia or Toyota's launch of its Prius hybrid car in the United States. For a specific brand or product, the goal may be to create a promotional campaign or pricing strategy to get more consumers to purchase.

Let's examine Medtronic's five-year plan to reach the "affordable and reliable" segment of the pacemaker market:

- *Set marketing and product goals.* The chances of new-product success are increased by specifying both market and product goals. Based on their market research showing the need for a reliable yet affordable pacemaker, Medtronic executives set the following as their goal: Design and market such a pacemaker in the next three years that could be manufactured in China for the Asian market.
- *Select target markets.* The Champion pacemaker will be targeted at cardiologists and medical clinics performing heart surgery in India, China, and other Asian countries.
    - *Find points of difference.* **Points of difference** are those characteristics of a product that make it superior to competitive substitutes. Just as a competitive advantage is a unique strength of an entire organization compared to its competitors, points of difference are unique characteristics of one of its products that make it superior to competitive products it faces in the marketplace. For the Champion pacemaker, the key points of difference are *not* the state-of-the-art features that drive up production costs and are important to only a minority of patients. Instead, they are high quality, long life, reliability, ease of use, and low cost.
    - *Position the product.* The pacemaker will be "positioned" in cardiologists' and patients' minds as a medical device that is high

The Champion: Medtronic's high-quality, long-life, low-cost heart pacemaker for Asian market segments.

recruit 招收，招募，征召；pacemakers 心脏起搏器；promotional 促销的。

FIGURE 2–8
The 4 Ps elements of the marketing mix must be blended to produce a cohesive marketing program.

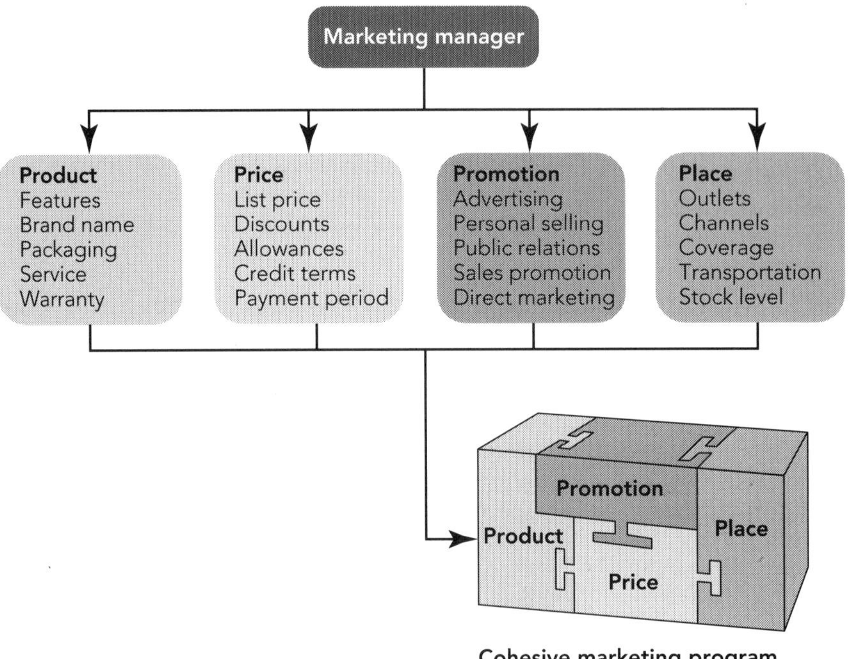

quality and reliable with a long, nine-year life. The name Champion was selected after testing acceptable names among doctors in India, China, Pakistan, Singapore, and Malaysia. So step 2 provides a solid foundation to use in developing the marketing program, step 3 in the planning phase of the strategic marketing process.

第三步：制定营销方案 第二步的活动告诉了营销经理哪些是目标顾客，企业提供的产品能够满足顾客的哪些需要——战略营销过程的“谁”与“什么”。计划阶段的第三步“怎样”则涉及方案的营销组合开发以及预算问题。

Step 3: Marketing Program Activities in step 2 tell the marketing manager which customers to target and which customer needs the firm's product offerings can satisfy—the *who* and *what* aspects of the strategic marketing process. The *how* aspect—step 3 in the planning phase—involves developing the program's marketing mix (the 4 Ps) and its budget. Figure 2–8 shows that each marketing mix element is combined to provide a cohesive marketing program. The five-year marketing plan of Medtronic's Champion pacemaker includes these marketing mix activities:

- *Product strategy.* Offer a Champion brand heart pacemaker with features needed by Asian patients.
- *Price strategy.* Manufacture the Champion to control costs so that it can be priced below $1,000 (in U.S. dollars)—an affordable price for Asian markets.
- *Promotion strategy.* Feature demonstrations at cardiologist and medical conventions across Asia to introduce the Champion and highlight the device's features and application.
- *Place (distribution) strategy.* Search out, utilize, and train reputable medical device distributors across Asia to call on cardiologists and medical clinics.

Putting this marketing program into effect requires that the firm commit time and money to it in the form of a sales forecast (see Chapter 5) and budget that must be approved by top management.

learning review

8. What are the three steps of the planning phase of the strategic marketing process?
9. What are points of difference and why are they important?

activities 活动，行动；element 要素，基本部分；combine（使）合并，（使）综合；cohesive 有黏着力的，紧密结合的。

战略营销过程的实施阶段

The Implementation Phase of the Strategic Marketing Process

LO6

As shown in Figure 2–6, the result of the tens or hundreds of hours spent in the planning phase of the strategic marketing process is the firm's marketing plan. Implementation, the second phase of the strategic marketing process, involves carrying out the marketing plan that emerges from the planning phase. If the firm cannot put the marketing plan into effect—in the implementation phase—the planning phase was a waste of time.

There are four components of the implementation phase: (1) obtaining resources, (2) designing the marketing organization, (3) developing planning schedules, and (4) actually executing the marketing program designed in the planning phase. Kodak provides a case example.

Kodak's new Zi6 pocket video camera can upload its videos to YouTube.

Obtaining Resources In 2003, Kodak announced a bold plan to reenergize the film marketer for the new age of digital cameras and prints. Kodak needed huge sums of cash to implement the plan. So by early 2009, it had sold or transformed several of its SBUs that provided over $300 billion to develop and market new products, such as the exciting Zi6 pocket video camera, which takes HD quality videos that can be uploaded to YouTube.

Designing the Marketing Organization A marketing program needs a marketing organization to implement it. Figure 2–9 shows the organization chart of a typical manufacturing firm, giving some details of the marketing department's structure. Four managers of marketing activities are shown to report to the vice president of marketing. Several regional sales managers and an international sales manager may report to the manager of sales. The product or brand managers and their subordinates help plan, implement, and evaluate the marketing plans for their offerings. However, the entire marketing organization is responsible for converting these marketing plans to reality as part of the corporate marketing team.

Developing Planning Schedules To implement marketing plans, members of the marketing department hold meetings to identify the tasks that need to be done, the

FIGURE 2–9
Organization of a typical manufacturing firm, showing a breakdown of the marketing department.

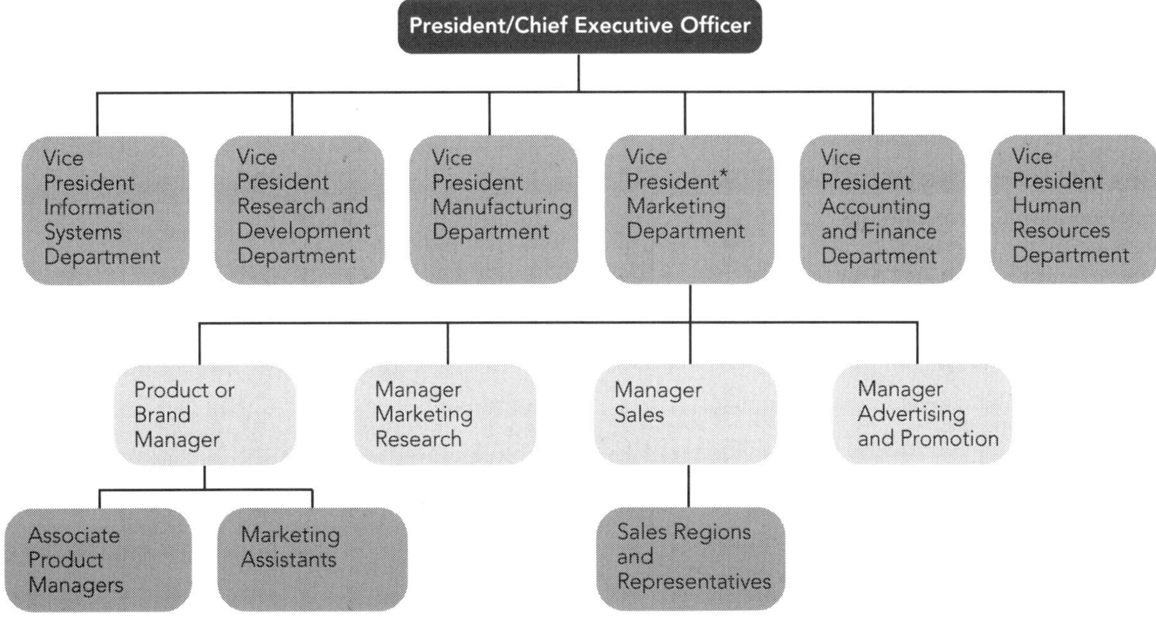

implementation 履行，实施；emerge 形成，兴起，出现；subordinate 隶属的，从属的，下级的。

time to allocate to each one, the people responsible, and the deadlines for their accomplishment. In most cases, each team member works on different parts of the plan.

Executing the Marketing Program Marketing plans are meaningless pieces of paper without effective execution of those plans. This effective execution requires attention to detail for both marketing strategies and marketing tactics. A **marketing strategy** is the means by which a marketing goal is to be achieved, usually characterized by a specified target market and a marketing program to reach it. The term implies both the end sought (target market) and the means to achieve it (marketing program). At this marketing strategy level, Kodak will seek to increase sales of digital cameras, ink-jet printers, and digital picture frames.

To implement a marketing program successfully, hundreds of detailed decisions are often required. These decisions, called **marketing tactics**, are detailed day-to-day operational decisions essential to the overall success of marketing strategies. At Kodak, writing ads and setting prices for its new lines of digital cameras are examples of marketing tactics.

战略营销过程的评价阶段
The Evaluation Phase of the Strategic Marketing Process

The evaluation phase of the strategic marketing process seeks to keep the marketing program moving in the direction set for it (see Figure 2–6). Accomplishing this requires the marketing manager to (1) compare the results of the marketing program with the goals in the written plans to identify deviations and (2) act on these deviations—correcting negative deviations and exploiting positive ones.

Comparing Results with Plans to Identify Deviations Suppose you are on a Kodak task force in 2003 responsible for making plans through 2010. You observe that Kodak's sales revenues from 1998 through 2003, or AB in Figure 2–10, exhibit a very flat trend. Extending the 1998–2003 trend to 2010 along BC shows very flat sales revenues, a totally unacceptable, no-growth strategy.

Kodak's growth target of 5 to 6 percent annually, the line BD in Figure 2–10, would give sales revenues of $16 billion in 2006 and $20 billion in 2010. This reveals a wedge-shaped shaded gap in the figure. Planners call this the *planning gap*, the difference between the projection of the path to reach a new goal (line BD) and the projection of the path of the results of a plan already in place (line BC). The ultimate purpose of the firm's marketing program is to "fill in" this planning gap—in the case

FIGURE 2–10
The evaluation phase of the strategic marketing process requires that the organization compare actual results with goals to identify and act on deviations to fill in its "planning gap." The text describes how Kodak hopes to fill in its planning gap by 2010.

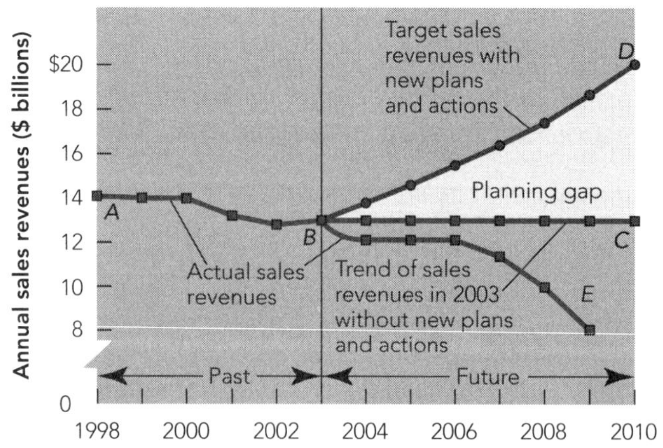

imply 暗指，暗示；tactics 战术。

To help fill in its planning gap, Kodak is pursuing opportunities for sales of digital cameras in France.

of your Kodak task force, to move its future sales revenue line from the no-growth line BC up to the challenging target of line BD. But poor performance can result in actual sales revenues being far less than the targeted levels, the actual situation faced by Kodak in 2009 (line BE), where sales were expected to be about $8 billion. This is the essence of evaluation: comparing actual results with goals set.

In this example, the Kodak task force in 2003 used trend extrapolation to project the historic trend through 2010. But as shown by the discrepancy between line BC (the trend extrapolation) and BE (Kodak's actual annual sales revenues), serious forecasting problems can occur. In this case, Kodak failed to anticipate the drastic decline in sales of its film and film cameras.

Acting on Deviations When evaluation shows that actual performance failed to meet expectations, managers need to take corrective actions. Two possible Kodak midcourse corrections for both positive and negative deviations from targets illustrate these management actions your Kodak task force might take in 2009:

- *Exploiting a positive deviation.* If Kodak's innovative digital cameras sell better than expected, Kodak might try to move quickly to offer these to international customers—such as those in France.
- *Correcting a negative deviation.* However, if Panasonic is able to surpass Kodak in global market share of digital cameras, Kodak may need to reduce prices.

Kodak also might (1) develop more feature-laden digital cameras that use its proprietary sensor technologies that improve image (picture) quality to (2) launch a new aggressive global marketing program that integrates its digital camera images into its Kodak digital picture frame.

learning review

10. What is the implementation phase of the strategic marketing process?
11. How do the goals set for a marketing program in the planning phase relate to the evaluation phase of the strategic marketing process?

LEARNING OBJECTIVES REVIEW

LO1 *Describe two kinds of organizations and the three levels of strategy in them.*
An organization is a legal entity of people who share a common mission. There are two kinds. One is a business firm that is a privately owned organization that serves its customers to earn a profit so that it can survive. The other is a nonprofit, nongovernmental organization that serves its customers but does not have profit as a goal. Most large business firms and nonprofit organizations are divided into three levels of strategy: (*a*) the corporate level, where top management directs overall strategy for the entire organization; (*b*) the strategic business unit level, where managers set a more specific strategic direction for their businesses to set value-creating opportunities; and (*c*) the functional level, where groups of specialists actually create value for the organization.

LO2 *Describe how core values, mission, organizational culture, business, and goals are important to organizations.*
Organizations exist to accomplish something for someone. To give organizations direction and focus, they continuously assess their core values, mission, organizational culture, business, and goals. Today's organizations specify their foundation, set a direction, and formulate strategies—"why," "what," and "how" factors, respectively. Core values are thc organization's fundamental, passionate, and enduring principles that guide its conduct over time—what Enron forgot when it lost sight of its responsibilities to its stakeholders. The organization's mission is a statement of its function in society, often identifying its customers, markets, products, and technologies. Organizational culture is a set of values, ideas, attitudes, and norms of behavior that is learned and shared among the members of an

historic 历史（性）的，具有重大历史意义的；aggressive 有闯劲的，积极进取的。

organization. To answer the question, "What business are we in?" an organization defines its "business"—the clear, broad, underlying industry category or market sector of its offering. Finally, the organization's goals (or objectives) are statements of an accomplishment of a task to be achieved, often by a specific time.

LO3 *Explain why managers use marketing dashboards and metrics.*
Marketing managers use marketing dashboards to visually display on a single computer screen the essential information to make a decision to take an action or further analyze a problem. This information consists of key performance measures of a product category, such as sales or market share, and is known as a marketing metric, which is a measure of the quantitative value or trend of a marketing activity or result. Most organizations tie their marketing metrics to the quantitative objectives established in their marketing plan, which is a road map for the marketing activities of an organization for a specified future time period, such as one year or five years.

LO4 *Discuss how an organization assesses where it is now and seeks to be.*
Managers of an organization ask two key questions to set a strategic direction. The first question, "Where are we now?" requires an organization to (*a*) reevaluate its competencies to ensure that its special capabilities still provide a competitive advantage; (*b*) assess its present and prospective customers to ensure they have a satisfying customer experience—the central goal of marketing today; and (*c*) analyze its current and potential competitors from a global perspective to determine whether it needs to redefine its business.

The second question, "Where do we want to go?" requires an organization to set a specific direction and allocate resources to move it in that direction. Business portfolio and diversification analyses help an organization do this. Managers use business portfolio analysis to assess its strategic business units (SBUs), product lines, or individual products as though they were a collection of separate investments (cash cows, stars, question marks, and dogs) to determine the amount of cash each should receive. Diversification analysis is a tool that helps managers use one or a combination of four strategies to increase revenues: market penetration (selling more of an existing product to existing markets); market development (selling an existing product to new markets); product development (selling a new product to existing markets); and diversification (selling new products to new markets).

LO5 *Explain the three steps of the planning phase of the strategic marketing process.*
An organization uses the strategic marketing process to allocate its marketing mix resources to reach its target markets. This process is divided into three phases: planning, implementation, and evaluation. The planning phase consists of: (*a*) a situation (SWOT) analysis, which involves taking stock of where the firm or product has been recently, where it is now, and where it is headed. This assessment focuses on the organization's internal factors (strengths and weaknesses) and the external forces and trends affecting it (opportunities and threats); (*b*) a market-product focus through market segmentation—grouping buyers into segments with common needs and similar responses to marketing programs—and goal setting, which in part requires creating points of difference—those characteristics of a product that make it superior to competitive substitutes; and (*c*) a marketing program that specifies the budget and activities (marketing strategies and tactics) for each marketing mix element.

LO6 *Describe the elements of the implementation and evaluation phases of the strategic marketing process.*
The implementation phase of the strategic marketing process carries out the marketing plan that emerges from the planning phase. It has four key elements: (*a*) obtaining resources; (*b*) designing the marketing organization to perform product management, marketing research, sales, and advertising and promotion activities; (*c*) developing schedules to identify the tasks that need to be done, the time that is allocated to each one, the people responsible for each task, and the deadlines for each task's accomplishment; and (*d*) executing the marketing strategies, which are the means by which marketing goals are to be achieved, and their associated marketing tactics, which are the detailed day-to-day operational decisions of a firm's marketing strategies. These are the marketing program actions a firm takes to achieve the goals set forth in its marketing plan.

The evaluation phase of the strategic marketing process seeks to keep the marketing program moving in the direction that was established in the marketing plan. This requires the marketing manager to compare the results from the marketing program with the marketing plan's goals to (*a*) identify deviations or "planning gaps" and (*b*) take corrective actions to exploit positive deviations or correct negative ones.

FOCUSING ON KEY TERMS

business
business portfolio analysis
competitive advantage
core values
corporate level
cross-functional teams
diversification analysis
functional level
goals
market segmentation
market share
marketing dashboard
marketing metric
marketing plan
marketing strategy
marketing tactics
mission
objectives
organizational culture
points of difference
profit
situation analysis
strategic business unit (SBU)
strategic marketing process
strategy
SWOT analysis

APPLYING MARKETING KNOWLEDGE

1 *(a)* Using Medtronic as an example, explain how a mission statement gives it a strategic direction. *(b)* Create a mission statement for your own career.
2 What competencies best describe (*a*) your college or university and (*b*) your favorite restaurant?
3 Why does a product often start as a question mark and then move counterclockwise around the BCG's growth-share matrix shown in Figure 2–4?
4 Select one strength, one weakness, one opportunity, and one threat from the Ben & Jerry's SWOT analysis shown in Figure 2–7. Suggest an action that a marketing manager there might take to address each factor.
5 What is the main result of each of the three phases of the strategic marketing process? (*a*) planning, (*b*) implementation, and (*c*) evaluation.
6 The goal-setting step in the planning phase of the strategic marketing process sets quantified objectives for use in the evaluation phase. What does a manager do if measured results are below objectives? Above objectives?

building your marketing plan

1 U sing Chapter 2 give focus to your marketing plan by (*a*) writing your mission statement in 25 words or less, (*b*) listing three nonfinancial goals and three financial goals, (*c*) writing your competitive advantage in 35 words or less, and (*d*) doing a SWOT analysis table.
2 Draw a simple organization chart for your organization.

video case 2 BP: Transforming Its Strategy "Beyond Petroleum"

"We want to get people to drive an extra block or cut across an extra lane of traffic to choose BP over its competitors," claims Ann Hand, senior vice president—Global Brand Marketing and Innovation (photo below).

BP, formerly known as British Petroleum, is one of the world's largest producers and marketers of petroleum products. Through innovative marketing and with a focus on the environment, BP has been transforming itself into a consumer-centric provider of energy products and services that are broader than just oil and gas.

KEY ELEMENTS IN BP'S "BEYOND PETROLEUM" TRANSFORMATION

Increased energy demand due to the growing economies of both the developed and developing countries as well as supply constraints have caused oil prices to rise sharply during the past few decades. This, along with the heightened awareness of global climate change in the late 1990s, created an opportunity for BP to transform its mission statement to the following:

> Our business is about finding, producing, and marketing the natural energy resources on which the modern world depends.

BP then reorganized itself primarily into two strategic performance (i.e., business) units to support its mission. These "SPUs" consist of activities related to the (1) discovery and production of oil and natural gas and (2) refining and marketing of petroleum products.

BP also identified and evaluated many opportunities to increase its sales and profits. One strategy was through acquisitions. During the late 1990s, BP invested $120 billion to add competitors Amoco, ARCO, and

Castrol to its business portfolio. BP now produces about 3 percent of the planet's oil and gas, operates in over 100 countries around the world, and serves 13 million customers per day at 24,600 retail sites, including 12,300 stations in the United States. The benefits to its stakeholders: BP global sales now exceed $360 billion.

In 2000, BP introduced a new brand identity to reflect the integrated company it had become. The BP shield and Amoco torch were replaced by a new Helios logo that more appropriately reflects BP's corporate and retail brand image as a green, environmentally friendly company. Because a brand image communicates the brand's essence—an emotional tie between the company and its customers—it provides confidence to customers: They know they can get high-quality gas, conveniently purchase food and beverages, and travel onwards refreshed. Thus, BP is not just about gasoline—it goes "beyond petroleum."

Within its refining and marketing SPU, BP sells gasoline at its branded retail gas stations, which include the BP, Amoco Ultimate, Wild Bean Café, BP Connect, and BP Express brands (eastern United States) and the ARCO and *am/pm* brands (western United States). In the near term, BP's retail strategy will focus on high-growth metropolitan areas in the United States through new and franchised service stations. In the long term, BP plans to transform the retail gasoline landscape with its new Helios House and Helios Power strategies.

BP'S FOUR CORE VALUES

BP specifies four core values to express the way the organization does business and help translate the mission into practical action:

- *Progressive:* BP is always looking for new and better ways to conduct business. It has developed a relationship with Ford to build hydrogen vehicles and fueling stations in California, Michigan, and elsewhere. BP also has reformulated its BP Amoco Ultimate fuel to reduce air pollutants.
- *Innovative:* Through the creative approaches of employees, and the development and application of cutting-edge drilling technology, BP seeks breakthrough solutions for its customers.
- *Green:* BP is committed to environmental leadership—the proactive and responsible treatment of the planet's natural resources and developing lower carbon emission energy sources. As a result, BP now stores its gasoline in double-skinned tanks to prevent spills and leaks.
- *Performance-driven:* BP sets the global standards of performance on financial and environmental dimensions, as well as safety, growth, and customer and employee satisfaction.

HELIOS HOUSE: TRANSFORMING BP'S GASOLINE RETAILING

Since 1977, the percentage of gasoline stations in the United States that also contain a convenience store has gone from 5 percent to more than 50 percent. To support the demand for convenience store offerings, BP developed a very successful convenience store concept called *am/pm*. This branded offering was created and tested on ARCO sites in the western United States; in the future, *am/pm* will partner with the BP retail brand and penetrate the eastern United States.

Currently, the *am/pm* stores sell both fuel and more than 2,000 convenience items (snacks, beverages, necessities, etc.). Sales from the more than 1,000 *am/pm* stores now exceed $6 billion; both the number and sales revenues are expected to grow significantly during the next several years as BP transforms many of its existing gas stations into *am/pm* stores.

In early 2007, BP launched a two-part strategy to change the way consumers think about its gas stations. One part was Helios House, a new-look gasoline station located in Los Angeles that will serve as a living laboratory to test ideas in a real environment (photo below). Ann Hand, who manages BP's $280 million global marketing programs, was instrumental in the planning and implementation of Helios House. Becoming operational during April 2007, Helios House was designed to be eco-friendly from the top down. The building itself was constructed from recycled, sustainable, and nontoxic materials. Moreover, its canopy has 90 solar panels to generate its own electricity. The roof is covered with grass to reduce the building's heating and cooling needs and has rain collectors to irrigate the surrounding drought-tolerant landscape. The facility also has energy-efficient lighting, using one-fifth less energy than a traditional gas station. As a result of these and other design features, Helios House became the first gas station to be certified as green by the U.S. Green Building Council.

bp

Helios House also offers customers (1) clean, well-maintained restrooms, (2) friendly "green team" employees who will not only greet customers with a smile but also check their cars' tire pressure to ensure proper inflation—which boosts gas mileage, and (3) tips on creating a green lifestyle through its www.thegreencurve.com Web site. According to Kathy Seegebrecht, BP's U.S. advertising manager, "Helios House will serve as a place where BP can have a conversation with its customers about green ideas and how its gas station can play a part in creating a better environment. It was designed to serve as a beacon to inspire the employees and franchisees through the U.S."

Helios House is *not* a prototype of BP's station of the future. However, it will be an incubator of green ideas that can be implemented among its existing and new stations. It is just too costly to replace 25,000 existing stations throughout the world. Seegebrecht concludes, "Helios House is showing us that in a more brand-conscious world, where we all want the best of everything, people might actually want a better gas station." How successful has the Helios House been? "The site has nearly doubled its fuel volumes."

HELIOS POWER: BP'S PROMOTION OF ITS GASOLINE RETAILING

The second part of BP's strategy was a promotional campaign to transform BP's retail brand image at its locations in the United States. Buying gasoline is a low involvement purchase and consumers have low expectations regarding their purchase experiences. Armed with that consumer insight, BP created and executed the $45 million Helios Power advertising and brand-building campaign, which is an extension of BP's "Beyond Petroleum" corporate campaign that began in the early 2000s. The Helios Power campaign consisted of the following marketing tactics:

- *"A little better" tagline.* BP customers can expect to receive "a little better" experience at its service stations and other retail outlets compared to those of its competitors. Hand elaborates, "In this market, a little better means a lot. People see refueling as a necessary and unpleasant chore. However, BP can be cleaner and friendlier, and that's why people will choose us rather than our competitors." And this choice will be made on an emotional basis because customers "like what we stand for."
- *Animated TV ads.* These feature a family of characters (the Lighthouse family, the Babies, and the Beeps) and a catchy tune designed to reinforce the emotional appeal of the BP brand. The TV ads aired during some of the top U.S. TV shows (*American Idol, Ugly Betty*) and also had exposure on YouTube. The purposes of the ads were to generate awareness of and an emotional connection to the BP brand and its offerings.
- *In-store give-aways.* At the launch in April 2007, environmentally friendly paper bags, T-shirts with a fun new look from the campaign, kids activity books and trading cards featuring the campaign characters, and sunflower seed packets were handed out to customers throughout the entire network of BP stations.
- *Unique Web site.* The www.alittlebettergasstation.com Web site features the "Gas Mania" interactive game, selected animations, ringtones, screensavers, a sweepstakes, and the TV ads.
- *Street teams.* BP and Ford teamed up to promote the use of BP's Ultimate gasoline in Ford's new Edge automobile. Videos featuring groups of college-aged students were created to showcase the BP brand in Florida and the ARCO brand in California.

Questions

1 (*a*) What is BP's "Helios" strategy? (*b*) How does this strategy relate to BP's mission and core values?

2 Conduct a SWOT (strengths, weaknesses, opportunities, and threats) analysis for BP's "Helios" initiative—looking forward globally to the next three years.

3 What are some ways BP could use to effectively communicate its "Helios" strategy to consumers?

4 What are the long-term benefits to (*a*) society and (*b*) BP of its "Helios" initiative?

5 Looking at BP's Helios Power marketing strategy and its "street team" marketing tactic: (*a*) What objectives would you set for this tactic? (*b*) How would you propose BP measure the results?

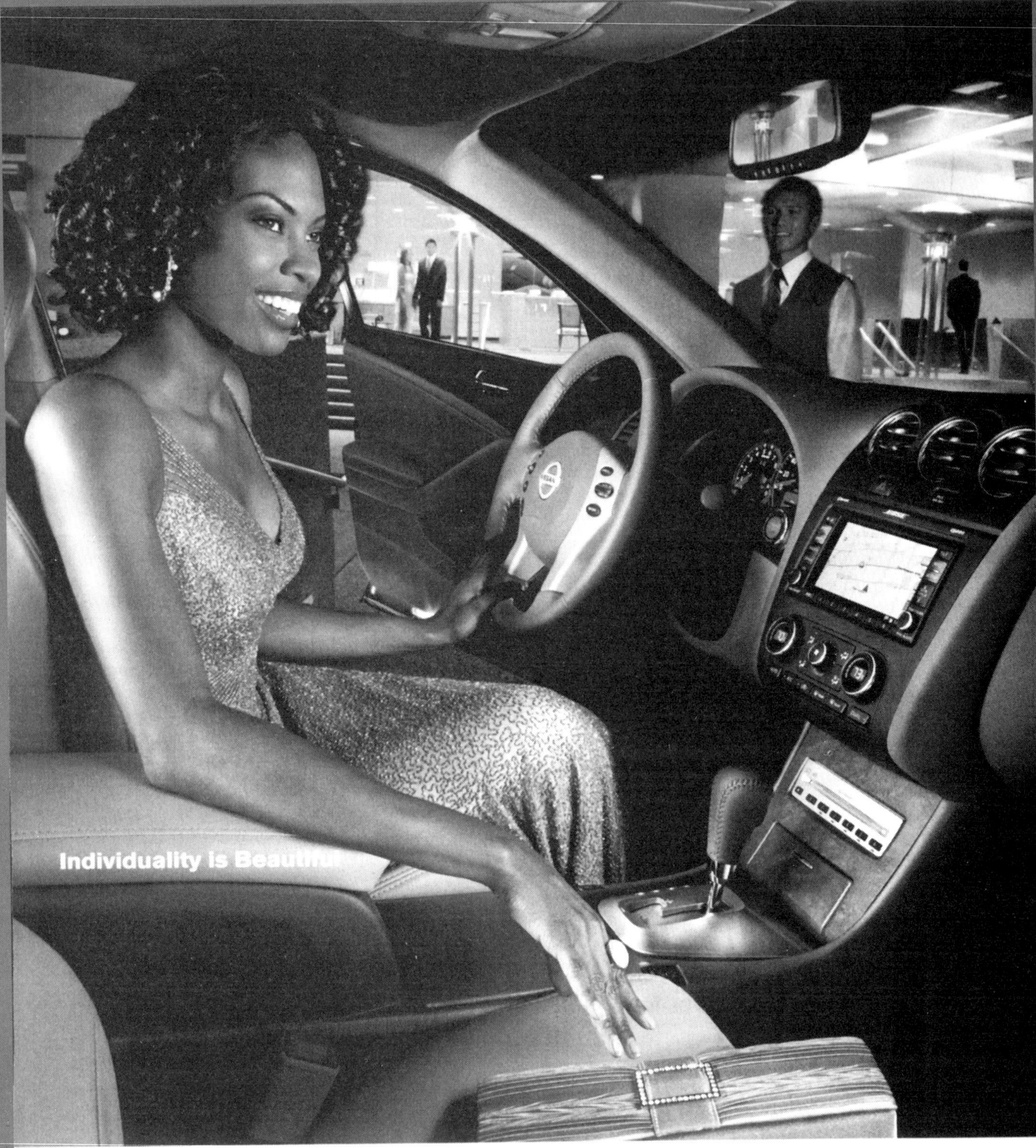

3 了解消费者行为
Understanding Consumer Behavior

LEARNING OBJECTIVES

After reading this chapter you should be able to:

LO1 Describe the stages in the consumer purchase decision process.

LO2 Distinguish among three variations of the consumer purchase decision process: routine, limited, and extended problem solving.

LO3 Identify major psychological influences on consumer behavior.

LO4 Identify the major sociocultural influences on consumer behavior.

受启发的汽车制造商知道客户重视什么
ENLIGHTENED CARMAKERS KNOW WHAT CUSTOM(H)ERS VALUE

Who buys 68 percent of new cars? Who influences 83 percent of new-car-buying decisions? Women. Yes, women.

Women are a driving force in the U.S. automobile industry. Enlightened carmakers have hired women designers, engineers, and marketing executives to better understand and satisfy this valuable car buyer and influencer. What have they learned? Women and men think and feel differently about key elements of the new-car-buying decision process and experience.

- *The sense of styling.* Women and men care about styling. For men, styling is more about a car's exterior lines and accents. Women are more interested in interior design and finishes. Designs that fit their proportions, provide good visibility, offer ample storage space, and make for effortless parking are particularly important.
- *The need for speed.* Both sexes want speed, but for different reasons. Men think about how many seconds it takes to get from zero to 60 miles per hour. Women want to feel secure that the car has enough acceleration to outrun an 18-wheeler trying to pass them on a freeway entrance ramp.
- *The substance of safety.* Safety for men is about features that help avoid an accident, such as antilock brakes and responsive steering. For women, safety is about features that help to survive an accident, including passenger airbags and reinforced side panels.
- *The shopping experience.* The new-car-buying experience differs between men and women. Generally, men decide upfront what car they want and set out alone to find it. By contrast, women approach it as an intelligence-gathering expedition. They actively seek information and postpone a purchase decision until all options have been evaluated. Women frequently visit auto-buying Web sites, read car-comparison articles, and scan car advertisements. Still, recommendations of friends and relatives matter most. Women typically shop three dealerships before making a purchase decision—one more than men. While only a third of women say that price is the most influential when they shop for a new car, 71 percent say price determines the final decision.

Carmakers have learned that women, more than men, dislike the car-buying experience. In particular, women dread the price negotiations that are often involved in buying a new car. Not surprisingly, 76 percent of women car buyers take a man with them to finalize the terms of sale.

---

automobile 汽车；exterior 外观，外部；substance 物质，材料；surprisingly 惊人地，出人意外地；finalize（尤指经与他人讨论）最后确定，最终敲定。

本章研究的是**消费者行为**，即人们购买和使用产品与服务过程中的行动，包括购前购后所发生的心理与社会过程。

This chapter examines **consumer behavior**, the actions a person takes in purchasing and using products and services, including the mental and social processes that come before and after these actions. This chapter shows how the behavioral sciences help answer questions such as why people choose one product or brand over another, how they make these choices, and how companies use this knowledge to provide value to consumers.

消费者购买决策过程和购买体验
CONSUMER PURCHASE DECISION PROCESS AND EXPERIENCE

隐藏在可见的购买行为背后的是重要的决策过程，这必须予以调查分析。一个购买者在购买某种产品和服务过程中所经历的阶段称为**购买决策过程**。这一过程分为5个阶段（见图3-1）：认识问题、搜集信息、评估方案、决定购买和购后行为。

Behind the visible act of making a purchase lies an important decision process and consumer experience that must be investigated. The stages a buyer passes through in making choices about which products and services to buy is the **purchase decision process**. This process has the five stages shown in Figure 3–1: (1) problem recognition, (2) information search, (3) alternative evaluation, (4) purchase decision, and (5) postpurchase behavior.

认识问题：感知需要
Problem Recognition: Perceiving a Need

Problem recognition, the initial step in the purchase decision, is perceiving a difference between a person's ideal and actual situations big enough to trigger a decision. This can be as simple as finding an empty milk carton in the refrigerator; noting, as a first-year college student, that your high school clothes are not in the style that other students are wearing; or realizing that your notebook computer may not be working properly.

In marketing, advertisements or salespeople can activate a consumer's decision process by showing the shortcomings of competing (or currently owned) products. For instance, an advertisement for a new generation smart phone could stimulate problem recognition because it emphasizes "maximum use from one device."

搜集信息：寻求价值
Information Search: Seeking Value

After recognizing a problem, a consumer begins to search for information, the next stage in the purchase decision process. First, you may scan your memory for previous experiences with products or brands. This action is called *internal search*. For frequently purchased products such as shampoo and conditioner, this may be enough.

外部信息的主要来源有：(1)个人来源，如消费者信任的亲朋好友；(2)公共来源，包括各种产品评比组织如《消费者报告》、相关政府部门或电视台的"消费者节目"；(3)商业来源，如从广告、公司网站、推销人员以及商店现场展示等处搜集信息。

Or a consumer may undertake an *external search* for information. This is needed when past experience or knowledge is insufficient, the risk of making a wrong purchase decision is high, and the cost of gathering information is low. The primary sources of external information are: (1) *personal sources*, such as relatives and friends whom the consumer trusts; (2) *public sources*, including various product-rating organizations such as *Consumer Reports*, government agencies, and TV "consumer programs"; and (3) *marketer-dominated sources*, such as information from sellers including advertising, company Web sites, salespeople, and point-of-purchase displays in stores.

FIGURE 3–1
The purchase decision process consists of five stages.

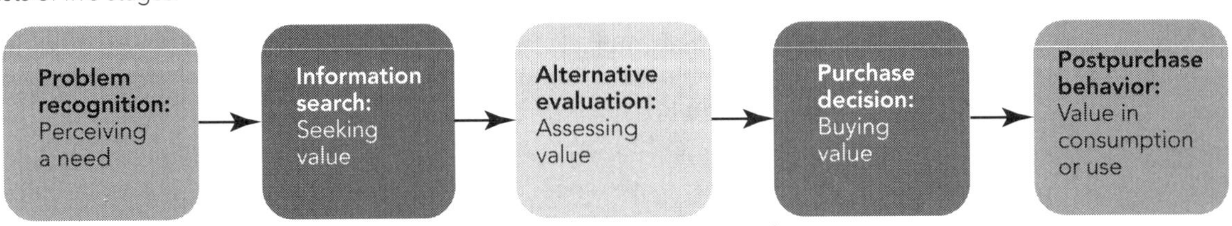

---

investigate 调查，审查；carton（装食物或饮料的）塑料盒，硬纸盒；emphasize 强调，重视。

BRAND	MODEL	RETAIL PRICE	DISPLAY	NAVIGATION	VOICE QUALITY	BATTERY LIFE	CAMERA RESOLUTION (in megapixels)
Apple	iPhone 3GS	$200	Excellent	Excellent	Fair	Excellent	3.1
BlackBerry	Storm 9530	150	Very Good	Very Good	Fair	Very Good	3.1
HTC	Touch Diamond	200	Very Good	Very Good	Fair	Good	3.1
Palm	Pre	200	Very Good	Excellent	Fair	Good	3.1
LG	Incite	80	Good	Good	Fair	Very Good	3.1
T-Mobile	G1	150	Very Good	Excellent	Fair	Very Good	3.1
Samsung	Blackjack II	50	Good	Good	Good	Excellent	1.9

Rating: Excellent, Very Good, Good, Fair, Poor

FIGURE 3–2
Consumer Reports' evaluation of smart phones

Consumer Reports
www.consumerreports.org

Suppose you consider buying a new smart phone. You will probably tap several of these information sources: friends and relatives, advertisements, brand and company Web sites, and stores carrying these phones (for demonstrations). You might study the comparative evaluation of selected smart phones appearing in *Consumer Reports*, a portion of which appears in Figure 3–2.

评估方案：价值评估

Alternative Evaluation: Assessing Value

The information search stage clarifies the problem for the consumer by (1) suggesting criteria to use for the purchase, (2) yielding brand names that might meet the criteria, and (3) developing consumer value perceptions. Given only the information shown in Figure 3–2, which selection criteria would you use in buying a smart phone? Would you use price, display quality, navigation or ease of use, battery life, camera resolution, or some other combination of these or other criteria?

For some of you, the information provided may be inadequate because it does not contain all the factors you might consider when evaluating smart phones. These factors are a consumer's **evaluative criteria**, which represent both the objective attributes of a brand (such as display) and the subjective ones (such as prestige) you use to compare different products and brands. Firms try to identify and capitalize on both types of criteria to create the best value for the money paid by you and other consumers. These criteria are often displayed in advertisements.

Consumers often have several criteria for evaluating brands. Knowing this, companies seek to identify the most important evaluative criteria that consumers use when judging brands. For example, among the evaluative criteria shown in the columns of Figure 3–2, suppose you use three in considering smart phones: (1) a retail price of $200 or less, (2) very good or excellent display quality, and (3) excellent navigation. These criteria establish the brands in your **consideration set**—the group of brands that a consumer would consider acceptable from among all the brands of which he

clarify 阐明，阐释，说明；inadequate 不充分的，不足的，不够好的；establish 建立，创立。

or she is aware in the product class. Your evaluative criteria result in three brands and their respective models (Apple iPhone 3GS, Palm Pre, and T-Mobile G1) in your consideration set. If these alternatives are unsatisfactory, you can change your evaluative criteria to create a different consideration set of models and brands. For example, the availability of a memory card or USB slot to download pictures might join the list of evaluative criteria if you take a lot of pictures and want to email them from your PC.

购买决策：购买价值
Purchase Decision: Buying Value

Having examined the alternatives in the consideration set, you are almost ready to make a purchase decision. Two choices remain: (1) from whom to buy and (2) when to buy. For a product like a smart phone, the information search process probably involved visiting retail stores, seeing different brands in catalogs, and viewing a smart phone on a seller's Web site. The choice of which seller to buy from will depend on such considerations as the terms of sale, your past experience buying from the seller, and the return policy. Often a purchase decision involves a simultaneous evaluation of both product attributes and seller characteristics. For example, you might choose the second-most preferred smart phone brand at a store or Web site with a liberal refund and return policy versus the most preferred brand with more conservative policies.

Deciding when to buy is determined by a number of factors. For instance, you might buy sooner if one of your preferred brands is on sale or its manufacturer offers a rebate. Other factors such as the store atmosphere, pleasantness or ease of the shopping experience, salesperson assistance, time pressure, and financial circumstances could also affect whether a purchase decision is made or postponed.

Use of the Internet to gather information, evaluate alternatives, and make buying decisions adds a technological dimension to the consumer purchase decision process and buying experience.

购后行为：消费或使用价值
Postpurchase Behavior: Value in Consumption or Use

After buying a product, the consumer compares it with his or her expectations and is either satisfied or dissatisfied. If the consumer is dissatisfied, marketers must determine whether the product was deficient or consumer expectations were too high. Product deficiency may require a design change. If expectations are too high, perhaps the company's advertising or the salesperson oversold the product's features and benefits.

Sensitivity to a customer's consumption or use experience is extremely important in a consumer's value perception. For example, research on telephone services provided by Sprint and AT&T indicates that satisfaction or dissatisfaction affects consumer value perceptions. Studies show that satisfaction or dissatisfaction affects consumer communications and repeat-purchase behavior. Satisfied buyers tell three other people about their experience. Dissatisfied buyers complain to nine people. Satisfied buyers also tend to buy from the same seller each time a purchase occasion arises. The financial impact of repeat-purchase behavior is signficant, as described in the accompanying Marketing Matters box.

A satisfactory or unsatisfactory consumption or use experience is an important factor in postpurchase behavior. Marketer attention to this stage can pay huge dividends as described in the text.

Firms such as General Electric (GE), Johnson & Johnson, Coca-Cola, and British Airways focus attention on postpurchase behavior to maximize customer satisfaction and retention. These firms, among many others, now provide toll-free telephone numbers, offer liberalized return and refund policies, and engage in extensive staff training to handle complaints, answer questions, record suggestions, and solve consumer problems. For example, GE has a database that stores 750,000 answers about 8,500 of its models in

alternative 可供选择的，可供替代的；dimension 方面，部分。

Marketing Matters > > > > > customer value

The Value of a Satisfied Customer to the Company

Customer satisfaction and experience underlie the marketing concept. But how much is a satisfied customer worth?

This question has prompted firms to calculate the financial value of a satisfied customer over time. Frito-Lay, for example, estimates that the average loyal consumer in the Southwestern United States eats 21 pounds of snack chips a year. At a price of $2.50 a pound, this customer spends $52.50 annually on the company's snacks such as Lays and Ruffles potato chips, Doritos and Tostitos tortilla chips, and Fritos corn chips. Exxon estimates that a loyal customer will spend $500 annually for its branded gasoline, not including candy, snacks, oil, or repair services purchased at its gasoline stations. Kimberly-Clark reports that a loyal customer will buy 6.7 boxes of its Kleenex tissues each year and will spend $994 on facial tissues over 60 years, in today's dollars.

These calculations have focused marketer attention on the buying experience, customer satisfaction, and retention. Ford Motor Company set a target of increasing customer retention—the percentage of Ford owners whose next car is also a Ford—from 60 percent to 80 percent. Why? Ford executives say that each additional percentage point is worth a staggering $100 million in profits.

This calculation is not unique to Ford. Research shows that a 5 percent improvement in customer retention can increase a company's profits by 70 to 80 percent.

120 product lines to handle 3 million calls annually. Such efforts produce positive post-purchase communications among consumers and foster relationship building between sellers and buyers.

Often a consumer is faced with two or more highly attractive alternatives, such as a BlackBerry or Samsung smart phone. If you choose a BlackBerry, you might think, "Should I have purchased the Samsung?" This feeling of postpurchase psychological tension or anxiety is called **cognitive dissonance**. To alleviate it, consumers often attempt to applaud themselves for making the right choice. So after your purchase, you may seek information to confirm your choice by asking friends questions like, "Don't you like my new phone?" or by reading ads of the brand you chose. You might even look for negative features about the brand you didn't buy and decide that the Samsung headset didn't feel right. Firms often use ads or follow-up calls from salespeople in this postpurchase behavior stage to comfort buyers that they made the right decision. For many years, Buick ran an advertising campaign with the message, "Aren't you really glad you bought a Buick?"

消费者有时候并不完全经过购买决策过程的5个阶段，他们会跳过一个或多个阶段，这取决于**参与度**，即某项购买对消费者个人、社会以及经济上的相对重要程度。高度参与的购买一般有3个特点：要购买的产品（1）比较昂贵；（2）具有很强的个性化色彩；（3）能够体现一个人的社会地位。

参与度与决策类型

Consumer Involvement and Problem-Solving Variations

LO2

Sometimes consumers don't engage in the five-stage purchase decision process. Instead, they skip or minimize one or more stages depending on the level of **involvement**, the personal, social, and economic significance of the purchase to the consumer. High-involvement purchase occasions typically have at least one of three characteristics: The item to be purchased (1) is expensive, (2) can have serious personal consequences, or (3) could reflect on one's social image. For these occasions,

alleviate 减轻，缓解；significance 重要性，意义。

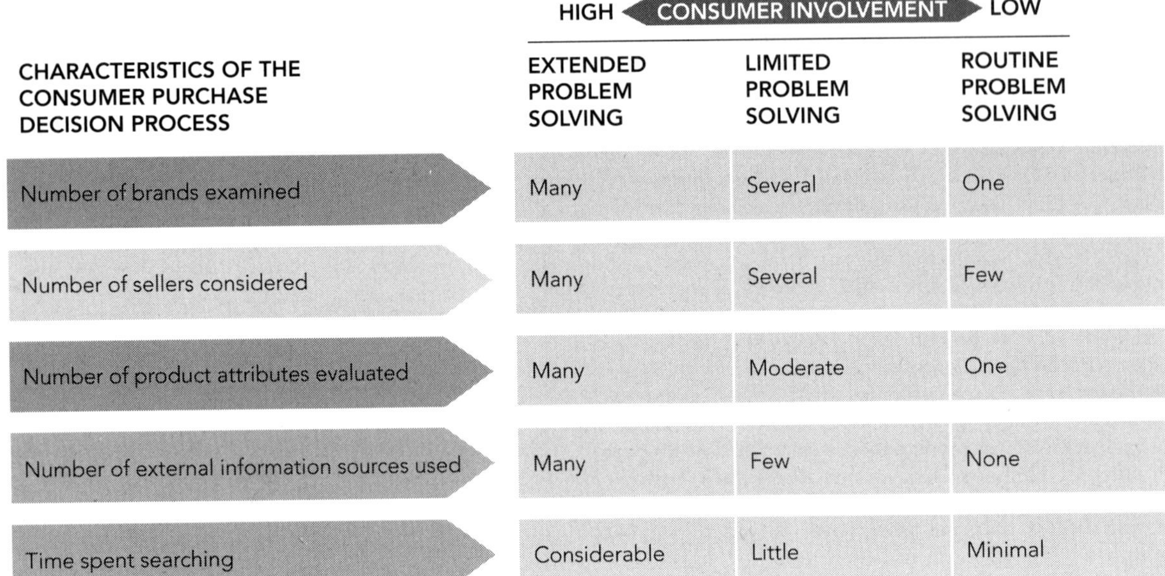

FIGURE 3–3
Comparison of problem-solving variations: extended problem solving, limited problem solving, and routine problem solving.

consumers engage in extensive information search, consider many product attributes and brands, form attitudes, and participate in word-of-mouth communication. Low-involvement purchases, such as toothpaste and soap, barely involve most of us, but audio and video systems and automobiles are very involving.

There are three general variations in the consumer purchase decision process based on consumer involvement and product knowledge. Figure 3–3 shows some of the important differences between the three problem-solving variations.

Extended Problem Solving In extended problem solving, each of the five stages of the consumer purchase decision process is used, including considerable time and effort on external information search and in identifying and evaluating alternatives. Several brands are in the consideration set, and these are evaluated on many attributes. Extended problem solving exists in high-involvement purchase situations for items such as automobiles and audio systems.

Limited Problem Solving In limited problem solving, consumers typically seek some information or rely on a friend to help them evaluate alternatives. Several brands might be evaluated using a moderate number of attributes. Limited problem solving might be used in choosing a toaster, a restaurant for lunch, and other purchase situations in which the consumer has little time or effort to spend.

Routine Problem Solving For products such as table salt and milk, consumers recognize a problem, make a decision, and spend little effort seeking external information and evaluating alternatives. The purchase process for such items is virtually a habit and typifies low-involvement decision making. Routine problem solving is typically the case for low-priced, frequently purchased products.

Involvement and Marketing Strategy Low and high consumer involvement has important implications for marketing strategy. If a company markets a low-involvement product and its brand is a market leader, attention is placed on (1) maintaining product quality, (2) avoiding stockout situations so that buyers don't substitute a competing brand, and (3) repetitive advertising messages that reinforce

toothpaste 牙膏；typically 通常，一般地；implication 暗示，暗指，含意。

What does this ad for Campbell's V8 vegetable juice have to do with getting it into a consumer's consideration set? Read the text to find out.

a consumer's knowledge or assures buyers they made the right choice. Market challengers have a different task. They must break buying habits and use free samples, coupons, and rebates to encourage trial of their brand. Advertising messages will focus on getting their brand into a consumer's consideration set. For example, Campbell's V8 vegetable juice advertising message—"I could have had a V8!"—is targeted at consumers who routinely purchase fruit juices and soft drinks. Marketers can also link their brand attributes with high-involvement issues. Hershey's does this by linking consumption of Hershey's Extra Dark™ Chocolate with improved blood pressure and blood vessel function in addition to a great taste.

Marketers of high-involvement products know that their consumers constantly seek and process information about objective and subjective brand attributes, form evaluative criteria, rate product attributes in various brands, and combine these ratings for an overall brand evaluation—like that described in the smart phone purchase decision. Market leaders ply consumers with product information through advertising and personal selling and create chat rooms and communities on their company or brand Web sites. Market challengers capitalize on this behavior through comparative advertising that focuses on existing product attributes and often introduce novel evaluative criteria for judging competing brands. Challengers also benefit from Internet search engines such as Microsoft Bing and Google that assist buyers of high-involvement products.

环境影响
Situational Influences

购买环境通常会影响到购买决策过程。有五种**环境因素**会影响购买决策过程:(1)购买任务;(2)社会环境;(3)物质环境;(4)时间条件;(5)目前状况。购买任务是进行购买决策的主要原因。

Often the purchase situation will affect the purchase decision process. Five **situational influences** have an impact on the purchase decision process: (1) the purchase task, (2) social surroundings, (3) physical surroundings, (4) temporal effects, and (5) antecedent states. The purchase task is the reason for engaging in the decision. Information searching and evaluating alternatives may differ depending on whether the purchase is a gift, which often involves social visibility, or for the buyer's own use. Social surroundings, including the other people present when a purchase decision is made, may also affect what is purchased. Consumers accompanied by children buy about 40 percent more items than consumers shopping by themselves. Physical surroundings such as decor, music, and crowding in retail stores may alter how purchase decisions are made. Temporal effects such as time of day or the amount of time available will influence where consumers have breakfast and lunch and what is ordered. Finally, antecedent states, which include the consumer's mood or the amount of cash on hand, can influence purchase behavior and choice. For example, consumers with credit cards purchase more than those with cash or debit cards.

Figure 3–4 on the next page shows the many influences that affect the consumer purchase decision process. The decision to buy a product also involves important psychological and sociocultural influences. These two influences are covered in the remainder of this chapter. Marketing mix influences are described in Chapters 7 through 14.

learning review

1. What is the first stage in the consumer purchase decision process?
2. The brands a consumer considers buying out of the set of brands in a product class of which the consumer is aware is called the ____________.
3. What is the term for postpurchase anxiety?

---

routinely 例行地，常规地，通常地；comparative 相对的，比较而言的。

FIGURE 3–4
Influences on the consumer purchase decision process come from both internal and external sources.

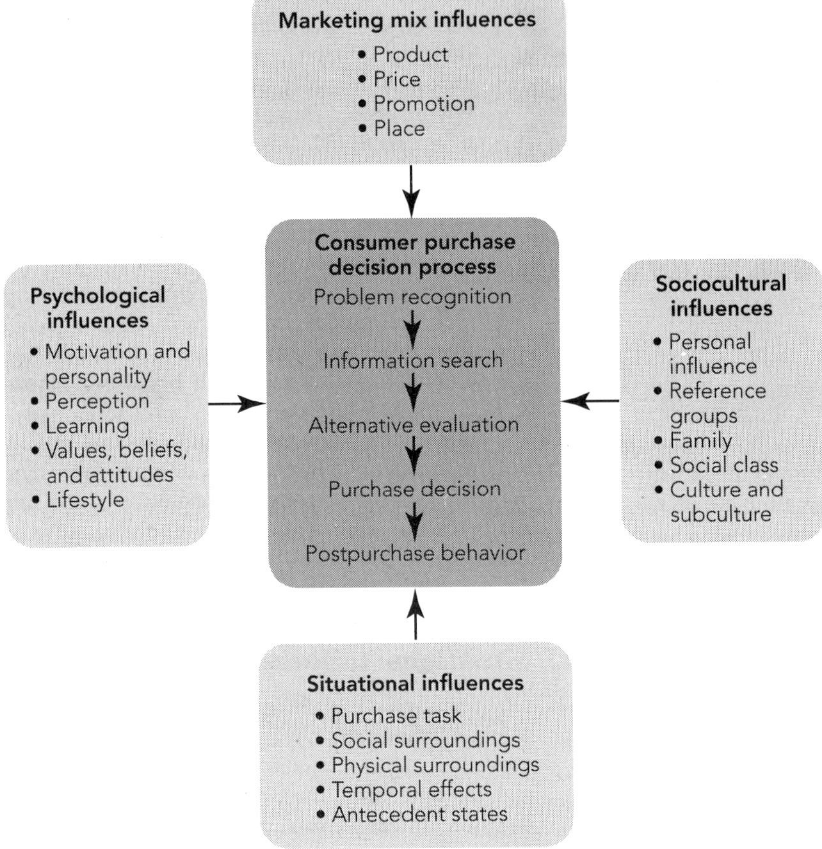

消费者行为的心理影响
PSYCHOLOGICAL INFLUENCES ON CONSUMER BEHAVIOR

心理学家帮助营销者了解消费者的购买原因以及购买方式，尤其是诸如动机、个性、感知、学习、价值观、信念、态度以及生活方式等概念对于解释购买过程、指导营销活动大有裨益。

LO3

Psychology helps marketers understand why and how consumers behave as they do. In particular, psychological concepts such as motivation and personality; perception; learning; values, beliefs, and attitudes; and lifestyle are useful for interpreting buying processes and directing marketing efforts.

动机与个性
Motivation and Personality

Motivation and personality are two familiar psychological concepts that have specific meanings and marketing implications. These concepts are closely related and are used to explain why people do some things and not others.

动机　**动机**是刺激一个人采取行动以满足自己需要的驱动力。由于消费者需要是营销观念的核心，因此营销者必须尽量唤起这些需要。

Motivation **Motivation** is the energizing force that stimulates behavior to satisfy a need. Because consumer needs are the focus of the marketing concept, marketers try to arouse these needs.

An individual's needs are boundless. People possess physiological needs for basics such as water, shelter, and food. They also have learned needs, including self-esteem, achievement, and affection. Psychologists point out that these needs may be hierarchical; that is, once physiological needs are met, people seek to satisfy their learned needs.

Figure 3–5 shows one need hierarchy and classification scheme that contains five need classes. *Physiological needs* are basic to survival and must be satisfied first.

---

motivation 动机；individual 个体的。

FIGURE 3–5
The hierarchy of needs is based on the idea that motivation comes from a need. If a need is met, it's no longer a motivator, so a higher-level need becomes the motivator. Higher-level needs demand support of lower-level needs.

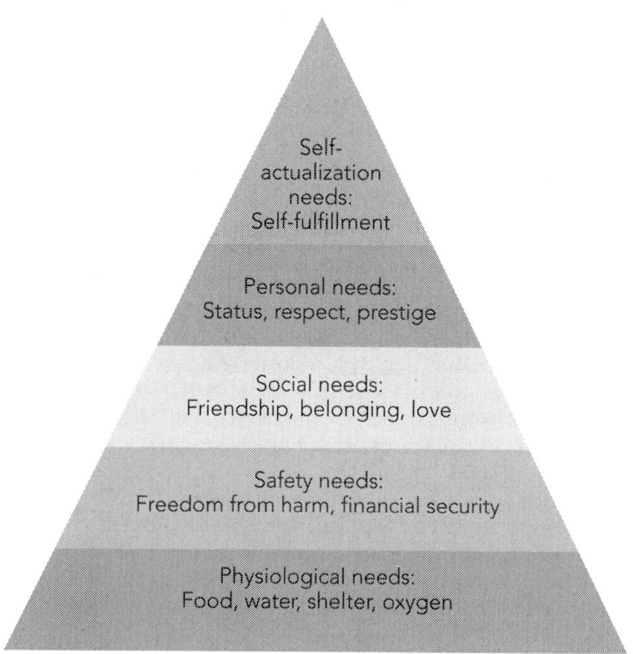

A Red Lobster advertisement featuring a seafood salad attempts to activate the need for food. *Safety needs* involve self-preservation as well as physical and financial well-being. Smoke detector and burglar alarm manufacturers focus on these needs, as do insurance companies and retirement plan advisors. *Social needs* are concerned with love and friendship. Dating services, such as Match.com and eHarmony, and fragrance companies try to arouse these needs. *Personal needs* include the need for achievement, status, prestige, and self-respect. The American Express Platinum Card and Brooks Brothers Clothiers appeal to these needs. Sometimes firms try to arouse multiple needs to stimulate problem recognition. Michelin has combined safety with parental love to promote tire replacement for automobiles. *Self-actualization needs* involve personal fulfillment. For example, a long-running U.S. Army recruiting program invited enlistees to "Be all you can be."

个性　动机是一种能够驱动消费者产生某种有目的行为的力量，而消费者的个性则起到了引导和指示行为的作用。**个性**是指一个人的一贯行为或面临同样情况时的反应。

Personality While motivation is the energizing force that makes consumer behavior purposeful, a consumer's personality guides and directs behavior. **Personality** refers to a person's consistent behaviors or responses to recurring situations.

Although many personality theories exist, most identify *key traits*—enduring characteristics within a person or in his or her relationship with others. Such traits include assertiveness, extroversion, compliance, dominance, and aggression, among others. These traits are inherited or formed at an early age and change little over the years. Research suggests that compliant people prefer known brand names and use more mouthwash and toilet soaps. Aggressive types use razors, not electric shavers, apply more cologne and aftershave lotions, and purchase signature goods such as Gucci, Yves St. Laurent, and Donna Karan as an indicator of status.

These personality characteristics are often revealed in a person's **self-concept**, which is the way people see themselves and the way they believe others see them. Marketers recognize that people have an actual self-concept and an ideal self-concept. The actual self refers to how people actually see themselves. The ideal self describes how people would like to see themselves. These two self-images are reflected in the products and brands a person buys, including automobiles, home appliances and furnishings, magazines, consumer electronics, clothing, grooming and leisure products, and frequently, the stores a person shops. The importance of self-concept is summed

multiple 多种的；fulfillment 完成，履行，实现；characteristic 特色，特点，特征。

Making Responsible Decisions > > > > > > > ethics

The Ethics of Subliminal Messages

For about 50 years, the topic of subliminal perception and the presence of subliminal messages and images embedded in commercial communications have sparked heated debate.

The Federal Communications Commission has denounced subliminal messages as deceptive. Still, consumers spend $50 million a year for subliminal messages designed to help them raise their self-esteem, quit smoking, or lose weight. Almost two-thirds of U.S. consumers think subliminal messages are present in commercial communications; about half are firmly convinced that this practice can cause them to buy things they don't want.

Subliminal messages are not illegal in the United States, however, and marketers are often criticized for pursuing opportunities to create these messages in both electronic and print media. A book by August Bullock, *The Secret Sales Pitch: An Overview of Subliminal Advertising,* is devoted to this topic. Bullock identifies images and advertisements that he claims contain subliminal messages and describes techniques that can be used for conveying these messages.

Do you believe that a marketer's attempts to implant subliminal messages in electronic and print media are a deceptive practice and unethical, regardless of their intent?

up by a senior marketing executive at Lenovo, a global supplier of notebook computers: "The notebook market is getting more like cars. The car you drive reflects you, and notebooks are becoming a form of self-expression as well."

感 知

Perception

一个人把卡迪拉克看成是成功的标志，而另一个人可能认为它是一种炫耀，这就是**感知**的结果，即个人用以选择、组织和解释信息，形成一个具有某种含义的世界图像的过程。

One person sees a Cadillac as a mark of achievement; another sees it as ostentatious. This is the result of **perception**—the process by which an individual selects, organizes, and interprets information to create a meaningful picture of the world.

Selective Perception Because the average consumer operates in a complex environment, the human brain attempts to organize and interpret information with a process called *selective perception*, a filtering of exposure, comprehension, and retention. *Selective exposure* occurs when people pay attention to messages that are consistent with their attitudes and beliefs and ignore messages that are inconsistent. Selective exposure often occurs in the postpurchase stage of the consumer decision process, when consumers read advertisements for the brand they just bought. It also occurs when a need exists—you are more likely to "see" a McDonald's advertisement when you are hungry rather than after you have eaten a pizza.

Selective comprehension involves interpreting information so that it is consistent with your attitudes and beliefs. A marketer's failure to understand this can have disastrous results. For example, Toro introduced a small, lightweight snowblower called the Snow Pup. Even though the product worked, sales failed to meet expecta-

reflects 反映，表现，显示；perception 感觉，知觉，感受，体会。

Why does Clorox tout the Good Housekeeping seal for its Fresh Step cat litter? Why does Mary Kay, Inc. offer a free sample of its Velocity brand fragrance through its Web site? The answers appear in the text.

The Clorox Company
www.freshstep.com

Mary Kay, Inc.
www.marykay.com

tions. Why? Toro later found out that consumers perceived the name to mean that Snow Pup was a toy or too light to do any serious snow removal. When the product was renamed Snow Master, sales increased sharply.

Selective retention means that consumers do not remember all the information they see, read, or hear, even minutes after exposure to it. This affects the internal and external information search stage of the purchase decision process. This is why furniture and automobile retailers often give consumers product brochures to take home when they leave the showroom.

Because perception plays an important role in consumer behavior, it is not surprising that the topic of subliminal perception is a popular item for discussion. **Subliminal perception** means that you see or hear messages without being aware of them. The presence and effect of subliminal perception on behavior is a hotly debated issue, with more popular appeal than scientific support. Indeed, evidence suggests that such messages have limited effects on behavior. If these messages did influence behavior, would their use be an ethical practice? (See the accompanying Making Responsible Decisions box.)

可感知风险 在购买某项产品或服务的过程中，感知发挥着重要作用。**可感知风险**是消费者无法预知一项购买的效果但是又相信某种产品或服务存在潜在不良后果而感受到的一种焦虑。

Perceived Risk Perception plays a major role in the perceived risk in purchasing a product or service. **Perceived risk** represents the anxiety felt because the consumer cannot anticipate the outcomes of a purchase but believes there may be negative consequences. Examples of possible negative consequences are the size of the financial outlay required to buy the product (Can I afford $500 for those skis?), the risk of physical harm (Is bungee jumping safe?), and the performance of the product (Will the whitening toothpaste work?). A more abstract form is psychosocial (What will my friends say if I get a tattoo?). Perceived risk affects information

subliminal 下意识的，潜意识的；anxiety 忧虑，焦虑，不安；financial 财政的，金融的，财务的。

search, because the greater the perceived risk, the more extensive the external search stage is likely to be.

Recognizing the importance of perceived risk, companies develop strategies to reduce the consumer's risk and encourage purchases. These strategies and examples of firms using them include the following:

- *Obtaining seals of approval:* The Good Housekeeping seal for Fresh Step cat litter.
- *Securing endorsements from influential people:* Endorsements for Promise soft spread from 9 out of 10 cardiologists.
- *Providing free trials of the product:* Samples of Mary Kay's Velocity fragrance.
- *Giving extensive usage instructions:* Clairol hair coloring.
- *Providing warranties and guarantees:* Kia Motors' 10-year, 100,000-mile warranty.

学 习
Learning

Much consumer behavior is learned. Consumers learn which information sources to consult for information about products and services, which evaluative criteria to use when assessing alternatives, and, more generally, how to make purchase decisions. **Learning** refers to those behaviors that result from (1) repeated experience and (2) reasoning.

行为学习 行为学习是当处于一种曾重复经历过的情景下时所产生的自动反应过程。关于一个人如何从重复经历中学习，需要把握 4 个核心变量：驱动、提示、反应与强化。驱动是一种能够促使人们采取行动的需要，如饥饿；提示是一种能被消费者所感知的刺激物或标志；反应是消费者为了满足驱动而采取的行动；而强化是一种回报。

Behavioral Learning *Behavioral learning* is the process of developing automatic responses to a situation built up through repeated exposure to it. Four variables are central to how consumers learn from repeated experience: drive, cue, response, and reinforcement. A *drive* is a need that moves an individual to action. Drives, such as hunger, might be represented by motives. A *cue* is a stimulus or symbol perceived by consumers. A *response* is the action taken by a consumer to satisfy the drive, whereas a *reinforcement* is the reward. Being hungry (drive), a consumer sees a cue (a billboard), takes action (buys a sandwich), and receives a reward (it tastes great!).

Marketers use two concepts from behavioral learning theory. *Stimulus generalization* occurs when a response elicited by one stimulus (cue) is generalized to another stimulus. Using the same brand name for different products is an application of this concept, such as Tylenol Cold & Flu and Tylenol P.M. *Stimulus discrimination* refers to a person's ability to perceive differences in stimuli. Consumers' tendency to perceive all light beers as being alike led to Budweiser Light commercials that distinguished between many types of "light beers" and Bud Light.

认知学习 消费者学习也可以来自非直接体验，如通过思考、推理以及心智问题解决方式。这种学习称为认知学习，是指将两种或多种想法联系在一起或根据简单观察到的他人行为的结果来调整自己的行为。

Cognitive Learning Consumers also learn through thinking, reasoning, and mental problem solving without direct experience. This type of learning, called *cognitive learning*, involves making connections between two or more ideas or simply observing the outcomes of others' behaviors and adjusting your own accordingly. Firms also influence this type of learning. Through repetition in advertising, messages such as "Advil is a headache remedy" attempt to link a brand (Advil) and an idea (headache remedy) by showing someone using the brand and finding relief.

品牌忠诚 学习对营销者而言也非常重要，因为它与习惯形成（这是常规购买决策的基础）密切相关，而习惯又与品牌忠诚密切相关。所谓**品牌忠诚**，是指对某一品牌产品抱有一种偏爱态度并持续购买。品牌忠诚源于以前行为的正面强化。

Brand Loyalty Learning is also important to marketers because it relates to habit formation—the basis of routine problem solving. Furthermore, there is a close link between habits and **brand loyalty**, which is a favorable attitude toward and consistent purchase of a single brand over time. Brand loyalty results from the positive reinforcement of previous actions. A consumer reduces risk and saves time by consistently purchasing the same brand of shampoo and has favorable results—healthy,

perceived 觉察，理解；reinforcement 增强，加强，加固；habit 习惯。

Attitudes toward Colgate Total toothpaste and Hellmann's Real Mayonnaise were successfully changed by these ads. How? Read the text to find out how marketers can change consumer attitudes toward products and brands.

Colgate-Palmolive
www.colgate.com

Hellmann's
www.hellmanns.com

态度形成 **态度**是对某一事物或某类事物所表现出的一贯喜欢或厌恶的倾向。态度的形成源于我们成长过程中习得的价值观和信念。价值观因人而异。

shining hair. There is evidence of brand loyalty in many commonly purchased products in the United States and the global marketplace. However, the incidence of brand loyalty appears to be declining in North America, Western Europe, and Japan.

价值观、信念与态度
Values, Beliefs, and Attitudes

Values, beliefs, and attitudes play a central role in consumer decision making and related marketing actions.

Attitude Formation An **attitude** is a "learned predisposition to respond to an object or class of objects in a consistently favorable or unfavorable way." Attitudes are shaped by our values and beliefs, which are learned. Values vary by level of specificity. We speak of American core values, including material well-being and humanitarianism. We also have personal values, such as thriftiness and ambition. Marketers are concerned with both but focus mostly on personal values. Personal values affect attitudes by influencing the importance assigned to specific product attributes. Suppose thriftiness is one of your personal values. When you evaluate cars, fuel economy (a product attribute) becomes important. If you believe a specific car brand has this attribute, you are likely to have a favorable attitude toward it.

Beliefs also play a part in attitude formation. **Beliefs** are a consumer's subjective perception of how a product or brand performs on different attributes. Beliefs are based on personal experience, advertising, and discussions with other people. Beliefs about product attributes are important because, along with personal values, they create the favorable or unfavorable attitude the consumer has toward certain products, services, and brands.

---

thriftiness 节俭，节约；ambition 雄心，抱负，野心。

Going Online

Are You an Experiencer? An Achiever?: Identifying Your VALS Profile

The VALS™ system run by SRI Consulting Business Intelligence has identified eight unique consumer segments based on a person's primary motivation and resources. The text provides a brief description of each segment.

Do you wish to know your VALS profile? If you do, respond to the questions on the VALS survey at www.sric-bi.com. Simply click "VALS Survey." In addition to obtaining your profile in real time, you can examine the characteristics of your and other profiles in greater detail.

Attitude Change Marketers use three approaches to try to change consumer attitudes toward products and brands, as shown in the following examples.

1. *Changing beliefs about the extent to which a brand has certain attributes.* To allay mothers' concerns about ingredients in its mayonnaise, Hellmann's successfully communicated the product's high Omega 3 content which is essential to human health.
2. *Changing the perceived importance of attributes.* Pepsi-Cola made freshness an important product attribute when it stamped freshness dates on its cans. Before doing so, few consumers considered cola freshness an issue. After Pepsi spent about $25 million on advertising and promotion, a consumer survey found that 61 percent of cola drinkers believed freshness dating was an important attribute.
3. *Adding new attributes to the product.* Colgate-Palmolive included a new antibacterial ingredient, tricloson, in its Colgate Total toothpaste and spent $100 million marketing the brand. The result? Colgate replaced Crest as the market leader for the first time in 25 years.

消费者生活方式
Consumer Lifestyle

生活方式是指体现人们如何利用其时间与资源、认为生活中什么是重要的，以及如何看待自己和周围世界的一种生活模式。对消费者生活方式的分析称为心理分析，即洞察消费者的需要和欲望。

Lifestyle is a mode of living that is identified by how people spend their time and resources, what they consider important in their environment, and what they think of themselves and the world around them. The analysis of consumer lifestyles, called *psychographics*, provides insights into consumer needs and wants. Lifestyle analysis has proven useful in segmenting and targeting consumers for new and existing products and services (see Chapter 6).

Psychographics, the practice of combining psychology, lifestyle, and demographics, is often used to uncover consumer motivations for buying and using products and services. A prominent psychographic system is VALS from SRI Consulting Business Intelligence (SRIC-BI). The VALS system identifies eight consumer segments based on (1) their primary motivation for buying and having certain products and services and (2) their resources.

According to SRIC-BI researchers, consumers are motivated to buy products and services and seek experiences that give shape, substance, and satisfaction to their lives. But not all consumers are alike. Consumers are inspired by one of three primary motivations—ideals, achievement, and self-expression—that give meaning to their self or the world and govern their activities. The different levels of resources

ingredient 要素，因素；freshness 新近的，最近的；motivation 动力，诱因。

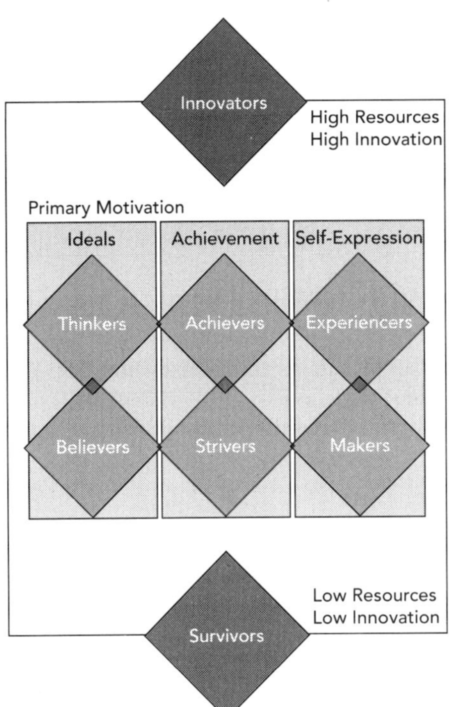

The VALS classification system places consumers with abundant resources—psychological, physical, and material means and capacities—near the top of the chart and those with minimal resources near the bottom. The chart segments consumers by their basis for decision making: ideals, achievement, or self-expression. The boxes intersect to indicate that some categories may be considered together. For instance, a marketer may categorize Thinkers and Believers together.

enhance or constrain a person's expression of his or her primary motivation. A person's resources include psychological, physical, demographic, and material capacities such as income, self-confidence, and risk-taking. Before reading further, visit the VALS Web site shown in the accompanying Going Online box. Complete the short survey to learn which segment best describes you.

The VALS system seeks to explain why and how consumers make purchase decisions.

- *Ideals-motivated groups.* Consumers motivated by ideals are guided by knowledge and principle. *Thinkers* are mature, reflective, and well-educated people who value order, knowledge, and responsibility. They are practical consumers, deliberate information-seekers, who value durability and functionality in products over styling and newness. *Believers*, with fewer resources, are conservative, conventional people with concrete beliefs based on traditional, established codes: family, religion, community, and the nation. They choose familiar products and brands, favor American-made products, and are generally brand loyal.
- *Achievement-motivated groups.* Consumers motivated by achievement look for products and services that demonstrate success to their peers or to a peer group they aspire to. These consumers include *Achievers*, who have a busy, goal-directed lifestyle and a deep commitment to career and family. Image is important to them. They favor established, prestige products and services and are interested in time-saving devices given their hectic schedules. *Strivers* are trendy, fun-loving, and less self-confident than Achievers. They also have lower levels of education and household income. Money defines success for them. They favor stylish products and are as impulsive as their financial circumstances permit.
- *Self-expression-motivated groups.* Consumers motivated by self-expression desire social or physical activity, variety, and risk. *Experiencers* are young, enthusiastic, and impulsive consumers who become excited about new possibilities but are equally quick to cool. They savor the new, the offbeat, and the risky. Their energy finds an outlet in exercise, sports, outdoor recreation, and social activities. Much of their income is spent on fashion items, entertainment, and socializing and particularly on looking good and having the latest things. *Makers*, with fewer resources, express themselves and experience the world by working on it—raising children or fixing a car. They are practical people who have constructive skills, value self-sufficiency, and are unimpressed by material possessions except those with a practical or functional purpose.
- *High- and low-resource groups.* Two segments stand apart. *Innovators* are successful, sophisticated, take-charge people with high self-esteem and abundant resources of all kinds. Image is important to them, not as evidence of power or status, but as an expression of cultivated tastes, independence, and character. They are receptive to new ideas and technologies. Their lives are characterized by variety. *Survivors*, with the least resources of any segment, focus on meeting basic needs (safety and security) rather than fulfilling desires. They represent a modest market for most products and services and are loyal to favorite brands, especially if they can be purchased at a discount.

Each of these segments exhibits unique media preferences. Experiencers and Strivers are the most likely to visit Internet chat rooms. Innovators, Thinkers, and Achievers tend to read business and news magazines such as *Fortune and Time*. Makers read automotive magazines. Believers are the heaviest readers of *Reader's Digest*. GeoVALS™ estimates the percentage of each VALS group by zip code.

constrain 约束，限制，强迫；deliberate 考虑，熟思，研究，讨论；prestige 声望，威望，威信；circumstance 境况，境遇。

learning review

4. The problem with the Toro Snow Pup was an example of selective ____________.
5. What three attitude-change approaches are most common?
6. What does *lifestyle* mean?

消费者行为的社会文化影响
SOCIOCULTURAL INFLUENCES ON CONSUMER BEHAVIOR

Sociocultural influences, which evolve from a consumer's formal and informal relationships with other people, also exert a significant impact on consumer behavior. These involve personal influence, reference groups, family influence, social class, culture, and subculture.

个人影响
Personal Influence

A consumer's purchases are often influenced by the views, opinions, or behaviors of others. Two aspects of personal influence are very important to marketing: opinion leadership and word-of-mouth activity.

意见领袖　**意见领袖**是指能够对他人产生直接或间接社会影响的人。

Opinion Leadership Individuals who exert direct or indirect social influence over others are called **opinion leaders**. Opinion leaders are considered to be knowledgeable about or users of particular products and services, so their opinions influences others' choices. Opinion leadership is widespread in the purchase of cars and trucks, entertainment, clothing and accessories, club membership, consumer electronics, vacation locations, food, and financial investments. A study by *Popular Mechanics* magazine identified 18 million opinion leaders who influence the purchases of some 85 million consumers for do-it-yourself products.

About 10 percent of U.S. adults are opinion leaders. Identifying, reaching, and influencing opinion leaders is a major challenge for companies. Some firms use

Firms use actors or athletes as spokespersons to represent their products, such as Cindy Crawford and Michael Phelps for OMEGA watches.

OMEGA
www.omegawatches.com

significant 重要的，有意义的；widespread 普遍的，广泛的。

Marketing Matters > > > > > > customer value

BzzAgent—The Buzz Experience

Have you recently heard about a new product, movie, Web site, book, or restaurant from someone you know . . . or a complete stranger? If so, you may have had a word-of-mouth experience.

Marketers recognize the power of word of mouth. The challenge has been to harness that power. BzzAgent Inc. does just that. Its worldwide volunteer army of over 600,000 natural-born talkers channel their chatter toward products and services they deem authentically worth talking about. "Our goal is to capture honest word of mouth," says David Balter, BzzAgent's founder, "and to build a network that turns passionate customers into brand evangelists."

BzzAgent's method is simple. Once a client signs on with Bzz-Agent, the company searches its "agent" database for those who match the demographic and psychographic profile of the target market for a client's offering. Agents then can sign up for a buzz campaign and receive a sample product and a training manual for buzz-creating strategies. Each time an agent completes an activity, he or she is expected to file an online report describing the nature of the buzz and its effectiveness. BzzAgent coaches respond with encouragement and feedback on additional techniques.

Agents keep the products they promote. They also earn points redeemable for books, CDs, and other items by filing detailed reports. Who are the agents? About 65 percent are older than 25, 70 percent are women, and two are Fortune 500 CEOs. All are gregarious and genuinely like the product or service, otherwise they wouldn't participate in the buzz campaign.

Estée Lauder, Monster.com, Anheuser-Busch, Penguin Books, Lee jeans, Arby's, Nestlé, Hershey Foods, and Volkswagen have used BzzAgent. But BzzAgent's buzz isn't cheap, and not everything is buzz worthy. Deploying 1,000 agents on a 12-week campaign can cost a company $95,000, exclusive of product samples. BzzAgent researches a product or service before committing to a campaign and rejects about 80 percent of the companies that seek its service. It also refuses campaigns for politicians, religious groups, and certain products, such as firearms. Interested in BzzAgent? Visit its Web site at www.bzzagent.com.

---

sports figures or celebrities as spokespersons to represent their products, such as actor Cindy Crawford and swimmer Michael Phelps for OMEGA watches. Others promote their products in media believed to reach opinion leaders. Still others use more direct approaches. For example, a carmaker recently invited influential community leaders and business executives to test-drive its new models. Some 6,000 accepted the offer, and 98 percent said they would recommend their tested car. The company estimated that the number of favorable recommendations totaled 32,000.

口碑　通过言谈交流而产生的对人的影响称为**口碑**。对消费者而言，口碑是最有力和最可信的信息来源，因为这些信息一般来自于比较信任的朋友。

Word of Mouth The influencing of people during conversations is called **word of mouth**. Word of mouth is the most powerful and authentic information source for consumers because it typically involves friends viewed as trustworthy. According to a recent study, 67 percent of U.S. consumer product sales are directly based on word-of-mouth activity among friends, family, and colleagues.

The power of personal influence has prompted firms to promote positive and retard negative word of mouth. For instance, "teaser" advertising campaigns are run in advance of new-product introductions to stimulate conversations. Other techniques such as advertising slogans, music, and humor also heighten positive word of mouth. Many commercials shown during the Super Bowl are created expressly to initiate conversations about the advertisements and featured product or service the next day. Increasingly, companies recruit and deploy people to produce *buzz*—popularity created by consumer word of mouth. Read the accompanying Marketing Matters box to learn how this is done by BzzAgent.

celebrity（尤指娱乐界的）名人，明星；authentic 可信的，可靠的，权威性的；deploy 有效地利用，调动。

On the other hand, rumors about Kmart (snake eggs in clothing), McDonald's (worms in hamburgers), Corona Extra beer (contaminated beer), and Snickers candy bars in Russia (a cause of diabetes) have resulted in negative word of mouth, none of which was based on fact. Overcoming or neutralizing negative word of mouth is difficult and costly. Marketers have found that supplying factual information, providing toll-free numbers for consumers to call the company, and giving appropriate product demonstrations have proven helpful.

The power of word of mouth has been magnified by the Internet through online forums, chat rooms, blogs, bulletin boards, and Web sites. In fact, Ford uses special software to monitor online messages and find out what consumers are saying about its vehicles.

参照群体

Reference Groups

参照群体是指被某一个人视为自我评价基础或个人标准来源的一群人。参照群体之所以影响消费者购买是因为他们影响着能够帮助消费者确立标准的信息、态度和渴望程度。

Reference groups are people to whom an individual looks as a basis for self-appraisal or as a source of personal standards. Reference groups affect consumer purchases because they influence the information, attitudes, and aspiration levels that help set a consumer's standards. For example, one of the first questions one asks others when planning to attend a social occasion is, "What are you going to wear?" Reference groups influence the purchase of luxury products but not necessities—reference groups exert a strong influence on the brand chosen when its use or consumption is highly visible to others.

Consumers have many reference groups, but three groups have clear marketing implications. A *membership group* is one to which a person actually belongs, including fraternities and sororities, social clubs, and the family. Such groups are easily identifiable and are targeted by firms selling insurance, insignia products, and charter vacations. An *aspiration group* is one that a person wishes to be a member of or wishes to be identified with, such as a professional society. Firms frequently rely on spokespeople or settings associated with their target market's aspiration group in their advertising. A *dissociative group* is one that a person wishes to maintain a distance from because of differences in values or behaviors.

家庭影响

Family Influence

Family influences on consumer behavior result from three sources: consumer socialization, passage through the family life cycle, and decision making within the family or household.

消费者社会化 人们借以获得必要的消费技能、知识与态度的过程称为**消费者社会化**。

Consumer Socialization The process by which people acquire the skills, knowledge, and attitudes necessary to function as consumers is **consumer socialization.** Children learn how to purchase (1) by interacting with adults in purchase situations and (2) through their own purchasing and product usage experiences. Research shows that children evidence brand preferences at age two, and these preferences often last a lifetime. This knowledge prompted the licensing of the well-known Craftsman brand name to MGA Entertainment for its children's line of My First Craftsman power tools; Time, Inc., to launch *Sports Illustrated for Kids*; and Yahoo! and America Online to offer special areas where young audiences can view their children's menu—Yahoo! Kids and Kids Only, respectively.

家庭生命周期 在生命的不同阶段，消费者的行为与购买活动也不一样。**家庭生命周期**概念描述的是一个家庭从组建到消失过程的不同阶段，每一阶段都伴随着特定的购买行为。

Family Life Cycle Consumers act and purchase differently as they go through life. The **family life cycle** concept describes the distinct phases that a family progresses through from formation to retirement, each phase bringing with it identifiable purchasing behaviors. Figure 3–6 illustrates the traditional progression as well as contemporary variations of the family life cycle. Today, the *traditional family*—

factual 与事实有关的，真实的；initiate 开始，创始，发起；aspiration 抱负，志向，渴望；fraternities 社团，团体。

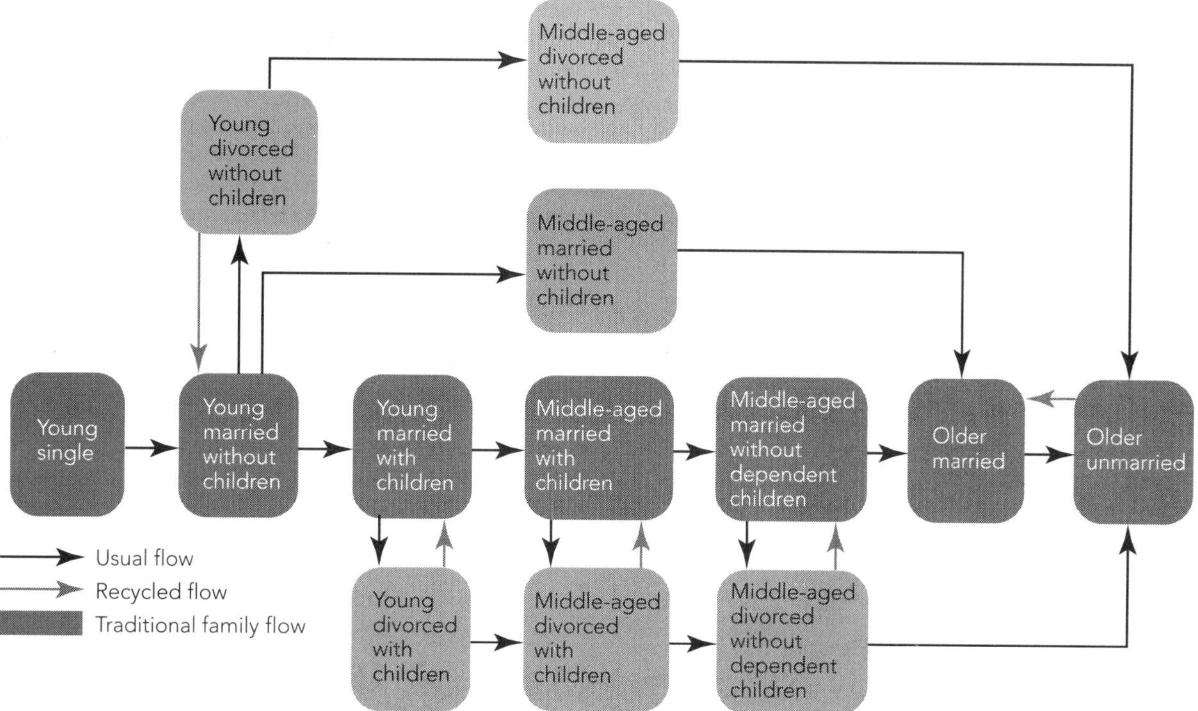

FIGURE 3–6
Modern family life cycle stages and flows. Can you identify people you know in different stages? Do they follow the purchase patterns described in the text?

married couple with children younger than 18 years—constitutes just 22 percent of all U.S. households. The remaining 78 percent of U.S. households include single parents, unmarried couples, divorced, never-married, or widowed individuals, and older married couples whose children no longer live at home.

Young singles' buying preferences are for nondurable items, including prepared foods, clothing, personal care products, and entertainment. They represent a target market for recreational travel, automobile, and consumer electronics firms. Young married couples without children are typically more affluent than young singles because usually both spouses are employed. These couples exhibit preferences for furniture, housewares, and gift items for each other. Young marrieds with children are driven by the needs of their children. They make up a sizable market for life insurance, various children's products, and home furnishings. Single parents with children are the least financially secure of households with children. Their buying preferences are often affected by a limited economic status and tend toward convenience foods, child care services, and personal care items.

Middle-aged married couples with children are typically better off financially than their younger counterparts. They are a significant market for leisure products and home improvement items. Middle-aged couples without children typically have a large amount of discretionary income. These couples buy better home furnishings, status automobiles, and financial services. Persons in the last two phases—older married and older unmarried—make up a sizable market for prescription drugs, medical services, vacation trips, and gifts for younger relatives.

家庭决策 1/3 的购买决策过程会受到家庭的影响。有两种类型的家庭决策：单方支配型与共同决策型。共同决策型指绝大部分决策是由夫妻双方共同做出的。单方支配型是指由丈夫或妻子一方负责决策。

Family Decision Making A third influence in the decision-making process occurs within the family. Two decision-making styles exist: spouse-dominant and joint decision making. With a joint decision-making style, most decisions are made by both husband and wife. Spouse-dominant decisions are those for which either the husband or the wife is mostly responsible. Research indicates that wives tend to have more say when purchasing groceries, children's toys, clothing, and medicines.

furnishing 家具，设备；prescription 处方，药方。

Husbands tend to be more influential in home and car maintenance purchases. Joint decision making is common for cars, vacations, houses, home appliances and electronics, and medical care. As a rule, joint decision making increases with the education of the spouses.

Roles of individual family members in the purchase process are another element of family decision making. Five roles exist: (1) information gatherer, (2) influencer, (3) decision maker, (4) purchaser, and (5) user. Family members assume different roles for different products and services. This knowledge is important to firms. For example, 89 percent of wives either influence or make outright purchases of men's clothing. Knowing this, Haggar Clothing, a menswear marketer, advertises in women's magazines such as *Vanity Fair* and *Redbook*. Even though women are often the grocery decision maker, they are not necessarily the purchaser. More than 40 percent of all food-shopping dollars are spent by male customers.

Increasingly, preteens and teenagers are the information gatherers, influencers, decision makers, and purchasers of products and services for the family, given the prevalence of working parents and single-parent households. Children under 12 directly influence more than $365 billion in annual family purchases. Teenagers influence another $650 billion and spend $200 million of their own money annually. These figures help explain why, for example, Nabisco, Johnson & Johnson, Hewlett-Packard, Apple, Kellogg, P&G, Sony, and Oscar Mayer, among countless other companies, spend more than $55 billion annually in electronic and print media that reach preteens and teens.

社会阶层
Social Class

社会阶层是指其成员具有相似价值观、兴趣、行为的相对持久的同类社会群体。一个人的职业、收入来源（而非收入水平）、受教育程度决定着其所属的社会阶层。

A more subtle influence on consumer behavior than direct contact with others is the social class to which people belong. **Social class** may be defined as the relatively permanent, homogeneous divisions in a society into which people sharing similar values, interests, and behavior can be grouped. A person's occupation, source of income (not level of income), and education determine his or her social class. Generally speaking, three major social class categories exist—upper, middle, and lower—with subcategories within each. This structure has been observed in the United States, Great Britain, Western Europe, and Latin America.

The Haggar Clothing Co. recognizes the important role women play in the choice of men's clothing. The company directs a large portion of its advertising toward women because they influence and purchase men's clothing.

Haggar Clothing Co.
www.haggar.com

maintenance 定期维修，检修，保养；prevalence 盛行；relatively 相当地，相对地。

To some degree, persons within social classes exhibit common values, attitudes, beliefs, lifestyles, and buying behaviors. Compared with the middle classes, people in the lower classes have a more short-term time orientation, think in concrete rather than abstract terms, and see fewer personal opportunities. Members of the upper classes focus on achievements and the future and think in abstract or symbolic terms.

Companies use social class as a basis for identifying and reaching particularly good prospects for their products and services. For instance, JCPenney has historically appealed to the middle classes. *New Yorker* magazine reaches the upper classes. In general, people in the upper classes are targeted by companies for items such as financial investments, expensive cars, and formal evening wear. The middle classes represent a target market for home improvement centers, automobile parts stores, and personal hygiene products. Firms also recognize differences in media preferences among classes: lower and working classes prefer tabloid magazines; middle classes read fashion, romance, and celebrity (*People*) magazines; and upper classes tend to subscribe to literary, travel, and news magazines.

文化与亚文化
Culture and Subculture

从属于某一大群体文化或国家文化、具有其独特价值观、观念与态度的较小群体文化称为**亚文化**。

Subgroups within the larger, or national, culture with unique values, ideas, and attitudes are referred to as **subcultures**. Various subcultures exist within the American culture. The three largest racial/ethnic subcultures in the United States are Hispanics, African Americans, and Asian Americans. Collectively, they are expected to account for one in four U.S. consumers and spend about $3.4 trillion for goods and services in 2013. Each group exhibits sophisticated social and cultural behaviors that affect buying patterns.

Why does Best Foods advertise its Mazola Corn Oil in Spanish? Read the text for the answer.

Mazola Corn Oil
www.mazola.com

Hispanic Buying Patterns Hispanics represent the largest racial/ethnic subculture in the United States in terms of population and spending power. About 50 percent of Hispanics in the United States are immigrants, and the majority are under the age of 25. One-third of Hispanics are younger than 18.

Research on Hispanic buying practices has uncovered several consistent patterns:

1. Hispanics are quality and brand conscious. They are willing to pay a premium price for premium quality and are often brand loyal.
2. Hispanics prefer buying American-made products, especially those offered by firms that cater to Hispanic needs.
3. Hispanic buying preferences are strongly influenced by family and peers.
4. Hispanics consider advertising a credible product information source, and U.S. firms spend more than $4 billion annually on advertising to Hispanics.
5. Convenience is not an important product attribute to Hispanic homemakers with respect to food preparation or consumption, nor is low caffeine in coffee and soft drinks, low fat in dairy products, and low cholesterol in packaged foods.

Despite some consistent buying patterns, marketing to Hispanics has proven to be a challenge for two reasons. First, the Hispanic subculture is diverse and composed of Mexicans, Puerto Ricans, Cubans, and others of Central and South American ancestry. Cultural differences among these nationalities often affect product preferences. For example, Campbell Soup Company sells its Casera

orientation（岗前、学前、课前等的）情况介绍，培训，训练；hygiene 卫生学，健康法，卫生；subculture 亚文化（模式）；consistent 一致的，吻合的，不矛盾的。

line of soups, beans, and sauces using different recipes to appeal to Puerto Ricans on the East Coast and Mexicans in the Southwest. Second, a language barrier exists, and commercial messages are frequently misinterpreted when translated into Spanish. Volkswagen learned this lesson when the Spanish translation of its "Drivers Wanted" slogan suggested "chauffeurs wanted." The Spanish slogan was changed to "*Agarra calle*," a slang expression that can be loosely translated as "let's hit the road."

Sensitivity to the unique needs of Hispanics by firms has paid huge dividends. For example, Metropolitan Life Insurance is the largest insurer of Hispanics. Goya Foods dominates the market for ethnic food products sold to Hispanics. Best Foods' Mazola Corn Oil captures two-thirds of the Hispanic market for this product category. Time, Inc., has more than 750,000 subscribers to its *People en Español*.

African American women represent a large market for health and beauty products. Cosmetic companies such as Bonne Bell Cosmetics, Inc., actively seek to serve this market.

Bonne Bell Cosmetics, Inc
www.bonnebell.com

African American Buying Patterns African Americans have the second-largest spending power of the three racial/ethnic subcultures in the United States. Consumer research on African American buying patterns has focused on similarities and differences with Caucasians. When socioeconomic status differences between African Americans and Caucasians are removed, there are more similarities than points of difference. Differences in buying patterns are greater within the African American subculture, due to levels of socioeconomic status, than between African Americans and Caucasians of similar status.

Even though similarities outweigh differences, there are consumption patterns that do differ between African Americans and Caucasians. For example, African Americans spend far more than Caucasians on boy's clothing, rental goods, and audio equipment. Adult African Americans are twice as likely to own a pager and spend twice as much for online services, on a per capita basis, than Caucasians. African American women spend three times more on health and beauty products than Caucasian women. Furthermore, the typical African American family is five years younger than the typical Caucasian family. This factor alone accounts for some of the observed differences in preferences for clothing, music, shelter, cars, and many other products, services, and activities. Finally, it must be emphasized that, historically, African Americans have been deprived of employment and educational opportunities in the United States. Both factors have resulted in income disparities between African Americans and Caucasians, which influence purchase behavior.

Recent research indicates that while African Americans are price conscious, they are strongly motivated by quality and choice. They respond more to products such as apparel and cosmetics and advertising that appeal to their African American pride and heritage as well as address their ethnic features and needs regardless of socioeconomic status.

亚裔亚文化群体由中国人、日本人、菲律宾人、韩鲜人、亚裔印度人以及来自东南亚和太平洋岛国的人所组成。亚裔群体所包含的人种如此之多以至于很难对他们的购买模式进行概括。对亚裔群体所做的消费者调查显示，应将个人和家庭分成两部分：同化的亚裔精通英语，受过高等教育，拥有专业与管理职位，他们的消费模式与典型的美国消费者非常相似；未被同化的亚裔，这部分人是新移民过来的，他们仍保留着本国的语言和风俗习惯。

Asian American Buying Patterns About 70 percent of Asian Americans are immigrants. Most are under the age of 30.

The Asian subculture is composed of Chinese, Japanese, Filipinos, Koreans, Asian Indians, people from Southeast Asia, and Pacific Islanders. The diversity of the Asian subculture is so great that generalizations about buying patterns of this group are difficult to make. Consumer research on Asian Americans suggests that individuals and families divide into two groups. *Assimilated* Asian Americans are conversant in English, highly educated, hold professional and managerial positions, and exhibit buying patterns very much like the typical American consumer. *Nonassimilated* Asian Americans are recent immigrants who still cling to their native languages and customs.

The diversity of Asian Americans evident in language, customs, and tastes requires marketers to be sensitive to different Asian nationalities. For example, Anheuser-

sensitivity 敏感，敏感度；consumption 消费；generalization 概括，概论，归纳。

This advertisement featured NBA basketball star Yao Ming and ran in Asian-language print publications nationwide, focusing on Asian Americans.

McDonald's Corporation
www.mcdonalds.com

Busch's agricultural products division sells eight varieties of California-grown rice, each with a different Asian label to cover a range of nationalities and tastes. The company's advertising also addresses the preferences of Chinese, Japanese, and Koreans for different kinds of rice bowls. McDonald's actively markets to Asian Americans. According to a company executive, "We recognize diversity in this market. We try to make our messages in the language they prefer to see them." Recently, McDonald's launched an advertising campaign that emphasized the company's Chicken Select product for Chinese, Vietnamese, and Korean consumers.

Studies show that the Asian American subculture as a whole is characterized by hard work, strong family ties, appreciation for education, and median family incomes exceeding those of any other ethnic group. This subculture is also the most entrepreneurial in the United States, as evidenced by the number of Asian-owned businesses. These qualities led Metropolitan Life Insurance to identify Asian Americans as a target for insurance following the company's success in marketing to Hispanics.

learning review

7. What are the two primary forms of personal influence?
8. Marketers are concerned with which types of reference groups?
9. What two challenges must marketers overcome when marketing to Hispanics?

LEARNING OBJECTIVES REVIEW

LO1 *Describe the stages in the consumer purchase decision process.*

The consumer purchase decision process consists of five stages. They are problem recognition, information search, alternative evaluation, purchase decision, and postpurchase behavior. Problem recognition is perceiving a difference between a person's ideal and actual situation big enough to trigger a decision. Information search involves remembering previous purchase experiences (internal search) and external search behavior such as seeking information from other sources. Alternative evaluation clarifies the problem for the consumer by (*a*) suggesting the evaluative criteria to use for the purchase, (*b*) yielding brand

agricultural 农业的，农用的；exceeding 超过，超出（某数量、数字等）。

names that might meet the criteria, and (*c*) developing consumer value perceptions. The purchase decision involves the choice of an alternative, including from whom to buy and when to buy. Postpurchase behavior involves the comparison of the chosen alternative with a consumer's expectations, which leads to satisfaction or dissatisfaction and subsequent purchase behavior.

LO2 *Distinguish among three variations of the consumer purchase decision process: routine, limited, and extended problem solving.*
Consumers don't always engage in the five-stage purchase decision process. Instead, they skip or minimize one or more stages depending on the level of involvement—the personal, social, and economic significance of the purchase. For low-involvement purchase occasions, consumers engage in routine problem solving. They recognize a problem, make a decision, and spend little effort seeking external information and evaluating alternatives. For high-involvement purchase occasions, each of the five stages of the consumer purchase decision process is used, including considerable time and effort on external information search and in identifying and evaluating alternatives. With limited problem solving, consumers typically seek some information or rely on a friend to help them evaluate alternatives.

LO3 *Identify major psychological influences on consumer behavior.*
Psychology helps marketers understand why and how consumers behave as they do. In particular, psychological concepts such as motivation and personality; perception; learning; values, beliefs, and attitudes; and lifestyle are useful for interpreting buying processes. Motivation is the energizing force that stimulates behavior to satisfy a need. Personality refers to a person's consistent behaviors or responses to recurring situations. Perception is the process by which an individual selects, organizes, and interprets information to create a meaningful picture of the world. Consumers filter information through selective exposure, comprehension, and retention.

Much consumer behavior is learned. Learning refers to those behaviors that result from (*a*) repeated experience and (*b*) reasoning. Brand loyalty results from learning. Values, beliefs, and attitudes are also learned and influence how consumers evaluate products, services, and brands. A more general concept is lifestyle. Lifestyle, also called psychographics, combines psychology and demographics and focuses on how people spend their time and resources, what they consider important in their environment, and what they think of themselves and the world around them.

LO4 *Identify the major sociocultural influences on consumer behavior.*
Sociocultural influences, which evolve from a consumer's formal and informal relationships with other people, also affect consumer behavior. These involve personal influence, reference groups, the family, social class, culture, and subculture. Opinion leadership and word-of-mouth behavior are two major sources of personal influence on consumer behavior. Reference groups are people to whom an individual looks as a basis for self-approval or as a source of personal standards. Family influences on consumer behavior result from three sources: consumer socialization, passage through the family life cycle, and decision making within the family or household. A more subtle influence on consumer behavior than direct contact with others is the social class to which people belong. Persons within social classes tend to exhibit common values, attitudes, beliefs, lifestyles, and buying behaviors. Finally, a person's culture and subculture have been shown to influence product preferences and buying patterns.

FOCUSING ON KEY TERMS

attitude
beliefs
brand loyalty
cognitive dissonance
consideration set
consumer behavior
consumer socialization
evaluative criteria
family life cycle
involvement
learning
lifestyle
motivation
opinion leaders
perceived risk
perception
personality
purchase decision process
reference groups
self-concept
situational influences
social class
subcultures
subliminal perception
word of mouth

APPLYING MARKETING KNOWLEDGE

1 Review Figure 3–2, which shows the smart phone attributes identified by *Consumer Reports*. Which attributes are important to you? What other attributes might you consider? Which brand would you prefer?

2 Suppose research at Panasonic reveals that prospective buyers are anxious about buying high-definition television sets. What strategies might you recommend to the company to reduce consumer anxiety?

3 A Porsche salesperson was taking orders on new cars because he was unable to satisfy the demand with the limited number of cars in the showroom and lot. Several persons had backed out of the contract within two weeks of signing the order. What explanation can you give for this behavior, and what remedies would you recommend?

4 Which social class would you associate with each of the following items or actions: (*a*) tennis club membership, (*b*) an arrangement of plastic flowers in the kitchen, (*c*) *True Romance* magazine, (*d*) *Smithsonian* magazine, (*e*) formally dressing for dinner frequently, and (*f*) being a member of a bowling team.

5 Assign one or more levels of the hierarchy of needs and the motives described in Figure 3–5 to the following products: (*a*) life insurance, (*b*) cosmetics, (*c*) *The Wall Street Journal*, and (*d*) hamburgers.

6 With which stage in the family life cycle would the purchase of the following products and services be most closely identified: (*a*) bedroom furniture, (*b*) life insurance, (*c*) a Caribbean cruise, (*d*) a house mortgage, and (*e*) children's toys?

7 "The greater the perceived risk in a purchase situation, the more likely that cognitive dissonance will result." Does this statement have any basis given the discussion in the text? Why?

building your marketing plan

To do a consumer analysis for the product—the good, service, or idea—in your marketing plan:

1 Identify the consumers who are most likely to buy your product—the primary target market—in terms of (*a*) their demographic characteristics and (*b*) any other kind of characteristics you believe are important.

2 Describe (*a*) the main points of difference of your product for this group and (*b*) what problem they help solve for the consumer, in terms of the first stage in the consumer purchase decision process in Figure 3–1.

3 Identify the one or two key influences for each of the four outside boxes in Figure 3–4: (*a*) marketing mix, (*b*) psychological, (*c*) sociocultural, and (*d*) situational influences.

This consumer analysis will provide the foundation for the marketing mix actions you develop later in your plan.

video case 3 Best Buy: Using Customer Centricity to Connect with Consumers

"So much of our business success comes down to understanding consumer behavior," explains Joe Brandt, a store service manager at one of Best Buy's newest stores. "What we do is we try to keep our ear to the railroad tracks. In essence, we listen to the customer to be able to change on a dime when a customer wants us to tailor that experience a certain way and provide certain shopping experiences and certain services.

"Consumers look at a lot of different things," Joe added. "They look at brands, shopability of the store, how easy it is to navigate the store, how pleasant the employees are, price, and how we take care of the customer." Overall there are many factors that "customers look at when they're making a purchase decision."

THE COMPANY

Best Buy is the world's largest consumer electronics retailer with 1,172 stores, 140,000 employees, and $35.9 billion in revenue. Its U.S. and Canadian market share is almost 20 percent, far ahead of rivals Circuit City, Wal-Mart, and Costco.

Best Buy operates superstores that provide a limited number of product categories with great depth within the categories. The retailer sells consumer electronics, home office products, appliances, entertainment software, and related services. In addition to its U.S. and Canadian stores, Best Buy has recently opened stores in China and has announced plans to open stores in Puerto Rico, Mexico, and Turkey. Best Buy also offers its products online through bestbuy.com, and design and installation services through Geek Squad and Magnolia Audio and Video.

Best Buy began as The Sound of Music, a small specialty audio retailer, in 1966. A tornado severely damaged one of its stores in 1981. Instead of closing the store for repairs, Dick Schulze, the owner, had a tornado sale in which more goods were brought in from its other stores and prices were slashed. The sale was so successful that it was repeated the following two years. "When the tornado hit, we decided to market to the community as a whole, and get electronics out there to everybody. We geared ourselves up to win by understanding what consumers want in technology," said Joe Brandt. In 1983, The Sound of Music changed its name to Best Buy and opened its first superstore.

The company continued to grow as the consumer electronics category exploded in the 1980s and 1990s. Based on consumer feedback, Best Buy moved away from the traditional sales approach in 1989 by eliminating commissioned sales representatives. This move was embraced by customers, but questioned by some suppliers and Wall Street analysts who thought it would reduce sales and profits. Best Buy's approach was successful at generating growth in stores and revenues. However, company expenses increased and profits declined. When growth of the consumer electronics market slowed and mass marketers such as Wal-Mart, Target, Costco, and Sam's Club became competitors, Best Buy considered changes to its approach.

Best Buy began to differentiate itself from the mass marketers by offering more services, delivery, and installation. Instead of selling individual products, it concentrated on selling entire systems. The acquisition of Geek Squad to provide in-store, home, and office computer services and Magnolia Home Theater to provide complete audio and home theater systems reflect these changes. These additions significantly increased profit and insulated the company from discount store competition. Responding to customer needs and competitive changes was an important part of Best Buy's strategy.

ADOPTING "CUSTOMER CENTRICITY" AT BEST BUY

When Dick Schulze stepped down as CEO, his successor, Brad Anderson, began looking for new ideas to continue the company's growth. He invited Larry Seldon of Columbia University to present his theory of "customer centricity." Seldon's theory suggested that some customers account for a disproportionate amount of a firm's sales and profits. Anderson adapted the theory to try to understand the needs and behaviors of specific types of customers, or segments. Initial research identified five segments:

- **Barry:** The affluent professional who wants the best technology and entertainment, and who demands excellent service.
- **Jill:** The prototypical "soccer mom" who is a busy suburban mom who wants to enrich her children's lives with technology and entertainment.
- **Carrie and Buzz:** The "early adopter," active, younger customer who wants the latest technology and entertainment.
- **Ray:** The "practical adopter" who is a family man who wants technology that improves his life through technology and entertainment.
- **Small business:** The customer who runs his or her own business and has specific needs relating to growing sales and increasing the profitability of the business.

Best Buy used "lab" stores to test product offerings, store designs, and service offerings targeted at each segment. Successful offerings and designs were then expanded to a larger number of pilot stores that would undergo significant physical changes and require substantial new training of sales associates. The cost of applying customer centricity to a store was often as much as $600,000. Early results were impressive as customer centricity stores reported sales much higher than the chain average. As Best Buy began rapid conversion of hundreds of Best Buy stores to the centricity formats, however, expenses increased and profits declined.

THE ISSUES

The impact of Best Buy's new approach on profitability led the company to continue to adapt its ideas about customers. One consideration, for example, was that the "Jill" segment should be broadened to include all females. Research showed that women spend $68 billion on consumer electronics each year and influence 89 percent of all purchases. Unfortunately, females did not embrace the Best Buy experience, largely because its stores were male-oriented in merchandise, appearance, and staffing. "Men and women shop very differently," observes Brandt. Men "typically love the technology" and they like to "play with it" while women are "looking for a knowledgeable person who can answer their questions in a simple manner." To address this problem Best Buy began to implement many changes that would make Best Buy *the* place for women to shop (and work!).

Today, Best Buy is trying a variety of new approaches. Its stores, for example, are being changed to be more appealing to women. Store layout has been changed to include larger aisles, softer colors, less noise, and reduced visibility of boxes and extra stock. In addition, Best Buy now offers women, and all customers, a personal shopping assistant who will walk a customer through the store, demonstrate how the products function, and arrange for delivery and installation after the sale. Best Buy has also created rooms that resemble a home in the store to show customers exactly how the products will look when they are installed. According to Brandt, "We try to personalize the experience as much as possible, and we really try to build a relationship. Once we do that we have the opportunity to really listen and answer questions that customers have." Best Buy is undertaking other initiatives as well. It created the Women's Leadership Forum (WOLF) to develop female leaders within the company. Early results have yielded an increase in applications and a decline in turnover. Overall, these changes appear to be working. Best Buy has observed an increase in its female market share in consumer electronics!

In the future Best Buy's customer centricity efforts will continue to focus on understanding consumer behavior and improving the customer experience. Brandt explains: "Customer centricity, in simple terms, is listening to the customer, putting the customer at the forefront of everything we do. That is, whatever shopping experience that they are looking for, we gear our company and our structure to satisfy that need as much as possible."

Questions

1 How has an understanding of consumer behavior helped Best Buy grow from a small specialty audio retailer to the world's largest consumer electronics retailer?

2 What were the advantages and disadvantages of using "customer centricity" to create five segments of Best Buy customers?

3 How are men and women different in their consumer behavior when they are shopping in a Best Buy store?

4 What are two or three (*a*) objective evaluative criteria and (*b*) subjective evaluative criteria female consumers use when shopping for electronics at Best Buy?

5 What challenges does Best Buy face in the future?

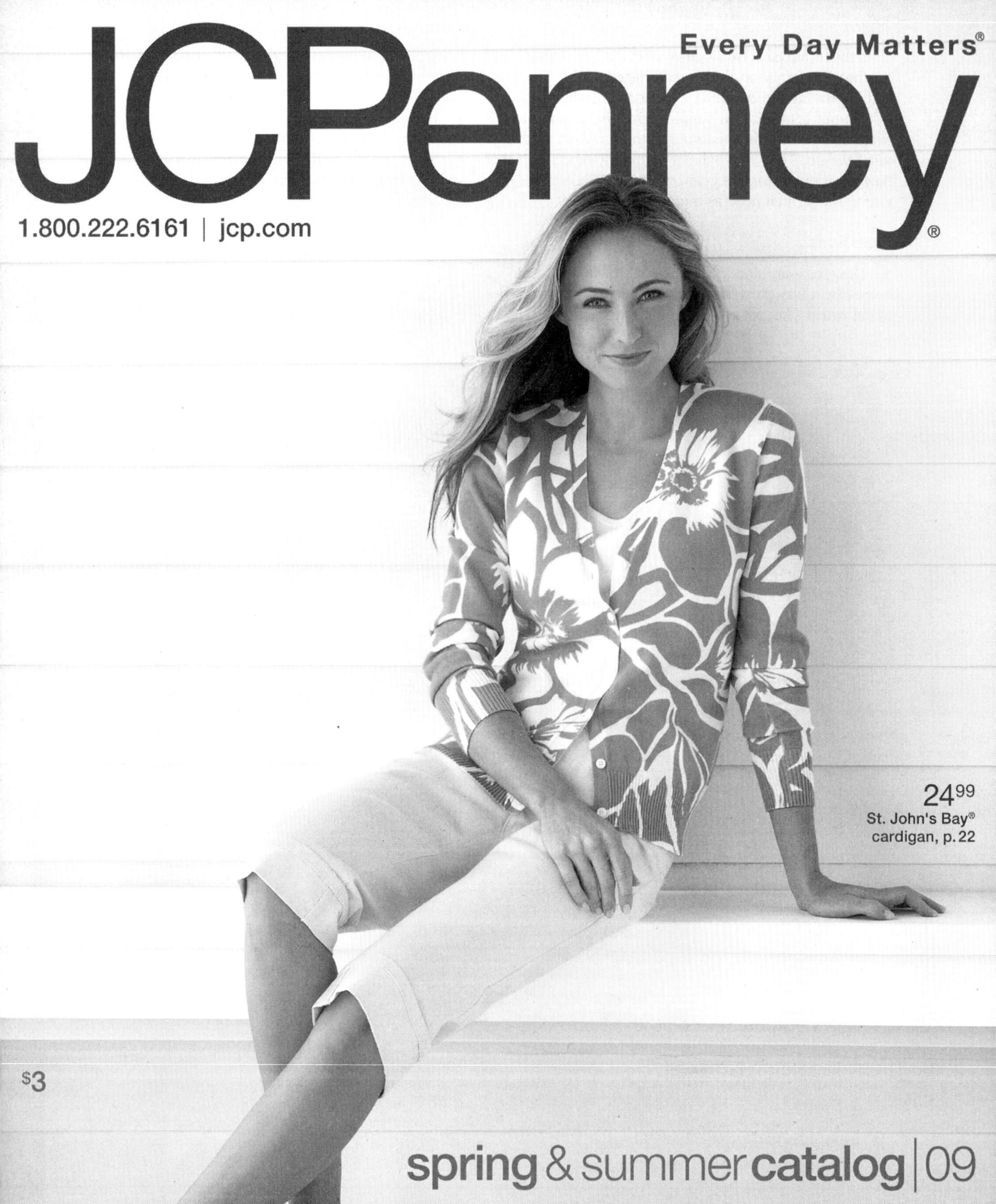
JCPenney
Every Day Matters®
1.800.222.6161 | jcp.com
24.99
St. John's Bay®
cardigan, p. 22
$3
spring & summer catalog | 09

4

了解客户组织
Understanding Organizations as Customers

采购也是市场营销！彭尼公司采购纸张
BUYING IS MARKETING, TOO! PURCHASING PUBLICATION PAPER AT JCPENNEY

LEARNING OBJECTIVES

After reading this chapter you should be able to:

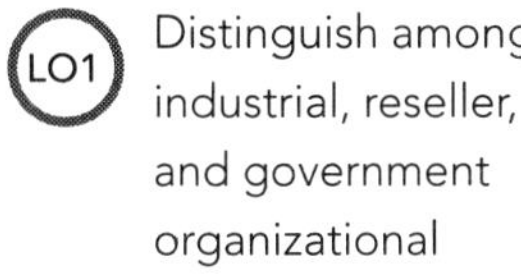

LO1 Distinguish among industrial, reseller, and government organizational markets.

LO2 Describe the key characteristics of organizational buying that make it different from consumer buying.

LO3 Explain how buying centers and buying situations influence organizational purchasing.

LO4 Recognize the importance and nature of online buying in industrial, reseller, and government organizational markets.

Kim Nagele views paper differently than most people do. As the senior procurement agent at JCPMedia, he and a team of purchasing professionals buy more than 260,000 tons of publication paper annually at a cost of hundreds of millions of dollars.

JCPMedia is the print and paper purchasing arm for JCPenney, the fifth-largest retailer in the United States and the largest catalog merchant of general merchandise in the Western Hemisphere. Paper is serious business at JCPMedia, which buys publication paper for JCPenney catalogs, newspaper inserts, and direct-mail pieces. Some 10 companies from around the world including Verso Paper in the United States, Catalyst Paper Inc. in Canada, Norski Skog in Norway, and UPM-Kymmene Inc. in Finland, supply paper to JCPMedia.

The choice of paper and suppliers is also a significant business decision given the sizable revenue and expense consequences. Therefore, JCPMedia paper buyers work closely with JCPenney marketing personnel and within budget constraints to assure that the right quality and quantity of publication paper is purchased at the right price point for the millions of catalogs, newspaper inserts, and direct-mail pieces distributed every year.

In addition to paper quality and price, buyers formally evaluate supplier capabilities, often by extended visits to supplier facilities. These include a supplier's capacity to deliver on time selected grades of paper from specialty items to magazine papers, the availability of specific types of paper to meet printing deadlines, and ongoing environmental programs. For example, a supplier's forestry management and sustainability practices are considered in the JCPMedia buying process.

The next time you thumb through a JCPenney catalog, newspaper insert, or direct-mail piece, notice the paper. Considerable effort and attention was given to its selection and purchase by Kim Nagele and JCPMedia paper buyers.

Purchasing paper for JCPMedia is one example of organizational buying. This chapter examines types of organizational buyers; key characteristics of organizational buying, including online buying; different buying situations; unique aspects of the organizational buying process; and typical buying procedures and decisions in today's organizational markets.

---

merchandise 商品，货物；sustainability 可持续性。

组织市场的性质与规模
THE NATURE AND SIZE OF ORGANIZATIONAL MARKETS

Understanding organizational markets and buying behavior is a necessary prerequisite for effective business marketing. **Business marketing** is the marketing of goods and services to companies, governments, or not-for-profit organizations for use in the creation of goods and services that they can produce and market to others. Because over half of all U.S. business school graduates take jobs in firms that engage in business marketing, it is important to understand the characteristics of organizational buyers and their buying behavior.

组织采购者是指那些为了自己使用或再销售而购买商品和服务的制造商、批发商、零售商和政府机构。

Organizational buyers are those manufacturers, wholesalers, retailers, and government agencies that buy goods and services for their own use or for resale. For example, these organizations buy computers and telephone services for their own use. However, manufacturers buy raw materials and parts that they reprocess into the finished goods they sell. Wholesalers and retailers resell the goods they buy without reprocessing them. Organizational buyers include all buyers in a nation except ultimate consumers. These organizational buyers purchase and lease large volumes of capital equipment, raw materials, manufactured parts, supplies, and business services. In fact, because they often buy raw materials and parts, process them, and sell the upgraded product several times before it is purchased by the final organizational buyer or ultimate consumer, the total annual purchases of organizational buyers are far greater than those of ultimate consumers. IBM alone buys nearly $40 billion in goods and services each year for its own use or resale.

Organizational buyers are divided into three markets: (1) industrial, (2) reseller, and (3) government. Each market is described next.

产业市场
Industrial Markets

这些工业企业以某种方式对所采购的产品和服务进行再加工，然后再销售给下游购买者。

There are about 7.2 million firms in the industrial, or business, market. These *industrial firms* in some way reprocess a product or service they buy before selling it again to the next buyer. This is certainly true of Corning, Inc., which transforms an exotic blend of materials to create optical fiber capable of carrying much of the telephone traffic in the United States on a single strand. It is also true (if you stretch your imagination) of a firm selling services, such as a bank that takes money from its depositors, reprocesses it, and "sells" it as loans to borrowers.

The importance of services in the United States today is emphasized by the composition of industrial markets. Companies that primarily sell physical goods (manufacturers; mining; construction; and farms, timber, and fisheries) represent 25 percent of all the industrial firms. The services market sells diverse services such as legal advice, auto repair, and dry cleaning. Along with finance, insurance, and real estate businesses, and transportation, communication, public utility firms, and not-for-profit organizations, service companies represent 75 percent of all industrial firms. Because of the size and importance of service companies and not-for-profit organizations (such as the American Red Cross), services marketing is discussed in detail in Chapter 9.

中间商市场
Reseller Markets

Wholesalers and retailers that buy physical products and resell them again without any reprocessing are *resellers*. In the United States there are almost 2 million retailers and 430,000 wholesalers. In Chapters 10 through 12 we shall see how manufacturers use wholesalers and retailers in their distribution ("place") strategies as channels through which their products reach ultimate consumers. In this chapter, we look at these resellers mainly as organizational buyers in terms of (1) how they make their own buying decisions and (2) which products they choose to carry.

---

manufacturers 生产商，制造商；equipment 设备，装备；emphasized 强调，重视。

The Orion lunar spacecraft to be designed, developed, tested, and evaluated by Lockheed Martin Corp. is an example of a purchase by a government unit, namely the National Aeronautics and Space Administration (NASA). Read the text to find out how much NASA will pay for the Orion lunar spacecraft.

Lockheed Martin Corporation
www.lockheedmartin.com

政府市场
Government Markets

政府部门是指为了服务选民而购买产品与服务的联邦政府、州政府以及地方政府机构。

Government units are the federal, state, and local agencies that buy goods and services for the constituents they serve. There are about 89,500 of these government units in the United States. These purchases include the $3.9 billion the National Aeronautics and Space Administration (NASA) intends to pay to Lockheed Martin to develop and produce the Orion lunar spacecraft scheduled for launch in 2014 as well as lesser amounts spent by local school and sanitation districts.

全球组织市场
Global Organizational Markets

Industrial, reseller, and government markets also exist on a global scale. International trade statistics indicate that the largest exporting industries in the United States focus on organizational buyers, not ultimate consumers. Capital equipment (such as construction equipment, computers, and telecommunications) and industrial supplies (such as machine parts) account for about 46 percent of all U.S. product exports.

The majority of world trade involves exchange relationships that span the globe. Consider the ingredients found in Kellogg's popular Nutri-Grain cereal bar. Kellogg buyers purchase ingredients from farmers, food processors, and wholesalers in eight countries on three continents.

衡量国内市场、全球产业市场、中间商市场和政府市场
MEASURING DOMESTIC AND GLOBAL INDUSTRIAL, RESELLER, AND GOVERNMENT MARKETS

The measurement of industrial, reseller, and government markets is an important first step for a firm interested in gauging the size of one, two, or all three of these markets in the United States and around the world. This task has been made easier with the **North American Industry Classification System (NAICS)**. The NAICS provides common industry definitions for Canada, Mexico, and the United States, which

scheduled（价格、细节或条件等的）一览表，明细表，清单；gauging（常指用某种仪器）测量，测定，算出。

makes it easier to measure economic activity in the three member countries of the North American Free Trade Agreement (NAFTA). The NAICS replaced the Standard Industrial Classification (SIC) system, a version of which has been in place for more than 50 years in the three NAFTA member countries. The SIC neither permitted comparability across countries nor accurately measured new or emerging industries. Furthermore, the NAICS is consistent with the International Standard Industrial Classification of All Economic Activities, published by the United Nations, to facilitate measurement of global economic activity.

The NAICS groups economic activity to permit studies of market share, demand for goods and services, import competition in domestic markets, and similar studies. It designates industries with a numerical code in a defined structure. A six-digit coding system is used. The first two digits designate a sector of the economy, the third digit designates a subsector, and the fourth digit represents an industry group. The fifth digit designates a specific industry and it is the most detailed level at which comparable data is available for Canada, Mexico, and the United States. The sixth digit designates individual country-level national industries. Figure 4–1 shows a breakdown within the information industries sector (code 51) to illustrate the classification scheme.

The NAICS permits a firm to find the NAICS codes of its present customers and then obtain NAICS-coded lists for similar firms. Also, it is possible to monitor NAICS categories to determine the growth in various sectors and industries to identify promising marketing opportunities. However, the NAICS has an important limitation. Five-digit national industry codes are not available for all three countries because the respective governments will not reveal data when too few organizations exist in a category.

A further refinement in the measurement of organizational markets is the *North American Product Classification System* (NAPCS). The NAPCS provides a classification system for products and services that is consistent across Canada, Mexico, and the United States and international classification systems, such as the Central Product Classification System of the United Nations. The NAICS and NAPCS represent the continued effort toward economic integration in North America and the world.

FIGURE 4–1
NAICS breakdown for information industries sector: NAICS code 51 (abbreviated)

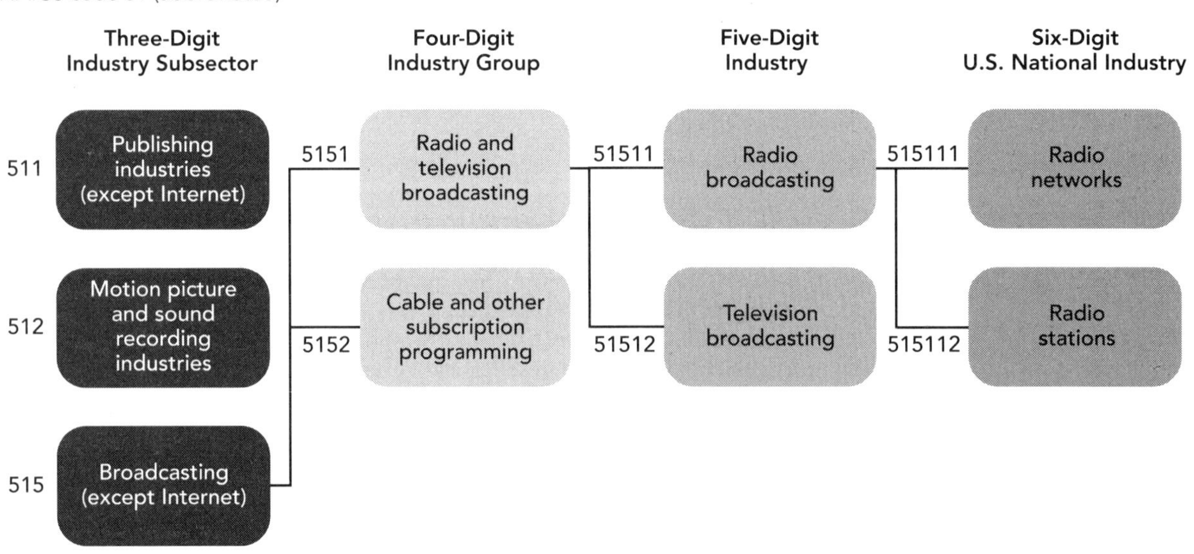

domestic 国内的，本国的；designate 指派，选派，委任；refinement 完善，修正，改进。

learning review	1. What are the three main types of organizational buyers? 2. What is the North American Industry Classification System (NAICS)?

组织采购的特点
CHARACTERISTICS OF ORGANIZATIONAL BUYING

LO2

Organizations are different from individuals, so buying for an organization is different from buying for yourself or your family. In both cases the objective in making the purchase is to solve the buyer's problem—to satisfy a need or want. But unique objectives and policies of an organization put special constraints on how it makes buying decisions. Understanding the characteristics of organizational buying is essential in designing effective marketing programs to reach these buyers. Key characteristics of organizational buying are listed in Figure 4–2 and discussed next.

消费者对某种产品和服务的需求受价格与供应状况以及消费者个人偏好与可任意支配收入的影响。通过比较可以看出，产业需求是衍生出来的。所谓**衍生需求**是指由消费者的最终需求驱动或衍生出来的对某些工业产品和服务的需求。

需求特点
Demand Characteristics

Consumer demand for products and services is affected by their price and availability and by consumers' personal tastes and discretionary income. By comparison, industrial demand is derived. **Derived demand** means that the demand for industrial products and services is driven by, or derived from, demand for consumer products and services. For example, the demand for Weyerhaeuser's pulp and paper products is based on consumer demand for newspapers, FedEx packages, and disposable diapers. Derived demand is based on expectations of future consumer demand. For

FIGURE 4–2
Key characteristics and dimensions of organizational buying behavior

CHARACTERISTICS	DIMENSIONS
Market characteristics	• Demand for industrial products and services is derived. • Few customers typically exist, and their purchase orders are large.
Product or service characteristics	• Products or services are technical in nature and purchased on the basis of specifications. • Many of goods purchased are raw and semifinished. • Heavy emphasis is placed on delivery time, technical assistance, and postsale service.
Buying process characteristics	• Technically qualified and professional buyers follow established purchasing policies and procedures. • Buying objectives and criteria are typically spelled out, as are procedures for evaluating sellers and their products or services. • There are multiple buying influences, and multiple parties participate in purchase decisions. • There are reciprocal arrangements, and negotiation between buyers and sellers is commonplace. • Online buying over the Internet is widespread.
Marketing mix characteristics	• Direct selling to organizational buyers is the rule, and distribution is very important. • Advertising and other forms of promotion are technical in nature. • Price is often negotiated, evaluated as part of broader seller and product or service qualities, and frequently affected by quantity discounts.

comparison 比较，对照；expectation 期待，期望，预期。

instance, Whirlpool buys parts for its washers and dryers in anticipation of consumer demand, which is affected by the replacement cycle for these products and by consumer income.

订单量或采购数量
Size of the Order or Purchase

The size of the purchase involved in organizational buying is typically much larger than that in consumer buying. The dollar value of a single purchase made by an organization often runs into thousands or millions of dollars. For example, Siemens Energy & Automation's Airport Logistics Division was awarded a $28 million contract to build a baggage handling and security system for JetBlue Airways' terminal at John F. Kennedy International Airport. With so much money at stake, most organizations place constraints on their buyers in the form of purchasing policies or procedures. Buyers must often get competitive bids from at least three prospective suppliers when the order is above a specific amount, such as $5,000. When the order is above an even higher amount, such as $50,000, it may require the review and approval of a vice president or even the president of the company. Knowing how order size affects buying practices is important in determining who participates in the purchase decision and makes the final decision, and the length of time required to arrive at a purchase agreement.

潜在购买者数量
Number of Potential Buyers

Firms selling consumer products or services often try to reach thousands or millions of individuals or households. For example, your local supermarket or bank probably serves thousands of people. Kellogg tries to reach 80 million North American households with its breakfast cereals and probably succeeds in selling to a third or half of these in any given year. Firms selling to organizations are often restricted to far fewer buyers. Gulfstream Aerospace Corporation can sell its business jets to a few thousand organizations throughout the world, and Goodyear sells its original equipment tires to fewer than 10 car manufacturers.

组织采购目标
Organizational Buying Objectives

组织采购产品和服务只有一个主要原因：帮助它们实现目标。对企业而言，采购目标一般是通过降低成本或增加销售额而提高利润。

Organizations buy products and services for one main reason: to help them achieve their objectives. For business firms the buying objective is usually to increase profits through reducing costs or increasing revenues. For example, 7-Eleven buys automated inventory systems to increase the number of products that can be sold through its convenience stores and to keep them fresh. Nissan Motor Company switched its advertising agency because it expects the new agency to devise a more effective ad campaign to help it sell more cars and increase revenues. To improve executive decision making, many firms buy advanced computer systems to process data. The objectives of nonprofit firms and government agencies are usually to meet the needs of the groups they serve. Recognizing the high costs of energy, Sylvania promotes to prospective buyers cost savings and increased profits made possible by its fluorescent and halogen lights.

Many companies today have broadened their buying objectives to include an emphasis on buying from minority- and women-owned suppliers and vendors. Companies such as Pitney Bowes, PepsiCo, Coors, and JCPenney report that sales, profits, and customer satisfaction have increased because of their minority- and women-owned supplier and vendor initiatives. Learn about Procter & Gamble's commitment to and success of its supplier diversity efforts in the accompanying Going Online box. Other companies include environmental initiatives. For example, Lowe's and Home Depot no longer purchase lumber from companies that harvest timber from the world's endangered forests. Successful business market-

anticipation 期待着，预计到；competitive 竞争的，角逐的；prospective 盼望中的，预期的，有希望的。

Going Online

Supplier Diversity Is a Fundamental Business Strategy at Procter & Gamble

"Supplier diversity is no longer an issue of social conscience," says A. G. Lafley, chairman of the board, president, and chief executive officer at Procter & Gamble, Inc. "It is a fundamental business strategy." At P&G, purchases from minority- and women-owned suppliers are targeted to reach $2.5 billion by 2010 . . . and for good reason.

Minority- and women-owned suppliers deliver a competitive advantage to P&G. They (1) provide innovative and new ways to help P&G deliver greater value to its consumers; (2) help P&G achieve greater cost efficiencies; and (3) assist P&G in finding new ways to market its brands to consumers.

To learn more about P&G's supplier diversity initiatives and hear from many of its minority- and women-owned suppliers, visit the P&G Web site at www.pg.com/supplier diversity and watch the video titled, "Economic Inclusion: A Corporate Commitment."

---

ers recognize that understanding buying objectives is a necessary first step in marketing to organizations.

组织采购标准
Organizational Buying Criteria

在采购过程中，组织必须设定用以评价潜在供应商及其所售产品的主要采购标准。**组织采购标准**是衡量供应商的产品与服务以及供应商本身实力的一系列客观属性。

In making a purchase, the buying organization must weigh key buying criteria that apply to the potential supplier and what it wants to sell. **Organizational buying criteria** are the objective attributes of the supplier's products and services and the capabilities of the supplier itself. These criteria serve the same purpose as the evaluative criteria used by consumers and described in Chapter 3. The most commonly used criteria are: (1) price, (2) ability to meet the quality specifications required for the item, (3) ability to meet required delivery schedules, (4) technical capability, (5) warranties and claim policies in the event of poor performance, (6) past performance on previous contracts, and (7) production facilities and capacity. Suppliers that meet or exceed these criteria create customer value.

Organizational buyers who purchase products and services in the global marketplace often supplement their buying criteria with supplier ISO 9000 standards certification. **ISO 9000** standards, developed by the International Standards Organization (ISO) in Geneva, Switzerland, refer to standards for registration and certification of a manufacturer's quality management and assurance system based on an on-site audit of practices and procedure. The 3M Co., which buys and markets its products globally, has over 80 percent of its manufacturing and service facilities ISO 9000 certified. This certification also gives 3M confidence in the consistent quality of its suppliers' manufacturing systems and products.

目前，许多组织采购者开始从自己制定采购标准转向与潜在供应商协商，共同确定具体规格。这种行动称为**供应商开发**，即组织采购者通过协商，建立起与供应商的合作关系，从而规范供应商的产品、服务与能力，以更好地满足采购者及其顾客的需要。

Many organizational buyers today are transforming their buying criteria into specific requirements that are communicated to prospective suppliers. This practice, called **supplier development**, involves the deliberate effort by organizational buyers to build relationships that shape suppliers' products, services, and capabilities to fit a buyer's needs and those of its customers. Consider Deere & Company, the maker of John Deere farm, construction, and lawn-care equipment. Deere employs supplier-development engineers who work full-time with the company's suppliers to improve their efficiency and quality and reduce their costs. According to a Deere senior executive, "Their quality, delivery, and costs are, after all, our quality, delivery, and costs." Read the Marketing Matters box on the next page to learn how Harley-Davidson emphasizes supplier collaboration in its product design.

With many U.S. manufacturers using a *just-in-time* (JIT) inventory system that reduces the inventory of production parts to those to be used within hours or days, on-time delivery is becoming an even more important buying criterion and, in some instances, a requirement. Caterpillar trains its key suppliers in JIT inventory system

---

criteria（判定的）标准，准则；registration 注册，登记；inventory 储备，存货。

Marketing Matters > > > > > > customer value

Harley-Davidson's Supplier Collaboration Creates Customer Value . . . and a Great Ride

It's nice to be admired. Harley-Davidson's well-deserved reputation for innovation, product quality, and talented management and employees has made it a perennial member of *Fortune* magazine's list of "America's Most Admired Companies."

Harley-Davidson is also respected by suppliers for the way it collaborates with them in product design. According to Jeff Bluestein, the company's chairman: "We involve our suppliers as much as possible in future products, new-product development, and get them working with us." Emphasis is placed on quality benchmarks, cost control, delivery schedules, and technological innovation as well as building mutually beneficial, long-term relationships. Face-to-face communication is encouraged, and many suppliers have personnel stationed at Harley-Davidson's Product Development Center.

The relationship between Harley-Davidson and Milsco Manufacturing is a case in point. Milsco has been the sole source of original equipment motorcycle seats and a major supplier of aftermarket parts and accessories, such as saddlebags, for Harley-Davidson since 1934. Milsco engineers and designers work closely with their Harley counterparts in the design of each year's new products.

The notion of a mutually beneficial relationship is expressed by Milsco's manager of industrial design: "Harley-Davidson refers to us as stakeholders, someone who can win or lose from a successful or failed program. We all share responsibility toward one another." He also notes that Harley-Davidson is not Milsco's only customer. It is simply the customer that he most respects.

---

and conducts supplier seminars on how to diagnose, correct, and implement continuous quality improvement programs. The just-in-time inventory system is discussed further in Chapter 11.

买卖关系与供应伙伴关系
Buyer–Seller Relationships and Supply Partnerships

Another distinction between organizational and consumer buying behavior lies in the nature of the relationship between organizational buyers and suppliers. Specifically, organizational buying is more likely to involve complex negotiations concerning delivery schedules, price, technical specifications, warranties, and claim policies. These negotiations also can last for an extended period. This was the case when the Lawrence Livermore National Laboratory acquired two IBM supercomputers—each with capacity to perform 360 trillion mathematical operations per second—at a cost of $290 million.

组织采购中还存在一种互惠行为。**互惠**是一种产业购买行为，指两个组织同意彼此采购对方的产品和服务。美国司法部并不赞成互惠采购，因为它限制了自由市场的正常运转。然而，目前这种互惠行为仍然存在，并且确实限制了组织采购者选择供应商的灵活性。

Reciprocal arrangements also exist in organizational buying. **Reciprocity** is an industrial buying practice in which two organizations agree to purchase each other's products and services. The U.S. Justice Department disapproves of reciprocal buying because it restricts the normal operation of the free market. However, the practice exists and can limit the flexibility of organizational buyers in choosing alternative suppliers.

Long-term contracts are also prevalent. For instance, Kraft Foods, Inc. is spending $1.7 billion over seven years for global information technology services provided by Electronic Data Systems. Hewlett-Packard has a 10-year, $3 billion contract to manage Procter & Gamble's information technology in 160 countries.

In some cases, buyer–seller relationships evolve into supply partnerships. A **supply partnership** exists when a buyer and its supplier adopt mutually beneficial

diagnose 诊断，确诊，判断，断定；reciprocity 互惠，互换。

Making Responsible Decisions >>>>> sustainability

Sustainable Procurement for Sustainable Growth

Manufacturers, retailers, wholesalers, and governmental agencies are increasingly sensitive to how their buying decisions affect the environment. Concerns about the depletion of natural resources; air, water, and soil pollution; and the social consequences of economic activity have given rise to the concept of sustainable procurement. Sustainable procurement aims to integrate environmental considerations into all stages of an organization's buying process with the goal of reducing the impact on human health and the physical environment.

Starbucks is a pioneer and worldwide leader in sustainable procurement. The company's attention to quality coffee extends to its coffee growers located in more than 20 countries. This means that Starbucks pays coffee farmers a fair price for the beans; that the coffee is grown in an ecologically sound manner; and that Starbucks invests in the farming communities where its coffees are produced. In this way, Starbucks focuses on the sustainable growth of its suppliers.

objectives, policies, and procedures for the purpose of lowering the cost or increasing the value of products and services delivered to the ultimate consumer. Intel, a manufacturer of microprocessors and the "computer inside" of most personal computers, is an example. Intel supports its suppliers by offering them quality management programs and by investing in supplier equipment that produces fewer product defects and boosts supplier productivity. Suppliers, in turn, provide Intel with consistent high-quality products at a lower cost for its customers, the makers of personal computers, and finally you, the ultimate customer. Retailers, too, have forged partnerships with their suppliers. Wal-Mart has such a relationship with Procter & Gamble for ordering and replenishing P&G's products in its stores. By using computerized cash register scanning equipment and direct electronic linkages to P&G, Wal-Mart can tell P&G what merchandise is needed, along with how much, when, and to which store to deliver it on a daily basis.

Supply partnerships often include provisions for what is called *sustainable procurement*. This buying practice is described in the accompanying Making Responsible Decisions box. Because supply partnerships also involve the physical distribution of goods, they are again discussed in Chapter 11 in the context of supply chain management.

采购中心：一个跨职能团体
The Buying Center: A Cross-Functional Group

LO3 对于小批量常规购买而言，通常由单个采购人员或采购经理单独决策即可。然而在许多情况下，组织中会有若干人参与采购过程。我们把在购买决策方面目标一致、风险共担，并具备相关知识的一些人所组成的团体称为**采购中心**。

For routine purchases with a small dollar value, a single buyer or purchasing manager often makes the purchase decision alone. In many instances, however, several people in the organization participate in the buying process. The individuals in this group, called a **buying center**, share common goals, risks, and knowledge important to a purchase decision. For most large multistore chain resellers, such as Sears, 7-Eleven convenience stores, Target, or Safeway, the buying center is highly formalized and is called a *buying committee*. However, most industrial firms or government units use informal groups of people or call meetings to arrive at buying decisions.

The importance of the buying center requires that a firm marketing to many industrial firms and government units understand the structure, technical and business functions represented, and behavior of these groups. Four questions provide guidance in understanding the buying center in these organizations: Which individuals

equipment 设备，装备；productivity 生产力，生产率，生产能力；merchandise 商品，货物。

are in the buying center for the product or service? What is the relative influence of each member of the group? What are the buying criteria of each member? How does each member of the group perceive our firm, our products and services, and our salespeople?

Answers to these questions are difficult to come by. This is particularly true when dealing with industrial firms, resellers, and governments outside the United States. For example, U.S. firms are often frustrated by the fact that Japanese buyers "ask a thousand questions" but give few answers, sometimes rely on third-party individuals to convey views on proposals, are prone to not "talk business," and often say "yes" to be courteous when they mean "no."

People in the Buying Center The composition of the buying center in a given organization depends on the specific item being bought. Although a buyer or purchasing manager is almost always a member of the buying center, individuals from other functional areas are included, depending on what is to be purchased. In buying a million-dollar machine tool, the president (because of the size of the purchase) and the production vice president or manager would probably be members. For key components to be included in a final manufactured product, a cross-functional group of individuals from research and development (R&D), engineering, and quality control are likely to be added. For new word-processing equipment, experienced secretaries who will use the equipment would be members. Still, a major question in penetrating the buying center is finding and reaching the people who will initiate, influence, and actually make the buying decision.

Roles in the Buying Center Researchers have identified five specific roles that an individual in a buying center can play. In some purchases the same person may perform two or more of these roles.

- 使用者，即组织中实际使用所购产品或服务的人，如秘书就是新购文字处理设备的使用者。
- 影响者，即可以影响采购决策的人，他们一般协助确定采购产品的具体规格。

Effective marketing to organizations requires an understanding of buying centers and their role in purchase decisions.

- *Users* are the people in the organization who actually use the product or service, such as a secretary who will use a new word processor.
- *Influencers* affect the buying decision, usually by helping define the specifications for what is bought. The information systems manager would be a key influencer in the purchase of a new mainframe computer.
- *Buyers* have formal authority and responsibility to select the supplier and negotiate the terms of the contract. Kim Nagele performs this role as senior procurement agent at JCPMedia as described in the chapter opening example.
- *Deciders* have the formal or informal power to select or approve the supplier that receives the contract. In routine orders the decider is usually the buyer or purchasing manager; in important technical purchases it is more likely to be someone from R&D, engineering, or quality control. The decider for a key component being incorporated in a final manufactured product might be any of these three people.
- *Gatekeepers* control the flow of information in the buying center. Purchasing personnel, technical experts, and secretaries can all keep salespeople or information from reaching people performing the other four roles.

Buying Situations and the Buying Center The number of people in the buying center largely depends on the specific buying situation. Researchers who have studied organizational buying identify three types of buying situations, called **buy classes**. These buy classes vary from the routine reorder, or *straight rebuy*, to the completely new purchase, termed *new buy*.

perceive 注意到，察觉，意识到；functional 职能的；rebuy 再次购买。

In between these extremes is the *modified rebuy*. Some examples will clarify the differences.

- *New buy*. Here the organization is a first-time buyer of the product or service. This involves greater potential risks in the purchase, so the buying center is enlarged to include all those who have a stake in the new buy. Procter & Gamble's purchase of a multimillion-dollar fiber-optic network from Corning, Inc., for its corporate offices in Cincinnati, represented a new buy.
- *Straight rebuy*. Here the buyer or purchasing manager reorders an existing product or service from the list of acceptable suppliers, probably without even checking with users or influencers from the engineering, production, or quality control departments. Office supplies and maintenance services are usually obtained as straight rebuys.
- *Modified rebuy*. In this buying situation the users, influencers, or deciders in the buying center want to change the product specifications, price, delivery schedule, or supplier. Although the item purchased is largely the same as with the straight rebuy, the changes usually necessitate enlarging the buying center to include people outside the purchasing department.

- 直接重购。指采购人员或采购经理从原有供应商处再次购买现有产品和服务，而不必经过来自工程、制造或质量控制部门的使用者或影响者的审核。
- 修正重购。在该采购类型中，采购中心的使用者、影响者和决策者将调整采购方案，改变产品规格、价格、送货日期或供应商。

Figure 4–3 summarizes how buy classes affect buying center tendencies.

The marketing and sales strategies of the sellers facing each of these three buying situations can vary greatly because the importance of personnel from functional areas such as purchasing, engineering, production, and R&D often varies with (1) the type of buying situation and (2) the stage of the purchasing process. If it is a new buy for the manufacturer, you should be prepared to act as a consultant to the buyer, work with technical personnel, and expect a long time for a buying decision to be reached. However, if the manufacturer has bought the item from you before (a straight or modified rebuy), you might emphasize a competitive price and a reliable supply in meetings with the purchasing agent.

FIGURE 4–3
The buying situation affects buying center behavior in different ways. Understanding these differences can pay huge dividends.

BUYING CENTER DIMENSION	BUY-CLASS SITUATION		
	NEW BUY	STRAIGHT REBUY	MODIFIED REBUY
People involved	Many	One	Two to three
Decision time	Long	Short	Moderate
Problem definition	Uncertain	Well-defined	Minor modifications
Buying objective	Good solution	Low-priced supplier	Low-priced supplier
Suppliers considered	New/present	Present	Present
Buying influence	Technical/operating personnel	Purchasing agent	Purchasing agent and others

modify 修改，变更，改进；necessitate 使成为必需，需要。

learning review

3. What one department is almost always represented by a person in the buying center?
4. What are the three types of buying situations or buy classes?

制定组织采购流程
CHARTING THE ORGANIZATIONAL BUYING PROCESS

组织采购者与消费者一样，在挑选产品和服务时也要经过一个决策过程。**组织采购行为**是指组织用以确定产品与服务需要，并识别、评估与选择品牌和供应商的一种决策过程。

Organizational buyers, like consumers, engage in a decision process when selecting products and services. **Organizational buying behavior** is the decision-making process that organizations use to establish the need for products and services and identify, evaluate, and choose among alternative brands and suppliers. There are important similarities and differences between the two decision-making processes. To better understand the nature of organizational buying behavior, we first compare it with consumer buying behavior and then describe an actual organizational purchase in detail.

组织购买流程的步骤
Stages in the Organizational Buying Process

As shown in Figure 4–4 (and covered in Chapter 3), the five stages a student might use in buying a smart phone also apply to organizational purchases. However, comparing the two right-hand columns in Figure 4–4 reveals key differences. For example, when a smart phone manufacturer buys earbud headsets for its units from a supplier, more individuals are involved, supplier capability becomes more important, and the postpurchase evaluation behavior is more formalized.

The headset-buying decision process is typical of the steps made by organizational buyers. Let's now examine in detail the decision-making process for a more complex product—machine vision systems.

购买机器视觉系统
Buying a Machine Vision System

Machine vision is widely regarded as one of the keys to the factory of the future. The chief elements of a machine vision system are its optics, light source, camera, video processor, and computer software. Vision systems are mainly used for product inspection. They are also becoming important as one of the chief elements in the information feedback loop of systems that control manufacturing processes. Vision systems, selling for $25,000 to $250,000, are mostly sold to original equipment manufacturers (OEMs) who incorporate them in still larger industrial automation systems, which sell for millions of dollars. Companies worldwide are expected to spend more than $10 billion for machine vision systems in 2010.

Finding productive applications for machine vision involves the constant search for technology and designs that satisfy user needs. The buying process for machine vision components and assemblies is frequently a new buy because many machine vision systems contain elements that require some custom design. Let's track five purchasing stages that a company such as the Industrial Automation Division of Siemens, a large German industrial firm, would follow when purchasing components and assemblies for the machine vision systems it produces and installs.

Problem Recognition Sales engineers constantly canvass industrial automation equipment users such as American National Can, Ford Motor Company, Grumman Aircraft, and many Asian and European firms for leads on upcoming industrial automation projects. They also keep these firms current on Siemens' technology, products, and services. When a firm needing a machine vision capability identifies a project

alternative 备选的，备用的，其他的；capability 能力，素质；canvass 详细研究。

STAGE IN THE BUYING DECISION PROCESS	CONSUMER PURCHASE: SMART PHONE FOR A STUDENT	ORGANIZATIONAL PURCHASE: EARBUD HEADSET FOR A SMART PHONE
Problem recognition	Student doesn't like the features of the smart phone now owned and desires a new one.	Marketing research and sales departments observe that competitors are improving the earbud headsets for their smart phones. The firm decides to improve the earbud headsets on its own new models, which will be purchased from an outside supplier.
Information search	Student uses past experience, that of friends, ads, the Internet, and *Consumer Reports* to collect information and uncover alternatives.	Design and production engineers draft specifications for earbud headsets. The purchasing department identifies suppliers of earbud headsets.
Alternative evaluation	Alternative smart phones are evaluated on the basis of important attributes desired in a phone, and several stores are visited.	Purchasing and engineering personnel visit with suppliers and assess (1) facilities, (2) capacity, (3) quality control, and (4) financial status. They drop any suppliers not satisfactory on these factors.
Purchase decision	A specific brand of smart phone is selected, the price is paid, and the student leaves the store.	They use (1) quality, (2) price, (3) delivery, and (4) technical capability as key buying criteria to select a supplier. Then they negotiate terms and award a contract.
Postpurchase behavior	Student reevaluates the purchase decision, may return the phone to the store if it is unsatisfactory.	They evaluate suppliers using a formal vendor rating system and notify a supplier if the earbud headsets do not meet their quality standard. If the problem is not corrected, they drop the firm as a future supplier.

FIGURE 4–4
Comparing the stages in a consumer and organizational purchase decision process

合同签订之后，项目人员通常必须做出**自制—购买决策**，即评估零部件和成品是由公司自己制造还是从外部供应商处采购。

数据库中所有产品的价格、质量和送货时间先前都已经谈判过，而且其中许多产品还运用**价值分析**——对某一产品的设计、质量和性能进行系统化评估鉴定以降低采购成本——评估过。

that would benefit from Siemens' expertise, company engineers typically work with the firm to determine the kind of system required to meet the customer's need.

After a contract is won, project personnel must often make a **make-buy decision**—an evaluation of whether components and assemblies will be purchased from outside suppliers or built by the company itself. (Siemens produces many components and assemblies.) When these items are to be purchased from outside suppliers, the company engages in a thorough supplier search and evaluation process.

Information Search Companies such as Siemens employ a sophisticated process for identifying outside suppliers of components and assemblies. For standard items such as connectors, printed circuit boards, and components such as resistors and capacitors, the purchasing agent consults the company's purchasing databank, which contains information on hundreds of suppliers and thousands of products. All products in the databank have been prenegotiated as to price, quality, and delivery time, and many have been assessed using **value analysis**—a systematic appraisal of the design, quality, and performance of a product to reduce purchasing costs.

For one-of-a-kind components or assemblies such as new optics, cameras, and light sources, the company relies on its engineers to keep current on new developments in product technology. This information is often found in technical journals and industry magazines or at international trade shows where suppliers display their most recent innovations. In some instances, supplier representatives might be asked to make presentations to the buying center at Siemens. Such a group often consists

engineers 工程师，设计师；systematic 系统的；appraisal 评定，评价。

of a project engineer; several design, system, and manufacturing engineers; and a purchasing agent.

Alternative Evaluation The main buying criteria used to select machine vision suppliers and products are displayed in Figure 4–5. Product performance, a supplier's technical support, and ease of use are the three most frequently mentioned buying criteria for machine vision suppliers and products. Interestingly, price is among the least frequently mentioned. Typically, two or three suppliers for each standard component and assembly are identified from a **bidder's list**—a list of firms believed to be qualified to supply a given item. This list is generated from the company's purchasing databank as well as from engineering inputs. Specific items that are unique may be obtained from a single supplier after careful evaluation by the buying center.

一般而言，每一标准零部件和成品都会有两三个供应商入围**投标清单**，即采购者认为有资格供应既定项目的企业名单。这一清单可能来自于公司的采购数据库，也可能来自工程投标。对于某些特殊项目，采购中心可能会经过严格评估后独选一家企业作为供应商。

Firms selected from the bidder's list are sent a quotation request from the purchasing agent, describing the desired quantity, delivery date(s), and specifications of the components or assemblies. Suppliers are expected to respond within 30 days.

Purchase Decision Unlike the short purchase stage in a consumer purchase, the period from supplier selection to order placement to product delivery can take several weeks or even months. Even after bids for components and assemblies are submitted, further negotiation concerning price, performance, and delivery terms is likely. Sometimes conditions related to warranties, indemnities, and payment schedules have to be agreed on. The purchase decision is further complicated by the fact that two or more suppliers of the same item might be awarded contracts. This practice can occur when large orders are requested. Suppliers who are not chosen are informed why their bids were not selected.

Postpurchase Behavior As in the consumer purchase decision process, postpurchase evaluation occurs in the industrial purchase decision process, but it is formalized and often more sophisticated. All items purchased are examined in a formal product acceptance process. The performance of the supplier is also monitored and recorded. Performance on past contracts determines a supplier's chances of being asked to bid on future purchases, and poor performance may result in a supplier's name being dropped from the bidder's list.

This example of an organizational purchase suggests four lessons for marketers who want to increase their chances of selling products and services to organiza-

FIGURE 4–5
Product and supplier selection criteria for buying machine vision equipment emphasize factors other than price.

An optic component in a larger machine vision system for soft drink cans.

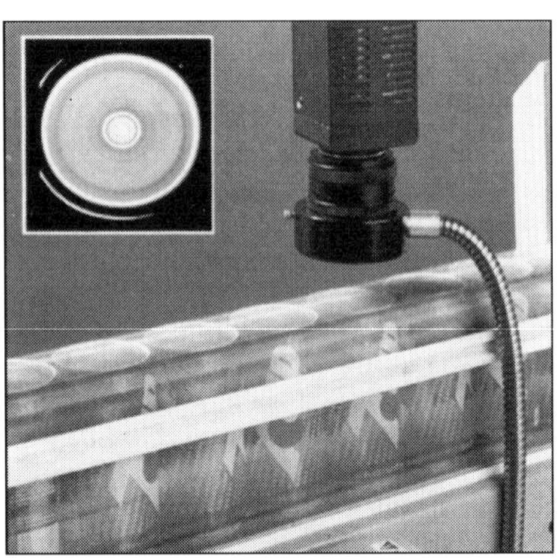

Percentage of machine vision buyers citing individual selection criteria.

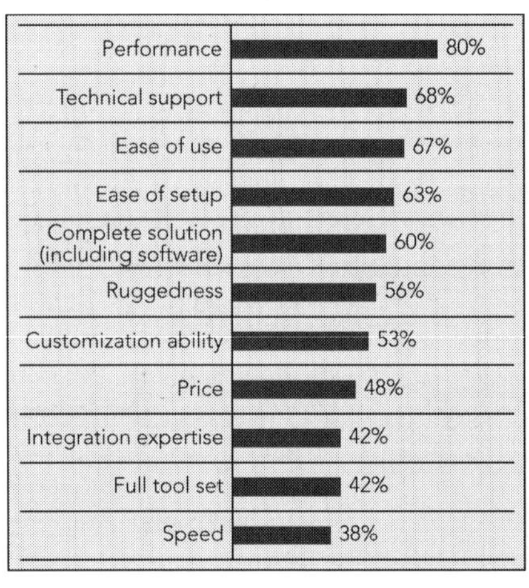

quotation 报价，开价；specifications 规格，具体要求。

tions. Firms selling to organizations must: (1) understand the organization's needs, (2) get on the right bidder's list, (3) find the right people in the buying center, and (4) provide value to organizational buyers.

learning review

5. What is a make-buy decision?
6. What is a bidder's list?

组织市场中的网上采购
ONLINE BUYING IN ORGANIZATIONAL MARKETS

Organizational buying behavior and business marketing continues to evolve with the application of Internet technology. Organizations dwarf consumers in terms of online transactions made, average transaction size, and overall purchase volume. In fact, organizational buyers account for about 80 percent of the global dollar value of all online transactions.

组织市场的网上采购发展迅猛
Prominence of Online Buying in Organizational Markets

Online buying in organizational markets is prominent for three major reasons. First, organizational buyers depend heavily on timely supplier information that describes product availability, technical specifications, application uses, price, and delivery schedules. This information can be conveyed quickly via Internet technology. Second, this technology has been shown to substantially reduce buyer order processing costs. At General Electric, online buying has cut the cost of a transaction from $50 to $100 per purchase to about $5. Third, business marketers have found that Internet technology can reduce marketing costs, particularly sales and advertising expense, and broaden their potential customer base for many types of products and services.

For these reasons, online buying is popular in all three kinds of organizational markets. For example, airlines electronically order over $400 million in spare parts from the Boeing Company each year. Customers of W. W. Grainger, a large U.S. wholesaler of maintenance, repair, and operating supplies, buy more than $425 million worth of these products annually online. Supply and service purchases totaling $650 million each year are made online by the Los Angeles County government.

Online buying can assume many forms. Organizational buyers can purchase directly from suppliers. For instance, a buyer might acquire a dozen desktop photocopiers from Xerox at www.xerox.com. This same buyer might purchase office furniture and supplies through a reseller such as Office Depot at www.officedepot.com. Increasingly, organizational buyers and business marketers are using e-marketplaces and online auctions to purchase and sell products and services.

电子市场：虚拟的组织市场
E-Marketplaces: Virtual Organizational Markets

组织采购的一个重大发展是创建了在线交易社区，即有效连接买卖双方组织的**电子市场**。这些在线社区有各种名称，如B2B 交易、电子交易平台，它们使信息、资金、产品和服务的实时交换成为可能。

A significant development in organizational buying has been the creation of online trading communities, called **e-marketplaces**, that bring together buyers and supplier organizations. These online communities go by a variety of names, including B2B exchanges and e-hubs, and make possible the real-time exchange of information, money, products, and services.

E-marketplaces can be independent trading communities or private exchanges. Independent e-marketplaces act as a neutral third party and provide an Internet technology trading platform and a centralized market that enable exchanges between buyers and sellers. They charge a fee for their service and exist in settings that have one or more of the following features: (1) thousands of geographically dispersed buyers and sellers, (2) volatile prices caused by demand and supply fluctuations,

evolve 进化，演变；prominent 重要的，杰出的，著名的；significant 数量相当大的，显著的；geographically 地理学上，在地理上。

Marketing Matters > > > > > entrepreneurship

eBay Means Business for Entrepreneurs

San Jose, California–based eBay Inc. is a true Internet phenomenon. By any measure, it is the predominant person-to-person trading community in the world. But there is more.

Now eBayBusiness offers a trading platform for over 23 million small businesses in the United States and even greater numbers around the world. Transactions on eBayBusiness exceed sales of $20 billion annually.

The eBayBusiness platform has proven to be a boon for small businesses. According to an eBay-commissioned survey conducted by ACNielsen, 82 percent of small businesses using eBayBusiness report that it helped their business grow and expand, 78 percent say it helped to reduce their costs, and 79 percent say their business had become more profitable. Additionally, eBayBusiness promotes entrepreneurship. According to the general manager of eBayBusiness, "Many of our sellers started their businesses specifically as a result of the ability to use eBay as their e-commerce platform."

Today, more than 724,000 Americans report that eBay is their primary or secondary source of income—up 68 percent from 2003 when 430,000 Americans were making some or all of their income selling on eBay. According to a spokesperson from the American Enterprise Institute for Public Policy Research, "The potential for entrepreneurs to realize success through eBay is significant."

(3) time sensitivity due to perishable offerings and changing technologies, and (4) easily comparable offerings between a variety of sellers.

Examples of independent e-marketplaces include PlasticsNet (plastics), Hospital Network.com (healthcare supplies and equipment), and Textile Web (garment and apparel products). Small business buyers and sellers, in particular, benefit from independent e-marketplaces. These e-marketplaces offer them an economical way to expand their customer base and reduce the cost of products and services. To serve entrepreneurs and the small business market in the United States, eBay launched eBayBusiness. Read the accompanying Marketing Matters box to learn more about this independent trading community.

大公司则更倾向于利用专属电子市场，与限定的供应商和顾客实现网络连接。专属电子市场侧重于使公司的交易更加顺畅。与独立电子市场相同，它们也为供求双方提供技术交易平台和集中交易市场。

Large companies tend to favor private exchanges that link them with their network of qualified suppliers and customers. Private exchanges focus on streamlining a company's purchase transactions with its suppliers and customers. Like independent e-marketplaces, they provide a technology trading platform and central market for buyer–seller interactions. They are not a neutral third party, however, but represent the interests of their owners. For example, Agentrics is an international business-to-business private exchange. It connects more than 250 retail customers with 80,000 suppliers. Its members include Best Buy, Campbell Soup, Costco, Radio Shack, Safeway, Target, Tesco, and Walgreens. The Global Healthcare Exchange engages in the buying and selling of health care products for over 1,400 hospitals and more than 100 health care suppliers, such as Abbott Laboratories, GE Medical Systems, Johnson & Johnson, Medtronic USA, and McKesson Corporation. Each of these private exchanges has saved their members over $2 billion since 2000 due to efficiencies in purchase transactions.

---

accompany 陪伴，陪同；streamlining 使（机构或过程）效率更高，精简；platform 平台。

组织市场的网上竞拍
Online Auctions in Organizational Markets

Online auctions have grown in popularity among organizational buyers and business marketers. Many e-marketplaces offer this service. Two general types of auctions are common: (1) a traditional auction and (2) a reverse auction. Figure 4–6 shows how buyer and seller participants and price behavior differ by type of auction. Let's look at each auction type more closely to understand the implications of each for buyers and sellers.

传统竞拍是指一个卖者给出欲售商品，邀请多个买者竞价购买。买者越多，价格越高。

In a **traditional auction** a seller puts an item up for sale and would-be buyers are invited to bid in competition with each other. As more would-be buyers become involved, there is an upward pressure on bid prices. Why? Bidding is sequential. Prospective buyers observe the bids of others and decide whether or not to increase the bid price. The auction ends when a single bidder remains and "wins" the item with its highest price. Traditional auctions are often used to dispose of excess merchandise. For example, Dell, Inc., sells surplus, refurbished, or closeout computer merchandise at its www.dellauction.com Web site.

反向竞拍与传统竞拍恰恰相反。**反向竞拍**是指一个买者公布所需产品与服务的清单，邀请多个卖者竞价销售。卖者越多，价格越低。

A reverse auction works in the opposite direction from a traditional auction. In a **reverse auction**, a buyer communicates a need for a product or service and would-be suppliers are invited to bid in competition with each other. As more would-be suppliers become involved, there is a downward pressure on bid prices for the buyer's business. Why? Like traditional auctions, bidding is sequential and prospective suppliers observe the bids of others and decide whether or not to decrease the bid price. The auction ends when a single bidder remains and "wins" the business with its lowest price. Reverse auctions benefit organizational buyers by reducing the cost of their purchases. As an example, United Technologies Corp., estimates that it has saved $600 million on the purchase of $6 billion in supplies using online reverse auctions.

Clearly, buyers welcome the lower prices generated by reverse auctions. Suppliers often favor reverse auctions because they give them a chance to capture business that they might not have otherwise had because of a long-standing purchase relationship between the buyer and another supplier. On the other hand, suppliers say reverse auctions put too much emphasis on prices, discourage consideration of other important buying criteria, and may threaten supply partnership opportunities.

FIGURE 4–6
Buyer and seller participants and price behavior differ by type of online auction. As an organizational buyer, would you prefer to participate in a traditional auction or a reverse auction?

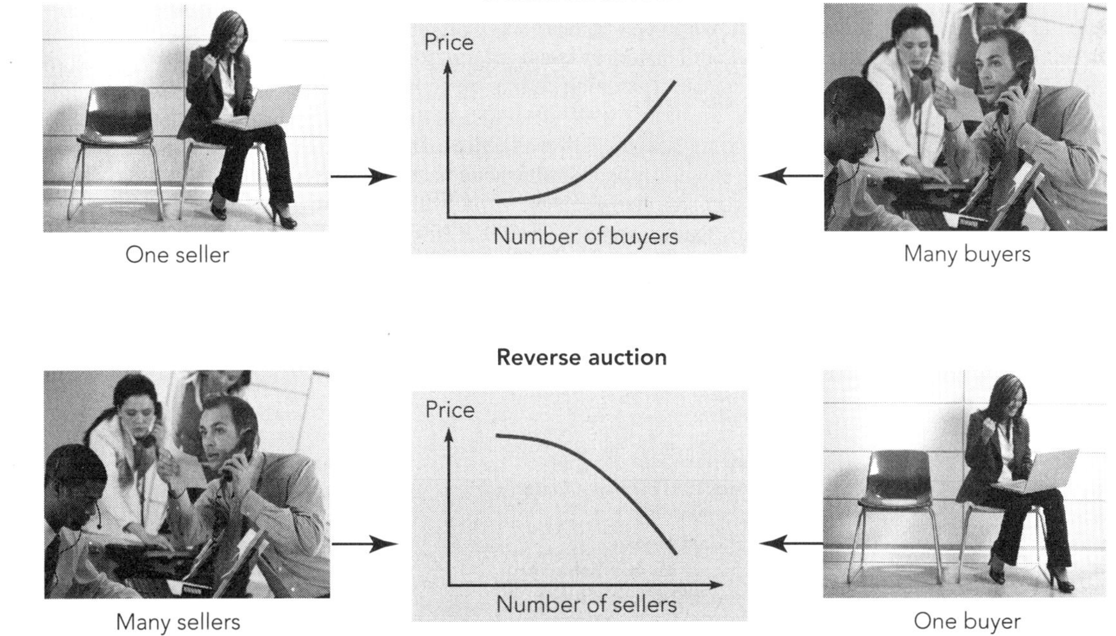

sequential 按次序的，顺序的，序列的；reverse 逆转，彻底改变（决定、政策、趋势等）。

learning review

7. What are e-marketplaces?
8. In general, which type of online auction creates upward pressure on bid prices and which type creates downward pressure on bid prices?

LEARNING OBJECTIVES REVIEW

LO1 *Distinguish among industrial, reseller, and government organizational markets.*

There are three different organizational markets: industrial, reseller, and government. Industrial firms in some way reprocess a product or service they buy before selling it to the next buyer. Resellers—wholesalers and retailers—buy physical products and resell them again without any reprocessing. Government agencies, at the federal, state, and local levels, buy goods and services for the constituents they serve. The North American Industry Classification System (NAICS) provides common industry definitions for Canada, Mexico, and the United States, which facilitates the measurement of economic activity for these three organizational markets.

LO2 *Describe the key characteristics of organizational buying that make it different from consumer buying.*

Seven major characteristics of organizational buying make it different from consumer buying. These include demand characteristics, size of the order or purchase, number of potential buyers, buying objectives, buying criteria, buyer–seller relationships and supply partnerships, and multiple buying influences within organizations. The organizational buying process itself is more formalized, more individuals are involved, supplier capability is more important, and the postpurchase evaluation behavior often includes performance of the supplier and the item purchased. Figure 4–4 details how the purchase of a smart phone differs between a consumer and organizational purchase. The example describing the purchase of machine vision systems by an industrial firm illustrates this process in greater depth.

LO3 *Explain how buying centers and buying situations influence organizational purchasing.*

Buying centers and buying situations have an important influence on organizational purchasing. A buying center consists of a group of individuals who share common goals, risks, and knowledge important to a purchase decision. A buyer or purchasing manager is almost always a member of a buying center. However, other individuals may affect organizational purchasing due to their unique roles in a purchase decision. Five specific roles that a person may play in a buying center include users, influencers, buyers, deciders, and gatekeepers. The specific buying situation will influence the number of people in and the different roles played in a buying center. For a routine reorder of an item—a straight rebuy situation—a purchasing manager or buyer will typically act alone in making a purchasing decision. When an organization is a first-time purchaser of a product or service—a new buy situation—a buying center is enlarged and all five roles in a buying center often emerge. A modified rebuy buying situation lies between these two extremes. Figure 4–3 offers additional insights into how buying centers and buying situations influence organization purchasing.

LO4 *Recognize the importance and nature of online buying in industrial, reseller, and government organizational markets.*

Organizations dwarf consumers in terms of online transactions made and purchase volume. Online buying in organizational markets is popular for three reasons. First, organizational buyers depend on timely supplier information that describes product availability, technical specifications, application uses, price, and delivery schedules. This information can be conveyed quickly via Internet technology. Second, this technology substantially reduces buyer order processing costs. Third, business marketers have found that Internet technology can reduce marketing costs, particularly sales and advertising expense, and broaden their customer base. Two developments in online buying have been the creation of e-marketplaces and online auctions. E-marketplaces provide a technology trading platform and a centralized market for buyer–seller transactions and make possible the real-time exchange of information, money, products, and services. These e-marketplaces can be independent trading communities, such as PlasticsNet, or private exchanges such as the Global Healthcare Exchange. Online traditional and reverse auctions represent a second major development. With traditional auctions, the highest-priced bidder "wins." Conversely, the lowest-priced bidder "wins" with reverse auctions.

FOCUSING ON KEY TERMS

bidder's list
business marketing
buy classes
buying center
derived demand
e-marketplaces
ISO 9000
make-buy decision
North American Industry Classification System (NAICS)
organizational buyers
organizational buying behavior
organizational buying criteria
reciprocity
reverse auction
supplier development
supply partnership
traditional auction
value analysis

APPLYING MARKETING KNOWLEDGE

1 Describe the major differences among industrial firms, resellers, and government units in the United States.

2 Explain how the North American Industry Classification System (NAICS) might be helpful in understanding industrial, reseller, and government markets, and discuss the limitations inherent in this system.

3 List and discuss the key characteristics of organizational buying that make it different from consumer buying.

4 What is a buying center? Describe the roles assumed by people in a buying center and what useful questions should be raised to guide any analysis of the structure and behavior of a buying center.

5 Effective marketing is of increasing importance in today's competitive environment. How can firms more effectively market to organizations?

6 A firm that is marketing multimillion-dollar wastewater treatment systems to cities has been unable to sell a new type of system. This setback has occurred even though the firm's systems are cheaper than competitive systems and meet U.S. Environmental Protection Agency (EPA) specifications. To date, the firm's marketing efforts have been directed to city purchasing departments and the various state EPAs to get on approved bidder's lists. Talks with city-employed personnel have indicated that the new system is very different from current systems and therefore city sanitary and sewer department engineers, directors of these two departments, and city council members are unfamiliar with the workings of the system. Consulting engineers, hired by cities to work on the engineering and design features of these systems and paid on a percentage of system cost, are also reluctant to favor the new system. (*a*) What roles do the various individuals play in the purchase process for a wastewater treatment system? (*b*) How could the firm improve the marketing effort behind the new system?

building your marketing plan

Your marketing plan may need an estimate of the size of the market potential or industry potential (see Chapter 6) for a particular product market in which you compete. Use these steps:

1 Define the product market precisely, such as ice cream.

2 Visit the NAICS Web site at www.census.gov.

3 Click "NAICS" and enter a keyword that describes your product market (e.g., ice cream).

4 Follow the instructions to the specific NAICS code and economic census data that details the dollar sales and provides the estimate of market or industry potential.

video case 4 Lands' End: Where Buyers Rule

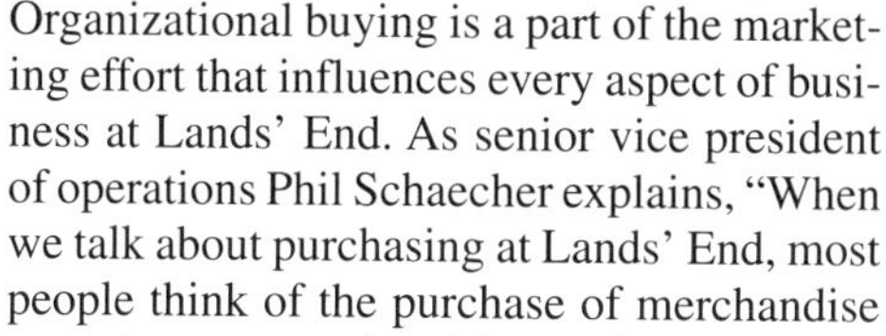

Organizational buying is a part of the marketing effort that influences every aspect of business at Lands' End. As senior vice president of operations Phil Schaecher explains, "When we talk about purchasing at Lands' End, most people think of the purchase of merchandise for resale, but we buy many other things aside from merchandise, everything from the simplest office supply to the most sophisticated piece of material-handling equipment." As a result, Lands' End has developed a sophisticated approach to organizational buying, which is one of the keys to its success.

THE COMPANY

The company started by selling sailboat equipment, duffle bags, rainsuits, and sweaters from a basement location in Chicago's old tannery district. In its first catalog, the company name was printed with a typing error—the apostrophe in the wrong place—but the fledgling company couldn't afford to correct and reprint it. So ever since, the company name has been Lands' End—with the misplaced apostrophe.

When the company outgrew its Chicago location, founder Gary Comer relocated it to Dodgeville, Wisconsin, where he had fallen in love with the rolling hills and changing seasons. The original business ideas were simple: "Sell only things we believe in, ship every order the day it arrives, and unconditionally guarantee everything." Over time, the company developed eight principles of doing business:

- Never reduce the quality of a product to make it cheaper.
- Price products fairly and honestly.
- Accept any return for any reason.

- Ship items in stock the day after the order is received.
- What is best for the customer is best for Lands' End.
- Place contracts with manufacturers who are cost-conscious and efficient.
- Operate efficiently.
- Encourage customers to shop in whatever way they find most convenient.

These principles became the guidelines for the company's dedicated local employees and helped create extraordinary expectations from Lands' End customers.

Today, Lands' End is one of the world's largest direct merchants of traditionally styled clothing for the family, soft luggage, and products for the home. The products are offered through catalogs, on the Internet, and in retail stores. In one year, Lands' End distributes more than 200 million catalogs designed for specific segments, including *The Lands' End Catalog, Lands' End Men, Lands' End Plus Size Collection, Lands' End Kids, Lands' End for School Uniforms, Lands' End Home,* and *Lands' End Business Outfitters*. In a typical day, catalog shoppers place more than 40,000 telephone calls to the company. The Lands' End Web site (www.landsend.com) also offers every Lands' End product and a wide variety of Internet shopping innovations such as a 3-D model customized to each customer (called My Virtual Model™); individually tailored clothes (called Lands' End Custom™); and a feature that allows customers to "chat" online directly with a customer service representative (called Lands' End Live™). Lands' End also operates stores in the United States, the United Kingdom, Germany, and Japan. Selected Lands' End merchandise is also sold in Sears stores, following the purchase of Lands' End by Sears in 2002.

The company's goal is to please customers with the highest levels of quality and service in the industry. Lands' End maintains the high quality of its products through several important activities. For example, the company works directly with mills and manufacturers to retain control of quality and design. "The biggest difference between Lands' End and some other retailers or catalog businesses is that we actually design all the product here and we do all the specifications. Therefore, the manufacturer is building that product directly to our specs, we are not buying off of somebody else's line," explains Joan Mudget, vice president of quality assurance. In addition, Lands' End tests its products for comfort and fit by paying real people (local residents and children) to "wear-test" and "fit-test" all types of garments.

Service has also become an important part of the Lands' End reputation. Customers expect prompt, professional service at every step—initiating the order, making selections, shipping, and follow-up (if necessary). Some of the ways Lands' End meets these expectations include offering the simplest guarantee in the industry—"Guaranteed. Period."—toll-free telephone lines open 24 hours a day, 364 days a year, continuous product training for telephone representatives, and two-day shipping. Lands' End operators even send personal responses to all e-mail messages, approximately 230,000 per year.

ORGANIZATIONAL BUYING AT LANDS' END

The sixth Lands' End business principle (described earlier) is accomplished through the company's organizational buying process. First, its buyers specify fabric quality, construction, and sizing standards, which typically exceed industry standards, for current and potential Lands' End products. Then the buyers literally search around the world for the best possible source of fabrics and products. Once a potential supplier is identified, one of the company's 150 quality assurance personnel makes an information-gathering visit. The purpose of the visit is to understand the supplier's values, to assess four criteria (economic, quality, service, and vendor), and to determine if the Lands' End standards can be achieved.

Lands' End evaluations of potential suppliers lead to the selection of what the company hopes will become long-term partners. As Mudget explains, "When we're looking for new manufacturers we are looking for the long term. I think one of the most interesting things is we're not out there looking for new vendors every year to fill the same products." In fact, Lands' End believes that the term *supplier* does not adequately describe the importance the company places on the relationships. Lands' End suppliers are viewed as allies, supporters, associates, colleagues, and stakeholders in the future of the company. Once an alliance is formed the product specifications and the performance on those specifications are regularly evaluated.

Lands' End buyers face a variety of buying situations. Straight rebuys involve reordering an existing product—such as shipping boxes—without evaluating or changing specifications. Modified rebuys involve changing some aspect of a previously ordered product—such as the collar of a knit shirt—based on input from consumers, retailers, or other people involved in the purchase decision. Finally, new buys involve first-time purchases—such as Lands' End addition of men's suits to its product line. The complexity of the process can vary with the type of purchase. Schaecher explains, "As you get more complicated in the purchase there are more things you look at to decide on a vendor."

FUTURE CHALLENGES FOR LANDS' END

Lands' End faces several challenges as it pursues improvements in its organizational buying process. First, new technologies offer opportunities for fast, efficient, and accurate communication with suppliers. Ed Smidebush, general inventory manager, describes a new system at Lands' End: "Our quick response system is a computerized system where we transmit electronically to our vendors each Sunday night, forecast information as well as stock positions and purchase order information so that on Monday morning this information will be incorporated directly into their manufacturing reports so that they can prioritize their production." Occasionally Lands' End must work with its suppliers to improve their technology and information system capabilities.

Another challenge for Lands' End is to anticipate changes in consumer interests. While it has many years of experience with retail consumers, preferences for colors, fabrics, and styles change frequently, requiring buyers to constantly monitor the marketplace. In addition, Lands' End's more recent offerings to corporate customers require constant attention "because business customers' wants and incentives, and the environment in which they're shopping, are very different from consumers at home," explains marketing manager Hilary Kleese.

Finally, Lands' End must anticipate the quantities of each of its products consumers are likely to order. To do this, historical information is used to develop forecasts. One of the best tests of their forecast accuracy is the holiday season, when Lands' End receives more than 100,000 calls each day. Having the right products available is important because, as every employee knows from Principle 4, every order must be shipped the day after it is received.

Questions

1 *(a)* Who is likely to comprise the buying center in the decision to select a new supplier for Lands' End? *(b)* Which of the buying center members are likely to play the roles of users, influencers, buyers, deciders, and gatekeepers?

2 *(a)* Which stages of the organizational buying decision process does Lands' End follow when it selects a new supplier? *(b)* What selection criteria does the company utilize in the process?

3 Describe purchases Lands' End buyers typically face in each of the three buying situations: straight rebuy, modified rebuy, and new buy.

AND THE
HALF-BLOOD
PRINCE
DARK SECRETS REVEALED
COMING SOON
WWW.HARRYPOTTER.CO.UK

5

营销调研：将消费者信息变成行动
Marketing Research: From Customer Insights to Actions

LEARNING OBJECTIVES

After reading this chapter you should be able to:

LO1 Identify the reason for conducting marketing research.

LO2 Describe the five-step marketing research approach that leads to marketing actions.

LO3 Explain how marketing uses secondary and primary data.

LO4 Discuss the uses of observations, questionnaires, panels, experiments, and newer data collection methods.

LO5 Explain how information technology and data mining lead to marketing actions.

LO6 Describe three approaches to developing a company's sales forecast.

试映和跟踪调研：怎样倾听消费者去降低电影风险
TEST SCREENINGS AND TRACKING STUDIES: HOW LISTENING TO CONSUMERS REDUCES MOVIE RISKS

Harry Potter and the Half Blood Prince, *Star Trek*, and *Transformers: Revenge of the Fallen* are movies that their studios count on for huge profits. But what can these studios do to try to reduce the costly risks of a movie's box-office failure?

What's in a Movie Name?

Fixing bad names for movies—such as *Shoeless Joe* and *Rope Burns*—can turn potential disasters into hugely successful blockbusters. Don't remember seeing these movies? Well, test screenings, a form of marketing research, found that moviegoers like you had problems with these titles. Here's what happened:

- Shown frequently on television now, *Shoeless Joe* became *Field of Dreams* because audiences thought Kevin Costner might be playing a homeless person.
- *Rope Burns* became *Million Dollar Baby* because audiences didn't like the original name. The movie won the 2005 Academy Award™ for Best Picture and starred Hilary Swank as a woman boxer and Clint Eastwood as her trainer.

Filmmakers want movie titles that are concise, grab attention, capture the essence of the film, and have no legal restrictions to reduce risk to both the studio and audiences—the same factors that make a good brand name.

Using Marketing Research to Reduce Movie Risks

Bad titles, poor scripts, temperamental stars, costly special effects, and several blockbuster movies released at the same time are just a few of the nightmares studios face. According to the latest data, today's films now average $107 million to produce and market. So studios try to reduce their risks by doing marketing research that includes conducting test screenings and using tracking studies.

Without reading ahead, think about the answers to these questions:

- Whom would you recruit for movie test screenings?
- What questions would you ask to help you edit or modify the title or other aspects of a film?

---

disaster 灾祸，祸患；blockbuster 轰动一时的电影，一度热卖的畅销书；release 发布，发表，公布。

Test screenings and tracking studies can help avoid potential dangers, such as improving movie titles, endings, and characters.

Virtually every major U.S. movie produced today uses test screenings to obtain the key reactions of consumers likely to be in the target audience. In test screenings, 300 to 400 prospective moviegoers are recruited to attend a "sneak preview" of a film before its release. After viewing the movie, the audience fills out an exhaustive survey to critique its title, plot, characters, music, and ending as well as the marketing program (posters, trailers, and so on) to identify improvements to make in the final edit.

Test screenings resulted in *Fatal Attraction* having one of the most commercially successful "ending-switches" of all time. In sneak previews, audiences liked everything but the ending, which had Alex (Glenn Close) committing suicide and framing Dan (Michael Douglas) as her murderer by leaving his fingerprints on the knife she used. The studio shot $1.3 million of new scenes for the ending that audiences eventually saw. The new ending for *Fatal Attraction* undoubtedly contributed to the movie's box-office success.

Figure 5–1 summarizes some key questions used in these test screenings both to select the people for the screenings and to obtain key reactions of those sitting in the screenings. Note how specific the studio's action is for each question asked. This is an example of effective, action-oriented marketing research.

Marketing researchers use tracking studies immediately before an upcoming film's release to forecast its opening week's box-office revenues. The tracking studies ask prospective target audience moviegoers who have seen at least six movies in the last year three key questions: (1) Are you aware of the film? (2) Are you interested in seeing the film? and (3) Will you see the film this week? Depending on the research results, the movie studio may run last-minute ads to increase awareness, interest, and attendance at the film. Industry "wisdom" says that the total U.S. box-office revenues will be two and one-half times the opening week's box office revenues.

This example shows how marketing research, the main topic of this chapter, links marketing strategy and decisive marketing actions. Also, marketing research is often used to help a firm develop its sales forecasts, the final topic of this chapter.

FIGURE 5–1
Marketing research questions asked in test screenings of movies. Note each kind of question leads to a specific action—a characteristic of effective marketing research.

POINT WHEN ASKED	KEY QUESTIONS	ACTION AND USE OF QUESTION
Before the test screening	• How old are you? • How frequently do you pay to see movies?	• Find people who fit the target audience profile for movie. • Find people who frequently attend movies.
After the test screening	• What do you think of the title? What title would you suggest? • Were any characters too distasteful? Who? How? • Did you like the ending? If not, how would you change it?	• Change movie title. • Change aspects of some characters in the movie. • Change or clarify ending of the movie.

moviegoer 常看电影的人，影迷；audience 观众，听众；awareness 警觉。

营销调研的角色
THE ROLE OF MARKETING RESEARCH

LO1

Let's look at (1) what marketing research is, (2) identify some difficulties with it, and (3) describe the five steps marketers use to conduct it.

什么是营销调研
What Is Marketing Research?

For how Fisher-Price does marketing research on young children who can't read, see the text.

Marketing research is the process of defining a marketing problem and opportunity, systematically collecting and analyzing information, and recommending actions. Although imperfect, marketers conduct marketing research to reduce risk of and thereby improve marketing decisions.

做好营销调研的挑战
The Challenges in Doing Good Marketing Research

Whatever the marketing issue involved—whether discovering consumer tastes or setting the right price—good marketing research is challenging. For example:

- Suppose your firm is developing a new product never before seen by consumers. Would consumers really know whether they are likely to buy a product that they have never thought about before?
- Imagine if you, as a consumer, were asked about your personal hygiene habits. Even though you know the answers, would you reveal them? When personal or status questions are involved, will people give honest answers?
- Will consumers' actual purchase behavior match their stated interest or intentions? Will they buy the same brand they say they will?

Marketing research must overcome these difficulties and obtain the information needed so that marketers can make reasonable estimates about what consumers want and will buy.

五步营销调研法
Five-Step Marketing Research Approach

LO2

决策是指从两个或两个以上方案中慎重选一的行为。我们每天都在做着许多决策。工作中为了分配任务，我们要从诸多方案中进行选择。上大学我们要选择课程。作为消费者我们要选择品牌。但是没有一种神奇的方法能保证选择肯定正确。

A **decision** is a conscious choice from among two or more alternatives. All of us make many such decisions daily. At work we choose from alternative ways to accomplish an assigned task. At college we choose from alternative courses. As consumers we choose from alternative brands. No magic formula guarantees correct decisions.

Managers and researchers have tried to improve the outcomes of decisions by using more formal, structured approaches to *decision making,* the act of consciously choosing from alternatives. The systematic marketing research approach used to collect information to improve marketing decisions and actions described in this chapter uses five steps and is shown in Figure 5–2 on the next page. Although the five-step approach described here focuses on marketing decisions, it provides a systematic checklist for making both business and personal decisions.

第一步：确定问题
STEP 1: DEFINE THE PROBLEM

Every marketing problem faces its own research challenges. For example, toy designers at Fisher-Price conduct marketing research to discover how children play, how

systematically 系统的；magic 魔力，魅力，神奇；formula 方案，方法；guarantee 保证，担保。

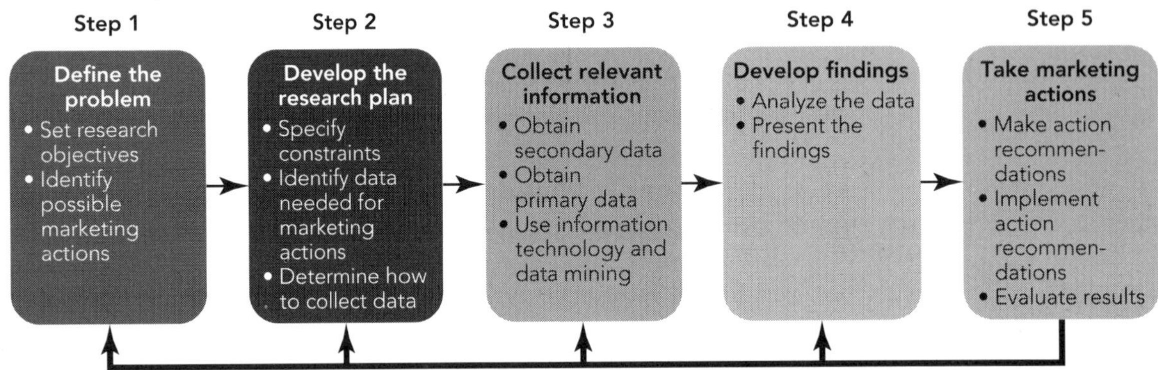

FIGURE 5–2
Five-step marketing research approach leading to marketing actions. Lessons learned from past research mistakes are fed back to improve each of the steps.

they learn, and what they like to play with. As part of its marketing research, Fisher-Price invites children to play at its state-licensed nursery school in East Aurora, New York. From behind one-way mirrors, toy designers and marketing researchers watch the children use—and abuse—toys, which helps the firm develop better products.

The original model of a classic Fisher-Price toy, the Chatter Telephone™, was simply a wooden phone with a dial that rang a bell. However, observers noted that the children kept grabbing the receiver like a handle to pull the phone along behind them, so a designer added wheels, a noisemaker, and eyes that bobbed up and down.

A careful look at Fisher-Price's toy marketing research shows the two key elements of defining a problem: setting the research objectives and identifying possible marketing actions.

设定调研目标
Set the Research Objectives

Research objectives are specific, measurable goals the decision maker—in this case, an executive at Fisher-Price—seeks to achieve in conducting the marketing research. For Fisher-Price, the immediate research objective was to decide whether to market the old or new telephone design.

In setting these research objectives, marketers have to be clear on the purpose of the research that leads to marketing actions. The three main types of marketing research, with examples explained in more detail later in the chapter, are:

1. *Exploratory research* provides ideas about a relatively vague problem. General Mills discovered that the initial version of its Hamburger Helper wasn't satisfactory for many consumers, so it interviewed them to get ideas to improve the product.
2. *Descriptive research* generally involves trying to find the frequency that something occurs or the extent of a relationship between two factors. So when General Mills wants to study how loyal consumers are to its Wheaties, it can obtain data on the number of households buying Wheaties and competitive products.
3. *Causal research*, the most sophisticated, tries to determine the extent to which the change in one factor changes another one. In the Fisher-Price example discussed next, changing the toy designs is related to changes in the amount of time children play with the toy. Experiments and test markets, discussed later, are examples of causal research.

The wheels, noisemaker, and bobbing eyes on Fisher-Price's hugely successful Chatter Telephone resulted from careful marketing research on children.

明确可行的营销行动
Identify Possible Marketing Actions

Effective decision makers develop specific **measures of success**, which are criteria or standards used in evaluating proposed solutions to the problem.

nursery 幼儿园，幼稚园；noisemaker 发出大声音的人，会高声喧闹的人。

Marketing research isn't perfect. Recently it correctly identified Cybertron Transformers as a "hot toy" . . .

. . . but missed on Hasbro's FurReal Friends Butterscotch Pony.

Different research outcomes—based on the measure of success—lead to different marketing actions. For the Fisher-Price problem, if a measure of success were the total time children spent playing with each of the two telephone designs, the results of observing them would lead to clear-cut actions as follows:

Measure of Success: Playtime	Possible Marketing Action
• Children spent more time playing with old design.	• Continue with old design; don't introduce new design.
• Children spent more time playing with new design.	• Introduce new design; drop old design.

One test of whether marketing research should be done is if different outcomes will lead to different marketing actions. If all the research outcomes lead to the same action—such as top management sticking with the older design regardless of what the observed children liked—the research is useless and a waste of money. In this case, research results showed that kids liked the new design, so Fisher-Price introduced its noisemaking pull-toy Chatter Telephone, which became a toy classic and has sold millions.

Each year, *FamilyFun* magazine has dozens of children—and their parents—evaluate hundreds of new toys from over 100 toy manufactures to select its Toy of the Year awards. Over the years, the magazine has been right on the money in selecting Barney the TV dinosaur, Tickle Me Elmo, and Fisher-Price's Love to Dance Bear™ as hot toys—ones that jumped off retailers' shelves. But as shown with the toys in the margin, even careful marketing research can sometimes overlook hot toys. Forecasting which toys are hot and will sell well is critical for retailers, which must place orders to manufacturers 8 to 10 months before holiday shoppers walk into their stores. Bad forecasts can lead to lost sales for understocks and severe losses for overstocks.

Marketing researchers know that defining a problem is an incredibly difficult task. For example, if the objectives are too broad, the problem may not be researchable. If they are too narrow, the value of the research results may be seriously lessened. This is why marketing researchers spend so much time defining a marketing problem precisely and writing a formal proposal that describes the research to be done.

第二步：制订调研计划
STEP 2: DEVELOP THE RESEARCH PLAN

The second step in the marketing research process requires that the researcher (1) specify the constraints on the marketing research activity, (2) identify the data needed for marketing decisions, and (3) determine how to collect the data.

列出约束条件
Specify Constraints

约束条件是指一项决策中对某一问题潜在解决方案的限制。

The **constraints** in a decision are the restrictions placed on potential solutions to a problem. Examples include the limitations on the time and money available to solve the problem. Thus, Fisher-Price might set two constraints on its decision to select either the old or new version of the Chatter Telephone: The decision must be made in 10 weeks and no research budget is available beyond that needed for collecting data in its nursery school.

确定营销行动所需资料
Identify Data Needed for Marketing Actions

Often marketing research studies wind up collecting a lot of data that are interesting but irrelevant for marketing decisions that result in marketing actions. In the

retailer 零售商，零售店；constraint 限制，束缚，约束；irrelevant 无关紧要的，不重要的。

Fisher-Price Chatter Telephone case, it might be nice to know the children's favorite colors, whether they like wood or plastic toys better, and so on. In fact, knowing answers to these questions might result in later modifications of the toy, but right now the problem is to select one of two toy designs. So this study must focus on collecting data that help managers make a clear choice between the two telephone designs.

决定如何收集资料
Determine How to Collect Data

Determining how to collect useful marketing research data is often as important as actually collecting the data—step 3 in the process, which is discussed later. Two key elements in deciding how to collect the data are (1) concepts and (2) methods.

概念　在营销领域，概念是指有关产品或服务的想法。为了掌握消费者对一款潜在新产品的反应，营销调研人员常常提出一个新产品概念，即公司可能生产销售的产品或服务的一种形象描绘或视觉描述。

方法　这里的方法是指用于收集资料，以解决全部或部分问题的途径。

Concepts In the world of marketing, *concepts* are ideas about products or services. To find out about consumer reaction to a potential new product, marketing researchers frequently develop a *new-product concept*, that is, a picture or verbal description of a product or service the firm might offer for sale. For example, Fisher-Price's addition of a noisemaker, wheels, and eyes to the basic design of its Chatter Telephone made the toy more fun for children and increased sales.

Methods *Methods* are the approaches that can be used to collect data to solve all or part of a problem. For example, if you are the marketing researcher at Fisher-Price responsible for the Chatter Telephone, you face a number of methods issues in developing your research plan, including the following:

- Can we actually ask three- or four-year-olds meaningful questions they can answer about their liking or disliking of the two designs?
- Are we better off not asking them questions but simply observing their behavior?
- If we simply observe the children's behavior, how can we do this in a way to get the best information without biasing the results?

Millions of other people have asked similar questions about millions of other products and services. How can you find and use the methods that other marketing researchers have found successful? Information on useful methods is available in tradebooks, textbooks, and handbooks that relate to marketing and marketing research. Some periodicals and technical journals, such as the *Journal of Marketing* and the *Journal of Marketing Research* both published by the American Marketing Association, summarize methods and techniques valuable in addressing marketing problems.

Special methods vital to marketing are (1) sampling and (2) statistical inference. For example, marketing researchers often use *sampling*, which is a technique to select a group of distributors, customers, or prospects and treating the information they provide as typical of all those in whom they are interested. They may then use *statistical inference* to generalize the results from the sample to much larger groups of distributors, customers, or prospects to help decide on marketing actions.

learning review

1. What is marketing research?
2. What is the five-step marketing research approach?
3. What are constraints, as they apply to developing a research plan?

modification 修改，变更，改进；concept 概念，观念；periodical（尤指学术）期刊。

第三步：收集相关信息
STEP 3: COLLECT RELEVANT INFORMATION

LO3

资料，即相关问题的事实和数据可以分为两个主要部分：二手资料和原始资料。**二手资料**是在当前计划开始之前就已被记录的事实和数据。

Collecting enough relevant information to make a rational, informed marketing decision sometimes simply means using your knowledge to decide immediately. At other times it entails collecting an enormous amount of information at great expense.

Figure 5–3 shows how the different kinds of marketing information fit together. **Data**, the facts and figures related to the problem, are divided into two main parts: secondary data and primary data. **Secondary data** are facts and figures that have already been recorded before the project at hand. As shown in Figure 5–3, secondary data divide into two parts—internal and external secondary data—depending on whether the data come from inside or outside the organization needing the research. **Primary data** are facts and figures that are newly collected for the project. Figure 5–3 shows that primary data can be divided into observational data, questionnaire data, and other sources of data.

二手资料：内部的
Secondary Data: Internal

Examples of internal secondary data include detailed sales breakdowns by product line, by region, by customer, and by sales representative, as well as customer inquiries and complaints. So internal secondary data are often the starting point for a new marketing research study because using this information can result in huge time and cost savings.

二手资料：外部的
Secondary Data: External

Published data from outside the organization are external secondary data. The U.S. Census Bureau publishes a variety of useful reports. Best known is the Census 2000, which is the most recent count of the U.S. population that occurs every 10 years. Recently, the Census Bureau began collecting data annually from a smaller number

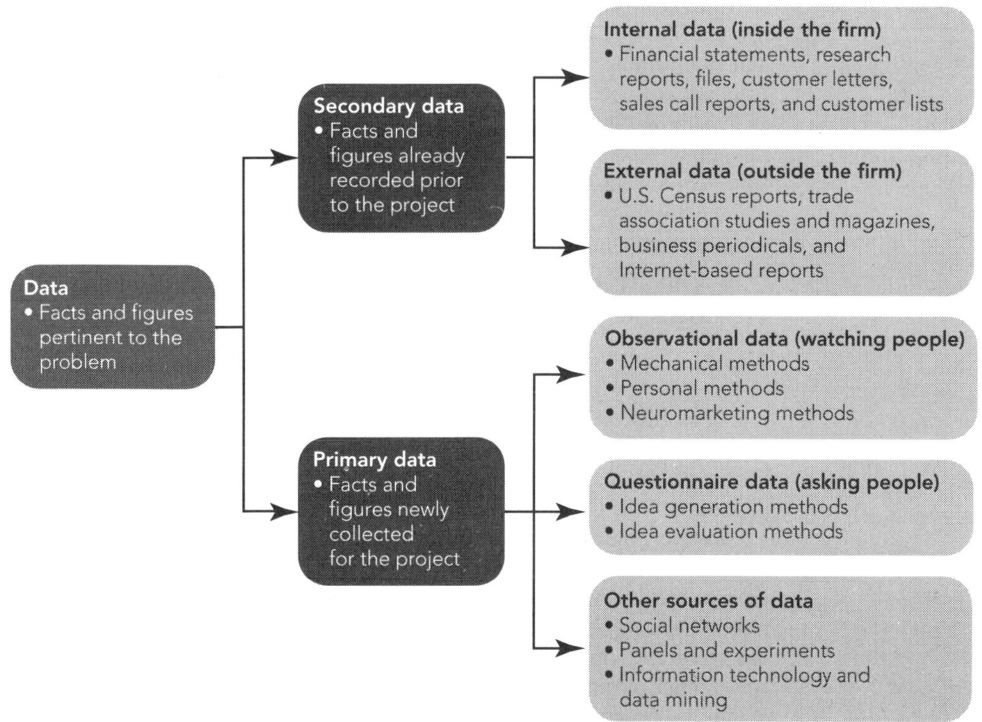

FIGURE 5–3
Types of marketing information. Researchers must choose carefully among these to get the best results, considering time and cost constraints.

observational 观察的，观测的；questionnaire 调查问卷，调查表。

Scanner data at supermarket checkout counters provide valuable information for marketing decisions.

of people through the American Community Survey. Both surveys contain detailed information on American households, such as the number of people per household and their age, sex, race/ethnic background, income, occupation, and education. Marketers use these data to identify characteristics and trends of ultimate consumers.

The Census Bureau also publishes the Economic Census, which is conducted every five years. These reports are vital to business firms selling products and services to organizations. The 2007 Economic Census contains data on the number and sales of establishments in the United States that produce a good or service based on its geography (states, counties, ZIP codes, etc.), industry sector (Manufacturing, Retail Trade, etc.), and North American Industry Classification System (NAICS) code. The Current Industrial Reports are periodic studies that provide data on the production quantity and shipment value of selected products. Finally, trade associations, universities, and business periodicals provide detailed data of value to market researchers and planners. These data are now available online via the Internet and can be identified and located using a search engine such as Google. The accompanying Going Online box provides examples.

Several market research companies pay households and businesses to record all their purchases using a paper or electronic diary. Such *syndicated panel* data economically answer questions that require consistent data collection over time, such as how many times did our customers buy our products this year compared to last year? One syndicated panel sample with almost 100,000 households gives each household an electronic wand to scan the bar codes on purchases it makes. Other examples of specialized syndicated services that provide a standard set of data on a regular basis are the Nielsen Media Research's TV ratings and the J. D. Power's automotive quality and customer satisfaction surveys.

Some data services provide comprehensive information on household demographics and lifestyle, product purchases, TV viewing behavior, and responses to coupon and free-sample promotions. Their advantage is that a single firm can collect, analyze, interrelate, and present all this information. For consumer product firms such as Procter & Gamble, sales data from various channels are critical to allocate scarce marketing resources. As a result, they use services such as Information Resources' InfoScan and ACNielsen's ScanTrack to collect product sales and coupon/free-sample redemptions that have been scanned at the checkout counters of supermarket, drug, convenience, and mass merchandise retailers.

二手资料的优缺点
Advantages and Disadvantages of Secondary Data

营销界有一条基本规则：先获得二手资料，然后再收集原始资料。二手资料有两个重要的优点：(1) 利用已被收集公布的资料可以节省大量时间；(2) 成本低，比如免费或便宜的普查报告。而且，二手资料提供的信息通常更详细，特别是美国普查局的资料。

A general rule among marketing people is to obtain secondary data first and then collect primary data. Two important advantages of secondary data are (1) the tremendous time savings because the data have already been collected and published or exist internally and (2) the low cost, such as free or inexpensive Census reports. Furthermore, a greater level of detail is often available through secondary data, especially U.S. Census Bureau data.

However, these advantages must be weighed against some significant disadvantages. First, the secondary data may be out of date, especially if they are U.S. Census data collected only every 5 or 10 years. Second, the definitions or categories might not be quite right for a researcher's project. For example, the age groupings or product categories might be wrong for the project. Also, because the data are collected for another purpose, they may not be specific enough for the project. In such cases it may be necessary to collect primary data.

household 家庭，一家人；geography 地理学；syndicate 辛迪加，企业联合组织，财团。

Going Online

Online Databases and Internet Resources Useful to Marketers

Information contained in online databases available via the Internet consists of indexes to articles in periodicals and statistical or financial data on markets, products, and organizations that are accessed either directly or via Internet search engines or portals through keyword searches.

Statistical and financial data on markets, products, and organizations include:

- *The Wall Street Journal* (www.wsj.com), CNBC (www.cnbc.com), and *Fox Business News* (www.foxbusiness.com) provide up-to-the-minute business news and security prices plus research reports on companies, industries, and countries.
- STAT-USA (www.stat-usa.gov) and the Census Bureau (www.census.gov) of the U.S. Department of Commerce provide information on U.S. business, economic, and trade activity collected by the federal government.

Portals and search engines include:

- USA.gov (www.usa.gov) is the portal to all U.S. government Web sites. Users click on links to browse by topic or enter keywords for specific searches.
- Google (www.google.com) is the most popular portal to the entire Internet. Users click on links to browse by topic or enter keywords for specific searches.

Some of these Web sites are accessible only if your educational institution has paid a subscription fee. Check with your institution's Web site.

learning review

4. What is the difference between secondary and primary data?
5. What are some advantages and disadvantages of secondary data?

原始资料：观察人们
Primary Data: Watching People

Observing people and asking them questions are the two principal ways to collect new or primary data for a marketing study. Facts and figures obtained by watching, either mechanically or in person, how people actually behave is the way marketing researchers collect **observational data**. Observational data can be collected by mechanical (including electronic), personal, or neuromarketing methods.

Mechanical Methods National TV ratings, such as those of Nielsen Media Research shown in Figure 5–4 on the next page are an example of mechanical observational data collected by a "people meter." The people meter is a box that (1) is attached to TV sets, VCRs, cable boxes, and satellite dishes in more than 25,000 homes across the country; (2) has a remote that operates the meter when a viewer begins and finishes watching a TV program; and (3) stores and then transmits the viewing information each night to Nielsen Media Research. Data are also collected using less sophisticated meters or TV diaries (a paper-pencil measurement system).

By 2011, Nielsen will implement a new measurement program dubbed the *Anytime Anywhere Media Measurement (A2/M2) Initiative*. The purpose of A2/M2 is to "follow the video" of 21st century viewers. New "active/passive" people meter technology will measure all types of TV viewing behavior from a variety of devices and sources: DVR (digital video recorders), VOD (video on demand), Internet-delivered TV shows on computers via iTunes, streaming media, mobile media devices (cell phones, iPods, etc.), as well as outside the home in bars, fitness clubs, airports, and so on.

On the basis of all these observational data, Nielsen Media Research then calculates the rating and share of each TV program. With 114.5 million TV households

principal 首要的，最主要的，最重要的；sophisticated（机器、装置等）高级的，精密的，（方法）复杂的。

FIGURE 5–4
Nielsen Television Index Ranking Report for network TV prime-time households, week of May 18–24, 2009. The difference of a few share points in Nielsen TV ratings affects the cost of a TV ad on a show and even whether the show remains on the air.

Rank	Program	Network	Rating	Share
1	*American Idol—Wednesday*	FOX	16.1	27
2	*American Idol—Tuesday*	FOX	13.5	22
3	*Dancing with the Stars—Results*	ABC	12.6	20
4	*Dancing with the Stars*	ABC	12.2	20
5	*The Mentalist*	CBS	10.4	16
6	*NCIS*	CBS	10.3	17
7	*Two and a Half Men*	CBS	9.9	15
8	*CSI: Miami*	CBS	8.9	15
9	*Criminal Minds*	CBS	8.7	14
10	*Rules of Engagement*	CBS	7.9	12

Source: Copyright 2009, The Nielsen Company. All times Eastern. Viewing estimates include live viewing and DVR playback on the same day, defined as 3 A.M. to 3 A.M. Rank is based on U.S. Household Rating % from Nielsen Media Research's National People Meter Sample.

in the United States, based on the 2000 U.S. Census, a single ratings point equals 1 percent, or 1,145,000 TV households. For TV viewing, a share point is the percentage of TV sets in use tuned to a particular program. Because TV and cable networks sell almost $65 billion annually in advertising and set advertising rates to advertisers on the basis of those data, precision in the Nielsen data is critical. Thus, a change of one percentage point in a rating can mean gaining or losing millions of dollars in advertising revenues because advertisers pay rates on the basis of the size of the audience for a TV program. So as Figure 5–4 shows, we might expect to pay more for a 30-second TV ad on *The Mentalist* than one on *CSI: Miami*. Broadcast and cable networks may change the time slot or even cancel a TV program if its ratings are consistently poor and advertisers are unwilling to pay a rate based on a higher guaranteed rating.

But TV advertisers today have a special problem: With about three out of four TV viewers skipping ads with TiVo or channel surfing during commercials, how many people are actually seeing their TV ad? Now services such as Nielsen Media Research and Media Check offer advertisers minute-by-minute measurement of how many viewers stay tuned during commercials. The viewership data in Figure 5–4 includes not only live TV but also programs taped on digital video recorders (DVRs). With these more precise measures of who is likely to see a TV ad, buying TV ads is becoming a lot more scientific.

Nielsen Online Ratings also uses an electronic meter to record Internet user behavior. These data are collected via a meter installed on computers by tracking the actual mouse clicks made by a large sample of 230,000 panelists in the U.S. as they surf the Internet. Nielsen Online Ratings identifies the top Web sites—or "brands"—that have the largest unique audiences and "active reach," which is the percent of total home and office users that visited the Web site. In 2009, the five most popular U.S. Web site brands were Google, Microsoft, Yahoo!, Facebook, and AOL.

What determines if *American Idol* stays on the air? For the importance of the TV "ratings game," see the text.

Personal Methods Observational data can take some strange twists. Jennifer Voitle, a laid-off investment bank employee with four advanced degrees, responded to an Internet ad and found a new career: *mystery shopper*. Companies pay mystery shoppers to check on the quality and pricing of their products and the integrity of and customer service provided by their employees. Jennifer

precision 精确，精密；consistently（行为、态度等）一贯的，一致的，始终如一的；electronic 电子化的，使用电子装置的。

Is this *really* marketing research? A *mystery shopper* at work.

gets paid to travel to exotic hotels, eat at restaurants, play golf, test-drive new cars, shop for clothes, and play arcade games. But her role posing as a customer gives her client unique marketing research information that can be obtained in no other way. Says Jennifer, "Can you believe they call this work?"

Watching consumers in person or videotaping them are two other observational approaches. For example, Procter & Gamble watched women do their laundry, clean the floor, put on makeup, and so on because they comprise 80 percent of its customers! And Gillette videotaped consumers brushing their teeth in their own bathrooms to see how they really brush—not just how they say they brush. The new-product result: Gillette's Oral-B CrossAction toothbrush.

Ethnographic research is a specialized observational approach in which trained observers seek to discover subtle behavioral and emotional reactions as consumers encounter products in their "natural use environment," such as in their home or car. Recently, Kraft launched Deli Creations, which are sandwiches made with its Oscar Mayer meats, Kraft cheeses, and Grey Poupon mustard, after spending several months with consumers in their kitchens. Kraft discovered that consumers wanted complete, ready-to-serve meals that are easy to prepare—and it had the products to create them.

人员观察是一种有效且有弹性的方法，但费用可能比较高，而且当不同的观察者对同一事件观察所得出结论不一致时，就不那么可靠。

Personal observation is both useful and flexible, but it can be costly and unreliable when different observers report different conclusions when watching the same event. And while observation can reveal *what* people do, it cannot easily determine *why* they do it. This is the principal reason for using neuromarketing and questionnaires, our next topics.

Neuromarketing Methods As a global brand expert, Martin Lindstrom has consulted for clients that market everything from chocolate and TV remote controls to toothpaste and iPod speakers. Not being satisfied with the results obtained from traditional marketing research, Lindstrom undertook a three-year, $7 million study that used brain scanning to analyze the buying processes of more than 2,000 participants. And how was his study different from traditional marketing research? Lindstrom merged neuroscience—the study of the brain—with marketing! His controversial findings using "neuromarketing" are summarized in his 2008 breakthrough book *Buy•ology*. Several of his findings appear in the Marketing Matters box on the next page.

原始数据：询问人们
Primary Data: Asking People

How many dozens of times have you filled out some kind of a questionnaire? Maybe a short survey at school or a telephone or e-mail survey to see if you are pleased with the service you received. Asking consumers questions and recording their answers is the second principal way of gathering information.

We can divide this primary data collection task into (1) idea generation methods and (2) idea evaluation methods, although they sometimes overlap and each has a number of special techniques. Each survey method results in valuable **questionnaire data**, which are facts and figures obtained by asking people about their attitudes, awareness, intentions, and behaviors.

Idea Generation Methods—Coming Up with Ideas In the past the most common way of collecting questionnaire data to generate ideas was through

obtain 得到，获得，实现；videotape 把……录在录像带上；behavioral 行为，特性，性能（的）；flexible 易变通的，适应性强的，灵活的。

Marketing Matters > > > > > > > > technology

Buy•ology: How "Neuromarketing" Is Trying to Understand Consumers

Is much of the more than $12 *billion* spent on traditional market research (focus groups, surveys, and so on) wasted? Brand guru Martin Lindstrom believes so. Why? Because 85 percent of consumers' thoughts, feelings, or preferences toward products, brands, and advertisements resides deep within the subconscious part of the brain and can't be understood using traditional techniques.

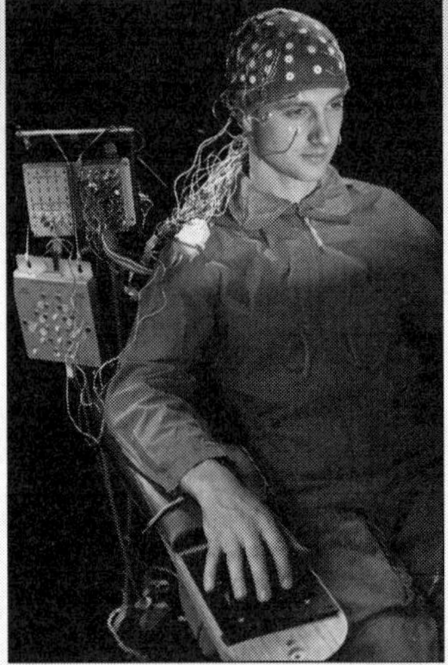

Lindstrom is a believer in the relatively new field of "neuromarketing," which uses high-tech brain scanning instruments to record the brain's responses to various marketing stimuli (package designs, brand logos, fragrances, TV ads, and so on) via the five senses (sight, sound, smell, touch, and taste). Two instruments are typically used when stimuli are presented: (1) An expensive, doughnut-shaped functional magnetic resonance imaging (fMRI) scanner, where different areas of the brain "light up" and can be mapped and (2) a less costly cap with dozens of sensors plugged into an electroencephalograph (EEG), where the real-time changes in brain wave patterns can be seen (see photo).

So why is neuromarketing important to marketers? Lindstrom draws these fascinating conclusions that could have a significant impact on current marketing actions:

- **Brand logos don't work.** Instead, brands should focus on indirect logo signals, such as shapes, sound, smell, color, and so on.
- **Ads with sex appeal don't sell.** Men in particular don't recall these types of ads nearly as much as nonsexually oriented ads.
- **Successful brands function like religion.** Participants' brains respond similarly to brand messages and religious icons.
- **Warning labels on cigarettes don't work.** Interestingly, the labels stimulate the area of the brain responsible for cravings.

So, what do you think about neuromarketing? Are you concerned that marketers will invade your privacy by influencing what you buy? Stay tuned!

an *individual interview*, which involves a single researcher asking questions of one respondent. This approach has many advantages, such as being able to probe for additional ideas using follow-up questions to a respondent's initial answers, but it is very expensive. Later in the chapter we'll discuss some alternatives.

Individual interviews have the advantage of enabling interviewers to ask probing follow-up questions about a respondent's answers.

General Mills sought ideas about why Hamburger Helper didn't fare well when introduced. Initial instructions called for cooking a half-pound of hamburger separately from the noodles or potatoes, which were later mixed with the hamburger. So General Mills researchers used a special kind of individual interview called *depth interviews* in which researchers ask lengthy, free-flowing kinds of questions to probe for underlying ideas and feelings. These depth interviews showed that consumers (1) didn't think it contained enough meat and (2) didn't want the hassle of cooking in two different pots. So the Hamburger Helper product manager changed the recipe to call for a full pound of meat and to allow users to prepare it in one dish. This marketing action converted a potential failure into a success.

Focus groups are informal sessions of 6 to 10 past, present, or prospective customers in which a discussion leader, or moderator, asks their opinions about the firm's and its competitors' products, how they use these products, and special needs they have that these products don't address. Often recorded and conducted in special interviewing rooms with a one-way mirror, these groups enable marketing researchers and managers to hear and watch consumer reactions. The informality and peer support in an effective focus group help uncover ideas that are often difficult to obtain with individual interviews. For example, 3M ran eight focus groups around the United States and heard consumers complain that standard steel wool pads scratched their

respondent（调查和问题的）回答者，答卷人；prospective 可能即将发生的。

Listening carefully in focus groups to student and instructor suggestions benefits this text, such as providing answers to the Learning Review questions.

expensive cookware. These interviews led to 3M's internationally successful Scotch-Brite® Never Scratch soap pad.

Finding "the next big thing" for consumers has become the obsession not only for consumer product firms but also for firms in many other industries. The result is that marketing researchers have come to rely on other—many would say bizarre—techniques than more traditional individual or focus group interviews. These "fuzzy front end" methods attempt early identification of elusive consumer tastes or trends. For example, Trend Hunter is a firm that seeks to anticipate and track "the evolution of cool." Trend hunting (or watching) is the practice of identifying "emerging shifts in social behavior," which are driven by changes in pop culture that can lead to new products. Trend Hunter has identified over 47,000 "micro trends" through its global network of 27,000 spotters and features several of these trends on its daily Trend Hunter TV broadcast via its Web site (see www.trendhunter.com/tv).

Idea Evaluation Methods—Testing an Idea In idea evaluation, the marketing researcher tries to test ideas discovered earlier to help the marketing manager recommend marketing actions. Idea evaluation methods often involve conventional questionnaires using personal, mail, telephone, fax, and online (e-mail or Internet) surveys of a large sample of past, present, or prospective consumers. In choosing among them, the marketing researcher balances the cost of the particular method against the expected quality of and speed with which the information is obtained. Personal interview surveys enable the interviewer to be flexible in asking probing questions or getting reactions to visual materials but are very costly. Mail surveys are usually biased because those most likely to respond have had especially positive or negative experiences with the product or brand. While telephone interviews allow flexibility, unhappy respondents may hang up on the interviewer, even with the efficiency of computer-assisted telephone interviewing (CATI). Fax surveys, a method in decline, are restricted to respondents having the technology.

Increasingly, marketing researchers have begun to use online (e-mail and Internet) surveys to collect primary data. The reason: Most consumers have an Internet connection and an e-mail account. Marketers can embed a survey in an e-mail sent to targeted respondents. When they open the e-mail, consumers can either see the survey or click on a link to access it from a Web site. Marketers can also ask consumers to complete a "pop up" survey in a separate window when they access an organization's Web site. Many organizations use this method to have consumers assess their products and services or evaluate the design and usability of their Web sites.

The advantages of online surveys are that the cost is relatively minimal and the turnaround time from data collection to report presentation is much quicker than the traditional methods discussed earlier. However, online surveys have serious drawbacks: Some consumers may view e-mail surveys as "junk" or "spam" and either do not receive them if they have a "spam blocker" or purposely or inadvertently delete them without opening. For Internet surveys, some consumers have a "pop-up blocker" that prohibits a browser from opening a separate window that contains the survey; thus, they may not be able to participate in the research. For both e-mail and Internet surveys, consumers can complete the survey multiple times, creating a significant bias in the results. This is especially true for online panels. Research firms, such as MarketTools that markets Zoomerang, have developed sampling technology to prohibit this practice.

在受访者家中进行个人访谈的高昂成本促使一种新的调查法迅猛发展起来，这就是商店拦截访谈法，即对那些在购物中心逛商场的消费者进行个人访谈。

The high cost of reaching respondents in their homes using personal interviews has led to a dramatic increase in the use of *mall intercept interviews*, which are personal interviews of consumers visiting shopping centers. These face-to-face

cookware 烹饪用具，炊具；participate 参与，参加。

1. What things are most important to you when you decide to eat out and go to a fast-food restaurant?

____

____

____

2. Have you eaten at a fast-food restaurant in the past month?

☐ Yes ☐ No

3. If you answered yes to question 2, how often do you eat fast food?

☐ Once a week ☐ 2 to 3 times a month ☐ Once a month or less

4. How important is it to you that a fast-food restaurant satisfies you on the following characteristics? [Check the box that describes your feelings for each item listed]

CHARACTERISTIC	VERY IMPORTANT	SOMEWHAT IMPORTANT	IMPORTANT	UNIMPORTANT	SOMEWHAT UNIMPORTANT	VERY UNIMPORTANT
• Taste of food	☐	☐	☐	☐	☐	☐
• Cleanliness	☐	☐	☐	☐	☐	☐
• Price	☐	☐	☐	☐	☐	☐
• Variety of menu	☐	☐	☐	☐	☐	☐

5. For each of the characteristics listed below, check the space on the scale that describes how you feel about Wendy's. Mark an X on only **one** of the five spaces listed for each item listed.

CHARACTERISTIC	CHECK THE SPACE THAT DESCRIBES THE DEGREE TO WHICH WENDY'S IS . . .						
• Taste of food	Tasty	____	____	____	____	____	Not tasty
• Cleanliness	Clean	____	____	____	____	____	Dirty
• Price	Inexpensive	____	____	____	____	____	Expensive
• Variety of menu	Broad	____	____	____	____	____	Narrow

FIGURE 5–5
To obtain the most valuable information from consumers, the Wendy's survey utilizes five different kinds of questions discussed in the text.

interviews reduce the cost of personal visits to consumers in their homes while providing the flexibility to show respondents visual cues such as ads or actual product samples. However, a critical disadvantage of mall intercept interviews is that the people selected for the interviews may not be representative of the consumers targeted, giving a biased result.

The foundation of all research using questionnaires is designing precise questions that get clear, unambiguous answers very efficiently. Figure 5–5 shows a number of formats for questions taken from a Wendy's survey that assessed fast-food restaurant preferences among present and prospective consumers. Question 1 is an example of an *open-ended question*, which allows respondents to express opinions, ideas, or behaviors in their own words without being forced to choose among alternatives that have been predetermined by a marketing researcher. This information is invaluable to marketers because it captures the "voice" of respondents, which is useful in understanding consumer behavior, identifying product benefits, or developing advertising messages. In contrast, *closed-end* or *fixed alternative questions* require respondents to select one or more response options from a set of predetermined choices. Question

unambiguous 不含糊的，清楚的，明白的；predetermine 预先决定。

6. Check one box that describes your agreement or disagreement with each statement listed below:

STATEMENT	STRONGLY AGREE	AGREE	DON'T KNOW	DISAGREE	STRONGLY DISAGREE
• Adults like to take their families to fast-food restaurants	☐	☐	☐	☐	☐
• Our children have a say in where the family chooses to eat	☐	☐	☐	☐	☐

7. How important are each of the following sources of information to you when selecting a fast-food restaurant to eat at? [Check one box for each source listed]

SOURCE OF INFORMATION	VERY IMPORTANT	SOMEWHAT IMPORTANT	NOT AT ALL IMPORTANT
• Television	☐	☐	☐
• Newspapers	☐	☐	☐
• Radio	☐	☐	☐
• Billboards	☐	☐	☐
• Flyers	☐	☐	☐

8. How often do you eat out at each of the following fast-food restaurants? [Check one box for each source listed]

RESTAURANT	ONCE A WEEK OR MORE	2 TO 3 TIMES A MONTH	ONCE A MONTH OR LESS
• Burger King	☐	☐	☐
• McDonald's	☐	☐	☐
• Wendy's	☐	☐	☐

9. Please answer the following questions about you and your household. [Check only one for each item]

a. What is your gender? ☐ Male ☐ Female

b. What is your marital status? ☐ Single ☐ Married ☐ Other (widowed, divorced, etc.)

c. How many children under age 18 live in your home? ☐ 0 ☐ 1 ☐ 2 ☐ 3 or more

d. What is your age? ☐ Under 25 ☐ 25–44 ☐ 45 or older

e. What is your total annual individual or household income?

☐ <$15,000 ☐ $15,000–49,000 ☐ $50,000 or more

FIGURE 5–5
(continued)

具有 3 个或更多选项的多项选择问题可以采用一个衡量尺度。问题 5 就采用了语义差异尺度，即采用五级分制方式，其中两端有一字或两字的表示反义的形容词。例如，在调查受访者对文迪餐馆的干净程度的感觉时，他可以从左端的尺度（干净）到右端尺度（不干净）之间的 5 个中介分级中选择一个级别。问题 6 采用的是李克特尺度，即要求受访者就某一事实给出他同意或不同意的程度。

2 is an example of a *dichotomous question*, the simplest form of a fixed alternative question that allows only a "yes" or "no" response.

A fixed alternative question with three or more choices uses a *scale*. Question 5 is an example of a question that uses a *semantic differential scale*, a five-point scale in which the opposite ends have one- or two-word adjectives that have opposite meanings. For example, depending on how clean the respondent feels that Wendy's is, he or she would check the left-hand space on the scale, the right-hand space, or one of the five intervening points. Question 6 uses a *Likert scale*, in which the respondent indicates the extent to which he or she agrees or disagrees with a statement.

The questionnaire in Figure 5–5 provides valuable information to the marketing researcher at Wendy's. Questions 1 to 8 inform him or her about the likes and dislikes in eating out, frequency of eating out at fast-food restaurants generally and at Wendy's specifically, and sources of information used in making decisions about fast-food restaurants. Question 9 gives details about the personal or household characteristics, which can be used in trying to segment the fast-food market, a topic discussed in Chapter 6.

scale 规模尺度；frequency 频率，发生次数。

Wendy's does marketing research continuously to discover changing customer wants.

Wendy's Restaurant
www.wendys.com

Figure 5–6 shows typical problems to guard against when wording questions to obtain meaningful answers from respondents. For example, in a question of whether you eat at fast-food restaurants regularly, the word *regularly* is ambiguous. Two people might answer "yes" to the question, but one might mean "once a day" while the other means "once or twice a month." Both answers appear as "yes" to the researcher who tabulates them, but they suggest that dramatically different marketing actions be directed to each of these two prospective consumers. Therefore, it is essential that marketing research questions be worded precisely so that all respondents interpret the same question similarly.

Electronic technology has revolutionized traditional concepts of interviews or surveys. Today, respondents can walk up to a kiosk in a shopping center, read questions off a screen, and key their answers into a computer on a touch screen. Even fully automated telephone interviews exist: An automated voice questions respondents over the telephone, who then key their replies on a touch-tone telephone.

原始数据：其他资源
Primary Data: Other Sources

Three other methods of collecting primary data exist that overlap somewhat with the observational or questionnaire methods just discussed. These involve using (1) social networks, (2) panels and experiments, and (3) information technology and data mining.

Social Networks At this moment, someone—maybe even you!—is communicating with someone else online using a social network. Many consumers use social networking Web sites such as Facebook, LinkedIn, and Twitter to communicate with and share opinions among friends, family, and other like-minded individuals around the world. Social networks allow for more intimate and frequent contact among people who share common interests—at a lower cost than other media.

Why is this important to marketers? Because consumers often share their opinions about the offerings they use or want on these social networking Web sites or in

FIGURE 5–6
Typical problems when wording questions

PROBLEM	SAMPLE QUESTION	EXPLANATION OF PROBLEM
Leading question	Why do you like Wendy's fresh meat hamburgers better than those of competitors?	Consumer is led to make statement favoring Wendy's hamburgers.
Ambiguous question	Do you eat at fast-food restaurants regularly? ☐ Yes ☐ No	What is meant by word *regularly*—once a day, once a month, or what?
Unanswerable question	What was the occasion for eating your first hamburger?	Who can remember the answer? Does it matter?
Two questions in one	Do you eat Wendy's hamburgers and chili? ☐ Yes ☐ No	How do you answer if you eat Wendy's hamburgers but not chili?
Nonmutually exclusive answers	What is your age? ☐ Under 20 ☐ 20–40 ☐ 40 and over	What answer does a 40-year-old check?

guard 警惕，提防；dramatically 戏剧性地，引人注目地；tabulate 将……制成表格，以表格形式排列。

How do marketers track information on social networks such as Facebook or Twitter? Why do they care? For the answers, see the text.

online blogs (a personal diary or commentary) and forums (a place to hold discussions that allows participants to post comments)—it's like an online version of word of mouth! As a result, marketing researchers increasingly want to glean information from these sites to "mine" their raw consumer-generated content in real time. When collected, transcribed, tabulated, and analyzed, this content may signal a trend in the marketplace that can lead to marketing actions. While most social networks are consumer-driven, not marketer-driven, some organizations have established their own brand-related social networks to obtain consumer insights about both the organization and its offerings, which can increase brand loyalty.

What's likely to happen in the future? For marketers such as Procter & Gamble (P&G) and Unilever, a much larger portion of their market research budgets will be allocated to online research such as social network data mining. They believe that social networks are more in touch with today's consumer lifestyles. Moreover, many consumers are frustrated with research methods such as focus groups, mail surveys, and telephone surveys. However, when relying on consumer-generated content, the sample of individuals from whom this content was gleaned may not be statistically representative of the marketplace.

Panels and Experiments Two special ways that observations and questionnaires are sometimes used are panels and experiments.

营销调研人员通常对同一批消费者连续跟踪衡量，以了解他们经过一段时间后是否改变了行为。

Marketing researchers often want to know if consumers change their behavior over time, so they take successive measurements of the same people. A *panel* is a sample of consumers or stores from which researchers take a series of measurements. For example, the NPD Group collects data about consumer purchases such as apparel, food, and electronics from its Online Panel, which consists of more than 3 million individuals worldwide. So a firm like General Mills can use descriptive research—counting the frequency of consumer purchases—to measure switching behavior from one brand of its breakfast cereal (Wheaties) to another (Cheerios) or to a competitor's brand (Kellogg's Special K). A disadvantage of panels is that the marketing research firm needs to recruit new members continually to replace those who drop out. These new recruits must match the characteristics of those they replace to keep the panel representative of the marketplace.

How might Wal-Mart have done early marketing research to help develop its supercenters, which have achieved international success? For its unusual research, see the text.

An *experiment* involves obtaining data by manipulating factors under tightly controlled conditions to test cause and effect, an example of causal research. The interest is in whether changing one of the independent variables (a cause) will change the behavior of the dependent variable that is studied (the result). In marketing experiments, the independent variables of interest—sometimes called the marketing *drivers*—are often one or more of the marketing mix elements, such as a product's features, price, or promotion (like advertising messages or coupons). The ideal dependent variable usually is a change in purchases (incremental unit or dollar sales) of individuals, households, or organizations. For example, food companies often use *test markets*, which offer a product for sale in a small geographic area to help evaluate potential marketing actions. So a test market is really a kind of marketing experiment to reduce risks. In 1988, Wal-Mart opened three experimental stand-alone supercenters to gauge consumer acceptance before deciding to open others. Today, Wal-Mart operates 2,500 supercenters around the world.

A potential difficulty with experiments is that outside factors (such as actions of competitors) can distort the results of an experiment and affect the dependent variable (such as sales). A researcher's task is to identify

transcribe 笔录，转写；manipulate 操作，使用，处理；distort（使）变形，（使）失真。

the effect of the marketing variable of interest on the dependent variable when the effects of outside factors in an experiment might hide it.

learning review

6. What is the difference between observational and questionnaire data?
7. Which survey provides the greatest flexibility for asking probing questions: mail, telephone, or personal interview?
8. What is the difference between a panel and an experiment?

LO5

Information Technology and Data Mining Today's marketing managers can be drowned in an ocean of data; they need to adopt strategies for dealing with complex, changing views of the competition, the market, and the consumer. The Internet and PC power help make sense out of this data ocean. The marketer's task is to convert this data ocean into useful information that leads to marketing actions.

Information technology involves operating computer networks that can store and process data. Today information technology can extract hidden information from large databases such as households' product purchases, TV viewing behavior, and responses to coupon or free-sample promotions. As noted earlier, firms such as Information Resources' InfoScan and AC Nielsen's ScanTrack collect this information through bar-code scanners at the checkout counters in supermarket, drug, convenience, and mass merchandise retailers in the United States.

Figure 5–7 shows how marketing researchers and managers use information technology to frame questions that provide answers leading to marketing actions. At the bottom of Figure 5–7 the marketer queries the databases in the information system with marketing questions needing answers. These questions go through statistical models that analyze the relationships that exist among the data. The databases form the core, or *data warehouse,* where the ocean of data is collected and stored. After the search of this data warehouse, the models select and link the pertinent data, often presenting them in tables and graphics for easy interpretation. Marketers can also use *sensitivity analysis* to query the database with "what if" questions to determine how a hypothetical change in a driver such as advertising can affect sales.

Traditional marketing research typically involves identifying possible drivers and then collecting data. For example, we might collect data to test the hypothesis that increasing couponing (the driver) during spring will increase trials by first-time buyers (the result).

In contrast, **data mining** is the extraction of hidden predictive information from large databases to find statistical links between consumer purchasing patterns and marketing actions. Some of these are common sense: Since many consumers buy peanut butter and grape jelly together, it may be a good idea to run a joint promotion between Skippy peanut butter and Welch's grape jelly. But would you have expected that men buying diapers in the evening sometimes buy a six-pack of beer as well? This is exactly what supermarkets discovered when they mined checkout data from scanners. So they placed diapers and beer near each other, then placed potato chips between them—and increased sales on all three items!

At 10 P.M. what is this man likely to buy besides these diapers? For the curious answer data mining gives, see the text.

On the near horizon: RFID technology using a "smart tag" microchip on the diapers and beer to tell whether they wind up in the same shopping bag—at 10 in the evening. Still, the success in data mining depends on

complex 复杂的，错综的；database 数据库，资料库，信息库。

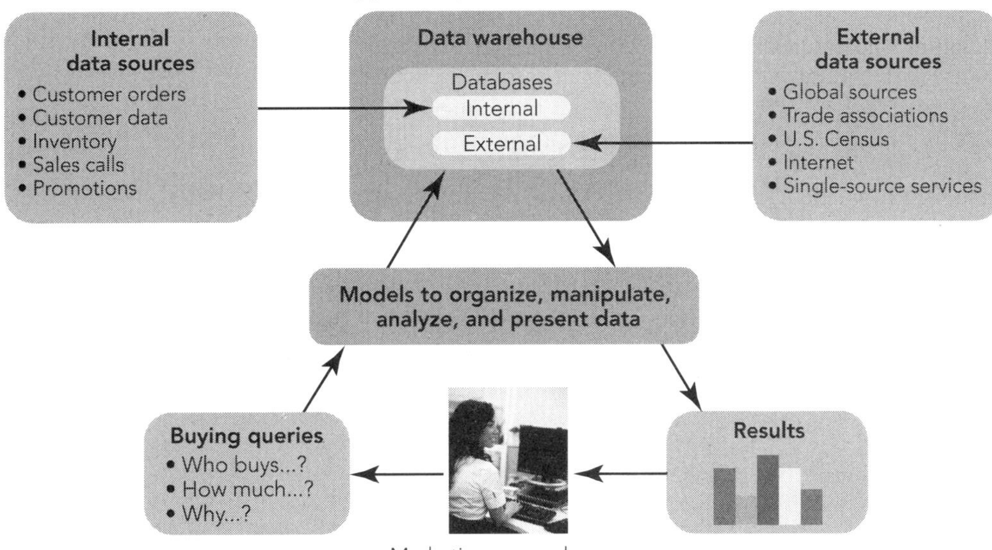

FIGURE 5–7
How marketing researchers and managers use information technology to turn information into action

the judgments of the marketing managers and researchers in how to select, analyze, and interpret the information.

原始数据的优点和缺点
Advantages and Disadvantages of Primary Data

Compared with secondary data, primary data have the advantage of being more specific to the problem being studied. The main disadvantages are that primary data are usually far more costly and time consuming to collect than secondary data.

第四步：提交结论
STEP 4: DEVELOP FINDINGS

How are sales doing? To see how marketers at Tony's Pizza assessed this question and the results, read the text.

Mark Twain once observed, "Collecting data is like collecting garbage. You've got to know what you're going to do with the stuff before you collect it." Thus, marketing data and information have little more value than garbage unless they are analyzed carefully and translated into logical findings, step 4 in the marketing research approach.

分析数据
Analyze the Data

Let's consider the case in early 2010 of Tony's Pizza and Teré Carral, the marketing manager responsible for the Tony's brand. We will use hypothetical data to protect Tony's proprietary information.

Teré is concerned about the limited growth in the Tony's brand over the past four years. She hires a consultant to collect and analyze data to explain what's going on with her brand and to recommend ways to improve its growth. Teré asks the consultant to put together a proposal that includes the answers to two key questions:

1. How are Tony's sales doing on a household basis? For example, are fewer households buying Tony's pizzas, or is each household buying fewer Tony's? Or both?
2. What factors might be contributing to Tony's very flat sales over the past four years?

interpret 解释，说明，阐释；primary 首先的，最早的，最初的。

Facts uncovered by the consultant are vital. For example, is the average household consuming more or less Tony's pizza than in previous years? Is Tony's flat sales performance related to a specific factor? With answers to these questions Teré can identify actions in her marketing plan and implement them over the coming year.

展示结果
Present the Findings

Findings should be clear and understandable from the way the data are presented. Managers are responsible for *actions*. Often it means delivering the results in clear pictures and, if possible, in a single page.

The consultant gives Teré the answers to her questions using the marketing dashboards in Figure 5–8, a creative way to present findings graphically. Let's look over the shoulders of Teré and the consultant while they interpret these findings:

- Figure 5–8A, Annual Sales—This shows the annual growth of the Tony's Pizza brand is stable but virtually flat from 2006 through 2009.
- Figure 5–8B, Average Annual Sales per Household—Look closely at this graph. At first glance, it may seem like sales in 2009 are *half* what they were in 2006, right? But be careful to read the numbers on the vertical axis. They show that household purchases of Tony's have been steadily declining over the

FIGURE 5–8
These marketing dashboards present findings to Tony's marketing manager that lead to recommendations and actions.
Source: Teré Carral, Tony's Pizza.

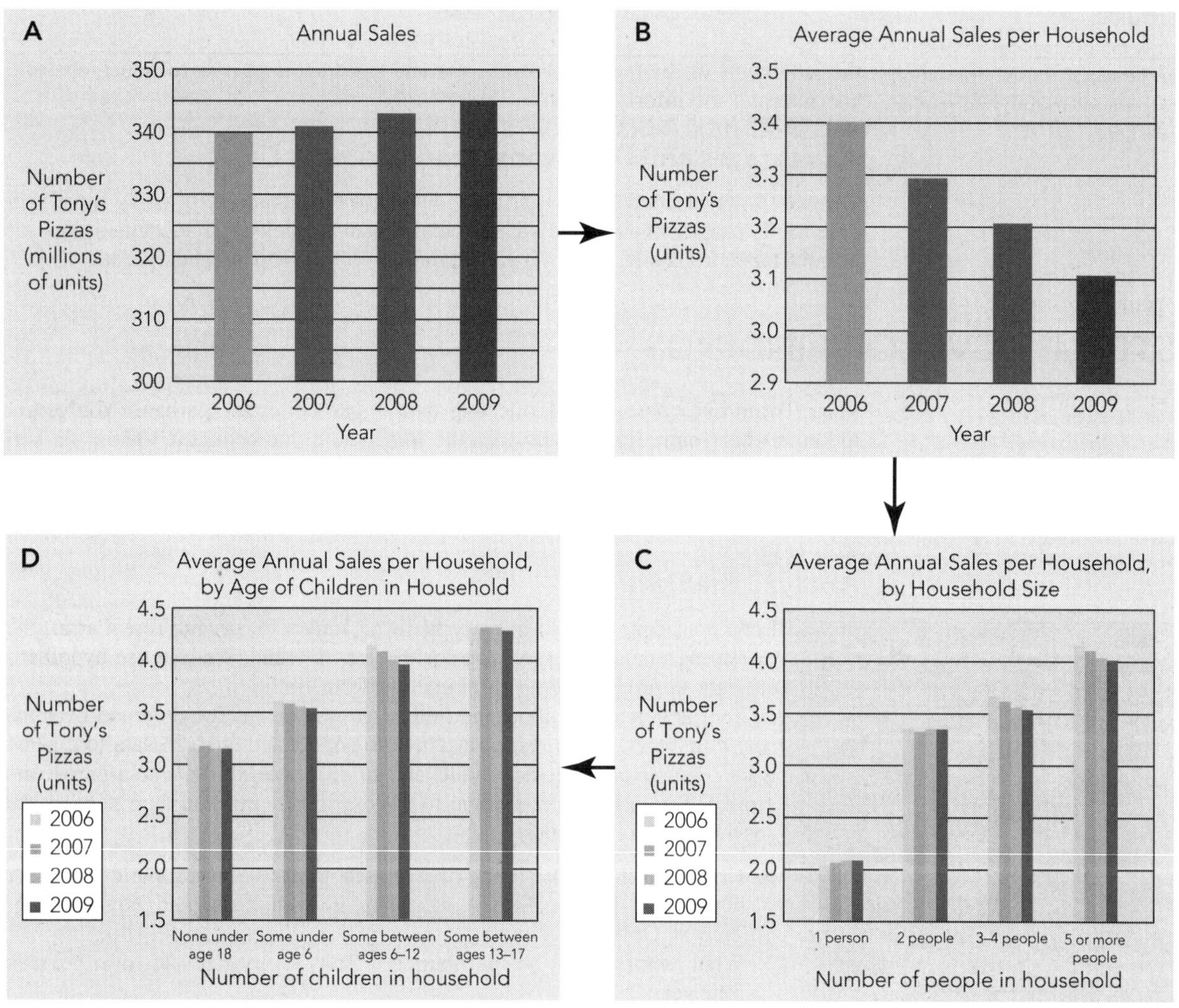

consultant 征求意见者，查阅者，咨询者；graphically 绘画的，绘图的，图像的。

past four years, from an average of 3.4 pizzas per household in 2006 to 3.1 pizzas per household in 2009. (Significant, but hardly a 50 percent drop.) Now the question is, if Tony's annual sales are stable, yet the average individual household is buying fewer Tony's pizzas, what's going on? The answer is, more households are buying pizzas—it's just that each household is buying fewer Tony's pizzas. That households aren't choosing Tony's is a genuine source of concern. But again, here's a classic example of a marketing problem representing a marketing opportunity. The number of households buying pizza is *growing*, and that's good news for Tony's.

- Figure 5–8C, Average Annual Sales per Household, by Household Size—This chart starts to show a source of the problem: Even though average sales of pizza to households with only one or two people is stable, households with three or four people and those with five or more are declining in average annual pizza consumption. Which households tend to have more than two people? Answer: Households *with children*. Therefore, we should look more closely at the pizza-buying behavior of households with children.
- Figure 5–8D, Average Annual Sales per Household, by Age of Children in the Household—The picture is becoming very clear now: The real problem is in the serious decline in average consumption in the households with younger children, especially in households with children in the 6- to 12-year-old age group.

Identifying a sales problem in households with children 6 to 12 years old is an important discovery, as Tony's sales are declining in a market segment that is known to be one of the heaviest in buying pizzas.

第五步：采取营销行动
STEP 5: TAKE MARKETING ACTIONS

Effective marketing research doesn't stop with findings and recommendations—someone has to identify the marketing actions, put them into effect, and monitor how the decisions turn out, which is the essence of step 5.

提出行动建议
Make Action Recommendations

Marketing research at Tony's Pizza helped develop this colorful, friendly ad targeted at families with 6 to 12 year olds.

Teré Carral, the marketing manager for Tony's Pizza, met with her team to convert the market research findings into specific marketing recommendations with a clear objective: Target households with children ages 6 to 12 to reverse the trend among this segment and gain strength in one of the most important segments in the frozen pizza category. Her recommendation is to develop:

- An advertising campaign that will target children 6 to 12.
- A monthly promotion calendar with this age group target in mind.
- A special event program reaching children 6 to 12.

实施行动建议
Implement the Action Recommendations

As her first marketing action, Teré undertakes advertising research to develop ads that appeal to children in the 6-to-12 age group and their families. The research shows that children like colorful ads with funny, friendly characters. She gives these research results to her advertising agency, which develops several sample ads for her review. Teré selects three that are tested on children to identify the most appealing one, which is then used in her next advertising campaign for Tony's Pizza. This is the ad at left.

recommendation 建议，提议，劝告；implement 履行，实施；agency 代理，机构。

评估结果
Evaluate the Results

Evaluating results is a continuing way of life for effective marketing managers. There are really two aspects of this evaluation process:

- 评估决策本身。主要是监测市场状况以确定该行动在将来是否仍然必要。
- 评估决策过程。用以提出建议的营销调研和分析是否有效？有什么缺陷？将来再出现类似情况时能予以改进吗？

- *Evaluating the decision itself.* This involves monitoring the marketplace to determine if action is necessary in the future. For Teré, is her new ad successful in appealing to 6-to-12-year-olds and their families? Are sales increasing to this target segment? The success of this strategy suggests Teré add more follow-up ads with colorful, funny, friendly characters.
- *Evaluating the decision process used.* Was the marketing research and analysis used to develop the recommendations effective? Was it flawed? Could it be improved for similar situations in the future? Teré and her marketing team must be vigilant for ways to improve the analysis and results—to learn lessons that might apply to future marketing research efforts at Tony's.

Again, systematic analysis does not guarantee success. But, as in the case of Tony's Pizza, it can improve a firm's success rate for its marketing decisions.

learning review

9. How does data mining differ from traditional marketing research?
10. In the marketing research for Tony's Pizza, what is an example of (*a*) a finding and (*b*) a marketing action?

销售预测技术
SALES FORECASTING TECHNIQUES

LO6

Forecasting or estimating potential sales is often a key goal in a marketing research study. Good sales forecasts are important for a firm as it schedules production. The term **sales forecast** refers to the total sales of a product that a firm expects to sell during a specified time period under specified environmental conditions and its own marketing efforts. For example, Betty Crocker might develop a sales forecast of 4 million cases of cake mix for U.S. consumers in 2011, assuming consumers' dessert preferences remain constant and competitors don't change prices.

Three main sales forecasting techniques are often used: (1) judgments of the decision maker, (2) surveys of knowledgeable groups, and (3) statistical methods.

决策者的判断
Judgments of the Decision Maker

Probably 99 percent of all sales forecasts are simply the judgment of the person who must act on the results of the forecast—the individual decision maker. *A direct forecast* involves estimating the value to be forecast without any intervening steps. Examples appear daily: How many quarts of milk should I buy? How much money should I get out of the ATM?

A *lost-horse forecast* involves starting with the last known value of the item being forecast, listing the factors that could affect the forecast, assessing whether they have a positive or negative impact, and making the final forecast. The technique gets its name from how you'd find a lost horse: go to where it was last seen, put yourself in its shoes, consider those factors that could affect where you might go (to the pond if you're thirsty, the hayfield if you're hungry, and so on), and go there.

How might a marketing manager at Under Armour forecast running shoe sales through 2012? Use a lost-horse forecast, as described in the text.

For example, in early 2009 Under Armour introduced its first line of running shoes. This required it to broaden its appeal from boys and young men who often used its knee pads and cleats in team sports to women, older

segment 部分，片段；schedule 工作计划，日程安排；environmental（个人）环境的，由个人环境产生的。

consumers, and casual athletes. Suppose an Under Armour marketing manager in early 2010 needs to make a sales forecast through 2012. She would take the known value of 2009 sales and list positive factors (good acceptance of its high-tech designs, great publicity) and the negative factors (the economic recession, competition from established name brands) to arrive at the final series of sales forecasts.

调查懂行的团体
Surveys of Knowledgeable Groups

If you wonder what your firm's sales will be next year, ask people who are likely to know something about future sales. Two common groups that are surveyed to develop sales forecasts are prospective buyers and the firm's salesforce.

A *survey of buyers' intentions forecast* involves asking prospective customers if they are likely to buy the product during some future time period. For industrial products with few prospective buyers, this can be effective. There are only a few hundred customers in the entire world for Boeing's large airplanes, so Boeing surveys them to develop its sales forecasts and production schedules.

A *salesforce survey forecast* involves asking the firm's salespeople to estimate sales during a coming period. Because these people are in contact with customers and are likely to know what customers like and dislike, there is logic to this approach. However, salespeople can be unreliable forecasters—painting too rosy a picture if they are enthusiastic about a new product and too grim a forecast if their sales quota and future compensation are based on it.

统计学方法
Statistical Methods

The best-known statistical method of forecasting is *trend extrapolation*, which involves extending a pattern observed in past data into the future. When the pattern is described with a straight line, it is *linear trend extrapolation*. Suppose that in early 2000 you were a sales forecaster for the Xerox Corporation and had actual sales data running from 1988 to 1999 (see Figure 5–9). Using linear trend extrapolation, you draw a line to fit the past sales data and project it into the future to give the forecast values shown for 2000 to 2012.

If in 2008 you want to compare your forecasts with actual results, you are in for a surprise—illustrating the strength and weakness of trend extrapolation. Trend extrapolation assumes that the underlying relationships in the past will continue into the future, which is the basis of the method's key strength: simplicity. If this assumption

FIGURE 5–9
Linear trend extrapolation of sales revenues at Xerox, made at the start of 2000

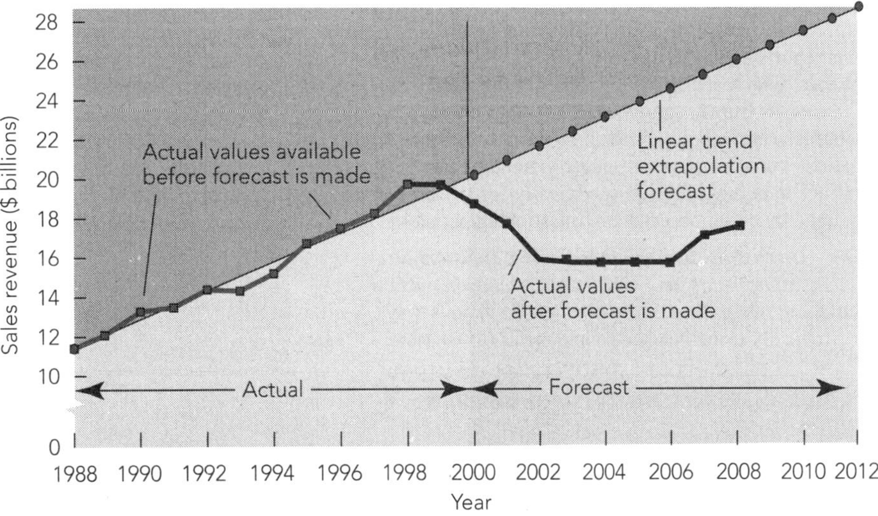

casual 临时的，非正式的；athlete 运动员，运动选手；recession 经济衰退，不景气。

proves correct, you have an accurate forecast. However, if this proves wrong, the forecast is likely to be wrong. In this case your forecasts from 2001 through 2007 were too high, as shown in Figure 5–9, largely because of fierce competition in the photocopying industry.

learning review

11. What are the three kinds of sales forecasting techniques?

12. How do you make a lost-horse forecast?

LEARNING OBJECTIVES REVIEW

LO1 *Identify the reason for conducting marketing research.*
To be successful, products and marketing programs must meet the wants and needs of potential customers. So marketing research reduces risk by providing the vital information to help marketing managers understand those wants and needs and translate them into marketing actions.

LO2 *Describe the five-step marketing research approach that leads to marketing actions.*
Marketing researchers engage in a five-step decision-making process to collect information that improves marketing decisions. The first step is to define the problem, which requires setting the research objectives and identifying possible marketing actions. The second step is to develop the research plan, which involves specifying the constraints, identifying data needed for marketing decisions, and determining how to collect the data. The third step is to collect the relevant information, which includes considering pertinent secondary data (both internal and external) and primary data (by observing and questioning consumers) as well as using information technology and data mining to trigger marketing actions. The fourth step is to develop findings from the marketing research data collected. This involves analyzing the data and presenting the findings of the research. The fifth and last step is to take marketing actions, which involves making and implementing the action recommendations.

LO3 *Explain how marketing uses secondary and primary data.*
Secondary data have already been recorded before the start of the project and consist of two parts: (*a*) internal secondary data, which originate from within the organization, such as sales reports and customer comments, and (*b*) external secondary data, which are created by other organizations, such as the U.S. Census Bureau (provides data on the country's population, manufacturers, retailers, and so on) or business and trade publications (provide data on industry trends, market size, etc.). Primary data are collected specifically for the project and are obtained by either observing or questioning people.

LO4 *Discuss the uses of observations, questionnaires, panels, experiments, and newer data collection methods.*
Marketing researchers observe people in various ways, such as electronically using Nielsen people meters to measure TV viewing behavior or personally using mystery shoppers or ethnographic techniques. A recent electronic innovation is neuromarketing—using high-tech brain scanning to record the responses of a consumer's brain to marketing stimuli like packages or TV ads. Questionnaires involve asking people questions (*a*) in person using interviews or focus groups or (*b*) via a questionnaire using a telephone, fax, print, e-mail, or an Internet survey. Panels involve a sample of consumers or stores that are repeatedly measured through time to see if their behaviors change. Experiments, such as test markets, involve measuring the effect of marketing variables such as price or advertising on sales. Collecting data from social networks like Facebook or Twitter is increasingly important because users can share their opinions about products and services with countless "friends" around the globe.

LO5 *Explain how information technology and data mining lead to marketing actions.*
Today's marketing managers are often overloaded with data—from internal sales and customer data to external data on TV viewing habits or grocery purchases from the scanner data at checkout counters. Information technology enables this massive amount of marketing data to be stored, accessed, and processed. The resulting databases can be queried using data mining to find statistical relationships useful for marketing decisions and actions.

LO6 *Describe three approaches to developing a company's sales forecast.*
One approach uses subjective judgments of the decision maker, such as direct or lost-horse forecasts. A direct forecast involves estimating the value to be forecast without any intervening steps. A lost horse forecast starts with the last known value of the item being forecast, listing the factors that could affect the forecast, assessing whether they have a positive or negative impact, and making the final forecast. Surveys of knowledgeable groups is a second method. It involves obtaining information such as the intentions of potential buyers or estimates of the salesforce. Statistical methods involving extending a pattern observed in past data into the future is a third example. The best-known statistical method is linear trend extrapolation.

FOCUSING ON KEY TERMS

constraints
data
data mining
decision
information technology
marketing research
measures of success
observational data
primary data
questionnaire data
sales forecast
secondary data

forecast 预测，预言。

APPLYING MARKETING KNOWLEDGE

1 Suppose your dean of admissions is considering surveying high school seniors about their perceptions of your school to design better informational brochures for them. What are the advantages and disadvantages of doing (*a*) telephone interviews and (*b*) an Internet survey of seniors requesting information about the school?

2 Nielsen Media Research obtains ratings of local TV stations in small markets by having households fill out diary questionnaires. These give information on (*a*) who is watching TV and (*b*) what program. What are the limitations of this questionnaire method?

3 The format in which information is presented is often vital. (*a*) If you were a harried marketing manager and queried your information system, would you rather see the results in tables or charts and graphs? (*b*) What are one or two strengths and weaknesses of each format?

4 Wisk detergent decides to run a test market to see the effect of coupons and in-store advertising on sales. The index of sales is as follows:

Element in Test Market	Weeks Before Coupon	Week of Coupon	Week after Coupon
Without in-store ads	100	144	108
With in-store ads	100	268	203

What are your conclusions and recommendations?

5 Suppose Fisher-Price wants to run a simple experiment to evaluate a proposed chatter telephone design. It has two different groups of children on which to run its experiment for one week each. The first group has the old toy telephone, whereas the second group is exposed to the newly designed pull toy with wheels, a noisemaker, and bobbing eyes. The dependent variable is the average number of minutes during the two-hour play period that one of the children is playing with the toy, and the results are as follows:

Element in Experiment	First Group	Second Group
Independent variable	Old design	New design
Dependent variable	13 minutes	62 minutes

Should Fisher-Price introduce the new design? Why?

6 (*a*) Why might a marketing researcher prefer to use secondary data rather than primary data in a study? (*b*) Why might the reverse be true?

7 Which of the following variables would linear trend extrapolation be more accurate for? (*a*) Annual population of the United States or (*b*) annual sales of cars produced in the United States by Ford. Why?

building your marketing plan

To help you collect the most useful data for your marketing plan, develop a three-column table:

1 In column 1, list the information you would ideally like to have to fill holes in your marketing plan.

2 In column 2, identify the source for each bit of information in column 1, such as an Internet search, talking to prospective customers, looking at internal data, and so forth.

3 In column 3, set a priority on information you will have time to spend collecting by ranking them: 1 = most important; 2 = next most important, and so forth.

video case 5 Ford Consulting Group, Inc.: From Data to Actions

"The fast pace of working as a marketing professional isn't getting any easier," agrees David Ford, as he talks with Mark Rehborg, Tony's Pizza brand manager. "The speed of communication, the availability of real-time market information, and the responsibility for a brand's profit make marketing one of the most challenging professional jobs today."

Mark responds, "Ten years ago, we could reach 80 percent of our target market with 3 television spots—but today, to reach the same 80 percent, we would have to buy 97 spots. We haven't the luxury to be complacent—our core consumer, the 6- to 12-year-old 'big kid,' is part of a savvy, wired culture that is changing rapidly."

DASHBOARDS: DATA INTO ACTIONS

David Ford, president of Ford Consulting Group (FCG), prepares business analysis, often in the form of a dashboard, to assist clients such as Tony's in translating the market and sales information into marketing actions. David works with Mark to grow Tony's sales and profit performance. Mark uses information to choose where to spend his funds to promote his products. Many times, the sales force requests additional promotion funds to help them hit their sales targets.

The information used most often for sales and promotion analysis comes from places like ACNielsen's ScanTrack and Information Resources' InfoScan (IRI) that summarize sales data from grocery stores and other outlets that scan purchases at the checkout.

FCG helps clients make sense of their existing information, *not* collect more information. The project that follows is typical of the work Ford Consulting Group (www.fordconsultinggroup.com) undertakes for a client. The data are hypothetical, but the situation is a very typical one in the grocery products industry. Here's a snapshot of some of the terms in the case:

- "You" have just come on the job, as the new marketing person.
- "NE" is the Northeastern sales region of Tony's.
- "SW, NW, SW" are the other sales regions.

PART 1: A TYPICAL QUESTION, ON A TYPICAL DAY

Let's dive into the background of a typical question you might face on a typical day. You are given two memos (one from Mark to you) as background.

You dig into data files and develop Table 1 that shows how Tony's is doing in the company's four sales regions and the entire United States on key marketing dimensions. Without reading further, take a deep breath and try to answer question 1.

PART 2: UNCOVERING THE TRUTH

Let's assume your analysis (question 1) shows the NE is a problem, so we need to understand what's going on in the NE. Further effort enables you to develop Table 2. It shows the situation for the four largest supermarket chains in the Northeast sales region that carry Tony's. Now answer question 2.

Questions

1 Study Table 1. (*a*) How does the situation in the Northeast compare with the other regions in the United States? (*b*) What are reasons that sales are soft? (*c*) Write a 150-word e-mail with attachments to Mark Rehborg, your boss, giving your answers to *b*.

2 Study Table 2. (*a*) What do you conclude from this information? (*b*) Summarize your conclusions in a 150-word e-mail with attachments to Mark, who needs them for a meeting tomorrow with Margaret, the Northeast sales region manager. (*c*) What marketing actions might your memo suggest?

> TO: Mark Rehborg, Tony's Brand Manager
> FROM: Steve Quam, Tony's Field Sales
> CC: Margaret Loiaza, NE Sales Region Manager
>
> RE: Feedback on Sales Call at Food-Fast
>
> Hi Mark—
>
> Our sales call at Food-Fast wasn't so great. They don't see how our Tony's is going to sell well enough to justify the additional shelf-space. I also talked to Margaret and she said that second quarter may be weaker than planned across all the NE, and I should give you a heads-up. She's on vacation this week. She's planning to schedule some time with you to talk about additional promotion money to do catch-up in the third quarter. She'll be there next week.
>
> Steve

> TO: You, the New Marketing Person
> FROM: Mark Rehborg, Tony's Brand Manager (Your Boss)
>
> RE: Small Project due Friday
>
> Hi You,
>
> Can you help out here? I've got a meeting with Margaret on Friday afternoon, and she's concerned that Food-Fast and the whole NE is going to need some additional promotion dollars.
>
> Lauretta started the analysis and was hurt in a kick-boxing accident yesterday and won't be back to work for a week. Her files are attached. Can you look through her files and summarize what's going on in the NE and the rest of the U.S.? Does Margaret need more promotion money?
>
> Let's discuss Friday A.M.
>
> Mark

TABLE 1. COMPARISON OF TONY'S PERFORMANCE, BY REGION

Region	Quarterly Change in Volume (%)	Distribution[a] (%)	Price ($)	Price Gap[b] ($)	Promotion Support[c] (%)	Promotion Volume[d] (%)
NE	3%	93%	$1.29	+8	7%	14%
SE	5	95	1.11	−1	9	16
NW	8	98	1.19	+1	8	15
SW	6	96	1.25	0	8	15
U.S.	6	97	1.19	0	8	15

[a] % of outlets carrying Tony's.
[b] Price gap = (Our price) − (Competitor's price).
[c] Promotion support = % of the time brand was promoted.
[d] Promotion volume = % of the volume sold on promotion.

TABLE 2. COMPARISON OF MAJOR SUPERMARKET CHAINS IN THE NORTHEAST

Super-Market Chain	Quarterly Change in Volume (%)	Distribution[a] (%)	Price ($)	Price Gap[b] ($)	Promotion Support[c] (%)	Promotion Volume[d] (%)
Save-a-lot	5%	95%	$1.39	+10	10%	19%
Food-Fast	0	90	1.28	−1	3	4
Get-Fresh	0	90	1.30	+1	3	4
Dollars-Off	7	97	1.34	+5	7	14

24/7 Customer Service 1.800.927.7671 • Español 1.888.927.4104

Cart

My Account • My Favorites | Help

Zappos.com ZETA POWERED by SERVICE

Free Shipping Both Ways!*
365-Day Return Policy

--Search-- Search
Search by: Size • Narrow Shoes • Wide Shoes • Popular Searches

Go to Zappos.com Classic
--Visit Our Other Sites--

View All Departments | Shoes | Clothing | Bags & Handbags | Watches | Sunglasses | New Arrivals | Brands | Women's | Men's | Kids'

Alphabetical Brand Index # A B C D E F G H I J K L M N O P Q R S T U V W X Y Z

Women's Shoes
- What's New
- Sandals
- Heels
- Boots
- Sneakers
- Slippers
- Flats
- Clogs & Mules
- **More Women's Shoes**

Men's Shoes
- What's New
- Boots
- Sneakers
- Oxfords
- Sandals
- Loafers
- Boat Shoes
- Slippers
- **More Men's Shoes**

Kids' Shoes
- What's New
- Sneakers
- Flats
- Sandals
- Boots
- First Walkers
- **More Kids' Shoes**

Women's Clothing
- What's New
- Tops
- Shorts
- Skirts
- Pants
- Jackets & Coats
- Swimsuits
- Sleepwear
- **More Women's Clothing**

Men's Clothing
- What's New
- Shirts
- Shorts
- Pants
- Jackets & Coats
- Suits
- Swimsuits
- Sleepwear
- **More Men's Clothing**

Kids' Clothing
- What's New
- Clothing Sets
- Shirts
- Shorts
- Pants
- Jackets & Coats
- Swimwear
- Baby One-Pieces
- **More Kids' Clothing**

Bags and Handbags
- Backpacks
- Messenger Bags
- Diaper Bags
- Laptop Bags
- Tote Bags
- Hobo Bags
- Shoulder Bags
- Clutch Bags
- **More Bags**

More Departments
- What's New
- Accessories
- Housewares
- Beauty
- Jewelry
- Watches
- Sporting Goods
- **More Departments**

FREE RETURNS · 365-DAY RETURN POLICY · 24/7 CUSTOMER SERVICE · 1.800.927.7671

Shopping Recommendations For You

Onitsuka Tiger by Asics
Ultimate 81
$66.95

Converse
All Star Core OX
$45.00

Converse
Chuck Taylor All Star Ox
$45.00

Sperry Top-Sider
Authentic Original
$64.95

Vans
Classic Slip-On Core Classics
$42.00

What's New At Zappos!

Women's

Zappos Top Sellers!

Women's

Find What You Need Quickly

By Gender

Special Interest

Specialty Site

The Zappos Culture

Learn about what inspires Zappos to provide the best service!

Zappos Core Values:
10 Values We Live By

Customer Testimonials:
Our Customers Connect

Enjoy Fun and A Little Weirdness:
Check out Zappos Blogs

The Zappos Experience:
Share Your Zappos Videos

Unique Customers:
Zappos Furry Customers
Zappos Customers In Training

Become a Part of Our Culture:
Careers at Zappos

Get Inspired:

Zappos.com POWERED by SERVICE

6

市场细分、确定目标市场与定位
Market Segmentation, Targeting, and Positioning

LEARNING OBJECTIVES

After reading this chapter you should be able to:

LO1 Explain what market segmentation is and when to use it.

LO2 Identify the five steps involved in segmenting and targeting markets.

LO3 Recognize the bases used to segment consumer and organizational markets.

LO4 Develop a market-product grid to identify a target market and recommend resulting actions.

LO5 Explain how marketing managers position products in the marketplace.

Zappos.com：通过市场细分和提供客户服务获得成功
ZAPPOS.COM: DELIVERING "WOW" THROUGH MARKET SEGMENTATION AND SERVICE

Tony Hsieh (opposite page) showed signs of being an entrepreneur early in life. He's now chief executive officer (CEO) of online retailer Zappos.com. The company name is derived from the Spanish word *zapatos,* which means shoes.

At age 12, Hsieh brought in several hundred dollars a month with his button-making business. In college, Hsieh sold pizzas out of his dorm room. Fellow entrepreneur Alfred Lin bought pizzas from Hsieh and then sold them by the slice to other students. And where is pizza-slice marketer Alfred Lin today? He's the chief operating officer at Zappos.com.

A Clear Market Segmentation Strategy

Hsieh, Lin, and founder Nick Swinmurn have given Zappos.com a clear, specific market segmentation strategy: Offer a huge selection of shoes to people who will buy them online. Recently Zappos.com has added lines of clothes, accessories, beauty, and housewares. This focus on the segment of online buyers generated over $1 billion in sales in 2008.

"With Zappos, the shoe store comes to you," says Pamela Leo, a New Jersey customer. "I can try the shoes in the comfort of my own home. . . . It's fabulous." Besides the in-home convenience, Zappos .com offers free shipping both ways. The choices for its online customers are staggering. A recent Zappos.com home page described "Today at Zappos" as 1,136 brands, with over 3 million products.

Delivering WOW Customer Service

Asked about Zappos.com, Hsieh says, "We try to spend most of our time on stuff that will improve customer-service levels." This customer-service obsession for its market segment of online customers means that all new Zappos.com employees—whether the chief financial officer or children's footwear buyer—go through four weeks of customer-loyalty training. Hsieh offers $2,000 to anyone completing the training who wants to leave Zappos.com. The theory: If you take the money and run, you're not right for Zappos.com. Few take the money!

Ten "core values" are the foundation for the Zappos.com culture, brand, and business strategies. Some examples:

#1. Deliver WOW through service. This focus on exemplary customer service encompasses all 10 core values.

#3. Create fun and a little weirdness. In a Zappos.com day, cowbells ring, parades appear, and modified-blaster gunfights arise.

---

entrepreneur 企业家；retailer 零售商，零售店。

#6. Build open and honest relationships with communications. Employees are told to say what they think.

The other Zappos.com core values appear on its Web site: www.Zappos.com.

The Zappos.com strategy illustrates successful market segmentation and targeting, the first topics in Chapter 6. The chapter ends with the topic of positioning the organization, product, or brand.

为何要细分市场
WHY SEGMENT MARKETS?

A business firm segments its markets so it can respond more effectively to the wants of groups of potential buyers and thus increase its sales and profits. Not-for-profit organizations also segment the clients they serve to satisfy client needs more effectively while achieving the organization's goals. Let's describe (1) what market segmentation is and (2) when to segment markets, sometimes using the Zappos.com segmentation strategy as an example.

市场细分意味着什么
What Market Segmentation Means

尽管人们具有不同的需要和欲望，但相对于如果他们没有需要和欲望而言，营销人员的工作仍然容易得多。**市场细分**是根据（1）具有相同的需要；（2）对某个营销行动会有相似的反应，来把潜在顾客分成不同群体。

People have different needs and wants, even though it would be easier for marketers if they didn't. **Market segmentation** involves aggregating prospective buyers into groups that (1) have common needs and (2) will respond similarly to a marketing action. **Market segments** are the relatively homogeneous groups of prospective buyers that result from the market segmentation process. Each market segment consists of people who are relatively similar to each other in terms of their consumption behavior.

The existence of different market segments has caused firms to use a marketing strategy of **product differentiation**. This strategy involves a firm using different marketing mix activities, such as product features and advertising, to help consumers perceive the product as being different and better than competing products. The perceived differences may involve physical features, such as size or color, or nonphysical ones, such as image or price.

Segmentation: Linking Needs to Actions The process of segmenting a market and selecting specific segments as targets is the link between the various buyers' needs and the organization's marketing program, as shown in Figure 6–1. Market segmentation is only a means to an end: to lead to tangible marketing actions that can increase sales and profitability.

Effective market segmentation does two key things: (1) forms meaningful groupings and (2) develops specific marketing mix actions. People or organizations should be grouped into a market segment according to the similarity of their needs and the benefits they look for in making a purchase. The market segments must relate to specific marketing actions that the organization can take. These actions may involve separate offerings or other aspects of the marketing mix, such as price, promotion, or distribution strategies.

FIGURE 6–1
Market segmentation links market needs to an organization's marketing program—specific marketing mix actions to satisfy those needs.

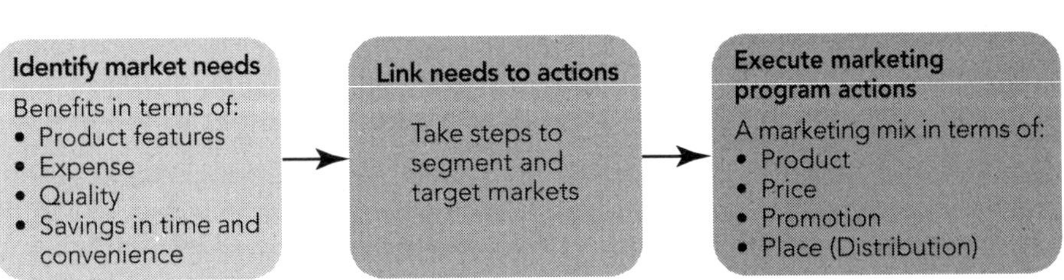

relatively 相当地，相对地；profitability 盈利的，有利润的，赚钱的。

Core value #3—"create fun and a little weirdness"—helped in naming Zappos .com one of the 2008 "Marketers of the Year" by *Advertising Age* magazine.

The Successful Zappos.com Footwear Segmentation Strategy The Zappos.com target customer segment consists of people who want (1) a wide selection of shoes, (2) to shop online in the convenience of their own home, and (3) to receive the guarantee of quick delivery and free returns. Zappos' actions include offering a huge inventory of shoes and other products, using an online selling strategy, and providing overnight delivery. This enables Zappos .com to create a positive customer experience and generate repeat purchases. On any given day, about 75 percent of Zappos.com shoppers are repeat customers.

With over 8 million customers and 5,000 calls daily to Zappos' service center, Zappos.com executives believe that the speed with which a customer receives an online purchase plays a big role in gaining repeat customers. The company will continue to stress this point of difference, made possible by stocking in its warehouse every item it sells. And if customers continue to associate Zappos.com with the absolute best service among online sellers with its footwear, clothing, and other offerings, both Zappos.com weirdness (its fifth core value) and its sales are on solid footing!

何时及如何细分市场

When and How to Segment Markets

只有当一家商业企业预计细分市场将增加销售量、利润和投资回报的时候，它才会花费人力物力来细分市场。如果所花费用超过所能带来的潜在销售额增长，公司就不应该去细分市场。有效市场细分有 3 种具体情形：(1) 单个产品和多个市场；(2) 多个产品和多个市场；(3) "单一市场" 或大规模定制。

The one-size-fits-all mass markets—like that for Tide laundry detergent of 40 years ago—no longer exist. The global marketing officer at Procter & Gamble, which markets Tide, says, "Every one of our brands is targeted." Welcome to today's customer relationship era that consists of market segmentation and target marketing.

A business goes to the trouble and expense of segmenting its markets when it expects that this will increase its sales, profit, and return on investment. When expenses are greater than the potentially increased sales from segmentation, a firm should not attempt to segment its market. Three specific segmentation strategies that illustrate this point are: (1) one product and multiple market segments, (2) multiple products and multiple market segments, and (3) "segments of one," or mass customization.

One Product and Multiple Market Segments When an organization produces only a single product or service and attempts to sell it to two or more market segments, it avoids the extra costs of developing and producing additional versions of the product. In this case, the incremental costs of taking the product into new market segments are typically those of a separate promotional campaign or a new channel of distribution.

These *different* covers for the *same* magazine issue show a very effective market segmentation strategy. For which specific one it is and why it works, see the text.

associate（使）发生联系，（使）联合，结交，联想；investment 投资；additional 额外的，附加的，添加的；detergent 洗涤剂，去垢剂。

Does Harry Potter appeal only to the English-speaking kids' segment? See the text about this amazing publishing success story.

Magazines and books are single products frequently directed to two or more distinct market segments. The *Sporting News Baseball Yearbook* uses 16 different covers featuring a baseball star from each of its regions in the United States. Harry Potter's phenomenal seven-book success is based both on author J. K. Rowling's fiction-writing wizardry and her publisher's creativity in marketing to preteen, teen, and adult segments of readers around the world. By 2008, more than 400 million Harry Potter books had been sold in 64 languages. In the United States, the books were often at the top of *The New York Times* fiction best-seller list—for adults. Although separate covers for magazines or separate advertisements for books are expensive, these expenses are minor compared with the costs of producing multiple versions of magazines or books for multiple age or geographic market segments.

Multiple Products and Multiple Market Segments Ford's different lines of cars, SUVs, and pickup trucks are each targeted at a different type of customer—examples of multiple products aimed at multiple market segments. Producing these different vehicles is clearly more expensive than producing only a single vehicle. But this strategy is very effective if it meets customers' needs better, doesn't reduce quality or increase price, and adds to Ford's sales revenues and profits.

Marketers increasingly emphasize a two-tier marketing strategy—what some call "Tiffany/Wal-Mart strategies." Many firms now offer different variations of the same basic offering to high-end and low-end segments. Gap's Banana Republic chain sells blue jeans for $58, whereas its Old Navy stores sell a slightly different version for $22.

Segments of One: Mass Customization American marketers are rediscovering today what their ancestors running the corner general store knew a century ago: Each customer has unique needs and wants, and desires special tender loving care. Economies of scale in manufacturing and marketing during the past century made mass-produced goods so affordable that most customers were willing to compromise their individual tastes and settle for standardized products. Today's Internet ordering and flexible manufacturing and marketing processes have made *mass customization* possible, which means tailoring goods or services to the tastes of individual customers on a high-volume scale.

Ann Taylor Stores Corporation's LOFT chain tries to reach value-conscious women with a casual lifestyle while its flagship Ann Taylor chain targets more sophisticated women. Do these store fronts convey this difference? For the potential dangers of this two-segment strategy, see the text.

---

frequently 经常性的，频繁的；vehicle 车辆，交通工具，运输工具；ancestor 祖宗，祖先。

Mass customization is the next step beyond *build-to-order* (BTO), manufacturing a product only when there is an order from a customer. Dell uses BTO systems that trim work-in-progress inventories and shorten delivery times to customers. To do this, Dell restricts its computer manufacturing line to only a few basic models that can be assembled in four minutes. This gives customers a good choice with quick delivery. But even this system falls a bit short of total mass customization because customers do not have an unlimited number of features they can choose from.

The Segmentation Trade-Off: Synergies versus Cannibalization

成功的产品差异化和市场细分的关键是在满足顾客个人需要与实现组织协同增效之间找到理想的平衡点。组织协同增效是指通过更有效地发挥组织的各个职能来实现顾客价值增值。“顾客价值增值”表现为许多形式：更多的产品、现有产品质量的提高、更低的价格、通过改进分销使产品更容易被得到，等等。因此，通过协同增效使顾客更加满意是评价一个组织营销是否成功的最终标准。

The key to successful product differentiation and market segmentation strategies is finding the ideal balance between satisfying a customer's individual wants and achieving *organizational synergy*, the increased customer value achieved through performing organizational functions such as marketing or manufacturing more efficiently. The "increased customer value" can take many forms: more products, improved quality on existing products, lower prices, easier access to products through improved distribution, and so on. So the ultimate criterion for an organization's marketing success is that customers should be better off as a result of the increased synergies.

The organization should also achieve increased revenues and profits from the product differentiation and market segmentation strategies it uses. When the increased customer value involves adding new products or a new chain of stores, the product differentiation–market segmentation trade-off raises a critical issue: Are the new products or new chain simply stealing customers and sales from the older, existing ones? This is known as *cannibalization*.

However, the lines between customer segments can often blur, which can lead to problems, such as the Ann Taylor flagship store competing with its LOFT outlets. The flagship Ann Taylor chain targets polished, sophisticated women while its sister Ann Taylor LOFT chain targets women wanting moderately priced, trendy, casual clothes they can wear to the office. The nightmare: Annual sales of the LOFT stores recently passed those of the Ann Taylor chain, which has struggled to reach its target customers. The result: More than 100 stores from both chains were to be closed by 2010.

learning review

1. Market segmentation involves aggregating prospective buyers into groups that have two key characteristics. What are they?
2. In terms of market segments and products, what are the three market segmentation strategies?

市场细分与确定目标市场的步骤
STEPS IN SEGMENTING AND TARGETING MARKETS

Figure 6–2 identifies the five-step process used to segment a market and select the target segments on which it wants to focus. Segmenting a market requires both detailed analysis and large doses of common sense and managerial judgment. So market segmentation is both science and art!

FIGURE 6–2
The five key steps in segmenting and targeting markets link market needs of customers to the organization's marketing program.

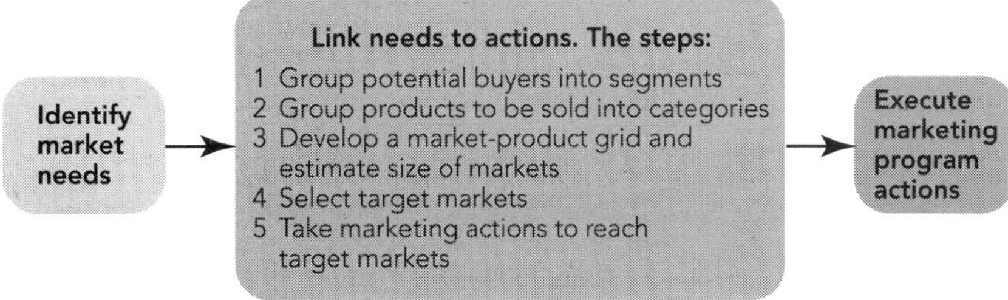

customization 用户化，专用化，定制；synergy 协同，配合。

This appliance includes everything from a small refrigerator, freezer, and microwave oven to a charging station for laptops and cell phones. To which market segment might this appeal? The answer appears in the text.

Mac-Gray Corporation
www.microfridge.com

Use market segmentation to choose target markets and take useful marketing actions for the Wendy's restaurant we assume you just bought. Your Wendy's is located next to a large urban university, one that offers both day and evening classes. Your restaurant offers the basic Wendy's fare: hamburgers, chicken and deli sandwiches, salads, French fries, and Frosty desserts. Even though you are part of a chain that has some restrictions on menu and décor, you are free to set your hours of business and to develop local advertising. How can market segmentation help?

步骤 1：对潜在购买者进行细分
Step 1: Group Potential Buyers into Segments

It's not always a good idea to segment a market. Grouping potential buyers into meaningful segments involves meeting some specific criteria that answer the questions, "Would segmentation be worth doing?" and "Is it possible?" If so, a marketer must find specific variables that can be used to create these various segments.

Criteria to Use in Forming the Segments A marketing manager should develop segments for a market that meet five essential criteria:

- *Simplicity and cost-effectiveness of assigning potential buyers to segments.* A marketing manager must be able to put a market segmentation plan into effect. This means identifying the characteristics of potential buyers in a market and then cost-effectively assigning them to a segment.
- *Potential for increased profit.* The best segmentation approach is the one that maximizes the opportunity for future profit and return on investment (ROI). If this potential is maximized without segmentation, don't segment. For nonprofit organizations, the criterion is the potential for serving clients more effectively.
- *Similarity of needs of potential buyers within a segment.* Potential buyers within a segment should be similar in terms of common needs that, in turn, leads to a common marketing action, such as product features sought or advertising media used.
- *Difference of needs of buyers among segments.* If the needs of the various segments aren't very different, combine them into fewer segments. A different segment usually requires a different marketing action that, in turn, means greater costs. If increased sales don't offset extra costs, combine segments and reduce the number of marketing actions.
- *Potential of a marketing action to reach a segment.* Reaching a segment requires a simple but effective marketing action. If no such action exists, don't segment.

Ways to Segment Consumer Markets Figure 6–3 shows four general bases of segmentation and the typical variables that can be used to segment U.S. consumer markets. These four segmentation bases are: (1) *geographic segmentation*, which is based on where prospective customers live or work (region, city size); (2) *demographic segmentation*, which is based on some *objective* physical (gender, race), measurable (age, income), or other classification attribute (birth era, occupation) of prospective customers; (3) *psychographic segmentation*, which is based on some subjective mental or emotional attributes (personality), aspirations (lifestyle), or needs of prospective customers; and (4) *behavioral segmentation*, which is based on some observable actions or attitudes by prospective customers—such as where

---

criteria（批评、判断等的）标准，准则（criterion 的名词复数）; characteristic 特色，特点，特征；attribute（人或物的）品质，特征。

they buy, what benefits they seek, how frequently they buy, and why they buy. Some examples are:

- *Geographic segmentation: Region.* Campbell's found that its canned nacho cheese sauce, which could be heated and poured directly onto nacho chips, was too spicy for Americans in the East and not spicy enough for those in the West and Southwest. The result: Today, Campbell's plants in Texas and California produce a hotter nacho cheese sauce than that produced in the other plants to serve their regions better.
- *Demographic segmentation: Household size.* More than half of all U.S. households are made up of only one or two persons, so Campbell's packages meals with only one or two servings—from Great Starts breakfasts to L'Orient dinners.
- *Psychographic segmentation: Lifestyle.* Nielsen Claritas' lifestyle segmentation is based on the belief that "birds of a feather flock together." Thus, people of similar lifestyles tend to live near one another, have similar interests, and buy similar offerings. This is of great value to marketers. Claritas' PRIZM classifies every household in the United States into one of 66 unique market segments. See the Going Online box on the next page for a profile of where you live.
- *Behavioral segmentation: Product features.* Understanding what features are important to different customers is a useful way to segment markets because it can lead directly to specific marketing actions, such as a new product, an ad campaign, or a distribution system. For example, college dorm residents frequently want to keep and prepare their own food to save money or have a

FIGURE 6–3
Segmentation bases, variables, and breakdowns for U.S. consumer markets. In selecting a segmentation variable, a marketing manager needs it to lead to a marketing action.

Basis of Segmentation	Segmentation Variables	Typical Breakdowns
Geographic	Region	Northeast; Midwest; South; West; etc.
	City size	Under 10,000; 10,000–24,999; 25,000–49,999; 50,000–99,999; etc.
	Statistical area	Metropolitan and micropolitan statistical areas; Census tract; etc.
	Media-television	210 designated market areas (DMA) in the U.S. (Nielsen)
	Density	Urban; suburban; small town; rural
Demographic	Gender	Male; female
	Age	Under 6 yrs; 6–11 yrs; 12–17 yrs; 18–24 yrs; 25–34 yrs; etc.
	Race/ethnicity	African American; Asian; Hispanic; White/Caucasian; etc.
	Life stage	Infant; preschool; child; youth; collegiate; adult; senior
	Birth era	Baby boomer (1946–1964); Generation X (1965–1976); etc.
	Household size	1; 2; 3–4; 5 or more
	Marital status	Never married; married; separated; divorced; widowed; domestic partner
	Income	Under $15,000; $15,000–$24,999; $25,000–$34,999; etc.
	Education	Some high school or less; high school graduate (or GED); etc.
	Occupation	Managerial & professional; technical, sales; farming; etc.
Psychographic	Personality	Gregarious; compulsive; extroverted; aggressive; ambitious; etc.
	Values (VALS2)	Innovators; Thinkers; Achievers; Experiencers; Believers; Strivers; etc.
	Lifestyle (Claritas PRIZM)	Blue Blood Estates; Single City Blues; etc. 66 total neighborhood clusters
	Needs	Quality; service; price/value; health; convenience; etc.
Behavioral	Retail store type	Department; specialty; outlet; convenience; mass merchandiser; etc.
	Direct marketing	Mail order/catalog; door-to-door; direct response; Internet
	Product features	Situation-specific; general
	Usage rate	Light user; medium user; heavy user
	User status	Nonuser; ex-user; prospect; first-time user; regular user
	Awareness/intentions	Unaware; aware; interested; intending to buy; purchaser; rejection

frequently 经常性的，频繁的；spicy 辛辣的，有刺激性的。

Going Online

What "Flock" Do You Belong to?

Who are your target customers? What are they like? Where do they live? How can you reach them? These questions are answered by Nielsen Claritas, whose PRIZM classifies every household into one of 66 demographically and behaviorally distinct neighborhood segments to identify lifestyles and purchase behavior within a defined geographic market area, such as zip code.

Want to know what your neighborhood is like? Go to claritas.com/MyBestSegments/Default.jsp and click the "You Are Where You Live" image. Then, type in your zip code (and security code) to find out what the most common segments are in your neighborhood. For a description of these segments, click the "Segment Look-Up" tab. Is this your "flock"?

late-night snack. However, their dorm rooms are often woefully short of space. MicroFridge understands this and markets a combination microwave, refrigerator, freezer, and charging station targeted to these students.

- *Behavioral segmentation: Usage rate.* **Usage rate** is the quantity consumed or patronage—store visits—during a specific period. It varies significantly among different customer groups. Airlines have developed frequent-flier programs to encourage passengers to use the same airline repeatedly to create loyal customers. This technique, sometimes called *frequency marketing*, focuses on usage rate. One key conclusion emerges about usage: In market segmentation studies, some measure of usage by, or sales obtained from, various segments is central to the analysis.

The Aberdeen Group recently analyzed which segmentation bases were used by the 20 percent most profitable organizations of the 220 surveyed. From highest to lowest, these were the segmentation bases they used:

- Geographic bases—88 percent.
- Behavioral bases—65 percent.
- Demographic bases—53 percent.
- Psychographic bases—43 percent.

The top 20 percent often use more than one of these bases in their market segmentation studies, plus measures such as purchase histories and usage rates of customers.

To obtain quarterly, projectable usage rate data to the U.S. national population for more than 450 consumer product categories, and 8,000+ brands, Experian Simmons continuously surveys over 25,000 adults each year. The purpose is to discover how the products and services they buy and the media they use relate to their behavioral, psychographic, and demographic characteristics. Figure 6–4 shows the results of a question Simmons asked about adult respondents' frequency of use (or patronage) of fast-food restaurants.

As shown by the arrow in the far right column of Figure 6–4, the importance of the segment increases as we move up the table. Among nonusers of these restaurants, prospects (who might become users) are more important than nonprospects (who are never likely to become users). Moving up the rows to users, it seems logical that light users of these restaurants (0 to 5 times per month) are important but less so than medium users (6 to 13 times per month), who, in turn, are a less important segment than the critical group: heavy users (14 or more times per month). The Actual

woefully 恶劣的，糟糕的，不合意的；microwave 微波，微波炉；patronage 光顾，惠顾。

Consumption column in Figure 6–4 shows how much of the total monthly usage of these restaurants is accounted for by heavy, medium, and light users.

使用率有时指的是 **80/20 法则**，即公司 80% 的销量来自于 20% 的顾客。80/20 法则中的百分比并不是要真正地、精确地固定在 80% 和 20% 上，而是说明公司的大部分销量由小部分顾客产生。

Usage rate is sometimes referred to in terms of the **80/20 rule**, a concept that suggests 80 percent of a firm's sales are obtained from 20 percent of its customers. The percentages in the 80/20 rule are not really fixed at exactly 80 percent and 20 percent but suggest that a small fraction of customers provides a large fraction of a firm's sales. For example, Figure 6–4 shows that the 45.4 percent of the U.S. population who are heavy users of fast-food restaurants provide 70.6 percent of the consumption volume. These high percentages are most likely due to the recession that began in late 2008 as consumers increasingly patronized fast food restaurants due to their inexpensive "value meal" offerings.

The Usage Index per Person column in Figure 6–4 emphasizes the importance of the heavy-user segment even more. Giving the light users (0 to 5 restaurant visits per month) an index of 100, the heavy users have an index of 640. In other words, for every $1.00 spent by a light user in one of these restaurants in a month, each heavy user spends $6.40. This is the reason that as a Wendy's restaurant owner, you want to focus most of your marketing efforts on reaching the highly attractive heavy-user market segment.

As part of its survey, Experian Simmons asked adults which fast-food restaurant(s) were (1) the sole or only restaurant, (2) the primary one, or (3) one of several secondary ones they patronized. As a Wendy's restaurant owner, the information depicted in Figure 6–5 on the next page should give you some ideas in developing a marketing program for your local market. For example, the Wendy's bar graph in Figure 6–5 shows that your sole (0.6 percent) and primary (17.2 percent) user segments are somewhat behind Burger King and far behind McDonald's. Thus, your challenge is to look at these two competitors and devise a marketing program to win customers from them.

The nonusers part of the Wendy's bar graph in Figure 6–5 also provides ideas. It shows that 13.8 percent of adult Americans don't go to fast-food restaurants in a typical month and are really nonprospects—unlikely to ever patronize your restaurant. However, 56.6 percent of nonusers are prospects who may be worth a targeted marketing program. These adults use the product category (fast food) but do not yet

FIGURE 6–4
Patronage of fast-food restaurants by adults 18 years and older. The table shows the critical importance of attracting heavy users and medium users to a fast-food restaurant.

User or Nonuser	Specific Segment	Number (1,000s)	Percentage	Actual Consumption (%)	Usage Index per Person	Importance of Segment
Users	Heavy users (14 + per month)	100,739	45.4%	70.6%	640	High
	Medium users (6–13 per month)	64,724	29.2	26.9	380	↑
	Light users (0–5 or per month)	22,051	9.9	2.4	100	
Total users		187,514	84.5	100.0	—	
Nonusers	Prospects	3,758	1.7	—	—	
	Nonprospects	30,569	13.8	—	—	↓
Total nonusers		34,327	15.5	—	—	Low
Total	Users + nonusers	221,841	100.0	—	—	

Source: Experian Simmons Spring 2009 Full-Year NCS/NHCS Choices 3 System Crosstabulation Report based on visits within the past 30 days.

column 柱状物；fraction 少量，小份，一点儿。

FIGURE 6–5
Comparison of various kinds of users and nonusers for Wendy's, Burger King, and McDonald's fast-food restaurants. This table gives a Wendy's restaurant a snapshot of its customers compared to those of its major competitors.

Percentage of respondents (adults, 18 and over)

	Wendy's	Burger King	McDonald's
Users: Sole restaurant	0.6%	0.8%	3.7%
Users: Primary restaurant	17.2%	23.5%	46.0%
Users: Secondary restaurant	11.8%	13.9%	11.4%
Nonusers: Prospects	56.6%	48.0%	25.1%
Nonusers: Nonprospects	13.8%	13.8%	13.8%

Source: Experian Simmons Spring 2009 Full-Year NCS/NHCS Choices 3 System Crosstabulation Report based on visits within the past 30 days.

patronize Wendy's. New menu items, such as the Coffee Toffee Twisted Frosty, or promotional strategies, such as the "Lessons in 3conomics" TV ad that introduces three sandwiches for 99¢ to beat the recession, may succeed in converting these prospects into users that patronize Wendy's.

Variables to Use in Forming Segments To analyze your Wendy's customers, you need to identify which variables to use to segment them. Because the restaurant is located near a large urban university, the most logical starting point for segmentation is really behavioral: Are the prospective customers students or nonstudents?

To segment the students, you could try a variety of (1) geographic variables, such as city or zip code, (2) demographic variables, such as gender, age, year in school, or college major, or (3) psychographic variables, such as personality or needs. But none of these variables really meets the five criteria listed previously—particularly, the fifth criterion about leading to a doable marketing action to reach the various segments. The bases of segmentation for the "students" segment really combines two variables: (1) where students live and (2) when they are on campus. This results in four "student" segments:

- Students living in dormitories (university residence halls, sororities, fraternities).
- Students living near the university in apartments.
- Day commuter students living outside the area.
- Night commuter students living outside the area.

What variables might Xerox use to segment organizational markets to respond to a firm's color copying problems? For the possible answer and related marketing actions, see the text.

The three main segments of "nonstudents" include:

- Faculty and staff members who work at the university.
- People who live in the area but aren't connected with the university.
- People who work in the area but aren't connected with the university.

People in each of these nonstudent segments aren't quite as similar as those in the student segments, which makes them harder to reach with a marketing program or action. Think about (1) whether the needs of all these segments are different and (2) how various advertising media can be used to reach these groups effectively.

Ways to Segment Organizational Markets A number of variables can be used to segment organizational markets (see Figure 6–6). For

patronize 光顾，惠顾；demographic 人口统计学的，人口统计的。

Basis of Segmentation	Segmentation Variables	Typical Breakdowns
Geographic	Global region or country Statistical area Density	European Union, South America, etc.; U.S., Japan, India, etc. Metropolitan and micropolitan statistical areas; Census tract; etc. Urban; suburban; small town; rural
Demographic	NAICS code NAICS sector Number of employees Annual sales	2 digit: Sector; 3 digit: subsector; 4 digit: industry group; etc. Agriculture, forestry (11); mining (21); utilities (22); etc. 1–99; 100–499; 500–999; 1,000–4,999; 5,000 + Under $1 million; $1 million–$9.9 million; $10 million–$49.9 million; etc.
	Number of locations	1–9; 10–49; 50–99; 100–499; 500–999; 1,000+
Behavioral	Kind Where used Application Purchase location Who buys Type of buy	Product; service Installation; component; supplies; etc. Office; production; etc. Centralized; decentralized Individual buyer; industrial buying group New buy; modified rebuy; straight rebuy

FIGURE 6–6
Segmentation bases, variables, and breakdowns for U.S. organizational markets. These variables are used in business-to-business marketing.

example, a product manager at Xerox responsible for its new line of color printers might use these segmentation bases and corresponding variables:

- *Geographic segmentation: Statistical area.* Firms located in a metropolitan statistical area might receive a personal sales call, whereas those in a micropolitan statistical area might be contacted by telephone.
- *Demographic segmentation: NAICS code.* Firms categorized by the North American Industry Classification System code as manufacturers that deal with customers throughout the world might have different document printing needs than do retailers or lawyers serving local customers.
- *Demographic segmentation: Number of employees.* The size of the firm is related to the volume of digital documents produced, so firms with varying numbers of employees might be specific target markets for different Xerox copier systems.
- *Behavioral segmentation: Usage rate.* Similar to this segmentation variable for consumer markets, features are often of major importance in organizational markets. So Xerox can target organizations needing fast printing, copying, and scanning in color—the benefits and features emphasized in the ad for its Xerox WorkCentre 7655 Color MFP system.

learning review

3. The process of segmenting and targeting markets is a bridge between which two marketing activities?
4. What is the difference between the demographic and behavioral bases of market segmentation?

步骤 2：将待售产品进行分类
Step 2: Group Products to Be Sold into Categories

What does your Wendy's restaurant sell? Of course you are selling individual products such as Frostys, hamburgers, and fries. But for marketing purposes you're really selling combinations of individual products that become a "meal." This distinction is critical, so let's discuss both (1) individual Wendy's products and (2) groupings of Wendy's products.

micropolitan 居住区；emphasize 强调，重视。

MARKET SEGMENT		PRODUCT OR INNOVATION								
GENERAL	GROUP WITH NEED	HOT 'N JUICY HAMBURGER (1969)	DRIVE-THRU (1970)	99¢ SUPER VALUE MEALS (1989)	SALAD SENSATIONS (2002)	E-PAY (2003)	ADULT COMBO MEALS (2004)	LOW TRANS FAT CHICKEN SANDWICHES (2006)	FRESCATA DELI SANDWICHES (2006)	BREAKFAST SANDWICHES (2007)
GENDER	Male	P	P	P	S	P	P	S	P	P
	Female				P	P	S	P	P	
NEEDS	Price/Value			P	S		P			
	Health-Conscious				P			P	P	
	Convenience	S	P		S	P	S			P
	Meat Lovers	P		S			P	S	S	S
UNIVERSITY AFFILIATION	Affiliated (Students, Faculty, Staff)	P	S	P	P	P	S	P	P	S
	Nonaffiliated (Residents, Workers)	S	P	S	S	S	P	S	S	P

Key: P = Primary market S = Secondary market

FIGURE 6–7
Wendy's new products and other innovations target specific market segments based on a customer's gender, needs, or university affiliation.

Individual Wendy's Products When Dave Thomas founded Wendy's in 1969, he offered only four basic items: "hot 'n juicy" hamburgers, Frosty Dairy Desserts (Frostys), French fries, and soft drinks. Since then, Wendy's has introduced many new products and innovations to compete for customers' fast-food dollars. Some of these are shown in Figure 6–7. New products include salads, low trans fat chicken sandwiches, and Frescata deli sandwiches. But there are also nonproduct innovations to increase consumer convenience like drive-thru services and E-Pay to enable credit card purchases.

Figure 6–7 also shows that each product or innovation is not targeted equally to all market segments based on gender, needs, or university affiliation. The cells in Figure 6–7 labeled "P" represent Wendy's primary target market segments when it introduced each product or innovation. The boxes labeled "S" represent the secondary target market segments that also bought these products or used these innovations. In some cases, Wendy's discovered that large numbers of people in a segment not originally targeted for a particular product or innovation bought it anyway.

Groupings of Wendy's Products: Meals Finding a means of grouping the products a firm sells into meaningful categories is as important as grouping customers into segments. If the firm has only one product or service, this isn't a problem. But when it has dozens or hundreds, these must be grouped in some way so buyers can relate to them. This is why department stores and supermarkets are organized into product groups, with the departments or aisles containing related merchandise. Likewise, manufacturers have product lines that are the groupings they use in the catalogs sent to customers.

What are the product groupings for your Wendy's restaurant? It could be the item purchased, such as, hamburgers, salads, a Frosty, and French fries. This is where judgment—the qualitative aspect of marketing—comes in. Customers really buy an eating experience—a meal occasion that satisfies a need at a particular time of day. So the product grouping that makes the most marketing sense is the five "meals" based on the time of day consumers buy them: breakfast, lunch, between-meal snack,

gender 性别；category 种类，类别。

dinner, and after-dinner snack. These groupings are more closely related to the way purchases are actually made and permit you to market the entire meal, not just your French fries or hamburgers.

步骤 3：开发市场—产品方格图并估计市场规模

Step 3: Develop a Market-Product Grid and Estimate the Size of Markets

LO4

A **market-product grid** is a framework to relate the market segments of potential buyers to products offered or potential marketing actions by an organization. In a complete market-product grid analysis, each cell in the grid can show the estimated market size of a given product sold to a specific market segment. Let's first look at forming a market-product grid for your Wendy's restaurant and then at estimating market sizes.

Forming a Market-Product Grid Developing a market-product grid means identifying and labeling the markets (or horizontal rows) and product groupings (or vertical columns), as shown in Figure 6–8. From our earlier discussion we've chosen to divide the market segments as students versus nonstudents, with subdivisions of each. The columns—or "products"—are really the meals (or eating occasions) customers enjoy at the restaurant.

Estimating Market Sizes Now the size of the market in each cell (the unique market-product combination) of the market-product grid must be estimated. For your Wendy's restaurant, this involves estimating the sales of each kind of meal expected to be sold to each student and nonstudent market segment.

The market size estimates in Figure 6–8 vary from a large market ("3") to no market at all ("0") for each cell in the market-product grid. These may be simple guesstimates if you don't have the time or money to conduct formal marketing research (as discussed in Chapter 5). But even such crude estimates of the size of specific markets using a market-product grid are helpful in determining which target market segments to select and which product groupings to offer.

步骤 4：选择目标市场

Step 4: Select Target Markets

A firm must take care to choose its target market segments carefully. If it picks too narrow a set of segments, it may fail to reach the volume of sales and profits it needs.

FIGURE 6–8
Selecting a target market for your Wendy's fast-food restaurant next to an urban university. The numbers show the estimated size of market in that cell, which leads to selecting the shaded target market.

	PRODUCTS: MEALS				
MARKET SEGMENTS	Break-fast	Lunch	Between-Meal Snack	Dinner	After-Dinner Snack
Student					
Dormitory	0	1	3	0	3
Apartment	1	3	3	1	1
Day commuter	0	3	2	1	0
Night commuter	0	0	1	3	2
Nonstudent					
Faculty or staff	0	3	1	1	0
Live in area	0	1	2	2	1
Work in area	1	3	0	1	0

Key: 3 = Large market; 2 = Medium market; 1 = Small market; 0 = No market.

framework 框架，构架；vertical 垂直的，直立的。

If it selects too broad a set of segments, it may spread its marketing efforts so thin that the extra expense exceeds the increased sales and profits.

选择目标市场所用的标准 市场细分过程中有两种不同的标准：（1）细分市场的标准（前面已讨论）；（2）选择目标市场的实际标准。即使经验丰富的营销经理也常常会混淆这两套不同的标准。在温蒂快餐店的例子中，可采用如下 5 个选择目标市场的实际标准：

- 市场规模
- 预期增长
- 竞争状况
- 到达细分市场的成本
- 与组织客观条件和资源的匹配状况

Criteria to Use in Selecting the Target Segments Two kinds of criteria in the market segmentation process are those used to (1) divide the market into segments (discussed earlier) and (2) actually pick the target segments. Even experienced marketing executives often confuse these two different sets of criteria. Five criteria can be used to select the target segments for your Wendy's restaurant:

- *Market size.* The estimated size of the market in the segment is an important factor in deciding whether it's worth going after. There is really no market for breakfasts among dormitory students (Figure 6–8), so you should not devote any marketing effort toward reaching this tiny segment.
- *Expected growth.* Although the size of the market in the segment may be small now, perhaps it is growing significantly or is expected to grow in the future. Sales of fast-food meals eaten outside the restaurants are projected to exceed those eaten inside. And Wendy's is the fast-food leader in average time to serve a drive-thru order—it is 16.7 seconds faster than McDonald's. This speed and convenience is potentially very important to night commuters in adult education programs.
- *Competitive position.* Is there a lot of competition in the segment now or is there likely to be in the future? The less the competition, the more attractive the segment is. For example, if the college dormitories announce a new policy of "no meals on weekends," this segment is suddenly more promising for your restaurant. Wendy's recently introduced E-Pay pay-by-credit-card service at its restaurants to keep up with this new service at McDonald's.
- *Cost of reaching the segment.* A segment that is inaccessible to a firm's marketing actions should not be pursued. For example, the few nonstudents who live in the area may not be reachable with ads in newspapers or other media. As a result, do not waste money trying to advertise to them.
- *Compatibility with the organization's objectives and resources.* If your Wendy's restaurant doesn't yet have the cooking equipment to make breakfasts and has a policy against spending more money on restaurant equipment, then don't try to reach the breakfast segment. As is often the case in marketing decisions, a particular segment may appear attractive according to some criteria and very unattractive according to others.

How can Wendy's target different market segments like late-night customers or commuting college students? For the answer, see the text and Figure 6–9.

Choose the Segments Ultimately, a marketing executive has to use these criteria to choose the segments for special marketing efforts. As shown in Figure 6–8, let's assume you've written off the breakfast product grouping for two reasons: It's too small a market and it's incompatible with your objectives and resources. In terms of competitive position and cost of reaching the segment, you choose to focus on the four student segments and *not* the three nonstudent segments (although you're certainly not going to turn away business from the nonstudent segments!). This combination of market-product segments—your target market—is shaded in Figure 6–8.

步骤 5：实施营销行动到达目标市场

Step 5: Take Marketing Actions to Reach Target Markets

The purpose of developing a market-product grid is to trigger marketing actions to increase sales and profits. This means that someone must develop and execute an action plan in the form of a marketing program.

dormitory（大学等的）学生宿舍；inaccessible 达不到的，难到达的，不可（或不易）进入的；grid 方格图。

Your Immediate Wendy's Segmentation Strategy With your Wendy's restaurant you've already reached one significant decision: There is a limited market for breakfast, so you won't open for business until 10:30 A.M. In fact, Wendy's first attempt at a breakfast menu was a disaster and was discontinued in 1986. Wendy's evaluates possible new menu items continuously to compete not only with McDonald's and Burger King but also with a complex array of convenience stores and gas stations that sell repeatable packaged foods as well as new "easy-lunch" products.

Another essential decision is where and what meals to advertise to reach specific market segments. An ad in the student newspaper could reach all the student segments, but you might consider this approach too expensive and want a more focused effort to reach smaller segments. If you choose three segments for special actions (Figure 6–9), advertising actions to reach them might include:

- *Day commuters* (an entire market segment). Run ads inside commuter buses and put flyers under the windshield wipers of cars in parking lots used by day commuters. These ads and flyers promote all the meals at your restaurant to a single segment of students, a horizontal cut through the market-product grid.
- *Between-meal snacks* (directed to all four student markets). To promote eating during this downtime for your restaurant, offer "Ten percent off all purchases between 2:00 and 4:30 P.M. during winter quarter." This ad promotes a single meal to all four student segments, a vertical cut through the market-product grid.
- *Dinners to night commuters.* The most focused of all three campaigns, this ad promotes a single meal to the single segment of night commuter students. The campaign might consist of a windshield flyer offering a free Frosty with the coupon when the person buys a drive-thru meal between 5 P.M. and 8 P.M.

Depending on how your advertising actions work, you can repeat, modify, or drop them and design new campaigns for other segments you deem are worth the effort. This advertising example is just a small piece of a complete marketing program for your Wendy's restaurant. And Wendy's focus on the late-night customers shown in its

FIGURE 6–9
Advertising actions to market various meals to a range of possible market segments of students

MARKET SEGMENTS	PRODUCTS: MEALS			
	Lunch	Between-Meal Snack	Dinner	After-Dinner Snack
Dormitory students	1	3	0	3
Apartment students	3	3	1	1
Day commuter students	3	2	1	0
Night commuter students	0	1	3	2

Ads in buses; flyers under windshield wipers of cars in parking lots

Ad campaign: "Ten percent off all purchases between 2:00 and 4:30 P.M. during winter quarter"

Ad on flyer under windshield wipers of cars in night parking lots: "Free Frosty with this coupon when you buy a drive-thru meal between 5:00 P.M. and 8:00 P.M."

Key: 3 = Large market; 2 = Medium market; 1 = Small market; 0 = No market.

disaster 彻底的失败，不幸；windshield（汽车等的）风挡，挡风玻璃。

ad on page 234 has been successful because customers like that the late-night pickup window is open until midnight or later.

Future Strategies for Your Wendy's Restaurant Changing customer tastes and competition mean you must alter your strategies when necessary. This involves looking at (1) what Wendy's headquarters is doing, (2) what competitors are doing, and (3) what might be changing in the area served by your restaurant.

Wendy's headquarters recently announced an aggressive new marketing program that includes:

- Targeting 25-to-49-year-old customers, not just 18-to-24-year-old ones.
- Positioning Wendy's as a lower-cost fast-food chain.
- Responding to the 2009 recession by aggressively marketing three 99-cent sandwiches.
- Introducing new menu items as the chain breaks into the breakfast market again.

The Wendy's strategy has been remarkably successful.

But other competitors such as McDonald's and Burger King are not sitting still, and you must be aware of their strategies. For example, in 2009 McDonald's actively promoted its lower-priced items that customers perceive as having good value, such as its Dollar Menu loaded with "choice choices." Also, individual McDonald's restaurants were given the flexibility to change prices in light of local demand. And Burger King rolled out its $1.39 BK Burger Shots™—"tiny flame-broiled burgers."

With these corporate Wendy's plans and new actions from competitors, maybe you'd better rethink your market segmentation decisions on hours of operation and breakfasts. Also, if new businesses have moved into your area, what about a new strategy to reach people that work in the area? Or a new promotion for the night owls and early birds—the 12 A.M. to 5 A.M. customers—that now generate one-sixth of revenues at some McDonald's restaurants?

How has Apple moved from its 1977 Apple II to today's Mac Pro? The Marketing Matters box and text discussion provide insights into Apple's current market segmentation strategy.

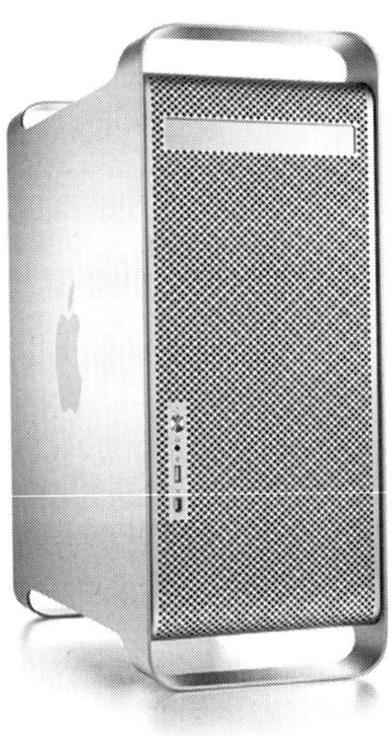

Apple's Ever-Changing Segmentation Strategy Steve Jobs and Steve Wozniak didn't realize they were developing today's multibillion-dollar PC industry when they invented the Apple I in a garage on April Fool's Day in 1976. Hobbyists, the initial target market, were not interested in the product. However, when the Apple II was displayed at a computer trade show in 1977, consumers loved it and Apple Computer was born. Typical of young companies, Apple focused on its products and had little concern for its markets. Its creative, young engineers were often likened to "Boy Scouts without adult supervision."

Steve Jobs left Apple in 1985, the company languished, and it constantly altered its market-product strategies. When Steve Jobs returned in 1997, he detailed his vision for a reincarnated Apple by describing a new market segmentation strategy that he called the "Apple Product Matrix." This strategy consisted of developing two general types of computers (desktops and portables) targeted at two general kinds of market segments—the consumer and professional sectors.

In most segmentation situations, a single product does not fit into an exclusive market niche. Rather, product lines and market segments overlap. So Apple's market segmentation strategy enables it to offer different products to meet the needs of different market segments, as shown in the Marketing Matters box.

市场—产品协同增效：一种权衡
Market-Product Synergies: A Balancing Act

Recognizing opportunities for key synergies—that is, efficiencies—is vital to success in selecting target market segments and making marketing decisions. Market-product grids illustrate where such synergies can be found. How? Let's consider Apple's

headquarters 总部，总公司；competitor 竞争者，对手；languish 中落，衰败，衰落。

Marketing Matters > > > > > > > > > technology

Apple's Segmentation Strategy—Camp Runamok No Longer

Camp Runamok was the nickname given to Apple in the early 1980s because the innovative company had no coherent series of product lines directed at identifiable market segments. Today, Apple has targeted its various lines of Macintosh computers at specific market segments, as shown in the accompanying market-product grid. Because the market-product grid shifts as a firm's strategy changes, the one here is based on Apple's product lines in late-2009. The grid suggests the market segmentation strategy Steve Jobs is using to compete in the digital age.

MARKETS		COMPUTER PRODUCTS					
Sector	Segment	Mac Pro	MacBook Pro	iMac	MacBook	MacBook Air	Mac Mini
Consumer	Individuals	✓	✓	✓	✓	✓	✓
	Small/home office	✓	✓	✓	✓	✓	
	Students			✓	✓		✓
	Teachers		✓	✓			
Professional	Medium/large business	✓	✓	✓		✓	
	Creative	✓	✓	✓			
	College faculty	✓	✓	✓		✓	
	College staff			✓	✓		✓

market-product grid in the accompanying Marketing Matters box and examine the difference between marketing synergies and product synergies shown there.

- *Marketing synergies.* Running horizontally across the grid, each row represents an opportunity for efficiency in terms of a market segment. Were Apple to focus on just one group of consumers, such as the medium/large business segment, its marketing efforts could be streamlined. Apple would not have to spend time learning about the buying habits of students or college faculty. So it could probably create a single ad to reach the medium/large business target segment (the yellow row), highlighting the only products they'd need to worry about developing: the Mac Pro, the MacBook Pro, the iMac, and the MacBook Air. Although clearly not Apple's strategy today, new firms often focus only on a single customer segment.
- *Product synergies.* Running vertically down the market-product grid, each column represents an opportunity for efficiency in research and development (R&D) and production. If Apple wanted to simplify its product line, reduce R&D and production expenses, and manufacture only one computer, which might it choose? Based on the market-product grid, Apple might do well to focus on the iMac (the orange column), because every segment purchases it.

Marketing synergies often come at the expense of product synergies because a single customer segment will likely require a variety of products, each of which will

synergy 协同增效作用，协同作用；horizontally 水平的，横的。

have to be designed and manufactured. The company saves money on marketing but spends more in production. Conversely, if product synergies are emphasized, marketing will have to address the concerns of a wide variety of consumers, which costs more time and money. Marketing managers responsible for developing a company's product line must balance both product and marketing synergies as they try to increase the company's profits.

learning review

5. What factor is estimated or measured for each of the cells in a market-product grid?
6. What are some criteria used to decide which segments to choose for targets?
7. How are marketing and product synergies different in a market-product grid?

产品定位
POSITIONING THE PRODUCT

LO5

产品定位是指相对于竞争品而言，本产品的重要属性在消费者心目中的地位。

When a company introduces a new product, a decision critical to its long-term success is how prospective buyers view it in relation to those products offered by its competitors. **Product positioning** refers to the place a product occupies in consumers' minds on important attributes relative to competitive products. By understanding where consumers see a company's product or brand today, a marketing manager can seek to change its future position in their minds. This requires **product repositioning**, *changing* the place a product occupies in a consumer's mind relative to competitive products.

产品定位的两种途径
Two Approaches to Product Positioning

Marketers follow two main approaches to positioning a new product in the market. *Head-to-head positioning* involves competing directly with competitors on similar product attributes in the same target market. Using this strategy, Dollar rental car competes directly with Avis and Hertz.

Differentiation positioning involves seeking a less-competitive, smaller market niche in which to locate a brand. McDonald's tried to appeal to the health-conscious segment when it introduced the low-fat McLean Deluxe hamburger to avoid competing directly with Wendy's and Burger King. However, it was eventually dropped from the menu. Companies also follow a differentiation positioning strategy among brands within their own product line to minimize the cannibalization of a brand's sales or market shares.

Marketing managers often convert their positioning ideas for the product or brand into a succinct written positioning statement. The positioning statement not only is used internally within the marketing department but also for others, outside it, such as research and development engineers or advertising agencies.

利用感知图进行产品定位
Product Positioning Using Perceptual Maps

A key to positioning a product or brand effectively is discovering the perceptions of its potential customers. In determining its positioning in the minds of customers, companies take four steps:

1. Identify the important attributes for a product or brand class.
2. Discover how target customers rate competing products or brands with respect to these attributes.

---

conversely 相反地，反过来说；occupy 占领，占据，侵占；cannibalization 销售再分配。

More "zip" for chocolate milk? The text and Figure 6–11 describe how American dairies have successfully repositioned chocolate milk to appeal to American adults.

3. Discover where the company's product or brand is on these attributes in the minds of potential customers.
4. Reposition the company's product or brand in the minds of potential customers.

From these data, it is possible to develop a **perceptual map**, a means of displaying or graphing in two dimensions the location of products or brands in the minds of consumers to enable a manager to see how consumers perceive competing products or brands, as well as its own product or brand. The firm can then develop marketing actions to move its product or brand to an ideal position.

再定位巧克力牛奶（给成人）的感知图

A Perceptual Map to Reposition Chocolate Milk for Adults

Recently U.S. dairies were struggling to increase milk sales. So they hit on a wild idea: Try to reposition chocolate milk in the minds of American adults to increase their sales revenues. Let's use the four steps above to show how dairies repositioned chocolate milk for American adults:

1. *Identify the important attributes (or scales) for adult drinks.* Research reveals the key attributes adults use to judge various drinks are (*a*) low versus high nutrition and (*b*) children's drinks versus adult drinks, as shown by the two axes in Figure 6–10.
2. *Discover how adults see various competing drinks.* Locate various adult drinks on these axes, as shown in Figure 6–10.
3. *Discover how potential customers see chocolate milk.* Figure 6–10 shows adults see chocolate milk as moderately nutritious (on the vertical axis) but as mainly a child's drink (on the horizontal axis).
4. *Reposition chocolate milk to make it more appealing to adults.* Looking at the circled letters in Figure 6–10, to which one should the dairies try to move chocolate milk to increase sales?

What actions did dairies take? They repositioned chocolate milk to the location of the star shown in the perceptual map in Figure 6–11 on the next page, the position of letter "B" in Figure 6–10. Their arguments are nutritionally powerful. For women,

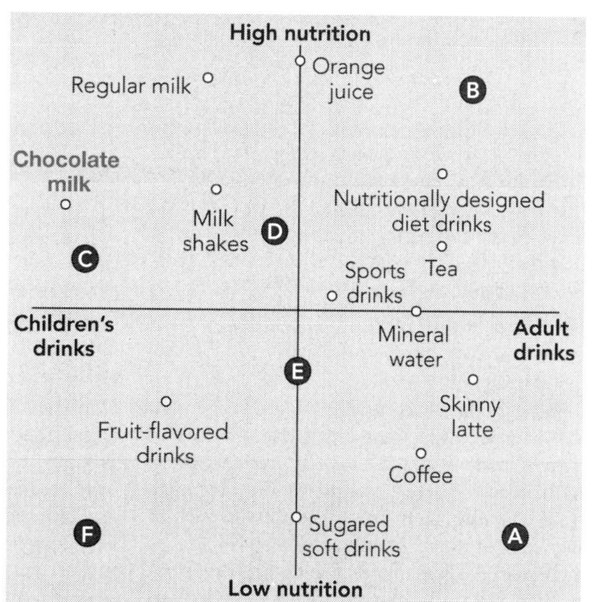

FIGURE 6–10
A perceptual map of the location of beverages in the minds of American adults. Toward which letter would you try to move the perception of chocolate milk to make it more appealing to these adults?

perceptual 理解的，感知的；revenue 收益，所得；reposition 再定位，重新定位（产品或服务）。

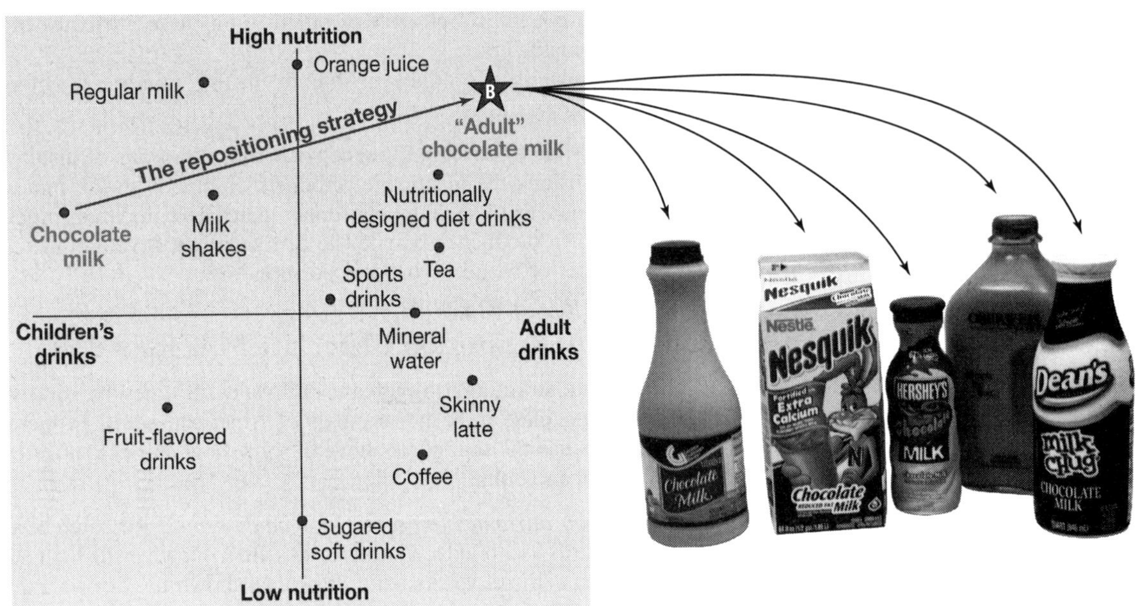

FIGURE 6–11
The strategy American dairies are using to reposition chocolate milk to reach adults: Have adults view chocolate milk both as more nutritional and "more adult."

chocolate milk provides calcium, critically important in female diets. And dieters get a more filling, nutritious beverage than with a soft drink for about the same calories.[21] The result: Chocolate milk sales increased dramatically, much of it because of adult consumption.[22] Part of this is due to giving chocolate milk "nutritional respectability" for adults, but another part is due to the innovative packaging that enables many new chocolate milk containers to fit in a car's cup holders.

learning review

8. What is the difference between product positioning and product repositioning?
9. Why do marketers use perceptual maps in product positioning decisions?

LEARNING OBJECTIVES REVIEW

LO1 *Explain what market segmentation is and when to use it.*
Market segmentation involves aggregating prospective buyers into groups that (*a*) have common needs and (*b*) will respond similarly to a marketing action. Organizations go to the expense of segmenting their markets when it increases their sales, profits, and ability to serve customers better.

LO2 *Identify the five steps involved in segmenting and targeting markets.*
Step 1 is to group potential buyers into segments. Buyers within a segment should have similar characteristics to each other and respond similarly to marketing actions like a new product or a lower price. Step 2 involves putting related products to be sold into meaningful groups. In step 3, organizations develop a market-product grid with estimated sizes of markets in each of the market-product cells of the resulting table. Step 4 involves selecting the target market segments on which the organization should focus. Step 5 involves taking marketing mix actions—often in the form of a marketing program—to reach the target market segments.

LO3 *Recognize the bases used to segment consumer and organizational markets.*
Bases used to segment consumer markets include geographic, demographic, psychographic, and behavioral ones. Organizational markets use the same bases except for psychographic ones.

LO4 *Develop a market-product grid to identify a target market and recommend resulting actions.*
Organizations use five key criteria to segment markets, whose groupings appear in the rows of the market-product grid. Groups of related products appear in the columns. After estimating the size of market in each cell in the grid, they select the target market segments on which to focus. They then identify marketing mix actions—often in a marketing program—to reach the target market most efficiently.

dramatically 戏剧性地，引人注目地。

LO5 *Explain how marketing managers position products in the marketplace.*
Marketing managers often locate competing products on two-dimensional perceptual maps to visualize the products in the minds of consumers. They then try to position new products or reposition existing products in this space to attain the maximum sales and profits.

FOCUSING ON KEY TERMS

80/20 rule
market-product grid
market segmentation
market segments
perceptual map
product differentiation
product positioning
product repositioning
usage rate

APPLYING MARKETING KNOWLEDGE

1 What variables might be used to segment these consumer markets? (*a*) lawn mowers, (*b*) frozen dinners, (*c*) dry breakfast cereals, and (*d*) soft drinks.
2 What variables might be used to segment these industrial markets? (*a*) industrial sweepers, (*b*) photocopiers, (*c*) computerized production control systems, and (*d*) car rental agencies.
3 In Figure 6–8, the dormitory market segment includes students living in college-owned residence halls, sororities, and fraternities. What market needs are common to these students that justify combining them into a single segment in studying the market for your Wendy's restaurant?
4 You may disagree with the estimates of market size given for the rows in the market-product grid in Figure 6–8. Estimate the market size, and give a brief justification for these market segments: (*a*) dormitory students, (*b*) day commuters, and (*c*) people who work in the area.
5 Suppose you want to increase revenues for your fast-food restaurant even further. Referring to Figure 6–9, what advertising actions might you take to increase revenues from (*a*) dormitory students, (*b*) dinners, and (*c*) after-dinner snacks from night commuters?
6 Locate these drinks on the perceptual map in Figure 6–10: (*a*) cappuccino, (*b*) beer, and (*c*) soy milk?

building your marketing plan

Your marketing plan (*a*) needs a market-product grid to focus your marketing efforts and also (*b*) leads to a forecast of sales for the company. Use these steps:
1 Define the market segments (the rows in your grid) using the bases of segmentation used to segment consumer and organizational markets.
2 Define the groupings of related products (the columns in your grid).
3 Form your grid and estimate the size of market in each market-product cell.
4 Select the target market segments on which to focus your efforts with your marketing program.
5 Use the information and the lost-horse forecasting technique to make a sales forecast (company forecast).

video case 6 Prince Sports, Inc.: Tennis Racquets for Every Segment

"Over the last decade we've seen a dramatic change in the media to reach consumers," says Linda Glassel, vice president of sports marketing and brand image of Prince Sports, Inc.

PRINCE SPORTS IN TODAY'S CHANGING WORLD

"Today—particularly in reaching younger consumers—we're now focusing so much more on social marketing and social networks, be it Facebook, Twitter, MySpace, and internationally with Hi5, Bebo, and Orkut," she adds.

Linda Glassel's comments are a snapshot look at what Prince Sports faces in the changing world of tennis in the 2010s.

Prince Sports is a racquet sports company whose portfolio of brands includes Prince (tennis, squash, and badminton), Ektelon (racquetball), and Viking (platform/paddle tennis). Its complete line of tennis products alone is astounding: more than 150 racquet models; more than

50 tennis strings; over 50 footwear models; and countless types of bags, apparel, and other accessories.

Prince prides itself on its history of innovation in tennis—including inventing the first "oversize" and "longbody" racquets, the first "synthetic gut" tennis string, and the first "Natural Foot Shape" tennis shoe. Its challenge today is to continue to innovate to meet the needs of all levels of tennis players.

"One favorable thing for Prince these days is the dramatic growth in tennis participation—higher than it's been in many years," says Nick Skally (center in the photo below), senior marketing manager. A recent study by the Sporting Goods Manufacturers confirms this point: Tennis participation in the U.S. was up 43 percent from 2000 to 2008—the fastest growing traditional individual sport in the country.

TAMING TECHNOLOGY TO MEET PLAYERS' NEEDS

Every tennis player wants the same thing: to play better. But they don't all have the same skills, or the same ability to swing a racquet fast. So adult tennis players fall very broadly into three groups, each with special needs:

- *Those with shorter, slower strokes.* They want maximum power in a lightweight frame.
- *Those with moderate to full strokes.* They want the perfect blend of power and control.
- *Those with longer, faster strokes.* They want greater control with less power.

To satisfy all these needs in one racquet is a big order.

"When we design tennis racquets, it involves an extensive amount of market research on players at all levels," explains Tyler Herring, Global Business Director for Performance Tennis Racquets. In 2005, Prince's research led it to introduce its breakthrough O^3 technology. "Our O^3 technology solved an inherent contradiction between racquet speed and sweet spot," he says. Never before had a racquet been designed that simultaneously delivers faster racquet speed with a dramatically increased "sweet spot." The "sweet spot" in a racquet is the middle of the frame that gives the most power and consistency when hitting. In 2009 Prince introduced their latest evolution of the O^3 platform called EXO^3. Its newly patented design suspends the string bed from the racquet frame—thereby increasing the sweet spot by up to 83 percent while reducing frame vibration up to 50 percent.

SEGMENTING THE TENNIS MARKET

"The three primary market segments for our tennis racquets are our performance line, our recreational line, and our junior line," says Herring. He explains that within each of these segments Prince makes difficult design trade-offs to balance (1) the price a player is willing to pay, (2) what playing features (speed versus spin, sweet spot versus control, and so on) they want, and (3) what technology can be built into the racquet for the price point.

Within each of these three primary market segments, there are at least two sub-segments—sometimes overlapping! Figure 1 gives an overview of Prince's market segmentation strategy and identifies sample racquet models. The three right-hand columns show the design variations of length, unstrung weight, and head size. The table shows the complexities Prince faces in converting its technology into a racquet with physical features that satisfy players' needs.

DISTRIBUTION AND PROMOTION STRATEGIES

"Prince has a number of different distribution channels—from mass merchants like Wal-Mart and Target, to sporting goods chains, to smaller specialty tennis shops," says Nick Skally. For the large chains Prince contributes co-op advertising for their in-store circulars, point-of-purchase displays, in-store signage, consumer brochures, and even "space planograms" to help the retailer plan the layout of Prince products in their tennis area. Prince aids for small tennis specialty shops include a supply of demo racquets, detailed catalogs, posters, racquet and string guides, merchandising fixtures, and hardware, such as racquet hooks and footwear shelves, in addition to other items. Prince also provides these shops with "player standees," which are corregated life-size cut outs of professional tennis players.

Prince reaches tennis players directly through its Web site (www.princetennis.com), which gives product information, tennis tips, and the latest tennis news. Besides using social networks like Facebook and Twitter, Prince runs ads in regional and national tennis publications, and develops advertising campaigns for online sites and broadcast outlets.

In addition to its in-store activities, advertising, and online marketing, Prince invests heavily in its Teaching

Pro program. These sponsored teaching pros receive all the latest product information, demo racquets, and equipment from Prince, so they can truly be Prince ambassadors in their community. Aside from their regular lessons, instructors and teaching professionals hold local "Prince Demo events" around the country to give potential customers a hands-on opportunity to see and try various Prince racquets, strings, and grips.

Prince also sponsors over 100 professional tennis players who appear in marquee events such as the four Grand Slam tournaments (Wimbledon and the Australian, French, and U.S. Opens). TV viewers can watch Russia's Maria Sharapova walk onto a tennis court carrying a Prince racquet bag or France's Gael Monfils hit a service ace using his Prince racquet.

Where is Prince headed in the 2010s? "As a marketer, one of the biggest challenges is staying ahead of the curve," says Glassel. And she stresses, "It's learning, it's studying, it's talking to people who understand where the market is going."

Questions

1 In the 2010s what trends in the environmental forces (social, economic, technological, competitive, and regulatory) (*a*) work for and (*b*) work against success for Prince Sports in the tennis industry?

2 Because sales of Prince Sports in tennis-related products depends heavily on growth of the tennis industry, what marketing activities might it use in the U.S. to promote tennis playing?

3 What promotional activities might Prince use to reach (*a*) recreational players and (*b*) junior players?

4 What might Prince do to help it gain distribution and sales in (*a*) mass merchandisers like Target and Wal-Mart and (*b*) specialty tennis shops?

5 In reaching global markets outside the U.S. (*a*) what are some criteria that Prince should use to select countries in which to market aggressively, (*b*) what three or four countries meet these criteria best, and (*c*) what are some marketing actions Prince might use to reach these markets?

FIGURE 1

Prince Targets Racquets at Specific Market Segments

Market Segments			Product Features in Racquet			
Main Segments	**Sub-Segments**	**Segment Characteristics (Skill level, age)**	**Brand Name**	**Length (Inches)**	**Unstrung Weight (Ounces)**	**Head Size (Sq. In.)**
Performance	Precision	For touring professional players wanting great feel, control, and spin	EXO^3 Ignite 95	27.0	11.8	95
	Thunder	For competitive players wanting a bigger sweet spot and added power	EXO^3 Red 95	27.25	9.9	105
Recreational	Small head size	Players looking for a forgiving racquet with added control	AirO Lightning MP	27.0	9.9	100
	Larger head size	Players looking for a larger sweet spot and added power	AirO Maria Lite OS	27.0	9.7	110
Junior	More experienced young players	Ages 8 to 15; somewhat shorter and lighter racquets than high school adult players	AirO Team Maria 23	23.0	8.1	100
	Beginner	Ages 5 to 11; much shorter and lighter racquets; tennis balls with 50% to 75% less speed for young beginners	Air Team Maria 19	19.0	7.1	82

nano shoots video.

Introducing the new iPod nano.
Now with video recording,
a larger screen, and FM radio.

Buy now

Shop online now and get free shipping or pick one up Thursday at the Apple Retail Store.

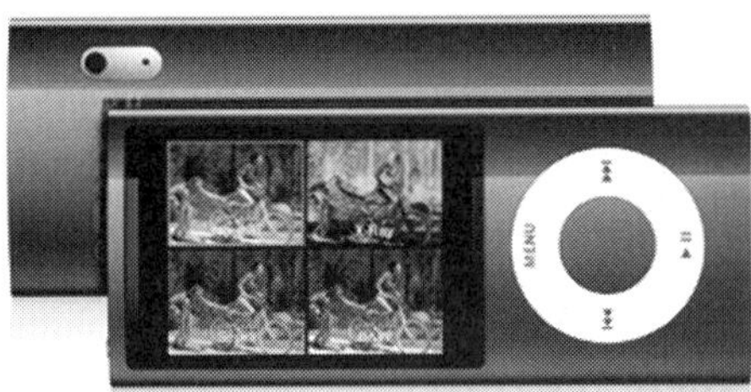

Video recording with effects

The new video camera in iPod nano lets you shoot video—even with video effects—wherever you are. Yet the new iPod nano is still the same ultraportable size. Learn more ›

Genius Mixes

Genius acts as your personal DJ, searching your iTunes library to find songs that go great together, then organizing them into mixes you'll love. All automatically.
Learn more ›

FM radio with Live Pause

7

开发新产品和服务
Developing New Products and Services

LEARNING OBJECTIVES

After reading this chapter you should be able to:

LO1 Recognize the various terms that pertain to products and services.

LO2 Identify the ways in which consumer and business products and services can be classified.

LO3 Explain the significance of "newness" in new products and services as it relates to the degree of consumer learning involved.

LO4 Describe the factors contributing to a new product's or service's success or failure.

LO5 Explain the purposes of each step of the new-product process.

苹果公司的新产品创新机器
APPLE'S NEW-PRODUCT INNOVATION MACHINE

The stage in front of an auditorium is empty except for a desk with an iMac and a huge screen with a large white logo. Then in walks a legend ready for his magic shows in his black turtleneck, jeans, and gray New Balance sneakers.

Apple's Innovation Machine

The legend, of course, is Steve Jobs (opposite page), co-founder and CEO of Apple, Inc. *Fortune* rated Apple as the world's most admired company in 2009 and *BusinessWeek* has perennially rated it as the world's most innovative. The magic shows Jobs has put on over the years have introduced many of Apple's market-changing innovations, such as the:

- Apple II—the first commercial personal computer.
- Macintosh—the first personal computer with a mouse and a graphical user interface.
- iPod—the first commercially successful MP3 digital music player.
- MacBook Air—the world's thinnest notebook that uses a solid state drive instead of a hard disk.
- iPhone 3GS—the revolutionary multi-touch mobile phone and media player.
- iPod nano with Built-in Video Camera—the digital media player that includes a video camera to shoot and play video or enables the user to upload it to a computer and view it on YouTube. The 2009 iPod nano comes in nine different colors and has an FM radio as well as a pedometer. And the larger color display makes it even easier to view images and video. The price? Only $149 for the 8Gb model, similar to what other pocket video cameras cost!

The Evolutionary iPod nano and Revolutionary iPod touch

The evolutionary iPod nano, first introduced in 2005 and now in its fifth generation, has sold over 100 million units as of September 2009, making it the most popular media player in the world. Moreover, the iPod family (iPod shuffle, iPod nano, iPod classic, and iPod touch) has sold over 220 million units since the iPod's launch in October 2001. "With iPod, Apple has invented a whole new category of digital music

---

auditorium（剧院或音乐厅的）观众席；perennially 经常出现地，长期地。

player. . . [and] listening to music will never be the same again," said Steve Jobs. This prophetic statement back in 2001 has certainly come true! And what about the revolutionary iPod touch that was launched in 2007? Its multi-touch graphical user interface, which was borrowed from the iPhone, has "buttons" that are transforming the device into an exciting portable game machine!

The life of an organization depends on how it conceives, produces, and markets *new* products (goods, services, and ideas), the topic of this chapter. Chapter 8 discusses the process of managing *existing* products, services, and brands.

什么是产品和服务
WHAT ARE PRODUCTS AND SERVICES?

The essence of marketing is in developing products and services to meet buyer needs. A **product** is a good, service, or idea consisting of a bundle of tangible and intangible attributes that satisfies consumers' needs and is received in exchange for money or something else of value. Let's look more carefully at the meanings of goods, services, and ideas.

观察商品、服务和理念
A Look at Goods, Services, and Ideas

商品具有消费者可以用五官感知的属性。

A *good* has tangible attributes that a consumer's five senses can perceive. For example, Apple's latest iPhone 3GS can be touched and its features can be seen and heard. A good also may have intangible attributes consisting of its delivery or warranties and embody more abstract concepts, such as becoming healthier or wealthier. Goods can also be divided into nondurable goods and durable goods. A *nondurable* good is an item consumed in one or a few uses, such as food products and fuel. A *durable* good is one that usually lasts over many uses, such as appliances, cars, and mobile phones. This classification method also provides direction for marketing actions. For example, nondurable goods such as Wrigley's gum rely heavily on consumer advertising. In contrast, costly durable goods, such as cars, generally emphasize personal selling.

Services are intangible activities or benefits that an organization provides to satisfy consumers' needs in exchange for money or something else of value. Services have become a significant part of the U.S. economy, exceeding 40 percent of its gross domestic product. Hence, a good may be the breakfast cereal you eat, whereas a service may be a tax return an accountant fills out for you.

Finally, in marketing, an *idea* is a thought that leads to an action such as a concept for a new invention, or getting people out to vote.

Throughout this book *product* generally includes not only physical goods but services and ideas as well. When *product* is used in its narrower meaning of "goods," it should be clear from the example or sentence.

产品分类
Classifying Products

消费品是由最终消费者购买的产品，而工业品也被称为B2B商品、**工业品**或组织机构用品，是直接或间接地用于提供再销售产品的产品。

Two broad categories of products widely used in marketing relate to the type of user. **Consumer products** are products purchased by the ultimate consumer, whereas **business products** (also called *B2B products or industrial products*) are products that organizations buy that assist in providing other products for resale. But some products can be considered both consumer and business items. For example, an Apple iMac computer can be sold to consumers for personal use or to business firms for office use. Each classification results in different marketing actions. Viewed as a consumer product, the iMac would be sold through its retail stores or directly from its Web site. As a business product, an Apple salesperson might contact a firm's purchasing department directly and offer discounts for multiple purchases.

intangible 无形的；perceive 注意到，察觉，意识到；nondurable 非耐用的。

The iPhone's innovative touch screen emerged after Apple engineers studied tablet PCs, portable computers using touch screens.

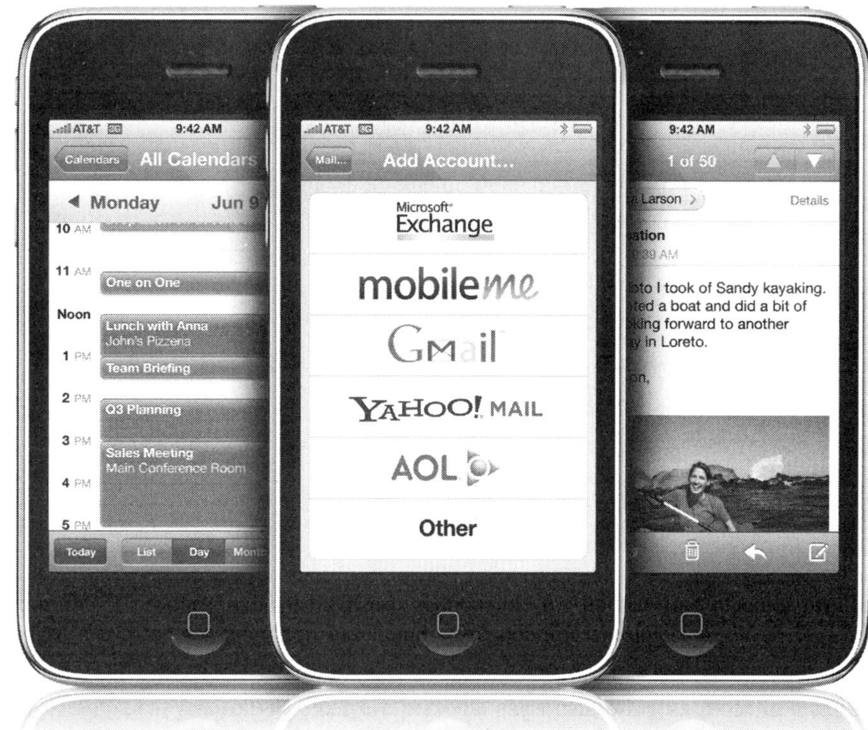

Consumer Products The four types of consumer products shown in Figure 7–1 on the next page differ in terms of the (1) effort the consumer spends on the decision, (2) attributes used in making the purchase decision, and (3) frequency of purchase. **Convenience products** are items that the consumer purchases frequently, conveniently, and with a minimum of shopping effort. **Shopping products** are items for which the consumer compares several alternatives on criteria such as price, quality, or style. **Specialty products** are items that the consumer makes a special effort to search out and buy. **Unsought products** are items that the consumer does not know about or knows about but does not initially want.

便利品是指消费者购买频繁、方便且不费多少精力的产品。**选购品**是指消费者购买根据价格、质量或式样等指标与相关产品比较的产品。**特殊品**是指消费者在选择和购买过程中专门付出努力的产品。**非渴求品**是指并不了解或者即便了解但一开始也不想要的产品。

Figure 7–1 shows how each type of consumer product stresses different marketing mix actions, degrees of brand loyalty, and shopping effort. But how a consumer product is classified depends on the individual. One woman may view a camera as a shopping product and visit several stores before deciding on a brand, whereas her friend may view a camera as a specialty product and will make a special effort to buy only a Nikon.

Business Products A major characteristic of business products is that their sales are often the result of *derived demand*; that is, sales of business products frequently result (or are derived) from the sale of consumer products. For example, as consumer demand for Ford cars (a consumer product) increases, the company may increase its demand for paint spraying equipment (a business product).

Business products may be classified as components or support products. *Components* are items that become part of the final product. These include raw materials such as grain or lumber, as well as assemblies or parts, such as a Ford car

conveniently 方便的，便利的；component 成分，零件；spray 在……上喷涂料（或油漆）。

BASIS OF COMPARISON	TYPE OF CONSUMER PRODUCT			
	CONVENIENCE PRODUCT	SHOPPING PRODUCT	SPECIALTY PRODUCT	UNSOUGHT PRODUCT
Product	Toothpaste, cake mix, hand soap, ATM cash withdrawal	Cameras, TVs, briefcases, airline tickets	Rolls-Royce cars, Rolex watches, heart surgery	Burial insurance, thesaurus
Price	Relatively inexpensive	Fairly expensive	Usually very expensive	Varies
Place (distribution)	Widespread; many outlets	Large number of selective outlets	Very limited	Often limited
Promotion	Price, availability, and awareness stressed	Differentiation from competitors stressed	Uniqueness of brand and status stressed	Awareness is essential
Brand loyalty of consumers	Aware of brand but will accept substitutes	Prefer specific brands but will accept substitutes	Very brand loyal; will not accept substitutes	Will accept substitutes
Purchase behavior of consumers	Frequent purchases; little time and effort spent shopping	Infrequent purchases; needs much comparison shopping time	Infrequent purchases; needs extensive search and decision time	Very infrequent purchases; some comparison shopping

FIGURE 7–1
How a consumer product is classified significantly affects which products consumers buy and the marketing strategies used.

engine or car door hinges. *Support products* are items used to assist in producing other goods and services. These include:

- *Installations*, such as buildings and fixed equipment.
- *Accessory equipment*, such as tools and office equipment.
- *Supplies*, such as stationery, paper clips, and brooms.
- *Industrial services*, such as maintenance, repair, and legal services.

Strategies to market business products reflect both the complexities of the product involved (paper clips versus computer-machine tools) and the buy-class situations discussed in Chapter 4.

A broad product line can benefit both consumers and retailers. The text shows how Little Remedies' product line does this.

产品项目、产品线和产品组合
Product Items, Product Lines, and Product Mixes

Most organizations offer a range of products and services to consumers. A **product item** is a specific product that has a unique brand, size, or price. For example, Ultra Downy softener for clothes comes in several different sizes. Each size is a separate *stock keeping unit* (SKU), which is a unique identification number that defines an item for ordering or inventory purposes.

A **product line** is a group of product or service items that are closely related because they satisfy a class of needs, are used together, are sold to the same customer group, are distributed through the same outlets, or fall within a given price range. Nike's product lines include shoes and clothing, whereas the Mayo Clinic's service lines consist of inpatient hospital care and outpatient physician services. Each product line has its own marketing strategy.

hinge（门等的）铰链，合页；physician 医生，内科医生。

Using Marketing Dashboards
Which States Are Underperforming?

In 2008, you started your own company to sell a nutritious, high-energy snack you developed. It is now January 2011. As a marketer, you ask yourself, "How well is my business growing?"

Your Challenge The snack is sold in all 50 states. Your goal is 10 percent annual growth. To begin 2011, you want to quickly solve any sales problems that occurred during 2010. You know that states whose sales are stagnant or in decline are offset by those with greater than 10 percent growth.

Studying a table of the sales and percent change versus a year ago in each of the 50 states would work but be very time consuming. A good graphic is better. You choose the following marketing metric, where "sales" are measured in units:

$$\text{Annual \% sales change} = \frac{(\text{2010 Sales} - \text{2009 Sales}) \times 100}{\text{2009 Sales}}$$

You want to act quickly to improve sales. In your map, growth that is greater than 10 percent is green, 0 to 10 percent growth is orange, and decline is red. Notice that you (1) picked a metric and (2) made your own rules that green is good, orange is bad, and red is very bad.

Your Findings You see that sales growth in the Northeastern states is weaker than the 10 percent target, and sales are actually declining in many of the states.

Annual Percentage Change in Unit Volume, by State

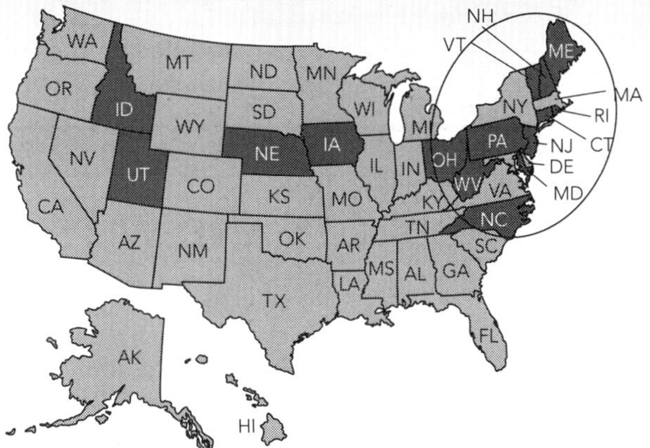

Your Action Marketing is often about grappling with sales shortfalls. You'll need to start by trying to identify and correct the problems in the largest volume states that are underperforming—in this case in the northeastern United States.

You'll want to do marketing research to see if the problem starts with (1) an external factor such as changing consumer tastes or (2) an internal factor such as a breakdown in your distribution system.

The Little Remedies® product line consists of more than a dozen nonprescription medicines for infants and young children sold in a family of creative packages. A broad product line enables both consumers and retailers to simplify their buying decisions. If a family has a good experience with one Little Remedies product, it might buy another one in the line. And an extensive line enables Little Remedies to obtain distribution chains such as Babies "Я" Us and Wal-Mart, avoiding the need for retailers to deal with many different suppliers.

Many firms offer a **product mix** that consists of all of the product lines offered by an organization. For example, Cray Inc. has a small product mix of three supercomputer lines that are sold mostly to governments and large businesses. Fortune Brands, however, has a large product mix that includes product lines such as sporting equipment (Titleist golf balls) and plumbing supplies (Moen faucets).

营销信息板如何提高新产品的性能
How Marketing Dashboards Can Improve New-Product Performance

The Using Marketing Dashboards box shows how marketers measure actual market performance versus the goals set in new-product planning. It shows that you have set a goal of 10 percent annual growth for the new snack you developed. You choose a marketing metric of "annual % sales change"—to measure the annual growth rate from 2009 to 2010 for each of the 50 states. Your special concerns in the marketing

plumbing（建筑物的）水管装置，水暖设备。

dashboard are the states shown in red, where sales have actually declined. As shown in the box, having identified the Northeastern United States as a problem region, you conduct in-depth marketing research to lead to corrective actions.

learning review

1. What are the four main types of consumer products?
2. What is the difference between a product line and a product mix?
3. What marketing metric might you use in a marketing dashboard to discover which states have weak sales?

新产品及其成败原因
NEW PRODUCTS AND WHY THEY SUCCEED OR FAIL

LO3

New products are the lifeblood of a company and keep it growing, but the financial risks can be large. Before discussing how new products reach the market, we'll begin by looking at *what* a new product is.

何谓新产品
What Is a New Product?

The term *new* is difficult to define. Is Sony's PlayStation 3 *new* when there was a PlayStation 2? Is Nintendo's Wii *new* when its GameCube launch goes back to 2001? What does *new* mean for new-product marketing? Newness from several points of view are discussed next.

如果一款产品的功能与现有产品不同，我们可以认为它是新产品。

Newness Compared with Existing Products If a product is functionally different from existing products, it can be defined as new. Sometimes this newness is revolutionary and creates a whole new industry, as in the case of the Apple II computer. At other times additional features are added to an existing product to try to make it appeal to more customers. And as microprocessors now appear not only in computers and cell phones but also in countless applications in vehicles and

As you read the discussion about what *new* means in new-product development, think about how it affects the marketing strategies of Sony and Nintendo in their *new* video-game console launches.

dashboard 仪表板，仪表盘；functionally 工作（或运转）方式的，功能性的。

appliances, consumers' lives get far more complicated. This proliferation of extra features—sometimes called "feature bloat"—overwhelms many consumers. The Marketing Matters box on the next page describes how founder Richard Stephens and his Geek Squad work to address the rise of feature bloat.

The text describes the potential benefits and dangers of an incremental innovation such as Purina's Elegant Medleys, its restaurant-inspired food for cats.

Newness in Legal Terms The U.S. Federal Trade Commission (FTC) advises that the term *new* be limited to use with a product up to six months after it enters regular distribution. The difficulty with this suggestion is in the interpretation of the term *regular distribution*.

Newness from the Organization's Perspective Successful organizations view newness and innovation in their products at three levels. At the lowest level, which usually involves the least risk, is a product line extension. This is an incremental improvement of an existing product for the company. For example, Purina added its "new" line of Elegant Medleys®, a "restaurant-inspired food for cats," to its existing line of 50 varieties of its Fancy Feast® gourmet cat food. This has the potential benefit of adding new customers but the twin dangers of increasing expenses and cannibalizing its existing line.

At the next level is a significant jump in the innovation or technology, such as from a regular landline telephone to a cell phone. The third level is true innovation, a truly revolutionary new product, such as the first Apple computer in 1976. Effective new-product programs in large firms deal at all three levels.

Newness from the Consumer's Perspective A fourth way to define new products is in terms of their effects on consumption. This approach classifies new products according to the degree of learning required by the consumer, as shown in Figure 7–2.

With a *continuous innovation*, consumers don't need to learn new behaviors. Toothpaste manufacturers can add new attributes or features like "whitens teeth" or "removes plaque," as when they introduce a new or improved product. But the extra features in the new toothpaste do not require buyers to learn new tooth-brushing behaviors, so it is a continuous innovation. The benefit of this simple innovation is that effective marketing mainly depends on generating awareness and not needing to reeducate customers.

FIGURE 7–2
The degree of "newness" in a new product affects the amount of learning effort consumers must exert to use the product and the resulting marketing strategy.

LOW ← Degree of New Consumer Learning Needed → HIGH

BASIS OF COMPARISON	CONTINUOUS INNOVATION	DYNAMICALLY CONTINUOUS INNOVATION	DISCONTINUOUS INNOVATION
Definition	Requires no new learning by consumers	Disrupts consumer's normal routine but does not require totally new learning	Requires new learning and consumption patterns by consumers
Examples	New improved shaver or detergent	Electric toothbrush, compact disc player, and automatic flash unit for cameras	VCR, digital video recorder, electric car
Marketing strategy	Gain consumer awareness and wide distribution	Advertise points of difference and benefits to consumers	Educate consumers through product trial and personal selling

proliferation 激增，剧增；landline 固定电话；generate 形成，造成。

Marketing Matters > > > > > > > > technology

Feature Bloat: Geek Squad to the Rescue!

Adding more features to a product to satisfy more consumers seems like a no-brainer strategy.

Feature Bloat

In fact, most marketing research with potential buyers of a product done *before* they buy shows they say they *do want* more features in the product. It's when the new product gets home that the "feature bloat" problems occur—often overwhelming the consumer with mind-boggling complexity.

Computers pose a special problem for homeowners because there's no in-house technical assistance like that existing in large organizations. Also, to drive down prices of home computers, usually little customer support service is available. Ever call the manufacturer's toll-free "help" line? One survey showed that 29 percent of the help-line callers wound up swearing at the customer service representative and 21 percent just screamed.

The Geek Squad to the Rescue

Computer feature bloat has given rise to what TV's *60 Minutes* says is "the multibillion-dollar service industry populated by the very people who used to be shunned in the high-school cafeteria: Geeks like Robert Stephens!"

More than a decade ago he turned his geekiness into the Geek Squad—a group of technically savvy people who can fix almost any computer problem. "There's usually some frantic customer at the door pointing to some device in the corner that will not obey," Stephens explains.

"The biggest complaint about tech support people is rude, egotistical behavior," says Stephens. So he launched the Geek Squad to show some friendly humility by having team members work their wizardry while:

1. Showing genuine concern to customers.
2. Dressing in geeky white shirts, black clip-on ties, and white socks, a "uniform" borrowed from NASA engineers.
3. Driving to customer homes or offices in black-and-white VW "geekmobiles."

Do customers appreciate the 6,000-person Geek Squad, now owned by Best Buy? Robert Stephens answers by explaining, "People will say, 'They saved me . . . they saved my data.'" This includes countless college students working on their papers or theses with data lost somewhere in their computers—"data they promised themselves they'd back up next week."

For how the kind of innovation present in this ketchup bottle affects the marketing strategy, see the text.

With a *dynamically continuous innovation*, only minor changes in behavior are required. Heinz launched its EZ Squirt Ketchup in an array of unlikely hues—from green and orange to pink and teal—with kid-friendly squeeze bottles and nozzles. Encouraging kids to write their names on hot dogs or draw dinosaurs on burgers as they use this new product requires only minor behavioral changes. So the marketing strategy here is to educate prospective buyers on the product's benefits, advantages, and proper use.

A *discontinuous innovation* involves making the consumer learn entirely new consumption patterns to use the product. Have you bought a wireless router for your computer? Congratulations if you installed it yourself! Recently, one-third of those bought at Best Buy were returned because they were too complicated to set up—the problem with a discontinuous innovation. So marketing efforts for discontinuous innovations usually involve not only gaining initial consumer awareness but also educating consumers on both the benefits and proper use of the innovative product, activities that can cost millions of dollars—and maybe rely on Geek Squad help.

产品成败原因
Why Products Succeed or Fail

We all know the giant product successes—such as Apple's iPhone, Google, and CNN. Yet the thousands of product failures every year that slide quietly into oblivion cost American businesses billions of dollars. Ideally, a new product needs a precise

dynamically 动态的，发展变化的；discontinuous 不连续的，断续的；entirely 完全地，完整地，全部地。

New-product success or failure? For the special problems these two products face, see the text.

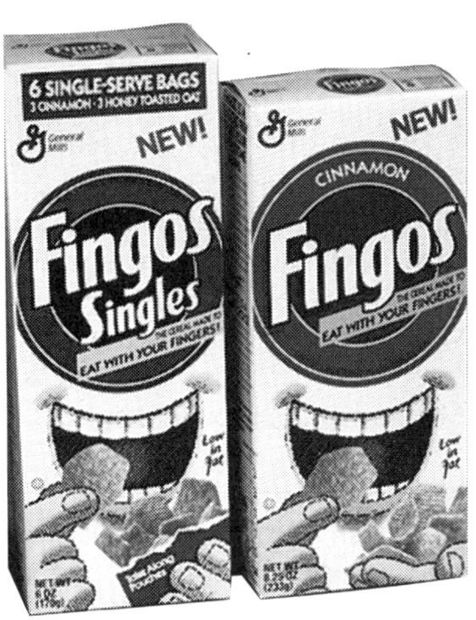

protocol, a statement that, before product development begins, identifies: (1) a well-defined target market; (2) specific customers' needs, wants, and preferences; and (3) what the product will be and do.

Research suggests that it takes about 3,000 raw unwritten ideas to produce a single commercially successful new product. To learn marketing lessons and convert potential failures to successes, we can analyze why new products fail and then study several failures in detail. As we go through the new-product process later in the chapter, we can identify ways such failures might have been avoided—admitting that hindsight is clearer than foresight.

LO4

Marketing Reasons for New-Product Failures Both marketing and nonmarketing factors contribute to new-product failures. Using the research results from several studies on new-product success and failure, we can identify critical marketing factors—which sometimes overlap—that often separate new-product winners and losers:

1. 差异点不明晰。

1. *Insignificant point of difference.* Research shows that a distinctive point of difference is the single most important factor for a new product to defeat competitive ones—having superior characteristics that deliver unique benefits to the user. In the mid-1990s, General Mills introduced Fingos, a sweetened cereal flake about the size of a corn chip. Consumers were supposed to snack on them dry, but they didn't. The point of difference was not important enough to get consumers to stop eating competing snacks such as popcorn and potato chips.

2. 产品开发之前市场与产品界定不完善。

3. 在关键因素上对消费者需要不敏感。

Lessons from new-product failures: Why might consumers not buy a tissue to kill sneezing germs (below) . . .

2. *Incomplete market and product protocol before product development starts.* Without this protocol, firms try to design a vague product for a phantom market. Developed by Kimberly-Clark, Avert Virucidal tissues contained vitamin C derivatives scientifically designed to kill cold and flu germs when users sneezed, coughed, or blew their noses into them. It failed in test market. People didn't believe the claims and were frightened by the "cidal" in the brand name, which they connected to words like *suicidal*. A big part of Avert's failure was its lack of a product protocol that clearly defined how it would satisfy consumer wants and needs.
3. *Not satisfying customer needs on critical factors.* Overlapping somewhat with point 1, this factor stresses that problems on one or two critical factors can kill the product, even though the general quality is high. For example, the Japanese, like the British, drive on the left side of the road. Until 1996, U.S. carmakers

avoid 避免，防止（坏事发生）; critical 极重要的，关键的 ; hindsight 后见之明，事后聪明 ; vague 含糊的，不明确的。

sent Japan few right-hand-drive cars—unlike German carmakers who exported right-hand-drive models in several of their brands.

. . . or a spray to get rid of scary creatures from a child's bedroom (above)? Answers appear in the text.

4. **Bad timing.** This results when a product is introduced too soon, too late, or when consumer tastes are shifting dramatically. Bad timing gives new-product managers nightmares. Microsoft, for example, introduced its Zune player a few years after Apple launched its iPod and other competitors offered new MP3 players.
5. *Too little market attractiveness.* The ideal is a large target market with high growth and real buyer need. But often the target market is too small or competitive to warrant the huge expenses necessary to reach it. OUT! International's Hey! There's A Monster In My Room spray was designed to rid scary creatures from a kid's bedroom and had a bubble-gum fragrance. While a creative and cute product, the brand name probably kept the kids awake at night more than their fear of the monsters because it implied the monster was still hiding in the bedroom. Also, was this a real market?
6. *Poor product quality.* This factor often results when a product is not thoroughly tested. The costs to an organization for poor quality can be staggering and include the labor, materials, and other expenses to fix the problem—not to mention the lost sales, profits, and market share that usually result. For example, after Microsoft launched its Xbox 360 video game console, millions began to experience the "red ring of death." The problem: The consoles' microprocessors ran too hot, causing them to "pop off" their motherboards. Microsoft had to set aside $1.1 billion to extend its warranty and fix any affected console for free—costing it future sales and reducing its market share lead in the multi-billion dollar market over rivals Sony and Nintendo.
7. *Poor execution of the marketing mix: brand name, package, price, promotion, distribution.* Somewhere in the marketing mix there can be a showstopper that kills the product. Introduced by Gunderson & Rosario, Inc., Garlic Cake was supposed to be served as an hors d'oeuvre with sweet breads, spreads, and meats, but somehow the company forgot to tell this to potential consumers. Garlic Cake died because consumers were left to wonder just what a Garlic Cake is and when on earth a person would want to eat it.
8. *No economical access to buyers.* Grocery products provide an example. Today's mega-supermarkets carry more than 30,000 different SKUs. With about 20,000 new packaged goods (food, beverage, health and beauty aids, household, and pet items) introduced each year, the cost to gain access to retailer shelf space is huge. Because shelf space is judged in terms of sales per square foot, Thirsty Dog! (a zesty beef-flavored, vitamin-enriched, mineral-loaded, lightly carbonated bottled water for your dog) must displace an existing product on the supermarket shelves, a difficult task with the high sales per square foot demands of these stores. Thirsty Dog! failed to generate enough sales to meet these requirements.

4. 糟糕的时间安排。
5. 市场吸引力太小。
6. 产品质量太差。
7. 名称、包装、定价、促销、分销等营销组合实施不力。
8. 缺乏经济的销售渠道。

Simple marketing research should have revealed the problems. Developing successful new products may sometimes involve luck, but more often it involves having a product that really meets a need and has significant points of difference over competitive products.

What Were They Thinking? Organizational Problems in New-Product Failure A number of other organizational problems can cause new-product disasters. Key ones—some that overlap—include:

1. *Not really listening to the "voice of the consumer."* Product managers may believe they "know better" than their customers or feel they "can't afford" the valuable marketing research that could uncover problems.
2. *Skipping stages in the new-product process.* Although details may vary, the seven-stage new-product process discussed in the next section is a sequence

1. 没有真正地倾听"消费者的声音"。
2. 在新产品开发过程中省略步骤。

attractiveness 吸引力；imply 暗指，暗示；retailer 零售商，零售店。

Marketing Matters > > > > > > > > technology

From Idea to Launch: Stage-Gate® Processes in New-Product Development

In the 1960s, the National Aeronautics and Space Administration (NASA) developed an engineering phase-review process to keep its missile and satellite programs on schedule. Today's Stage-Gate® process is adapted from NASA's system, but it covers all the business steps in converting a new-product idea to its commercialization launch—the idea-to-launch sequence.

The Stage-Gate process incorporates ideas uncovered by studying best practices of exemplary new-product-development projects and teams as they drive their projects to market quickly and effectively. The system is a series of stages, with each stage consisting of a set of activities whose purpose is to improve the project outcome.

Stage-Gate gets its name because preceding each stage in the new-product development is a "gate." Team members (the gatekeepers) make the key "go/kill" decision at each gate in the sequence to commit the resources required to move the project forward. Two important problems can cause ineffective gates:

- *Gates can lack teeth.* The gate review meetings are held, but bad projects aren't killed, often for the groupthink reason discussed in the text.
- *Gates can be hollow.* Go decisions are made, but inadequate resources are committed to ensure success.

Too often the project emphasis is simply getting through each gate to move into the next stage.

Today firms such as Procter & Gamble and Johnson & Johnson have a clearer innovation goal: To win in the marketplace with a successful new product—not simply go through the Stage-Gate process.

---

used in some form by most large organizations. Skipping a stage often leads to disaster. This is why many firms have a "gate" to ensure that one step is completed satisfactorily before going on to the next step, as discussed in the Marketing Matters box.

3. 当设计糟糕的产品推向市场以快速获得利润。
4. 在任务小组或委员会会议中存在"群体思维"。
5. 没有从过去的失败中吸取关键教训。

3. *Pushing a poorly conceived product into the market to generate quick revenue.* Today's marketing managers are under incredible pressure from top management to meet quarterly revenue targets. This focus on speed often results in overlooking the network of services needed to support the physical product.
4. *Encountering "groupthink" in task force and committee meetings.* Someone in the new-product planning meeting knows or suspects the product concept is a dumb idea. But that person is afraid to speak up for fear of being cast as a "negative thinker" and "not a team player" and then being ostracized from real participation in the group. And a strong public commitment to a new product by its key advocate may make it difficult to kill the product even when new negative information comes to light.
5. *Not learning critical takeaway lessons from past failures.* The easiest lessons are from "intelligent failures"—ones that happen early in the new-product process. At this point these failures are less expensive and immediately give better understanding of customers' wants and needs.

Many of these organizational problems cause the eight marketing reasons for new-product failure listed above.

learning review

4. What kind of innovation would an improved electric toothbrush be?
5. Why can an "insignificant point of difference" lead to new-product failure?
6. How might using the Stage-Gate process reduce the chances of skipping a stage in new-product development?

satisfactorily 令人满意地；ostracize 排斥，排挤。

新产品开发过程
THE NEW-PRODUCT PROCESS

LO5

Finding ways to stimulate American innovation and provide jobs is a vital concern to federal and state governments, business firms, and citizens alike. Organizations conduct global searches to find the scientists and engineers that can achieve the creative breakthroughs needed for new high-tech products. For example, Chinese, Indian, Russian, and other immigrant engineers represent half the total number of engineers in California's Silicon Valley.

To develop new products efficiently, companies such as General Electric and 3M use a specific sequence of steps to make their products ready for market. Figure 7–3 shows the **new-product process**, the seven stages an organization goes through to identify business opportunities and convert them to a salable good or service.

第一阶段：新产品战略开发
Stage 1: New-Product Strategy Development

对公司来说，**新产品战略开发**是根据公司总体目标界定新产品角色的阶段。

For companies, **new-product strategy development** is the stage of the new-product process that defines the role for a new product in terms of the firm's overall objectives. During this stage, the firm uses both a SWOT analysis and environmental scanning to assess its strengths and weaknesses relative to the trends it identifies as opportunities or threats. The outcome not only defines the vital "protocol" for each new-product idea but also identifies the strategic role it might serve in the firm's portfolio.

New-product development in services, such as buying a stock or airline ticket or watching a Major League Baseball game, is often difficult. Why? Because services are intangible and performance-oriented. Nevertheless, service innovations can have a huge impact on our lives. For example, the online brokerage firm E*TRADE has revolutionized the financial services industry through its online trading.

A Major League Baseball park is a study in new-product innovation. If you visit Turner Field, home of the Atlanta Braves, you may be in for a shock about what's going on besides baseball on the field. There's the members-only 755 club—honoring Hank Aaron's home run total—and the Chophouse bar and grill for 20-somethings and a big playground sponsored by Cartoon Network. Each of these attractions become part of the customer experience that the team wants its fans to enjoy—and the attractions are almost as important as fielding a winning team.

A visit to watch an Atlanta Braves baseball game is often a lot more than the game itself. As described in the text, it may involve a meal at the Chophouse or many other services.

portfolio 证券投资组合；intangible 无形的，不易捉摸的，难以确定的。

FIGURE 7–3
Carefully using the seven stages in the new-product process increases the chances of new-product success.

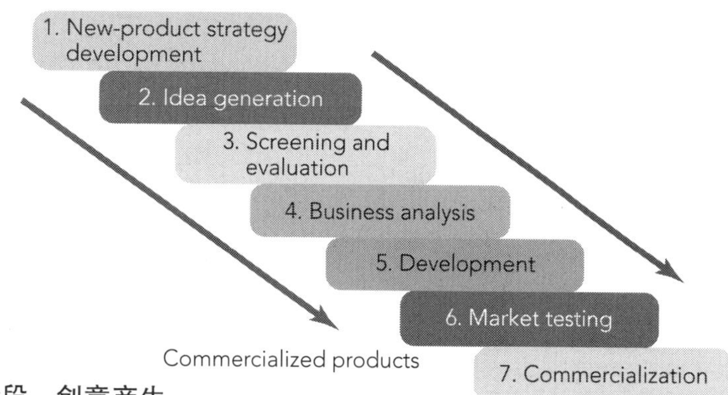

第二阶段：创意产生
Stage 2: Idea Generation

Idea generation is the stage of the new-product process that develops a pool of concepts as candidates for new products, building upon the previous stage's results. Many forward-looking companies have discovered their own organization is not generating enough useful new-products ideas. This has led to *open innovation*, in which an organization finds and executes creative new-product ideas by developing strategic relationships with outside individuals and organizations. This section contains examples of open innovation relationships.

Customer and Supplier Suggestions Firms ask their salespeople to talk to customers and ask their purchasing personnel to talk to suppliers to discover new-product ideas. Whirlpool gets ideas from customers on ways to standardize components so that it can cut the number of different product platforms to reduce costs. Business researchers emphasize that firms must actively involve customers and suppliers in the new-product development process. This means the focus should be on what the new product will actually *do* for them rather than simply *what they want*.

企业调研人员强调，公司必须积极将顾客和供应商纳入产品开发过程中来。这通常意味着要将重心锁定在新产品确实能做什么上而不是仅仅想做什么上。

A. G. Lafley, CEO of Procter & Gamble (P&G), gave his executives a *revolutionary* thought: "Look outside the company for solutions to problems rather than insisting P&G knows best." When he ran P&G's laundry detergent business, he had to redesign the laundry boxes so they were easier to open. Why? While consumers *said* P&G's laundry boxes were "easy to open," cameras they agreed to have installed in their laundry rooms showed they opened the boxes with *screwdrivers*!

Employee and Co-Worker Suggestions Employees should be encouraged to suggest new-product ideas through suggestion boxes. The idea for Nature Valley granola bars from General Mills came when one of its marketing managers observed co-workers bringing granola to work in plastic bags.

Auto industry studies show that women buy about two-thirds of all vehicles and influence about 85 percent of all sales. However, many auto-makers do marketing research on car-loving, "gear-head" guys to get ideas on new-car features. To bridge the gender gap, Volvo obtained ideas on new-car features from all-female focus groups from its Swedish workforce. It then named a five-woman team of Volvo managers to design a "concept car"—what the auto industry uses to test new designs, technical innovations, and consumer reactions. One innovative feature: when pressing an ignition key button, the car's gull-wing doors pop open and the steering wheel pulls in so the driver can enter the car more easily.

Would women *really* help design this car? For how Volvo said "yes," see the text.

Research and Development Laboratories Another source of new products is a firm's own research and development laboratories.

generation 产生；screwdriver 螺丝刀，螺丝起子；workforce 劳动力，劳动人口。

Going Online

IDEO—the Innovation Lab Superstar in Designing New Products

The Apple mouse. The Palm V PDA. The Crest Neat Squeeze toothpaste dispenser. The Steelecase Leap adjustable office chair. These are just some of the thousands of new products designed by IDEO, an innovation lab you've probably never heard of but benefit from everyday.

For David Kelley, co-founder of IDEO, product design is really "industrial design" and includes both artistic and functional elements. And to foster this creativity, IDEO allows its designers and engineers much freedom—its offices look like schoolrooms; employees can hang their bicycles from the ceiling; there are rubber-band fights; and on Monday mornings, there are show-and-tell sessions.

Fresh Express asked IDEO to design an innovative single-serve package for salads. IDEO's solution (photo): A five-section package—one large section for the salad greens and four smaller ones for proteins, dressings, and so on—each section sealed in plastic.

Visit IDEO's Web site (www.ideo.com) to view its recent inventions and innovations for clients such as McDonald's self-ordering kiosk, the Zyliss' Mandolin fruit and vegetable slicer, LifePort's kidney transporter, Pepsi's High Visibility vending machine, and Nike's all-terrain sunglasses.

Apple is a world leader in new-product development in computers and electronics. Apple is also world-class in *industrial design*, an applied art that improves the aesthetics and usefulness of mass-produced products for users. Apple's sleek iPhone and iMac models came out of its Apple Industrial Design Group, which is driven by the obsessive concerns of Steve Jobs for cutting-edge industrial design in all the company's products. But even Apple sometimes goes outside its own labs—for example, when it found its original "mouse" at IDEO.

Professional R&D laboratories that are outside the walls of large corporations are sources of open innovation and provide new-product ideas. Labs at Arthur D. Little helped put the "crunch" in the Quaker Oats Company's Cap'n Crunch cereal and the flavor in Carnation's Instant Breakfast. As described in the Going Online box, IDEO is a world-class new-product development firm, having designed more than 4,000 of them.

Brainstorming sessions conducted at IDEO can generate 100 new ideas in an hour. IDEO's "shop-a-long" visits with client firms let their managers experience firsthand what one of its customers does. A sample recommendation from a shop-a-long with managers from a large U.S. health maintenance organization who actually could play the part of a patient: Make examining rooms larger to enable the nervous patient to have a friend or relative in the room while waiting for the doctor.

Competitive Products Analyzing the competition can lead to new-product ideas. For six months, the Marriott Corporation sent a six-person intelligence team to travel and stay at economy hotels around the country. The team assessed the competitions' strengths and weaknesses on everything from the soundproof qualities of the rooms to the softness of the towels. Marriott then budgeted $500 million for a new economy hotel chain—Fairfield Inns.

Universities, Inventors, and Smaller Firms Many firms look for outside visionaries that have inventions or innovative ideas that can become products. Some sources of this open innovation strategy include:

- *Universities.* Many universities have technology transfer centers that often partner with business firms to commercialize faculty inventions. The first-of-its-kind carbonated yogurt Go-Gurt Fizzix was launched in late 2007 as a result

session 开会，会议；commercialize 商业化。

Gary Schwartzberg partnered with Kraft Foods to get his cream cheese-filled bagels in stores across the United States.

筛选与评估是新产品开发过程中对新产品创意进行内部和外部评估，以剔除那些不值得进一步开发部分的阶段。

of General Mills partnering with Brigham Young University to license the university's patent to put the "fizz" into the yogurt.

- *Inventors.* Many lone inventors and entrepreneurs develop brilliant new-product ideas—like Gary Schwartzberg's tube-shaped bagel filled with cream cheese. A portable breakfast for the on-the-go person, the innovative bagel couldn't get widespread distribution. So Schwartzberg sold his idea to Kraft Foods, Inc., which now markets its Bagel-Fuls filled with Kraft's best-selling Philadelphia cream cheese in supermarkets across the United States.
- *Smaller, nontraditional firms.* Small technology firms and even small, nontraditional firms in adjacent industries provide creative advances. General Mills partnered with Weight Watchers to develop Progresso Light soups, the first consumer packaged product in any grocery category to carry the Weight Watchers endorsement with a 0 points value per serving.

Great ideas can come from almost anywhere—the challenge is recognizing them.

第三阶段：筛选与评估

Stage 3: Screening and Evaluation

Screening and evaluation is the stage of the new-product process that internally and externally evaluates new-product ideas to eliminate those that warrant no further effort.

Internal Approach A firm's employees evaluate the technical feasibility of a proposed new-product idea to determine whether it meets the objectives defined in the new-product strategy development step. For example, 3M scientists develop many world-class innovations in the company's labs. A recent innovation was its microreplication technology—one that has 3,000 tiny gripping "fingers" per square inch. An internal assessment showed 3M that this technology could be used to improve the gripping of golf or work gloves.

Organizations that develop service-dominated offerings need to ensure that employees have the commitment and skills to meet customer expectations and sustain customer loyalty—an important criterion in screening a new-service idea. This is the essence of **customer experience management (CEM)**, which is the process of managing the entire customer experience within the firm. Marketers must consider employees' interactions with customers so that the new services are consistently delivered and experienced, clearly differentiated from other service offerings, and relevant and valuable to the target market.

External Approach Firms use *concept tests*, external evaluations with consumers that consist of preliminary testing of a new-product idea rather than an actual product. Generally, these tests are more useful with minor modifications of existing products than with new, innovative products with which consumers are not familiar. Concept tests rely on written descriptions of the product but may be augmented with sketches, mock-ups, or promotional literature. Key questions for concept testing include: How does the customer perceive the product? Who would use it? and How would it be used?

learning review

7. What is the new-product strategy development stage in the new-product process?
8. What are the main sources of new-product ideas?
9. How do internal and external screening and evaluation approaches differ?

nontraditional 非传统的，不符合传统的；endorsement 赞同，支持；eliminate 消除，淘汰。

第四阶段：商业分析
Stage 4: Business Analysis

How do you print ink-jet images on Pringles chips safely and inexpensively? The text describes how a global search found the critical technology.

Business analysis specifies the features of the product and the marketing strategy needed to bring it to market and make financial projections. This is the last checkpoint before significant resources are invested to create a *prototype*—a full-scale operating model of the product. The business analysis stage assesses the total "business fit" of the proposed new product with the company's mission and objectives—from whether the product can be economically developed and manufactured to the marketing strategy needed to have it succeed in the marketplace.

This process requires not only detailed financial projections but also assessments of the marketing and product synergies related to the company's existing operations. Will the new product require a lot of new machinery to produce it or can we use unused capacity of existing machines? Will the new product cannibalize sales of our existing products or increase revenues by reaching new market segments? Can the new product be protected with a patent or copyright? Financial projections of expected profits require estimates of expected prices per unit and units sold, as well as detailed estimates of the costs of R&D, production, and marketing.

For services, business analysis must consider *capacity management*, integrating the service component of the marketing mix with efforts to influence consumer demand. Most services are perishable and have a limited capacity due to the inseparability of the service from its provider. Therefore, a service provider must manage the availability of the offering so that demand matches capacity over the duration of the demand cycle (one day, a week, and so on). For example, airlines and mobile phone service providers use *off-peak pricing* to charge different prices for different times of the day or week to reflect the variations in demand for their services. This enables them to maximize profit.

第五阶段：开发
Stage 5: Development

Development is the stage of the new-product process that turns the idea on paper into a prototype. This results in a demonstrable, producible product that involves not only manufacturing the product but also performing laboratory and consumer tests to ensure it meets the standards established for it in the protocol. Moreover, the new product must be able to be manufactured at reasonable cost with the required quality.

A brainstorming session at Procter & Gamble produced the idea of printing pop culture images on its Pringles chips. But how do you print sharp images—like those for *Spider-Man 3*—using edible dyes on millions of chips? Internal development would be too long and costly, so P&G circulated a description of its unusual printing need globally. A university professor in Bologna, Italy, had invented an ink-jet method for printing edible images on cakes and cookies. In less than a year, P&G adapted the process and launched its new "Pringle Prints"—at a fraction of the time and cost internal development would have taken.

Does this Google home page look like a no-brainer to design? To read how Google designers spend thousands of hours to provide "favorable user experiences," see the text and Marketing Matters box.

For services, developing customer service delivery expectations is critical. This involves analyzing the entire sequence of steps or "service encounters" that make up the service to study the points of interaction between consumers and the service provider. High-contact services such as hotels, car rental agencies, and Web sites use this approach to enhance customer relationships. That white, plain-vanilla Google home page may look like it was designed by a child. But the Marketing Matters box describes how Google's Marissa Mayer has spent thousands of hours and done countless experiments to get exactly the right "feel" for Google's millions of users.

Safety tests are also critical for when the product isn't used as planned. To make sure seven-year-olds can't bite Barbie's

---

checkpoint 关卡，检验点；prototype 原型，样品，样本。

Marketing Matters > > > > > > > customer value

Marissa Mayer: The Talent Behind Google's Familiar *White* Home Page

Unknown to you, Google Employee No. 20, Marissa Mayer, probably impacts your life at least 5 or 10 times a week.

The New York Times calls her the "gatekeeper of Google's home page," the one person who "controls the look, feel, and functionality of the Internet's most heavily trafficked search engine." Virtually every new design or feature—from the color of the Google tool bar to the exact words on a Google page—needs her stamp of approval. The very clear, very plain, very white Google home page reflects Mayer's passion about obtaining a favorable user experience. Her job title: vice president of search products and user experience.

At Google, Mayer has introduced over 100 products and features, such as Google News, Gmail, and Image Search. Sounding like a combination English teacher and art instructor, Mayer sets the design standards for Google. Many of these are based on her internal Google experiments to measure user preferences. Her precise design rules include:

- Avoid first- and second-person pronouns.
- Write "Google" instead of "we."
- Don't switch tenses.
- Avoid italics because they are hard to read on a computer screen.

And beyond the grammar lessons, there are also precise design and graphic arts guidelines: "If you want to make the design on the page simpler, take away one of these: A type of font, a color, or an image."

An engineer, Mayer has a Google life that goes far beyond pronouns and colors of Google's Web pages. As *The New York Times* notes, "She oversees 200 product managers who in turn supervise 3,000 engineers, or more than 10 percent of Google's work force." Comments one colleague, "She functions at the executive level but is just as comfortable at the engineer level."

head off and choke, Mattel clamps her foot in steel jaws in a test stand and then pulls on her head with a wire. Similarly, car manufacturers have done extensive safety tests by crashing their cars into concrete walls.

第六阶段：市场测试
Stage 6: Market Testing

Market testing is the stage of the new-product process that involves exposing actual products to prospective consumers under realistic purchase conditions to see if they will buy. Often a product is developed, tested, refined, and then tested again to get consumer reactions through either test marketing or simulated test markets.

During development, laboratory tests like this one on Barbie result in safer dolls and toys for children.

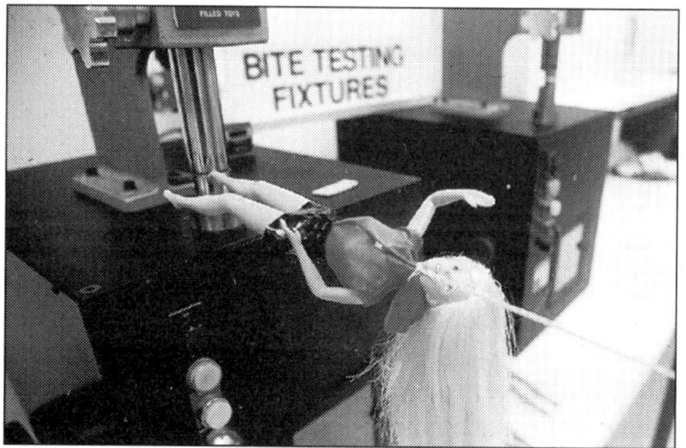

Test Marketing *Test marketing* involves offering a product for sale on a limited basis in a defined area. This test is done to determine whether consumers will actually buy the product and to try different ways of marketing it. Only about a third of the products tested do well enough to go on to the next stage. These market tests are usually conducted in cities that are viewed as being representative of U.S. consumers like the six shown in Figure 7–4 on the next page. Of these cities, Wichita Falls, Texas, most closely matches the U.S. average found in the 2000 Census. Other criteria used in selecting test market cities include cable systems to deliver different ads to different homes,

realistic 现实的。

Demographic Characteristic	USA	Wichita Falls, TX
2000 population	281.4 mil.	140,518
Median age (years)	35.3	33.6
% of family households with children under 18	32.8%	33.8%
% Hispanic or Latino of any race	12.5%	11.8%
% African American	12.3%	9.6%
% Asian American	3.6%	1.7%
% Native American	1.5%	1.7%

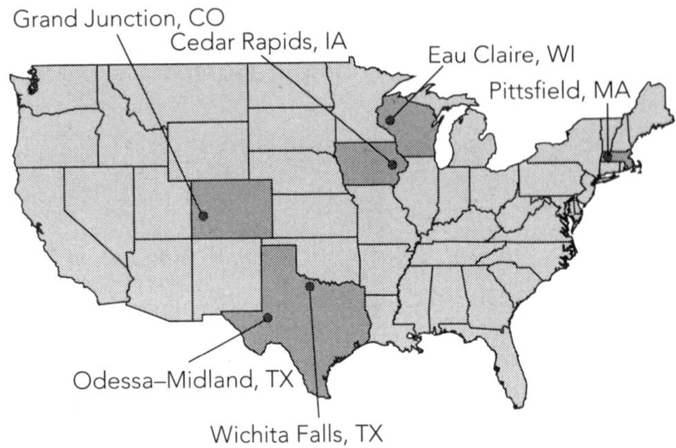

FIGURE 7–4
Six important U.S. test markets and the "demographics winner": the Wichita Falls, Texas, metropolitan statistical area

and tracking systems such as those of ACNielsen to measure sales resulting from different advertising campaigns. The 2010 Census will probably reveal different U.S. cities that better represent the national average demographic characteristics. These cities will become the new preferred test market cities.

This information indicates potential sales volume and market share in the test area. Companies also use market tests to check other elements of the marketing mix, such as price, level of advertising support, and distribution. Because market tests are so time consuming and expensive and can alert competitors to a firm's plans, some firms skip test markets or use simulated test markets.

Simulated Test Markets Because of the time, cost, and confidentiality problems of test markets, consumer packaged goods companies often turn to *simulated* (or *laboratory*) *test markets (STM)*, a technique that simulates a full-scale test market but in a limited fashion. STMs are often run in shopping malls, where consumers are questioned to identify who uses the product class being tested. Next, willing participants are questioned on usage, reasons for purchase, and important product attributes. Qualified persons are then shown TV commercials or print ads for the test product along with competitors' advertising. Finally, they are given money to make a decision to buy or not buy the firm's product—or the competitors' product—from a real or simulated store environment.

Commercializing a new French fry: To learn how Burger King's improved French fries confronted McDonald's fries, see the text.

When Test Markets Don't Work Not all products can use test marketing. Test marketing a service is very difficult because it is intangible and consumers can't see what they are buying. For example, how do you test market a new building for an art museum?

Similarly, test markets for expensive consumer products such as cars or costly industrial products such as jet engines are impractical. For these products, reactions of potential buyers to mockups or one-of-a-kind prototypes are all that is feasible.

第七阶段：商业化
Stage 7: Commercialization

Finally, the product is brought to the point of **commercialization**—the stage of the new-product process that positions and launches a new product in full-scale production and sales. Companies proceed very carefully at the commercialization stage because this is the most expensive stage for most new products. If competitors introduce a product that leapfrogs the firm's own new product or if cannibalization of its own existing products looks significant, the firm may halt the new-product launch permanently.

Countless other questions arise. Should we make an advance announcement of the new-product introduction to stimulate interest and potential sales? Do we need to add new salespeople? Do the salespeople need extra training?

demographic 人口统计学的，人口统计的；confidentiality 机密；commercialization 商业化，商品化。

大公司利用地方性展览，来逐步将新产品推向美国各个地区，这使得生产水平和营销活动能够逐步建立，从而将新产品失败的风险降到最低。

Large companies use *regional rollouts*, introducing the product sequentially into geographical areas of the United States, to allow production levels and marketing activities to build up gradually to minimize the risk of new-product failure. Grocery product manufacturers and telephone service providers are examples of firms that use this strategy.

Burger King's French Fries: The Complexities of Commercialization Burger King's "improved French fries" are an example of what can go wrong at the commercialization stage. In the fast-food industry, McDonald's French fries are the gold standard against which all other fries are measured. Burger King decided to take on McDonald's fries and spent millions of R&D dollars developing a starch-coated fry designed to retain heat longer and add crispiness. This crispiness was even defined: "An audible crunch that should be present for seven or more chews!"

A 100-person team set to work and developed the starch-coated fry that beat McDonald's fries in taste tests, 57 percent to 35 percent, with 8 percent having no opinion. After "certifrying" 300,000 managers and employees on the new frying procedures, the fries were launched with a $70 million marketing budget. The launch turned into disaster. The reason: The new fry proved too complicated to get right day after day in Burger King restaurants, except under ideal conditions, and was dropped.

Effective cross-functional teams at Hewlett-Packard have reduced new-product development times significantly—often with the aid of "fences."

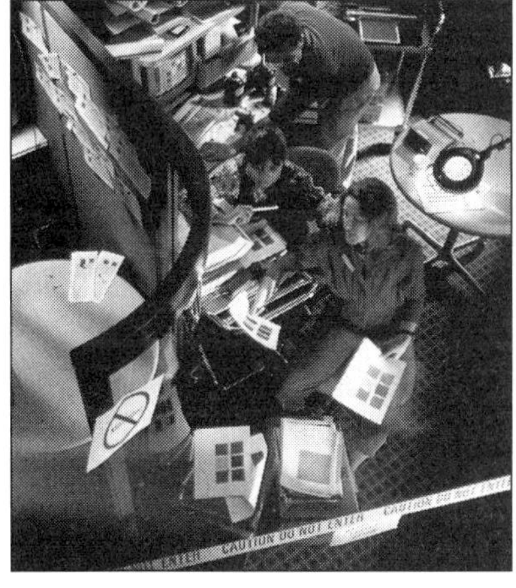

The Special Risks in Commercializing Grocery Products New grocery products pose special commercialization problems. Because shelf space is so limited, many supermarkets require a *slotting fee* for new products, a payment a manufacturer makes to place a new item on a retailer's shelf. This can run to several million dollars for a single product. But there's even another potential expense. If a new grocery product does not achieve a predetermined sales target, some retailers require a *failure fee*, a penalty payment a manufacturer makes to compensate a retailer for sales its valuable shelf space failed to make. These costly slotting fees and failure fees are further examples of why large grocery product manufacturers use regional rollouts.

Speed as a Factor in New-Product Success In recent years, companies have discovered that speed or *time to market* (TtM) is often vital in introducing a new product. Recent studies have shown that high-tech products coming to market on time are far more profitable than those arriving late. So some companies—such as Sony, BMW, 3M, and Hewlett-Packard—have overlapped the sequence of stages described in this chapter.

With this approach, termed *parallel development*, cross-functional team members who conduct the simultaneous development of both the product and the production process stay with the product from conception to production. This has enabled Hewlett-Packard to reduce the development time for notebook computers from 12 to 7 months. In software development, *fast prototyping* uses a "do it, try it, fix it" approach—encouraging continuing improvement even after the initial design. To speed up time to market, many large companies are building "fences" around their new product teams to keep them from getting bogged down in red tape.

learning review

10. How does the development stage of the new-product process involve testing the product inside and outside the firm?
11. What is a test market?
12. What is the commercialization of a new product?

rollout 首次展示；complicated 复杂的，难懂的，难处理的。

LEARNING OBJECTIVES REVIEW

LO1 *Recognize the various terms that pertain to products and services.*

A product is a good, service, or idea consisting of a bundle of tangible and intangible attributes that satisfies consumers and is received in exchange for money or something else of value.

A good has tangible attributes that a consumer's five senses can perceive and intangible ones such as warranties; a laptop computer is an example. Goods can also be divided into nondurable goods, which are consumed in one or a few uses, and durable goods, which usually last over many uses. Services are intangible activities or benefits that an organization provides to satisfy consumer needs in exchange for money or something else of value, such as an airline trip. An idea is a thought that leads to a product or action, such as eating healthier foods.

LO2 *Identify the ways in which consumer and business products and services can be classified.*

By type of user, the major distinctions are consumer products, which are products purchased by the ultimate consumer, and business products, which are products that assist in providing other products for resale.

Consumer products can be broken down based on the effort involved in the purchase decision process, marketing mix attributes used in the purchase, and the frequency of purchase: (*a*) convenience products are items that consumers purchase frequently and with a minimum of shopping effort; (*b*) shopping products are items for which consumers compare several alternatives on selected criteria; (*c*) specialty products are items that consumers make special efforts to seek out and buy; and (*d*) unsought products are items that consumers do not either know about or initially want.

Business products can be broken down into (*a*) components, which are items that become part of the final product, such as raw materials or parts, and (*b*) support products, which are items used to assist in producing other goods and services and include installations, accessory equipment, supplies, and industrial services.

Services can be classified in terms of whether they are delivered by (*a*) people or equipment, (*b*) business firms or nonprofit organizations, or (*c*) government agencies.

Firms can offer a range of products, which involve decisions regarding the product item, product line, and product mix.

LO3 *Explain the significance of "newness" in new products and services as it relates to the degree of consumer learning involved.*

From the important perspective of the consumer, "newness" is often seen as the degree of learning that a consumer must engage in to use the product. With a continuous innovation, no new behaviors must be learned. With a dynamically continuous innovation, only minor behavioral changes are needed. With a discontinuous innovation, consumers must learn entirely new consumption patterns.

LO4 *Describe the factors contributing to a new product's or service's success or failure.*

A new product or service often fails for these marketing reasons: (*a*) insignificant points of difference, (*b*) incomplete market and product protocol before product development starts, (*c*) not satisfying customer needs on critical factors, (*d*) bad timing, (*e*) too little market attractiveness, (*f*) poor product quality, (*g*) poor execution of the marketing mix, and (*h*) no economical access to buyers.

LO5 *Explain the purposes of each step of the new-product process.*

The new-product process consists of seven stages a firm uses to develop a salable good or service: (*a*) New-product strategy development involves defining the role for the new product within the firm's overall objectives. (*b*) Idea generation involves developing a pool of concepts from consumers, employees, basic R&D, and competitors to serve as candidates for new products. (*c*) Screening and evaluation involves evaluating new product ideas to eliminate those that are not feasible from a technical or consumer perspective. (*d*) Business analysis involves defining the features of the new product, developing the marketing strategy and marketing program to introduce it, and making a financial forecast. (*e*) Development involves not only producing a prototype product but also testing it in the lab and on consumers to see that it meets the standards set for it. (*f*) Market testing involves exposing actual products to prospective consumers under realistic purchasing conditions to see if they will buy the product. (*g*) Commercialization involves positioning and launching a product in full-scale production and sales with a specific marketing program.

FOCUSING ON KEY TERMS

business analysis
business products
commercialization
consumer products
convenience products
customer experience management (CEM)
development
idea generation
market testing
new-product process
new-product strategy development
product
product item
product line
product mix
protocol
screening and evaluation
services
shopping products
specialty products
unsought products

APPLYING MARKETING KNOWLEDGE

1 Products can be classified as either consumer or business goods. How would you classify the following products? (*a*) Johnson's baby shampoo, (*b*) a Black & Decker two-speed drill, and (*c*) an arc welder.

2 Are Nature Valley Granola bars and Eddie Bauer hiking boots convenience, shopping, specialty, or unsought products?

3 Based on your answer to question 2, how would the marketing actions differ for each product and the classification to which you assigned it?

4 In terms of the behavioral effect on consumers, how would a computer, such as an Apple iMac, be classified? In light of this classification, what actions would you suggest to the manufacturers of these products to increase their sales in the market?

5 What methods would you suggest to assess the potential commercial success for the following new products? (*a*) a new, improved ketchup; (*b*) a three-dimensional television system that took the company 10 years to develop; and (*c*) a new children's toy on which the company holds a patent.

6 Concept testing is an important step in the new-product process. Outline the concept tests for (*a*) an electrically powered car and (*b*) a new loan payment system for automobiles that is based on a variable interest rate. What are the differences in developing concept tests for products as opposed to services?

building your marketing plan

In fine-tuning the product strategy for your marketing plan, do these two things:

1 Develop a simple three-column table in which (*a*) market segments of potential customers are in the first column and (*b*) the one or two key points of differences of the product to satisfy the segment's needs are in the second column.

2 In the third column of your table, write ideas for specific new products for your business in each of the rows in your table.

video case 7 Activeion Cleaning Solutions: Marketing a High-Tech Cleaning Gadget

If a company told you it was marketing a handheld, on-demand cleaning gadget that also sanitizes, eliminating greater than 99.9 percent of harmful bacteria—and uses simply the tap water from your faucet—what would you think?

You'd probably think it was just another overly hyped gadget involving false, exaggerated claims and featured on late-night infomercials!

That's exactly the problem that Activeion Cleaning Solutions, a small startup company with a revolutionary technology, faced in late 2009. Let's have you give the company some *pro bono* (free!) marketing advice.

THE TECHNOLOGY: SAFE, SMART, SUSTAINABLE CLEANING

Activeion Cleaning Solutions is a privately held technology company created to revolutionize the cleaning industry through the manufacturing, marketing, and distribution of advanced technologies and products that address the ever-growing need for sustainable cleaning.

In 2008, Activeion licensed a new chemical-free cleaning technology from a mid-sized industrial company using the technology on the large scrubbing machines it sells to factories and warehouses. Other forms of the base chemical-free cleaning technology are used in hospitals for wound cleaning, in food-processing plants for sanitizing produce, and in pharmaceutical plants for maximizing cleanliness. Activeion decided to miniaturize these large, expensive versions of the technology, integrate the technology into a portable handheld sprayer, and market it to commercial cleaning professionals, as well as consumers, at a reasonable price.

The technology makes use of the energy stored in water molecules. First, tap water is passed through a membrane to create oxygen-rich micro-bubbles. Next, this water passes through an electrical charge to separate it into acidic and alkaline ionized or "activated" water. Because dirt and grime are naturally charged themselves, they are attracted to the activated water, which then breaks down the dirt and grime, lifts them from the surface, and enables the resulting dirt and grime particles to be wiped away easily.

Effective on a range of surfaces—from glass and stainless steel to wood and carpet—*R&D Magazine* named the technology as one of the most technologically significant developments of 2008. Through the innovation, cleaning professionals can meet the demand for green cleaning without the negative environmental and health concerns associated with producing, packaging, transporting, using, and disposing of traditional cleaning chemicals.

PRODUCTS AND MARKETS

In 2009 Activeion Cleaning Solutions introduced the Ionator for professional commercial cleaners as well as a consumer version for homes.

"The benefits from the Ionator are dramatic," explains Scott Beine, custodial manager for the Target Center Arena in Minneapolis, Minnesota, and a believer in the technology. "With its activated water-cleaning process, we've been able to eliminate most general-purpose cleaning products, thereby providing health and safety benefits to our custodial staff and building occupants."

The most stunning benefit of the Ionator is in the environmental area. It avoids the problems associated with traditional chemical detergents and their related packaging, which must be produced, transported, and then disposed of into the waste stream. The Ionator also can replace the hundreds of millions of chemical-laden cleaning bottles used—and disposed of—everyday, around the world. On April 22, 2009 Ellen DeGeneres featured the product on her "Earth Day" show—calling it one of the best green products available. The Ionator is now priced at $299.

Markets for the Ionator range from schools and hospitals to hotels and restaurants—virtually anywhere traditional, general-purpose cleaning chemicals are in use. There are millions of these locations in the United States that use general purpose cleaning chemicals.

To reach consumers, the company has recently introduced a version for home use, selling at about half the price of the commercial Ionator. This product seeks to reach the 117 million single-family homes, especially those with families interested in creating a safer, healthier, more sustainable living space.

BENEFITS

"We believe we have a fantastic story to tell," says Amber Arnseth, product marketing manager for Activeion. She lists the key benefits Activeion technology offers both professional cleaners and consumers:

- *Safety*. By converting tap water into a powerful cleaner and sanitizer, the Ionator eliminates cleaning chemicals. The technology is one of the only cleaning products in the world without a health-related warning label.
- *Simplicity*. Just fill with tap water and go! This is the ultimate form of "cleaning on the go" that so many households and cleaning professionals want and need. There's nothing to add, mix, or batch (it's portable)—just spray, clean, and wipe dry whenever and wherever there's a spill or a mess (it's on-demand).
- *Sustainability*. In a carbon footprint analysis, the University of Tennessee/Eco-Form compared cleaning with the Ionator to cleaning with traditional general-purpose chemicals. It found significant benefits to using the Ionator. It not only reduces environmental problems but also significantly reduces energy consumption.
- *Savings*. With a technology that works as well as or better than existing general-purpose cleaning chemicals, the Ionator eliminates the purchasing, storing, refilling, and managing of toxic cleaning supplies most organizations face today when they clean. The Grand Haven (Michigan) Area Public School District reports savings of over $20,000 annually by converting to the Ionator. Many other testimonials just like this one exist.
- *Fun*. In a recent blogging event with the Silicon Valley Moms group (www.svmoms.com), virtually all bloggers reported the same: The Ionator is cool, it helps make cleaning fun, and kids love using it because of the futuristic green glow and the buzzing sound.

CHALLENGES

Despite the numerous benefits, introducing a new, disruptive technology comes with challenges. "Almost everyone who hears about our product and technology loves the promise of what it can do," says Arnseth. "Yet we know it won't be easy to get people to convert."

Among the obvious challenges:

- *Defining "clean."* Aside from the removal of visible dirt and grime, how can one tell if a surface is clean? Or if harmful bacteria have been eliminated? Chemical companies mitigate this challenge by adding scents, bubbles, and colors—to "signal" clean.

- *Assessing new technology risk.* It's difficult enough to introduce any new technology to a fast-paced, short-attention-spanned world—much less a technology that is seemingly so unbelievable. Consumers are notoriously finicky in adopting new technologies.
- *Defining a new category.* The category of "high-tech cleaning gadgets for everyday, hard-surface, cleaning on-the-go throughout the home" does not exist today. Activeion is creating a new category in the marketplace—which has historically been one of the most difficult of marketing objectives.

Welcome to the challenges of bringing a new technology into the world!

Questions

1 What are the major points of difference for the Activeion portable handheld cleaning and sanitizing devices for (*a*) business users and (*b*) households?

2 From information in the case and a visit to the Activeion Web site (www.activeion.com), what are the characteristics of the main target markets for the Activeion cleaning tools among (*a*) business users and (*b*) households?

3 Look again at the eight key reasons for new product success and failure in the chapter. Using a five-point scale (5 = very favorable, 3 = neutral, 1 = very unfavorable), evaluate (*a*) the Ionator for business users and (*b*) the consumer version for households on each of the eight reasons and briefly justify your answers.

4 When introducing the consumer version for households, (*a*) identify three key target markets, (*b*) suggest media you might use to reach them, and (*c*) create one or two simple messages to communicate the product's points of difference.

5 What other handheld applications could Activeion pursue for its technology?

SERENA
SERENA

G2
LESS CALORIES
FOR MORE ATHLETES™

8

成功的产品和品牌管理
Managing Successful Products and Brands

LEARNING OBJECTIVES

After reading this chapter you should be able to:

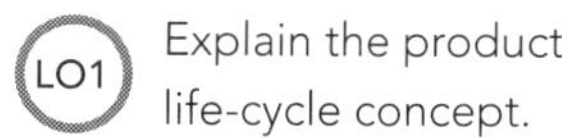

LO1 Explain the product life-cycle concept.

LO2 Identify ways that marketing executives manage a product's life cycle.

LO3 Recognize the importance of branding and alternative branding strategies.

LO4 Describe the role of packaging, labeling, and warranties in the marketing of a product.

佳得乐公司：满足难以抑制的渴望
GATORADE: QUENCHING THE ACTIVE THIRST WITHIN YOU

Why is the thirst for Gatorade unquenchable? Look no further than constant product improvement and masterful brand development.

Like Kleenex in the tissue market, Jell-O among gelatin desserts, and iPod for digital music players, Gatorade is synonymous with sports drinks. Concocted in 1965 at the University of Florida as a rehydration beverage for the school's football team, the drink was coined "Gatorade" by an opposing team's coach after watching his team lose to the Florida Gators in the Orange Bowl. The name stuck, and a new beverage product class was born. Stokely-Van Camp Inc. bought the Gatorade formula in 1967 and commercialized the product. The original Gatorade had one flavor—lemon-lime.

The Quaker Oats Company acquired Stokely-Van Camp in 1983 and quickly increased Gatorade sales through a variety of means. More flavors were added. Multiple package sizes were offered using different containers. Distribution expanded from convenience stores and supermarkets to mass merchandisers such as Wal-Mart. Consistent advertising and promotion effectively conveyed the product's unique performance benefits and links to athletic competition. International opportunities were vigorously pursued. Today, Gatorade is sold in more than 80 countries in North America, Europe, Latin America, the Middle East, Africa, Asia, and Australia and has become a global brand.

Masterful brand management spurred Gatorade's success. Gatorade Frost® was introduced in 1997 and aimed at expanding the brand's reach beyond organized sports to other usage occasions. Gatorade Fierce® appeared in 1999. In the same year, Gatorade entered the bottled-water category with Propel Fitness Water, a lightly flavored water fortified with vitamins. The Gatorade Performance Series was introduced in 2001, featuring a Gatorade Energy Bar, Gatorade Energy Drink, and Gatorade Nutritional Shake.

Brand development accelerated after PepsiCo Inc. purchased Quaker Oats and the Gatorade brand in 2001. Gatorade All Stars, designed for teens, and Gatorade Xtremo, developed with a bilingual label for Latino consumers, were launched in 2002. Gatorade X-Factor followed in 2003. In 2005, Gatorade Endurance Formula was created for serious runners, construction workers, and other people doing long, sweaty workouts. Gatorade Rain, a lighter tasting version of regular Gatorade, arrived in 2006. In 2007, Gatorade AM, with no caffeine, debuted for the morning workout consumer. Gatorade Tiger, named for Tiger Woods, and a low-calorie Gatorade called G2 were successfully marketed in 2008.

---

masterful 巧妙的，熟练的，精彩的，精湛的；tissue 面巾纸，手巾纸；accelerate 加快，加速。

G2's new "Everyday Athletic" campaign has been a resounding success. Gatorade's marketing performance is a direct result of continuous product improvement and masterful brand management.

Gatorade
www.Gatorade.com

In 2009, Gatorade executives unleashed a bevy of enhanced beverages in bold new packaging. "Just like any good athlete, Gatorade is taking it to the next level," said Sarah Rob O'Hagan, Gatorade's chief marketing officer. "Whether you're in it for the win, for the thrill or for better health, if your body is moving, Gatorade sees you as an athlete, and we're inviting you into the brand." According to a company announcement, "The new Gatorade attitude would be most visible through a total packaging redesign." For example, Gatorade Thirst Quencher now displays the letter G front and center along with the brand's iconic bolt. "For Gatorade, G represents the heart, hustle, and soul of athleticism and will become a badge of pride for anyone who sweats, no matter where they're active"

To differentiate the range of Gatorade offerings from the traditional Gatorade Thirst Quencher, newly enhanced beverages conveyed the attitude of a tough-love coach or personal trainer through in-your-face names on the label and nutrition benefits inside. Gatorade Fierce is now Bring It™, Gatorade X-Factor is now Be Tough™, Gatorade AM is now Shine On™, and Gatorade Rain is now No Excuses™. Additionally, Gatorade Tiger was updated to emphasize its new focus benefit derived from the product's reformulation. Some 45 years after its creation, Gatorade remains a vibrant multibillion-dollar growth brand with seemingly unlimited potential.

The marketing of Gatorade illustrates continuous product development and masterful brand management in a dynamic marketplace. This chapter shows how the actions taken by Gatorade executives exemplify those made by successful marketers.

制定产品生命周期
CHARTING THE PRODUCT LIFE CYCLE

产品同人一样具有生命周期。**产品生命周期**概念描述了一个新产品在市场中所经历的不同阶段：导入期、成长期、成熟期和衰退期（如图 11-1）。

Products, like people, are viewed as having a life cycle. The concept of the **product life cycle** describes the stages a new product goes through in the marketplace: introduction, growth, maturity, and decline (Figure 8–1). The two curves shown in this figure, total industry sales revenue and total industry profit, represent the sum of sales revenue and profit of all firms producing the product. The reasons for the changes in each curve and the marketing decisions involved are detailed in the following pages.

导入期
Introduction Stage

产品生命周期的导入期是产品初次进入预计目标市场的时期。在该时期，销售额增长缓慢，利润微薄。缺乏利润常常是由于产品开发中的巨额投资成本造成的。

The introduction stage of the product life cycle occurs when a product is introduced to its intended target market. During this period, sales grow slowly, and profit is minimal. The lack of profit is often the result of large investment costs in product development, such as the millions of dollars spent by Gillette to develop the Gillette Fusion razor shaving system. The marketing objective for the company at this stage is to create consumer awareness and stimulate *trial*—the initial purchase of a product by a consumer.

Companies often spend heavily on advertising and other promotion tools to build awareness and stimulate product trial among consumers in the introduction stage. For example, Gillette budgeted $200 million in advertising to introduce the Fusion

unleashed 释放，放纵……而出；bevy（人）群；enhance 提高，增加，加强；beverage 饮料。

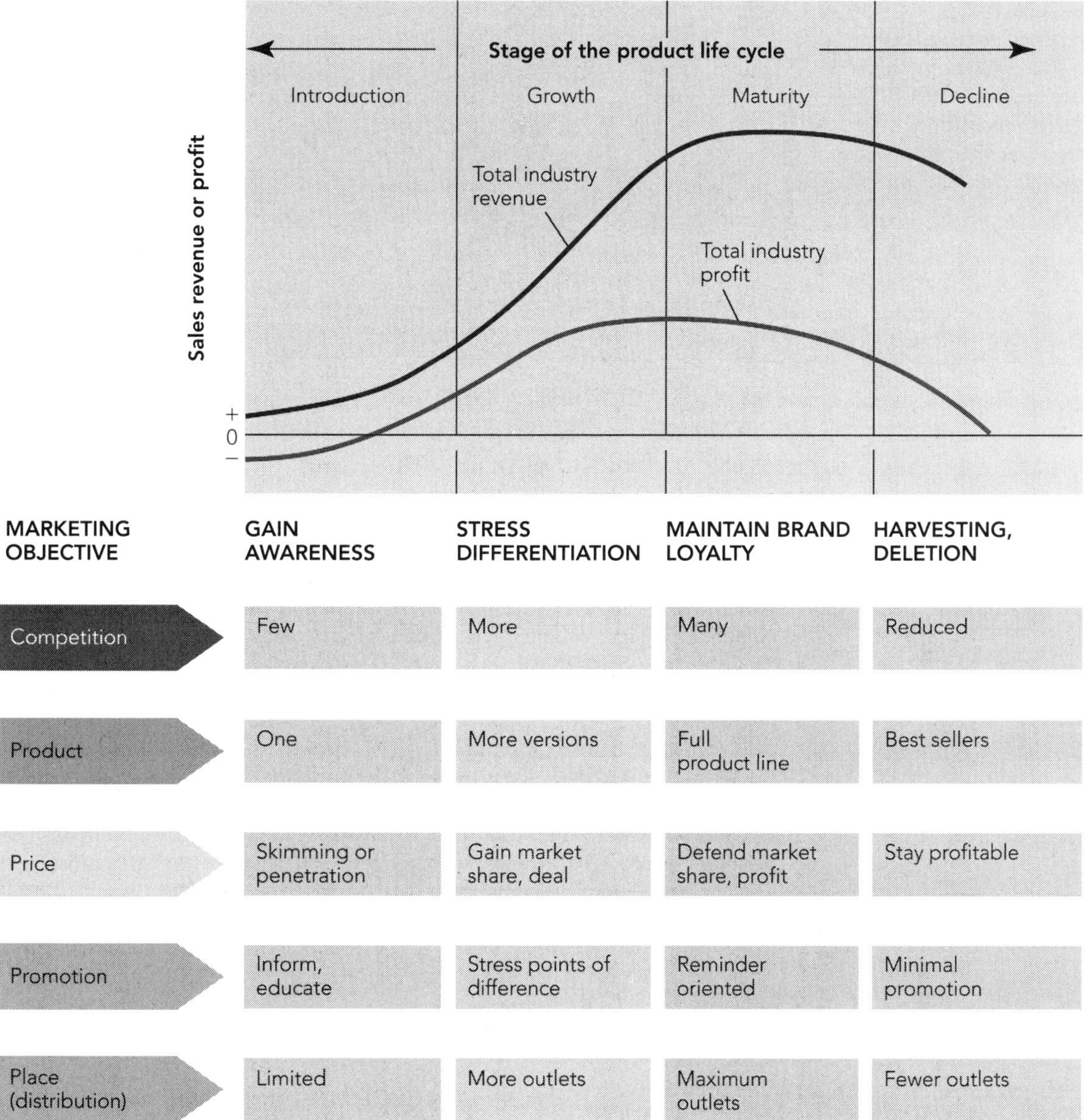

FIGURE 8–1
How stages of the product life cycle relate to a firm's marketing objectives and marketing mix actions

shaving system to male shavers. The result? Over 60 percent of male shavers became aware of the new razor within six months and 26 percent tried the product.

Advertising and promotion expenditures in the introduction stage are often made to stimulate *primary demand*, the desire for the product class rather than for a specific brand, since there are few competitors with the same product. As more competitors launch their own products and the product progresses along its life cycle, company attention is focused on creating *selective demand*, the preference for a specific brand.

Other marketing mix variables also are important at this stage. Gaining distribution can be a challenge because channel intermediaries may be hesitant to carry a new product. Also, a company often restricts the number of variations of the product to ensure control of product quality. Remember that the original Gatorade came in only one flavor.

During introduction, pricing can be either high or low. A high initial price may be used as part of a *skimming* strategy to help the company recover the costs of

shaver 电动剃须刀；hesitant 犹豫的，迟疑的。

FIGURE 8–2
Product life cycle for the stand-alone fax machine for business use: 1970–2012. All four product life-cycle stages appear: introduction, growth, maturity, and decline.

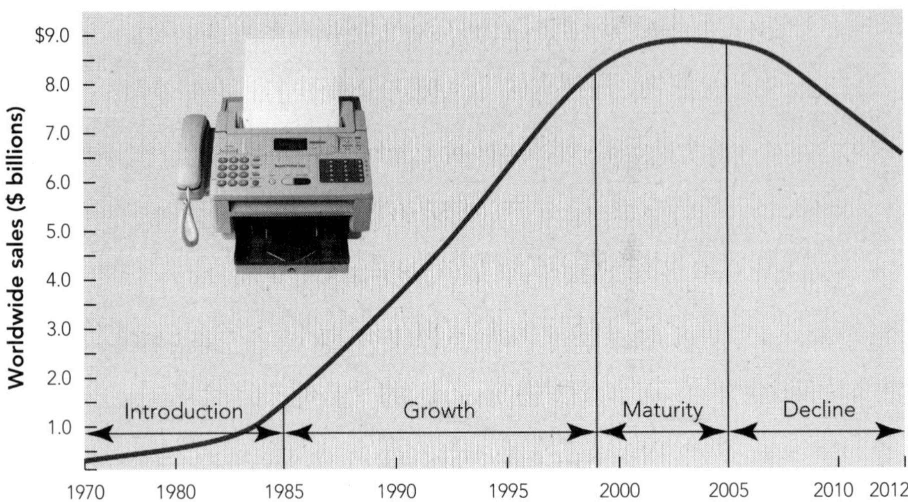

development as well as capitalize on the price insensitivity of early buyers. A master of this strategy is 3M. According to a 3M manager, "We hit fast, price high, and get the heck out when the me-too products pour in." High prices tend to attract competitors eager to enter the market because they see the opportunity for profit. To discourage competitive entry, a company can price low, referred to as *penetration pricing*. This pricing strategy helps build unit volume, but a company must closely monitor costs.

Figure 8–2 charts the stand-alone fax machine product life cycle for business use in the United States from the early 1970s to 2012. As shown, sales grew slowly in the 1970s and early 1980s after Xerox pioneered the first portable fax machine. Fax machines were first sold direct to businesses by company salespeople and were premium priced. The average price for a fax machine in 1980 was a hefty $12,700. Those fax machines were primitive by today's standards. They contained mechanical parts, not electronic circuitry, and offered few features seen in today's models.

Several product classes are in the introductory stage of the product life cycle. These include pocket video cameras and electric-powered automobiles.

成长期
Growth Stage

产品生命周期的第二个阶段是成长期，其特征是销售额迅速增长。在这一阶段，竞争者开始出现。

The growth stage of the product life cycle is characterized by rapid increases in sales. It is in this stage that competitors appear. For example, Figure 8–2 shows the dramatic increase in sales of fax machines from 1986 to 1998. The number of companies selling fax machines also increased, from one in the early 1970s to four in the late 1970s to seven manufacturers in 1983, which sold nine brands. By 1998 there were some 25 manufacturers and 60 brands from which to choose.

The result of more competitors and more aggressive pricing is that profit usually peaks during the growth stage. For instance, the average price for a fax machine plummeted from $3,300 in 1985 to $500 in 1995. At this stage, advertising shifts emphasis to stimulating selective demand; product benefits are compared with those of competitors' offerings for the purpose of gaining market share.

在成长期，产品销售量的增长率也有所提高，因为有更多的消费者试用或使用该产品，而且使用后感到满意又再次购买的重复购买者的比例也有所提高。

Product sales in the growth stage grow at an increasing rate because of new people trying or using the product and a growing proportion of *repeat purchasers*—people who tried the product, were satisfied, and bought again. For the Gillette Fusion razor, over 60 percent of men who tried the razor adopted the product permanently. For successful products, the ratio of repeat to trial purchases grows as the product moves through the life cycle. Durable fax machines meant that replacement purchases were

insensitivity 不敏感，不敏感性；penetration 渗透，穿透。

Electric automobiles made by General Motors are in the introductory stage of the product life cycle. Digital cameras produced by OLYMPUS are in the growth stage. Each product and company faces unique challenges based on its product life-cycle stage.

General Motors Company
www.gm.com

OLYMPUS America, Inc.
www.olympusamerica.com

rare. However, it became common for more than one machine to populate a business as the machine's use became more widespread.

Changes appear in the product in the growth stage. To help differentiate a company's brand from competitors, an improved version or new features are added to the original design, and product proliferation occurs. Changes in fax machines included (1) models with built-in telephones; (2) models that used plain, rather than thermal, paper for copies; and (3) models that integrated electronic mail.

In the growth stage, it is important to gain as much distribution for the product as possible. In the retail store, for example, this often means that competing companies fight for display and shelf space. Expanded distribution in the fax industry is an example. Early in the growth stage, just 11 percent of office machine dealers carried this equipment. By the mid-1990s, more than 70 percent of these dealers sold fax equipment, and distribution was expanded to other stores selling electronic equipment.

Numerous product classes or industries are in the growth stage of the product life cycle. Examples include smart phones and digital cameras.

成熟期
Maturity Stage

The maturity stage is characterized by a slowing of total industry sales or product class revenue. Also, marginal competitors begin to leave the market. Most consumers who would buy the product are either repeat purchasers of the item or have tried and abandoned it. Sales increase at a decreasing rate in the maturity stage as fewer new buyers enter the market. Profit declines due to fierce price competition among many sellers, and the cost of gaining new buyers at this stage rises.

在成熟期，因为新进入市场的购买者减少，销售增长率开始下降，诸多卖者之间的激烈价格竞争加上赢得新购买者的成本支出也会导致利润下降。

Marketing attention in the maturity stage is often directed toward holding market share through further product differentiation and finding new buyers. Fax machine

thermal 热的，保热的，温热的；maturity 成熟，完备；marginal 边的，边缘的。

Marketing Matters > > > > > > customer value

Will E-mail Spell Extinction for Fax Machines?

Technological substitution that creates value for customers often causes the decline stage in the product life cycle. Will e-mail replace fax machines?

This question has been debated for years. Even though e-mail continues to grow with broadening Internet access, millions of fax machines are still sold each year. Industry analysts estimate that the number of e-mail mailboxes worldwide will grow to 2.5 billion in 2012. However, the phenomenal popularity of e-mail has not brought fax machines to extinction. Why? The two technologies do not directly compete for the same messaging applications.

E-mail is used for text messages, and faxing is predominately used for communicating formatted documents by business users. Fax usage is expected to increase through 2010, even though unit sales of fax machines have declined on a worldwide basis. Internet technology and e-mail may eventually replace facsimile technology and paper and make fax machines extinct, but not in the immediate future.

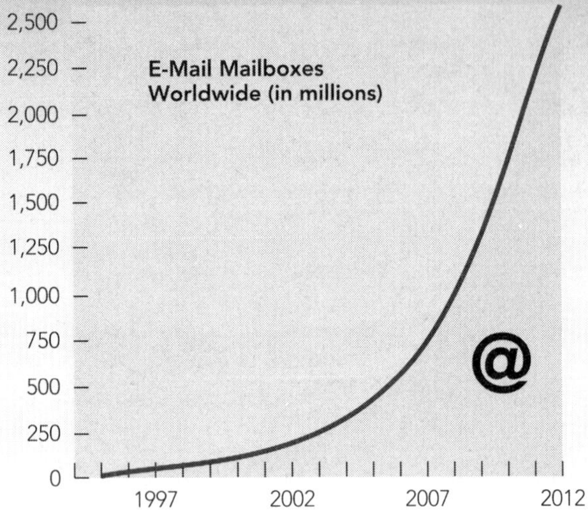

manufacturers developed Internet-enabled multifunctional models with new features such as scanning, copying, and color reproduction. They also designed fax machines suitable for small and home businesses, which today represent a substantial portion of sales. Still, a major consideration in a company's strategy in this stage is to control overall marketing cost by improving promotional and distribution efficiency.

Fax machines entered the maturity stage in the late 1990s. At the time, about 90 percent of industry sales were captured by five producers (Hewlett-Packard, Brother, Sharp, Lexmark, and Samsung), reflecting the departure of marginal competitors. By 2004, 200 million stand-alone fax machines were installed throughout the world, sending more than 120 billion faxes annually.

Numerous product classes and industries are in the maturity stage of their product life cycle. These include soft drinks and DVD players.

衰退期
Decline Stage

The decline stage occurs when sales drop. Fax machines for business use moved to this stage in early 2005 and the average price for a fax machine had sunk below $100. Frequently, a product enters this stage not because of any wrong strategy on the part of companies, but because of environmental changes. For example, digital music players pushed compact discs into decline in the recorded music industry. Will Internet technology and e-mail make fax machines extinct any time soon? The accompanying Marketing Matters box offers one perspective on this question.

处于衰退期的产品所消耗的管理时间和财务资源往往要大于其潜在收益。公司可以运用放弃和收获两种策略来处理衰退期的产品。

Products in the decline stage tend to consume a disproportionate share of management and financial resources relative to their future worth. A company will follow one of two strategies to handle a declining product: deletion or harvesting.

Deletion Product *deletion*, or dropping the product from the company's product line, is the most drastic strategy. Because a residual core of consumers still consume or use a product even in the decline stage, product elimination decisions are not taken lightly. For example, Sanford Corporation continues to sell its Liquid Paper correction fluid for use with typewriters in the era of word-processing equipment.

multifunctional 多功能的，起多功能作用的；elimination 根除，淘汰。

Harvesting A second strategy, *harvesting*, is when a company retains the product but reduces marketing costs. The product continues to be offered, but salespeople do not allocate time in selling nor are advertising dollars spent. The purpose of harvesting is to maintain the ability to meet customer requests. Coca-Cola, for instance, still sells Tab, its first diet cola, to a small group of die-hard fans. According to Coke's CEO, "It shows you care. We want to make sure those who want Tab, get Tab."

产品生命周期的四个方面
Four Aspects of the Product Life Cycle

分析产品生命周期需要关注几个方面：(1) 周期长度；(2) 销售曲线形状；(3) 不同产品层级的变化情况；(4) 消费者对产品的采用状况。

Some important aspects of product life cycles are (1) their length, (2) the shape of their sales curves, (3) how they vary with different levels of products, and (4) the rate at which consumers adopt products.

Length of the Product Life Cycle There is no set time that it takes a product to move through its life cycle. As a rule, consumer products have shorter life cycles than business products. For example, many new consumer food products such as Frito-Lay's Baked Lay's potato chips move from the introduction stage to maturity in 18 months. The availability of mass communication vehicles informs consumers quickly and shortens life cycles. Also, technological change tends to shorten product life cycles as new-product innovation replaces existing products.

Shape of the Product Life Cycle The product life-cycle sales curve shown in Figure 8–1 is the *generalized life cycle*, but not all products have the same shape to their curve. In fact, there are several life-cycle curves, each type suggesting different marketing strategies. Figure 8–3 shows the shape of life-cycle sales curves for four different types of products: high-learning, low-learning, fashion, and fad products.

A *high-learning product* is one for which significant customer education is required and there is an extended introductory period (Figure 8–3A). It may surprise you, but personal computers had this life-cycle curve. Consumers in the 1980s had to learn the benefits of owning the product or be educated in a new way of performing familiar tasks. Convection ovens for home use required consumers to learn a new way of cooking and alter familiar recipes used with conventional ovens. As a result, these ovens spent years in the introductory period.

In contrast, sales for a *low-learning product* begin immediately because little learning is required by the consumer, and the benefits of purchase are readily understood

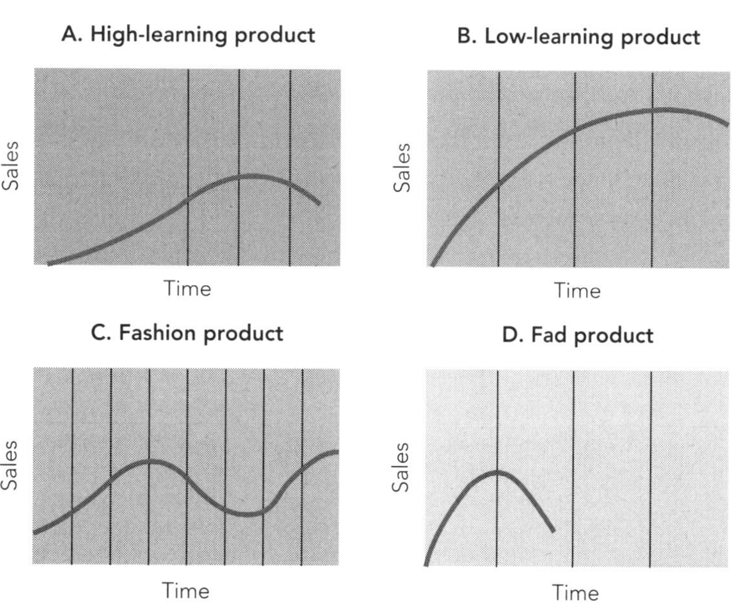

FIGURE 8–3
Alternative product life-cycle curves based on product types. Note the long introduction stage for a high-learning product compared with a low-learning product. Read the text for an explanation of different product life-cycle curves.

allocate 分配，分派；immediately 立即，马上。

(Figure 8–3B). This product often can be easily imitated by competitors, so the marketing strategy is to broaden distribution quickly. In this way, as competitors rapidly enter, most retail outlets already have the innovator's product. It is also important to have the manufacturing capacity to meet demand. A successful low-learning product is Gillette's Fusion razor. This product achieved $1 billion in worldwide sales in less than three years.

A *fashion product* (Figure 8–3C) is a style of the times. Life cycles for fashion products frequently appear in women's and men's apparel. Fashion products are introduced, decline, and then seem to return. The length of the cycles may be months, years, or decades. Consider women's hosiery. Product sales have been declining for years. Women consider it more fashionable to not wear hosiery—bad news for Hanes brands, the leading marketer of women's sheer hosiery. According to an authority on fashion, "Companies might as well let the fashion cycle take its course and wait for the inevitable return of pantyhose."

A *fad* experiences rapid sales on introduction and then an equally rapid decline (Figure 8–3D). These products are typically novelties and have a short life cycle. They include car tattoos sold in Southern California and described as the first removable and reusable graphics for automobiles, and vinyl dresses and fleece bikinis made by a Minnesota clothing company.

The Product Level: Class and Form The product life cycle shown in Figure 8–1 is a total industry or product class sales curve. Yet, in managing a product it is important to often distinguish among the multiple life cycles (class and form) that may exist. **Product class** refers to the entire product category or industry, such as prerecorded music. **Product form** pertains to variations within the product class. For prerecorded music, product form exits in the technology used to provide the music such as cassette types, compact discs, and digital music players. Figure 8–4 shows the life cycles for these three product forms.

产品生命周期依赖于对消费者的销售状况。并非所有消费者都在产品导入期购买产品，生

The Life Cycle and Consumers The life cycle of a product depends on sales to consumers. Not all consumers rush to buy a product in the introductory stage, and the shapes of the life-cycle curves indicate that most sales occur after the

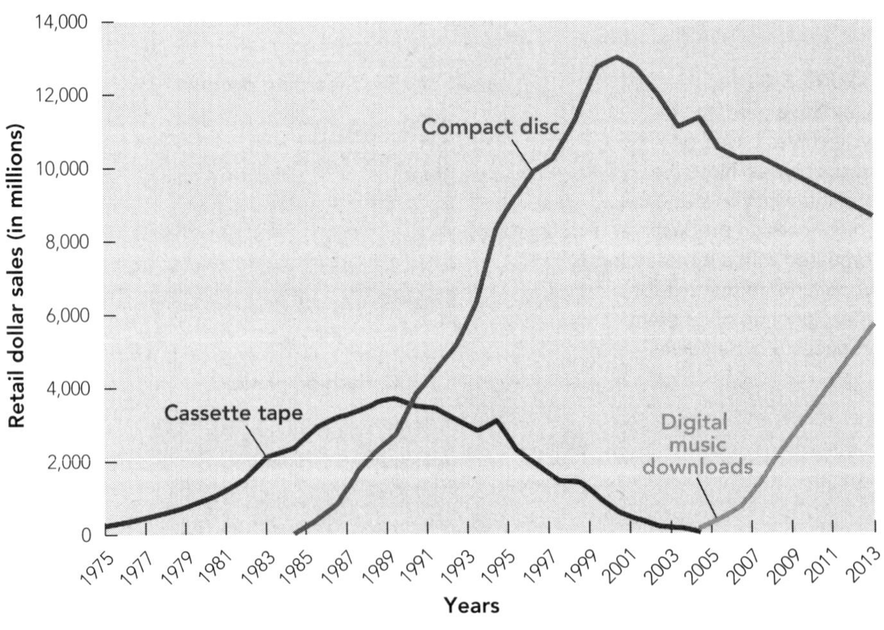

FIGURE 8–4
Prerecorded music product life cycles by product form illustrate the effect of technology on sales. Do you remember the cassette tape?

hosiery 袜类；inevitable 不可避免的，必然发生的；pantyhose 袜裤，长筒袜裤。

FIGURE 8–5
Five categories and profiles of product adopters. For a product to be successful, it must be purchased by innovators and early adopters.

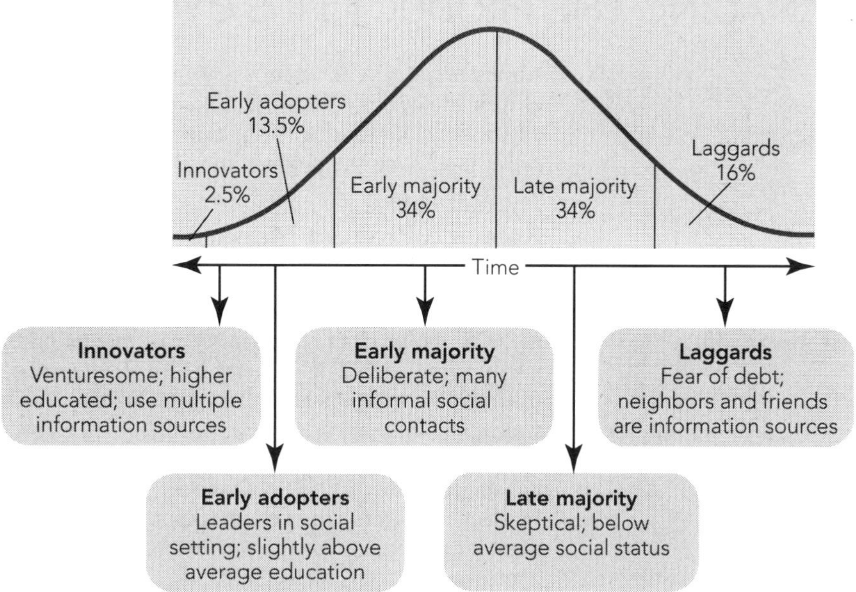

命周期曲线的形状显示，大多数销售是发生在产品已经进入市场一段时间之后。从本质上说，一个产品在大众中扩散、传播的过程，我们称之为创新扩散。

product has been on the market for some time. In essence, a product diffuses, or spreads, through the population, a concept called the *diffusion of innovation*.

Some people are attracted to a product early. Others buy it only after they see their friends or opinion leaders with the item. Figure 8–5 shows the consumer population divided into five categories of product adopters based on when they adopt a new product. Brief profiles accompany each category. For any product to be successful, it must be purchased by innovators and early adopters. This is why manufacturers of new pharmaceuticals try to gain adoption by respected hospitals, clinics, and physicians. Once accepted by innovators and early adopters, the adoption of new products moves on to the early majority, late majority, and laggard categories.

有些因素会影响到消费者是否采用某一新产品。抑制一个新产品进入导入期的一般原因是使用壁垒（产品不符合现有习惯）、价值壁垒（产品未能提供改变消费行为的激励）、风险壁垒（身体的、经济的、社会的）以及心理壁垒（文化差异和形象问题）。

Several factors affect whether a consumer will adopt a new product or not. Common reasons for resisting a product in the introduction stage are usage barriers (the product is not compatible with existing habits), value barriers (the product provides no incentive to change), risk barriers (physical, economic, or social), and psychological barriers (cultural differences or image).

Companies attempt to overcome these barriers in numerous ways. They provide warranties, money-back guarantees, extensive usage instructions, demonstrations, and free samples to stimulate initial trial of new products. For example, software developers offer demonstrations downloaded from the Internet. Cosmetic consumers can browse through the Cover Girl ColorMatch system on its Web site to find out how certain makeup products will look. Free samples are one of the most popular means to gain consumer trial. In fact, 71 percent of consumers consider a sample to be the best way to evaluate a new product.

learning review

1. Advertising plays a major role in the ______________ stage of the product life cycle, and ______________ plays a major role in maturity.
2. How do high-learning and low-learning products differ?
3. What are the five categories of product adopters?

diffuse 扩散；pharmaceutical 制药的，配药的；category 种类，类别；warranty 保证，担保。

产品生命周期管理
MANAGING THE PRODUCT LIFE CYCLE

An important task for a firm is to manage its products through the successive stages of their life cycles. This section describes the role of the product manager who is usually responsible for this and presents three ways to manage a product through its life cycle: modifying the product, modifying the market, and repositioning the product.

产品经理的角色
Role of a Product Manager

产品经理有时也称为品牌经理，其负责管理一个密切相关的产品或品牌家族的营销工作。

The product manager, sometimes called a *brand manager*, manages the marketing efforts for a close-knit family of products or brands. Introduced by Procter & Gamble in 1928, the product manager style of marketing organization is used by consumer goods firms, including General Mills and PepsiCo, and by industrial firms such as Intel and Hewlett-Packard. The U.S. Postal Service employs product managers as well.

All product managers are responsible for managing existing products through the stages of the life cycle. Some are also responsible for developing new products. Product managers' marketing responsibilities include developing and executing a marketing program for the product line described in an annual marketing plan and approving ad copy, media selection, and package design.

Harley-Davidson redesigned some of its motorcycle models to feature smaller hand grips, a lower seat, and an easier-to-pull clutch lever to create a more comfortable ride for women. According to Genevieve Schmitt, founding editor of WomenRidersNow.com, "They realize that women are an up-and-coming segment and that they need to accommodate them."

Harley-Davidson, Inc.
www.harley-davidson.com

Product managers also engage in extensive data analysis related to their products and brands. Sales, market share, and profit trends are closely monitored. Managers often supplement these data with two measures: (1) a category development index (CDI) and (2) a brand development index (BDI). These indexes help to identify strong and weak market segments (usually demographic or geographic segments) for specific consumer products and brands and provide direction for marketing efforts. The calculation, visual display, and interpretation of these two indexes for Hawaiian Punch are described in the Using Marketing Dashboards box.

调整产品
Modifying the Product

Product modification involves altering a product's characteristic, such as its quality, performance, or appearance, to increase the product's value to customers and increase sales. Wrinkle-free and stain-resistant clothing made possible by nanotechnology revolutionized the men's and women's apparel business and stimulated industry sales of casual pants, shirts, and blouses. Nokia's global leadership position among cell phone handset manufacturers is due to continuous product modification. For example, Nokia offers a cell phone handset that plays music, displays maps, takes pictures, surfs the Internet, and holds a 3.5-inch screen for watching TV and playing video games. Nokia's effort is called *product bundling*—the sale of two or more separate products in one package. In this case, the Nokia handset integrates seven separate products: telephone, camera, computer, video game player, GPS, television, and MP3 player in one handset package.

New features, packages, or scents can be used to change a product's characteristics and give the sense of a revised product. Procter & Gamble revamped Pantene shampoo and conditioner with a new vitamin formula and relaunched the brand with a multimillion-dollar advertising and promotion campaign. The result? Pantene, a brand first introduced in the 1940s, is now the top-selling shampoo and conditioner in the United States in an industry with more than 1,000 competitors.

调整市场
Modifying the Market

With **market modification** strategies, a company tries to find new customers, increase a product's use among existing customers, or create new use situations.

annual 年度的，全年的；selection 选拔，挑选，选择；vitamin 维生素，维他命。

Using Marketing Dashboards

Knowing Your CDI and BDI

Where are sales for my product category and brand strongest and weakest? Data related to this question are displayed in a marketing dashboard using two indexes: (1) category development index and (2) brand development index.

Your Challenge You have joined the marketing team for Hawaiian Punch, the top fruit punch drink sold in the United States. The brand has been marketed to mothers with children under 12 years old. The majority of Hawaiian Punch sales are in gallon and 2-liter bottles. Your assignment is to examine the brand's performance and identify growth opportunities for the Hawaiian Punch brand among households that consume prepared fruit drinks (the product category).

Your marketing dashboard displays a category development index and a brand development index provided by a syndicated marketing research firm. Each index is based on the calculations below:

$$\text{Category Development Index (CDI)} = \frac{\text{Percent of a product category's total U.S. sales in a market segment}}{\text{Percent of the total U.S. population in a market segment}} \times 100$$

$$\text{Brand Development Index (BDI)} = \frac{\text{Percent of a brand's total U.S. sales in a market segment}}{\text{Percent of the total U.S. population in a market segment}} \times 100$$

A CDI over 100 indicates above-average product category purchases by a market segment. A number under 100 indicates below-average purchases. A BDI over 100 indicates a strong brand position in a segment; a number under 100 indicates a weak brand position.

You are interested in CDI and BDI displays for four household segments that consume prepared fruit drinks: (1) households without children; (2) households with children 6 years old or under; (3) households with children aged 7 to 12; and (4) households with children aged 13 to 18.

Your Findings The BDI and CDI measures displayed below show that Hawaiian Punch is consumed by households with children, and particularly households with children under age 12. The Hawaiian Punch BDI is over 100 for both segments—not surprising since the brand is marketed to these segments. Households with children 13 to 18 years old evidence high fruit drink consumption with a CDI over 100. But Hawaiian Punch is relatively weak in this segment with a BDI under 100.

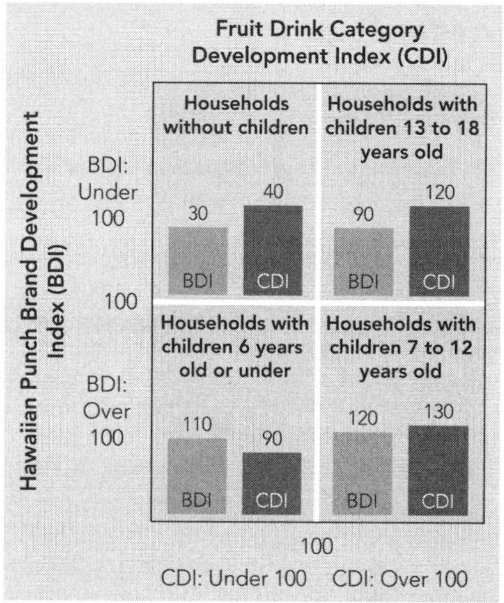

Your Action An opportunity for Hawaiian Punch exists among households with children 13 to 18 years old—teenagers. You might propose that Hawaiian Punch be repositioned for teens. In addition, you might recommend that Hawaiian Punch be packaged in single-serve cans or bottles to attract this segment, much like soft drinks. Teens might also be targeted for advertising and promotions.

Finding New Customers Produce companies have begun marketing and packaging prunes as dried plums to attract younger buyers. Harley-Davidson has tailored a marketing program to encourage women to take up biking, thus doubling the number of potential customers for its motorcycles.

Increasing a Product's Use Promoting more frequent usage has been a strategy of Campbell Soup Company. Because soup consumption rises in the winter and declines during the summer, the company now advertises more heavily in warm months to encourage consumers to think of soup as more than a cold-weather food.

dried 干燥的，干缩的；consumption 消费。

Similarly, the Florida Orange Growers Association advocates drinking orange juice throughout the day rather than for breakfast only.

Creating a New Use Situation Finding new uses for an existing product has been the strategy behind Dockers, the U.S. market leader in casual pants. Originally intended as a single pant for every situation, Dockers now promotes different looks for different usage situations: work, weekend, dress, and golf.

产品重新定位
Repositioning the Product

为了增加销售量，一个公司通常会对产品和产品线进行重新定位。产品重新定位就是改变产品在消费者心目中与其他竞争产品相对的位置。公司可以通过改变营销组合四要素中的一个或多个要素实现产品重新定位。

Often a company decides to reposition its product or product line in an attempt to bolster sales. *Product repositioning* changes the place a product occupies in a consumer's mind relative to competitive products. A firm can reposition a product by changing one or more of the four marketing mix elements. Four factors that trigger the need for a repositioning action are discussed next.

Reacting to a Competitor's Position One reason to reposition a product is because a competitor's entrenched position is adversely affecting sales and market share. New Balance, Inc. successfully repositioned its athletic shoes to focus on fit, durability, and comfort rather than competing head-on against Nike and Adidas on fashion and professional sports. The company offers an expansive range of shoes and it networks with podiatrists, not sport celebrities.

Reaching a New Market When Unilever introduced iced tea in Britain, sales were disappointing. British consumers viewed it as leftover hot tea, not suitable for drinking. The company made its tea carbonated and repositioned it as a cold soft drink to compete as a carbonated beverage and sales improved. Johnson & Johnson effectively repositioned St. Joseph aspirin from one for infants to an adult low-strength aspirin to reduce the risk of heart problems or strokes.

Catching a Rising Trend Changing consumer trends also lead to repositioning. Growing consumer interest in foods that offer health and dietary benefits is an example. Many products have been repositioned to capitalize on this trend. Quaker

The Milk Processor Education Program (MilkPEP) promotes the nutritional qualities of milk, notably vitamin D, in its advertising.

The Milk Processor Education Program
www.whymilk.com

reposition 重新定位（产品或服务）; occupy 占领，占据; dietary 饮食的，有关饮食的。

Making Responsible Decisions >>>>>>>> ethics

Consumer Economics of Downsizing—Get Less, Pay More

For more than 30 years, Starkist put 6.5 ounces of tuna into its regular-sized can. Today, Starkist puts 6.125 ounces of tuna into its can, but charges the same price. Frito-Lay (Doritos and Lay's snack chips), Procter & Gamble (Pampers and Luvs disposable diapers), Nestlé (Poland Spring and Calistoga bottled waters) have whittled away at package contents 5 to 10 percent while maintaining their products' package size, dimensions, and prices. Kimberly-Clark cut its retail price on its jumbo pack of Huggies diapers from $13.50 to $12.50, but reduced the number of diapers per pack from 48 to 42. Georgia-Pacific reduced the content of its Brawny paper towel six-roll pack by 20 percent without lowering the price.

Consumer advocates charge that downsizing the content of packages while maintaining prices is a subtle and unannounced way of taking advantage of consumer buying habits. They also say downsizing is a price increase in disguise and deceptive, but legal. Manufacturers argue that this practice is a way of keeping prices from rising beyond psychological barriers for their products.

Is downsizing an unethical practice if manufacturers do not inform consumers that the package contents are less than they were previously?

Oats makes the FDA-approved claim that oatmeal, as part of a low-saturated-fat, low-cholesterol diet, may reduce the risk of heart disease. Calcium-enriched products, such as Kraft American cheese and Uncle Ben's Calcium Plus rice, emphasize healthy bone structure for children and adults. Weight-conscious consumers have embraced low-fat and low-calorie diets in growing numbers. Today, most food and beverage companies offer reduced-fat and low-calorie versions of their products.

在产品重新定位中，公司可以改变其提供给购买者的价值，进而实现价值升级或价值降级。**价值升级**是指通过增添附加性能或采用高质量原料来提高产品或产品线价值。

Changing the Value Offered In repositioning a product, a company can decide to change the value it offers buyers and trade up or down. **Trading up** involves adding value to the product (or line) through additional features or higher-quality materials. Michelin, Bridgestone, and Goodyear have done this with a "run-flat" tire that can travel up to 50 miles at 55 miles per hour after suffering total air loss. Dog food manufacturers, such as Ralston Purina, also have traded up by offering super-premium foods based on "life-stage nutrition." Mass merchandisers, such as Target and JCPenney, can trade up by adding a designer clothes section to their stores.

Trading down involves reducing the number of features, quality, or price. For example, airlines have added more seats, thus reducing legroom, and limited snack service. Trading down exists when companies engage in *downsizing*—reducing the package content without changing package size and maintaining or increasing the package price. Firms are criticized for this practice, as described in the Making Responsible Decisions box.

learning review

4. How does a product manager help manage a product's life cycle?
5. What does "creating a new use situation" mean in managing a product's life cycle?
6. Explain the difference between trading up and trading down in repositioning.

oatmeal 燕麦片；emphasize 强调，重视。

BRANDING AND BRAND MANAGEMENT

LO3

产品营销中一个基本的决策就是**品牌化**，即组织运用一个名字、短语、图案、符号或其组合以使自己的产品与竞争产品区别开来。**品牌名称**是用以区分一个销售者产品和服务的任何词汇、"设计"（图案、声音、形状或颜色）或它们的组合。

A basic decision in marketing products is **branding**, in which an organization uses a name, phrase, design, symbols, or combination of these to identify its products and distinguish them from those of competitors. A **brand name** is any word, device (design, sound, shape, or color), or combination of these used to distinguish a seller's goods or services. Some brand names can be spoken, such as a Gatorade or Rollerblade. Other brand names cannot be spoken, such as the colored apple (the *logotype* or *logo*) that Apple puts on its machines and in its ads. A **trade name** is a commercial, legal name under which a company does business. The Coca-Cola Company is the trade name of that firm.

A **trademark** identifies that a firm has legally registered its brand name or trade name so the firm has its exclusive use, thereby preventing others from using it. In the United States, trademarks are registered with the U.S. Patent and Trademark Office and protected under the Lanham Act. A well-known trademark can help a company advertise its offerings to customers and develop their brand loyalty.

Because a good trademark can help sell a product, *product counterfeiting*, which involves low-cost copies of popular brands not manufactured by the original producer, is a serious problem. Counterfeit products can steal sales from the original manufacturer or harm the company's reputation. U.S. companies lose between $200 billion and $250 billion each year to counterfeit products. To counteract counterfeiting, the U.S. government passed the *Stop Counterfeiting in Manufactured Goods Act* (2006), which makes counterfeiters subject to 20-year prison sentences and $15 million in fines.

Consumers may benefit most from branding. Recognizing competing products by distinct trademarks allows them to be more efficient shoppers. Consumers can recognize and avoid products with which they are dissatisfied, while becoming loyal

Can you describe the brand personality traits for these two brands?

got2b
www.got2b.com

Degree Fine Fragrance Collection
www.degree.com

distinguish 区分，辨别，分清；registered 注册的，登记过的；counterfeiting 仿造的，假冒的。

to other, more satisfying brands. As discussed in Chapter 3, brand loyalty often eases consumers' decision making by eliminating the need for an external search.

品牌个性与品牌资产
Brand Personality and Brand Equity

产品经理认识到，品牌不仅可以提供产品认知，而且也有助于使自己的产品与竞争产品区分开来。成功塑造的品牌都呈现出一种**品牌个性**，即使品牌名称与某些人类个性特征相联系。

Product managers recognize that brands offer more than product identification and a means to distinguish their products from competitors. Successful and established brands take on a **brand personality**, a set of human characteristics associated with a brand name. Research shows that consumers often assign personality traits to products—traditional, romantic, rugged, sophisticated, rebellious—and choose brands that are consistent with their own or desired self-image. Marketers can and do imbue a brand with a personality through advertising that depicts a certain user or usage situation and conveys certain emotions or feelings to be associated with the brand. For example, the personality traits associated with Coca-Cola are all-American and real; with Pepsi, young and exciting; and with Dr Pepper, nonconforming and unique. The traits often linked to Harley-Davidson are masculinity, defiance, and rugged individualism.

Brand name importance to a company has led to a concept called **brand equity**, the added value a brand name gives to a product beyond the functional benefits provided. This value has two distinct advantages. First, brand equity provides a competitive advantage. The Sunkist brand implies quality fruit. The Disney name defines children's entertainment. A second advantage is that consumers are often willing to pay a higher price for a product with brand equity. Brand equity, in this instance, is represented by the premium a consumer will pay for one brand over another when the functional benefits provided are identical. Gillette razors and blades, Bose audio systems, Duracell batteries, and Louis Vuitton luggage all enjoy a price premium arising from brand equity.

Creating Brand Equity Brand equity doesn't just happen. It is carefully crafted and nurtured by marketing programs that forge strong, favorable, and unique customer associations and experiences with a brand. Brand equity resides in the minds of consumers and results from what they have learned, felt, seen, and heard about a brand over time. Marketers recognize that brand equity is not easily or quickly achieved. Rather, it arises from a sequential building process consisting of four steps (see Figure 8–6).

- The first step is to develop positive brand awareness and an association of the brand in consumers' minds with a product class or need to give the brand an identity. Gatorade and Kleenex have achieved this in the sports drink and facial tissue product classes, respectively.
- Next, a marketer must establish a brand's meaning in the minds of consumers. Meaning arises from what a brand stands for and has two dimensions—a functional, performance-related dimension and an abstract, imagery-related dimension. Nike has done this through continuous product development and improvement and its links to peak athletic performance in its integrated marketing communications program.
- The third step is to elicit the proper consumer responses to a brand's identity and meaning. Here attention is placed on how consumers think and feel about a brand. Thinking focuses on a brand's perceived quality, credibility, and superiority relative to other brands. Feeling

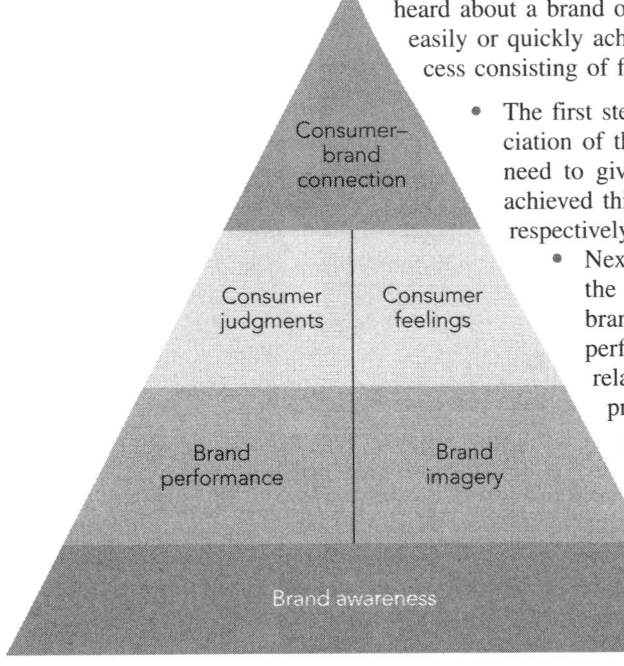

FIGURE 8–6
The customer-based brand equity pyramid shows the four-step building process that forges strong, favorable, and unique customer associations with a brand.

eliminate 排除，消除；sophisticated 复杂的，精致的；rebellious 叛逆的，不听话的。

Ralph Lauren has a long-term licensing agreement with Luxottica Group, S.P.A. of Milan for the design, production, and worldwide distribution of prescription frames and sunglasses under the Ralph Lauren brand. The agreement is an ideal fit for both companies. Ralph Lauren is a leader in the design, marketing, and distribution of premium lifestyle products. Luxottica is the global leader in the premium and luxury eyewear sector.

Luxottica Group, S.P.A.
www.luxottica.com

Ralph Lauren Corporation
www.ralphlauren.com

relates to the consumer's emotional reaction to a brand. Michelin elicits both responses for its tires. Not only is Michelin thought of as a credible and superior-quality brand, but consumers also acknowledge a warm and secure feeling of safety, comfort, and self-assurance without worry or concern about the brand.

- The final, and most difficult, step is to create a consumer–brand connection evident in an intense, active loyalty relationship between consumers and the brand. A deep psychological bond characterizes a consumer–brand connection and the personal identification customers have with the brand. Brands that have achieved this status include Harley-Davidson, Apple, and eBay.

Valuing Brand Equity Brand equity also provides a financial advantage for the brand owner. Successful, established brand names, such as Gillette, Nike, Gatorade, and Nokia, have an economic value in the sense that they are intangible assets. The recognition that brands are assets is apparent in the decision to buy and sell brands. For example, Triarc Companies bought the Snapple brand from Quaker Oats for $300 million and sold it three years later to Cadbury Schweppes for $900 million. This example illustrates that brands, unlike physical assets that depreciate with time and use, can appreciate in value when effectively marketed. However, brands can lose value when they are not managed properly. Consider the purchase and sale of Lender's Bagels. Kellogg bought the brand for $466 million only to sell it to Aurora Foods for $275 million three years later following deteriorating sales and profits.

品牌资产可以带来具有财务收益的许可机会。**品牌许可**是指一家公司（许可方）允许另一家公司（被许可方）通过缴纳特许费的形式在产品或服务中使用其品牌名称或商标而签署的协议。

Financially lucrative brand licensing opportunities arise from brand equity. **Brand licensing** is a contractual agreement whereby one company (licensor) allows its brand name(s) or trademark(s) to be used with products or services offered by another company (licensee) for a royalty or fee. For example, Playboy earns more than $260 million licensing its name and logo for merchandise. Disney makes billions of dollars each year licensing its characters for children's toys, apparel, and games. Licensing fees for Winnie the Pooh alone exceed $3 billion annually.

Successful brand licensing requires careful marketing analysis to assure a proper fit between the licensor's brand and the licensee's products. World-renowned designer Ralph Lauren earns over $140 million each year by licensing his Ralph Lauren, Polo, and Chaps brands for dozens of products, including paint by Glidden, furniture by Henredon, footwear by Rockport, eyewear by Luxottica, and fragrances by L'Oreal. Mistakes, such as Kleenex diapers, Bic perfume, and Domino's fruit-favored bubble gum, are a few examples of poor matches and licensing failures.

---

evident 明显的，明白的。

Going Online

Have an Idea for a Brand or Trade Name? Check It Out

More than a million brand names or trade names are registered with the U.S. Patent and Trademark Office. Thousands more are registered each year.

An important step in choosing a brand or trade name is to determine whether the name has been already registered. The U.S. Patent and Trademark Office (www.uspto.gov) offers a valuable service by allowing individuals and companies to quickly check to see if a name has been registered.

Do you have an idea for a brand or trade name for a new snack, software package, retail outlet, or service? Check to see if the name has been registered by clicking "Trademarks," then "Search." Enter your brand name to find out if someone has registered your chosen name(s).

选择一个好品牌名称
Picking a Good Brand Name

We take brand names such as Red Bull, iPod, and Axe for granted, but it is often a difficult and expensive process to pick a good name. Companies will spend between $25,000 and $100,000 to identify and test a new brand name. Five criteria are mentioned most often when selecting a good brand name.

- 名称应该表明产品的利益。
- 名称应该便于记忆、与众不同且积极向上。
- 名称应该与公司和产品的形象相吻合。
- 名称不能违反法律和规章。
- 最后一点，名称应该简明且富有感情色彩。

- *The name should suggest the product benefits.* For example, Accutron (watches), Easy Off (oven cleaner), Glass Plus (glass cleaner), Cling-Free (antistatic cloth for drying clothes), Chevy Volt (electric car), and Tidy Bowl (toilet bowl cleaner) all clearly describe the benefits of purchasing the product.
- *The name should be memorable, distinctive, and positive.* In the auto industry, when a competitor has a memorable name, others quickly imitate. When Ford named a car the Mustang, Pintos, Colts, and Broncos soon followed. The Thunderbird name led to the Phoenix, Eagle, Sunbird, and Firebird.
- *The name should fit the company or product image.* Sharp is a name that can apply to audio and video equipment. Bufferin, Excedrin, Anacin, and Nuprin are scientific-sounding names, good for analgesics. Eveready, Duracell, and DieHard suggest reliability and longevity—two qualities consumers want in a battery.
- *The name should have no legal or regulatory restrictions.* Legal restrictions produce trademark infringement suits, and regulatory restrictions arise through improper use of words. For example, the U.S. Food and Drug Administration discourages the use of the word *heart* in food brand names. This restriction led to changing the name of Kellogg's Heartwise cereal to Fiberwise, and Clorox's Hidden Valley Ranch Take Heart Salad Dressing had to be modified to Hidden Valley Ranch Low-Fat Salad Dressing. Increasingly, brand names need a corresponding address on the Internet. This further complicates name selection because about 140 million domain names are already registered.
- *The name should be simple* (such as Bold laundry detergent, Axe deodorant and body spray, and Bic pens) *and should be emotional* (such as Joy and Obsession perfumes). In the development of names for international use, having a nonmeaningful brand name has been considered a benefit. A name such as Exxon does not have any prior impressions or undesirable images among a diverse world population of different languages and cultures. The 7Up name is another matter. In Shanghai, China, the phrase means "death through drinking" in the local dialect. Sales have suffered as a result.

Do you have an idea for a brand name? If you do, check to see if the name has been already registered with the U.S. Patent and Trademark Office by visiting its Web site described in the Going Online box.

---

memorable 显著的，难忘的；distinctive 有特色的，与众不同的；regulatory 具有监管权的，监管的。

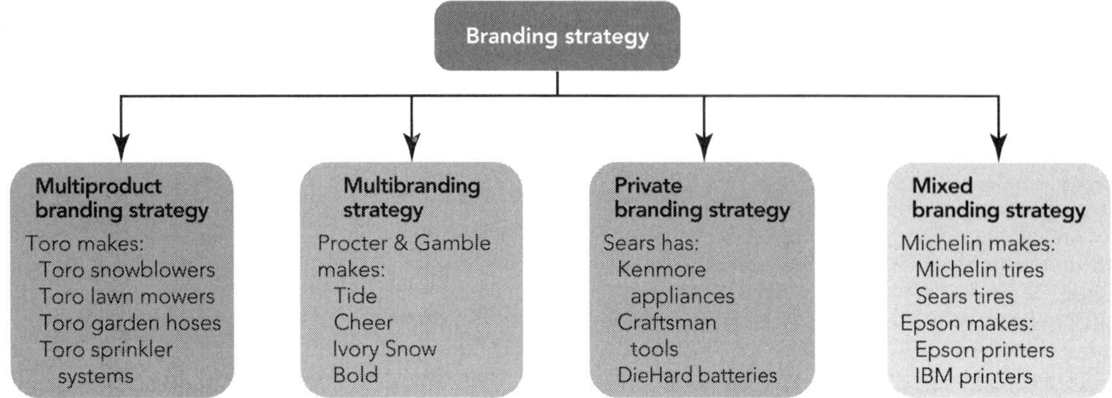

FIGURE 8–7
Alternative branding strategies are available to marketers. Each has advantages and disadvantages described in the text.

多产品统一品牌是指一个公司对一个产品大类中的所有产品都使用同一个品牌。这种方法有时称为家族品牌，当用公司商号做品牌时又称为公司品牌。

品牌战略
Branding Strategies

Companies can employ several different branding strategies, including multiproduct branding, multibranding, private branding, or mixed branding (see Figure 8–7).

Multiproduct Branding Strategy With **multiproduct branding**, a company uses one name for all its products in a product class. This approach is sometimes called *family branding* or *corporate branding* when the company's trade name is used. For example, Microsoft, General Electric, Samsung, Gerber, and Sony engage in corporate branding—the company's trade name and brand name are identical. Church & Dwight uses the Arm & Hammer family brand name for all its products featuring baking soda as the primary ingredient.

There are several advantages to multiproduct branding. Capitalizing again on brand equity, consumers who have a good experience with the product will transfer this favorable attitude to other items in the product class with the same name. Therefore, this brand strategy makes possible *product line extensions*, the practice of using a current brand name to enter a new market segment in its product class. Campbell Soup Company employs a multiproduct branding strategy with soup line extensions. It offers regular Campbell soup, home-cooking style, and chunky varieties and more than 100 soup flavors. This strategy can result in lower advertising and promotion costs because the same name is used on all products, thus raising the level of brand awareness. A risk with line extension is that sales of an extension may come at the expense of other items in the company's product line. Line extensions work best when they provide incremental company revenue by taking sales away from competing brands or attracting new buyers.

Some multiproduct branding companies employ *subbranding*, which combines a corporate or family brand with a new brand, to distinguish a part of its product line from others. Gatorade successfully used subbranding with the introduction of Gatorade G2. Similarly, Porsche successfully markets its higher-end Porsche Carrera and its lower-end Porsche Boxster.

A strong brand equity also allows for *brand extension*, the practice of using a current brand name to enter a different product class. For instance, equity in the Huggies family brand name has allowed Kimberly-Clark to successfully extend its name to a full line of baby and toddler toiletries. Honda's established name for motor vehicles has extended easily to snowblowers, lawn mowers, marine engines, and snowmobiles.

However, there is a risk with brand extensions. Too many uses for one brand name can dilute the meaning of a brand for consumers. Marketing experts claim this has happened to the Arm & Hammer brand given its use for toothpaste, laundry detergent, gum, cat litter, air freshener, carpet deodorizer, and antiperspirant.

---

multiproduct 多产品，多种产品；extension 延伸，扩大；equity 资产。

Kimberly-Clark was able to leverage the strong Huggies brand equity among mothers when it introduced a full line of baby and toddler toiletries first in the United States and then globally. The success of this brand extension strategy is evident in the $500 million in annual sales generated globally.

Kimberly-Clark Corporation
www.kimberly-clark.com

A variation on brand extensions is the practice of *co-branding*; the pairing of two brand names of two manufacturers on a single product. For example, Hershey Foods has teamed with General Mills to offer a co-branded breakfast cereal called Reese's Peanut Butter Puffs and with Nabisco to provide Chips Ahoy! cookies using Hershey's chocolate morsels. Co-branding benefits firms by allowing them to enter new product classes and capitalize on an already established brand name in that product class.

Multibranding Strategy Alternately, a company can engage in **multibranding**, which involves giving each product a distinct name. Multibranding is a useful strategy when each brand is intended for a different market segment. P&G makes Camay soap for those concerned with soft skin and Safeguard for those who want deodorant protection. Black & Decker markets its line of tools for the household do-it-yourselfer segment with the Black & Decker name but uses the DeWalt name for its professional tool line. Disney uses the Miramax and Touchstone Pictures names for films directed at adults and its Disney name for children's films.

Multibranding is applied in a variety of ways. Some companies array their brands on the basis of price-quality segments. Marriott International offers 15 hotel and resort brands, each suited for a particular traveler experience and budget. To illustrate, Marriott Marquis hotels and Vacation Clubs offer luxury amenities at a premium price. Marriott and Renaissance hotels offer medium- to high-priced accommodations. Courtyard hotels and TownPlace Suites appeal to economy-minded travelers, whereas the Fairfield Inn is for those on a very low travel budget.

Other multibrand companies introduce new product brands as defensive moves to counteract competition. Called *fighting brands*, their chief purpose is to confront competitor brands. For instance, Frito-Lay introduced Santitas brand tortilla chip to go head-to-head against regional tortilla chip brands that were biting into sales of its flagship Doritos and Tostitos brand tortilla chips. Ford launched its Fusion brand to halt the defection of Ford owners who were buying competitors' midsize cars. According to Ford's car group marketing manager, "Every year we're losing around 50,000 people from our products to competitors' midsize cars. We're losing Mustang, Focus, and Taurus owners. Fusion is our interceptor."

Compared with the multiproduct strategy, advertising and promotion costs tend to be higher with multibranding. The company must generate awareness among consumers and retailers for each new brand name without the benefit of any previous impressions. The advantages of this strategy are that each brand is unique to each market segment and there is no risk that a product failure will affect other products in the line. Still, some large multibrand firms have found that the complexity and expense of implementing this strategy can outweigh the benefits. For example, Unilever recently pruned its brands from some 1,600 to 400 through product deletion and sales to other companies.

一个公司可使用**自有品牌**，通常称为私有标签或中间商品牌，即制造商生产产品但以批发商或是零售商的品牌出售。

Private Branding Strategy A company uses **private branding**, often called *private labeling* or *reseller branding*, when it manufactures products but sells them under the brand name of a wholesaler or retailer. Rayovac, Paragon Trade Brands, and Ralcorp Holdings are major suppliers of private-label alkaline batteries, diapers, and grocery products, respectively. Radio Shack, Costco, Sears, Wal-Mart, and Kroger are large retailers that have their own brand names. Private branding is popular because it typically produces high profits for manufacturers and resellers. Consumers also buy them. It is estimated that one of every five items purchased at U.S. supermarkets, drugstores, and mass merchandisers bears a private brand.

deodorant 除臭的，防臭的；array 陈列，布置。

Black & Decker uses a multibranding strategy to reach different market segments. Black & Decker markets its tool line for the do-it-yourselfers with the Black & Decker name, but uses the DeWalt name for professionals.

Black & Decker
www.blackanddecker.com

Mixed Branding Strategy A fourth branding strategy is **mixed branding**, where a firm markets products under its own name(s) and that of a reseller because the segment attracted to the reseller is different from its own market. Beauty and fragrance marketer Elizabeth Arden is an example. The company sells its Elizabeth Arden brand through department stores and a line of skin care products at Wal-Mart with the "skinsimple" brand name. Companies such as Del Monte, Whirlpool, and Dial produce private brands of pet foods, home appliances, and soap, respectively, for resellers.

产品包装与标签
PACKAGING AND LABELING PRODUCTS

包装是产品的一个组成部分，包括盛放代售产品的容器以及传递产品信息的标签。**标签**是包装不可或缺的部分，其主要用来识别产品或品牌、生产者、生产时间与地点、使用方法以及产品内容与成分。

LO4

The **packaging** component of a product refers to any container in which it is offered for sale and on which label information is conveyed. A **label** is an integral part of the package and typically identifies the product or brand, who made it, where and when it was made, how it is to be used, and package contents and ingredients. To a great extent, the customer's first exposure to a product is the package and label and both are an expensive and important part of marketing strategy. For Pez Candy, Inc., the character head-on-a-stick plastic container that dispenses a miniature tablet candy is the central element of its marketing strategy as described in the Marketing Matters box.

运用包装与标签创造顾客价值和竞争优势
Creating Customer Value and Competitive Advantage through Packaging and Labeling

Packaging and labeling cost U.S. companies more than $120 billion annually and account for about 15 cents of every dollar spent by consumers for products. Despite

convey 传达，表达，传递；container 箱子，盒子。

Marketing Matters > > > > > > customer value

Creating Customer Value through Packaging—Pez Heads Dispense More Than Candy

Customer value can assume numerous forms. For Pez Candy, Inc. (www.pez.com), customer value manifests itself in some 450 Pez character candy dispensers. Each refillable dispenser ejects tasty candy tablets in a variety of flavors that delight preteens and teens alike in more than 60 countries.

Pez was formulated in 1927 by Austrian food mogul Edward Haas III and successfully sold in Europe as an adult breath mint. Pez, which comes from the German word for peppermint, *pfefferminz*, was originally packaged in a hygienic, headless plastic dispenser. Pez first appeared in the United States in 1953 with a headless dispenser, marketed to adults. After conducting extensive marketing research, Pez was repositioned with fruit flavors, repackaged with licensed character heads on top of the dispenser, and remarketed as a children's product in the mid-1950s. Since then, most top-level licensed characters and hundreds of other characters have become Pez heads. Consumers eat more than 3 billion Pez tablets annually in the United States alone, and company sales growth exceeds that of the candy industry as a whole.

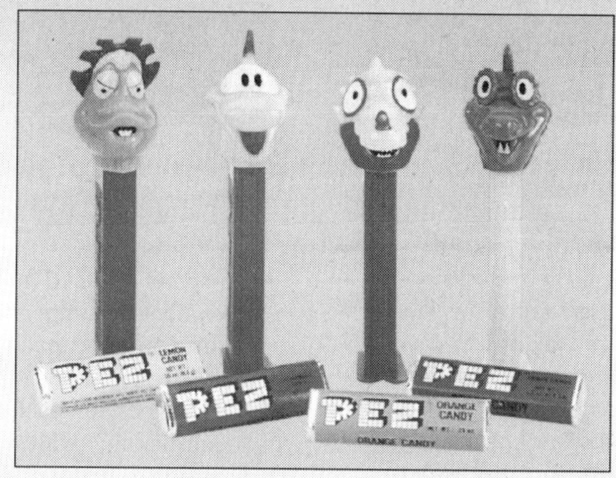

The unique Pez package dispenses a "use experience" for its customers beyond the candy itself, namely, fun. And fun translates into a 98 percent awareness level for Pez among teenagers and 89 percent among mothers with children. Pez has not advertised its product for years. With that kind of awareness, who needs advertising?

the cost, packaging and labeling are essential because both provide important benefits for the manufacturer, retailer, and ultimate consumer. Packaging and labeling also can provide a competitive advantage.

Communication Benefits A major benefit of packaging is the label information on it conveyed to the consumer, such as directions on how, where, and when to use the product and the source and composition of the product, which is needed to satisfy legal requirements of product disclosure. For example, the labeling system for packaged and processed foods in the United States provides a uniform format for nutritional and dietary information. Many packaged foods contain informative recipes to promote usage of the product. Campbell Soup estimates that the green bean casserole recipe on its cream of mushroom soup can accounts for $20 million in soup sales each year! Other information consists of seals and symbols, either government required or commercial seals of approval (such as the Good Housekeeping seal).

Quick. Name a soft drink.

Can you name this soft-drink brand? If you can, then the package has fulfilled its purpose.

Functional Benefits Packaging often plays a functional role, such as storage, convenience, protection, or product quality. Storing food containers is one example, and beverage companies have developed lighter and easier ways to stack products on shelves and in refrigerators. Examples

competitive 竞争的，角逐的；disclosure 公开，透露；functional 功能的。

Which chip stacks up better? Frito-Lay's launch of Lay's Stax potato crisps to compete against Procter & Gamble's Pringles illustrates the role of packaging in product and brand management.

include Coca-Cola beverage packs designed to fit neatly onto refrigerator shelves and Ocean Spray Cranberries' rectangular juice bottles that allow 10 units per package versus 8 of its former round bottles.

The convenience dimension of packaging is increasingly important. Kraft Miracle Whip salad dressing, Heinz ketchup, and Skippy Squeez'It peanut butter are sold in squeeze bottles; microwave popcorn has been a major market success; and Chicken of the Sea tuna and Folgers coffee are packaged in single-serving portions. Nabisco offers portion-control package sizes for the convenience of weight-conscious consumers. It offers 100-calorie packs of Oreos, Cheese Nips, and other products in individual pouches.

Consumer protection is another important function of packaging, including the development of tamper-resistant containers. Today, companies commonly use safety seals or pop-tops that reveal previous opening. But, no package is truly tamper resistant. U.S. law now provides for maximum penalties of life imprisonment and $250,000 fines for package tampering. Consumer protection through labeling exists in "open dating," which states the expected shelf life of the product.

Functional features of packaging also can affect product quality. Procter & Gamble's Pringles, with its cylindrical packaging, offers uniform chips, minimal breakage, and for some consumers, better value for the money than flex-bag packages for chips. Not to be outdone, Frito-Lay, the world's leading producer of snack chips, "stands up" to Pringles with its own line of Lay's Stax potato crisps. Consumers are the final judge of which chip stacks up better.

Perceptual Benefits A third component of packaging and labeling is the perception created in the consumer's mind. Package and label shape, color, and graphics distinguish one brand from another, convey a brand's positioning, and build brand equity. According to the director of marketing for L'eggs hosiery, "Packaging is important to the positioning and equity of the L'eggs brand." Why? Packaging and labeling have been shown to enhance brand recognition and facilitate the formation of strong, favorable, and unique brand associations. This logic applies to Celestial Seasonings' packaging and labeling, which uses delicate illustrations, soft and warm colors, and quotations about life to reinforce the brand's positioning as a New Age, natural herbal tea.

Successful marketers recognize that changes in packages and labels can update and uphold a brand's image in the customer's mind. Just Born, Inc., a candy manufacturer of such brands as Jelly Joes and Mike and Ike Treats, is a case in point. For many years these brands were sold in old-fashioned black-and-white packages. However, when the packaging was updated to four color, with animated grape and cherry characters, sales jumped 25 percent. Pepsi-Cola has embarked on a packaging change to uphold its image among teens and young adults. Beginning in 2007, Pepsi-Cola debuted new graphics on its cans and bottles every three or four weeks to reflect the "fun, optimistic, and youthful spirit" of the brand to its customers.

The distinctive design of Celestial Seasonings' tea boxes reinforces the brand's positioning as a New Age, natural herbal tea.

Because labels list a product's source, brands competing in the global marketplace can benefit from "country of origin or manufacture" perceptions. Consumers tend to have stereotypes about country-product pairings that they judge "best"—English tea, French perfume, Italian leather, and Japanese electronics—which can affect a brand's image.

---

beverage 饮料；facilitate 促进，使便利。

Increasingly, Chinese firms are adopting the English language and Roman letters for their brand labels. This is being done because of a common perception in many Asian countries that "things Western are good."

包装与标签的挑战和应对
Packaging and Labeling Challenges and Responses

Package and label designers face four challenges. They are: (1) the continuing need to connect with customers; (2) environmental concerns; (3) health, safety, and security issues; and (4) cost reduction.

Connecting with Customers Packages and labels must be continually updated to connect with customers. The challenge lies in creating aesthetic and functional design features that attract customer attention and deliver customer value in their use. If done right, the rewards can be huge.

For example, the marketing team responsible for Kleenex tissues converted its standard rectangular box into an oval shape with colorful seasonal graphics. Sales soared with this aesthetic change in packaging. After months of in-home research, Kraft product managers discovered that consumers often transferred Chips Ahoy! cookies to jars for easy access and to avoid staleness. The company solved both problems by creating a patented resealable opening on the top of the bag. The result? Sales of the new package doubled that of the old package with the addition of this functional feature.

随着全球范围内对不断增加的固体垃圾及缺乏切实可行的垃圾掩埋地点问题的广泛关注，包装材料的数量、构成及处理问题也日益引起人们的重视。

Environmental Concerns Because of widespread worldwide concern about the growth of solid waste and the shortage of viable landfill sites, the amount, composition, and disposal of packaging material continues to receive much attention. For example, PepsiCo, Coca-Cola, and Nestlé have decreased the amount of plastic in their beverage bottles to reduce solid waste. Recycling packaging material is another major thrust. Procter & Gamble now uses recycled cardboard in over 70 percent of its paper packaging. Its Spic and Span liquid cleaner is packaged in 100 percent recycled material. Other firms, such as Wal-Mart, are emphasizing the use of less packaging material. In 2008, the company began working with its 600,000 global suppliers to reduce overall packaging and shipping material by 5 percent by 2013.

European countries have been trendsetters concerning packaging guidelines and environmental sensitivity. Many of these guidelines now exist in provisions governing trade to and within the European Union. In Germany, 80 percent of packaging material must be collected, and 80 percent of this amount must be recycled or reused to reduce solid waste in landfills. U.S. firms marketing in Europe have responded to these guidelines and ultimately benefited U.S. consumers.

Health, Safety, and Security Issues A third challenge involves the growing health, safety, and security concerns of packaging materials. Today, most U.S. and European consumers believe companies should make sure products and their packages are safe and secure, regardless of the cost, and companies are responding in numerous ways. Most butane lighters sold today, like those made by Scripto, contain a child-resistant safety latch to prevent misuse and accidental fire. Child-proof caps on pharmaceutical products and household cleaners and sealed lids on food packages are now common. New packaging technology and materials that extend a product's *shelf life* (the time a product can be stored) and prevent spoilage continue to be developed with special applications for developing countries.

Cost Reduction About 80 percent of packaging material used in the world consists of paper, plastics, and glass. As the cost of these materials rises, companies are constantly challenged to find innovative ways to cut packaging costs while delivering value to their customers. As an example, Hewlett-Packard reduced the

---

reduction 减少，降低；aesthetic 美的，艺术的，美感的；rectangular 长方形的，矩形的。

size and weight of its Photosmart product package and shipping container. Through design and material changes, packaging material costs fell by more than 50 percent. Shipping costs per unit dropped 41 percent.

产品担保 PRODUCT WARRANTY

A final component for product consideration is the **warranty**, which is a statement indicating the liability of the manufacturer for product deficiencies. There are various types of product warranties with different implications for manufacturers and customers.

America's Best Warranty

Hyundai has made a commitment to offer the best automobile warranty for buyers.

Hyundai Motor America
www.hyundaiusa.com

Some companies like Hyundai, offer *express warranties*, which are written statements of liabilities. In recent years, the FTC has required greater disclosure on express warranties to indicate whether the warranty is a limited-coverage or full-coverage alternative. A *limited-coverage warranty* specifically states the bounds of coverage and, more important, areas of noncoverage. A *full warranty* has no limits of noncoverage. The *Magnuson-Moss Warranty/FTC Improvement Act* (1975) regulates the content of consumer warranties and so has strengthened consumer rights with regard to warranties. Increasingly, manufacturers are being held to *implied warranties*, which assign responsibility for product deficiencies to the manufacturer. Studies show that the type of warranty can affect a consumer's product evaluation. Brands with limited warranties tend to receive less positive evaluations compared with full-warranty items.

Warranties are also important in light of product liability claims. In the early part of the 20th century, the courts protected companies. The trend now is toward "strict liability" rulings, where a manufacturer is liable for any product defect, whether it followed reasonable research standards or not. This issue remains hotly contested between companies and consumer advocates.

Warranties represent much more to the buyer than just protection from negative consequences—they offer a significant marketing advantage for the producer. Sears has built a strong reputation for its Craftsman tool line with a simple warranty: If you break a tool, it's replaced with no questions asked. Zippo has an equally simple warranty: "If it ever fails, we'll fix it free."

learning review

7. What are the five criteria mentioned most often when selecting a good brand name?
8. What are the three major benefits of packaging and labeling?
9. What is the difference between an expressed and an implied warranty?

LEARNING OBJECTIVES REVIEW

LO1 *Explain the product life-cycle concept.*
The product life cycle describes the stages a new product goes through in the marketplace: introduction, growth, maturity, and decline. Product sales growth and profitability differ at each stage, and marketing managers have marketing objectives and marketing mix strategies unique to each stage based on consumer behavior and competitive factors. In the introductory stage, the need is to establish primary demand, whereas the growth stage requires selective demand strategies. In the maturity stage, the need is to maintain market share; the decline stage necessitates a deletion or harvesting strategy. Some important aspects of product life cycles are (*a*) their length, (*b*) the shape of the sales curve, (*c*) how they vary by product classes and forms, and (*d*) the rate at which consumers adopt products.

LO2 *Identify ways that marketing executives manage a product's life cycle.*
Marketing executives manage a product's life cycle three ways. First, they can modify the product itself by altering its characteristics, such as product quality, performance, or appearance. Second, they can modify the market by finding new customers for the product, increasing a product's use among existing customers, or creating new use situations for the product. Finally, they can reposition the product using any one or a combination of marketing mix elements. Four factors trigger a repositioning

warranty 保证，担保；deficiency 缺点，缺陷；implication 意义。

action. They include reacting to a competitor's position, reaching a new market, catching a rising trend, and changing the value offered to consumers.

LO3 *Recognize the importance of branding and alternative branding strategies.*
A basic decision in marketing products is branding, in which an organization uses a name, phrase, design, symbols, or a combination of these to identify its products and distinguish them from those of its competitors. Product managers recognize that brands offer more than product identification and a means to distinguish their products from competitors. Successful and established brands take on a brand personality and acquire brand equity—the added value a given brand name gives to a product beyond the functional benefits provided—that is crafted and nurtured by marketing programs that forge strong, favorable, and unique consumer associations with a brand. A good brand name should suggest the product benefits, be memorable, fit the company or product image, be free of legal restrictions, and be simple and emotional. Companies can and do employ several different branding strategies. With multiproduct branding, a company uses one name for all its products in a product class. A multibranding strategy involves giving each product a distinct name. A company uses private branding when it manufactures products but sells them under the brand name of a wholesaler or retailer. Finally, a company can employ mixed branding, where it markets products under its own name(s) and that of a reseller.

LO4 *Describe the role of packaging, labeling, and warranties in the marketing of a product.*
Packaging, labeling, and warranties play numerous roles in the marketing of a product. The packaging component of a product refers to any container in which it is offered for sale and on which label information is conveyed. Manufacturers, retailers, and consumers acknowledge that packaging and labeling provide communication, functional, and perceptual benefits. Contemporary packaging and labeling challenges include (*a*) the continuing need to connect with customers, (*b*) environmental concerns, (*c*) health, safety, and security issues, and (*d*) cost reduction. Warranties indicate the liability of the manufacturer for product deficiencies and are an important element of product and brand management.

FOCUSING ON KEY TERMS

brand equity
brand licensing
brand name
brand personality
branding
label
market modification
mixed branding
multibranding
multiproduct branding
packaging
private branding
product class
product form
product life cycle
product modification
trade name
trademark
trading down
trading up
warranty

APPLYING MARKETING KNOWLEDGE

1 Listed here are three different products in various stages of the product life cycle. What marketing strategies would you suggest to these companies? (*a*) Canon digital cameras—growth stage, (*b*) Hewlett Packard tablet computers—introductory stage, and (*c*) handheld manual can openers—decline stage.

2 It has often been suggested that products are intentionally made to break down or wear out. Is this strategy a planned product modification approach?

3 The product manager of GE is reviewing the penetration of trash compactors in American homes. After more than two decades in existence, this product is in relatively few homes. What problems can account for this poor acceptance? What is the shape of the trash compactor life cycle?

4 For years, Ferrari has been known as the manufacturer of expensive luxury automobiles. The company plans to attract the major segment of the car-buying market who purchase medium-priced automobiles. As Ferrari considers this trading-down strategy, what branding strategy would you recommend? What are the trade-offs to consider with your strategy?

5 The nature of product warranties has changed as the federal court system reassesses the meaning of warranties. How does the regulatory trend toward warranties affect product development?

building your marketing plan

For the product offering in your marketing plan,

1 Identify (*a*) its stage in the product life cycle and (*b*) key marketing mix actions that might be appropriate, as shown in Figure 8–1.

2 Develop (*a*) branding and (*b*) packaging strategies, if appropriate for your offering.

"We're fortunate right now at BMW in that all of our products are new and competitive," says Jim McDowell, vice president of marketing at BMW, as he explains BMW's product life cycle. "Now, how do you do that? You have to introduce new models over time. You have to logically plan out the introductions over time, so you're not changing a whole model range at the same time you're changing another model range."

BMW's strategy is to keep its products in the introduction and growth stages by periodically introducing new models in each of its product lines. In fact, in contrast to many auto manufacturers that launch a new model and then leave it unchanged, BMW works continually to improve its existing products. Explains McDowell, "Anyone can sell a lot of cars the first year, when a car is new. It is our challenge to constantly improve the car and to continuously find new innovative ways to market it."

BMW—THE COMPANY AND ITS PRODUCTS

BMW started in 1916 as a manufacturer of airplane engines. "When you look at our roundel, the BMW symbol, it is a blue-and-white circle," says McDowell, "that is meant to represent the spinning propeller on a plane, to remind us of our heritage." Since then the company has added motorcycle and automobile production. Today, BMW is one of the preeminent luxury car manufacturers in Europe, North America, and the world.

BMW produces several lines of cars including the 1, 3, 5, 6, and 7 series, the Z line of roadsters, the X line of "sport activity vehicles," and the M line of "motor sport" sedans. Currently, the United States, Germany, and the United Kingdom are BMW's largest markets. BMW introduced its 1 series—a compact car designed to compete with the Volkswagen Golf in Europe and the Rabbit in the United States—to attract a new younger audience. In addition BMW owns the MINI and Rolls-Royce brands. Combined sales of BMW, MINI, and Rolls-Royce exceed $59 billion and are expected to increase 40 percent by 2020. Reasons for the growing popularity of BMW include high-performance products, unique advertising, an award-winning Web site, innovations such as "smart" electronics that "learn" what the driver prefers, and new vehicles such as the V-series, which will compete with minivans.

PRODUCT LIFE CYCLE

BMW cars typically have a product life cycle of seven years. To keep products in the introductory and growth stages, BMW regularly introduces new models for each of its series to keep the entire series "new." For instance, with the 3 series, it will introduce the new sedan model one year, the new coupe the next year, then the convertible, then the station wagon, and then the sport hatchback. That's a new product introduction for five of the seven years of the product life cycle. McDowell explains, "So, even though we have seven-year life cycles, we constantly try to make the cars meaningfully different and new about every three years. And that involves adding features and other capabilities to the cars as well." How well does this strategy work? BMW often sees its best sales numbers in either the sixth or seventh year after the product introduction.

As global sales have increased, BMW has become aware of some international product life-cycle differences. For example, it has discovered that some competitive products have life cycles that are shorter or longer than seven years. In Sweden and Britain, automotive product life cycles are eight years, while in Japan they are typically only four years long.

BMW uses a system of "product advocates" to manage the marketing efforts of its product lines. McDowell explains that a series advocate would actually use and drive that series and would constantly be thinking "How can I better serve my customer?" In addition to modifying each model throughout the product life cycle, BMW modifies the markets it serves. For example, during the past 10 years BMW has expanded its market by appealing to a much larger percentage of women, African Americans, Asians, and Hispanics. BMW's positioning strategy is the same worldwide and that is to offer high-performance, luxury vehicles to individuals. "You won't find it as a taxi or a fleet car," says McDowell. Generally, once a model is positioned and introduced, BMW avoids trying to reposition it.

BRANDING

"BMW is fortunate—we don't have too much of a dilemma as to what we're going to call our cars." McDowell is referring to BMW's trademark naming system that consists of the product line number and the motor type. For example, the designation "328" tells you the car is in the 3 series and the engine is 2.8 liters in size. BMW has found this naming system to be clear and logical and can be easily understood around the world.

The Z, X, and M series don't quite fit in with this system. BMW had a tradition of building experimental, open-air cars and calling them Z's, so when one of them was selected for production, BMW decided to continue with the Z name. For the sport activity vehicles BMW also used a letter name—the X series—since the four-wheel-drive vehicle didn't fit with the sedan-oriented 1, 3, 5, 6, and 7 series. The M series has a 20-year history with BMW as the line with the luxury and racing-level performance. The lettered series now includes the Z4, X3, X5, M3, M5, and M6. Compared to the evocative names many car manufacturers choose to garner excitement for their new models, the BMW numbers and letters are viewed as a simple and effective branding strategy.

In the past BMW has built a brand personality for its vehicles with high-visibility product placements. BMW products, for example, have been featured in four James Bond films. Similarly, BMW hired master directors to create a series of Internet-based mini-movies called "The Hire"–which featured "the ultimate driving machine" and edgy actors. The movies were so successful and attracted so much attention from consumers and industry experts that the movies have been placed into the Museum of Modern Art. Other marketing programs that contribute to the BMW brand personality include the BMW Art Car Collection, created by internationally acclaimed artists; sponsorship of America's Cup and Formula 1 Series racing teams; and events such as the BMW Golf Club International tournament.

MANAGING THE PRODUCT THROUGH THE WEB—THE WAVE OF THE FUTURE

One of the ways BMW is improving its product offerings even further is through its innovative Web site (www.bmwusa.com). At the site, customers can learn about the particular models, e-mail questions, and request literature or test-drives from their local BMW dealership. What really sets BMW's Web site apart from other car manufacturers, though, is the ability for customers to configure a car to their own specifications (interior choices, exterior choices, engine, packages, and options) and then transfer that information to their local dealer. As Carol Burrows, product communications manager for BMW, explains, "The BMW Web site is an integrated part of the overall marketing strategy for BMW. The full range of products can be seen and interacted with online. We offer pricing options online. Customers can go to their local dealership via the Web site to further discuss costs for purchase of a car. And it is a distribution channel for information that allows people access to the information 24 hours a day at their convenience." The ultimate extravagance in buying a car is having everything customized to the owner's preferences. Today, 80 percent of European buyers and 30 percent of U.S. buyers use the BMW Web site to choose from 350 model variations, 500 options, 90 exterior colors, and 170 interior trims to create their perfect vehicle!

Questions

1 Compare the product life cycle described by BMW for its cars to the product life cycle shown in Figure 8–1. How are they (*a*) similar and (*b*) dissimilar?

2 Based on BMW's typical product life cycle, what marketing strategies are appropriate for the 3 series? The X5?

3 Which of the three ways to manage the product life cycle does BMW utilize with its products—modifying the product, modifying the market, or repositioning the product?

4 How would you describe BMW's branding strategy (manufacturer branding, private branding, or mixed branding)? Why?

5 Go to the BMW Web site (www.bmwusa.com) and design a car to your own specifications. How does this enable you as a customer to evaluate the product differently than would be otherwise possible?

CIRQUE DU SOLEIL®
KOOZA™
CIRQUE DU SOLEIL®

9 服务营销 Services Marketing

LEARNING OBJECTIVES

After reading this chapter you should be able to:

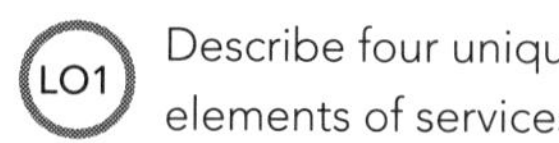

LO1 Describe four unique elements of services.

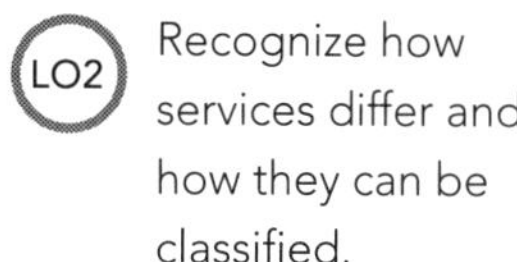

LO2 Recognize how services differ and how they can be classified.

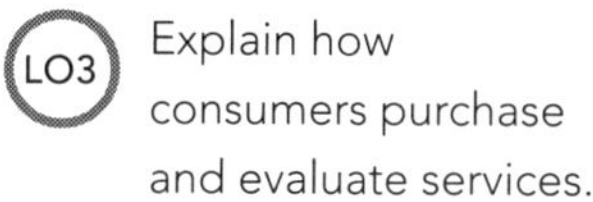

LO3 Explain how consumers purchase and evaluate services.

LO4 Develop a customer contact audit to identify service advantages.

LO5 Explain the role of the eight Ps in the services marketing mix.

LO6 Discuss the important roles of internal marketing and customer experience management in service organizations.

获得真正的服务
SERVICES GET REAL!

Have you recently heard someone use the words *fake* or *phony* or even *counterfeit*? It's a common concern of many consumers today and part of a growing trend that will change most services. As authors James Gilmore and Joseph Pine explain, "The more contrived the world seems, the more we all demand what is real." In their book, *Authenticity,* they suggest that what consumers really want are engaging, personal, memorable, and authentic offerings. Cirque du Soleil, for example, offers a completely new art form, but manages the perception of authenticity by combining the original elements of street performance, the circus, and live theater.

Our economy has shifted from the production of goods, to the delivery of services, and more recently, to the staging of experiences. The "experience economy" focuses on performing services that provide a unique experience. Disneyland, for example, was one of the first service organizations to recognize the importance of sights, sounds, tastes, aromas, and textures in creating experiences for consumers. Hard Rock Café and Planet Hollywood restaurants used a similar approach to sell dining experiences that included food, music, entertainment, and a fun environment. Many other companies such as Starbucks and Apple stores also have strategies designed to provide compelling experiences.

The growth of produced, sometimes contrived experiences, however, has led consumers to search for sincere, or authentic, offerings. Consumers are no longer content with affordable, high-quality purchases; they want offerings that reflect their self-image—who they are or who they aspire to be. How can service providers ensure that they are offering authentic experiences? There are many options!

First, services that facilitate customization increase authenticity. Creating custom playlists for iPods, for example, allows consumers to participate in the production process. Another option is to provide personal interaction rather than automation. ATMs, kiosks, credit card readers, and Web sites are not viewed as authentic. Geico advertisements address this issue by emphasizing that "insurance specialists are available 24/7." Authenticity can also result from a social process that allows consumers to share their interests. YouTube, MySpace, and Facebook are obvious outlets, although companies can create their own social networking opportunities. The advertising agency for Doritos, for example, created a contest to encourage consumers to submit their own TV commercial, and then ran the winning entry during the Super Bowl. Finally, institutions that provide services must manage any dimension of their reputation that might influence perceptions of authenticity.

Disneyland 迪斯尼乐园；authenticity 确实性，真实性。

If you look closely you'll see that many services are adding dimensions of authenticity. Nike's customization service, NIKEiD.com, allows customers to design shoes according to their exact preferences. Progressive Insurance provides personal attention by sending Immediate Response Vehicles to the site of an accident so an adjuster can handle emergencies, arrange for new transportation, and provide the policyholder with a check—in person. Retailers such as Bloomingdale's now facilitate the social aspects of shopping by providing dressing rooms large enough for friends and electronic mirrors that allow texting anyone whose opinion might be needed.

As the actions of Disneyland, Planet Hollywood, NikeiD, Progressive Insurance, Cirque du Soleil, and many others illustrate, the marketing of services is dynamic and exciting. In this chapter, we discuss how services differ from traditional products (goods), how consumers make purchase decisions, and the ways in which the marketing mix is used.

服务的独特性
THE UNIQUENESS OF SERVICES

服务是指一个组织提供给消费者的用以交换的无形活动或利益，比如航空旅行、理财咨询或汽车维修等。

Services are intangible activities or benefits (such as airline trips, financial advice, or automobile repair) that an organization provides to satisfy consumers' needs in exchange for money or something else of value.

Services have become a significant component of the global economy and one of the most important components of the U.S. economy. The World Trade Organization estimates that all countries exported merchandise valued at $13.5 trillion and commercial services valued at $3.2 trillion. In the United States, more than 42 percent of the gross domestic product (GDP) now comes from services. As shown in Figure 9–1, the value of services in the economy has increased more than 70 percent since 1990. Projections indicate that by 2016, goods-producing firms will employ 21.7 million people and service firms will employ more than 130 million. Services also

FIGURE 9–1
Services are now a larger part of the U.S. gross domestic product (GDP) than goods.

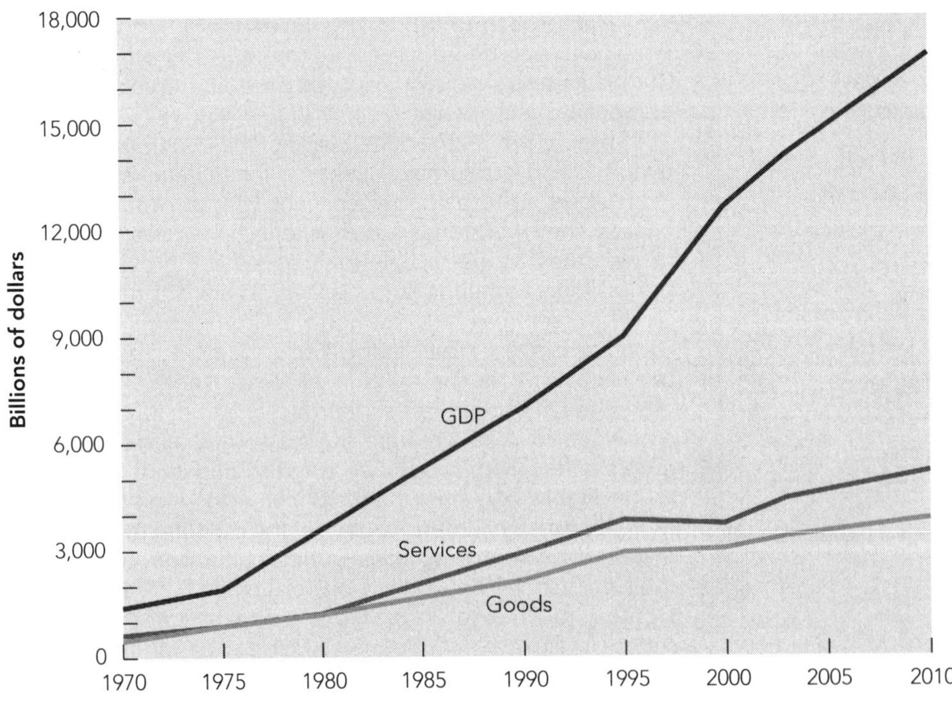

intangible 无形的；economy（国家或地区的）经济，经济体制。

represent a large export business—the $512 billion of services exports in 2009 is one of the few areas in which the United States has a trade surplus.

The growth of this sector is the result of increased demand for services that have been available in the past and the increasing interest in new services. Concierge services, for example, have been popular in hotels such as the Breakers in Palm Beach, Florida, which has a staff of 11 concierges, and the Ritz-Carlton, which offers concierges who specialize in technology support, shopping, and medical issues. Outside the hotel industry, Famous Friends Concierge service offers clients opportunities to fly on private jets with celebrities, private check-in at resorts, hard-to-get restaurant and nightclub reservations, and special event tickets. Concierge services are even available for daily lifestyle needs. Ace Concierge, for example, will schedule car maintenance, pick up and deliver dry cleaning, walk your dog, or even shop for groceries and gifts! Other new services include: The Luggage Club, which offers door-to-door luggage delivery to and from 220 countries; Virgin Galactic, which offers private space travel; and friendorfollow.com, which helps you determine if the people you are following on Twitter are also following you. These firms and many others like them are examples of the imaginative services that will play a role in our economy in the future.

服务4I
The Four I's of Services

服务有4个独特的要素：无形性、易变性、不可分离性和不可贮存性。这4个要素被称为**服务的4I**。

LO1

There are four unique elements to services—*intangibility, inconsistency, inseparability,* and *inventory*—referred to as the **four I's of services**.

Intangibility Services are intangible; that is, they can't be held, touched, or seen before the purchase decision. In contrast, before purchasing a traditional product, a consumer can touch a box of laundry detergent, kick the tire of an automobile, or sample a new breakfast cereal. Because services tend to be a performance rather than an object, they are much more difficult for consumers to evaluate. To help consumers assess and compare services, marketers try to make them tangible or show the benefits of using the service.

The Singapore Airlines ad shows the airline's new seats and emphasizes their size and other tangible benefits. American Express also provides tangible benefits by allowing cardmembers to earn points for redemption of airline tickets, electronics, and gift cards through its Membership Rewards® program.

Why do many services emphasize their tangible benefits? The answer appears in the text.

Singapore Airlines
www.singaporeair.com

American Express Co.
www.americanexpress.com

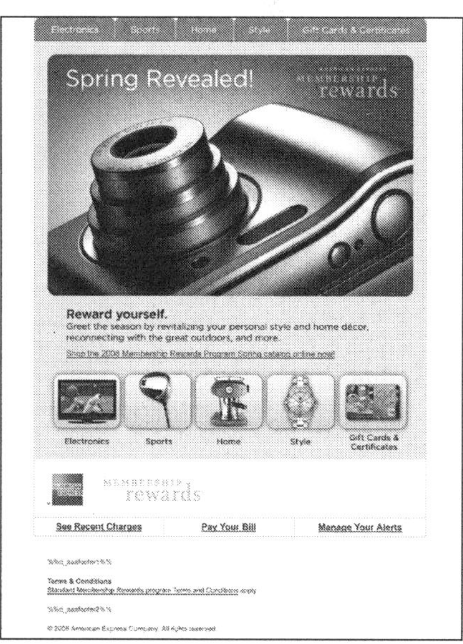

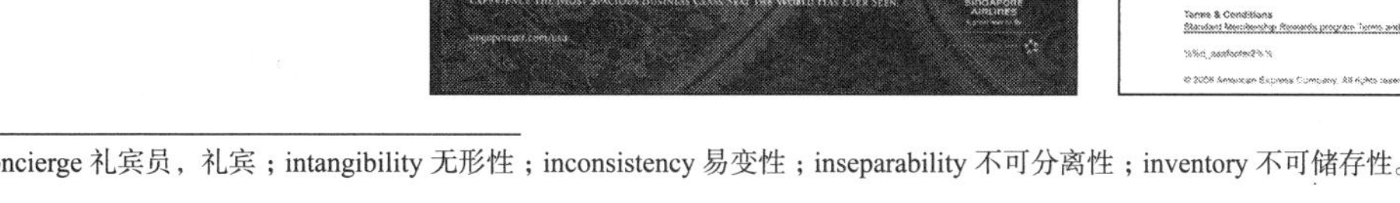

concierge 礼宾员，礼宾；intangibility 无形性；inconsistency 易变性；inseparability 不可分离性；inventory 不可储存性。

Inconsistency Developing, pricing, promoting, and delivering services is challenging because the quality of a service is often inconsistent. Because services depend on the people who provide them, their quality varies with each person's capabilities and day-to-day job performance. Inconsistency is much more of a problem in services than it is with tangible goods. Tangible products can be good or bad in terms of quality, but with modern production lines the quality will at least be consistent. On the other hand, one day the Philadelphia Phillies baseball team may have great hitting and pitching and look like a pennant winner and the next day lose by 10 runs. Or a soprano at New York's Metropolitan Opera may have a bad cold and give a less-than-perfect performance. Whether the service involves tax assistance at H&R Block or guest relations at the Ritz-Carlton, organizations attempt to reduce inconsistency through standardization and training.

Inseparability A third difference between services and goods, and related to problems of consistency, is inseparability. In most cases, the consumer cannot (and does not) separate the deliverer of the service from the service itself. For example, to receive an education, a person may attend a university. The quality of the education may be high, but if the student has difficulty interacting with instructors, finds counseling services poor, or does not receive adequate library or computer assistance, he or she may not be satisfied with the educational experience. Students' evaluations of their education will be influenced primarily by their perceptions of instructors, counselors, librarians, and other people at the university. Allstate's reminder that "You're in good hands" emphasizes the importance of its agents.

The amount of interaction between the consumer and the service provider depends on the extent to which the consumer must be physically present to receive the service. Some services such as haircuts, golf lessons, medical diagnoses, and food service require the customer to participate in the delivery of the services. Other services such as car repair, dry cleaning, and waste disposal process tangible objects with less involvement from the customer. Finally, services such as banking, consulting, and insurance can now be delivered electronically, often requiring no face-to-face customer interaction. While this approach can create value for consumers, a disadvantage of some *self-service technologies* such as ATMs, grocery store scanning

People play an important role in the delivery of many services.

Allstate
www.allstate.com

---

counseling 咨询服务，咨询，辅导；evaluation 评估，评价；interaction 合作，互动。

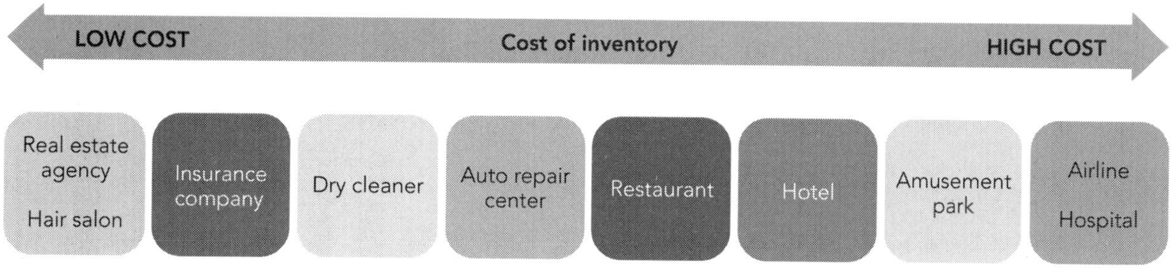

LOW COST — Cost of inventory — HIGH COST

Real estate agency / Hair salon	Insurance company	Dry cleaner	Auto repair center	Restaurant	Hotel	Amusement park	Airline / Hospital

FIGURE 9–2
Inventory carrying costs of services depend on the cost of employees and equipment.

stations, and self-service gas station pumps is that they are perceived as being less personal.

Inventory Inventory of services is different from that of goods. Inventory problems exist with goods because many items are perishable and because there are costs associated with handling inventory. With services, inventory carrying costs are more subjective and are related to **idle production capacity**, which is when the service provider is available but there is no demand. The inventory cost of a service is the cost of paying the person used to provide the service along with any needed equipment. If a physician is paid to see patients but no one schedules an appointment, the fixed cost of the idle physician's salary is a high inventory carrying cost. In some service businesses, however, the provider of the service is on commission (a Merrill Lynch stockbroker) or is a part-time employee (a clerk at Macy's). In these businesses, inventory carrying costs can be significantly lower or nonexistent because the idle production capacity can be cut back by reducing hours or having no salary to pay because of the commission compensation system. Figure 9–2 shows a scale of inventory carrying costs represented on the low end by real estate agencies and hair salons and on the high end by airlines and hospitals. The inventory carrying costs of airlines is high because of high-salaried pilots and very expensive equipment. In contrast, real estate agencies and hair salons have employees who work on commission and need little expensive equipment to conduct business. One reason service providers must maintain production capacity is because of the importance of time to today's customers.

服务连续体
The Service Continuum

在大多数情况下，4I 可以区分服务与商品，但是对于许多公司，我们却不能清楚区分它们究竟是属于服务性组织还是商品性组织。

LO2

The four I's differentiate services from goods in most cases, but many companies are not clearly service-based or good-based organizations. Is Hewlett-Packard a computer company or service business? Although Hewlett-Packard manufactures computers, printers, and other goods, many of the company's employees work in its services division providing systems integration, networking, consulting, education, and product support. What companies bring to the market ranges from the tangible to the intangible or good-dominant to service-dominant offerings referred to as the **service continuum** (Figure 9–3 on the next page).

Teaching, nursing, and the theater are intangible, service-dominant activities, and intangibility, inconsistency, inseparability, and inventory are major concerns in their marketing. Salt, neckties, and dog food are tangible goods, and the problems represented by the four I's are not relevant in their marketing. However, some businesses are a mix of intangible service and tangible good factors. A clothing tailor provides a service but also a good, the finished suit. How pleasant, courteous, and attentive the tailor is to the customer is an important component of the service, and how well the clothes fit is an important part of the product. As shown in Figure 9–3, a fast-food

perishable 易腐烂的，易变质的；significantly 显著地，明显地；necktie 领带，领结。

FIGURE 9–3
The service continuum shows how offerings can vary in their balance of goods and services.

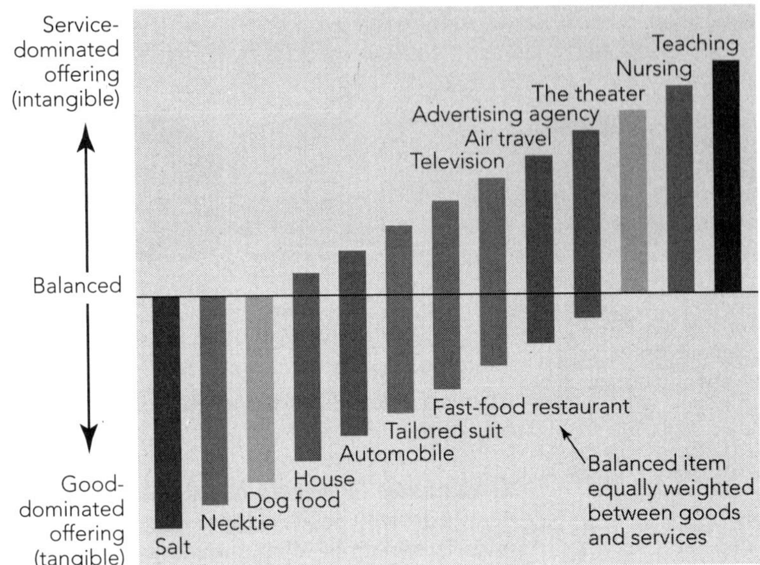

restaurant is about half tangible goods (the food) and half intangible services (courtesy, cleanliness, speed, and convenience).

For many businesses today it is useful to distinguish between their core product—either a good or a service—and supplementary services. A core service offering such as a bank account, for example, also has supplementary services such as deposit assistance, parking or drive-through availability, ATMs, and monthly statements. Supplementary services often allow service providers to differentiate their offering from competitors, and they may add value for consumers. While there are many potential supplementary services, key categories of supplementary services include consultation, finance, order taking, billing, and upgrades.

服务分类
Classifying Services

纵观全书，为了展现一个有组织的架构中的差异点与相似点，我们对营销组织、技能、观念都进行了分类。按照（1）服务是靠人还是靠设备传递，（2）是营利的还是非营利的以及（3）是否得到政府赞助，可以采用多种方法对服务进行分类。

Throughout this book, marketing organizations, techniques, and concepts are classified to show the differences and similarities in an organized framework. Services can also be classified in several ways, according to whether (1) they are delivered by people or equipment, (2) they are profit or nonprofit, or (3) they are government sponsored.

Delivery by People or Equipment As seen in Figure 9–4, many companies offer services. Professional services include management consulting firms such as Booz, Allen & Hamilton, or Accenture. Skilled labor is required to offer services such as Sears appliance repair or Sheraton catering service. Unskilled labor such as that used by Brinks store-security forces is also a service provided by people.

Equipment-based services do not have the marketing concerns of inconsistency because people are removed from the provision of the service. Electric utilities, for example, can provide service without frequent personal contact with customers. Motion picture theaters have projector operators that consumers never see. A growing number of customers use self-service technologies such as Home Depot's self checkout, Southwest Airlines' self check-in, and Schwab's online stock trading without interacting with any service employees.

Profit or Nonprofit Organizations Many organizations involved in services also distinguish themselves by their tax status as profit or nonprofit organiza-

tangible 有形的，切实的；supplementary 增补的，追加的。

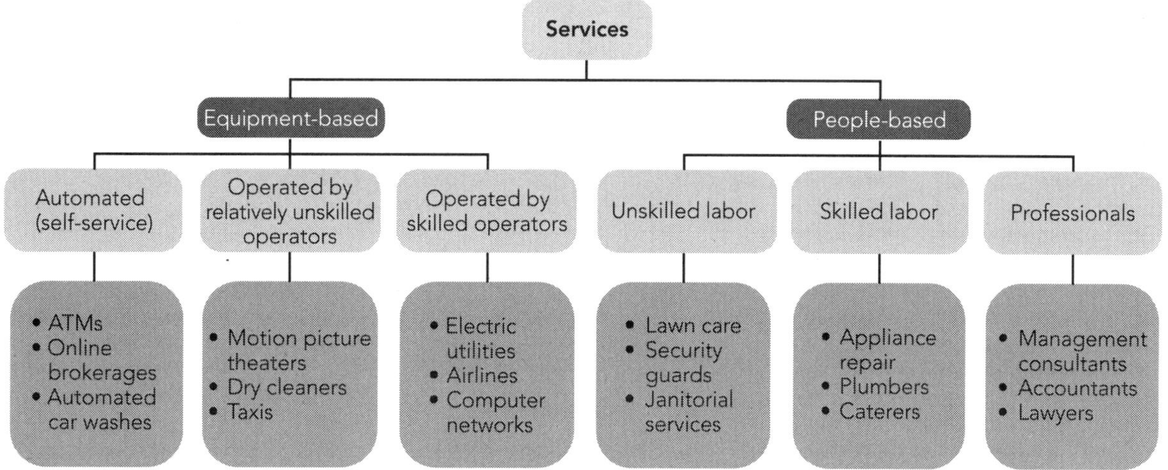

FIGURE 9–4
Services can be classified as equipment-based or people-based.

tions. In contrast to *profit organizations, nonprofit organizations'* excesses in revenue over expenses are not taxed or distributed to shareholders. When excess revenue exists, the money goes back into the organization's treasury to allow continuation of the service. Based on the corporate structure of the nonprofit organization, it may pay tax on revenue-generating holdings not directly related to its core mission. Nonprofit organizations in the United States now have expenditures of $1.9 trillion and employ 10 percent of the work force.

The United Way, Greenpeace, Outward Bound, The Salvation Army, and The Nature Conservancy are examples of nonprofit organizations. Historically, misconceptions have limited the use of marketing practices by such organizations. In recent years, however, nonprofit organizations have turned to marketing to help achieve their goals. The American Red Cross is a good example. To increase the organization's blood donor base, it recently hired an advertising agency to develop a campaign that includes advertising, direct marketing, public relations, and customer relationship management. Another agency was hired to focus on raising awareness in Hispanic communities through outdoor murals. Other promotional activities include

Nonprofit services often advertise.

Red Cross
www.redcross.org

United Nations Children's Fund
www.unicef.org

shareholder 股票持有人，股东；historically 从历史上看。

Marketing Matters > > > > > > customer value

Marketing Is a Must for 1.5 Million Nonprofits!

For many years "the M-word was not considered a good thing," explains Tom Peterson, the vice president for marketing at anti-poverty nonprofit Heifer International. As the 1.5 million charitable causes, universities, foundations, hospitals, and other nonprofits began to compete for members and donations, however, the need for marketing became apparent. The *Susan G. Komen for the Cure* organization has been one of the most successful to adapt. Its walks and races and partnerships with companies such as Yoplait, American Airlines, and Bank of America now generate more than $180 million annually and have allowed it to invest nearly $1 billion in cancer research and community outreach programs.

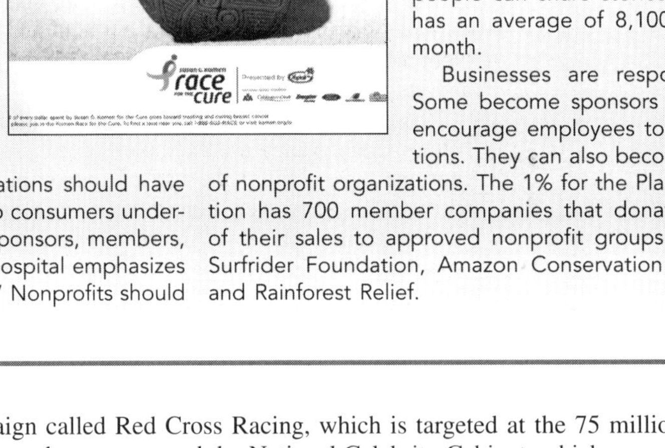

Nonprofit organizations should follow many of the same principles businesses use. First, they should create a specific and realistic mission statement. The Chicago Children's Museum's mission statement, for example, is "to create a community where play and learning connect." Second, the organizations should have a unique selling proposition that will help consumers understand what the organization will do for sponsors, members, or others. St. Jude Children's Research Hospital emphasizes that it is "Finding cures. Saving children." Nonprofits should also use common branding practices to select a name, logo, or tagline. The Museum of Modern Art's acronym "MoMA," the Komen pink ribbon logo, and the American Heart Association's tagline "Learn and Live" are all successful examples.

In the past many nonprofit organizations relied solely on free public service announcements for their communication. Now successful nonprofit budgets include advertising and Web-based tools to facilitate awareness and engagement. For example, the American Heart Association allocated $12 million to its advertising activities, which led to $40 million in contributions. Similarly, the March of Dimes created an online forum where people can share stories, and it now has an average of 8,100 posts each month.

Businesses are responding also. Some become sponsors of events or encourage employees to make donations. They can also become members of nonprofit organizations. The 1% for the Planet organization has 700 member companies that donate 1 percent of their sales to approved nonprofit groups such as the Surfrider Foundation, Amazon Conservation Association, and Rainforest Relief.

a campaign called Red Cross Racing, which is targeted at the 75 million NASCAR fans across the country, and the National Celebrity Cabinet, which currently includes Miley Cyrus, Pierce Brosnan, Heidi Klum, Eli Manning, and Patti LaBelle. The American Marketing Association Foundation recently began honoring extraordinary achievement in nonprofit marketing and recognized UNICEF for its "Tap Project" campaign that created 1 billion impressions about clean water. See the accompanying Marketing Matters box to learn about essential marketing activities for nonprofit organizations.

Government Sponsored A third way to classify services is based on whether they are government sponsored. Although there is no direct ownership and they are nonprofit organizations, governments at the federal, state, and local levels provide a broad range of services. The United States Postal Service, for example, has adopted many marketing activities. First-class postage revenue has declined as postal service customers have increased their use of the Internet to send e-mail, pay bills, and file taxes. Rather than fight the trend, however, the Postal Service is embracing the Internet. Its Web site, www.usps.com, allows consumers to buy stamps, arrange deliveries, and manage mailing lists online. In addition, new post office boxes are designed in a shoebox size to better meet the needs of consumers who shop for clothing and shoes online. Businesses can even buy stamps with their company brand and logo on them. The Postal Service's marketing activities are designed to allow it to compete

extraordinary 非凡的，优秀的，出色的；achievement 成就，成绩，功绩；stamp 邮票。

with UPS, FedEx, DHL, and foreign postal services for global package delivery business. Finally, you may have noticed that many post offices are now also retail outlets that sell collector stamps, Pony Express sweatshirts, and even neckties!

learning review

1. What are the four I's of services?
2. To eliminate service inconsistencies, companies rely on ________________ and ________________.
3. Would inventory carrying costs for an accounting firm with certified public accountants be (*a*) high, (*b*) low, or (*c*) nonexistent?

消费者如何购买服务
HOW CONSUMERS PURCHASE SERVICES

LO3

Colleges, hospitals, hotels, and even charities are facing an increasingly competitive environment. Successful service organizations, like successful product-oriented firms, must understand how the consumer makes a service purchase decision and quality evaluation and in what ways a company can present a differential advantage relative to competing offerings.

购买过程
The Purchase Process

Many aspects of services affect the consumer's evaluation of the purchase. Because services cannot be displayed, demonstrated, or illustrated, consumers cannot make a prepurchase evaluation of all the characteristics of services. Similarly, because service providers may vary in their delivery of a service, an evaluation of a service may change with each purchase. Figure 9–5 portrays how different types of goods and services are evaluated by consumers. Tangible goods such as clothing, jewelry, and furniture have *search* properties, such as color, size, and style, which can be determined before purchase. Services such as restaurants and child care have *experience* properties, which can be discerned only after purchase or during consumption. Finally, services provided by specialized professionals such as medical diagnoses and legal services have *credence* properties, or characteristics that the consumer may find impossible to evaluate even after purchase and consumption. To reduce the uncertainty created by these properties, service consumers turn to personal sources

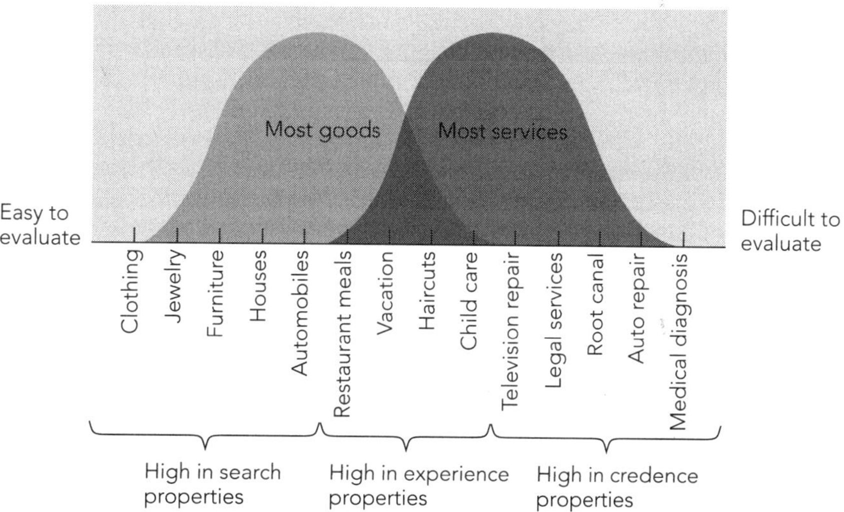

FIGURE 9–5
Consumers use search, experience, and credence properties to evaluate services.

demonstrate 展示，显示；discern 知道，了解。

of information such as early adopters, opinion leaders, and reference group members during the purchase decision process. The Mayo Clinic uses an organized, explicit approach called "evidence management" to present customers with concrete and convincing evidence of its strengths.

评估服务质量
Assessing Service Quality

一旦消费者尝试了服务，他将怎样评估呢？最主要的是将消费者对某项服务的预期与接受服务的实际体验进行比较。区别消费者预期与体验之间的差异可采用**缺口分析**方法。

Once a consumer tries a service, how is it evaluated? Primarily by comparing expectations about a service offering to the actual experience a consumer has with the service. Differences between the consumer's expectations and experience are identified through **gap analysis**. This type of analysis asks consumers to assess their expectations and experiences on dimensions of service quality such as those described in Figure 9–6. Expectations are influenced by word-of-mouth communications, personal needs, past experiences, and promotional activities, while actual experiences are determined by the way an organization delivers its service. The relative importance of the various dimensions of service quality varies by the type of service. What if someone is dissatisfied and complains? Recent studies suggest that customers who experience a "service failure" will increase their satisfaction if the service makes a satisfactory service recovery effort, although they may not increase their intent to repurchase. See the Going Online box for ideas about monitoring service failures.

顾客接触与关系营销
Customer Contact and Relationship Marketing

Consumers judge services on the entire sequence of steps that make up the service process. To focus on these steps, or "service encounters," a firm can develop a **customer contact audit**—a flowchart of the points of interaction between consumer and service provider. This is particularly important in high-contact services such as hotels, educational institutions, and automobile rental agencies. Figure 9–7 is a consumer contact audit for renting a car from Hertz. The interactions identified in a customer contact audit often serve as the basis for developing relationships with

FIGURE 9–6
There are five dimensions of service quality.

DIMENSION	DEFINITION	EXAMPLES OF QUESTIONS AIRLINE CUSTOMERS MIGHT ASK
Reliability	Ability to perform the promised service dependably and accurately	Is my flight on time?
Tangibles	Appearance of physical facilities, equipment, personnel, and communication materials	Are the gate, the plane, and the baggage area clean?
Responsiveness	Willingness to help customers and provide prompt service	Are the flight attendants willing to answer my questions?
Assurance	Knowledge and courtesy of employees and their ability to convey trust and confidence	Are the ticket counter attendants, flight attendants, and pilots knowledgeable about their jobs?
Empathy	Caring, individualized attention provided to customers	Do the employees determine if I have special seating, meal, baggage, transfer or rebooking needs?

evidence 证据，佐证，根据；institution 机构。

Going Online

How Can You Monitor Service Failure? Blog Watching!

Only 5 to 10 percent of dissatisfied customers choose to complain—the rest switch companies or make negative comments to other people. Increasingly, the forum for personal comments is on the Web through blogs or video sites. Domino's Pizza, for example, discovered that a negative video of two Domino's employees was viewed almost 1 million times on YouTube in just two days. Companies can monitor the postings for insights into service failures. Try using www.blogsearch.google.com or www.technorati.com to find blog entries about a service you know. There are also Web services such as www.buzzlogic.com and www.reputationdefender.com available to monitor blogs. Most public relations experts agree that it is best to respond to, rather than ignore, comments on the Web. Domino's posted a response on YouTube and created a Twitter account to try to counter the bad publicity and to answer questions. To find out what consumers are saying about your favorite brands try your own blog search now!

customers. Recent research suggests that authenticity and sincerity of the interactions affect the success of the relationships.

A Customer's Car Rental Activities A customer decides to rent a car and (1) contacts the rental company (see Figure 9–7). A customer service representative receives the information (2) and checks the availability of the car at the desired location. When the customer arrives at the rental site (3), the reservation system is again accessed, and the customer provides information regarding payment, address, and driver's license (4). A car is assigned to the customer (5), who proceeds by bus to the car pickup (6). On return to the rental location (7), the customer checks in (8),

FIGURE 9–7
Customer contact audit for a car rental (green shaded boxes indicate customer activity)

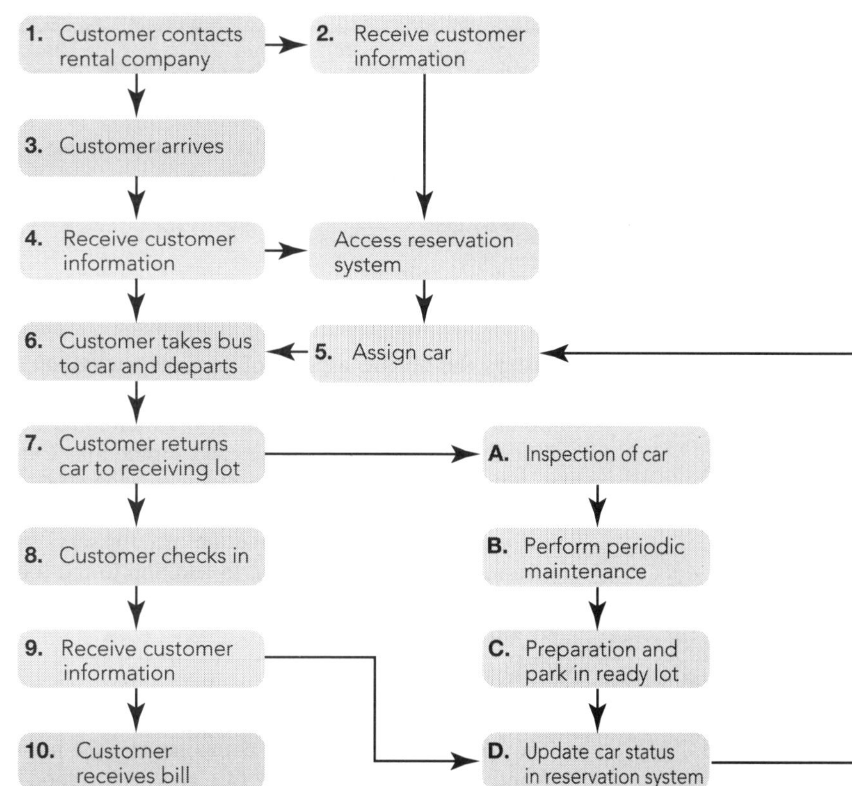

The Hertz Corporation
www.hertz.com

sincerity 诚恳，诚意。

a customer service representative collects information on mileage, gas consumption, and damages (9), and a bill is printed (10).

Each of the steps numbered 1 to 10 is a customer contact point where the tangible aspects of Hertz service are seen by the customer. Figure 9–7, however, also shows a series of steps lettered A to D that involve an inspection, maintenance, preparation for the next customer, and an update of the reservation system. These steps are essential in providing a clean, well-maintained car, but they are not points of customer interaction. To create a service advantage, Hertz must create a competitive advantage in the sequence of interactions with the customer. For example, Hertz has attempted to eliminate step 4 for some customers with its Hertz #1 Club—these customers simply show their drivers license and pick up the car's keys.

关系营销可以给消费者带来多种利益，比如持续得到固定服务者的服务、享受到定制化服务、由于重复购买而降低了不确定性的压力以及没有转换成本等。最近对消费者的调查显示，许多服务的消费者很愿意成为“关系客户”，他们要求关系应该实现忠诚度、利益、尊重隐私方面的协调，而且对将来服务提出了更高的预期。

Relationship Marketing The contact between a service provider and a customer represents a service encounter that is likely to influence the customer's assessment of the purchase. The number of encounters in a service experience may vary. Disney, for example, estimates that a park visitor will have 74 encounters with Disney employees in a single visit. These encounters represent opportunities to develop social bonds, or relationships, with customers. The relationship may also be developed through loyalty incentives such as airline frequent flyer programs. Relationship marketing provides several benefits for service customers including the continuity of a single provider, customized service delivery, reduced stress due to a repetitive purchase process, and an absence of switching costs. Recent surveys of consumers have indicated that while customers of many services are interested in being "relationship customers," they require that the relationship be balanced in terms of loyalty, benefits, and respect for privacy, and that there is a higher expectation of future use of the service. Understanding the service characteristics that lead to repeat purchases can help services managers allocate their resources to appropriate relationship marketing activities.

learning review

4. What are the differences between search, experience, and credence properties?
5. Hertz created its differential advantage at the points of ________________ in its customer contact audit.

服务营销管理
MANAGING THE MARKETING OF SERVICES

LO5

Just as the unique aspects of services necessitate changes in the consumer's purchase process, the marketing management process requires special adaptation. As we have seen in earlier chapters, the traditional marketing mix is composed of the four Ps: product, price, place, and promotion. Careful management of the four Ps is important when marketing services. However, the distinctive nature of services requires that other variables also be effectively managed by service marketers. The concept of an expanded marketing mix for services has been adopted by many service-marketing organizations. In addition to the four Ps, the services marketing mix includes people, physical environment, process, and productivity, or the **eight Ps of services marketing**.

产品（服务）
Product (Service)

The concepts of the product component of the marketing mix discussed in Chapters 7 and 8 apply equally well to Cheerios (a good) and to American Express (a

representative 代表，代理人；incentive 鼓励措施，激励机制；repetitive 重复多次的，反复性的。

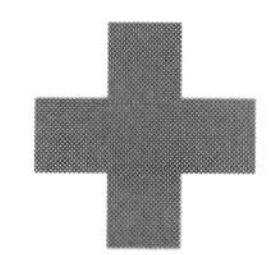

American Red Cross

Logos create service identities.

service). Managers of goods and services must design the product concept with the features and benefits desired by customers. An important aspect of the product concept is branding. Because services are intangible, and more difficult to describe, the brand name or identifying logo of the service organization is particularly important when a consumer makes a purchase decision. Therefore, service organizations, such as banks, hotels, rental car companies, and restaurants, rely on branding strategies to distinguish themselves in the minds of the consumers. Strong brand names and symbols are important for service marketers, not only as a means of differentiation, but also to convey an image of quality. A service firm with a well-established brand reputation will also find it easier to introduce new services than firms without a brand reputation.

Many services have undertaken creative branding activities. Hotels, for example, have begun to extend their branding efforts to consumers' homes through services such as *Hotels at Home*, which offers Westin's "Heavenly Bed," Hilton's bathrobes, and even artwork from Sheraton hotel rooms for consumers to buy and use at home. Look at the logos on this page to determine how successful some companies have been in branding their service with a name and symbol.

价 格
Price

In service businesses, price is referred to in many ways. Hospitals refer to *charges*; consultants, lawyers, physicians, and accountants to *fees*; airlines to *fares*; hotels to *rates*; and colleges and universities to *tuition*. Because of the intangible nature of services, price is often perceived by consumers as a possible indicator of the quality of the service. Do you expect higher quality from an expensive restaurant? Would you wonder about the quality of a $100 surgery? In many cases there may be few other available cues for the customer to judge, so price becomes very important as a quality indicator.

Pricing of services also goes beyond the traditional tasks of setting the selling price. When customers buy a service, they also consider nonmonetary costs, such as the mental and physical efforts required to consume the service. Service marketers must also try to minimize the effort required to purchase and use the service. Pricing also plays a role in balancing consumer demand for services. Many service businesses use **off-peak pricing**, which consists of charging different prices during different times of the day or during different days of the week to reflect variations in demand for the service. Airlines, for example, offer discounts for weekend travel, while movie theaters offer matinee prices.

Price influences perceptions of services.

地点（分销）
Place (Distribution)

Place or distribution is a major factor in developing a service marketing strategy because of the inseparability of services from the producer. Rarely are intermediaries involved in the distribution of a service; the distribution site and the service deliverer are the tangible components of the service. Until recently customers generally had to go to the service provider's physical location to purchase the service. Increased competition, however, has forced many service firms to consider the value of convenient distribution and to find new ways of distributing services to customers. Hairstyling chains such as Cost Cutters Family Hair Salon, tax preparation offices such as H&R Block, and accounting firms such as Ernst & Young all use multiple locations for the distribution of services. Technology is also being used to deliver services beyond the provider's physical locations. In the banking industry, for example, customers of participating banks using the Cirrus system

determine 确定，查明；perceive 察觉，发觉；indicator 指示物，指标。

can access any one of thousands of automatic teller machines throughout the United States. The availability of electronic distribution through the Internet also allows for global reach and coverage for a variety of services, including travel, education, entertainment, and insurance. With speed and convenience becoming increasingly important to customers when they select service providers, service firms can leverage the use of the Internet to deliver services on a 24/7 basis, in real time, on a global scale.

促 销
Promotion

The value of promotion, especially advertising, for many services is to show consumers the benefits of purchasing the service. It is valuable to stress availability, location, consistent quality, and efficient, courteous service, and to provide a physical representation of the service or a service encounter. The Accenture ad, for example, describes the benefits available to its customers—"High Performance. Delivered." The Space Adventures ad describes several benefits of spaceflight, such as traveling at 17,500 miles per hour and orbiting the Earth, and it provides a photo of the service encounter—a private astronaut in space! In most cases promotional concerns of services are similar to those of products.

Another form of promotion, *publicity*, has played a major role in the promotional strategy of many service organizations. Nonprofit organizations such public schools, religious organizations, and hospitals, for example, often use publicity to disseminate their messages. For many of these organizations the most common form of publicity is the *public service announcement* (PSA) because it is free. As discussed later in Chapter 14, however, using PSAs as the foundation of a promotion program is unlikely to be effective because the timing and location of the PSA are under the control of the medium, not the organization.

Personal selling, sales promotion, and direct marketing can also play an important role in services marketing. Service firm representatives, such as hotel employees handling check-in, or wait-staff in restaurants, are often responsible for selling their services. Similarly, sales promotions such as coupons, free trials, and contests are often effective tools for service firms. Finally, direct marketing activities are often used to reach specific audiences with interest in specific types of services. Increasingly, service firms are adopting an integrated marketing communications approach, similar to the approach used by many consumer packaged goods firms, to ensure that the

Services use promotional programs to communicate benefits and provide a representation of the service encounter.

Accenture
www.accenture.com

Space Adventures
www.spaceadventures.com

---

courteous 有礼貌的，谦恭的；orbiting 在……轨道上运行，环绕轨道运行。

many forms of promotion are providing a consistent message and contributing to a common objective.

人
People

LO6

Many services depend on people for the creation and delivery of the customer service experience. The nature of the interaction between employees and customers strongly influences the customer's perceptions of the service experience. Customers will often judge the quality of the service experience based on the performance of the people providing the service. This aspect of services marketing has led to a concept called internal marketing.

Internal marketing is based on the notion that a service organization must focus on its employees, or internal market, before successful programs can be directed at customers. Service firms need to ensure that employees have the attitude, skills, and commitment needed to meet customer expectations and to sustain customer loyalty. This idea suggests that employee development through recruitment, training, communication, coaching, management, and leadership are critical to the success of service organizations. Finally, many service organizations, such as educational institutions and athletic teams, must recognize that individual customer behavior may also influence the service outcome for other customers. These interactions suggest that the people element in services includes employees and all customers.

Once internal marketing programs have prepared employees for their interactions with customers, organizations can better manage the services they provide. **Customer experience management (CEM)** is the process of managing the entire customer experience with the company. CEM experts suggest that the process should be intentional and planned, consistent so that every experience is similar, differentiated from other service offerings, and relevant and valuable to the target market. Companies such as Disney, Southwest Airlines, the Ritz-Carlton, and Starbucks all manage the experience they offer customers. They integrate their activities to connect with customers at each contact point to move beyond customer relationships to customer loyalty. Zappos.com, an online shoe retailer, for example, requires that all employees complete a four-week customer loyalty training program to help deliver one of the company's core concepts—"Deliver WOW through service."

自然环境
Physical Environment

The appearance of the environment in which the service is delivered and where the firm and customer interact can influence the customer's perception of the service. The physical evidence of the service includes all the tangibles surrounding the service: the buildings, landscaping, vehicles, furnishings, signage, brochures, and equipment. Service firms need to manage physical evidence carefully and systematically to convey the proper impression of the service to the customer. This is sometimes referred to as impression, or evidence, management. For many services, the physical environment provides an opportunity for the firm to send consistent and strong messages about the nature of the service to be delivered.

过 程
Process

Process refers to the actual procedures, mechanisms, and flow of activities by which the service is created and delivered. The actual creation and delivery steps that the customer experiences provide customers with evidence on which to judge the service. These steps involve not only "what" gets created but also "how" it is created. The customer contact audit discussed earlier in the chapter is relevant to understanding the service process discussed here. The customer contact audit can serve as a basis for ensuring better service creation and delivery processes. Grease Monkey believes that it has the right process in the vehicle oil change and fluid exchange service

recruitment 招募，招聘；educational 教育的，与教育相关的；fluid 液体，流质。

FIGURE 9–8
Different prices and packages help match hotel demand to capacity.

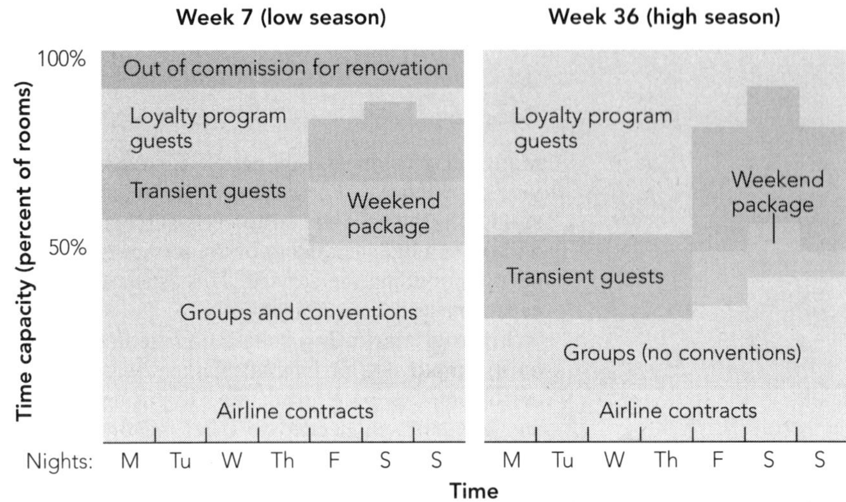

business. Customers do not need appointments, stores are open six days per week, the service is completed in 15–20 minutes, and a waiting room allows customers to read or work while the service is being completed.

生产率
Productivity

Most services have a limited capacity due to the inseparability of the service from the service provider and the perishable nature of the service. For example, to "buy" an appendectomy, a patient must be in the hospital at the same time as the surgeon and only one patient can be helped at that time. Similarly, no additional surgery can be conducted tomorrow because of an unused operating room or an available surgeon today—the service capacity is lost if it is not used. So the service component of the marketing mix must be integrated with efforts to influence consumer demand. This is referred to as **capacity management**.

Service organizations must manage the availability of the offering so that (1) demand matches capacity over the duration of the demand cycle (for example, one day, week, month, or year), and (2) the organization's assets are used in ways that will maximize the return on investment (ROI). Figure 9–8 shows how a hotel tries to manage its capacity during the high and low seasons. Differing price structures are assigned to each segment of consumers to help moderate or adjust demand for the service. Airline contracts fill a fixed number of rooms throughout the year. In the low season, when more rooms are available, tour packages at appealing prices are used to attract groups or conventions, such as an offer for seven nights in Orlando at a reduced price. Weekend packages are also offered to vacationers. In the high-demand season, groups are less desirable because guests who will pay high prices travel to Florida on their own. The accompanying Using Marketing Dashboards box demonstrates how JetBlue Airways uses a capacity management measure called *load factor* to assess its profitability.

未来的服务
SERVICES IN THE FUTURE

What can we expect from the services industry in the future? New and better services, of course, and an unprecedented variety of choices. Many of the changes will be the result of two factors: technological development and an expanding scope in the global economy.

Technological advances are rapidly changing the service industry. In fact, many of the likely changes in the United States are already occurring in Europe and Asia

appendectomy 阑尾切除术；unprecedented 前所未有的，无前例的。

Using Marketing Dashboards

Are JetBlue's Flights Profitably Loaded?

Capacity management is critical in the marketing of many services. For example, having the right number of airline seats or hotel rooms available at the right time, price, and place can spell the difference between a profitable or unprofitable service operation.

Airlines feature *load factor* as a capacity management measure on their marketing dashboards, along with two other measures; namely the *operating expense* per available seat flown one mile and the revenue generated by each seat flown one mile called *yield*. Load factor is the percentage of available seats flown one mile occupied by a paying customer.

These three measures combine to show airline operating income or loss per available seat flown one mile:

Operating income (loss) per available seat flown one mile
= [Yield × Load factor] − Operating expense

Your Challenge As a marketing analyst for New York City-based JetBlue Airways, you have been asked to determine the operating income or loss per available seat flown one mile for the first six months of 2010. In addition, you have been asked to determine what load factor JetBlue must reach to break even assuming its current yield and operating expense will not change in the immediate future.

Your Findings JetBlue's yield, load factor, and operating expense marketing dashboard displays are shown below.

You can conclude from these measures that JetBlue Airways posted about a 0.21¢ loss per available seat flown one mile in the first six months of 2010:

Operating loss per available seat flown one mile
= [9.83¢ × 82.1%] − 8.28¢ = −.2096¢

Assuming JetBlue's yield and operating expense will not change and using a little algebra, the airline's load factor will have to increase from 82.1 percent to 84.23 percent to break even:

Operating income (loss) per available seat flown one mile
= [9.83¢ × Load factor] − 8.28¢ = 0¢
Load factor = 84.23%

Your Action Assuming yield and operating expenses will not change, you should recommend that JetBlue consider revising its flight schedules to better accommodate traveler needs and advertise these changes. Consideration might be also given to how JetBlue utilizes its existing airplane fleet to serve its customers and produce a profit.

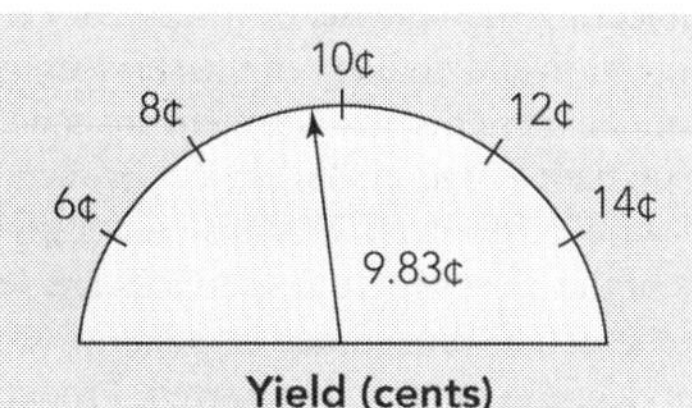

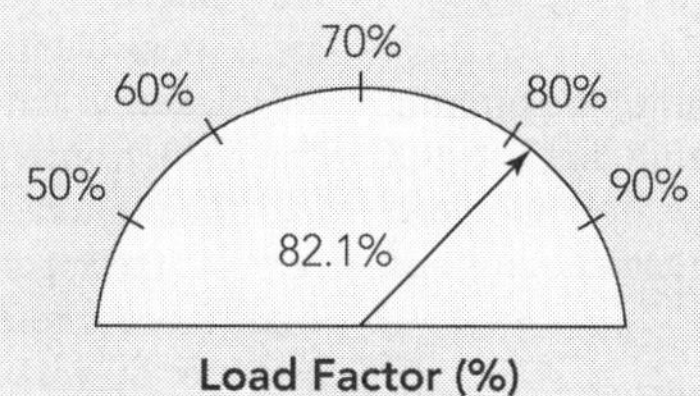

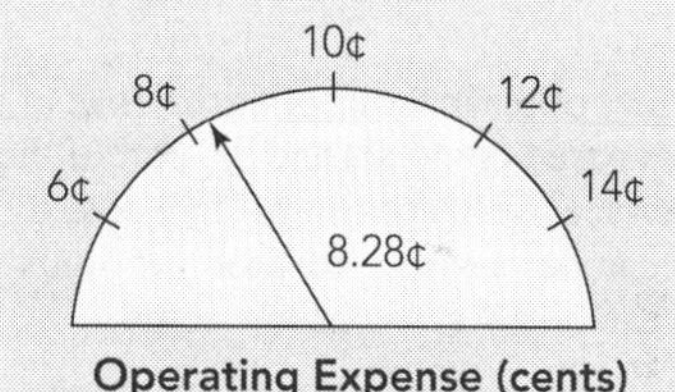

where new generations of technology have leapfrogged North America. The key elements of future services include mobility, convergence, personalization, and collaboration. Mobility will be provided by new generations of networks that will allow TV, GPS, high-speed data transfer, and audio programming on portable digital devices. Products such as the Apple iPhone are indications of the coming convergence of voice, video, and data in a single product. Personalization is also under way at services such as Amazon.com where past transactions are analyzed to customize information seen by customers. Technology-mediated personalization can increase the customers' perceptions of value; however, excessive attempts at personalization can also trigger privacy concerns. Finally, collaboration services that allow Web-conferencing, dating and matchmaking, and even remote involvement of friends when someone is shopping are coming!

An expanding scope of influence in the global economy is also changing the service industry. While the past decade has seen services grow to become the dominant part of the economy in the United States, the future is likely to see more emphasis on the global marketing of services and increasing attention to cross-cultural

generation（机械设备的设计和制造的）代；dominant 占支配（或统治）地位的，占优势的。

implications for services. Recent studies indicate that consumers in countries such as Australia, China, Germany, India, and the United States place varying emphasis on service quality and underscore the need to "think global and act local." Finally, some experts predict that the dominant view of economic exchange will shift from its current focus on goods and tangible resources to services and intangible attributes. Countries that expect to compete globally will need to invest in service industry growth and service innovation. In fact, recent research suggests that services marketing strategies create a competitive advantage and are very profitable.

learning review

6. How does a movie theater use off-peak pricing?
7. Matching demand with capacity is the focus of ______________ management.
8. What factors will influence future changes in services?

LEARNING OBJECTIVES REVIEW

LO1 *Describe four unique elements of services.*
The four unique elements of services—the four I's—are intangibility, inconsistency, inseparability, and inventory. Intangibility refers to the tendency of services to be a performance that cannot be held or touched, rather than an object. Inconsistency is a characteristic of services because they depend on people to deliver them, and people vary in their capabilities and in their day-to-day performance. Inseparability refers to the difficulty of separating the deliverer of the service (hair stylist) from the service itself (hair salon). Inventory refers to the need to have service production capability when there is service demand.

LO2 *Recognize how services differ and how they can be classified.*
Services differ in terms of the balance of the part of the offering that is based on goods and the part of the offering that is based on service. Services can be delivered by people or equipment, they can be provided by profit or nonprofit organizations, and they can be government sponsored.

LO3 *Explain how consumers purchase and evaluate services.*
Because services are intangible, prepurchase evaluation is difficult for consumers. To choose a service, consumers use search, experience, and credence qualities to evaluate the good and service elements of an offering. Once a consumer tries a service, it is evaluated by comparing expectations with the actual experience on five dimensions of quality—reliability, tangibles, responsiveness, assurance, and empathy. Differences between expectations and experience are identified through gap analysis.

LO4 *Develop a customer contact audit to identify service advantages.*
A customer contact audit is a flowchart of the points of interaction between a consumer and a service provider. The interactions identified in a customer contact audit often serve as the basis for developing relationships with customers.

LO5 *Explain the role of the eight Ps in the services marketing mix.*
The services marketing mix includes eight Ps. An important aspect of the product element is branding—the use of a brand name or logo to help consumers identify a service. Pricing is reflected in charges, fees, fares, and rates and can be used to influence perceptions of the quality of a service and to balance demand for services. Place (or distribution) is used to provide access and convenience. Promotional tools such as advertising and publicity are a means of communicating the benefits of a service. People are responsible for the creation and delivery of the service. Internal marketing and customer experience management are concepts that result from a focus on people within the service organization and their interactions with customers. Physical environment refers to the appearance of the place where the services are delivered. Process refers to the actual procedures, mechanisms, and activities by which a service is created and delivered. Productivity is related to the inseparability of the service from the service provider and is influenced by capacity management.

LO6 *Discuss the important roles of internal marketing and customer experience management in service organizations.*
Because the employee plays a central role in creating the service experience, and in building and maintaining relationships with customers, services have adopted a concept called internal marketing. This concept suggests that services need to ensure that employees (the internal market) have the attitude, skills, and commitment needed to meet customer expectations. Customer experience management is the process of managing the entire customer experience with the company to ensure customer loyalty.

FOCUSING ON KEY TERMS

capacity management
customer contact audit
customer experience management
eight Ps of services marketing
four I's of services
gap analysis
idle production capacity
internal marketing
off-peak pricing
service continuum
services

APPLYING MARKETING KNOWLEDGE

1 Explain how the four I's of services would apply to a Marriott Hotel.

2 Idle production capacity may be related to inventory or capacity management. How would the pricing component of the marketing mix reduce idle production capacity for (*a*) a car wash, (*b*) a stage theater group, and (*c*) a university?

3 Look back at the service continuum in Figure 9–3. Explain how the following points in the continuum differ in terms of consistency: (*a*) salt, (*b*) automobile, (*c*) advertising agency, and (*d*) teaching.

4 What are the search, experience, and credence properties of an airline for the business traveler and pleasure traveler? What properties are most important to each group?

5 Outline the customer contact audit for the typical deposit you make at your neighborhood bank.

6 How does off-peak pricing influence demand for services?

7 Draw the channel of distribution for the following services: (*a*) a restaurant, (*b*) a hospital, and (*c*) a hotel.

8 The text suggests that internal marketing is necessary before a successful marketing program can be directed at consumers. Why is this particularly true for service organizations?

9 Outline the capacity management strategies that an airline must consider.

10 In recent years, many service businesses have begun to provide their employees with uniforms. Explain the rationale behind this strategy in terms of the concepts discussed in this chapter.

building your marketing plan

In this section of your marketing plan you should distinguish between your core product—a good or a service—and supplementary services.

1 Develop an internal marketing program that will ensure that employees are prepared to deliver the core and supplementary services.

2 Conduct a customer contact audit and create a flowchart similar to Figure 9–7 to identify specific points of interaction with customers.

3 Describe marketing activities that will (*a*) address each of the four I's as they relate to your service and (*b*) encourage the development of relationships with your customers.

Add this as an appendix to your marketing plan and use the results in developing your marketing mix strategy.

video case 9 Philadelphia Phillies, Inc.: Sports Marketing 101

"Unfortunately we can't promise fans in the stands a win every game," laughs David Montgomery, president and chief executive officer of the Philadelphia Phillies, Inc. But in 2008 his Phillies came close enough to that: They beat the Tampa Bay Rays to win the World Series (photo).

Montgomery goes on to explain key elements of the Phillies' marketing strategy, starting with moving into its new Citizens Bank Park baseball stadium in 2004. "Bring everyone in closer. Have fans feel 'I'm not alone here; lots of others are in the seats. This is a *happening*!'" he says. Our new facility and the fact that it's a game played in summer out in the open air really takes you to a much broader audience," he says. "Our challenge is to appeal to all the segments in that audience." In the new baseball-only ballpark, every seat is angled toward home plate to give fans the best view of the action.

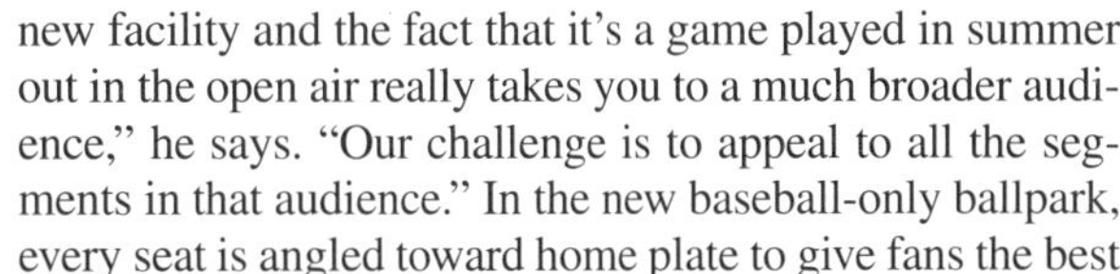

The new fan-friendly Phillies stadium is just one element in today's complex strategy to effectively market the Philadelphia Phillies to several different segments of fans—a far different challenge than in the past. A century ago Major League Baseball was pretty simple. You built a stadium. You hired the ballplayers. You printed tickets—hoping and praying a winning team would bring in fans and sell those tickets. And your advertising consisted of printing the team's home schedule in the local newspaper.

THE PHILLIES TODAY: APPEALS, SEGMENTS, AND ACTIVITIES

Baseball, like other sports, is a service whose primary benefit is entertainment. Marketing a Major League Baseball team is far different today.

"How do you market a product that is all over the board?" asks David Buck, the Phillies' vice president of marketing. He first gives a general answer to his question: "The ballpark experience is the key. As long as you project an image of a fun ballpark experience in everything you do, you're going to be in good shape. Our best advertising is word of mouth from happy fans." Next come the specifics. Marketing the appeal of a fun ballpark experience to all segments of fans is critical because the Phillies can't promise a winning baseball team.

Reaching the different segments of fans is a special challenge because each segment attends a game for different reasons and therefore will respond to different special promotions:

- *The diehards*. Intense baseball fans who are there to watch the strategy and see the Phillies win.
- *Kids 14 years and under*. At the game with their families, to get bat or bobble-head doll premiums, and have a "run-the-bases" day.
- *Women and men 15 years and older*. Special "days out," such as Mother's Day or Father's Day.
- *Seniors, 60 years and over*. A "stroll-the-bases" day.
- *The 20- and 30-somethings*. Meet friends at the ballpark and restaurants for a fun night out.
- *Corporate and community groups*. At the game to have fun but also to get to know members of their respective organizations better.

It's clear that not all fans are there for exactly the same "fun ballpark experience."

The "fun ballpark experience" today also goes beyond simply watching the Phillies play a baseball game. Fans at Citizens Bank Park can:

- Buy souvenirs at the Phanatic Attic, within the Majestic Clubhouse Store.
- Romp in the Phanatic Phun Zone, the largest soft-play area for kids in Major League Baseball.
- Test their skills in a pitching game.
- Stroll through Ashburn Alley (named for a famous Phillie), an outdoor food and entertainment area.
- Eat at McFadden's Restaurant and Saloon year round or Harry the K's Bar & Grill.

PROMOTIONAL ACTIVITIES

The range of the Phillies' promotional activities today is mind numbing. Before and during the season, the Phillies run a series of TV ads to generate and/or maintain fan interest. A recent ad campaign targeted kids by showing that the Phillies' players themselves are just like them. The tagline: "There's a little fan in all of us."

The Phillies also use "special promotion days," which typically increase fan attendance by 30 to 35 percent for a game, according to David Buck. These days often generate first-time visits by people who have never seen a Major League Baseball game. They generally fall into three categories: (1) theme nights, (2) event days, and (3) premium gift days.

Theme nights are devoted to special community groups or other fan segments. Examples include College Nights (fellow classmates, alumni, and faculty), dates for families of the military and law enforcement, Rooftop Thursdays (having a luau with friends on the stadium rooftop), among others. Event days can involve camera days where fans can have their photo taken with a favorite Phillies player. Or they can involve fireworks, an old-timers' game, or running or strolling the bases. Five "Dollar Dog Nights" during the season let fans eat as many hot dogs as they can for $1.

The Phillies premiums or giveaways are also directed at specific market segments. These premiums range from baseball caps, beach towels, and T-shirts to a Phillies team photo or bobble-head dolls. To control expenses, the Phillies try to keep the cost of the premiums in the range of $1 to $3.

Other promotional activities fall in both the traditional and nontraditional categories. Personal appearances at public and charity events by Phillies players and their wives, radio and TV ads, and special events paid for by sponsors have been used by baseball teams for decades. The "Phillies Ballgirls" involve a clearly new, nontraditional promotional activity. These 20 women are all college softball players and are ambassadors for the Phillies. Besides taking on other softball teams on the diamond, they make four or five appearances a week at charity events, schools, or golf outings. They also help promote the Phillies sense of social responsibility and its focus on recycling and the environment.

The Internet and social networks have revolutionized the Phillies media strategies. "I remember the days we used to mail press releases that took four or five days to get to recipients," says the Phillies vice president of communications, Bonnie Clark. Fans not only can order tickets on the team's Web site (www.phillies.com), but also can buy Phillies jerseys and caps and get the inside scoop on players—like who's going on the disabled list and so on. The social networks now have huge importance. "Six months after launching a Phillies Twitter, we have 7,400 followers," she says. "And we now have more than 190,000 Facebook friends."

Probably the best-known mascot in professional sports, the Phillie Phanatic is a Philadelphia legend. This oversized, green furry mascot has been around for over 25 years. It not only appears in the ballpark at all Phillies' home games, but also makes appearances at charity and public events year round. Or rather the *three* Phanatics do so, because the demand is too great for a single Phanatic. "The Phanatic is a great character because he doesn't carry wins or losses," says David Montgomery. "Fans young and old can relate to him . . . he makes you smile, makes you laugh, and adds to the enjoyment of the game."

BOTTOM LINE: REVENUES AND EXPENSES

"We're a private business that serves the public," David Montgomery points out. "And we've got to make sure our revenues more than cover our expenses." He identifies five key sources of revenues and the approximate annual percentages for each:

Sources of Revenue	Approx. %
1. Ticket sales (home and away games)	52%
2. National media (network TV and radio)	13
3. Local media (over-the-air TV, pay TV, radio)	13
4. Advertising (publications, co-sponsorship promotions)	12
5. Concessions (food, souvenirs, restaurants)	10
Total	100

Balanced against these revenues are some major expenses that include players' salaries (about $130 million) and salaries of more than 150 full-time employees. Other expenses are those for scouting and drafting 40 to 60 new players per year, operating six minor-league farm clubs, and managing a labor force of 400 persons for each of the Phillies' 81 regular-season home games at Citizens Bank Park.

David Montgomery never gets bored. "When I finished business school, I had to choose between a marketing research job at a large paper products company or marketing the Philadelphia Phillies," explains Montgomery, who started with the Phillies by selling season and group tickets. "And it was no real decision because there never has been one day on this job that wasn't different and exciting."

Questions

1 (*a*) What is the "product" that the Phillies market? (*b*) What "products" are the Phillies careful not to market?

2 How does the "quality" dimension in marketing the Philadelphia Phillies as an entertainment service differ from that in marketing a consumer product such as a breakfast cereal?

3 In terms of a social network marketing strategy, (*a*) what are the likely characteristics of the Phillies fans and (*b*) what should the Phillies' Facebook fan page contain?

4 Considering all five elements of the promotional mix (advertising, personal selling, public relations, sales promotion, and direct marketing), what specific promotional activities should the Phillies use? Which should be used off-season? During the season?

5 What kind of special promotion gift days (with premiums) and event days (no premiums) can the Phillies use to increase attendance by targeting these fan segments: (*a*) 14 and under, (*b*) 15 and over, (*c*) other special fan segments, and (*d*) all fans?

10

管理营销渠道与批发
Managing Marketing Channels and Wholesaling

卡拉威高尔夫：设计和提供优质的高尔夫商品
CALLAWAY GOLF: DESIGNING AND DELIVERING THE GOODS FOR GREAT GOLF

LEARNING OBJECTIVES

After reading this chapter you should be able to:

LO1 Explain what is meant by a marketing channel of distribution and why intermediaries are needed.

LO2 Distinguish among traditional marketing channels, electronic marketing channels, and different types of vertical marketing systems.

LO3 Describe the factors and considerations that affect a company's choice and management of a marketing channel.

LO4 Recognize how conflict, cooperation, and legal considerations affect marketing channel relationships.

What do Ernie Els, a world-class golf professional, and Justin Timberlake, a pop icon and avid amateur golfer, have in common? Both use Callaway Golf equipment, accessories, and apparel when playing their favorite sport.

With annual sales exceeding $1 billion annually, Callaway Golf is one of the most recognized and highly regarded companies in the golf industry. With its commitment to continuous product innovation and broad distribution in the United States and more than 100 countries worldwide, Callaway Golf has built a strong reputation for designing and delivering the goods for great golf for golfers of all skill levels, both amateur and professional.

Callaway Golf primarily markets its products through more than 15,000 on- and off-course golf retailers and sporting goods retailers, such as Golf Galaxy, Inc.; Dick's Sporting Goods, Inc.; and PGA Tour Superstores, that sell quality golf products and provide a level of customer service appropriate for the sale of such products. The company also has its own online store (Shop.Callawaygolf.com), which makes it a full-fledged multichannel marketer, and a successful one as well. The chief executive of PGA America called Callaway's online store "innovative in that it combines that old legacy relationship with the retail channel with the new innovation of the Web" soon after the online store was launched. Callaway's chief executive officer, George Fellows, says Callaway's online store is useful for consumers who are looking for accessories or apparel, and for those who know their preferred golf club specifications: "There are always going to be certain people that will not feel comfortable buying online. But for those that do feel comfortable, we really represent the most seamless process."

Callaway Golf considers its marketing channel partners a valued marketing asset. For example, when the company opened its online store, careful attention was placed on how Callaway Golf "could satisfy the consumer but do so in a way that didn't violate our relationships with our loyal trade partners," Fellows said. The solution? Callaway Golf has one of its retailers get credit for the sale. This retailer then fulfills a buyer's order within 24 hours. Consumers, retailers, and Callaway Golf all benefit from this arrangement.

This chapter focuses on marketing channels of distribution and why they are an important component in the marketing mix. It then shows how such channels benefit consumers and the sequence of firms that make up a marketing channel. Finally, it describes factors that influence the choice and management of marketing channels, including channel conflict, cooperation, and legal restrictions.

amateur 业余的，非职业的；equipment 设备，装备。

营销渠道的特性和重要性
NATURE AND IMPORTANCE OF MARKETING CHANNELS

Reaching prospective buyers, either directly or indirectly, is a prerequisite for successful marketing. At the same time, buyers benefit from distribution systems used by companies.

什么是分销渠道
What Is a Marketing Channel of Distribution?

LO1

你获得这些商品都通过了营销的分销渠道，或简称为**营销渠道**，这由营销过程中相关个人和公司所组成，它们负责将产品或服务传递给消费者或工业客户并被其使用和消费。

You see the results of distribution every day. You may have purchased Lay's Potato Chips at a 7-Eleven convenience store, a book online through Amazon.com, and Levi's jeans at Kohl's department stores. Each of these items was brought to you by a marketing channel of distribution, or simply a **marketing channel**, which consists of individuals and firms involved in the process of making a product or service available for use or consumption by consumers or industrial users.

Marketing channels can be compared with a pipeline through which water flows from a source to terminus. Marketing channels make possible the flow of goods from a producer, through intermediaries, to a buyer. Intermediaries go by various names (see Figure 10–1) and perform various functions. Some intermediaries actually purchase items from the seller, store them, and resell them to buyers. For example, Celestial Seasonings produces specialty teas and sells them to food wholesalers. The wholesalers then sell these teas to supermarkets and grocery stores, which, in turn, sell them to consumers. Other intermediaries such as brokers and agents represent sellers but do not actually take title to products—their role is to bring a seller and buyer together. Century 21 real estate agents are examples of this type of intermediary. The importance of intermediaries is made even clearer when we consider the functions they perform and the value they create for buyers.

中间商创造的价值
Value Is Created by Intermediaries

Few consumers appreciate the value created by intermediaries; however, producers recognize that intermediaries make selling goods and services more efficient because they minimize the number of sales contacts necessary to reach a target market.

FIGURE 10–1
A variety of terms is used for marketing intermediaries. They vary in specificity and use in consumer and business markets.

TERM	DESCRIPTION
Middleman	Any intermediary between manufacturer and end-user markets
Agent or broker	Any intermediary with legal authority to act on behalf of the manufacturer
Wholesaler	An intermediary who sells to other intermediaries, usually to retailers; term usually applies to consumer markets
Retailer	An intermediary who sells to consumers
Distributor	An imprecise term, usually used to describe intermediaries who perform a variety of distribution functions, including selling, maintaining inventories, extending credit, and so on; a more common term in business markets but may also be used to refer to wholesalers
 Dealer	A more imprecise term than *distributor* that can mean the same as distributor, retailer, wholesaler, and so forth

intermediary 中介，中间人；prerequisite 条件；industrial 工业的，从事工业的。

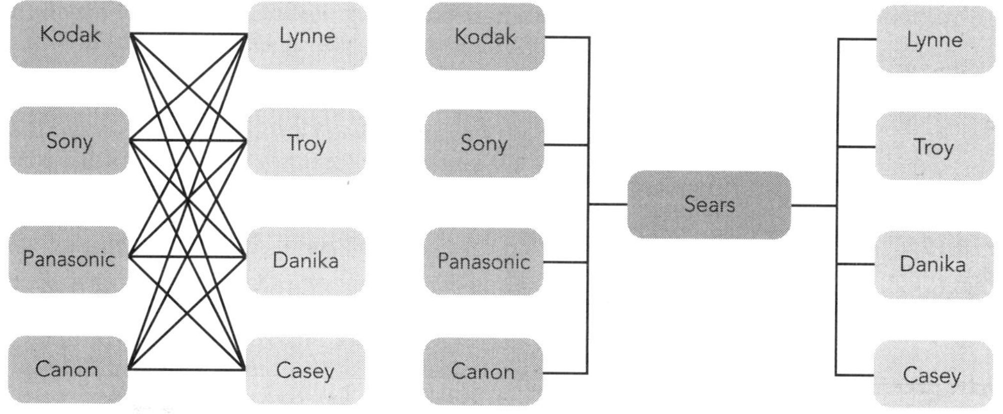

Contacts with no intermediaries
4 producers x 4 buyers = 16 contacts

Contacts with one intermediary
4 producers + 4 buyers = 8 contacts

FIGURE 10–2
Intermediaries minimize transactions and the cost of distribution for producers and customers.

Figure 10–2 shows a simple example of how this comes about in the digital camera industry. Without a retail intermediary (such as Sears), Kodak, Sony, Panasonic, and Canon would each have to make four contacts to reach the four buyers shown who are in the target market. However, each producer has to make only one contact when Sears acts as an intermediary. Equally important from a macromarketing perspective, the total number of industry transactions is reduced from 16 to 8, which reduces producer cost and hence benefits the customer.

Important Functions Performed by Intermediaries Intermediaries make possible the flow of products from producers to buyers by performing three basic functions (Figure 10–3). Intermediaries perform a *transactional function* that involves buying, selling, and risk taking because they stock merchandise in anticipation of sales. Intermediaries perform a *logistical function* evident in the gathering, storing, and dispersing of products (see Chapter 11 on supply chain and logistics management). Finally, intermediaries perform *facilitating functions*, which assist producers in making goods and services more attractive to buyers.

All three functions must be performed in a marketing channel, even though each channel member may not participate in all three. Channel members often negotiate

FIGURE 10–3
Marketing channel intermediaries perform three fundamental functions, each of which consists of different activities.

TYPE OF FUNCTION	ACTIVITIES RELATED TO FUNCTION
Transactional function	• *Buying*: Purchasing products for resale or as an agent for supply of a product • *Selling*: Contacting potential customers, promoting products, and seeking orders • *Risk taking*: Assuming business risks in the ownership of inventory that can become obsolete or deteriorate
Logistical function	• *Assorting*: Creating product assortments from several sources to serve customers • *Storing*: Assembling and protecting products at a convenient location to offer better customer service • *Sorting*: Purchasing in large quantities and breaking into smaller amounts desired by customers • *Transporting*: Physically moving a product to customers
Facilitating function	• *Financing*: Extending credit to customers • *Grading*: Inspecting, testing, or judging products, and assigning them quality grades • *Marketing information and research*: Providing information to customers and suppliers, including competitive conditions and trends

transaction 交易，业务；logistical 后勤方面的；facilitate 使便利。

Borders, a leading U.S. book retailer, works closely with book publishers. Read the text to learn how this is done.

Borders Group, Inc.
www.borders.com

about which specific functions they will perform. Borders, a leading U.S. book retailer with over 1,000 stores, is a case in point. It has agreements with major book publishers whereby they assume responsibility for recommending how to display books on its shelves, and providing information on new titles and consumer reading preferences in specific book categories. For example, HarperCollins has responsibility for cookbooks, Random House for children's books, and Pearson for computer books.

Consumers Also Benefit from Intermediaries

Consumers also benefit from intermediaries. Having the goods and services you want, when you want them, where you want them, and in the form you want them is the ideal result of marketing channels.

In more specific terms, marketing channels help create value for consumers through the four utilities described in Chapter 1: time, place, form, and possession. Time utility refers to having a product or service when you want it. For example, FedEx provides next-morning delivery. Place utility means having a product or service available where consumers want it, such as having a Texaco gas station located on a long stretch of lonely highway. Form utility involves enhancing a product or service to make it more appealing to buyers. Consider the importance of bottlers in the soft-drink industry. Coca-Cola and Pepsi-Cola manufacture the flavor concentrate (cola, lemon-lime) and sell it to bottlers—intermediaries—which then add sweetener and the concentrate to carbonated water and package the beverage in bottles and cans, which are then sold to retailers. Possession utility entails efforts by intermediaries to help buyers take possession of a product or service, such as having airline tickets delivered by a travel agency.

learning review

1. What is meant by a marketing channel?
2. What are the three basic functions performed by intermediaries?

渠道结构与组织
CHANNEL STRUCTURE AND ORGANIZATION

A product can take many routes on its journey from a producer to buyers. Marketers continually search for the most efficient route from the many alternatives available. As you'll see, there are some important differences between the marketing channels for consumer goods and those for business goods.

消费品与服务的营销渠道
Marketing Channels for Consumer Goods and Services

Figure 10–4 shows the four most common marketing channels for consumer goods and services. It also shows the number of levels in each marketing channel, as evidenced by the number of intermediaries between a producer and ultimate buyers. As the number of intermediaries between a producer and buyer increases, the channel is viewed as increasing in length. Thus, the producer → wholesaler → retailer → consumer channel is longer than the producer → consumer channel.

渠道 A 称为直接渠道，因为生产商与最终消费者直接交易。

Direct Channel Channel A represents a *direct channel* because a producer and ultimate consumers deal directly with each other. Many products and services are distributed this way. Many insurance companies sell their financial services using

alternative 可供选择的事物；delivery 交付，传递；enhance 提高。

FIGURE 10–4
Common marketing channels for consumer goods and services differ by the kind and number of intermediaries.

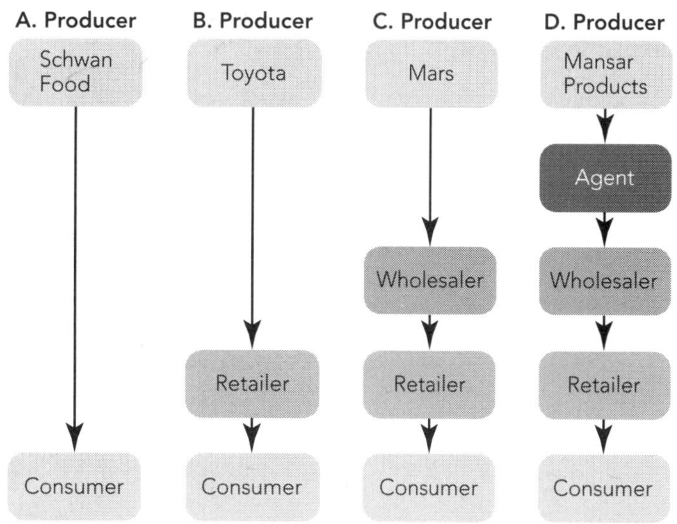

a direct channel and branch sales offices. The Schwan Food Company of Marshall, Minnesota markets a full line of frozen foods in 50 countries, including the United States, using route salespeople who sell from refrigerated trucks. Because there are no intermediaries with a direct channel, the producer must perform all channel functions.

剩下的三种渠道形式都属于间接渠道，因为在生产者和消费者之间增加了中间商，它们负责履行大量渠道职能。

Indirect Channel The remaining three channel forms are *indirect channels* because intermediaries are inserted between the producer and consumers and perform numerous channel functions. Channel B, with a retailer added, is most common when a retailer is large and can buy in large quantities from a producer or when the cost of inventory makes it too expensive to use a wholesaler. Automobile manufacturers such as Toyota use this channel, and a local car dealer acts as a retailer. Why is there no wholesaler? So many variations exist in the product that it would be impossible for a wholesaler to stock all the models required to satisfy buyers; in addition, the cost of maintaining an inventory would be too high. However, large retailers such as Sears, 7-Eleven, Staples, Safeway, and Home Depot buy in sufficient quantities to make it cost effective for a producer to deal with only a retail intermediary.

Adding a wholesaler in Channel C is most common for low-cost, low-unit value items that are frequently purchased by consumers, such as candy, confectionary items, and magazines. For example, Mars sells its line of candies to wholesalers in case quantities, who then break down (sort) the cases so that individual retailers can order in boxes or much smaller quantities.

Channel D, the most indirect channel, is employed when there are many small manufacturers and many small retailers, and an agent is used to help coordinate a large supply of the product. Mansar Products, Ltd., is a Belgian producer of specialty jewelry that uses agents to sell to wholesalers in the United States, which then sell to many small independent jewelry retailers.

工业品与服务的营销渠道
Marketing Channels for Business Goods and Services

The four most common channels for business goods and services are shown in Figure 10–5 on the next page. In contrast with channels for consumer products, business channels typically are shorter and rely on one intermediary or none at all because business users are fewer in number, tend to be more concentrated geographically, and buy in larger quantities (see Chapter 4).

refrigerate 冷藏，冷冻；manufacturer 制造商，制造厂；geographically 在地理上，地理学上。

FIGURE 10–5
Common marketing channels for business goods and services differ by the kind and number of intermediaries.

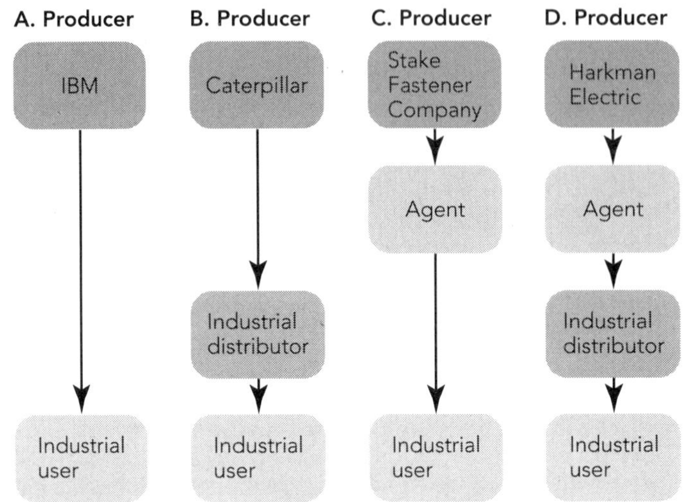

Direct Channel Channel A, represented by IBM's large, mainframe computer business, is a direct channel. Firms using this channel maintain their own salesforce and perform all channel functions. This channel is employed when buyers are large and well defined, the sales effort requires extensive negotiations, and the products are of high unit value and require hands-on expertise in terms of installation or use.

Indirect Channel Channels B, C, and D are indirect channels with one or more intermediaries to reach industrial users. In Channel B, an **industrial distributor** performs a variety of marketing channel functions, including selling, stocking, delivering a full product assortment, and financing. In many ways, industrial distributors are like wholesalers in consumer channels. Caterpillar uses industrial distributors to sell its construction and mining equipment in over 200 countries. In addition to selling, Caterpillar distributors stock 40,000 to 50,000 parts and service equipment using highly trained technicians.

Channel C introduces a second intermediary, an *agent*, who serves primarily as the independent selling arm of producers and represents a producer to industrial users. For example, Stake Fastener Company, a producer of industrial fasteners, has an agent call on industrial users rather than employing its own salesforce.

Channel D is the longest channel and includes both agents and distributors. For instance, Harkman Electric, a producer of electric products, uses agents to call on electrical distributors who sell to industrial users.

电子营销渠道
Electronic Marketing Channels

对消费品和工业品及服务而言，常用的营销渠道并不是到达市场的惟一路线。电子商务的发展为产品传递和顾客价值创造开辟了新的路径。

互动式电子技术已经使电子营销渠道成为可能。所谓**电子营销渠道**，是指借助互联网实现消费者或工业用户对产品与服务的使用消费。

These common marketing channels for consumer and business goods and services are not the only routes to the marketplace. Advances in electronic commerce have opened new avenues for reaching buyers and creating customer value.

Interactive electronic technology has made possible **electronic marketing channels**, which employ the Internet to make goods and services available for consumption or use by consumers or business buyers. A unique feature of these channels is that they combine electronic and traditional intermediaries to create time, place, form, and possession utility for buyers.

Figure 10–6 shows the electronic marketing channels for books (Amazon.com), automobiles (Autobytel.com), reservation services (Orbitz.com), and personal computers (Dell.com). Are you surprised that they look a lot like common consumer product marketing channels? An important reason for the similarity resides in channel functions detailed in Figure 10–3. Electronic intermediaries can and do perform

installation 安装，装置；primarily 主要地，根本地；distributor 分销商。

FIGURE 10–6
Consumer electronic marketing channels look much like those for consumer goods and services. Read the text to learn why.

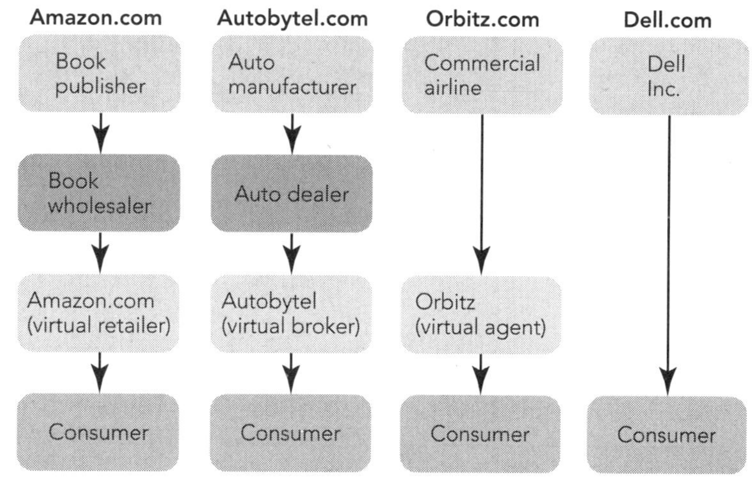

transactional and facilitating functions effectively and at a relatively lower cost than traditional intermediaries because of efficiencies made possible by information technology. However, electronic intermediaries are incapable of performing elements of the logistical function, particularly for products such as books and automobiles. This function remains with traditional intermediaries or with the producer, as evident with Dell, Inc., and its direct channel.

Many services can be distributed through electronic marketing channels, such as car rental reservations marketed by Alamo.com, financial securities by Schwab.com, and insurance by MetLife.com. However, many other services such as health care and auto repair still involve traditional intermediaries.

直接营销与多渠道营销
Direct and Multichannel Marketing

许多公司采用直销渠道使产品和服务抵达购买者。**直接营销渠道**可以使消费者在不与销售人员直接接触的情况下，通过与各种广告媒介的互动而购买产品。

Many firms also use direct and multichannel marketing to reach buyers. **Direct marketing channels** allow consumers to buy products by interacting with various advertising media without a face-to-face meeting with a salesperson. Direct marketing channels include mail-order selling, direct-mail sales, catalog sales, telemarketing, interactive media, and televised home shopping (the Home Shopping Network). Some firms sell products almost entirely through direct marketing. These firms include L.L. Bean (apparel) and Newegg.com (consumer electronics). Marketers such as Nestlé and Sunkist, in addition to using traditional channels composed of wholesalers and retailers, employ direct marketing through catalogs and telemarketing to reach more buyers. Direct marketing is covered in greater depth in Chapter 13.

Multichannel marketing is the *blending* of different communication and delivery channels that are *mutually reinforcing* in attracting, retaining, and building relationships with consumers who shop and buy in traditional intermediaries and online. Multichannel marketing seeks to integrate a firm's electronic and delivery channels. At Eddie Bauer, for example, every effort is made to make the apparel shopping and purchase experience for its customers the same in its retail stores, with its catalog, and at its Web site. According to an Eddie Bauer marketing manager, "We don't distinguish between channels because it's all Eddie Bauer to our customers."

Multichannel marketing also can leverage the value-adding capabilities of different channels. For example, retail stores can leverage their physical presence by allowing customers to pick up their online orders at a nearby store or return or exchange nonstore purchases if they wish. Catalogs can serve as shopping tools for online purchasing, as they do for store purchasing. Web sites can help consumers do their homework before visiting a store. Office Depot has leveraged its store, catalog, and Web site channels with impressive results. The company does more than $5 billion

security 证券；insurance 保险，保险业。

Eddie Bauer successfully engages in multichannel marketing through its 375 retail and outlet stores in North America, Japan, and Germany, its Web site, and catalog.

Eddie Bauer
www.eddiebauer.com

in online retail sales annually. Multichannel marketing is discussed further in Chapter 21 on interactive marketing.

双重分销与战略渠道联盟
Dual Distribution and Strategic Channel Alliances

在某些情况下，生产者会使用**双重分销**，即公司通过两种或以上不同类型的渠道向不同购买者销售同样产品。

In some situations, producers use **dual distribution**, an arrangement whereby a firm reaches different buyers by employing two or more different types of channels for the same basic product. For example, GE sells its large appliances directly to home and apartment builders but uses retail stores, including Lowe's home centers, to sell to consumers. In some instances, firms pair multiple channels with a multibrand strategy (see Chapter 8). This is done to minimize cannibalization of the firm's family brand and differentiate the channels. For example, Hallmark sells its Hallmark greeting cards through Hallmark stores and select department stores, and its Ambassador brand of cards through discount and drugstore chains.

A recent innovation in marketing channels is the use of **strategic channel alliances**, whereby one firm's marketing channel is used to sell another firm's products. An alliance between Kraft Foods and Starbucks is a case in point. Kraft distributes Starbucks coffee in U.S. supermarkets and internationally. Strategic alliances are popular in global marketing, where the creation of marketing channel relationships is expensive and time consuming. For example, General Mills and Nestlé have an extensive alliance that spans 130 international markets from Mexico to China. Read the Marketing Matters box so you won't be surprised when you are served Nestlé (not General Mills) Cheerios when traveling outside North America.

渠道中间商近览
A Closer Look at Channel Intermediaries

Channel structures for consumer and business products assume various forms based on the number and type of intermediaries. Knowledge of the roles played by these intermediaries is important for understanding how channels operate in practice.

The terms *wholesaler*, *agent*, and *retailer* have been used in a general fashion consistent with the meanings given in Figure 10–1. However, on closer inspection, a variety of specific types of intermediaries emerges. These intermediaries engage in wholesaling activities—those activities involved in selling products and services to

dualdistribution 双重分销；strategic channel alliances 战略渠道联盟；wholesaler 批发商；retailer 零售。

Marketing Matters > > > > > > customer value

Nestlé and General Mills—Cereal Partners Worldwide

Can you say Nestlé Cheerios *miel amandes*? Millions of French start their day with this European equivalent of General Mills' Honey Nut Cheerios, made possible by Cereal Partners Worldwide (CPW). CPW is a strategic alliance designed from the start to be a global business. It joined the cereal manufacturing and marketing capability of U.S.-based General Mills with the worldwide distribution clout of Swiss-based Nestlé.

From its headquarters in Switzerland, CPW first launched General Mills cereals under the Nestlé label in France, the United Kingdom, Spain, and Portugal in 1990. Today, CPW competes in 130 countries that span the globe.

The General Mills–Nestlé strategic channel alliance also increased the ready-to-eat cereal worldwide market share of these companies, which are already rated as the two best-managed firms in the world. CPW currently accounts for over 25 percent of global cereal sales with about $2 billion in annual revenue.

those who are buying for the purposes of resale or business use. Intermediaries engaged in retailing activities are discussed in detail in Chapter 12. Figure 10–7 on the next page describes the functions performed by major types of independent wholesalers.

商业批发商是对其所持商品拥有所有权的独立公司。

Merchant Wholesalers **Merchant wholesalers** are independently owned firms that take title to the merchandise they handle. They go by various names, including industrial distributor (described earlier). Most firms engaged in wholesaling activities are merchant wholesalers.

按照它们履行职能的多少，商业批发商可以分为全面服务批发商和有限服务批发商。

Merchant wholesalers are classified as either full-service or limited-service wholesalers, depending on the number of functions performed. Two major types of full-service wholesalers exist. *General merchandise* (or *full-line*) *wholesalers* carry a broad assortment of merchandise and perform all channel functions. This type of wholesaler is most prevalent in the hardware, drug, and clothing industries. However, these wholesalers do not maintain much depth of assortment within specific product lines. *Specialty merchandise* (or *limited-line*) *wholesalers* offer a relatively narrow range of products but have an extensive assortment within the product lines carried. They perform all channel functions and are found in the health foods, automotive parts, and seafood industries.

Four major types of limited-service wholesalers exist. *Rack jobbers* furnish the racks or shelves that display merchandise in retail stores, perform all channel functions, and sell on consignment to retailers, which means they retain the title to the products displayed and bill retailers only for the merchandise sold. Familiar products such as hosiery, toys, housewares, and health and beauty items are sold by rack jobbers. *Cash and carry wholesalers* take title to merchandise but sell only to buyers who call on them, pay cash for merchandise, and furnish their own transportation for merchandise. They carry a limited product assortment and do not make deliveries, extend credit, or supply market information. This wholesaler is common in electric supplies, office supplies, hardware products, and groceries.

general merchandise wholesaler 百货批发商；full-line 全线产品；Specialty merchandise wholesalers 专业批发商；limited-line 有限产品线。

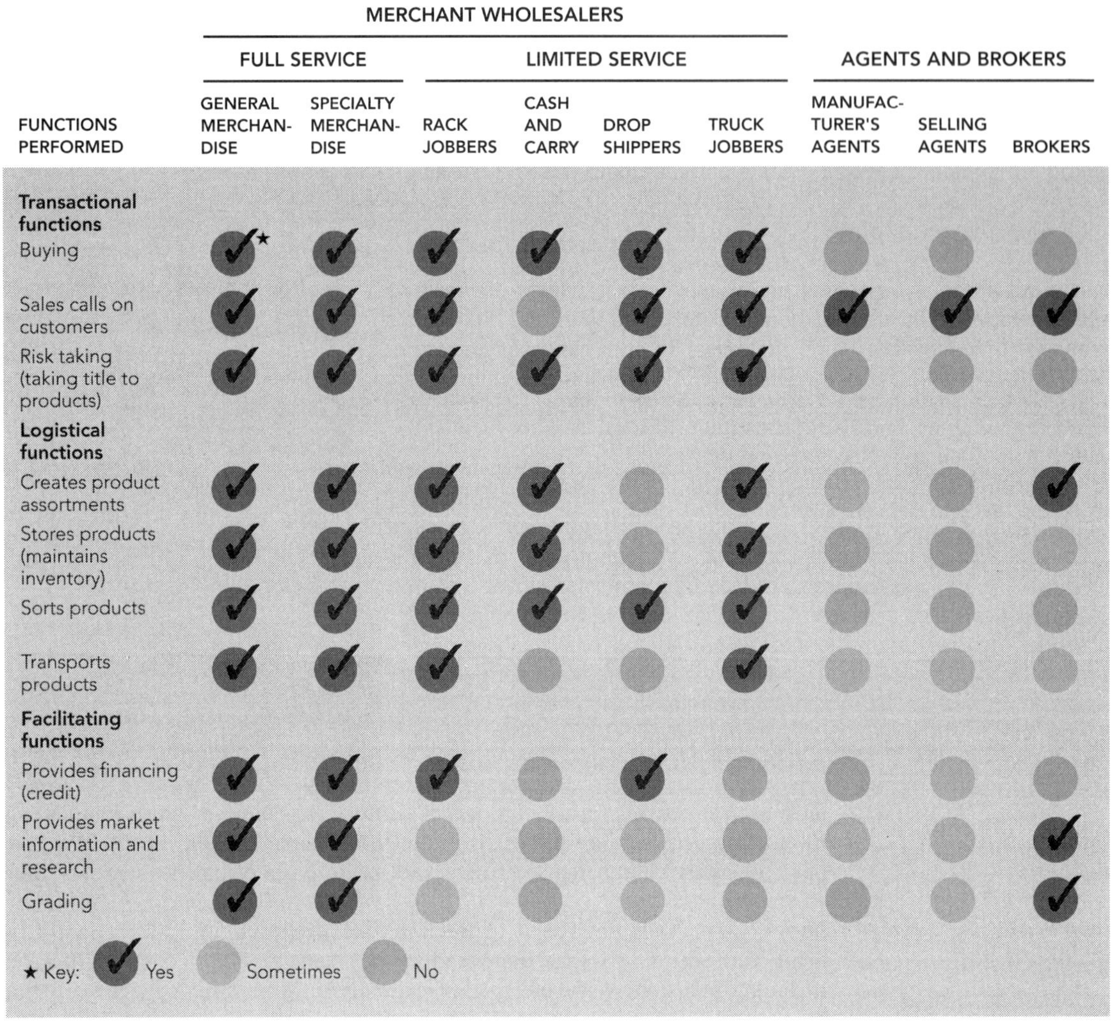

FUNCTIONS PERFORMED	MERCHANT WHOLESALERS: FULL SERVICE: GENERAL MERCHANDISE	MERCHANT WHOLESALERS: FULL SERVICE: SPECIALTY MERCHANDISE	MERCHANT WHOLESALERS: LIMITED SERVICE: RACK JOBBERS	MERCHANT WHOLESALERS: LIMITED SERVICE: CASH AND CARRY	MERCHANT WHOLESALERS: LIMITED SERVICE: DROP SHIPPERS	MERCHANT WHOLESALERS: LIMITED SERVICE: TRUCK JOBBERS	AGENTS AND BROKERS: MANUFACTURER'S AGENTS	AGENTS AND BROKERS: SELLING AGENTS	AGENTS AND BROKERS: BROKERS
Transactional functions									
Buying	Yes★	Yes	Yes	Yes	Yes	Yes	No	No	No
Sales calls on customers	Yes	Yes	Yes	No	Yes	Yes	Yes	Yes	Yes
Risk taking (taking title to products)	Yes	Yes	Yes	Yes	Yes	Yes	No	No	No
Logistical functions									
Creates product assortments	Yes	Yes	Yes	Yes	Sometimes	Yes	Sometimes	No	Yes
Stores products (maintains inventory)	Yes	Yes	Yes	Yes	Sometimes	Yes	No	No	Sometimes
Sorts products	Yes	Yes	Yes	Yes	Yes	Yes	No	No	No
Transports products	Yes	Yes	Yes	Sometimes	Sometimes	Yes	Sometimes	Sometimes	Sometimes
Facilitating functions									
Provides financing (credit)	Yes	Yes	Yes	No	Yes	No	No	Sometimes	No
Provides market information and research	Yes	Yes	Sometimes	No	Sometimes	No	Sometimes	Sometimes	Yes
Grading	Yes	Yes	Sometimes	No	Sometimes	No	No	Sometimes	Yes

★ Key: ✓ Yes; Sometimes; No

FIGURE 10–7
Functions performed by independent wholesaler types vary. Only full-service wholesalers perform all channel functions.

Drop shippers, or *desk jobbers*, are wholesalers that own the merchandise they sell but do not physically handle, stock, or deliver it. They simply solicit orders from retailers and other wholesalers and have the merchandise shipped directly from a producer to a buyer. Drop shippers are used for bulky products such as coal, lumber, and chemicals, which are sold in extremely large quantities. *Truck jobbers* are small wholesalers that have a small warehouse from which they stock their trucks for distribution to retailers. They usually handle limited assortments of fast-moving or perishable items that are sold for cash directly from trucks in their original packages. Truck jobbers handle products such as bakery items, dairy products, and meat.

与商业批发商不同，代理商和经纪人不具有商品所有权，且一般只履行较少的渠道职能。它们从服务佣金或服务费中获取利润，而商业批发商则是从销售自有商品中获利。

Agents and Brokers Unlike merchant wholesalers, agents and brokers do not take title to merchandise and typically perform fewer channel functions. They make their profit from commissions or fees paid for their services, whereas merchant wholesalers make their profit from the sale of the merchandise they own.

Manufacturer's agents and selling agents are the two major types of agents used by producers. **Manufacturer's agents**, or *manufacturer's representatives*, work for several producers and carry noncompetitive, complementary merchandise in an exclusive territory. Manufacturer's agents act as a producer's sales arm in a territory and are principally responsible for the transactional channel functions, primarily sell-

drop shippers 承运批发商；desk jobbers 批发商；manufacturer's representatives 生产商代表。

Century 21 has about 7,700 independently owned and operated broker offices in 68 countries and territories worldwide.

Century 21 Real Estate, LLC
www.century21.com

ing. They are used extensively in the automotive supply, footwear, and fabricated steel industries.

By comparison, **selling agents** represent a single producer and are responsible for the entire marketing function of that producer. They design promotional plans, set prices, determine distribution policies, and make recommendations on product strategy. Selling agents are used by small producers in the textile, apparel, food, and home furnishing industries.

Brokers are independent firms or individuals whose principal function is to bring buyers and sellers together to make sales. Brokers, unlike agents, usually have no continuous relationship with the buyer or seller but negotiate a contract between two parties and then move on to another task. Brokers are used extensively by producers of seasonal products (such as fruits and vegetables) and in the real estate industry.

A unique broker that acts in many ways like a manufacturer's agent is a food broker, representing buyers and sellers in the grocery industry. Food brokers differ from conventional brokers because they act on behalf of producers on a permanent basis and receive a commission for their services. For example, Nabisco uses food brokers to sell its candies, margarine, and Planters peanuts, but it sells its line of cookies and crackers directly to retail stores.

Manufacturer's Branches and Offices Unlike merchant wholesalers, agents, and brokers, manufacturer's branches and sales offices are wholly owned extensions of the producer that perform wholesaling activities. Producers assume wholesaling functions when there are no intermediaries to perform these activities, customers are few in number and geographically concentrated, or orders are large or require significant attention. A *manufacturer's branch office* carries a producer's inventory and performs the functions of a full-service wholesaler. A *manufacturer's sales office* does not carry inventory, typically performs only a sales function, and serves as an alternative to agents and brokers.

垂直营销体系与渠道伙伴关系
Vertical Marketing Systems and Channel Partnerships

传统营销渠道被描述为由独立生产商和中间商所组成的、从事商品和服务分销业务的一个松散网络。

The traditional marketing channels described so far represent a loosely knit network of independent producers and intermediaries brought together to distribute goods and services. However, other channel arrangements exist for the purpose of

Tiffany & Co. and H&R Block represent two different types of vertical marketing systems. Read the text to find out how they differ.

Tiffany & Co.
www.tiffany.com

H&R Block
www.hrblock.com

fabricate 制造，装配；selling agents 销售代理商；manufacturer's branch office 生产商分支机构。

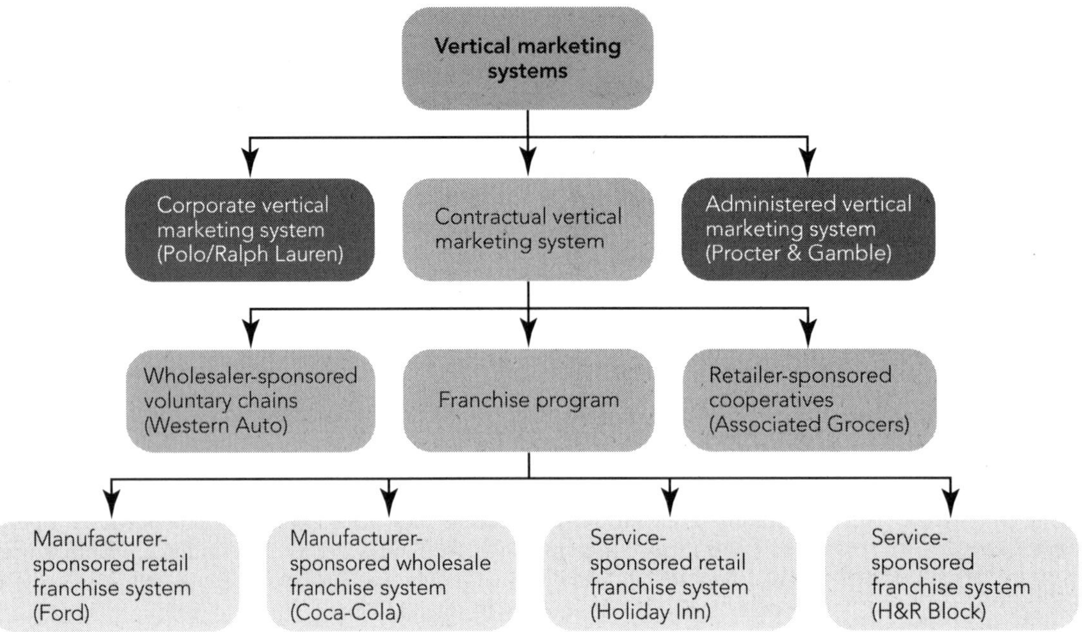

FIGURE 15–8
There are three major types of vertical marketing systems—corporate, contractual, and administered. Contractual systems are the most popular for reasons described in the text.

improving efficiency in performing channel functions and achieving greater marketing effectiveness. These arrangements are called vertical marketing systems and channel partnerships. **Vertical marketing systems** are professionally managed and centrally coordinated marketing channels designed to achieve channel economies and maximum marketing impact. Figure 10–8 depicts the major types of vertical marketing systems: corporate, contractual, and administered.

Corporate Systems The combination of successive stages of production and distribution under a single ownership is a *corporate vertical marketing system*. For example, a producer might own the intermediary at the next level down in the channel. This practice, called *forward integration*, is exemplified by Ralph Lauren, which manufactures clothing and also owns apparel shops. Other examples of forward integration include Goodyear, Apple, and Sherwin-Williams. Alternatively, a retailer might own a manufacturing operation, a practice called *backward integration*. For example, Kroger supermarkets operate manufacturing facilities that produce everything from aspirin to cottage cheese for sale under the Kroger label. Tiffany & Co., the exclusive jewelry retailer, manufactures about half of the fine jewelry items for sale through its 150 stores and boutiques worldwide.

Companies seeking to reduce distribution costs and gain greater control over supply sources or resale of their products pursue forward and backward integration. However, both types of integration increase a company's capital investment and fixed costs. For this reason, many companies favor contractual vertical marketing systems to achieve channel efficiencies and marketing effectiveness.

在契约型垂直营销体系下，独立生产公司与独立分销公司彼此签订契约，整合双方力量，以获得独自难以达到的更大的功能利益和营销成效。

Contractual Systems Under a *contractual vertical marketing system*, independent production and distribution firms integrate their efforts on a contractual basis to obtain greater functional economies and marketing impact than they could achieve alone. Contractual systems are the most popular among the three types of vertical marketing systems.

Three variations of contractual systems exist. *Wholesaler-sponsored voluntary chains* involve a wholesaler that develops a contractual relationship with small, independent retailers to standardize and coordinate buying practices, merchandising pro-

vertical marketing systems 垂直营销体系；forward integration 后向一体化。

grams, and inventory management efforts. With the organization of a large number of independent retailers, economies of scale and volume discounts can be achieved to compete with chain stores. IGA and Ben Franklin variety and craft stores represent wholesaler-sponsored voluntary chains. *Retailer-sponsored cooperatives* exist when small, independent retailers form an organization that operates a wholesale facility cooperatively. Member retailers then concentrate their buying power through the wholesaler and plan collaborative promotional and pricing activities. Examples of retailer-sponsored cooperatives include Associated Grocers and Ace Hardware.

The most visible variation of contractual systems is franchising. **Franchising** is a contractual arrangement between a parent company (a franchisor) and an individual or firm (a franchisee) that allows the franchisee to operate a certain type of business under an established name and according to specific rules.

Four types of franchise arrangements are most popular. *Manufacturer-sponsored retail franchise systems* are prominent in the automobile industry, where a manufacturer such as Ford licenses dealers to sell its cars subject to various sales and service conditions. *Manufacturer-sponsored wholesale systems* exist in the soft-drink industry, where Pepsi-Cola licenses wholesalers (bottlers) that purchase concentrate from Pepsi-Cola and then carbonate, bottle, promote, and distribute its products to retailers and restaurants. *Service-sponsored retail franchise systems* are provided by firms that have designed a unique approach for performing a service and wish to profit by selling the franchise to others. Holiday Inn, Avis, and McDonald's represent this franchising approach. *Service-sponsored franchise systems* exist when franchisors license individuals or firms to dispense a service under a trade name and specific guidelines. Examples include Snelling and Snelling, Inc., employment services and H&R Block tax services. Franchising is discussed further in Chapter 13.

相比较而言，管理型垂直营销体系是依靠一个渠道成员的规模和影响力而不是所有权来协调生产分销的各个连续阶段。

Administered Systems In comparison, *administered vertical marketing systems* achieve coordination at successive stages of production and distribution by the size and influence of one channel member rather than through ownership. Procter & Gamble, given its broad product assortment ranging from disposable diapers to detergents, is able to obtain cooperation from supermarkets in displaying, promoting, and pricing its products. Wal-Mart can obtain cooperation from manufacturers in terms of product specifications, price levels, and promotional support, given its position as the world's largest retailer.

渠道伙伴关系是指渠道成员之间建立的一种协议和程序，其目的是通过渠道实现向生产者订货并将产品实体分销给最终消费者。渠道伙伴关系的核心特征是实现了信息和沟通技术的共享，目的在于更好地服务顾客，降低履行渠道职能的时间与成本。

Channel Partnerships Increasingly, channel members are forging channel partnerships akin to supply partnerships described in Chapter 4. A **channel partnership** consists of agreements and procedures among channel members for ordering and physically distributing a producer's products through the channel to the ultimate consumer. A central feature of channel partnerships is the collaborative use of information and communication technology to better serve customers and reduce the time and cost of performing channel functions. Channel partnerships are elaborated upon in Chapter 11 on supply chain and logistics management.

learning review

3. What is the difference between a direct and an indirect channel?
4. Why are channels for business products typically shorter than channels for consumer products?
5. What is the principal distinction between a corporate vertical marketing system and an administered vertical marketing system?

retailer-sponsored cooperatives 零售商发起的合作体系；franchise 特许经营；channel partnership 渠道伙伴关系。

渠道选择与管理
CHANNEL CHOICE AND MANAGEMENT

Marketing channels not only link a producer to its buyers but also provide the means through which a firm implements various elements of its marketing strategy. Therefore, choosing a marketing channel is a critical decision.

渠道选择与管理的影响因素
Factors Affecting Channel Choice and Management

Environmental forces have broadened Tupperware Corporation's marketing channel.

Tupperware Corporation
www.tupperware.com

The final choice of a marketing channel by a producer depends on a number of factors that often interact with each other.

Environmental Factors Environmental factors have an important effect on the choice and management of a marketing channel. For example, Tupperware Corporation, a name synonymous with kitchen utensils and plastic storage containers sold at Tupperware parties, now also uses shopping mall kiosks and an online catalog to sell its wares. Changing family lifestyles with high employment among women prompted this action. Advances in the technology of growing, transporting, and storing perishable cut flowers has allowed Wal-Mart to buy from flower growers around the world. Wal-Mart's annual cut flower sales makes it the largest flower retailer in the world. The Internet has created new marketing channel opportunities for a variety of products, including consumer electronics, books, music, video, clothing, and accessory items.

Regulatory factors also influence channel choice, notably in global markets. Read the Marketing Matters box to learn how Avon responded to China's ban on direct selling and subsequent lifting of the ban.

Consumer Factors Consumer characteristics have a direct bearing on the choice and management of a marketing channel. Determining which channel is most appropriate is based on answers to fundamental questions such as: Who are potential customers? Where do they buy? When do they buy? How do they buy? What do they buy? These answers also indicate the type of intermediary best suited to reaching target buyers.

For example, Fila, a higher-end activewear apparel manufacturer that sold its product line through specialty athletic stores and pro shops, realized that it needed to broaden its market coverage. It signed a distribution agreement with Kohl's department stores for a line of moderately priced activewear bearing the Fila brand. According to a company spokesperson, "The (Fila) labels sell mainly to 14- to 24-year olds. (Kohl's) gives a chance to reach women between 25 and later 40s, the family consumer."

Product Factors In general, highly sophisticated products such as large, scientific computers, unstandardized products such as custom-built machinery, and products of high unit value, such as commercial aircraft, are distributed directly to buyers. Unsophisticated, standardized products with low unit value, such as table salt, are typically distributed through indirect channels. A product's stage in the life cycle also affects marketing channels. This was shown in the description of the fax machine product life cycle in Chapter 8.

Company Factors A firm's financial, human, or technological capabilities affect channel choice. For example, firms that are unable to employ a salesforce might use manufacturer's agents or selling agents to reach wholesalers or buyers. If a firm has multiple products for a particular target market, it might use a direct channel. Firms with a limited product line might use intermediaries to reach buyers.

---

sophisticate 精密；unstandardized 非标准化。

Marketing Matters > > > > > entrepreneurship

Avon Is Calling Again in China

What do you do when your marketing channel is banned by a government? Just ask executives at Avon, Inc., the world's largest cosmetic and beauty products direct selling company.

Avon pioneered direct selling in China in 1990. By 1998, the company had about 75,000 active independent representatives successfully selling its product line in China. The entrepreneurial spirit among Chinese women had proven to fit well with Avon's direct selling channel. Then, in April 1998, the Chinese State Council issued an order banning all forms of direct selling in China.

In response, Avon established a retail distribution network that grew to include some 6,300 independent beauty boutiques and over 1,000 cosmetic parlors in department stores across China by 2005. Then, in December 2005, direct selling was permitted in China provided companies met specific operating and licensing requirements. Avon was the first company to meet these standards and began recruiting representatives. By 2009, Avon had over 230,000 active representatives in China. Avon's retail network has been retained to offer after-sales services—including order pick-ups and product returns—and sell Avon products.

Andrea Jung, Avon's chairwoman and CEO, says the market in China could soon add $1 billion to the company's annual profit.

Company factors also influence a change in marketing strategy. Nike withdrew its Starter line of athletic shoes and apparel from Wal-Mart after the company decided it was "a business that did not play to Nike's strengths" and "did not provide the avenue for growth necessary for Nike to reach its target revenue of $23 billion by 2011."

渠道选择需考虑的问题
Channel Choice Considerations

Recognizing that numerous routes to buyers exist and also recognizing the factors just described, marketing executives typically consider three questions when choosing a marketing channel and intermediaries:

1. Which channel and intermediaries will provide the best coverage of the target market?
2. Which channel and intermediaries will best satisfy the buying requirements of the target market?
3. Which channel and intermediaries will be the most profitable?

实现最佳目标市场覆盖要求关注密度，即在一个既定地理区域内的商店数量，以及在分销渠道的零售层面上所利用中间商的类型。

Target Market Coverage Achieving the best coverage of the target market requires attention to the *density*—that is, the number of stores in a geographical area—and type of intermediaries to be used at the retail level of distribution. Three degrees of distribution density exist: intensive, exclusive, and selective.

Intensive distribution means that a firm tries to place its products and services in as many outlets as possible. Intensive distribution is usually chosen for convenience products or services such as candy, fast food, newspapers, and soft drinks. For example, Coca-Cola's retail distribution objective is to place its products "within an arm's reach of desire." Cash, yes cash, is distributed intensively by Visa. It operates over 1 million automatic teller machines in more than 170 countries.

Exclusive distribution is the extreme opposite of intensive distribution because only one retailer in a specified geographical area carries the firm's products. Exclusive distribution is typically chosen for specialty products or services, such as some women's fragrances, men's and women's apparel and accessories, and yachts. Gucci, one

withdrew 退出，撤回；density 密度。

Read the text to learn which buying requirements are satisfied by Jiffy Lube and PETCO.

Jiffy Lube International
www.jiffylube.com

PETCO
www.petco.com

of the world's leading luxury goods companies, uses exclusive distribution in the marketing of its Yves Saint Laurent, Sergio Rossi, Boucheron, Opium, and Gucci brands.

Selective distribution lies between these two extremes and means that a firm selects a few retailers in a specific geographical area to carry its products. Selective distribution weds some of the market coverage benefits of intensive distribution to the control over resale evident with exclusive distribution. For example, Dell, Inc., chose selective distribution when it decided to sell its products through U.S. retailers along with its direct channel. According to Michael Dell, the company's CEO, "There were plenty of retailers who said, 'sell through us,' but we didn't want to show up everywhere." The company now sells a limited range of its products through Wal-Mart, Best Buy, and Staples, an office-products retailer. Dell's decision was consistent with current trends. Today, selective distribution is the most common form of distribution intensity.

渠道设计第二个需要考虑的因素是，当购买者购买产品与服务时，公司要获得至少能满足他们某些利益的渠道和中间商通路。

Satisfying Buyer Requirements A second consideration in channel choice is gaining access to channels and intermediaries that satisfy at least some of the interests buyers might want fulfilled when they purchase a firm's products or services. These interests fall into four broad categories: (1) information, (2) convenience, (3) variety, and (4) pre- or postsale services. Each relates to customer experience.

Information is an important requirement when buyers have limited knowledge or desire specific data about a product or service. Properly chosen intermediaries communicate with buyers through in-store displays, demonstrations, and personal selling. Consumer electronics manufacturers such as Apple have opened their own retail outlets staffed with highly trained personnel to inform buyers how their products can better satisfy each customer's needs.

Convenience has multiple meanings for buyers, such as proximity or driving time to a retail outlet. For example, 7-Eleven stores, with more than 36,000 outlets worldwide, many of which are open 24 hours a day, satisfy this interest for buyers. Candy and snack-food firms benefit by gaining display space in these stores. For other consumers, convenience means a minimum of time and hassle. Jiffy Lube, which promises to change engine oil and filters quickly, appeals to this aspect of convenience. For those who shop on the Internet, convenience means that Web sites must be easy to locate and navigate, and image downloads must be fast. A commonly held view among Web site developers is the "eight second rule": Consumers

multiple 多重的；filter 过滤器。

Going Online

Visit an Apple Store to See What All the Excitement Is About

Interested in visiting an Apple store to see what all the excitement is about? Is one of Apple's 250-plus stores in the world situated near you? If you answered "yes" to the first question and "no" to the second, then log on to www.ifoapplestore.com/db. Here you will find exterior and interior photographs and video tours of various Apple stores. To learn whether an Apple store is planned for your area, visit this Web site to find announcements of grand openings.

will abandon their efforts to enter or navigate a Web site if download time exceeds eight seconds.

Variety reflects buyers' interest in having numerous competing and complementary items from which to choose. Variety is evident in the breadth and depth of products and brands carried by intermediaries, which enhances their attraction to buyers. Thus, manufacturers of pet food and supplies seek distribution through pet superstores such as PETCO and PetSmart, which offer a wide array of pet products.

Pre- or postsale services provided by intermediaries are an important buying requirement for products such as large household appliances that require delivery, installation, and credit. Therefore, Whirlpool seeks dealers that provide such services.

Steven Jobs' decision to distribute Apple products through company-owned stores was motivated by the failure of retailers to deliver on these four consumer interests for Apple. Visit the Web site in the Going Online box to learn more about Apple stores.

For the answer to how Schick became a razor and blade market share leader in Japan, read the text.

Schick
www.schick.com

Profitability The third consideration in choosing a channel is profitability, which is determined by the margins earned (revenue minus cost) for each channel member and for the channel as a whole. Channel cost is the critical dimension of profitability. These costs include distribution, advertising, and selling expenses associated with different types of marketing channels. The extent to which channel members share these costs determines the margins received by each member and by the channel as a whole.

Companies routinely monitor the performance of their marketing channels. Read the Using Marketing Dashboards box on the next page to see how Charlesburg Furniture views the sales and profit performance of its marketing channels.

营销渠道的全球因素
Global Dimensions of Marketing Channels

Marketing channels around the world reflect traditions, customs, geography, and the economic history of individual countries and societies. Even so, the basic marketing channel functions must be performed. But differences do exist and are illustrated by marketing channels in Japan, one of the world's largest economies and a major U.S. trade partner.

Intermediaries outside Western Europe and North America tend to be small, numerous, and often owner operated. Japan, for example, has less than one-half of

complementary 互补的，补充的；routinely 例行的，常规的。

Using Marketing Dashboards

Channel Sales and Profit at Charlesburg Furniture

Charlesburg Furniture is one of 1,000 wood furniture manufacturers in the United States. The company sells its furniture through furniture store chains, independent furniture stores, and department store chains in the southern United States. The company has traditionally allocated its marketing funds for cooperative advertising, in-store displays, and retail sales support on the basis of dollar sales by channel.

Your Challenge As the Vice President of Sales & Marketing at Charlesburg Furniture, you have been asked to review the company's sales and profit in its three channels and recommend a course of action. The question: Should Charlesburg Furniture continue to allocate its marketing funds on the basis of channel dollar sales or profit?

Your Findings Charlesburg Furniture tracks the sales and profit from each channel (and individual customer) and the three-year trend of sales by channel on its marketing dashboard. This information is displayed in the marketing dashboard below.

Several findings stand out. Furniture store chains and independent furniture stores account for 85.2 percent of Charlesburg Furniture sales and 93 percent of company profit. These two channels also evidence growth as measured by annual percentage change in sales. By comparison, department store chains annual percentage sales growth has declined and recorded negative growth in 2009. This channel accounts for 14.8 percent of company sales and 7 percent of company profit.

Your Action Charlesburg Furniture should consider abandoning the practice of allocating marketing funds solely on the basis of channel sales volume. The importance of independent furniture stores to Charlesburg's profitability warrants further spending, particularly given this channel's favorable sales trend. Doubling the percentage allocation for marketing funds for this channel may be too extreme, however. Rather, an objective-task promotional budgeting method should be adopted (see Chapter 13). Charlesburg Furniture might also consider the longer term role of department store chains as a marketing channel.

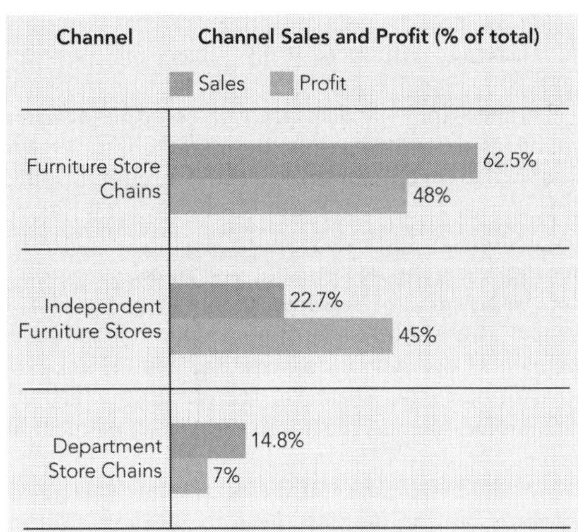

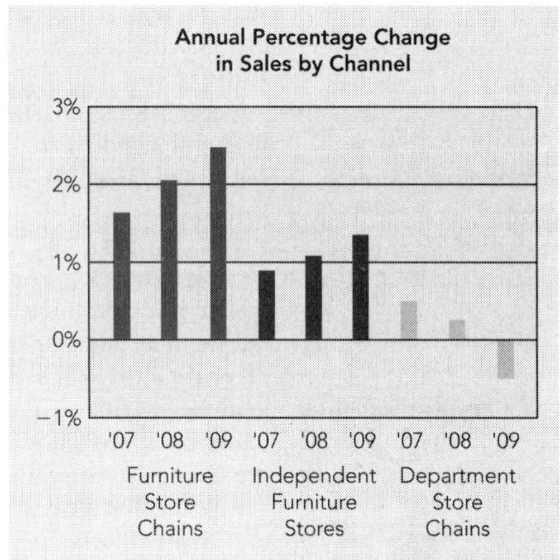

the population and a land mass less than 5 percent of the United States. However, Japan and the United States have about the same number of wholesalers and retailers. Why? Japanese marketing channels tend to include many intermediaries based on tradition and lack of storage space. As many as five intermediaries are involved in the distribution of soap in Japan compared with one or two in the United States.

storage 存储。

Understanding marketing channels in global markets is often a prerequisite to successful marketing. For example, Gillette attempted to sell its razors and blades through company salespeople in Japan as it does in the United States, thus eliminating wholesalers traditionally involved in marketing toiletries. However, Schick sold its razors and blades through the traditional Japanese channel involving wholesalers. The result? Schick achieved a commanding lead over Gillette in the Japanese razor and blade market.

Channel relationships also must be considered. In Japan, the distribution *keiretsu* (translated as "alignments") bonds producers and intermediaries together. The bond, through vertical integration and social and economic ties, ensures that each channel member benefits from the distribution alignment. The dominant member of the distribution *keiretsu*, which is typically a producer, has considerable influence over channel member behavior, including which competing products are sold by other channel members. Well-known Japanese companies such as Matsushita (electronics), Nissan and Toyota (automotive products), and Kirin (and other brewers and distillers) employ the distribution *keiretsu* extensively. Shiseido and Kanebo, for instance, influence the distribution of cosmetics through Japanese department stores.

渠道关系：冲突、合作与法律
Channel Relationships: Conflict, Cooperation, and Law

LO4

Unfortunately, because channels consist of independent individuals and firms, there is always potential for disagreements concerning who performs which channel functions, how profits are allocated, which products and services will be provided by whom, and who makes critical channel-related decisions. These channel conflicts necessitate measures for dealing with them. Sometimes they result in legal action.

Channel conflict is sometimes visible to consumers. Read the text to learn what antagonized independent Goodyear tire dealers.

Goodyear Tire and Rubber Company
www.goodyear.com

Sources of Conflict in Marketing Channels **Channel conflict** arises when one channel member believes another channel member is engaged in behavior that prevents it from achieving its goals. Two types of conflict occur in marketing channels: vertical conflict and horizontal conflict.

Vertical conflict occurs between different levels in a marketing channel—for example, between a manufacturer and a wholesaler or retailer or between a wholesaler and a retailer. Three sources of vertical conflict are most common. First, conflict arises when a channel member bypasses another member and sells or buys products direct, a practice called **disintermediation**. This conflict emerged when Jenn-Air, a producer of kitchen appliances, decided to terminate its distributors and sell directly to retailers. Second, disagreements over how profit margins are distributed among channel members produce conflict. This happened when the world's biggest music company, Universal Music Group, adopted a pricing policy for CDs that squeezed the profit margins for specialty music retailers. A third conflict situation arises when manufacturers believe wholesalers or retailers are not giving their products adequate attention. For example, Nike stopped shipping popular sneakers such as Nike Shox NZ to Foot Locker in retaliation for the retailer's decision to give more shelf space to shoes costing under $120.

Horizontal conflict occurs between intermediaries at the same level in a marketing channel, such as between two or more retailers (Target and Kmart) or two or more wholesalers that handle the same manufacturer's brands. Two sources of horizontal conflict are common. First,

keiretsu 企业集团（源自于日本）; channel conflict 渠道冲突 ; vertical conflict 垂直冲突 ; disintermediation 去中介化 ; horizontal conflict 水平冲突。

horizontal conflict arises when a manufacturer increases its distribution coverage in a geographical area. For example, a franchised Lexus dealer in Chicago might complain to Toyota that another franchised Lexus dealer has located too close to its dealership. Second, dual distribution causes conflict when different types of retailers carry the same brands. For instance, Goodyear tire dealers became irate when Goodyear Tire Company decided to sell its brands through Sears, Wal-Mart, and Sam's Clubs. Many switched to competing tire makers.

Securing Cooperation in Marketing Channels Conflict can have destructive effects on the workings of a marketing channel, so it is necessary to secure cooperation among channel members.

Channel Captain One means is through a **channel captain**, a channel member that coordinates, directs, and supports other channel members. Channel captains can be producers, wholesalers, or retailers. P&G assumes this role because it has a strong consumer following in brands such as Crest, Tide, and Pampers. Therefore, it can set policies or terms that supermarkets will follow. McKesson, a pharmaceutical drug wholesaler, is a channel captain because it coordinates and supports the product flow from numerous small drug manufacturers to drugstores and hospitals nationwide. Wal-Mart and Office Depot are retail channel captains because of their strong consumer image, number of outlets, and purchasing volume.

Channel Influence A firm becomes a channel captain because it is the channel member with the ability to influence the behavior of other members. Influence can take four forms. First, economic influence arises from the ability of a firm to reward other members given its strong financial position or customer franchise. Microsoft Corporation and Wal-Mart have such influence. Expertise is a second source of influence. For example, American Hospital Supply helps its customers (hospitals) manage inventory and streamline order processing for hundreds of medical supplies. Third, identification with a particular channel member can create influence for that channel member. For instance, retailers may compete to carry the Ralph Lauren line, or clothing manufacturers may compete to be carried by Neiman Marcus, Nordstrom, or Bloomingdale's. In both instances, the desire to be identified with a channel member gives that firm influence over others. Finally, influence can arise from the legitimate right of one channel member to direct the behavior of other members. This situation would occur under contractual vertical marketing systems where a franchisor can legitimately direct how a franchisee behaves. Other means for securing cooperation in marketing channels rest in the different variations of vertical marketing systems.

Channel influence can be used to gain concessions from other channel members. For instance, some large supermarket chains expect manufacturers to pay allowances, in the form of cash or free goods, to stock and display their products. Some manufacturers call these allowances "extortion" as described in the Making Responsible Decisions box.

营销渠道的冲突一般通过渠道成员的谈判或影响而予以解决。有时候冲突也会导致法律纠纷问题。因此，了解影响渠道战略和实践的法律限制知识非常重要。

Legal Considerations Conflict in marketing channels is typically resolved through negotiation or the exercise of influence by channel members. Sometimes conflict produces legal action. Therefore, knowledge of legal restrictions affecting channel strategies and practices is important. Some restrictions like vertical price fixing and price discrimination. However, other legal considerations unique to marketing channels warrant attention.

In general, suppliers can select whomever they want as channel intermediaries and may refuse to deal with whomever they choose. However, the Federal Trade Commission and the Justice Department monitor channel practices that restrain competition, create monopolies, or otherwise represent unfair methods of competition

channel captain 渠道首领；restriction 限制，限定；monopoly 垄断。

Making Responsible Decisions ethics

Pay to Play: The Ethics of Slotting Allowances

Have you ever wondered why your favorite cookies are no longer to be found at your local supermarket? Or that delicious tortilla chip you like to serve at parties is missing from the shelf and replaced by another brand?

Blame it on slotting allowances. Some large supermarket chains demand slotting allowances from food manufacturers, paid in the form of money or free goods to stock and display products. These allowances, which can run up to $25,000 per item per store for a supermarket chain, cost U.S. food makers about $1 billion annually. Not surprisingly, slotting allowances have been labeled "ransom," "extortional allowances," and "commercial bribery" by manufacturers because they already pay supermarkets $25 billion a year in "trade dollars" to promote and discount their products. Small food manufacturers, in particular, view slotting allowances as an economic barrier to distribution for their products. Supermarket operators see these allowances as a reasonable cost of handling business for manufacturers. Incidentally, Wal-Mart and Costco do not solicit slotting allowances from manufacturers.

Is the practice of charging slotting allowances unethical behavior?

under the Sherman Act (1890) and the Clayton Act (1914). Six channel practices have received the most attention (see Figure 10–9).

双重分销尽管不属于非法，但在某些情况下仍被视为是限制竞争行为。最常见的情况是，一家制造商通过其纵向一体化的渠道分销产品，但这就与也销售公司产品的独立批发商和零售商展开了竞争。

Dual distribution, although not illegal, can be viewed as anticompetitive in some situations. The most common situation arises when a manufacturer distributes through its own vertically integrated channel in competition with independent wholesalers and retailers that also sell its products. If the manufacturer's behavior is viewed as an attempt to lessen competition by eliminating wholesalers or retailers, then such action would violate both the Sherman and Clayton Acts.

Vertical integration is viewed in a similar light. Although not illegal, this practice is sometimes subject to legal action under the Clayton Act if it has the potential to lessen competition or foster monopoly.

The Clayton Act specifically prohibits exclusive dealing and tying arrangements when they lessen competition or create monopolies. *Exclusive dealing* exists when a supplier requires channel members to sell only its products or restricts distributors from selling directly competitive products. *Tying arrangements* occur when a supplier requires a distributor purchasing some products to buy others from the supplier. These arrangements often arise in franchising. They are illegal if the tied products could be purchased at fair market values from other suppliers at desired quality standards of the franchiser. *Full-line forcing* is a special kind of tying arrangement. This practice involves a supplier requiring that a channel member carry its full line of products in order to sell a specific item in the supplier's line.

Even though a supplier has a legal right to choose intermediaries to carry and represent its products, a *refusal to deal* with existing channel members may be illegal

FIGURE 10–9
Channel strategies and practices are affected by legal restrictions. The Clayton Act and the Sherman Act restrict specific strategies and practices.

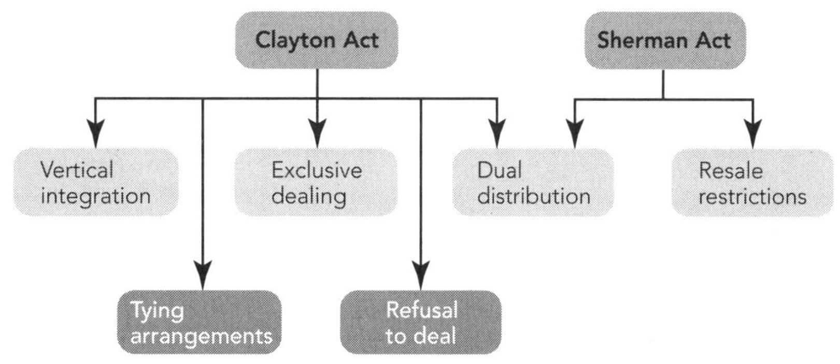

dual distribution 双重分销；vertical integration 纵向一体化；exclusive dealing 独家经销。

under the Clayton Act. *Resale restrictions* refer to a supplier's attempt to stipulate to whom distributors may resell the supplier's products and in what specific geographical areas or territories they may be sold. These practices have been prosecuted under the Sherman Act. Today, however, the courts apply the "rule of reason" in such cases and consider whether such restrictions have a "demonstrable economic effect."

learning review

6. What are the three questions marketing executives consider when choosing a marketing channel and intermediaries?
7. What are the three degrees of distribution density?
8. What is meant by exclusive dealing?

LEARNING OBJECTIVES REVIEW

LO1 *Explain what is meant by a marketing channel of distribution and why intermediaries are needed.*
A marketing channel of distribution, or simply a marketing channel, consists of individuals and firms involved in the process of making a product or service available for use or consumption by consumers or industrial users. Intermediaries make possible the flow of products from producers to buyers by performing three basic functions. The transactional function involves buying, selling, and risk taking because intermediaries stock merchandise in anticipation of sales. The logistical function involves the gathering, storing, and dispensing of products. The facilitating function assists producers in making goods and services more attractive to buyers. The performance of these functions by intermediaries creates time, place, form, and possession utility for consumers.

LO2 *Distinguish among traditional marketing channels, electronic marketing channels, and different types of vertical marketing systems.*
Traditional marketing channels describe the route taken by products and services from producers to buyers. This route can range from a direct channel with no intermediaries, because a producer and ultimate consumers deal directly with each other, to indirect channels where intermediaries (agents, wholesalers, distributors, or retailers) are inserted between a producer and consumer and perform numerous channel functions. Electronic marketing channels employ the Internet to make goods and services available for consumption or use by consumer or business buyers. Vertical marketing systems are professionally managed and centrally coordinated marketing channels designed to achieve channel economics and maximum marketing impact. There are three major types of vertical marketing systems (VMS). A corporate VMS combines successive stages of production and distribution under a single ownership. A contractual VMS exists when independent production and distribution firms integrate their efforts on a contractual basis to obtain greater functional economies and marketing impact than they could achieve alone. An administered VMS achieves coordination at successive stages of production and distribution by the size and influence of one channel member rather than through ownership.

LO3 *Describe the factors and considerations that affect a company's choice and management of a marketing channel.*
Four factors affect a company's choice and management of a marketing channel. These are environmental factors, consumer factors, product factors, and company factors, all of which interact with each other. Recognizing that numerous routes to buyers exist and also recognizing the factors just described, marketers consider three questions when choosing and managing a marketing channel and intermediaries. First, which channel and intermediaries will provide the best coverage of the target market? Marketers typically choose one of three levels of market coverage: intensive, selective, or exclusive distribution. Second, which channel and intermediaries will best satisfy the buying requirements of the target market? These buying requirements fall into four categories: information, convenience, variety, and attendant services. Finally, which channel and intermediaries will be the most profitable? Here marketers look at the margins earned (revenues minus cost) for each channel member and for the channel as a whole.

LO4 *Recognize how conflict, cooperation, and legal considerations affect marketing channel relationships.*
Because marketing channels consist of independent individuals and firms, there is always potential for conflict which sometimes results in legal action. So channel members try to find ways to cooperate for their mutual benefit. Two types of conflict occur in marketing channels. Vertical conflict occurs between different levels in a marketing channel, for example, between a manufacturer and a wholesaler or retailer, or between a wholesaler and a retailer. Horizontal conflict occurs between intermediaries at the same level in a marketing channel, such as between two retailers or two or more wholesalers that handle the same manufacturer's brands. Because conflict can have destructive effects on the workings of a marketing channel, channel members seek ways to cooperate. One way is through a channel captain—a channel member that coordinates, directs, and supports other channel members. A firm becomes a channel captain because of its ability to influence the behavior of other channel members. Nevertheless, channel conflict can result in legal action. The most common legal actions arise from channel practices that restrain competition, create monopolies, or represent unfair methods of competition.

---

resale restrictions 转售限制。

FOCUSING ON KEY TERMS

brokers
channel captain
channel conflict
channel partnership
direct marketing channels
disintermediation
dual distribution
electronic marketing channels
exclusive distribution
franchising
industrial distributor
intensive distribution
manufacturer's agents
marketing channel
merchant wholesalers
multichannel marketing
selective distribution
selling agents
strategic channel alliances
vertical marketing systems

APPLYING MARKETING KNOWLEDGE

1 A distributor for Celanese Chemical Company stores large quantities of chemicals, blends these chemicals to satisfy requests of customers, and delivers the blends to a customer's warehouse within 24 hours of receiving an order. What utilities does this distributor provide?

2 Suppose the president of a carpet manufacturing firm has asked you to look into the possibility of bypassing the firm's wholesalers (who sell to carpet, department, and furniture stores) and selling direct to these stores. (*a*) What caution would you voice on this matter, and (*b*) what type of information would you gather before making this decision?

3 What type of channel conflict is likely to be caused by dual distribution, and what type of conflict can be reduced by direct distribution? Why?

4 How does the channel captain idea differ among corporate, administered, and contractual vertical marketing systems with particular reference to the use of the different forms of influence available to firms?

5 Comment on this statement: "The only distinction among merchant wholesalers and agents and brokers is that merchant wholesalers take title to the products they sell."

6 (*a*) How do specialty, shopping, and convenience goods generally relate to intensive, selective, and exclusive distribution? (*b*) Give a brand name that is an example of each goods-distribution matchup.

7 How would you respond to the statement: "Marketing channels with the highest sales always produce the highest profit."

building your marketing plan

Does your marketing plan involve selecting channels and intermediaries? If the answer is no, read no further and do not include this element in your plan. If the answer is yes:

1 Identify which channel and intermediaries will provide the best coverage of the target market for your product or service.

2 Specify which channel and intermediaries will best satisfy the important buying requirements of the target market.

3 Determine which channel and intermediaries will be the most profitable.

4 Select your channel(s) and intermediary(ies).

video case 10 Act II Microwave Popcorn: The Surprising Channel

"We developed the technology that launched the microwave popcorn business and helped make ACT II the number one brand in the world," says Jack McKeon, president of Golden Valley Microwave Foods, a division of ConAgra Foods, Inc. "But we were also lucky along the way, as we backed into what has become one of the biggest distribution channels in the industry today, one that no one ever saw coming." Founded in 1978, ACT II is a global leader in producing and marketing microwave popcorn. But it hasn't always been easy.

THE LAUNCH: THE IDEA AND THE TECHNOLOGY

In the mid-1980s, only about 15 percent of U.S. households had microwave ovens, so launching a microwave foods business was risky. ACT II's initial marketing research turned up two key points of difference or benefits that people wanted in their microwave popcorn: (1) fewer unpopped kernels and (2) good popping results in all types of microwave ovens, even low-powered ovens—the kind that many households with microwaves had at the time. ACT II's research and development (R&D) staff successfully addressed these wants by developing a microwave popcorn bag utilizing a thin strip of material laminated between layers of paper, which focused the microwave energy to produce high-quality popped corn, regardless of an oven's power. This breakthrough significantly increased the size of the microwave popcorn market (and is still used in all microwave popcorn bags today). Using its revolutionary package, ACT II was introduced in 1984.

THE LUCKY DAY: BOTH CAPITAL AND MASS MERCHANDISERS

From 1978 until it became public in September 1986, ACT II was privately owned. Like most start-ups, ACT II was severely undercapitalized due to the cost of developing and introducing the brand. As a result, ACT II needed a partner to help develop the business. Its solution was to enter into a licensing agreement to share its technology for packaging microwave popcorn with one of the largest food manufacturers in the industry. The licensing partner would sell the popcorn under its own brand name in grocery stores and supermarkets. In turn, ACT II agreed it would not distribute its ACT II brand in U.S. grocery stores or supermarkets for 10 years. This meant that ACT II had to find other channels of distribution in which to sell its microwave popcorn.

For the next 10 years, the company developed many new channels. ACT II products were sold through vending machines, video stores (Blockbuster), institutions (movie theaters, colleges, military bases), drugstores (Walgreen's, Rite-Aid, CVS/Pharmacy), warehouse club stores (e.g., Sam's Club, Costco, BJ's), and convenience stores (7-Eleven, Circle K). "But the huge opportunity we discovered and developed was the mass merchandiser channel through chains like Wal-Mart and Target," says McKeon. "ACT II microwave popcorn was the first item of any kind to sell a million units in a week for Target, and that happened in 1987. Wal-Mart, too, was on the front end of this market and today is the top seller of microwave popcorn in any channel, selling far more popcorn than the leading grocery chains. Mass merchandisers now account for over a third of all the microwave popcorn sold in the U.S. They created the ACT II business as we know it today, and it was accomplished without a dime of conventional consumer promotions. That's one of the really unique parts of the ACT II story."

THE SITUATION TODAY

In the United States, more than 90 percent of households own microwave ovens. In addition, more than 60 percent of households are microwave popcorn consumers who spent more than $665 million on the product category in 2008. Orville Redenbacher's popcorn, also owned by ConAgra Foods, is now the market share leader with $142 million in sales while ACT II is #5 with $59 million in sales. "Our marketing research shows ACT II is especially strong in young families with kids," says Frank Lynch, vice president of marketing at Golden Valley. This conjures up an image of Mom and Dad watching a movie on TV with the kids and eating ACT II popcorn, a picture

close to reality. "ACT II has good market penetration in almost all age, income, urban versus rural, and ethnic segments," he continues.

"From the beginning, ACT II has been a leader in the microwave popcorn industry," says McKeon, "and we plan to continue that record." As evidence, he cites a number of ACT II "firsts":

- First mass-marketed microwave popcorn.
- First flavored microwave popcorn.
- First microwave popcorn tub.
- First fat-free microwave popcorn.
- First extra-butter microwave popcorn.
- First one-step sweetened microwave popcorn.

This list highlights a curious market segmentation phenomenon that has emerged in the last five years—the no-butter versus plenty-of-butter consumers. Originally, popcorn was seen as junk food. Later studies by nutritionists pointed out its health benefits: low calories and high fiber. This caused ACT II to introduce its low-fat popcorn to appeal to the health-conscious segment of consumers. However, when it comes to eating popcorn while watching a movie at home on TV, the more butter on their popcorn, the better. Recently, much of the growth in popcorn sales has been in the spoil-yourself-with-a lot-of-butter-on-your-popcorn segment.

Because of these diverse consumer tastes in popcorn, ACT II has developed a variety of popcorn products around its brand. Besides the low-fat and extra butter versions, these include the original flavors (natural, butter, and Kettle Corn), sweet glazed products (Caramel Corn and Buttery Cinnamon), and popcorn in tubs, mini-bags, and balls.

ACT II is positioned as unpretentious, fun, and youthful—a great product at a reasonable price. By stressing value, ACT II is responding to today's growing value consciousness of consumers seeking quality products at reasonable prices. These strategies have enabled ACT II to remain a leader in the microwave popcorn market.

OPPORTUNITIES FOR FUTURE GROWTH

For many years, the growth of the microwave popcorn industry closely followed the growth of household ownership of microwave ovens—from under 20 percent to more than 90 percent. But now, with a microwave oven in virtually every U.S. home, ACT II is trying to identify new market segments, new products, and innovative ways to appeal to all the major marketing channels.

In the United States, ACT II's strategy must include finding creative ways to continue to work with existing channels where it has special strength, such as the mass merchandiser channel. It also needs to further develop opportunities in the grocery store and supermarket channel. Now that the 10-year restriction on sales in grocery stores and supermarkets has expired, distribution through wholesalers that reach grocery stores and supermarkets is possible.

Global markets also present opportunities. ACT II has followed the penetration of microwave ovens in countries around the world, and used brokers to help gain distribution in those markets. However, foreign markets represent foreign tastes, something that does not always lend itself to standardized products. United Kingdom consumers, for example, think of popcorn as a candy or child's food rather than the salty snack it is in the United States. Even in DisneylandParis, France, American-style popcorn is absent, as French consumers sprinkle sugar on their popcorn. On the other hand, Swedes like theirs very buttery while many Mexicans like jalapeno-flavored popcorn.

Questions

1 Visit ACT II's Web site at www.ACTII.com and examine the assortment of products offered today. Are the assortment or the packaging related to its distribution channels or the segments they serve?

2 Use Figure 10–4 to create a description of the channels of distribution used for ACT II popcorn today.

3 Compared to selling through the nongrocery channels, what kind of product, price, and promotion strategies might ConAgra Foods use to reach the grocery channel more effectively?

4 What special marketing issues does ConAgra Foods face as it pursues growth in global markets?

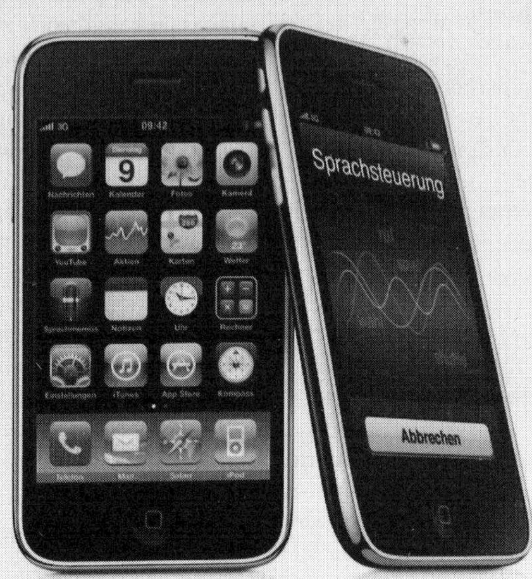
Sprachsteuerung
Abbrechen

11

消费者驱动的供应链与物流管理
Customer-Driven Supply Chain and Logistics Management

苹果公司：向全世界供应 IPHONE（3G）
APPLE INC.: SUPPLYING THE IPHONE 3G TO THE WORLD

LEARNING OBJECTIVES
After reading this chapter you should be able to:

LO1 Recognize the relationship between marketing channels, logistics, and supply chain management.

LO2 Describe how a company's supply chain aligns with its marketing strategy.

LO3 Identify the major logistics cost and customer service factors that managers consider when making supply chain decisions.

LO4 Describe the key logistics functions in a supply chain.

Apple excels in innovation . . . in global supply chain management. Yes, that's right, global supply chain management! Why?

Consider this. On July 11, 2008, the iPhone 3G was simultaneously launched in 21 countries regions: Australia, Austria, Belgium, Canada, Denmark, Finland, Germany, Chinese Hong Kong, Ireland, Italy, Japan, Mexico, the Netherlands, New Zealand, Norway, Portugal, Spain, Sweden, Switzerland, the United Kingdom, and the United States (1 million units were sold during the first weekend). Then, on August 22, 2008, the phone was introduced in 22 more countries: Argentina, Chile, Colombia, Czech Republic, Ecuador, El Salvador, Estonia, Greece, Guatemala, Honduras, Hungary, India, Liechtenstein, Macau, Paraguay, Peru, the Philippines, Poland, Romania, Singapore, Slovakia, and Uruguay. By late 2009, Apple expected to have its iPhone 3GS available in 70 countries with over 30 million units sold.

This feat was made possible by a carefully orchestrated supply chain consisting of no fewer than 10 component suppliers from three countries that produced circuit boards, tough-screen controllers, digital camera modules, video processing chips, and a host of other components. All of these were assembled, stored, and delivered to Apple's Shenzhen, China, facility to Apple Stores and authorized dealers in 70 countries in sufficient quantities to satisfy the enormous demand for the iPhone 3G. Not surprisingly, Apple was recognized by its peers as having the world's top supply chain in 2008.

Welcome to the critical world of customer-driven supply chain and logistics management. The essence of the problem is simple: It makes no sense to have brilliant marketing programs to sell world-class products if the products aren't available at the right time, at the right place, and in the right form and condition that customers want them.

This chapter describes the significance of supply chains and logistics management to the practice of marketing. In particular, attention is placed on the necessary alignment between supply chain management and marketing strategy, the trade-offs managers make between total distribution costs and customer service, and the increased application of information in managing the physical flow of goods to the final customer. Finally, the importance of reclaiming recyclable and reusable materials from customers for repair, remanufacturing, redistribution, and disposal is addressed in the context of reverse logistics.

供应链和物流管理的重要性
SIGNIFICANCE OF SUPPLY CHAIN AND LOGISTICS MANAGEMENT

We often hear or use the term *distribution* but seldom appreciate its significance in marketing. U.S. companies spend $560 billion transporting raw materials and finished goods each year, another $332 billion on material handling, warehousing, storage, and holding inventory, and $40 billion managing the distribution process, including the cost of information technology. Worldwide, these activities and investments cost companies about $3.4 trillion each year. In this section, we highlight contemporary perspectives on distribution, including supply chains and logistics, and describe the linkage between supply chain management and marketing strategy.

把营销渠道、物流与供应链管理联系起来
Relating Marketing Channels, Logistics, and Supply Chain Management

所谓**物流**，是指尽量以最低成本实现在适当时间、适当地点获得适当数量的适当产品的一系列活动。而这些活动的实施则称为**物流管理**，即以成本效益为原则，以满足顾客要求为目的，对原材料、在制品、产成品以及相关信息从供应地到消费地的流动进行组织管理的实践。

A marketing channel relies on logistics to make products available to consumers and industrial users, a point emphasized in Chapter 10. **Logistics** involves those activities that focus on getting the right amount of the right products to the right place at the right time at the lowest possible cost. The performance of these activities is **logistics management**, the practice of organizing the *cost-effective flow* of raw materials, in-process inventory, finished goods, and related information from point of origin to point of consumption to satisfy *customer requirements*.

Three elements of this definition deserve emphasis. First, logistics deals with decisions needed to move a product from the source of raw materials to consumption, or the *flow* of the product. Second, those decisions have to be made in a *cost-effective* manner. While it is important to drive down logistics costs, there is a limit—the third point of emphasis. A firm needs to drive down logistics costs as long as it can deliver expected *customer service*, which means satisfying customer requirements. The role of management is to see that customer needs are satisfied in the most cost-effective manner. When properly done, the results can be spectacular.

For example, Procter & Gamble set out to meet the needs of consumers more effectively by collaborating and partnering with its suppliers and retailers to ensure that the right products reached store shelves at the right time and at a lower cost. The effort was judged a success when, during an 18-month period, P&G's retail customers recorded a $65 million savings in logistics costs while customer service increased.

The Procter & Gamble experience is not an isolated incident. Today, logistics management is embedded in a broader view of distribution, consistent with the emphasis on supply and channel partnering described in Chapters 4 and 10. Companies now recognize that getting the right items needed for consumption or production to the right place at the right time in the right condition at the right cost is often beyond their individual capabilities and control. Instead, collaboration, coordination, and information sharing among manufacturers, suppliers, and distributors are necessary to create a seamless flow of goods and services to customers. This perspective is represented in the concept of a supply chain and the practice of customer-driven supply chain management.

供应链与营销渠道
Supply Chains versus Marketing Channels

A **supply chain** is a sequence of firms that perform activities required to create and deliver a product or service to ultimate consumers or industrial users. It differs from a marketing channel in terms of membership. A supply chain includes suppliers that provide raw material inputs to a manufacturer as well as the wholesalers and retailers that deliver products to you. The management process is also different.

---

logistics 物流；customer requirements 顾客要求。

FIGURE 11–1
Relating logistics management and supply chain management to supplier networks and marketing channels

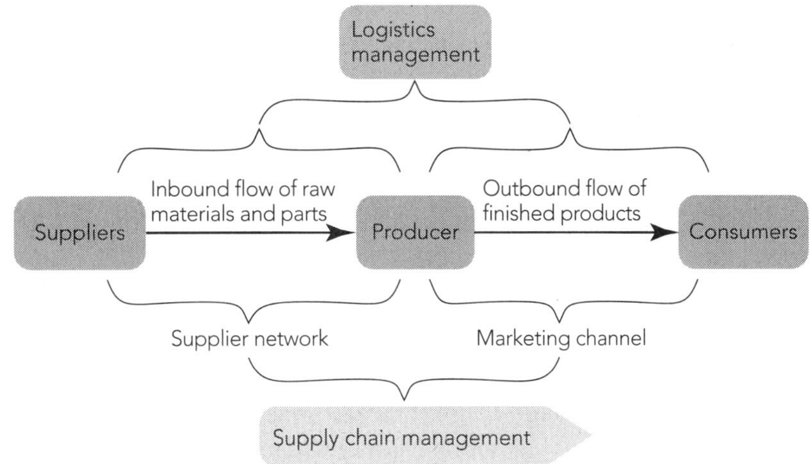

供应链管理是指以创造和传递能为消费者提供价值的对一条供应链上各公司间的信息与物流活动所进行的整合与组织。产品和服务为目的，

Supply chain management is the integration and organization of information and logistics activities *across firms* in a supply chain for the purpose of creating and delivering products and services that provide value to ultimate consumers. The relation among marketing channels, logistics management, and supply chain management is shown in Figure 11–1. An important feature of customer-driven supply chain management is its application of sophisticated information technology that allows companies to share and operate systems for order processing, transportation scheduling, and inventory and facility management.

全球供应商和供应链
Global Suppliers and Supply Chains

All companies are members of one or more supply chains. Supply chains span the globe; few companies rely only on domestic suppliers today.

Global suppliers provide ingredients in processed food, materials and parts in cars and trucks, components in consumer electronics, textiles and dyes in clothing—and the list goes on. For example, more than 80 percent of the active pharmaceutical ingredients in prescription and over-the-counter drugs sold in the United States are produced overseas, with the majority coming from manufacturers in India and China. Even a simple product like a cereal bar contains additives and ingredients from around the world (see Figure 11–2).

FIGURE 11–2
Cereal bars sold in stores and vending machines everywhere seem as American as apple pie—but their ingredients and additives come from all over the world thanks to global suppliers and supply chains. Enjoy your Kellogg's Nutri-Grain cereal bar!

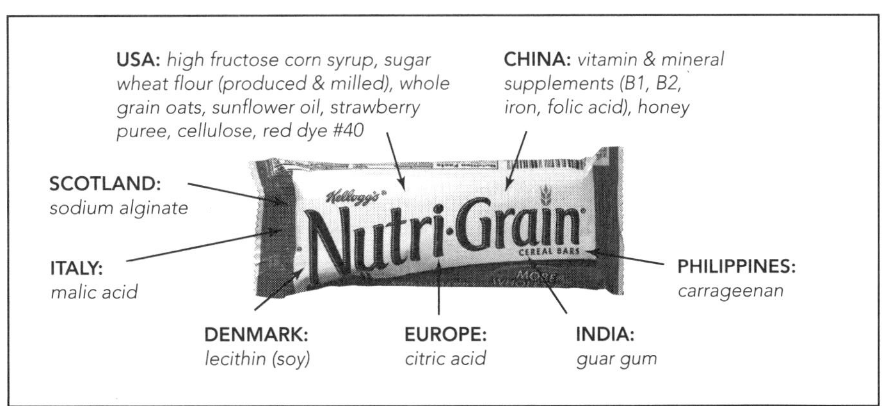

supply chain management 供应链管理；across firms 跨企业。

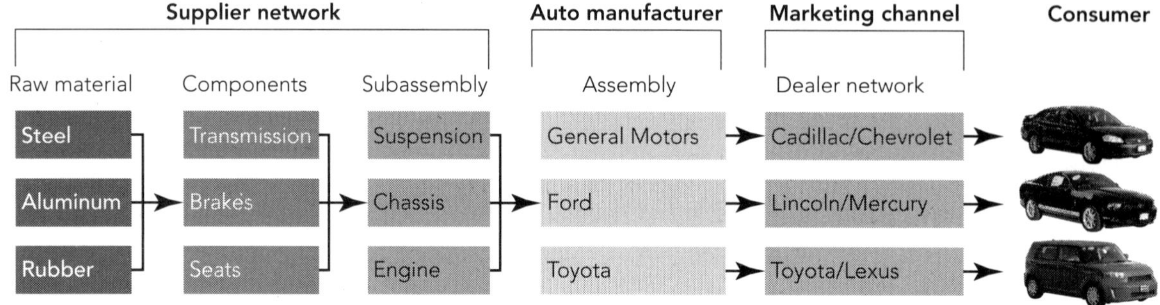

FIGURE 11–3
The automotive supply chain includes thousands of firms that provide the 5,000 or so electronic components and parts in a typical car.

采购、装配并运送一辆新轿车：汽车的供应链
Sourcing, Assembling, and Delivering a New Car: The Automotive Supply Chain

A supply chain is essentially a sequence of linked suppliers and customers in which every customer is, in turn, a supplier to another customer until a finished product reaches the final consumer. Even a simplified supply chain diagram for carmakers shown in Figure 11–3 illustrates how complex a supply chain can be. A carmaker's supplier network includes thousands of firms worldwide that provide the 5,000 or so electronic components and parts in a typical automobile. They provide items ranging from raw materials, such as steel and rubber, to components, including transmissions, tires, brakes, and seats, to complex subassemblies and assemblies evident in chassis and suspension systems that make for a smooth, stable ride. Coordinating and scheduling material and component flows for their assembly into actual automobiles by carmakers is dependent on logistical activities, including transportation, order processing, inventory control, materials handling, and information technology.

A central link is the carmaker supply chain manager, who is responsible for translating customer requirements into actual orders and arranging for delivery dates and financial arrangements for car dealers. This is not an easy task given different consumer preferences and how much consumers are willing to pay. To appreciate the challenge facing supply chain managers, visit the Volkswagen Web site described in the Going Online box, and assemble your own Jetta based on your preferences and price.

Logistical aspects of the automobile marketing channel are also an integral part of the supply chain. Major responsibilities include transportation (which involves the selection and oversight of external carriers—trucking, airline, railroad, and shipping companies—for cars and parts to dealers), the operation of distribution centers, the management of finished goods inventories, and order processing for sales. Supply chain managers also play an important role in the marketing channel. They work with car dealers to ensure that the right automobiles are delivered to different locations. In addition, they make sure that spare and service parts are available so that dealers can meet the car maintenance and repair needs of consumers. All of this is done with the help of information technology that links the entire automotive supply chain. What does all of this cost? Logistics costs represent 25 percent to 30 percent of the retail price of a typical new car.

供应链管理与营销战略
SUPPLY CHAIN MANAGEMENT AND MARKETING STRATEGY

The automotive supply chain illustration shows how information and logistics activities are integrated and organized across firms to create and deliver a car for you. What's missing from this illustration is the linkage between a specific company's supply chain and its marketing strategy. Just as companies have different marketing strategies, they also design and manage supply chains differently. The goals to be

sequence 序列；scheduling 安排，计划；automotive 汽车的。

Going Online

Build Your Own Jetta with a Mouse

Supply chain managers are responsible for having the right products at the right place at the right time at the right price for customers. In the automotive industry, this task is complex given the variety of car options available.

To appreciate the challenge, visit the Volkswagen Web site at www.VW.com. Click the link and choose a model such as a Jetta. Then click the "Start Building" button to select your trim, color, interior, and options. You will immediately obtain the manufacturer's suggested retail price (MSRP).

This easy task for you represents a sizable undertaking for a VW supply manager. You may not realize it, but VW comes in thousands of versions, including dealer-installed options you might want. A supply of these items has to be at the VW dealer for installation when you pick up your new car.

achieved by a firm's marketing strategy determine whether its supply chain needs to be more responsive or efficient in meeting customer requirements.

联合供应链与营销战略
Aligning a Supply Chain with Marketing Strategy

There are a variety of supply chain configurations, each of which is designated to perform different tasks well. Marketers today recognize that the choice of a supply chain follows from a clearly defined marketing strategy and involves three steps:

1. *Understand the customer.* To understand the customer, a company must identify the needs of the customer segment being served. These needs, such as a desire for a low price or convenience of purchase, help a company define the relative importance of efficiency and responsiveness in meeting customer requirements.
2. *Understand the supply chain.* Second, a company must understand what a supply chain is designed to do well. Supply chains range from those that emphasize being responsive to customer requirements and demand to those that emphasize efficiency with a goal of supplying products at the lowest possible delivered cost.
3. *Harmonize the supply chain with the marketing strategy.* Finally, a company needs to ensure that what the supply chain is capable of doing well is consistent with the targeted customer's needs and its marketing strategy. If a mismatch exists between what the supply chain does particularly well and a company's marketing strategy, the company will either need to redesign the supply chain to support the marketing strategy or change the marketing strategy. Read the Marketing Matters box on the next page to learn how IBM overhauled its complete supply chain to support its marketing strategy.

1. 理解顾客。为了理解顾客，一个公司必须明确其所服务的顾客群的需要。这些需要（比如追求购买的低价格或便利性）有助于公司明确在满足顾客要求方面效率性与反应性的相对重要程度。
2. 理解供应链。第二，一个公司必须明白如何设计一个运行良好的供应链。供应链既要强调对顾客要求和需求反应灵敏，又要实现以最低传递成本提供产品的效率。
3. 协调供应链与营销策略。最后，一个公司要保证其供应链的有效运营与目标顾客的需求和公司的营销战略协调一致。如果供应链的运营与公司的营销战略不匹配，则公司要么需要重新设计供应链以支持营销战略，要么需要改变营销战略。

How are these steps applied and how are efficiency and responsive considerations built into a supply chain? Let's look at how two well-known companies—Dell and Walmart—have harmonized their supply chain and marketing strategy.

戴尔：反应性的供应链
Dell: A Responsive Supply Chain

The Dell marketing strategy primarily targets customers who desire having the most up-to-date computer systems customized to their needs. These customers are also

configuration 结构；overhaul 彻底改造。

Marketing Matters > > > > > > customer value

IBM's Integrated Supply Chain—Delivering a Total Solution for Its Customers

IBM is one of the world's great business success stories because of its ability to reinvent itself to satisfy shifting customer needs in a dynamic global marketplace. The company's transformation of its supply chain is a case in point.

Beginning in 2001, IBM set about to build a single integrated supply chain that would handle raw material procurement, manufacturing, logistics, customer support, order entry, and customer fulfillment across all of IBM—something that had never been done before. Why would IBM undertake this task? According to IBM's CEO, Samuel J. Palmisano, "You cannot hope to thrive in the IT industry if you are a high-cost, slow-moving company. Supply chain is one of the new competitive battlegrounds. We are committed to being the most efficient and productive player in our industry."

The task wasn't easy. With factories in 10 countries, IBM buys 2 billion parts a year from 33,000 suppliers, offers 78,000 products available in 3 million possible variations, moves over 2 billion pounds of machines and parts annually, processes 1.7 million customer orders annually in North America alone, and operates in 150 countries. Yet with surprising efficiency, IBM overhauled its supply chain from raw material sourcing to postsales support.

Today, IBM is uniquely poised to configure and deliver a tailored mix of hardware, software, and service to provide a total solution for its customers. Not surprisingly, IBM's integrated supply chain is now heralded as one of the best in the world!

---

willing to: (1) wait to have their customized computer system delivered in a few days, rather than picking out a model at a retail store, and (2) pay a reasonable, though not the lowest, price in the marketplace. Given Dell's customer segment, the company has the option of adopting an efficient or responsive supply chain.

An efficient supply chain may use inexpensive, but slower, modes of transportation, emphasize economies of scale in its production process by reducing the variety of system configurations offered, and limit its assembly and inventory storage facilities to a single location, say Austin, Texas, where the company is headquartered. If Dell opted only for efficiency in its supply chain, it would be difficult if not impossible to satisfy its target customer's desire for rapid delivery and a wide variety of customizable products. Dell instead opted for a responsive supply chain. It relies on more expensive express transportation for receipt of components from suppliers and delivery of finished products to customers. The company achieves product variety and manufacturing efficiency by designing common platforms across several products and using common components. Moreover, Dell has invested heavily in information technology to link itself with suppliers and customers.

沃尔玛：高效的供应链
Walmart: An Efficient Supply Chain

Now let's consider Walmart. Walmart's marketing strategy is to be a reliable, lower-price retailer for a wide variety of mass consumption consumer goods. This strategy favors an efficient supply chain designed to deliver products to consumers at the lowest possible cost. Efficiency is achieved in a variety of ways. For instance, Walmart keeps relatively low inventory levels, and most is stocked in stores available for sale, not in warehouses gathering dust. The low inventory arises from Walmart's innovative use of *cross-docking*—a practice that involves unloading products from suppliers, sorting products for individual stores, and quickly reloading products onto its trucks for a particular store. No warehousing or storing of products occurs, except for a few hours or, at most, a day. Cross-docking allows Walmart to operate only a small number of distribution centers to service its vast network of Walmart Stores, Supercenters, Neighborhood Markets, Marketside, and Sam's Clubs, which contributes to efficiency. On the other hand, the company runs its own fleet of trucks to

headquartered 以……为总部所在地的；cross-docking 接驳式转运。

Dell and Walmart emphasize responsiveness and efficiency in their supply chains, respectively. The text details how they do this.

Dell, Inc.
www.dell.com

Walmart, Inc.
www.walmartstores.com

service its stores. This does increase cost and investment, but the benefits in terms of responsiveness justify the cost in Walmart's case.

Walmart has invested much more than its competitors in information technology to operate its supply chain. The company feeds information about customer requirements and demand from its stores back to its suppliers, which manufacture only what is being demanded. This large investment has improved the efficiency of Walmart's supply chain and made it responsive to customer needs.

Three lessons can be learned from these two examples. First, there is no one best supply chain for every company. Second, the best supply chain is the one that is consistent with the needs of the customer segment being served and complements a company's marketing strategy. And finally, supply chain managers are often called upon to make trade-offs between efficiency and responsiveness on various elements of a company's supply chain.

learning review

1. What is the principal difference between a marketing channel and a supply chain?
2. The choice of a supply chain involves what three steps?

顾客驱动的供应链中信息和物流管理的目标
OBJECTIVE OF INFORMATION AND LOGISTICS MANAGEMENT IN A CUSTOMER-DRIVEN SUPPLY CHAIN

供应链中信息和物流管理的目标是以最小的物流成本传递最大的顾客服务。

The objective of information and logistics management in a customer-driven supply chain is to minimize logistics costs while delivering maximum customer service. The Dell and Walmart examples highlighted how two well-known companies have realized this objective by different means. An important similarity between these two companies is that both use information to leverage logistics activities, reduce logistics costs, and improve customer service.

信息对供应链的反应速度与效率的影响
Information's Role in Supply Chain Responsiveness and Efficiency

Information consists of data and analysis regarding inventory, transportation, distribution facilities, and customers throughout the supply chain. Continuing advances in information technology make it possible to track logistics activities and customer service variables and manage them for efficiency and responsiveness. For example, information on customer demand patterns allows pharmaceutical companies such as Eli Lilly and GlaxoSmithKline to produce and stock drugs in anticipation of customer needs. This improves supply chain responsiveness because customers will find the drugs when and where they want them. Demand information improves supply chain efficiency because pharmaceutical firms are better able to meet customer needs and produce, transport, and store the required amount of inventory.

minimize 最小化；maximum 最大化；pharmaceutical 制药的，配药的。

Hewlett-Packard is a leader in the application of information technology to supply chain management.

Hewlett-Packard
www.hp.com

A variety of technologies are used to transmit and manage information in a supply chain. An **electronic data interchange (EDI)** combines proprietary computer and telecommunication technologies to exchange electronic invoices, payments, and information among suppliers, manufacturers, and retailers. When linked with store scanning equipment and systems, EDI provides a seamless electronic link from a retail checkout counter to suppliers and manufacturers. EDI is commonly used in retail, apparel, transportation, pharmaceutical, grocery, health care, and insurance industries, as well as by local, state, and federal government agencies. About 95 percent of the companies listed in the Fortune 1000 use EDI. At Hewlett-Packard, for example, 1 million EDI transactions are made every month.

还有一种技术称为外联网，这是一种基于互联网的网络，可以实现制造商与其供应商、分销商，有时候是其他合作伙伴（如广告代理机构）之间安全可靠的 B2B 交流。

Another technology is the *extranet*, which is an Internet-based network that permits secure business-to-business communication between a manufacturer and its suppliers, distributors, and sometimes other partners (such as advertising agencies). Extranets are less expensive and more flexible to operate than EDI because of their connection to the public Internet. This technology is prominent in private electronic exchanges described in Chapter 4. For example, Whirlpool's private exchange allows it to fulfill retailer orders quickly and inexpensively and better match appliance demand and supply.

Whereas EDI and extranets transmit information, other technologies help manage information in a supply chain. Enterprise resource planning (ERP) technology and supply chain management software track logistics cost and customer service variables, both of which are described next.

总物流成本概念

Total Logistics Cost Concept

For our purposes, **total logistics cost** includes expenses associated with transportation, materials handling and warehousing, inventory, stockouts (being out of inven-

electronic data interchange(EDI) 电子数据交换；extranet 外联网；total logistics cost 总物流成本。

FIGURE 11–4
How total logistics cost varies with the number of warehouses used based on inventory costs and transportation costs. The goal is to minimize total logistics cost.

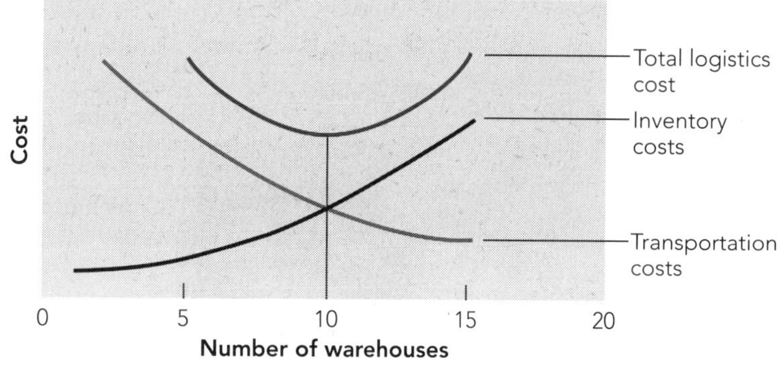

tory), order processing, and return goods handling. Many of these costs are interrelated so changes in one will impact the others. For example, as the firm attempts to minimize its transportation costs by shipping in larger quantities, it will also experience an increase in inventory levels. Larger inventory levels will not only increase inventory costs but should also reduce stockouts. It is important, therefore, to study the impact on all of the logistics decision areas when considering a change.

Figure 11–4 provides a graphic example. An oft-used supply chain strategy is for a firm to have a number of warehouses, which receive shipments in large quantities and then redistribute smaller shipments to local customers. As the number of warehouses increases, inventory costs rise and transportation costs fall. That is, more inventory is warehoused, but it is transported in volume closer to customers. The net effect is to minimize the total costs of logistics shown in Figure 11–4 by having 10 warehouses. This means the total cost curve is minimized at a point where neither of the two individual cost elements is at a minimum but the overall system is.

Studying its total logistics cost has had revolutionary consequences for National Semiconductor, which produces computer chips. In two years, it cut its standard delivery time 47 percent, reduced distribution costs 2.5 percent, and increased sales 34 percent by shutting down six warehouses around the world and air-freighting its microchips from its huge distribution center in Singapore. It does this even though it has six factories in Israel, Britain, and the United States. National also discovered that a lot of its chips were actually profit-losers, and it cut the number of products it sells by 45 percent, thereby simplifying logistics and increasing profits.

顾客服务概念
Customer Service Concept

如果把一条供应链比作一个流，那么其终点或说产出就是传递给顾客的服务。然而，服务成本可能很高昂。

If a supply chain is a *flow*, the end of it—or *output*—is the service delivered to customers. However, service can be expensive. One company found that to increase on-time delivery from a 95 percent rate to a 100 percent rate tripled total logistics costs. Higher levels of service require tactics such as more inventory to reduce stockouts, more expensive transportation to improve speed and lessen damage, and double or triple checking of orders to ensure correctness. A firm's goal should be to provide superior customer service while controlling logistics costs. Customer service is now seen not merely as an expense but as a means to increase customer satisfaction and sales. For example, a 3M survey about customer service among 18,000 European customers in 16 countries revealed surprising agreement in all countries about the importance of customer service. Respondents stressed factors such as condition of product delivered, on-time delivery, quick delivery after order placement, and effective handling of problems.

从供应链含义来看，**顾客服务**是指物流管理在时间、可靠性、沟通及便利性方面满足用户的能力。

Within the context of a supply chain, **customer service** is the ability of logistics management to satisfy users in terms of time, dependability, communication, and convenience. As suggested by Figure 11–5 on the next page, a supply chain manager's key task is to balance these four customer service factors against total logistics cost factors.

shipment 运输的货物；redistribute 重新分配，再分配。

FIGURE 11–5
Supply chain managers balance total logistics cost factors against customer service factors.

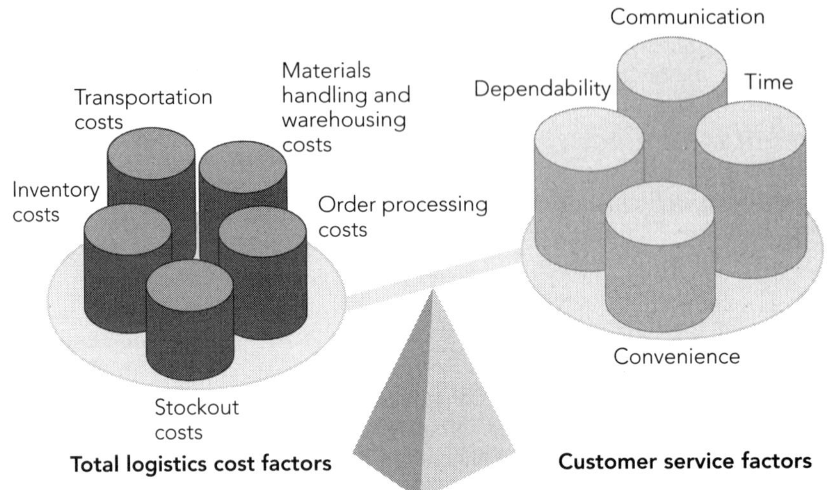

在供应链设置中，时间指某一商品的**前置期**，即从一款商品的订货到收到货物并准备使用或出售所间隔的时间。它也指订货处理周期或补货期，相对于消费者而言，这对零售商或批发商更加重要。

Time In a supply chain setting, time refers to **lead time** for an item, which means the lag from ordering an item until it is received and ready for use or sale. This is also referred to as *order cycle time* or *replenishment time* and may be more important to retailers or wholesalers than consumers. The various elements that make up the typical order cycle include recognition of the need to order, order transmittal, order processing, documentation, and transportation. A current emphasis in supply chain management is to reduce lead time so that customer inventory levels may be minimized. Another emphasis is to make the process of reordering and receiving products as simple as possible, often through electronic data and inventory systems called **quick response** or **efficient consumer response** delivery systems. These inventory management systems reduce the retailer's lead time for receiving merchandise, thereby lowering a retailer's inventory investment, improving customer service levels, and reducing logistics expense (see the Marketing Matters box). The order processing portion of lead time will be discussed later in this chapter.

Dependability Dependability is the consistency of replenishment. This is important to all firms in a supply chain and to consumers. It can be broken into three elements: consistent lead time, safe delivery, and complete delivery. Consistent service allows planning (such as appropriate inventory levels). Inconsistencies create surprises. Intermediaries may be willing to accept longer lead times if they know about them in advance and can thus make plans. While surprise delays may shut down a production line, early deliveries will be almost as troublesome because of the problems of storing the extra inventory. Dependability is essential for the just-in-time inventory strategies discussed at the end of the chapter.

Communication Communication is a two-way link between buyer and seller that helps in monitoring service and anticipating future needs. Status reports on orders are a typical example of improved communication between buyer and seller. The increased communication capability of transportation carriers has enhanced the accuracy of such tracing information and improved the ability of buyers to schedule shipments. Note, however, that such information is still reactive and is not a substitute for consistent on-time deliveries. Therefore, some firms have partnered with firms specializing in logistics in an effort to institutionalize a more proactive flow of useful information. Unisys, a major technology firm, relies on DHL's global service parts logistics system to enable monitoring, management, and inventory level reporting across regions of the world. This system provides timely information about the status of orders throughout the Unisys supply chain from multiple suppliers.

---

lead time 前置期；order cycle time 订货处理周期；replenishment time 补货期；quick response 快速反应；efficient consumer response 有效的顾客反应。

Marketing Matters > > > > > > > > technology

For Fashion and Food Merchandising, Haste Is as Important as Taste

Fashion and food have a lot in common. Both depend a lot on taste and both require timely merchandising. By its nature, fashion dictates that suppliers and retailers be able to adjust to new styles, colors, and different seasons. Fashion retailers need to identify what's hot, so it can be ordered quickly, and what's not, to avoid markdowns. Saks employs a *quick response* delivery system for fashion merchandise. Saks' point-of-sale scanner system records each day's sales. When stock falls below a minimum level, the system automatically generates a replenishment order. Vendors of fashion merchandise, such as Donna Karan (DKNY), receive an electronic order, which is processed within 48 hours.

Food marketers and retailers use the term *efficient consumer response* to describe their replenishment systems. All major food companies, including General Mills, Del Monte, Heinz, Nestlé, and Beatrice Foods, and many supermarket chains such as Kroger, Safeway, and A&P rely on electronic replenishment systems to minimize stockouts of popular items and overstocks of slow-moving items. Lowered retailer inventories and efficient logistics practices have been projected to save U.S. grocery shoppers $30 billion a year.

Convenience The concept of convenience means that there should be a minimum of effort on the part of the buyer in doing business with the seller. Is it easy for the customer to order? Are the products available from many outlets? Does the buyer have to buy huge quantities of the product? Will the seller arrange all necessary details, such as transportation? The seller must concentrate on removing unnecessary barriers to customer convenience. This customer service factor has promoted the use of vendor-managed inventory practices discussed later in the chapter.

顾客服务标准
Customer Service Standards

能够有效管理供应链的企业通常制定了一系列书面的顾客服务标准。这些标准成为努力的目标，并树立了衡量结果的标杆，从而便于实现有效控制。

Firms that operate effective supply chains usually develop a set of written customer service standards. These serve as objectives and provide a benchmark against which results can be measured for control purposes. In developing these standards, information is collected on customers' needs. It is also necessary to know what competitors offer as well as the willingness of customers to pay a bit more for better service. After these and similar questions are answered, realistic standards are set and an ongoing monitoring program is established. The examples below suggest that customer service standards will differ by type of firm.

Type of Firm	Customer Service Standard
Wholesaler	At least 98 percent of orders filled accurately
Manufacturer	Order cycle time of no more than five days
Retailer	Returns accepted within 30 days
Airline	At least 90 percent of arrivals on time
Trucker	A maximum of 5 percent loss and damage per year
Restaurant	Lunch served within five minutes of order

Effective customer service can yield substantial returns. The head of IBM's integrated supply chain group estimates that a 1 percent increase in customer service

concentrate 专心于，注意；monitoring 监控，监视，监督。

Using Marketing Dashboards

Diagnosing Out-of-Stocks and On-Time Delivery for Organic Produce

Supply chain managers recognize that out-of-stocks mean lost sales. And poor on-time delivery is often the culprit. These measures are routinely compared on a weekly or monthly basis against a numerical standard and each other.

Your Challenge You have just joined Superior Supermarkets as a distribution analyst. Superior Supermarkets is a 150-store chain that serves small cities and towns in the south central United States through its own distribution center. During your first meeting with the vice president of distribution, the topic of produce out-of-stocks arose. Specifically, organic produce (fresh fruits and vegetables) out-of-stocks had increased. Out-of-stocks are calculated as follows:

$$\text{Out-of-Stocks (\%)} = \frac{\text{Number of outlets where a brand or product is listed but unavailable}}{\text{Total number of outlets where a brand or product is listed}}$$

Poor on-time delivery of produce was the suspected reason for the rise in out-of-stocks. On-time delivery is calculated as follows:

$$\text{On-Time Delivery (\%)} = \frac{\text{Number of deliveries achieved in the time frame promised}}{\text{Total number of deliveries initiated in a time period}}$$

Your challenge is to examine whether on-time delivery performance might be the reason for the organic produce out-of-stocks situation at Superior Supermarkets.

Your Findings Superior Supermarkets monitors out-of-stocks and on-time delivery on a monthly basis. A 3 percent out-of-stock standard and a 98 percent on-time delivery standard have been set by the company. Monthly results for organic produce are displayed on the company's marketing dashboard shown below.

Clearly, the downward trend in on-time delivery corresponds with the upward trend in out-of-stocks for organic produce.

Your Action As a distribution analyst, you might recommend that the transportation department needs to improve its performance. However, the issue might reach deeper into the order cycle time for organic produce. Recall that order cycle time includes the recognition of the need to place, transmit, process, document, and transport the order. The actual *cause* of out-of-stocks might reside in the four prior elements of order cycle time and not just transportation.

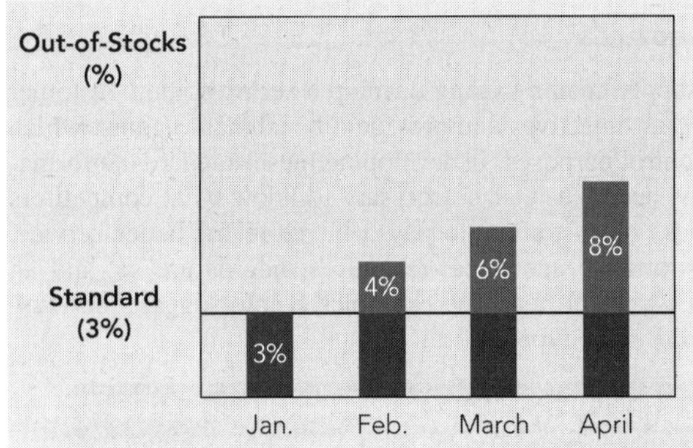

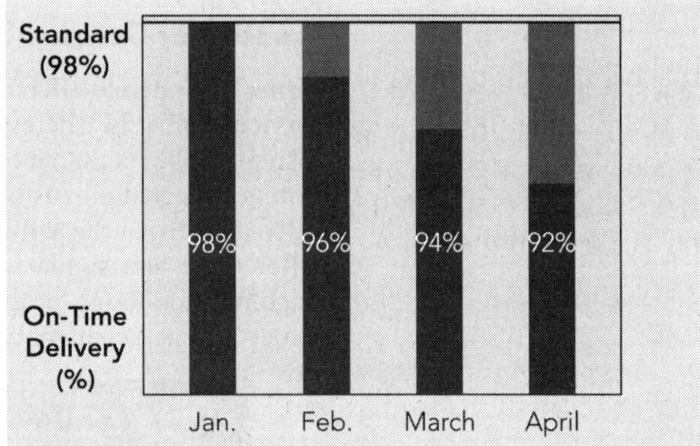

satisfaction translates into \$2 billion to \$3 billion of additional revenue to his company.

Companies rely on marketing dashboards to monitor customer service standards. Read the Using Marketing Dashboards box to see one application and interpretation of the link between out-of-stocks and on-time delivery.

---

additional 额外的，附加的。

learning review

3. The objective of information and logistics management in a supply chain is to _______________.
4. How does consumer demand information increase supply chain responsiveness and efficiency?
5. What is the relationship between the number of warehouses a company operates, its inventory costs, and its transportation costs?

供应链中物流的关键职能
KEY LOGISTICS FUNCTIONS IN A SUPPLY CHAIN

The four key logistic functions in a supply chain include (1) transportation, (2) warehousing and materials handling, (3) order processing, and (4) inventory management. These functions have become so complex and interrelated that many companies have outsourced them to third-party logistics providers.

Third-party logistics providers are firms that perform most or all of the logistics functions that manufacturers, suppliers, and distributors would normally perform themselves. Today, 77 percent of manufacturers listed in the Fortune 500 outsource one or more logistics functions, at least on a limited basis. Ryder Systems, UPS Supply Chain Solutions, FedEx Supply Chain Services, DHL, and Penske Logistics are just a few of the companies that specialize in handling logistics functions for their clients.

The four major logistics functions and the involvement of third-party logistics providers are described next.

FedEx Supply Chain Services and Ryder Systems are two third-party logistics providers that perform most or all of the logistics functions that manufacturers, suppliers, and distributors would normally perform.

FedEx Supply Chain Services
www.fedex.com

Ryder Systems
www.ryder.com

Third-party logistics providers 第三方物流提供商。

运 输
Transportation

LO4

Transportation provides the movement of goods necessary in a supply chain. There are five basic modes of transportation: railroads, motor carriers, air carriers, pipelines, and water carriers, and modal combinations involving two or more modes, such as truck trailers on a rail flatcar.

All transportation modes can be evaluated on six basic service criteria:

- *Cost.* Charges for transportation.
- *Time.* Speed of transit.
- *Capability.* What can be realistically carried with this mode.
- *Dependability.* Reliability of service regarding time, loss, and damage.
- *Accessibility.* Convenience of the mode's routes (such as pipeline availability).
- *Frequency.* Scheduling.

Figure 11–6 summarizes the relative service advantages and disadvantages of five modes of transportation available.

Railroads Railroads typically carry heavy, bulky items over long distances. Railroads can carry larger shipments than trucks (in terms of total weight per vehicle), but their routes are less extensive. Services include unit trains and intermodal service. A *unit train* is dedicated to one commodity (often coal), using permanently coupled cars that run a continuous loop from a single origin to a single destination and back. Even though the train returns empty, the process captures enough operating efficiencies to make it one of the lowest-cost transportation alternatives available. Unit trains keep to a specific schedule so that the customers can plan on reliable delivery, and they usually carry products that can be loaded and unloaded quickly and automatically.

Railroads also apply the unit train concept to *intermodal transportation*, which involves combining different transportation modes to get the best features of each. The result is a service that attracts high-value freight, which would normally go by

FIGURE 11–6
Advantages and disadvantages of five modes of transportation

TRANSPORTATION MODE	RELATIVE ADVANTAGES	RELATIVE DISADVANTAGES
Railroads	• Full capability • Extensive routes • Low cost	• Some reliability, damage problems • Not always complete pickup and delivery • Sometimes slow
Motor carriers	• Complete pickup and delivery • Extensive routes • Fairly fast	• Size and weight restrictions • Higher cost • More weather sensitive
Air carriers	• Fast • Low damage • Frequent departures	• High cost • Limited capabilities
Pipeline	• Low cost • Very reliable • Frequent departures	• Limited routes (accessibility) • Slow
Water carriers	• Low cost • Huge capacities	• Slow • Limited routes and schedules • More weather sensitive

capability 负载；dependability 可靠性；accessibility 可及性；frequency 频率；intermodal transportation 联合运输。

truck. The most popular combination is truck-rail, called *piggyback* or *trailer on flatcar (TOFC)*. The other popular use of an intermodal combination is associated with export/import traffic and uses containers in place of trailers. These containers can be loaded on ships, trains, and truck trailers. So in terms of the on-land segment of international shipments, a container is handled the same way as a trailer. Containers are used in international trade because they use less space on oceangoing vessels.

Motor Carriers In contrast to the railroad industry, the for-hire motor carrier industry is composed of many small firms, including independent truckers and firms that own their own trucks for transporting their own products.

The greatest advantage of motor carriers is the complete door-to-door service. Trucks can go almost anywhere there is a road, and with the design of specialized equipment, they can carry a variety of products. Their physical limitations are size and weight restrictions enforced by the states. Trucks have the reputation for maintaining a better record than rail for loss and damage and providing faster, more reliable service, especially for shorter distances. As a result, trucks carry higher-value goods that are time-sensitive and expensive to carry in inventory. The trade-off is that truck rates are substantially higher than rail rates.

Air Carriers and Express Companies Air freight is costly, but its speed may create savings in lower inventory. The items that can be carried are limited by space constraints and are usually valuable, time-sensitive, and lightweight, such as perishable flowers, clothing, and electronic parts. Specialized firms provide ground support in terms of collecting shipments and delivering them to the air terminal. When air freight is handled by major airlines—such as American, United, or Delta—it is often carried as cargo using the excess luggage space of scheduled passenger flights.

货运转运商是指那些将小件散装货集中成整装货，然后通常以低等费率雇佣承运者进行运送转移的公司。

Freight Forwarders *Freight forwarders* are firms that accumulate small shipments into larger lots and then hire a carrier to move them, usually at reduced rates. Recall that transportation companies provide rate incentives for larger quantities. Forwarders collect many small shipments consigned to a common destination and pay the carrier the lower rate based on larger volume, so they often convert shipments that are less-than-truckload (LTL) into full truckloads, thereby receiving better shipping rates. The rates charged by the forwarder to the individual shippers, in turn, are somewhat less than the small quantity rate, and the difference is the forwarder's margin. In general, the shipment receives improved service at lower cost.

仓储和物料搬运
Warehousing and Materials Handling

Warehouses may be classified in one of two ways: (1) storage warehouses and (2) distribution centers. In *storage warehouses*, products are intended to come to rest for some period of time, as in the aging of products or in storing household goods. *Distribution centers*, on the other hand, are designed to facilitate the timely movement of goods and represent a very important part of a supply chain. They represent the second most significant cost in a supply chain after transportation.

Distribution centers not only allow firms to hold their stock in decentralized locations but are also used to facilitate sorting and consolidating products from different manufacturing plants or suppliers. For example, a distribution center operated by ODW Logistics, Inc., a third-party logistics provider, provides these services. Pioneer Electronics, Inc., relies on ODW not just for warehousing and distribution, but for basic assembly as well. ODW employees put plasma television sets and stereo speakers delivered separately from China in a single box with receivers from Thailand, other smaller parts from around the world, and installation instructions. The boxes are then shipped to the home-theater sections of Walmart stores and Best

piggyback 背负式装运；railer on flatcar（TOFC）平板拖车；freight forwarders 货运代理人；storage warehouses 仓储仓库；distribution centers 配送中心。

Amazon.com operates 30 highly automated warehouses in the United States, Europe, and Asia.

Amazon.com
www.amazon.com

物料搬运是仓库运营中的一个关键环节，指货物在仓库或制造车间的移进移出或内部移动等短距离转运。物料搬运中存在两个主要问题，即较高的劳动力成本和较高的丢失破损率。

Buy. Some physical transformation can also take place in distribution centers such as mixing or blending ingredients, labeling, and repackaging. Paint companies such as Sherwin-Williams and Benjamin Moore use distribution centers for this purpose. In addition, distribution centers may serve as manufacturers' sales offices, described in Chapter 10, and order processing centers.

Materials handling, which involves moving goods over short distances into, within, and out of warehouses and manufacturing plants, is a key part of warehouse operations. The two major problems with this activity are high labor costs and high rates of loss and damage. Every time an item is handled, there is a chance for loss or damage. Common materials handling equipment includes forklifts, cranes, and conveyors. Today, materials handling in warehouses is automated by using computers and robots to reduce the cost of holding, moving, and recording inventories.

订单处理
Order Processing

There are several stages in the processing of an order, and a failure at any one of them can cause a problem with the customer. The process starts with transmitting the order by a variety of means such as the Internet, an extranet, or electronic data interchange. This is followed by entering the order in the appropriate databases and sending the information to those needing it. For example, a regional warehouse is notified to prepare an order. After checking inventory, a new quantity may need to be reordered from the production line, or purchasing may be requested to reorder from a vendor. If the item is currently out of stock, a *back order* is created, and the whole process of keeping track of a small part of the original order must be managed. In addition, credit may have to be checked for some customers, all docu-

materials handling 材料搬运；back order 待发货，延期交货。

United Airlines Cargo provides fast, global delivery, often utilizing containers.

United Airlines
www.unitedcargo.com

mentation for the order must be prepared, transportation must be arranged, and an order confirmation must be sent. Order processing systems are evaluated in terms of speed and accuracy.

Electronic order processing has replaced manual processing for most large companies. For example, 96 percent of IBM's purchase transactions with suppliers are conducted on the Internet. Kiwi Brands, the Douglassville, Pennsylvania, marketer of Kiwi shoe polish, Endust, and Behold, receives 75 percent of its retailers' purchase orders via EDI. The company has also implemented financial EDI, sending invoices to retailers and receiving payment order/remittance advice documents and electronic funds transfer (EFT) payments. Shippers as well are linked to the system, allowing Kiwi to receive shipment status messages electronically.

库存管理
Inventory Management

Inventory management is one of the primary responsibilities of the supply chain manager. The major problem is maintaining the delicate balance between too little and too much. Too little inventory may result in poor service, stockouts, brand switching, and loss of market share; too much leads to higher costs because of the money tied up in inventory and the chance that it may become obsolete.

一般而言，保留库存是基于以下几点：（1）可以减缓由于预测需求的不确定性而带来的供需不一致矛盾；（2）可以为那些希望随需随供的顾客提供更好的服务；（3）促进生产效率的提高；（4）防止供应商涨价；（5）争取采购和运输折扣；（6）避免公司受到罢工和物资短缺等偶然因素的影响。

Reasons for Inventory Traditionally, carrying inventory has been justified on several grounds: (1) to offer a buffer against variations in supply and demand, often caused by uncertainty in forecasting demand; (2) to provide better service for those customers who wish to be served on demand; (3) to promote production efficiencies; (4) to provide a hedge against price increases by suppliers; (5) to promote purchasing and transportation discounts; and (6) to protect the firm from contingencies such as strikes and shortages.

However, companies today view inventory as something to be moved, not stored, and more of a liability than an asset. The traditional justification for inventory has resulted in excessive inventories that have proven costly to maintain. Consider the U.S. automobile industry. Despite efforts to streamline its supply chain, industry analysts estimate that $230 billion worth of excess inventory piles up annually in the form of unused raw materials, parts waiting to be delivered, and vehicles sitting on dealers' lots.

electronically 电子地；contingency 意外事故，偶发事件。

Did you know Microsoft Corporation is also involved in supply chain management? This advertisement features Microsoft Dynamics and its just-in-time solution for supply chain management.

Microsoft Dynamics
www.microsoft.com/dynamics

Inventory Costs Specific inventory costs are often hard to detect because they are difficult to measure and occur in many different parts of the firm. A classification of inventory costs includes the following:

- *Capital costs.* The opportunity costs resulting from tying up funds in inventory instead of using them in other, more profitable investments; these are related to interest rates.
- *Inventory service costs.* Items such as insurance and taxes that are present in many states.
- *Storage costs.* Warehousing space and materials handling.
- *Risk costs.* Possible loss, damage, pilferage, perishability, and obsolescence.

Storage costs, risk costs, and some inventory service costs vary according to the characteristics of the item inventoried. For example, perishable products or highly seasonal items have higher risk costs than a commodity type product such as lumber. Capital costs are always present and are proportional to the *values* of the item and prevailing interest rates. The costs of carrying inventory vary with the particular circumstances but quite easily could range from 10 to 35 percent for different firms.

Supply Chain Inventory Strategies Conventional wisdom a decade ago was that a firm should protect itself against uncertainty by maintaining a reserve inventory at each of its production and stocking points. This has been described as a "just-in-case" philosophy of inventory management and led to unnecessary high levels of inventory. In contrast is the **just-in-time (JIT) concept**, which is an inventory supply system that operates with very low inventories and requires fast, on-time delivery. When parts are needed for production, they arrive from suppliers "just in

capital costs 资本成本；inventory service costs 库存服务成本；storage costs 存储成本；risk costs 风险成本；just-in-time (JIT) concept 即时生产概念。

Making Responsible Decisions > > > > sustainability

Reverse Logistics and Green Marketing Go Together at Hewlett-Packard: Recycling e-Waste

Between 20 and 50 million tons of electronic waste find their way to landfills around the world annually. Americans alone are expected to discard 400 million analog TV sets and computer monitors and Japanese consumers will trash 610 million cell phones in 2010. The result? Landfills are seeping lead, chromium, mercury, and other toxins, prevalent in digital debris, into the environment.

Fortunately, Hewlett-Packard has taken it upon itself to act responsibly and address this issue through its highly regarded reverse logistics program. Hewlett-Packard has recycled computer and printer hardware since 1987 and is an industry leader in this practice. The company's recycling service is available today in more than 40 countries, regions, and territories. By 2010, Hewlett-Packard will have recycled over 1 billion pounds of used products to be refurbished for resale or donation or for recovery of materials.

The recycling effort at Hewlett-Packard is also part of the company's Design for Supply Chain program. Among other initiatives in this program, emphasis is placed on product and packaging changes to reduce reverse supply chain and environmental costs. For example, design changes have increased the recycling of its popular ink-jet supplies by 25 percent.

time," which means neither before nor after they are needed. Note that JIT is used in situations where demand forecasting is reliable, such as when supplying an automobile production line, and is not suitable for inventories that are to be stored over significant periods of time.

电子数据交换和电子信息技术的出现，以及要求对补充库存做出更快反应的持续压力也改变了供应链中供应商和顾客的交易方式。这是一种被称为**供应商管理库存**的管理系统，供应商凭借该系统以决定顾客（如零售商）所需产品的数量和种类并自动配送适当产品。

Electronic data interchange and electronic messaging technology coupled with the constant pressure for faster response time in replenishing inventory have also changed the way suppliers and customers do business in a supply chain. The approach, called **vendor-managed inventory (VMI)**, is an inventory-management system whereby the *supplier* determines the product amount and assortment a customer (such as a retailer) needs and automatically delivers the appropriate items.

Campbell Soup's system illustrates how VMI works.[20] Campbell first establishes EDI links with retailers. Every morning, retailers electronically inform the company of their demand for all Campbell products and the inventory levels in their distribution centers. Campbell uses that information to forecast future demand and determine which products need replenishment based on upper and lower inventory limits established with each retailer. Trucks leave the Campbell shipping plant that afternoon and arrive at the retailer's distribution centers with the required replenishments the same day.

闭环分析：逆向物流
CLOSING THE LOOP: REVERSE LOGISTICS

The flow of products in a supply chain does not end with the ultimate consumer or industrial user. Companies today recognize that a supply chain can work in reverse.

vendor-managed inventory(VMI) 供应商管理库存。

逆向物流是指从产品消费点回收可再循环再利用的物料、需要退货、返工或维修的产品，并进行再制造、再分配或处理的过程。

Reverse logistics is a process of reclaiming recyclable and reusable materials, returns, and reworks from the point of consumption or use for repair, remanufacturing, redistribution, or disposal. The effect of reverse logistics can be seen in the reduced waste in landfills and lowered operating costs for companies. The Making Responsible Decisions box on the previous page describes the successful reverse logistics initiative at Hewlett-Packard.

Companies such as Kodak (reusable cameras), Motorola and Nokia (return and reuse of cell phones), and Caterpillar, Xerox, and IBM (remanufacturing and recycling) have implemented acclaimed reverse logistics programs. Other firms have enlisted third-party logistics providers to handle this process along with other supply chain functions. GNB Technologies, Inc., a manufacturer of lead-acid batteries for automobiles and boats, has outsourced much of its supply chain activity to UPS Supply Chain Services. The company contracts with UPS to manage its shipments between plants, distribution centers, recycling centers, and retailers. This includes movement of both new batteries and used products destined for recycling and covers both truck and railroad shipments. This partnership along with the initiatives of other battery makers has paid economic and ecological dividends. By recycling 90 percent of the lead from used batteries, manufacturers have kept the demand for new lead in check, thereby holding down costs to consumers. Also, solid waste management costs and the environmental impact of lead in landfills are reduced.

learning review

6. What are the basic trade-offs between the five modes of transportation?
7. What types of inventory should use storage warehouses and which type should use distribution centers?
8. What are the strengths and weaknesses of a just-in-time system?

LEARNING OBJECTIVES REVIEW

LO1 *Recognize the relationship between marketing channels, logistics, and supply chain management.*

A marketing channel relies on logistics to make products available to consumers and industrial users. Logistics involves those activities that focus on getting the right amount of the right products to the right place at the right time at the lowest possible cost. The performance of these activities is logistics management—the practice of organizing the cost-effective flow of raw materials, in-process inventory, finished goods, and related information from point of origin to point of consumption to satisfy customer requirements.

A supply chain is a sequence of firms that perform activities required to create and deliver a product or service to ultimate consumers or industrial users. It differs from a marketing channel in terms of membership. A supply chain includes suppliers that provide raw material inputs to a manufacturer as well as the wholesalers and retailers that deliver products. The management process is also different. Supply chain management is the integration and organization of information and logistics activities across firms in a supply chain for the purpose of creating and delivering products and services that provide value to consumers.

LO2 *Describe how a company's supply chain aligns with its marketing strategy.*

A company's supply chain follows from a clearly defined marketing strategy. The alignment of a company's supply chain with its marketing strategy involves three steps. First, a supply chain must reflect the needs of the customer segment being served. Second, a company must understand what a supply chain is designed to do well. Supply chains range from those that emphasize being responsive to customer requirements and demands to those that emphasize efficiency with the goal of supplying products at the lowest possible delivered cost. Finally, a supply chain must be consistent with the targeted customer's needs and the company's marketing strategy. The Dell and Wal-Mart examples in the chapter illustrate how this alignment is achieved by two well-known companies.

LO3 *Identify the major logistics cost and customer service factors that managers consider when making supply chain decisions.*

Companies strive to provide superior customer service while controlling logistics cost. The major customer service factors include the length of time between orders and deliveries, dependability in replenishing inventory, communication between buyers and sellers, and convenience in buying from the seller. Logistics cost factors include transportation, materials handling and warehousing, order processing, inventory, and stockouts.

LO4 *Describe the key logistics functions in a supply chain.*

The four key logistics functions in a supply chain include transportation, warehousing and materials handling, order process-

reverse logistics 逆向物流。

ing, and inventory management. Transportation provides the movement of goods necessary in a supply chain. The five major transportation modes are railroads, motor carriers, air carriers, pipelines, and water carriers. Warehousing and materials handling include the storing, sorting, and handling of products at storage warehouses or distribution centers. Order processing includes order receipt, delivery, invoicing, and collection from customers. Inventory management involves minimizing inventory-carrying costs while maintaining sufficient stocks of products to satisfy anticipated customer needs. Two popular inventory management practices are just-in-time (JIT) and vendor-managed inventory (VMI) systems.

FOCUSING ON KEY TERMS

customer service
efficient consumer response
electronic data interchange (EDI)
just-in-time (JIT) concept
lead time
logistics
logistics management
quick response
reverse logistics
supply chain
supply chain management
third-party logistics providers
total logistics cost
vendor-managed inventory (VMI)

APPLYING MARKETING KNOWLEDGE

1 List several companies to which logistical activities might be unimportant. Also list several whose focus is only on the inbound or outbound side.

2 What are some types of businesses in which order processing may be among the paramount success factors?

3 List the customer service factors that would be vital to buyers in the following types of companies: (*a*) manufacturing, (*b*) retailing, (*c*) hospitals, and (*d*) construction.

4 Name some cases when extremely high service levels (e.g., 99 percent) would be warranted.

5 Name the mode of transportation that would be the best for the following products: (*a*) farm machinery, (*b*) cut flowers, (*c*) frozen meat, and (*d*) coal.

6 The auto industry is a heavy user of the just-in-time concept. Why? What other industries would be good candidates for its application? What do they have in common?

7 Look again at Figure 11–4. Explain why as the number of warehouses increases, (*a*) inventory costs rise and (*b*) transportation costs fall.

8 What relationship would you expect to see between a company's on-time delivery percentage and its out-of-stock percentage?

building your marketing plan

Does your marketing plan involve a product? If the answer is no, read no further and do not include this element in your plan. If the answer is yes:

1 If inventory is involved, (*a*) identify the three or four major kinds of inventory needed for your organization (retail stock, finished products, raw materials, supplies, and so on), and (*b*) suggest ways to reduce their costs.

2 (*a*) Rank the four customer service factors (time, dependability, communication, and convenience) from most important to least important from your customers' point of view, and (*b*) identify actions for the one or two most important to serve customers better.

video case 11 Amazon: Delivering the Goods . . . Millions of Times a Day

"The new economy means that the balance of power has shifted toward the consumer," explains Jeff Bezos, CEO of Amazon.com, Inc. The global online retailer is a pioneer of fast, convenient, low-cost virtual shopping that has attracted millions of consumers. Of course, while Amazon has changed the way many people shop, the company still faces the traditional and daunting task of creating a seamless flow of deliveries to its customers—often millions of times each day.

THE COMPANY

Bezos started Amazon.com with a simple idea: to use the Internet to transform book buying into the fastest, easiest, and most enjoyable shopping experience possible.

The company was incorporated in 1994 and opened its virtual doors in July 1995. At the forefront of a huge growth of dot-com businesses, Amazon pursued a get-big-fast business strategy. Sales grew rapidly and Amazon began adding products and services other than books. In fact, Amazon soon set its goal on being the world's most customer-centric company, where customers can find and discover anything they might want to buy online!

Today Amazon claims to have the "Earth's Biggest Selection™" of products and services in the following categories: Books; Movies, Music & Games; Digital Downloads; Kindle; Computers & Office; Electronics; Home & Garden; Grocery, Health & Beauty; Toys, Kids & Baby; Clothing, Shoes & Jewelry; Sports & Outdoors; and Tools, Auto & Industrial. Other services allow customers to:

- Search for a product or brand using all or part of its name.
- Place orders with one click using "Buy Now with 1-Click" button.
- Receive personalized recommendations based on past purchases through opt-in e-mails.

These products and services have attracted millions of people around the globe. This has made Amazon.com, along with its international sites in Canada, the United Kingdom, Germany, Japan, France, and China, the leading online retailer.

Despite its incredible success with consumers and continuing growth in sales, Amazon.com found it difficult to be profitable. Many industry observers questioned the viability of online retailing and Amazon's business model. Then, in 2002, Amazon shocked many people by becoming profitable. The company has remained profitable. There are a variety of explanations for the turnaround. Generally, Bezos suggests that "efficiencies allow for lower prices, spurring sales growth across the board, which can be handled by existing facilities without much additional cost." More specifically, the facilities Bezos is referring to are the elements of its supply chain, which are one of the most complex and expensive aspects of the company's business.

SUPPLY CHAIN AND LOGISTICS MANAGEMENT AT AMAZON.COM

What happens after an order is submitted on Amazon's Web site but before it arrives at the customer's door? A lot. Amazon.com maintains huge distribution, or "fulfillment," centers where it keeps inventory of millions of products. This is one of the key differences between Amazon.com and some of its competitors—it actually stocks products. So Amazon must manage the flow of products from its 15 million suppliers to its distribution and customer service centers with the flow of customer orders from the distribution centers to individuals' homes or offices.

The process begins with the suppliers. "Amazon's goal is to collaborate with our suppliers to increase efficiencies and improve inventory turnover," explains Jim Miller, vice president of supply chain at Amazon.com. "We want to bring to suppliers the kind of interactive relationship that has inspired customers to shop with us." For example, Amazon is using software to more accurately forecast purchasing patterns by region, which allows it to give its suppliers better information about delivery dates and volumes. Before the development of this software, 12 percent of incoming inventory was sent to the wrong location, leading to lost time and delayed orders. Now only 4 percent of the incoming inventory is mishandled.

At the same time, Amazon has been improving the part of the process that sorts the products into the individual orders. Jeffrey Wilke, Amazon's senior vice president of operations, says, "We spent the whole year really focused on increasing productivity." Again, technology has been essential. "The speed at which telecommunications networks allow us to pass information back and forth has enabled us to do the real-time work that we keep talking about. In the past, it would have taken too long to get this many items through a system," explains Wilke. Once the order is in the system, computers ensure that all items are included in the box before it is taped and labeled. A network of trucks and regional postal hubs then conclude the process with delivery of the order.

The success of Amazon's logistics and supply chain management activities may be most evident during the year-end holiday shopping season. Amazon received orders for 37.9 million items between November 9 and December 21 one year, including orders for 450,000 Harry Potter books and products, and orders for 36,000 items placed just before the holiday delivery deadline. Well over 99 percent of the orders were shipped and delivered on time.

AMAZON'S CHALLENGES

Despite all of Amazon's recent improvements, logistics experts estimate that the company's distribution centers are operating at approximately 40 percent of their capacity. This situation suggests that Amazon must reduce its capacity or increase its sales.

Several sales growth options are possible. First, Amazon can continue to pursue growth through sales of hundreds of thousands of electronic books, magazines, and newspapers through its new Kindle devices and store. The 6" Kindle 2 is capable of storing 1,500 publications while the 9.7" Kindle DX can hold over 3,500. Second, Amazon can continue its expansion into new product and service categories. Recently, it launched its Outdoor Recreation store—the latest in over a dozen such categories. This approach would prevent Amazon from becoming a niche merchant and position it as a true online retail department store. Third, Amazon can increase the availability of products from other retailers through its Amazon WebStore. These retailers can create a customized, branded Web site that uses Amazon eCommerce technology. Finally, Amazon can pursue a strategy of providing access to its existing operations for other retailers through its Fulfillment by Amazon (FBA) service. Online retailers store their products at Amazon's distribution centers and when they sell a product—Amazon ships it!

Amazon.com has come a long way toward proving that online retailing can work. Its logistics and supply chain management activities have provided Amazon with a cost-effective and efficient distribution system that combines automation and communication technology with superior customer service. To continue its drive to increase future sales, profits, and customer service, Amazon acquired Zappos.com in mid-2009. According to Bezos, "We see great opportunities for both companies to learn from each other and create even better experiences for our customers."

Questions

1 How do Amazon.com's logistics and supply chain management activities help the company create value for its customers?

2 What systems did Amazon develop to improve the flow of products from suppliers to Amazon distribution centers? What systems improved the flow of orders from the distribution centers to customers?

3 Why will logistics and supply chain management play an important role in the future success of Amazon.com?

GLOBAL
globalcomputer.com

CYBER MONDAY
MADNESS
1 DAY SALE!
CLICK HERE

Search over 100,000 Products in Stock...

Deal Alerts via RSS

We are open 24 hours a day, 7 days a week. **Call us at 888-845-6225**
WHEN CALLING USE **PRIORITY CODE:** GLOEM609

12 零 售 Retailing

LEARNING OBJECTIVES

After reading this chapter you should be able to:

LO1 Identify retailers in terms of the utilities they provide.

LO2 Explain the alternative ways to classify retail outlets.

LO3 Describe the many methods of nonstore retailing.

LO4 Classify retailers in terms of the retail positioning matrix, and specify retailing mix actions.

LO5 Explain changes in retailing with the wheel of retailing and the retail life cycle concepts.

星期一有 8400 万消费者会在网上购物，你是其中一个吗

84 MILLION CONSUMERS WERE SHOPPING ONLINE ON CYBER MONDAY. WERE YOU ONE OF THEM?

Two of the biggest days of the retailing year are the Friday after Thanksgiving—Black Friday—and the Monday after Thanksgiving—Cyber Monday. The days are so popular for shoppers that retailers report more than $20 billion in sales on Black Friday and almost $1 billion in sales on Cyber Monday. The names have interesting histories. Black Friday was an accounting term used to suggest when retailers finally became profitable, and Cyber Monday was the result of consumers shopping from their broadband connections at work on their first day back after the holiday. The number of Cyber Monday shoppers has been growing dramatically. Are you one of them?

Several factors account for the growth in Cyber Monday shopping and online shopping in general. First, the number of fast Internet connections in homes and businesses has grown to about 100 million. Second, large retailers such as Amazon, Home Depot, and Walmart have given online shopping a lot of visibility. Many retailers now move their Friday in-store sales and promotions to their Web sites on Monday to attract the shoppers who didn't want to park, stand in line, or deal with crowds in the stores.

While retailers may encourage online shopping with promotions as simple as e-mail notifications, cyber shopping is also the result of many new, interesting, and exciting online approaches. OfficeMax, for example, drives traffic to its Web site with an online application called "Elf Yourself" that allows visitors to e-mail an animated elf to friends. New Web sites such as Mpire.com track the price of products like TVs, clothing, and books to let consumers know if prices are increasing or decreasing. Like.com provides a visual search engine that finds products that are similar in appearance—just draw a box around the product or part of the product that you like and the site shows other products that are similar! For many consumers, buying new products leads to selling old products, and sites such as gazelle.com now calculate the value of used products, offer users a price for the product, and even send a box to mail it. There is even an official Cyber Monday Web site where more than 500 retailers have special online offers!

Cyber Monday and online shopping are just a few examples of the many exciting changes occurring in retailing today. This chapter examines the critical role of retailing in the marketplace and the challenging decisions retailers face as they strive to create value for customers.

What types of products will consumers buy through catalogs, television, the Internet, or by telephone? In what type of store will consumers look for products they don't buy directly? How important is

visibility 能见度，可见性；occurring 事变，事件，事故。

the location of the store? Will customers expect services such as alterations, delivery, installation, or repair? What price should be charged for each product? These are difficult and important questions that are an integral part of retailing. In the channel of distribution, retailing is where the customer meets the product. It is through retailing that exchange (a central aspect of marketing) occurs. **Retailing** includes all activities involved in selling, renting, and providing products and services to ultimate consumers for personal, family, or household use.

零售的价值
THE VALUE OF RETAILING

Retailing is an important marketing activity. Not only do producers and consumers meet through retailing actions, but retailing also creates customer value and has a significant impact on the economy. To consumers, the value of retailing is in the form of utilities provided (Figure 12–1). Retailing's economic value is represented by the people employed in retailing as well as by the total amount of money exchanged in retail sales (Figure 12–2).

零售提供的消费者效用
Consumer Utilities Offered by Retailing

The utilities provided by retailers create value for consumers. Time, place, form, and possession utilities are offered by most retailers in varying degrees, but one utility is often emphasized more than others. Look at Figure 12–1 to see how well you can match the retailer with the utility being emphasized in the description.

FIGURE 12–1
Which retailer best provides which utilities?

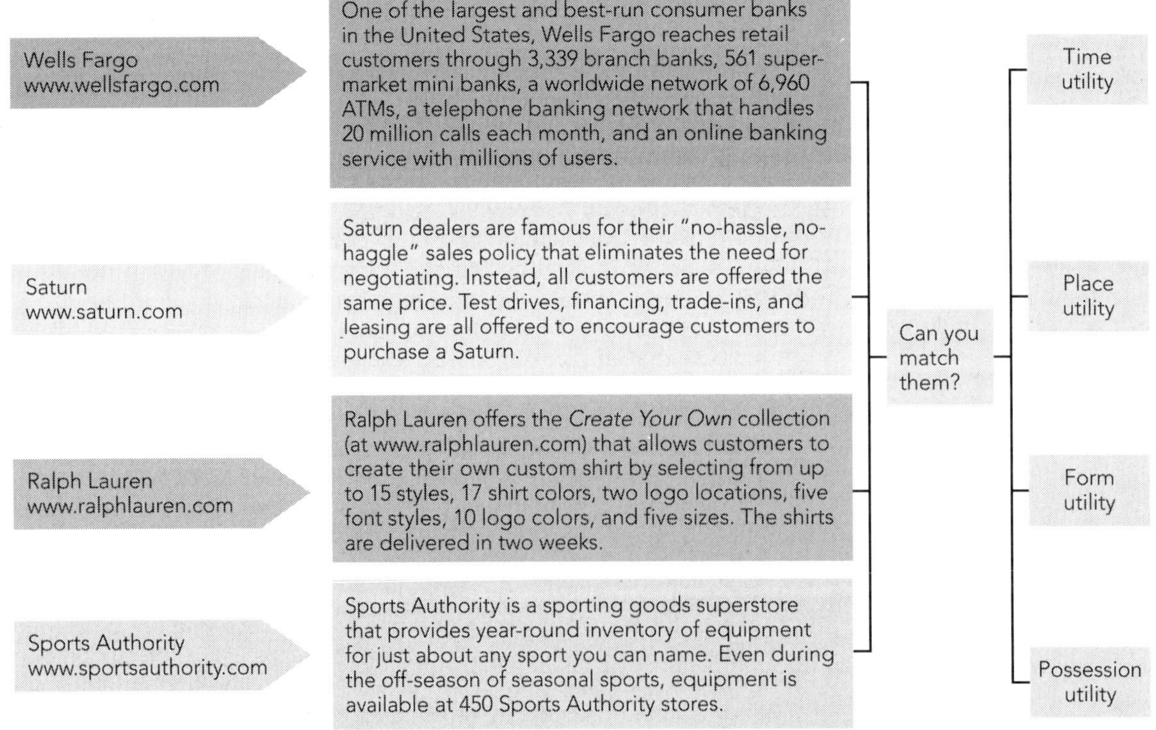

---

retailing 零售；utility 效用。

Type of retailer	Sales ($ billions)
Sporting goods, books, and music stores	87.3
Electronic stores	111.4
Furniture and home furnishing stores	118.7
Pharmacies and drugstores	198.4
Clothing and accessory stores	224.7
Nonstore retailers	303.4
Building material and hardware stores	337.2
Food services and drinking places	442.3
Gasoline stations	445.2
Food and beverage stores	560.6
General merchandise stores	576.4
Automotive dealers	919.3

0 200 400 600 800 1000
Sales ($ billions)

FIGURE 12–2
Are you surprised by the relative size of different types of retailers?

Providing mini banks in supermarkets, as Wells Fargo does, puts the bank's products and services close to the consumer, providing place utility. By providing financing or leasing and taking used cars as trade-ins, Saturn makes the purchase easier and provides possession utility. Form utility—production or alteration of a product—is offered by Ralph Lauren through its online *Create Your Own* program, which offers shirts that meet each customer's specifications. Finding the right sporting equipment during the off-season is the time utility provided by Sports Authority. Many retailers offer a combination of the four basic utilities. Some supermarkets, for example, offer convenient locations (place utility); are open 24 hours a day (time utility); customize purchases in the bakery, deli, and florist (form utility); and allow several payment and credit options (possession utility).

Tesco is one of the largest retailers outside the United States.

零售对全球经济的影响
The Global Economic Impact of Retailing

Retailing is important to the U.S. and global economies. Four of the 30 largest businesses in the United States are retailers (Walmart, Costco, Home Depot, and Target). Walmart's $405 billion in annual sales in 2008 surpassed the gross domestic product of all but 27 countries for that same year. Walmart, Costco, Home Depot, and Target together have more than 2.8 million employees—more than the combined populations of Jacksonville, Florida; El Paso, Texas; and Stockton, California. Figure 12–2 shows that many other retailers, including food stores, automobile dealers, and general merchandise outlets, are also significant contributors to the U.S. economy.

Outside the United States large retailers include Daiei in Japan, Carrefour in France, Metro Group in Germany, and Tesco in Britain. In emerging economies such as China and Mexico, a combination of local and global retailers is evolving. Walmart, for example, has more than 3,600 stores outside the United States, including stores in Brazil, China, Japan, Mexico, and the United Kingdom.

bakery 面包（或糕饼）店；florist 鲜花店，花坊。

learning review

1. When Ralph Lauren makes shirts to a customer's exact preferences, what utility is provided?
2. Two measures of the impact of retailing in the global economy are ______________ and ________________.

零售业态分类
CLASSIFYING RETAIL OUTLETS

LO2

首先是**所有权形式**，即根据商店是个体所有、公司连锁还是契约系统来区分零售。其次是**服务水平**，即向顾客提供服务的程度。这可分为三个层次，自助服务、有限服务与全面服务。最后是**商品线**，即一个商店中所经营商品种类的多少以及款式。

For manufacturers, consumers, and the economy, retailing is an important component of marketing that has several variations. Because of the large number of alternative forms of retailing, it is easier to understand the differences among retail institutions by recognizing that outlets can be classified in several ways. First, **form of ownership** distinguishes retail outlets based on whether individuals, corporate chains, or contractual systems own the outlet. Second, **level of service** is used to describe the degree of service provided to the customer. Three levels of service are provided by self-, limited-, and full-service retailers. Finally, the type of **merchandise line** describes how many different types of products a store carries and in what assortment. The alternative types of outlets are discussed in greater detail in the following pages. For many consumers today, each of the types of outlets discussed are viewed in terms of their environmentally friendly, or green, activities. The accompanying Making Responsible Decisions box gives examples of the green activities of several retailers.

所有权形式
Form of Ownership

There are three general forms of retail ownership—individual, corporate chain, and contractual system.

Independent Retailer One of the most common forms of retail ownership is the independent business owned by an individual. Independent retailers account for most of the 1.1 million retail establishments in the United States and include hardware stores, convenience stores, clothing stores, and computer and software stores. In addition, there are 29,600 jewelry stores, 21,100 florists, and 43,100 sporting good and hobby stores. The advantage of this form of ownership for the owner is that he or she can be his or her own boss. More than 50 percent of all retail establishments have four or fewer employees. For customers, the independent store can offer convenience, personal service, and lifestyle compatibility.

Corporate Chain A second form of ownership, the corporate chain, involves multiple outlets under common ownership. Many of the department store names you may know—Bon Marche, Lazurus, Burdines, Famous Barr, Filenes, Foleys, and Marshall Field's—are now one of 810 Macy's stores nationwide. Macy's Inc. also owns 40 Bloomingdale's, which compete with other chainstores such as Saks Fifth Avenue and Neiman Marcus.

In a chain operation, centralization in decision making and purchasing is common. Chain stores have advantages in dealing with manufacturers, particularly as the size of the chain grows. A large chain can bargain with a manufacturer to obtain good service or volume discounts on orders. Target's large volume makes it a strong negotiator with manufacturers of most products. The buying power of chains is seen when consumers compare chain store prices with other types of stores. Consumers also benefit in dealing with chains because there are multiple outlets with similar merchandise and consistent management policies.

form of ownership 所有权形式；level of service 服务水平；merchandise line 产品线。

Making Responsible Decisions >>>> sustainability

Environmentally Friendly Retailing Takes Off!

Sustainability has been a topic of interest for some retailers for many years. Recently, however, it has become a movement for the entire industry. What happened? A combination of factors contributed to the change: environmental consciousness among consumers has reached an all-time high, publicity related to global warming has increased, "green" has become an important element of company image and reputation, and most environmental initiatives save retailers money!

When consumers learned that food packaging creates 50 percent of all household waste, they added packaging to their purchase decision criteria. Walmart responded by requiring its suppliers to trim one square inch of packaging from its toy lines and reduced packaging by 3,500 tons. Electronics retailer Best Buy recently began using solar energy in some of its stores with the goal of reducing CO_2 emissions by 8 percent by 2012. Mountain Equipment company is building on its green image by collecting rainwater to water grass at the store and to use in its toilets. When Home Depot switched its in-store light fixture displays to compact fluorescent light bulbs it saved $16 million per year. Other companies are using motion detectors to turn lights on and off, improving the fuel economy of delivery vehicles, and designing "zero waste" stores.

Are your favorite retailers "green"? Do sustainability efforts influence your purchase decisions?

Retailing has become a high-tech business for many large chains. Walmart, for example, has developed a sophisticated inventory management and cost control system that allows rapid price changes for each product in every store. In addition, stores such as Walmart and Target are implementing pioneering new technologies such as radio frequency identification (RFID) tags to improve the quality of information available about products.

Contractual Systems Contractual systems involve independently owned stores that band together to act like a chain. The three kinds described in Chapter 10 are retailer-sponsored cooperatives, wholesaler-sponsored voluntary chains, and franchises. One retailer-sponsored cooperative is the Associated Grocers, which consists of neighborhood grocers that all agree with several other independent grocers to buy their goods directly from food manufacturers. In this way, members can take advantage of volume discounts commonly available to chains and also give the impression of being a large chain, which may be viewed more favorably by some consumers. Wholesaler-sponsored voluntary chains such as Independent Grocers' Alliance (IGA) try to achieve similar benefits.

Subway is a popular business-format franchisor.

As noted in Chapter 10, in a franchise system an individual or firm (the franchisee) contracts with a parent company (the franchisor) to set up a business or retail outlet. The franchisor usually assists in selecting the location, setting up the store or facility, advertising, and training personnel. The franchisee usually pays a onetime franchise fee and an annual royalty, usually tied to franchise's sales. There are two general types of franchises: *business-format franchises*, such as McDonald's, Radio Shack, and Subway, and *product-distribution franchises*,

contractual 契约的；business-format franchises 经营模式特许；product-distribution franchises 产品分销特许。

such as a Ford dealership or a Coca-Cola distributor. In business-format franchising, the franchisor provides step-by-step procedures for most aspects of the business and guidelines for the most likely decisions a franchisee will face.

Franchising is attractive because it offers an opportunity for people to enter a well-known, established business for which managerial advice is provided. Also, the franchise fee may be less than the cost of setting up an independent business. The International Franchise Association recently reported that there are 909,000 franchised businesses in the United States, which generate $880 billion in annual sales and employ more than 11 million people. Franchising is popular in international markets also: more than half of all U.S. franchisors have operations in other countries. What is the fastest growing franchise? Subway now has 29,612 locations, including 7,927 stores outside the United States.

Franchise fees paid to the franchisor can range from $15,000 for a Subway franchise to $45,000 for a McDonald's restaurant franchise. When the fees are combined with other costs such as real estate and equipment, however, the total investment can be much higher. Franchisees also pay an ongoing royalty fee that ranges from 2 percent for a Sonic Drive In to 12.5 percent for a McDonald's. Figure 12–3 shows the top five franchises, as rated by *Entrepreneur* magazine, based on factors such as size, financial strength, stability, years in business, and costs. By selling franchises, an organization reduces the cost of expansion but loses some control. A good franchisor, however, will maintain strong control of the outlets in terms of delivery and presentation of merchandise and try to enhance recognition of the franchise name.

服务水平
Level of Service

Even though most customers perceive little variation in retail outlets by form of ownership, differences among retailers are more obvious in terms of level of service. In some department stores, such as Loehmann's, very few services are provided. Some grocery stores, such as the Cub Foods chain, encourage customers to bag the food themselves and recycle their plastic bags. Other outlets, such as Neiman Marcus, provide a wide range of customer services from gift wrapping to wardrobe consultation.

自助服务要求顾客自己完成许多职能而零售店提供很少的服务。

Self-Service Self-service requires that the customers perform many functions and little is provided by the outlet. Warehouse clubs such as Costco, for example, are usually self-service, with all nonessential customer services eliminated. Similarly, most gas stations today are self-service. New forms of self-service are being developed at airlines, hotels, and even libraries! Lufthansa airline, for example, is installing 300 self-service check-in terminals that feature an integrated radio frequency identification (RFID) scanner to read passports or ID cards, in addition to allowing passengers to select seats, print boarding passes, and check baggage. Hilton Hotels now includes self-service kiosks in the lobby of each of its hotels. The kiosks allow guests to check in, print keys, check for messages, check out, print hotel receipts, and print airline boarding passes. The Palm Beach County library system is mov-

FIGURE 12–3
The top five franchises in the United States vary from sandwich restaurants to tax preparation services.

Franchise	Type of Business	Total Start-up Cost	Number of Franchises
Subway	Sandwich restaurant	$78,600–$238,300	29,612
McDonald's	Fast-food restaurant	$950,200–$1,800,000	25,465
Liberty Tax Service	Tax preparation service	$53,800–$66,900	2,579
Sonic Drive In Restaurants	Drive-In restaurant	$1,200,000–$3,200,000	2,768
InterContinental Hotels	Hotel	Variable	3,498

entrepreneur 企业家；eliminate 消除，剔除。

Breadth: Number of different product lines

Depth: Number of items within each product line	Shoes	Appliances	CDs	Men's clothing
	Nike running shoes Florsheim dress shoes Sperry boat shoes Adidas tennis shoes	General Electric dishwashers Panasonic microwave ovens Whirlpool washers Frigidaire refrigerators	Classical Rock Jazz Country R & B Rap	Suits Ties Jackets Overcoats Socks Shirts

FIGURE 12–4
Stores vary in terms of the breadth and depth of their merchandise lines.

ing in the same direction; it is adding self-service checkout machines to each of its branches. In general, the trend is toward retailing experiences that make customers co-creators of the value they receive.

有限服务网点提供一些诸如信贷和商品退货等服务，但不提供服装定制等服务。

Limited Service Limited-service outlets provide some services, such as credit and merchandise return, but not others, such as clothing alterations. General merchandise stores such as Walmart, Kmart, and Target are usually considered limited service outlets. Customers are responsible for most shopping activities, although salespeople are available in departments such as consumer electronics, jewelry, and lawn and garden.

Full Service Full-service retailers, which include most specialty stores and department stores, provide many services to their customers. Neiman Marcus, Nordstrom, and Saks Fifth Avenue, for example, all rely on better service to sell more distinctive, higher-margin goods and to retain their customers. Nordstrom offers a wide variety of services, including free exchanges, easy returns, credit cards through Nordstrom bank, a live help line, an online gift finder, catalogs, a four-level loyalty program called Nordstrom Fashion Rewards, and an online beauty specialist. Some Nordstrom stores also offer a "Personal Touch" department, which provides shopping assistants for consumers who need help with style, color, and size selection, and a concierge service for assistance with anything else. Nordstrom stores typically have 50 percent more salespeople on the floor than similarly sized stores, and the salespeople are renowned for their professional and personalized attention to customers. Nordstrom also offers e-mail and RSS feeds to notify customers when new merchandise is available.

商品线类型
Type of Merchandise Line

Retail outlets also vary by their merchandise lines, the key distinction being the breadth and depth of the items offered to customers (see Figure 12–4). **Depth of product line** means the store carries a large assortment of each item, such as a shoe store that offers running shoes, dress shoes, and children's shoes. **Breadth of product line** refers to the variety of different items a store carries, such as appliances and CDs.

Staples is the category killer in office supplies.

Depth of Line Stores that carry a considerable assortment (depth) of a related line of items are limited-line stores. Sports Authority sporting goods stores carry considerable depth in sports equipment ranging from weight-lifting accessories to running shoes. Stores that carry tremendous depth in one primary line of merchandise are single-line stores. Victoria's Secret, a nationwide chain, carries great depth in women's lingerie. Both limited- and single-line stores are often referred to as *specialty outlets*.

Specialty discount outlets focus on one type of product, such as electronics (Best Buy), office supplies (Staples), or books (Barnes and Noble) at very competitive

depth of product line 产品线的深度；breadth of product line 产品线的宽度。

	Hypermarket	Supercenter
Region of Popularity	Europe	United States
Average size	90,000–300,000 sq. ft.	100,000–215,000 sq. ft.
Number of products	20,000–80,000	35,000
Annual revenue	$100,000,000 per store	$60,000,000 per store

FIGURE 12–5
Hypermarkets are popular in Europe, and supercenters are popular in the U.S.

prices. These outlets are referred to in the trade as *category killers* because they often dominate the market. Best Buy, for example, is the largest consumer electronics retailer with more than 1,000 stores, and Staples is the leader in office supplies.

Breadth of Line Stores that carry a broad product line, with limited depth, are referred to as *general merchandise stores*. For example, large department stores such as Dillard's, Macy's, and Neiman Marcus carry a wide range of different types of products but not unusual sizes. The breadth and depth of merchandise lines are important decisions for a retailer. Traditionally, outlets carried related lines of goods. Today, however, **scrambled merchandising**, offering several unrelated product lines in a single store, is common. The modern drugstore carries food, camera equipment, magazines, paper products, toys, small hardware items, and pharmaceuticals. Supermarkets rent videos, print photos, and sell flowers.

A form of scrambled merchandising, the **hypermarket**, has been successful in Europe. These hypermarkets are large stores (more than 200,000 square feet) based on a simple concept: offer "everything under one roof," eliminating the need to stop at more than one location. The stores provide variety, quality, and low price for groceries and general merchandise. Carrefour, one of the largest hypermarket retailers, has 1,163 hypermarkets, including 218 in France, 160 in Spain, and 71 in Poland. The growth of hypermarkets may be slowing in Europe, however, as the availability of smaller discount stores in more convenient locations has increased. The concept is growing in popularity outside of Europe though; in China, for example, Carrefour, RT-Mart, and Geant are expanding the hypermarket format.

In the United States, retailers discovered that shoppers were uncomfortable with the huge size of hypermarkets. They developed a variation of the hypermarket called the *supercenter*, which combines a typical merchandise store (approximately 70,000 square feet) with a full-size grocery store. Walmart, Kmart, and Target are now using the concept very successfully. Walmart currently operates 2,700 supercenters in the United States and plans to open 100 to 200 new stores each year in the near future. Supercenters have seen an increase in popularity in the United States as the changes in the economy have encouraged shoppers to save money by buying in bulk. Figure 12–5 shows the differences between the supercenter and hypermarket concepts.

混合经营便利了消费者，因为这避免了消费者在一次购物中的停留次数。然而对许多零售商来说，这种经营策略意味着会在不同类型的零售店之间产生竞争，即**业内竞争**。

Scrambled merchandising is convenient for consumers because it eliminates the number of stops required in a shopping trip. However, for the retailer this merchandising policy means there is competition between very dissimilar types of retail outlets, or **intertype competition**. A local bakery may compete with a department store, discount outlet, or even a local gas station. Scrambled merchandising and intertype competition make it more difficult to be a retailer.

learning review

3. Centralized decision making and purchasing are an advantage of ______________ ownership.
4. What are some examples of new forms of self-service retailers?
5. Would a shop for big men's clothes carrying pants in sizes 40 to 60 have a broad or deep product line?

scrambled merchandising 跨行业销售；hypermarket 特级市场；intertype competition 非行业竞争。

无店铺零售
NONSTORE RETAILING

LO3

Most of the retailing examples discussed earlier in the chapter, such as corporate chains, department stores, and limited- and single-line specialty stores, involve store retailing. Many retailing activities today, however, are not limited to sales in a store. Nonstore retailing occurs outside a retail outlet through activities that involve varying levels of customer and retailer involvement. Figure 12–6 shows six forms of nonstore retailing: automatic vending, direct mail and catalogs, television home shopping, online retailing, telemarketing, and direct selling.

Vending machines offer many products found in convenience stores.

自动售货
Automatic Vending

Nonstore retailing includes vending machines, which make it possible to serve customers when and where stores cannot. Machine maintenance, operating costs, and location leases can add to the cost of the products, so prices in vending machines tend to be higher than those in stores. About 48 percent of the products sold from vending machines are cold beverages, another 19 percent are candy and snacks, and 10 percent is food. Many new types of products are quickly becoming available in vending machines. Best Buy now uses vending machines to sell cell phone and computer accessories, digital cameras, flash drives, and other consumer electronics products in airports. Similarly, YoNaturals uses vending machines to distribute healthy and organic snacks in schools, health clubs, and hospitals in 135 U.S. cities. The 11.5 million vending machines currently in use in the United States generate more than $46 billion in annual sales.

Improved technology is making vending machines easier to use by reducing the need for cash. In the United States, about 17,500 machines currently accept credit cards or PayPass cards and many more will be equipped with card readers soon. In Japan, Korea, and the Philippines consumers use cell phones that transmit payments to vending machines via an infrared beam or a radio wave. Another improvement in vending machines is the trend toward "green" machines that

FIGURE 12–6
Many types of retailers do not have stores.

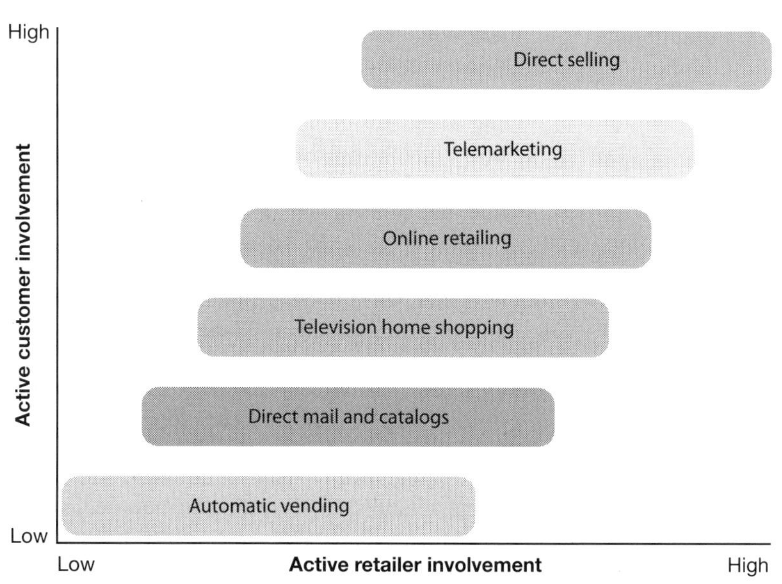

automatic 自动的，自动化的；transmit 传达，传输。

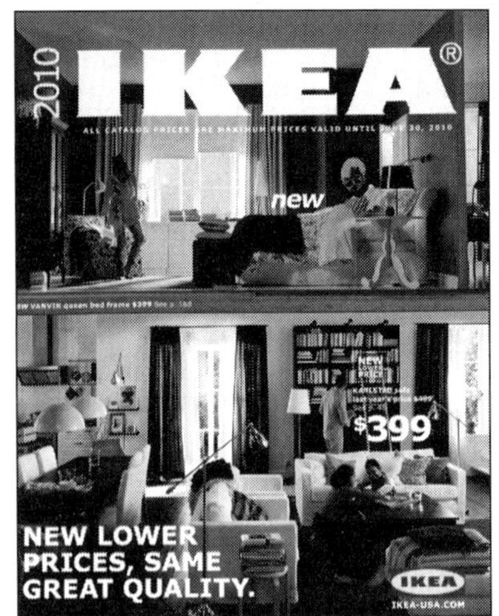

Specialty catalogs appeal to market niches.

consume less energy by using more efficient compressors, more efficient lighting, and better insulation. Vending machines are popular with consumers; recent consumer satisfaction research indicates that 82 percent of consumers believe purchasing from a vending machine is equal to or superior to a store purchase.

直邮与目录
Direct Mail and Catalogs

直邮和目录零售具有吸引力，这是因为它免去了商店和营业员的成本。

Direct-mail and catalog retailing is attractive because it eliminates the cost of a store and clerks. For example, it costs a traditional retail store $34 to acquire a new customer, whereas catalog customers are acquired for approximately $14. In addition, direct mail and catalogs improve marketing efficiency through segmentation and targeting, and they create customer value by providing a fast and convenient means of making a purchase. The average U.S. household now receives 18 direct-mail items or catalogs each week. The Direct Marketing Association estimates that direct-mail and catalog retailing creates 1.7 million jobs and $1.9 trillion in sales. Direct-mail and catalog retailing is popular outside of the United States also. Furniture retailer IKEA delivered 198 million copies of its catalog in 27 languages to 35 countries last year.

Several factors have had an impact on direct-mail and catalog retailing in recent years. The influence of large retailers such as IKEA, Crate and Barrel, JCPenney, and others has been positive as their marketing activities have increased the number and variety of products consumers purchase through direct mail and catalogs. Higher paper costs and increases in postage rates, the growing interest in do-not-mail legislation, the concern for "green" mailings and catalogs, and the possibility of the U.S. Postal Service reducing delivery to five days, however, have caused direct-mail and catalog retailers to search for ways to improve their efficiency and provide additional customer value. One approach has been to focus on proven customers rather than prospective customers. Some merchants, such as Williams-Sonoma, reduce mailings to zip codes that have not been profitable. Another successful approach used by many catalog retailers is to send specialty catalogs to market niches identified in their databases. L.L. Bean, for example, has developed an individual catalog for fly-fishing enthusiasts.

New, creative forms of direct-mail and catalog retailing are also being developed. Some retailers are investing in new technologies such as the intelligent mail bar code that will provide much more information about mail and catalog delivery at a lower cost. Other innovations include digital catalogs that are searchable, in PDF

catalog 目录，目录册；eliminate 消除，剔除。

format, and embedded with links to complementary products. You will also see merchants using direct mail and catalogs to direct customers to personalized URLs (PURLs, such as www.JohnSmith.offer.com), which are Web pages preloaded with information and offerings specific to an individual. To recognize companies that successfully integrate their direct-mail and catalog activities with other marketing activities, *Multichannel Merchant* magazine evaluates hundreds of entries to select the winners of the Multichannel Merchant Awards in 18 categories. Recent winners might be retailers you already know. They include L.L. Bean, The Republic of Tea, Ebags, and Harry and David.

电视家庭购物
Television Home Shopping

Television home shopping is possible when consumers watch a shopping channel on which products are displayed; orders are then placed over the telephone or the Internet. Currently, the three largest programs are QVC, HSN, and ShopNBC. QVC ("quality, value, convenience") broadcasts live 24 hours each day, 364 days a year and reaches 166 million cable and satellite homes in the United States, United Kingdom, Germany, Japan, and Italy. The company generates sales of $7 billion from its 50 million customers by offering more than 1,150 products each week, answering 181 million telephone calls, and shipping more than 166 million packages each year. The television home shopping channels offer apparel, jewelry, cooking, home improvement products, electronics, toys, and even food. Of all these products, the best-selling item ever was a Dell personal computer.

Television home shopping programs serve millions of customers each year.

In the past, television home shopping programs have attracted mostly 40- to 60-year-old women. To begin to attract a younger audience, QVC has invited celebrities onto the show. For example, Ellen DeGeneres has been on the show promoting her collection of holistic pet care products and supermodel Heidi Klum has been a host selling her line of jewelry. Broadcasting from remote locations such as Yankee Stadium and airing live acts such as LeAnn Rimes also help attract new customers. The shopping programs are also using other forms of retailing. QVC now has three types of retail stores: a studio store at its headquarters, QVC@THE MALL in Minnesota's Mall of America, and four outlet stores. Similarly, the Home Shopping Network now offers retail experiences on TV, online, in catalogs, and in stores. Finally, several television shopping programs are developing online video platforms, which may attract as many as 50 percent of all new customers, and interactive technology that allows viewers to place orders with their remote control rather than the telephone.

网上零售

Online Retailing

网上零售允许消费者通过互联网搜索、估价和订购产品。对许多消费者来说，这种零售方式的优势在于可以24小时进行、可以比较产品、可以在家私下购买、可以多样选择。对网上购买者的研究表明，男性比女性更愿意使用网上购买。

Online retailing allows consumers to search for, evaluate, and order products through the Internet. For many consumers the advantages of this form of retailing are the 24-hour access, the ability to comparison shop, in-home privacy, and variety. Studies of online shoppers indicated that men were initially more likely than women to buy something online. As the number of online households increased, however, the profile of online shoppers changed to include all shoppers. In addition, the number of online retailers grew rapidly for several years and then declined as many stand-alone, Internet-only businesses failed or consolidated. Today, traditional and online retailers—"bricks and clicks"—are melding, using experiences from both approaches to create better value and experiences for customers. Walmart (www.walmart.com) recently introduced "site-to-store" service that allows customers to order online and

---

Multichannel Merchant《多渠道商业》杂志；consolidate 合并，被兼并。

Going Online

For Some Consumers, Shopping Is a Game!

If you love shopping, particularly for bargains, there are several new Web sites and shopping services for you. Gilt.com, Ideeli.com, HauteLook.com and RueLaLa.com all send text messages announcing limited-time "flash sales" on luxury goods. Consumers then log on to the Web site to make their purchases. Alexandra Wilson, co-founder of Gilt.com, reports that one of the company's messages sold 600 dresses in six minutes!

A variation of these sites is the Web retailer TextBuyIt, a service that allows shoppers to text a product name, universal product code, or ISBN number from a mobile phone and receive price comparison information without getting on the Web.

For some consumers these new services make shopping fun, engaging, even a game! Quick, check your phone for information about the next flash sale!

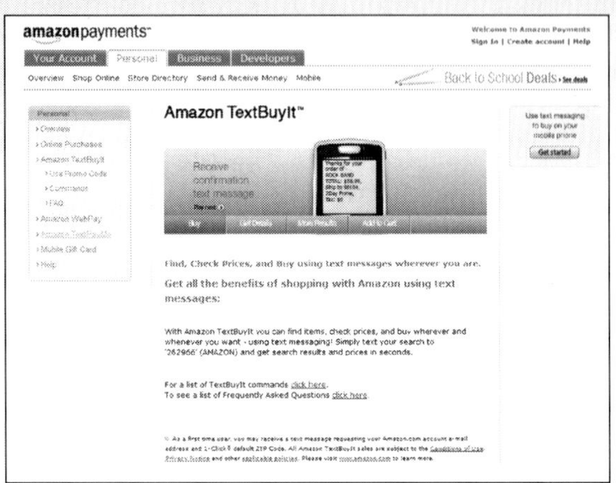

pick up the order without a shipping fee at the store of their choice. Experts predict that online sales will reach $335 billion by 2012.

Online retail purchases can be the result of several very different approaches. First, consumers can pay dues to become a member of an online discount service such as www.netMarket.com. The service offers tens of thousands of products and more than 1,200 brand names at very low prices to its 25 million subscribers. Another approach to online retailing is to use a shopping "bot" such as www.mysimon.com. This site searches the Internet for a product specified by the consumer and provides a report on the locations of the best prices available. Consumers can also use the Internet to go directly to online malls (www.fashionmall.com), apparel retailers (www.gap.com), bookstores (www.amazon.com), computer manufacturers (www.dell.com), grocery stores (www.peapod.com), music and video stores (www.tower.com), and travel agencies (www.travelocity.com). A final approach to online retailing is the online auction, such as www.ebay.com, where consumers bid on more than 50,000 categories of products. See the Going Online box for a description of new forms of online and mobile shopping.

One of the biggest problems online retailers face is that nearly two-thirds of online shoppers make it to "checkout" and then leave the Web site to compare shipping costs and prices on other sites. Of the shoppers who leave, 70 percent do not return. One way online retailers are addressing this issue is to offer consumers a comparison of competitors' offerings. At Allbookstores.com, for example, consumers can use a "comparison engine" to compare prices with Amazon.com, Barnesandnoble.com, and as many as 25 other bookstores. Experts suggest that online retailers should think of their Web sites as dynamic billboards and be visible to search engines if they are to attract and retain customers.

Shopping "bots" like mysimon.com find the best prices for products consumers specify.

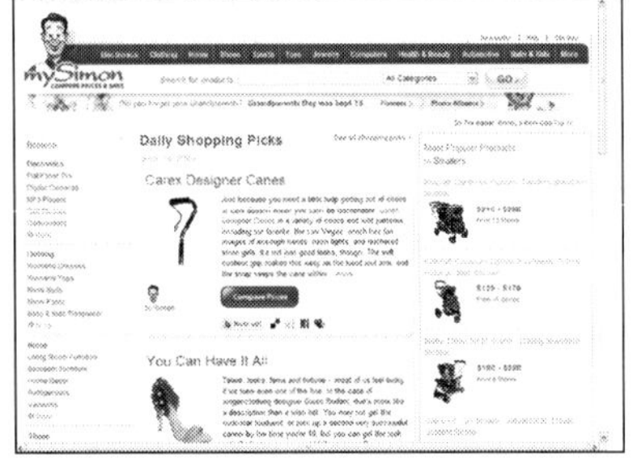

Online retailers are also trying to improve the online retailing experience by adding experiential or interactive activities to their Web sites. Similarly, car manufacturers such as BMW, Mercedes, and Jaguar encourage Web site visitors to "build" a vehicle by selecting interior and exterior colors, packages, and options and then view the customized virtual car. In addition, the merger of television home shopping and online retailing will be possible through TV-based Internet platforms such as Microsoft's MSN TV2, which

category 种类，类别；billboard 广告牌，告示牌。

Consumers can easily access the Internet in many locations today.

uses an Internet appliance attached to a television to connect to the Internet. Owning a television or a computer isn't a necessity for online retailing, however, as many hotels, bars, libraries, airports, and other public locations offer Internet kiosks. In China, the world's largest population of Internet users (253 million), consumers can shop online in more than 185,000 Internet cafes.

电话营销
Telemarketing

另一种无店铺零售方式是**电话营销**，就是利用电话联系消费者并直接销售。虽然两种技术常常一起使用，但与直接邮寄相比，电话营销常被看做是一种更高效的确定目标消费者的方式。

Another form of nonstore retailing, called **telemarketing**, involves using the telephone to interact with and sell directly to consumers. Compared with direct mail, telemarketing is often viewed as a more efficient means of targeting consumers. Insurance companies, brokerage firms, and newspapers have often used this form of retailing as a way to cut costs but still maintain access to their customers. According to the Direct Marketing Association, annual telemarketing sales exceed $330 billion.

The telemarketing industry has recently gone through dramatic changes as a result of new legislation related to telephone solicitations. Issues such as consumer privacy, industry standards, and ethical guidelines have encouraged discussion among consumers, Congress, the Federal Trade Commission, and businesses. The result was legislation that created the National Do-Not-Call registry (www.donotcall.gov) for consumers who do not want to receive telephone calls related to company sales efforts. Currently, there are more than 157 million phone numbers on the registry. Companies that use telemarketing have already adapted by adding compliance software to ensure that numbers on the list are not called. In addition, some firms are considering shifting their telemarketing budgets to direct-mail and door-to-door techniques.

直接销售
Direct Selling

Direct selling, sometimes called door-to-door retailing, involves direct sales of goods and services to consumers through personal interactions and demonstrations in their home or office. A variety of companies, including familiar names such as Avon, Fuller Brush, Mary Kay Cosmetics, and World Book, have created an industry with more than $110 billion in worldwide sales by providing consumers with personalized service and convenience. In the United States, there are more than 15 million direct salespeople working full-time and part-time in 70 product categories.

Growth in the direct-selling industry is the result of two trends. First, many direct selling retailers are expanding into markets outside of the United States. Avon, for example, has 5.8 million sales representatives in 100 countries. More than 77 percent of Amway's $10.7 billion in sales now comes from outside the United States. Similarly, other retailers such as Herbalife and Electrolux are rapidly expanding into new markets. Direct selling is likely to continue to grow in markets where the lack of effective distribution channels increases the importance of door-to-door convenience

telemarketing 电话销售；rapidly 快速地，迅速地。

and where the lack of consumer knowledge about products and brands will increase the need for a person-to-person approach.

The second trend is the growing number of companies that are using direct selling to reach consumers who prefer one-on-one customer service and a social shopping experience rather than online shopping or big discount stores. The Direct Selling Association reports that the number of companies using direct selling has increased by 30 percent in the past five years. Pampered Chef, for example, has 60,000 independent sales reps who sell the company's products at in-home kitchen parties. Interest among potential sales representatives has grown during the recent economic downturn as people seek independence and control of their work activities.

learning review

6. Successful catalog retailers often send ______________ catalogs to ______________ markets identified in their databases.
7. How are retailers increasing consumer interest and involvement in online retailing?
8. Where are direct selling retail sales growing? Why?

零售战略
RETAILING STRATEGY

This section describes how a retailer develops and implements a retailing strategy. Research suggests that factors related to market and competitor characteristics may influence strategic choices and that the combination of choices is an important consideration for retailers. Figure 12–7 identifies the relationship between strategy, positioning, and the retailing mix.

零售商店的定位
Positioning a Retail Store

LO4

The classification alternatives presented in the previous sections help determine one store's position relative to its competitors. The **retail positioning matrix** is a matrix developed by the MAC Group, Inc., a management consulting firm. This matrix positions retail outlets on two dimensions: breadth of product line and value added. As defined previously, *breadth of product line* is the range of products sold through each outlet. The second dimension, *value added*, includes elements such as location

FIGURE 12–7
Elements of a retailing strategy

retail positioning matrix 零售定位矩阵；value added 附加价值。

FIGURE 12–8
Four positioning strategies for retailers

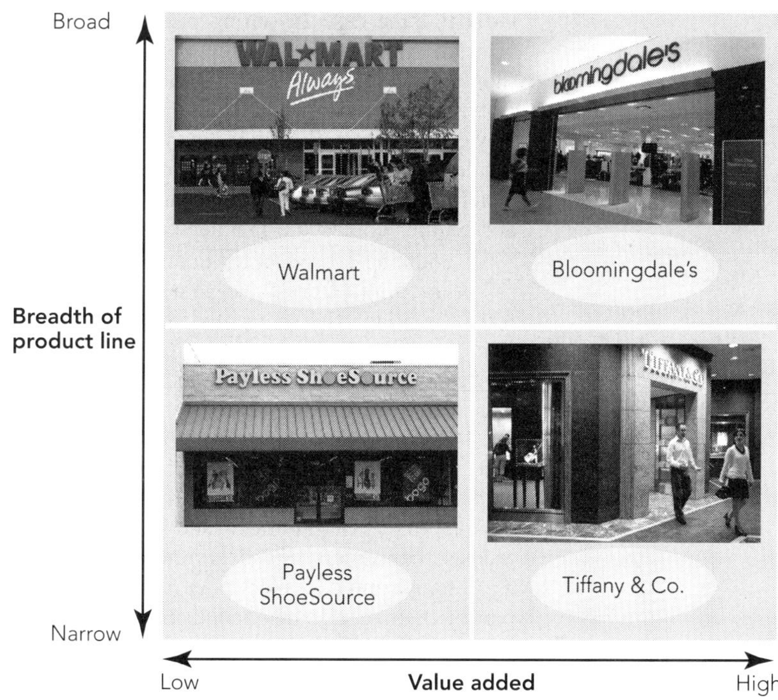

(as with 7-Eleven stores), product reliability (as with Holiday Inn or McDonald's), or prestige (as with Saks Fifth Avenue or Brooks Brothers).

The retail positioning matrix in Figure 12–8 shows four possible positions. An organization can be successful in any position, but unique strategies are required within each quadrant. Consider the four stores shown in the matrix:

1. Bloomingdale's has high value added and a broad product line. Retailers in this quadrant pay great attention to store design and product lines. Merchandise often has a high margin of profit and is of high quality. The stores in this position typically provide high levels of service.
2. Walmart has low value added and a broad line. Walmart and similar firms typically trade a lower price for increased volume in sales. Retailers in this position focus on price with low service levels and an image of being a place for good buys.
3. Tiffany & Co. has high value added and a narrow line. Retailers of this type typically sell a very restricted range of products that are high in status and quality. Customers are also provided with high levels of service.
4. Payless ShoeSource has low value added and a narrow line. Such retailers are specialty mass merchandisers. Payless ShoeSource, for example, carries athletic shoes at a discount. These outlets appeal to value-conscious consumers. Economies of scale are achieved through centralized advertising, merchandising, buying, and distribution. Stores are usually the same in design, layout, and merchandise; hence they are often referred to as "cookie-cutter" stores.

零售组合
Retailing Mix

在制定零售战略时，管理者一般要实施**零售组合**，即与管理店铺和店内商品有关的一切活动。与营销组合类似，零售组合包括零售定价、商店位置、零售传播以及所售商品。

In developing retailing strategy, managers work with the **retailing mix**, which includes activities related to managing the store and the merchandise in the store. The retailing mix is similar to the marketing mix and includes retail pricing, store location, retail communication, and merchandise.

centralize 使集中；retailing mix 零售组合。

加成是指零售商应该对一件产品所支出成本基础上加价多少以形成最终销售价。零售商先是决定最初加成，但等到产品销售时，它们会采用维持加成。最初加成是商品最初售价与零售商成本之间的差额。如果产品销售不如预期那样快速，就会降低价格。最终售价与零售商成本之间的差额就是维持加成，也被称作毛利。

Retail Pricing In setting prices for merchandise, retailers must decide on the markup, markdown, and timing for markdowns. The *markup* refers to how much should be added to the cost the retailer paid for a product to reach the final selling price. Retailers decide on the *original markup*, but by the time the product is sold, they end up with a *maintained markup*. The original markup is the difference between retailer cost and initial selling price. When products do not sell as quickly as anticipated, their price is reduced. The difference between the final selling price and retailer cost is the maintained markup, which is also called the *gross margin*.

Discounting a product, or taking a *markdown*, occurs when the product does not sell at the original price and an adjustment is necessary. Often new models or styles force the price of existing models to be marked down. Discounts may also be used to increase demand for complementary products. For example, retailers might take a markdown on CD players to increase sales of CDs or reduce the price of cake mix to generate frosting purchases. The *timing* of a markdown can be important. Many retailers take a markdown as soon as sales fall off to free up valuable selling space and cash. However, other stores delay markdowns to discourage bargain hunters and maintain an image of quality. There is no clear answer, but retailers must consider how the timing might affect future sales. Research indicates that frequent promotions increase consumers' ability to remember regular prices.

Although most retailers plan markdowns, many retailers use price discounts as a part of their regular merchandising policy. Walmart and Home Depot, for example, emphasize consistently low prices and eliminate most markdowns with a strategy often called *everyday low pricing*. Because consumers often use price as an indicator of product quality, however, the brand name of the product and the image of the store become important decision factors in these situations. Another strategy, *everyday fair pricing*, is advocated by retailers that may not offer the lowest price but try to create value for customers through service and the total buying experience. Consumers often use the prices of *benchmark* or *signpost* items, such as a can of Coke, to form an overall impression of the store's prices. In addition, price is the most likely to influence consumers' assessment of merchandise value. When store prices are based on rebates, retailers must be careful to avoid negative consumer perceptions if the rebate processing time is long (e.g., six weeks).

A special issue for retailers trying to keep prices low is shrinkage, or breakage, theft, and fraud by customers and employees. The National Retail Federation estimates that the average retailer loses 1.6 percent of sales to shrinkage each year. Fraudulent returns alone account for $15 billion. About 50 percent of retail shrinkage is due to employee theft. Some retailers have noticed an increase in theft and fraud as economic conditions have declined. In general, the issue has increased retailers' interest in new technical and surveillance techniques to reduce shrinkage.

Off-price retailing is a retail pricing practice that is used by retailers such as T.J. Maxx, Burlington Coat Factory, and Ross Stores. **Off-price retailing** involves selling brand-name merchandise at lower than regular prices. The difference between the off-price retailer and a discount store is that off-price merchandise is bought by the retailer from manufacturers with excess inventory at prices below wholesale prices. The discounter, however, buys at full wholesale price but takes less of a markup than do traditional department stores. Because of this difference in the way merchandise is purchased by the retailer, selection at an off-price retailer is unpredictable, and searching for bargains has become a popular activity for many consumers. "It's more like a sport than it is like ordinary shopping," says Christopher Boring of Columbus, Ohio's Retail Planning Associates. Savings to the consumer at off-price retailers are reported as high as 70 percent off the prices of a traditional department store.

T.J. Maxx is a popular off-price retailer.

original markup 最初加成；maintained markup 维持加成；gross margin 毛利润；off-price retailing 低价零售。

Off 5th provides an outlet for excess merchandise from Saks Fifth Avenue.

There are several variations of off-price retailing. One is the *warehouse club*. These large stores (100,000 to 140,000 square feet) are rather stark outlets with no elaborate displays, customer service, or home delivery. They require an annual membership fee (ranging from $30 to $100) for the privilege of shopping there. While a typical Walmart stocks 30,000 to 60,000 items, warehouse clubs carry 4,000 to 8,000 items and usually stock just one brand of appliance or food product. Service is minimal, and customers usually pay by cash or check. Customers are attracted by the ultralow prices and surprise deals on selected merchandise, although several of the clubs have recently started to add ancillary services such as optical shops and pharmacies to differentiate themselves from competitors. The major warehouse clubs in the United States include Walmart's Sam's Club, BJ's Wholesale Club, and Costco's Warehouse Club. Sales of these off-price retailers have grown to approximately $200 billion annually.

A second variation is the *outlet store*. Factory outlets, such as Van Heusen Factory Store, Bass Shoe Outlet, and Gap Factory Store, offer products for 25 to 30 percent off the suggested retail price. Manufacturers use the stores to clear excess merchandise and to reach consumers who focus on value shopping. Retail outlets such as Nordstrom Rack and Off 5th (Saks Fifth Avenue outlet) allow retailers to sell excess merchandise and still maintain an image of offering merchandise at full price in their primary store. The number of factory outlet centers has decreased recently as factory outlet stores are competing with the sales in mall and discount stores. In markets such as China, however, the outlet concept is still growing.

A third variation of off-price retailing is offered by *single-price*, or *extreme value*, *retailers* such as Family Dollar, Dollar General, and Dollar Tree. These stores average about 6,000 square feet in size and attract customers who want value and a "corner store" environment rather than a large supercenter experience. Some experts predict extraordinary growth of these types of retailers. Dollar General, for example, already has 8,000 stores in 35 states and plans to open more.

Store Location A second aspect of the retailing mix involves deciding where to locate the store and how many stores to have. Department stores, which started downtown in most cities, have followed customers to the suburbs, and in recent years more stores have been opened in large regional malls. Most stores today are near several others in one of five settings: the central business district, the regional center, the community shopping center, the strip mall, or the power center.

中央商业区是最古老的零售环境，是一个市区的聚集区。

The **central business district** is the oldest retail setting, the community's downtown area. Until the regional outflow to suburbs, it was the major shopping area, but the suburban population has grown at the expense of the downtown shopping area. Consumers often view central business district shopping as less convenient because of lack of parking, higher crime rates, and exposure to the weather. Many cities such as Louisville, Denver, and San Antonio have implemented plans to revitalize shopping in central business districts by attracting new offices, entertainment, and residents to downtown locations.

地区购物中心由 50~150 个商店构成，主要吸引在方圆 5~10 英里内工作或生活的顾客。

Regional shopping centers consist of 50 to 150 stores that typically attract customers who live or work within a 5- to 10-mile range. These large shopping areas often contain two or three *anchor stores*, which are well-known national or regional stores such as Sears, Saks Fifth Avenue, and Bloomingdale's. The largest variation of a regional center is the West Edmonton Mall in Alberta, Canada. The shopping center is a conglomerate of more than 800 stores, 21 movie theaters, the world's largest indoor amusement park, 110 restaurants, and a 354-room Fantasyland hotel.

A more limited approach to retail location is the **community shopping center**, which typically has one primary store (usually a department store branch) and often

outlet store 工厂直销店；single-price 单一价格；extreme value 极端价值；central business district 中央商业区。

about 20 to 40 smaller outlets. Generally, these centers serve a population of consumers who are within a 10- to 20-minute drive.

Not every suburban store is located in a shopping mall. Many neighborhoods have clusters of stores, referred to as a **strip mall**, to serve people who are within a 5- to 10-minute drive. Gas station, hardware, laundry, grocery, and pharmacy outlets are commonly found in a strip mall. Unlike the larger shopping centers, the composition of these stores is usually unplanned. A variation of the strip mall is called the **power center**, which is a huge shopping strip with multiple anchor (or national) stores such as Home Depot, Best Buy, or JCPenney. Power centers are seen as having the convenient location found in many strip malls and the additional power of national stores. These large strip malls often have two to five anchor stores and often contain a supermarket, which brings the shopper to the power center on a weekly basis.

Retail Communication A retailer's communication activities can play an important role in positioning a store and creating its image. While the traditional elements of communication and promotion are discussed in Chapter 14 on advertising, the message communicated by the many other elements of the retailing mix are also important.

Deciding on the image of a retail outlet is an important retailing mix factor that has been widely recognized and studied since the late 1950s. Pierre Martineau described image as "the way in which the store is defined in the shopper's mind," partly by its functional qualities and partly by an aura of psychological attributes. In this definition, *functional* refers to mix elements such as price ranges, store layouts, and breadth and depth of merchandise lines. The psychological attributes are the intangibles such as a sense of belonging, excitement, style, or warmth. Image has been found to include impressions of the corporation that operates the store, the category or type of store, the product categories in the store, the brands in each category, merchandise and service quality, and the marketing activities of the store.

Closely related to the concept of image is the store's atmosphere or ambience. Many retailers believe that sales are affected by layout, color, lighting, and music in the store as well as by how crowded it is. In addition, the physical surroundings that influence customers may affect the store's employees. In creating the right image and atmosphere, a retail store tries to attract its target audience with what those consumers seek from the buying experience, so the store will fortify the beliefs and the emotional reactions buyers are seeking. While store image perceptions can exist independently of shopping experiences, consumers' shopping experiences can also influence store perceptions.

Merchandise A final element of the retailing mix is the merchandise offering. Managing the breadth and depth of the product line requires retail buyers who are familiar with the needs of the target market and the alternative products available from the many manufacturers that might be interested in having a product available in the store. A popular approach to managing the assortment of merchandise today is called **category management**. This approach assigns a manager the responsibility for selecting all products that consumers in a market segment might view as substitutes for each other, with the objective of maximizing sales and profits in the category. For example, a category manager might be responsible for shoes in a department store or paper products in a grocery store.

当前流行的一种管理商品品类的方法是**目录管理**。该方法是安排一位经理负责挑选出某细分市场中消费者认为可相互替代的所有产品，其目的在于实现该目录产品的销售额和利润最大化。

Many retailers are developing an advanced form of category management called *consumer marketing at retail* (CMAR). Recent surveys show that, as part of their CMAR programs, retailers are conducting research, analyzing the data to identify shopper problems, translating the data into retailing mix actions, executing shopper-friendly in-store programs, and monitoring the performance of the merchandise. Walmart, for example, has used the approach to test baby-product and dollar-product categories. Grocery stores such as Safeway and Kroger use the approach to deter-

strip mall 沿公路商业区；power center 能量中心；category management 品类管理。

Using Marketing Dashboards

Why Apple Stores May Be the Best in the United States!

How effective is my retail format compared to other stores? How are my stores performing this year compared to last year? Information related to this question is often displayed in a marketing dashboard using two measures: (1) sales per square foot, and (2) same store sales growth.

Your Challenge You have been assigned to evaluate the Apple store retail format. The store's simple, inviting, and open atmosphere has been the topic of discussion among many retailers. Apple, however, is relatively new to the retailing business and many experts have been skeptical of the format. To allow an assessment of Apple stores, use *sales per square foot* as an indicator of how effectively retail space is used to generate revenue and *same store sales growth* to compare the increase in sales of stores that have been open for the same period of time. The calculations for these indicators are:

$$\text{Sales per square foot} = \frac{\text{Total sales}}{\text{Selling area in square feet}}$$

Same store sales growth

$$= \frac{\text{Store sales in year 2} - \text{Store sales in year 1}}{\text{Store sales in year 1}}$$

Your Findings You decide to collect sales information for Saks, Neiman Marcus, Best Buy, Tiffany, and Apple stores to allow comparisons with other successful retailers. The information you collect allows the calculation of *sales per square foot* and *same store growth* for each store. The results are then easy to compare in the graphs below.

Your Action The results of your investigation indicate that Apple stores' sales per square foot are higher than any of the comparison stores at $4,000. In addition, Apple's same store growth rate of 45 percent is higher than all of the other stores. You conclude that the elements of Apple's format are very effective and even indicate that Apple may currently be the best retailer in the United States.

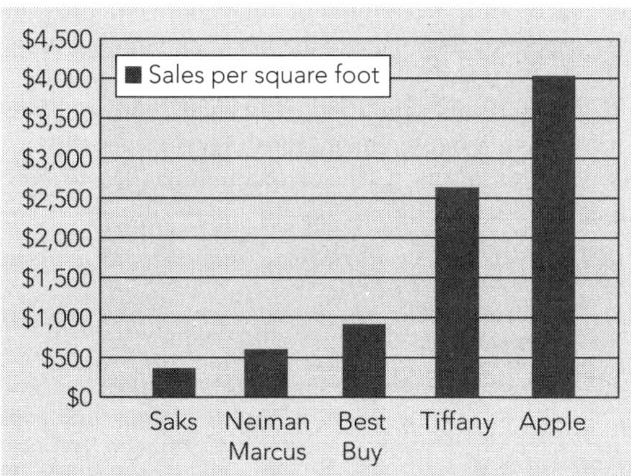

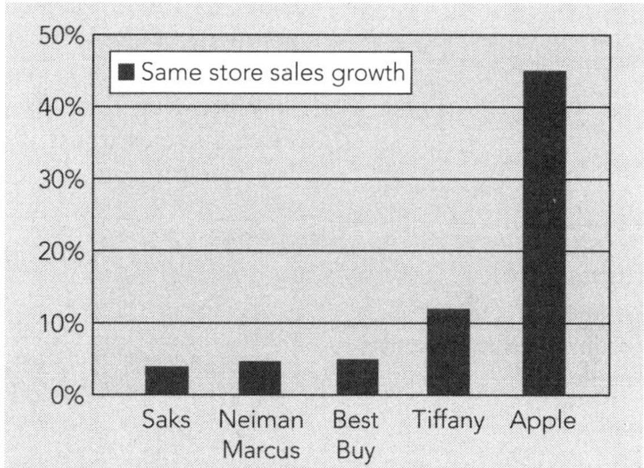

mine the appropriate mix of brand name and private-label products. Specialty retailer Barnes & Noble recently won a best practice award for its application of the approach to the selection, presentation, and promotion of magazines.

Retailers have a variety of marketing metrics that can be used to assess the effectiveness of a store or retail format. First, there are measures related to customers such as the number of transactions per customer, the average transaction size per customer, the number of customers per day or per hour, and the average length of a store visit. Second, there are measures related to products such as number of returns, inventory turnover, inventory carrying cost, and average number of items per transaction. Finally, there are financial measures, such as gross margin, sales per employee, return on sales, and markdown percentage. The two most popular measures for retailers are *sales per square foot* and *same store sales growth*. The Using Marketing Dashboards box describes the calculation of these measures for Apple stores.

sales per square foot 每平方英尺的销售额；same store sales growth 同一商店的增长速度。

learning review	9. What are the two dimensions of the retail positioning matrix? 10. How does original markup differ from maintained markup? 11. A huge shopping strip mall with multiple anchor stores is a ________ center.

零售的渠道性质
THE CHANGING NATURE OF RETAILING

LO5

Retailing is the most dynamic aspect of a channel of distribution. New types of retailers are always entering the market, searching for a new position that will attract customers. The reason for this continual change is explained by two concepts: the wheel of retailing and the retail life cycle.

零售轮
The Wheel of Retailing

零售轮描述了新型零售业态是如何进入市场的。

The **wheel of retailing** describes how new forms of retail outlets enter the market. Usually they enter as low-status, low-margin stores such as a drive-in hamburger stand with no indoor seating and a limited menu (Figure 12–9, box 1). Gradually these outlets add fixtures and more embellishments to their stores (in-store seating, plants, and chicken sandwiches as well as hamburgers) to increase the attractiveness for customers. With these additions, prices and status rise (box 2). As time passes, these outlets add still more services and their prices and status increase even further (box 3). These retail outlets now face some new form of retail outlet that again appears as a low-status, low-margin operator (box 4), and the wheel of retailing turns as the cycle starts to repeat itself.

When Ray Kroc started the first McDonald's in 1955, it opened shortly before lunch and closed just after dinner, offering a limited menu for the two meals without any inside seating for customers. Over time, the wheel of retailing has led to new

FIGURE 12–9
The wheel of retailing describes how retail outlets change.

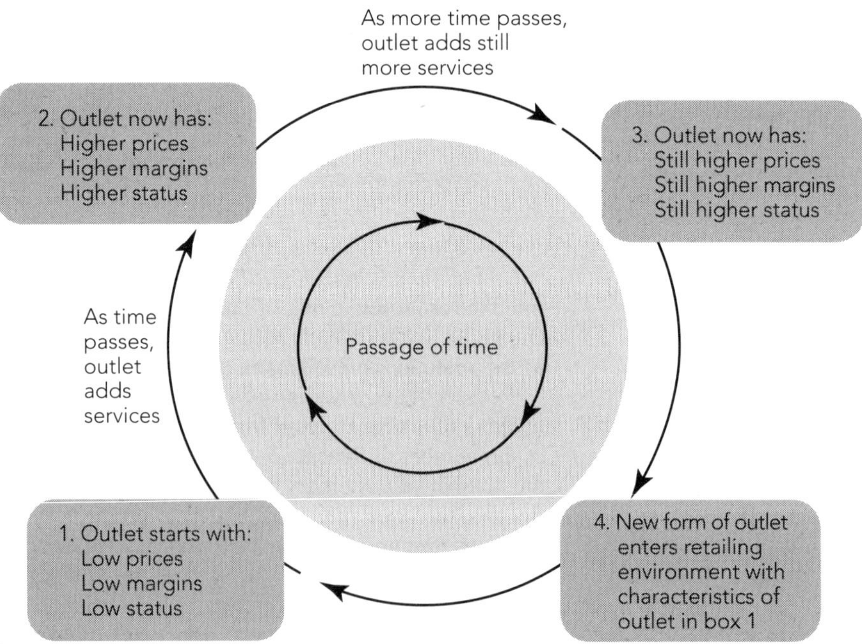

wheel of retailing 零售轮。

Outlets such as Checkers enter the wheel of retailing as low-status, low-margin stores.

products and services. In 1975, McDonald's introduced the Egg McMuffin and turned breakfast into a fast-food meal. Today, McDonald's has an extensive menu, seating, and services such as wireless Internet connections and McCafé premium coffee. For the future, McDonald's is testing new products such as fried chicken biscuits, frying oil without trans fats, and fruit smoothies; new formats such as seating "zones" for different types of customers; and 24/7 "always open" hours.

The changes are leaving room for new forms of outlets such as Checkers Drive-In Restaurants. The chain opened fast-food stores that offered only basics—burgers, fries, and cola, a drive-through window, and no inside seating—and now has more than 800 stores. The wheel is turning for other outlets too—Boston Market has added pick-up, delivery, and full-service catering to its original restaurant format, and it also provides Boston Market meal solutions through supermarket delis and Boston Market frozen meals in the frozen food sections. For still others, the wheel has come full circle. Taco Bell is now opening small, limited-offering outlets in gas stations, discount stores, or "wherever a burrito and a mouth might possibly intersect."

Discount stores were a major new retailing form in the 1960s and priced their products below those of department stores. As prices in discount stores rose in the 1980s, they found themselves overpriced compared with a new form of retail outlet—the warehouse club. Today, off-price retailers and factory outlets are offering prices even lower than warehouse clubs.

零售生命周期
The Retail Life Cycle

如产品一样，零售业态也经历一个成长与衰退的过程，这称为**零售生命周期**。

The process of growth and decline that retail outlets, like products, experience is described by the **retail life cycle**. Figure 12–10 shows the retail life cycle and the position of various current forms of retail outlets on it. Early growth is the stage

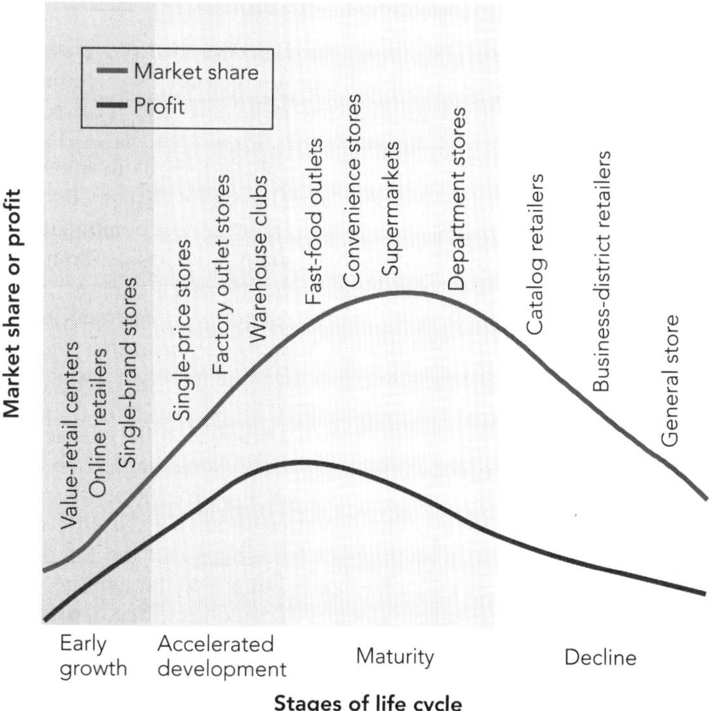

FIGURE 12–10
The retail life cycle describes stages of growth and decline for retail outlets.

biscuit 饼干；retail life cycle 零售生命周期。

of emergence of a retail outlet, with a sharp departure from existing competition. Market share rises gradually, although profits may be low because of start-up costs. In the next stage, accelerated development, both market share and profit achieve their greatest growth rates. Usually multiple outlets are established as companies focus on the distribution element of the retailing mix. In this stage, some later competitors may enter. Wendy's, for example, appeared on the hamburger chain scene almost 20 years after McDonald's had begun operation. The key goal for the retailer in this stage is to establish a dominant position in the fight for market share.

The battle for market share is usually fought before the maturity stage, and some competitors drop out of the market. In the wars among hamburger chains, Jack in the Box, Gino's Hamburgers, and Burger Chef used to be more dominant outlets. New retail forms such as Fatburger and In-N-Out Burger enter in the maturity stage, stores try to maintain their market share, and price discounting occurs.

The challenge facing retailers is to delay entering the decline stage in which market share and profit fall rapidly. Specialty apparel retailers, such as the Gap, Limited, Benetton, and Ann Taylor, have noticed a decline in market share after years of growth. To prevent further decline, these retailers will need to find ways of discouraging their customers from moving to low-margin, mass-volume outlets or high-price, high-service boutiques.

零售未来的变化
FUTURE CHANGES IN RETAILING

Two exciting trends in retailing—the growth of multichannel retailing and the increasing focus on customer experience management—are likely to lead to many changes for retailers and consumers in the future.

多渠道零售
Multichannel Retailing

每种模式都能使得零售商提供独特的利益，并满足各种顾客群体的特殊需要。每种模式都有许多成功的实践，未来的零售商可能将许多模式综合在一起，从而提供给顾客一种更宽的利益和体验范围并吸引更多的消费者。

The retailing formats described previously in this chapter represent an exciting menu of choices for creating customer value in the marketplace. Each format allows retailers to offer unique benefits and meet particular needs of various customer groups. While each format has many successful applications, retailers in the future are likely to combine many of the formats to offer a broader spectrum of benefits and experiences and to appeal to different segments of consumers. These **multichannel retailers** will utilize and integrate a combination of traditional store formats and nonstore formats such as catalogs, television, home shopping, and online retailing. Barnes & Noble, for example, created Barnesandnoble.com to compete with Amazon.com. Similarly, Office Depot has integrated its store, catalog, and Internet operations.

Integrated channels can make shopping simpler and more convenient. A consumer can research choices online or in a catalog and then make a purchase online, over the telephone, or at the closest store. In addition, the use of multiple channels allows retailers to reach a broader profile of customers. While online retailing may cannibalize catalog business to some degree, an online transaction costs about half as much to process as a catalog order. Multichannel retailers also benefit from the synergy of sharing information among the different channel operations. Online retailers, for example, have recognized that the Internet is more of a transactional medium than a relationship-building medium and are working to find ways to complement traditional customer interactions. The benefits of multichannel marketing are also apparent in the spending behavior of consumers as described in the Marketing Matters box.

accelerate 加快，加速；multichannel retailers 多渠道零售商。

Marketing Matters >>>>>> customer value

The Multichannel Marketing Multiplier

Multichannel marketing is the blending of different communication and delivery channels that are mutually reinforcing in attracting, retaining, and building relationships with consumers who shop and buy in the traditional marketplace and marketspace. Industry analysts refer to the complementary role of different communication and delivery channels as an *influence effect*.

Retailers that integrate and leverage their stores, catalogs, and Web sites have seen a sizable lift in yearly sales recorded from individual customers. Eddie Bauer is a good example. Customers who shop only one of its channels spend $100 to $200 per year. Those who shop in two channels spend $300 to $500 annually. Customers who shop all these channels—store, catalog, and Web site—spend $800 to $1,000 per year. Moreover, multichannel customers have been found to be *three times* as profitable as single-channel customers.

JCPenney has seen similar results. The company is a leading multichannel retailer and reports that a JCPenney customer who shops in all three channels—store, catalog, and Web site—spends *four to eight times* as much as a customer who shops in only one channel, as shown in the chart.

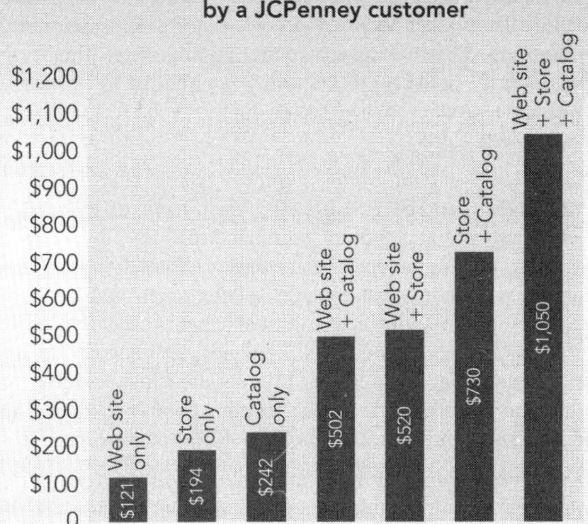

顾客体验管理
Managing the Customer Experience

Department stores are changing to create social retailing experiences. While many of those changes appeal to women and address the way women like to shop, retailers are also paying more attention to men and their shopping behavior. Men have typically been viewed as infrequent "mission shoppers" who go to a store only as a means of obtaining a product as efficiently as possible. Today's young men, however, are changing their shopping behavior. Recent research found that 84 percent of men said they purchase their own clothes, compared with just 65 percent four years ago. To appeal to men, many stores are creating stand-alone men's sections that combine clothes, accessories, and gadgets in one place. The new sections use "masculine" interior designs with simple colors, stainless-steel fixtures, and dark wood floors. Bloomingdale's in Manhattan has even added seating, sports magazines, and televisions to the men's areas. All of these changes are intended to create a better experience for male shoppers. As Jack Hruska, executive vice president at Bloomingdale's, explains, "We hope to make men feel more comfortable and at home by giving them a place to unwind while they are shopping."

learning review

12. According to the wheel of retailing, when a new retail form appears, how would you characterize its image?
13. Market share is usually fought out before the ______________ stage of the retail life cycle.
14. What is an influence effect?

infrequent 不频发的，很少发生的；president 总裁，董事长。

LEARNING OBJECTIVES REVIEW

LO1 *Identify retailers in terms of the utilities they provide.*
Retailers provide time, place, form, and possession utilities. Time utility is provided by stores with convenient time-of-day (e.g., open 24 hours) or time-of-year (e.g., seasonal sports equipment available all year) availability. Place utility is provided by the number and location of the stores. Possession utility is provided by making a purchase possible (e.g., financing) or easier (e.g., delivery). Form utility is provided by producing or altering a product to meet the customer's specifications (e.g., custom-made shirts).

LO2 *Explain the alternative ways to classify retail outlets.*
Retail outlets can be classified by their form of ownership, level of service, and type of merchandise line. The forms of ownership include independent retailers, corporate chains, and contractual systems that include retailer-sponsored cooperatives, wholesaler-sponsored voluntary chains, and franchises. The levels of service include self-service, limited-service, and full-service outlets. Stores classified by their merchandise line include stores with depth, such as sporting good specialty stores, and stores with breadth, such as large department stores.

LO3 *Describe the many methods of nonstore retailing.*
Nonstore retailing includes automatic vending, direct mail and catalogs, television home shopping, online retailing, telemarketing, and direct selling. The methods of nonstore retailing vary by the level of involvement of the retailer and the level of involvement of the customer. Vending, for example, has low involvement, whereas both the consumer and the retailer have high involvement in direct selling.

LO4 *Classify retailers in terms of the retail positioning matrix, and specify retailing mix actions.*
The retail positioning matrix positions retail outlets on two dimensions: breadth of product line and value added. There are four possible positions in the matrix—broad product line/low value added (Walmart), narrow product line/low value added (Payless Shoe Source), broad product line/high value added (Bloomingdale's), and narrow product line/high value added (Tiffany). Retailing mix actions are used to manage a retail store and the merchandise in a store. The mix variables include pricing, store location, communication activities, and merchandise. Two common forms of assessment for retailers are "sales per square foot" and "same store growth."

LO5 *Explain changes in retailing with the wheel of retailing and the retail life cycle concepts.*
The wheel of retailing concept explains how retail outlets typically enter the market as low-status, low-margin stores. Over time, stores gradually add new products and services, increasing their prices, status, and margins, and leaving an opening for new low-status, low-margin stores. The retail life cycle describes the process of growth and decline for retail outlets through four stages: early growth, accelerated development, maturity, and decline.

FOCUSING ON KEY TERMS

breadth of product line
category management
central business district
community shopping center
depth of product line
form of ownership
hypermarket
intertype competition
level of service
merchandise line
multichannel retailers
off-price retailing
power center
regional shopping centers
retail life cycle
retail positioning matrix
retailing
retailing mix
scrambled merchandising
strip mall
telemarketing
wheel of retailing

APPLYING MARKETING KNOWLEDGE

1 Discuss the impact of the growing number of dual-income households on (*a*) nonstore retailing and (*b*) the retail mix.

2 How does value added affect a store's competitive position?

3 In retail pricing, retailers often have a maintained markup. Explain how this maintained markup differs from original markup and why it is so important.

4 What are the similarities and differences between the product and retail life cycles?

5 How would you classify Walmart in terms of its position on the wheel of retailing versus that of an off-price retailer?

6 Develop a chart to highlight the role of each of the four main elements of the retailing mix across the four stages of the retail life cycle.

7 In Figure 12–8 Payless ShoeSource was placed on the retail positioning matrix. What strategies should Payless ShoeSource follow to move itself into the same position as Tiffany?

8 Breadth and depth are two important components in distinguishing among types of retailers. Discuss the breadth and depth implications of the following retailers discussed in this chapter: (*a*) Nordstrom, (*b*) Walmart, (*c*) L. L. Bean, and (*d*) Best Buy.

9 According to the wheel of retailing and the retail life cycle, what will happen to factory outlet stores?

10 The text discusses the development of online retailing in the United States. How does the development of this retailing form agree with the implications of the retail life cycle?

building your marketing plan

Does your marketing plan involve using retailers? If the answer is no, read no further and do not include a retailing element in your plan. If the answer is yes:

1 Use Figure 12–8 to develop your retailing strategy by (*a*) selecting a position in the retail positioning matrix and (*b*) specifying the details of the retailing mix.

2 Develop a positioning statement describing the breadth of the product line (broad versus narrow) and value added (low versus high).

3 Describe an appropriate combination of retail pricing, store location, retail communication, and merchandise assortment.

video case 12 Mall of America: Shopping and a Whole Lot More

"If you build it, they will come" not only worked in the movie *Field of Dreams* but also applies—big time—to Mall of America.

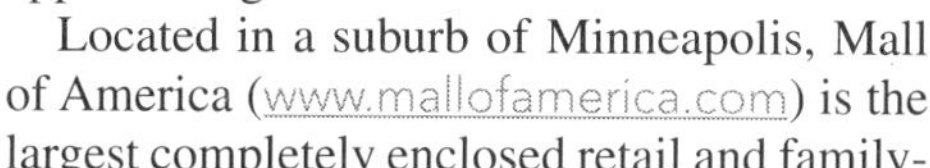

Located in a suburb of Minneapolis, Mall of America (www.mallofamerica.com) is the largest completely enclosed retail and family-entertainment complex in the United States. "We're more than a mall, we're a destination," explains Maureen Cahill, an executive at Mall of America. More than 100,000 people each day—40 million visitors each year—visit the one-stop complex offering retail shopping, guest services, convenience, a huge variety of entertainment, and fun for all. "Guest services" include everything from high school and college classrooms to a doctor's office and a wedding chapel.

THE CONCEPT AND CHALLENGE

The idea for the Mall of America came from the West Edmonton Mall in Alberta, Canada. The Ghermezian Brothers, who developed that mall, sought to create a unique mall that would attract not only local families but also tourists from the Upper Midwest, the nation, and even from abroad.

The two challenges for Mall of America: How can it (1) attract and keep the large number of retail establishments needed to (2) continue to attract even more millions of visitors than today? A big part of the answer is in Mall of America's positioning—"There is a place for fun in your life!"

THE STAGGERING SIZE AND OFFERINGS

Opened August 1992 amid tremendous worldwide publicity, Mall of America faced skeptics who had their doubts because of its size, its unique retail-entertainment mix, and the nationwide recession. Despite these concerns, it opened with more than 80 percent of its space leased and attracted more than 1 million visitors its first week.

Mall of America is 4.2 million square feet, the equivalent of 88 football fields. This makes it three to four times

the size of most other regional malls. It includes four anchor department stores: Nordstrom, Macy's, Bloomingdale's, and Sears. It also includes more than 520 specialty stores, from Brooks Brothers to DSW Shoe Warehouse. Approximately 36 percent of Mall of America's space is devoted to anchors and 64 percent to specialty stores. This makes the space allocation the reverse of most regional malls.

The retail-entertainment mix of Mall of America is incredibly diverse. For example, there are more than 100 apparel and accessory stores, 18 jewelry stores, and 33 shoe stores. Two food courts with 27 restaurants plus more than 30 other restaurants scattered throughout the building meet most food preferences of visitors. Another surprise: Mall of America is home to many "concept stores," where retailers introduce a new type of store or design. Because of its incredible size, the mall has 194 stores not found at competing regional malls. In addition, it has an entrepreneurial program for people with an innovative retail idea and limited resources. They can open a kiosk, wall unit, or small store for a specified time period or as a temporary seasonal tenant.

Unique features of Mall of America include:

- A seven-acre theme park with more than 50 attractions and rides, including a roller coaster, Ferris wheel, and games in a glass-enclosed, skylighted area with more than 400 trees.
- Underwater Adventures, where visitors are surrounded by sharks, stingrays, and sea turtles; can adventure among fish native to the north woods; and can discover what lurks at the bottom of the Mississippi River.
- Entertainment choices that include a 14-screen theater, A.C.E.S. Flight Simulation, NASCAR Silicon Motor Speedway, and Dinosaur Walk Museum.
- The LEGO Land Imagination Center, a 6,000-square-foot showplace with more than 30 full-sized models.

As a host to corporate events and private parties, Mall of America has a rotunda that opens to all four floors that facilitates presentations, demonstrations, and exhibits. Organizations such as PepsiCo, Visa-USA, and Chevrolet have used the facilities to gain shopper awareness. Mall of America is a rectangle with the anchor department stores at the corners and amusement park in the skylighted central area, making it easy for shoppers to understand and navigate. It has 12,550 free parking ramp spaces on site and another 7,000 spaces nearby during peak times.

THE MARKET

The Minneapolis–St. Paul metropolitan area is a market with more than 3 million people. A total of 30 million people live within a day's drive of Mall of America. A survey of its shoppers showed that 32 percent of the shoppers travel 150 miles or more and account for more than 50 percent of the sales revenues. Located three miles from the Minneapolis/St. Paul International Airport, Mall of America provides a shuttle bus from the airport every half hour. Light-rail service from the airport and downtown Minneapolis is also available.

Tourism accounts for 4 out of 10 visits to Mall of America. About 6 percent of visitors come from outside the United States. Some come just to see and experience Mall of America, while others take advantage of the cost savings available on goods (Japan) or taxes (Canada and states with sales taxes on clothing).

THE FUTURE: FACING THE CHALLENGES

Where does Mall of America head in the future?

"We just did a brand study and found that Mall of America is one of the most recognized brands in the world," Cahill says. "They might not know where we are sometimes, but they've heard of Mall of America and they know they want to come.

"What we've learned since 1992 is to keep the Mall of America fresh and exciting," she explains. "We're constantly looking at what attracts people and adding to that. We're adding new stores, new attractions, and new events. We hold more than 350 events a year and with everyone from Garth Brooks to Sarah Ferguson to N Sync."

Mall of America announced a plan for a 5.6 million-square-foot expansion, the area of another 117 football fields, connected by pedestrian skyway to the present building. "The second phase will not be a duplicate of what we have," Cahill says. "We have plans for at least three hotels, a performing arts center, a business office complex, an art or history museum, and possibly even a television broadcast facility." The expansion is expected to attract an additional 20 million visitors annually. In addition, the development is designed to exceed environmental certification standards.

One of the first elements of the expansion includes a now open 306,000-square-foot IKEA store. Other new elements will include a 13,000-square-foot restaurant called Cantina Corona, a 6,000-seat performing arts auditorium created by AEG, a 300,000-square-foot Bass Pro store, a 500-room hotel and a Mayo Clinic facility. All of these new additions and the many offerings of the current mall reinforce that Mall of America is a shopping destination and a whole lot more!

Questions

1 Why has Mall of America been such a marketing success so far?

2 What (*a*) retail and (*b*) consumer trends have occurred since Mall of America was opened in 1992 that it should consider when making future plans?

3 (*a*) What criteria should Mall of America use in adding new facilities to its complex? (*b*) Evaluate (*i*) retail stores, (*ii*) entertainment offerings, and (*iii*) hotels on these criteria.

4 What specific marketing actions would you propose that Mall of America managers take to ensure its continuing success in attracting visitors (*a*) from the local metropolitan area and (*b*) from outside of it?

TV Celebrity Food Games News Sports Mobile Shop

Shows Video HD Videos Watch & Chat Schedule Login Register

Social Viewing Room Lounge

Join A Social Viewing Room

Browse viewing rooms and connect with others to share

Join family, friends and fellow fans and watch your favorite episodes of your favorite shows together. Boo the latest villains on CSI: Miami and CSI: NY at the same time. LOL in unison at the same crazy antics on Worst Week and Gary UnMarried and toss tomatoes at your least favorite Survivor. Hop right into one of the rooms below, invite your friends and start socializing!

2 / 2

Gary Unmarried Gary And His Half Brother
Season 1: Episode 19
Full Episode (21:36)
Join Now

4 Fans in Room

Advertisement

View by myself

Other Rooms for This Show

Room 1	[3]	12 min. in
Room 2	[10]	2 min. in
Room 3	[2]	29 min. in
Room 4	[2]	25 min. in

Invite your friends

Feedback

Quick Quiz

00:12

How many days does Jeff say the game wil last?

33

39

55

Want your own avatar picture? **Register, it's free! | No, thanks**

Type here to comment

Survivor: Samoa - Episode 1
Air Date: 09/17/09
Full Episode 42:37

Twenty castaways are left to fend for themselves among Samoa's white sand beaches, lush green valleys and towering waterfalls.

13 整合营销传播与直接营销
Integrated Marketing Communications and Direct Marketing

LEARNING OBJECTIVES

After reading this chapter you should be able to:

- LO1 Discuss integrated marketing communication and the communication process.
- LO2 Describe the promotional mix and the uniqueness of each component.
- LO3 Select the promotional approach appropriate to a product's target audience, life-cycle stage, and characteristics, as well as stages of the buying decision and channel strategies.
- LO4 Describe the elements of the promotion decision process.
- LO5 Explain the value of direct marketing for consumers and sellers.

整合营销传播恰逢其时
INTEGRATED MARKETING COMMUNICATIONS USHERS IN THE 'AGE OF ENGAGE'

How would you characterize today's marketplace? For most consumers the answer is interactive and connected—through cell phones, computers, the Web, and social networks such as Facebook, MySpace, Twitter, LinkedIn, and Flickr. In this marketplace the key to communicating with consumers is to engage them—a perfect job for integrated marketing communications campaigns!

How can media engage consumers? The options are endless for traditional and new forms of media. TV networks, for example, now offer online video streams of many series. CBS recently created social viewing rooms at CBS.com for programs such as *CSI* and *Survivor*. The rooms allow viewers to chat about what they are watching and to offer critical reactions to the program. Senior Vice President Anthony Soohoo explains, "When people are online they want to engage in a different way, they want to share the experience." The audience for online viewing is now 162 million viewers, compared to the 282 million who watch on their television.

New forms of communicating with customers, such as social media, also offer opportunities to engage consumers. Recent research shows that 85 percent of consumers believe that companies should be interacting through social channels. Many companies create a branded presence such as a fan page within virtual communities such as Facebook or MySpace to generate word-of-mouth advertising. Some companies, such as Saturn, have even created their own online communities as showcases for their brands and products. One advantage of this medium is that it is less expensive than other forms of marketing, even though it may require constant monitoring by someone at the company or its advertising agency.

Many other media can also engage consumers today. When Disney created a contest for the chance to play a fantasy role at Disneyland, more than 10,000 people submitted videos! eBay Motors worked with the makers of a car racing game called "Grid" for Xbox 360, Playstation 3, and Nintendo so that the auction platform would be integrated into the game, and seen by a potential audience of 40 million game enthusiasts. Procter & Gamble used product placement to include its Crest Whitestrips in the movie *He's Just Not That into You*, and then passed out free samples at the exits of the movie theaters. E-mail, blogs, gift cards, magazines, and sweepstakes are also potential forms of media that can engage today's consumers.

The many types of promotion in these examples demonstrate the opportunity for engaging potential customers and the importance of integrating the various elements of a communication program.

---

audience 观众，听众；monitoring 监控，监视，监督。

Promotion represents the fourth element in the marketing mix. The promotional element consists of communication tools, including advertising, personal selling, sales promotion, public relations, and direct marketing. The combination of one or more of these communication tools is called the **promotional mix**. All of these tools can be used to: (1) inform prospective buyers about the benefits of the product, (2) persuade them to try it, and (3) remind them later about the benefits they enjoyed by using the product. In the past, marketers often viewed these communication tools as separate and independent. The advertising department, for example, often designed and managed its activities without consulting departments or agencies that had responsibility for sales promotion or public relations. The result was often an overall communication effort that was uncoordinated and, in some cases, inconsistent. Today, the concept of designing marketing communications programs that coordinate all promotional activities—advertising, personal selling, sales promotion, public relations, and direct marketing—to provide a consistent message across all audiences is referred to as **integrated marketing communications (IMC)**. In addition, by taking consumer expectations into consideration, IMC is a key element in a company's customer experience management strategy.

This chapter provides an overview of the communication process, a description of the promotional mix elements, several tools for integrating the promotional mix, and a process for developing a comprehensive promotion program. One of the promotional mix elements, direct marketing, is also discussed in this chapter. Chapter 14 covers advertising, sales promotion, and public relations.

传播过程
THE COMMUNICATION PROCESS

传播是向他人传递信息的过程，需要六大要素：信息源、信息、传播渠道、接收者以及编码和解码过程（图 13-1）。

LO1

Communication is the process of conveying a message to others and it requires six elements: a source, a message, a channel of communication, a receiver, and the processes of encoding and decoding (see Figure 13–1). The **source** may be a company or person who has information to convey. The information sent by a source, such as a description of a new cellular telephone, forms the **message**. The message is conveyed by means of a **channel of communication** such as a salesperson, advertising media, or public relations tools. Consumers who read, hear, or see the message are the **receivers**.

FIGURE 13–1
The communication process consists of six key elements.

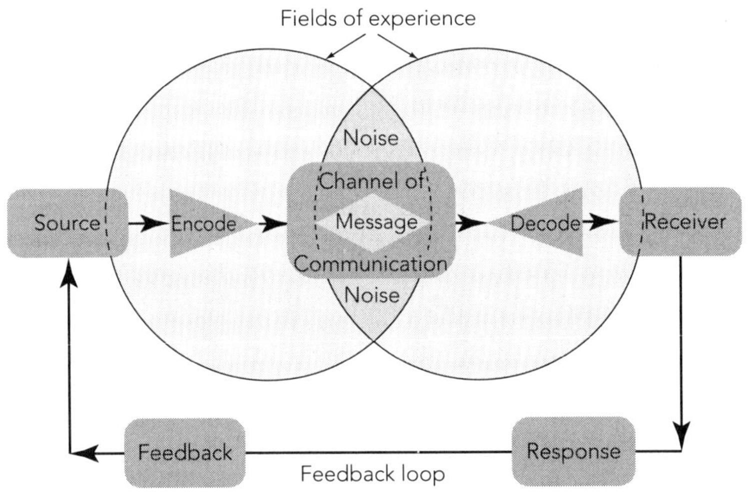

promotional mix 促销组合；integrated marketing communications（IMC）整合营销传播；channel of communication 传播渠道。

How would you decode this ad?

HUMMER
www.HUMMER.com

编码是信息发送者将某种观念转换成一系列符号的过程。**解码**正好相反，它是接受者获得一系列符号，即信息，并将它们转换成观念的过程。

编码和解码
Encoding and Decoding

Encoding and decoding are essential to communication. **Encoding** is the process of having the sender transform an idea into a set of symbols. **Decoding** is the reverse, or the process of having the receiver take a set of symbols, the message, and transform the symbols back to an idea. Look at the accompanying automobile advertisement: Who is the source, and what is the message?

Decoding is performed by the receivers according to their own frame of reference: their attitudes, values, and beliefs. HUMMER is the source and the advertisement is the message, which appeared in *BusinessWeek* magazine (the channel). How would you interpret (decode) this advertisement? The picture and text in the advertisement show that the source's intention is to generate interest in its product with the headline "Welcome to the open"—a statement the source believes will appeal to the readers of the magazine.

The process of communication is not always a successful one. Errors in communication can happen in several ways. The source may not adequately transform the abstract idea into an effective set of symbols, a properly encoded message may be sent through the wrong channel and never make it to the receiver, the receiver may not properly transform the set of symbols into the correct abstract idea, or finally, feedback may be so delayed or distorted that it is of no use to the sender. Although communication appears easy to perform, truly effective communication can be very difficult.

For the message to be communicated effectively, the sender and receiver must have a mutually shared **field of experience**—a similar understanding and knowledge they apply to the message. Figure 13–1 shows two circles representing the fields of experience of the sender and receiver, which overlap in the message. Some of the better-known message problems have occurred when U.S. companies have taken their messages to cultures with different fields of experience. Many misinterpretations

encoding 编码；decoding 解码；field of experience 经验域。

are merely the result of bad translations. For example, KFC made a mistake when its "finger-lickin' good" slogan was translated into Mandarin Chinese as "eat your fingers off!"

反 馈
Feedback

Figure 13–1 shows a line labeled *feedback loop*, which consists of a response and feedback. A **response** is the impact the message had on the receiver's knowledge, attitudes, or behaviors. **Feedback** is the sender's interpretation of the response and indicates whether the message was decoded and understood as intended. Chapter 14 reviews approaches called *pretesting* which ensure that messages are decoded properly.

噪 音
Noise

Noise includes extraneous factors that can work against effective communication by distorting a message or the feedback received (Figure 13–1). Noise can be a simple error, such as a printing mistake that affects the meaning of a newspaper advertisement or using words or pictures that fail to communicate the message clearly. Noise can also occur when a salesperson's message is misunderstood by a prospective buyer, such as when a salesperson's accent, use of slang terms, or communication style make hearing and understanding the message difficult.

learning review

1. What are the six elements required for communication to occur?
2. A difficulty for U.S. companies advertising in international markets is that the audience does not share the same ________________.
3. A misprint in a newspaper ad is an example of ________________.

促销要素
THE PROMOTIONAL ELEMENTS

广告、销售促进和公共关系这三种要素通常在面向潜在购买者群体时使用，故常被认为适用于大规模销售。

To communicate with consumers, a company can use one or more of five promotional alternatives: advertising, personal selling, public relations, sales promotion, and direct marketing. Figure 13–2 summarizes the distinctions among these five elements. Three of these elements—advertising, sales promotion, and public relations—are often said to use *mass selling* because they are used with groups of prospective buyers. In contrast, personal selling uses *customized interaction* between a seller and a prospective buyer. Personal selling activities include face-to-face, telephone, and interactive electronic communication. Direct marketing also uses messages customized for specific customers.

广 告
Advertising

Advertising is any paid form of nonpersonal communication about an organization, good, service, or idea by an identified sponsor. The *paid* aspect of this definition is important because the space for the advertising message normally must be bought. An occasional exception is the public service announcement, where the advertising time or space is donated. A full-page, four-color ad in *Time* magazine, for example, costs $273,750. The *nonpersonal* component of advertising is also important. Advertising involves mass media (such as TV, radio, and magazines), which are nonpersonal and do not have an immediate feedback loop as does personal selling.

response 反应；feedback 反馈；noise 噪音；nonpersonal 非人员的。

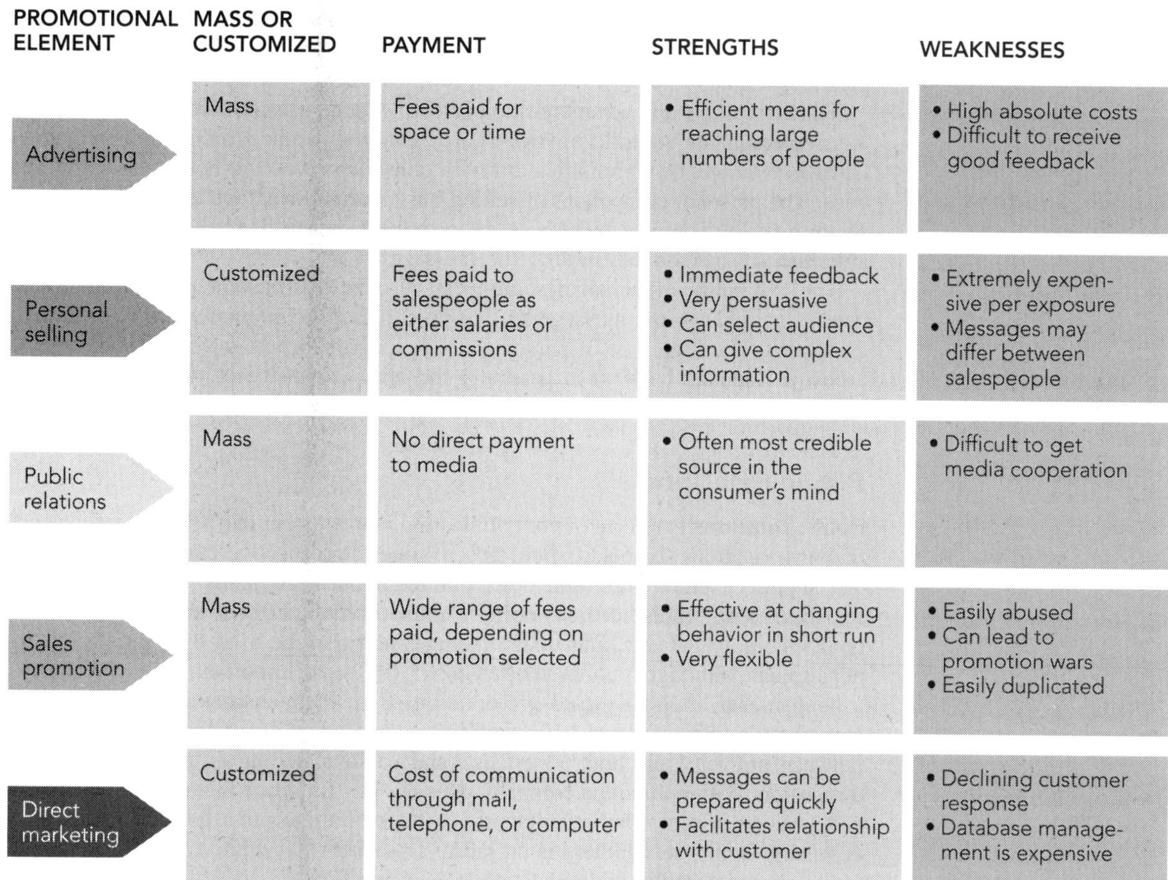

PROMOTIONAL ELEMENT	MASS OR CUSTOMIZED	PAYMENT	STRENGTHS	WEAKNESSES
Advertising	Mass	Fees paid for space or time	• Efficient means for reaching large numbers of people	• High absolute costs • Difficult to receive good feedback
Personal selling	Customized	Fees paid to salespeople as either salaries or commissions	• Immediate feedback • Very persuasive • Can select audience • Can give complex information	• Extremely expensive per exposure • Messages may differ between salespeople
Public relations	Mass	No direct payment to media	• Often most credible source in the consumer's mind	• Difficult to get media cooperation
Sales promotion	Mass	Wide range of fees paid, depending on promotion selected	• Effective at changing behavior in short run • Very flexible	• Easily abused • Can lead to promotion wars • Easily duplicated
Direct marketing	Customized	Cost of communication through mail, telephone, or computer	• Messages can be prepared quickly • Facilitates relationship with customer	• Declining customer response • Database management is expensive

FIGURE 13–2
The five elements of the promotional mix

So before the message is sent, marketing research plays a valuable role; for example, it determines that the target market will actually see the medium chosen and that the message will be understood.

There are several advantages to a firm using advertising in its promotional mix. It can be attention-getting—as with the Havaianas ad shown on the next page—and also can communicate specific product benefits to prospective buyers. By paying for the advertising space, a company can control *what* it wants to say and, to some extent, to *whom* the message is sent. Advertising also allows the company to decide *when* to send its message (which includes how often). The nonpersonal aspect of advertising also has its advantages. Once the message is created, the same message is sent to all receivers in a market segment. If the pictorial, text, and brand elements of an advertisement are properly pretested, an advertiser can ensure the ad's ability to capture consumers' attention and trust that the same message will be decoded by all receivers in the market segment.

Advertising has some disadvantages. As shown in Figure 13–2 and discussed in depth in Chapter 14, the costs to produce and place a message are significant, and the lack of direct feedback makes it difficult to know how well the message was received.

人员推销
Personal Selling

第二种主要促销方式是**人员推销**，即买卖双方之间进行的一

The second major promotional alternative is **personal selling**, which is the two-way flow of communication between a buyer and seller designed to influence a person's

personal selling 人员推销。

种双向沟通，目的在于影响某人或某团体的购买决策。

or group's purchase decision. Unlike advertising, personal selling is usually face-to-face communication between the sender and receiver. Why do companies use personal selling?

There are important advantages to personal selling, as summarized in Figure 13–2. A salesperson can control to *whom* the presentation is made, reducing the amount of *wasted coverage*, or communication with consumers who are not in the target audience. The personal component of selling has another advantage in that the seller can see or hear the potential buyer's reaction to the message. If the feedback is unfavorable, the salesperson can modify the message.

The flexibility of personal selling can also be a disadvantage. Different salespeople can change the message so that no consistent communication is given to all customers. The high cost of personal selling is probably its major disadvantage. On a cost-per-contact basis, it is generally the most expensive of the five promotional elements.

公共关系
Public Relations

Public relations is a form of communication management that seeks to influence the feelings, opinions, or beliefs held by customers, prospective customers, stockholders, suppliers, employees, and other publics about a company and its products or services. Many tools such as special events, lobbying efforts, annual reports, press conferences, RSS feeds, and image management may be used by a public relations department, although publicity often plays the most important role. **Publicity** is a nonpersonal, indirectly paid presentation of an organization, good, or service. It can take the form of a news story, editorial, or product announcement. A difference between publicity and both advertising and personal selling is the "indirectly paid" dimension. With publicity a company does not pay for space in a mass medium (such as television or radio) but attempts to get the medium to run a favorable story on the company. In this sense, there is an indirect payment for publicity in that a company must support a public relations staff.

An advantage of publicity is credibility. When you read a favorable story about a company's product (such as a glowing restaurant review), there is a tendency to

Advertising, public relations, and sales promotion are three elements of the promotional mix.

public relations 公共关系；publicity 宣传，广告。

believe it. Travelers throughout the world have relied on Frommer's guides such as *Australia from $60 a Day*. These books outline out-of-the-way, inexpensive restaurants and hotels, giving invaluable publicity to these establishments. Such businesses do not (nor can they) buy a mention in the guide.

The disadvantage of publicity relates to the lack of the user's control over it. A company can invite media to cover an interesting event such as a store opening or a new product release, but there is no guarantee that a story will result, if it will be positive, or who will be in the audience. Social media, such as blogs, have grown dramatically and allow uncontrollable public discussions of almost any company activity. Many public relations departments now focus on facilitating and responding to online discussions. McDonald's, for example, responds to comments about McDonald's products and promotions on its corporate social responsibility blog, *Open for Discussion*. Generally, publicity is an important element of most promotional campaigns, although the lack of control means that it is rarely the primary element. Research related to the sequence of IMC elements, however, indicates that publicity followed by advertising with the same message increases the positive response to the message.

销售促进
Sales Promotion

第四种促销要素是**销售促进**，即为激发消费者对某种商品或服务的购买兴趣而采取的一种短期性的价值优惠。销售促进通常与广告和人员推销配合使用，它可以面向中间商也可以直接面向最终消费者。

A fourth promotional element is **sales promotion**, a short-term inducement of value offered to arouse interest in buying a good or service. Used in conjunction with advertising or personal selling, sales promotions are offered to intermediaries as well as to ultimate consumers. Coupons, rebates, samples, and sweepstakes, such as the "Shop Smart for College" promotion, are just a few examples of sales promotions discussed later in this chapter.

The advantage of sales promotion is that the short-term nature of these programs (such as a coupon or sweepstakes with an expiration date) often stimulates sales for their duration. Offering value to the consumer in terms of a cents-off coupon or rebate may increase store traffic from consumers who are not store-loyal.

Sales promotions cannot be the sole basis for a campaign because gains are often temporary and sales drop off when the deal ends. Advertising support is needed to convert the customer who tried the product because of a sales promotion into a long-term buyer. If sales promotions are conducted continuously, they lose their effectiveness. Customers begin to delay purchase until a coupon is offered, or they question the product's value. Some aspects of sales promotions also are regulated by the federal government. These issues are reviewed in detail in Chapter 14.

直接营销
Direct Marketing

另一种促销方式是**直接营销**，即通过与消费者直接沟通，促使顾客做出订购、征询更多信息或光顾零售商店的反应。

Another promotional alternative, **direct marketing**, uses direct communication with consumers to generate a response in the form of an order, a request for further information, or a visit to a retail outlet. The communication can take many forms including face-to-face selling, direct mail, catalogs, telephone solicitations, direct response advertising (on television and radio and in print), and online marketing. Like personal selling, direct marketing often consists of interactive communication. It also has the advantage of being customized to match the needs of specific target markets. Messages can be developed and adapted quickly to facilitate one-to-one relationships with customers.

While direct marketing has been one of the fastest-growing forms of promotion, it has several disadvantages. First, most forms of direct marketing require a comprehensive and up-to-date database with information about the target market. Developing and maintaining the database can be expensive and time consuming. In addition, growing concern about privacy has led to a decline in response rates among some customer groups. Companies with successful direct marketing programs are sensitive

Open for Discussion 自由讨论；sales promotion 销售促进；direct marketing 直接营销。

to these issues and often use a combination of direct marketing alternatives together, or direct marketing combined with other promotional tools, to increase value for customers.

learning review

4. Explain the difference between advertising and publicity when both appear on television.
5. Cost per contact is high with the ______________ element of the promotional mix.
6. Which promotional element should be offered only on a short-term basis?

整合营销传播——开发促销组合
INTEGRATED MARKETING COMMUNICATIONS—DEVELOPING THE PROMOTIONAL MIX

A firm's promotional mix is the combination of one or more of the promotional tools it chooses to use. In putting together the promotional mix, a marketer must consider two issues. First, the balance of the elements must be determined. Should advertising be emphasized more than personal selling? Should a promotional rebate be offered? Would public relations activities be effective? Several factors affect such decisions: the target audience for the promotion, the stage of the product's life cycle, characteristics of the product, decision stage of the buyer, and even the channel of distribution. Second, because the various promotional elements are often the responsibility of different departments, coordinating a consistent promotional effort is necessary. A promotional planning process designed to ensure integrated marketing communications can facilitate this goal.

目标受众
The Target Audience

Promotional programs are directed to the ultimate consumer, to an intermediary (retailer, wholesaler, or industrial distributor), or to both. Promotional programs directed to buyers of consumer products often use mass media because the number of potential buyers is large. Personal selling is used at the place of purchase, generally the retail store. Direct marketing may be used to encourage first-time or repeat purchases. Combinations of many media alternatives are a necessity for some target audiences today. The Marketing Matters box describes how Generation Y consumers can be reached through mobile marketing programs.

Publications such as *Restaurant News* reach business buyers.

Advertising directed to business buyers is used selectively in trade publications, such as *Restaurant News* magazine for buyers of restaurant equipment and supplies. Because business buyers often have specialized needs or technical questions, personal selling is particularly important. The salesperson can provide information and the necessary support after sales.

Intermediaries are often the focus of promotional efforts. As with business buyers, personal selling is the major promotional ingredient. The salespeople assist intermediaries in making a profit by coordinating promotional campaigns sponsored by the manufacturer and by providing marketing advice and expertise. Intermediaries' questions often pertain to the allowed markup, merchandising support, and return policies.

---

coordinate 协调；sponsor 赞助。

Marketing Matters > > > > > > > > > technology

Mobile Marketing Reaches Generation Y, 32/7!

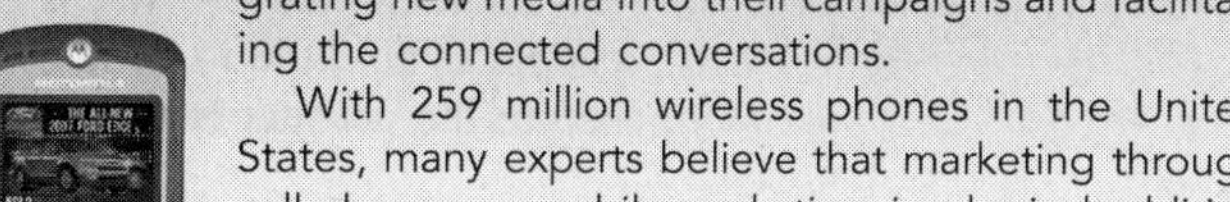

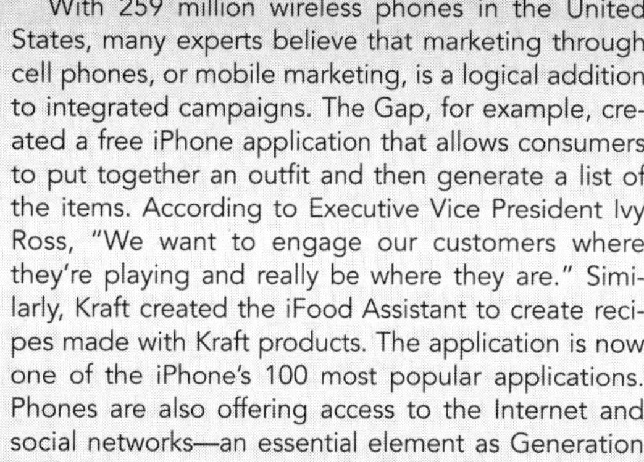

The marketplace is flooded with new forms of media. In addition to traditional media such as television, radio, magazines, and newspapers, marketers can now use cell phones, social networks, RSS feeds, blogs, and a variety of other means to deliver messages. To cope with the volume of messages, consumers have applied multitasking to media use. A recent study of television viewers, for example, found that 58 percent were instant messaging, e-mailing, texting, or talking on the phone while they watched TV. This simultaneous media use is so common it has created 32-hour "media days" for consumers.

Generation Y is particularly adept, as up to 72 percent of that group is "connected" while watching television. Since using a single medium alone is a thing of the past for young consumers, advertising agencies, broadcasters, cable and satellite providers, and retailers must change their views of consumers' ability to absorb and remember advertising messages. Marketers can still communicate with Generation Y, however, by integrating new media into their campaigns and facilitating the connected conversations.

With 259 million wireless phones in the United States, many experts believe that marketing through cell phones, or mobile marketing, is a logical addition to integrated campaigns. The Gap, for example, created a free iPhone application that allows consumers to put together an outfit and then generate a list of the items. According to Executive Vice President Ivy Ross, "We want to engage our customers where they're playing and really be where they are." Similarly, Kraft created the iFood Assistant to create recipes made with Kraft products. The application is now one of the iPhone's 100 most popular applications. Phones are also offering access to the Internet and social networks—an essential element as Generation Y members keep in touch with an average of 47 "friends."

Watch for other brands to try similar mobile programs, particularly for consumers who are connected multitaskers.

产品生命周期
The Product Life Cycle

LO3

All products have a product life cycle (see Chapter 8), and the composition of the promotional mix changes over the four life-cycle stages, as shown for Purina Dog Chow in Figure 13–3.

Introduction Stage Informing consumers in an effort to increase their level of awareness is the primary promotional objective in the introduction stage of the

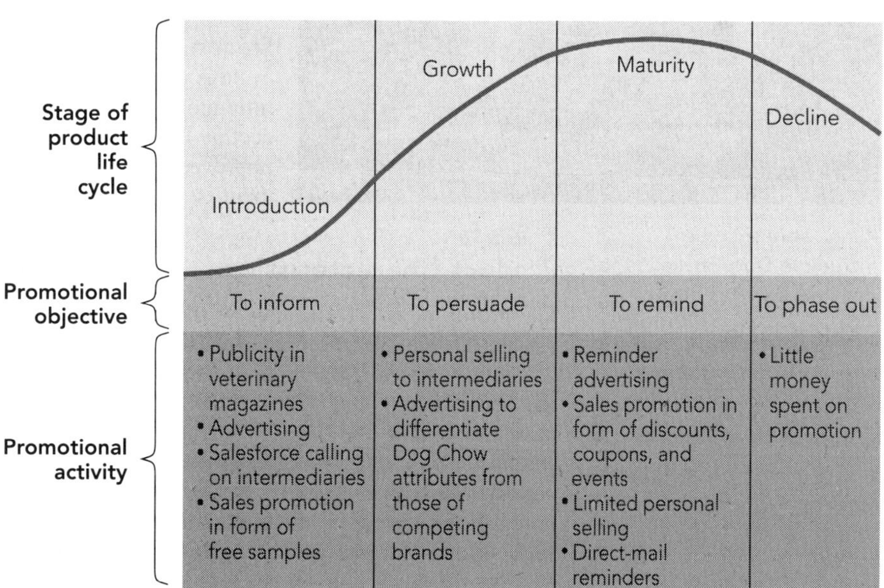

FIGURE 13–3
Promotional tools used over the product life cycle of Purina Dog Chow

introduction stage 导入期。

product life cycle. In general, all the promotional mix elements are used at this time, although the use of specific mix elements during any stage depends on the product and situation. News releases about Purina's new nutritional product are sent to veterinary magazines, trial samples are sent to registered dog owners, advertisements are placed in *Dog World* magazine, and the salesforce begins to approach supermarkets to get orders. Advertising is particularly important as a means of reaching as many people as possible to build awareness and interest. Publicity may even begin slightly before the product is commercially available.

Growth Stage The primary promotional objective of the growth stage is to persuade the consumer to buy the product—Purina Dog Chow—rather than substitutes, so the marketing manager seeks to gain brand preference and solidify distribution. Sales promotion assumes less importance in this stage, and publicity is not a factor because it depends on novelty of the product. The primary promotional element is advertising, which stresses brand differences. Personal selling is used to solidify the channel of distribution. For consumer products such as dog food, the salesforce calls on the wholesalers and retailers in hopes of increasing inventory levels and gaining shelf space. For business products, the salesforce often tries to get contractual arrangements to be the sole source of supply for the buyer.

Maturity Stage In the maturity stage, the need is to maintain existing buyers, and advertising's role is to remind buyers of the product's existence. Sales promotion, in the form of discounts and coupons offered to both ultimate consumers and intermediaries, is important in maintaining loyal buyers. In a test of one mature consumer product, it was found that 80 percent of the product's sales at this stage resulted from sales promotions. Sponsoring events can also help maintain loyalty. For the past 12 years, Purina has sponsored the Incredible Dog Challenge, which is now covered by ABC and is available as podcasts from the Purina Web site. Direct marketing actions such as direct mail are used to maintain involvement with existing customers and to encourage repeat purchases. Price cuts and discounts can also significantly increase a mature brand's sales. The salesforce at this stage seeks to satisfy intermediaries. An unsatisfied customer who switches brands is hard to replace.

Purina sponsors the Incredible Dog Challenge to maintain existing buyers.

Decline Stage The decline stage of the product life cycle is usually a period of phaseout for the product, and little money is spent in the promotional mix. The rate of decline can be rapid when a product is replaced by an improved or lower cost product, for example, or slow if there is a loyal group of customers.

产品属性
Product Characteristics

合理组合促销要素也要考虑到产品类别。要具体考虑产品的三个属性：复杂性、风险性及辅助服务。复杂性是指产品的技术复杂度及其由此引起的使用该产品所需的知识量。

The proper blend of elements in the promotional mix also depends on the type of product. Three specific characteristics should be considered: complexity, risk, and ancillary services. *Complexity* refers to the technical sophistication of the product and hence the amount of understanding required to use it. It's hard to provide much information in a one-page magazine ad or a 30-second television ad, so the more complex the product, the greater the emphasis on personal selling. Gulfstream asks potential customers to call their senior vice president in its ads. No information is provided for simple products such as Heinz ketchup.

A second element is the degree of risk represented by the product's purchase. *Risk* for the buyer can be assessed in terms of financial risk, social risk, and physi-

growth stage 成长期；maturity stage 成熟期；decline stage 衰退期；complexity 复杂性。

How do Gulfstream aircraft and Heinz ketchup differ on complexity, risk, and ancillary services?

Gulfstream
www.gulfstreamvsp.com

Heinz
www.heinz.com

cal risk. A private jet, for example, might represent all three risks—it is expensive, employees and customers may see and evaluate the purchase, and safety and reliability are important. Although advertising helps, the greater the risk, the greater the need for personal selling. Consumers are unlikely to associate any of these risks with ketchup.

The level of ancillary services required by a product also affects the promotional strategy. *Ancillary services* pertain to the degree of service or support required after the sale. This characteristic is common to many industrial products and consumer purchases. Who will provide maintenance for the plane? Advertising's role is to establish the seller's reputation. Direct marketing can be used to describe how a product or service can be customized to individual needs. However, personal selling is essential to build buyer confidence and provide evidence of customer service.

购买决策阶段
Stages of the Buying Decision

Knowing the customer's stage of decision making can also affect the promotional mix. Figure 13–4 on the next page shows how the importance of the promotional elements varies with the three stages in the consumer purchase decision process.

Prepurchase Stage In the prepurchase stage, advertising is more helpful than personal selling because advertising informs the potential customer of the existence of the product and the seller. Sales promotion in the form of free samples also can play an important role to gain low-risk trial. When the salesperson calls on the customer after heavy advertising, there is some recognition of what the salesperson represents. This is particularly important in industrial settings in which sampling of the product is usually not possible.

Purchase Stage At the purchase stage, the importance of personal selling is highest, whereas the impact of advertising is lowest. Sales promotion in the form of coupons, deals, point-of-purchase displays, and rebates can be very helpful in encouraging demand. In this stage, although advertising is not an active influence

ancillary services 附加服务；customize 定制，定做。

FIGURE 13–4
How the importance of promotional elements varies during the stages of the consumer purchase decision process

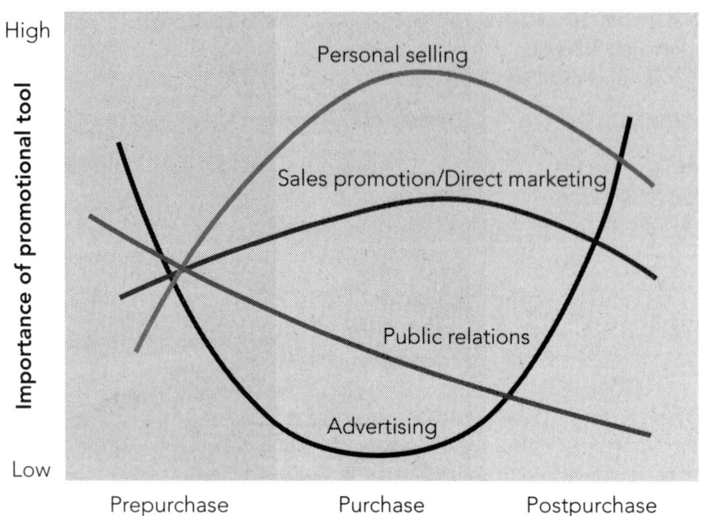

on the purchase, it is the means of delivering the coupons, deals, and rebates that are often important. Recent research indicates that direct marketing activities shorten the time consumers take to adopt a product or service.

Postpurchase Stage In the postpurchase stage, the salesperson is still important. In fact, the more personal contact after the sale, the more the buyer is satisfied. Advertising is also important to assure the buyer that the right purchase was made. Advertising and personal selling help reduce the buyer's postpurchase anxiety. Sales promotion in the form of coupons and direct marketing reminders can help encourage repeat purchases from satisfied first-time triers. Public relations plays a small role in the postpurchase stage.

渠道战略
Channel Strategies

Chapter 10 discussed the channel flow from a producer to intermediaries to consumers. Achieving control of the channel is often difficult for the manufacturer, and promotional strategies can assist in moving a product through the channel of distribution. This is where a manufacturer has to make an important decision about whether to use a push strategy, pull strategy, or both in its channel of distribution.

Why does this ad suggest readers should "Ask Your Doctor"? For the answer, see the text.

Push Strategy Figure 13–5A shows how a manufacturer uses a **push strategy**, directing the promotional mix to channel members to gain their cooperation in ordering and stocking the product. In this approach, personal selling and sales promotions play major roles. Salespeople call on wholesalers to encourage orders and provide sales assistance. Sales promotions, such as case discount allowances (20 percent off the regular case price), are offered to stimulate demand. By pushing the product through the channel, the goal is to get channel members to push it to their customers.

Ford Motor Company, for example, provides support and incentives for its 3,700 Ford and Lincoln-Mercury dealers. Through a multi-level program, Ford provides incentives to reward dealers for meeting sales goals. Dealers receive an incentive when they are near a goal, another when they reach a goal, and a larger incentive if they exceed sales projections. Ford also offers

push strategy 推动式策略。

FIGURE 13–5
A comparison of push and pull promotional strategies

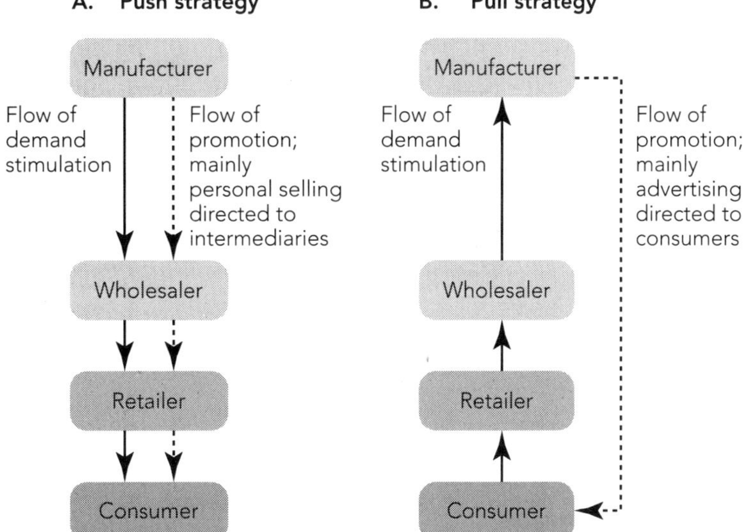

some dealers special incentives for maintaining superior facilities or improving customer service. All of these actions are intended to encourage Ford dealers to "push" the Ford products through the channel to consumers.

Pull Strategy In some instances, manufacturers face resistance from channel members who do not want to order a new product or increase inventory levels of an existing brand. As shown in Figure 13–5B, a manufacturer may then elect to implement a **pull strategy** by directing its promotional mix at ultimate consumers to encourage them to ask the retailer for a product. Seeing demand from ultimate consumers, retailers order the product from wholesalers and thus the item is pulled through the intermediaries. Pharmaceutical companies, for example, now spend more than $5 billion annually on *direct-to-consumer* prescription drug advertising, to complement traditional personal selling and free samples directed only at doctors. The strategy is designed to encourage consumers to ask their doctor for a specific drug by name—pulling it through the channel. Successful campaigns such as the print ad which says, "Ask your doctor if Zetia is right for you," can have dramatic effects on the sales of a product.

learning review

7. Describe the promotional objective for each stage of the product life cycle.
8. At what stage of the consumer purchase decision process is the importance of personal selling highest? Why?
9. Explain the differences between a push strategy and a pull strategy.

制定营销整合传播方案
DEVELOPING AN IMC PROGRAM

由于媒体成本很高，促销决策必须通过一套系统方法慎重地做出。类似于战

Because media costs are high, promotion decisions must be made carefully, using a systematic approach. Paralleling the planning, implementation, and evaluation steps described in the strategic marketing process (Chapter 2), the promotion decision process is divided into (1) developing, (2) executing, and (3) assessing the promotion

pull strategy 拉动式策略。

FIGURE 13–6
The promotion decision process includes planning, implementation, and evaluation.

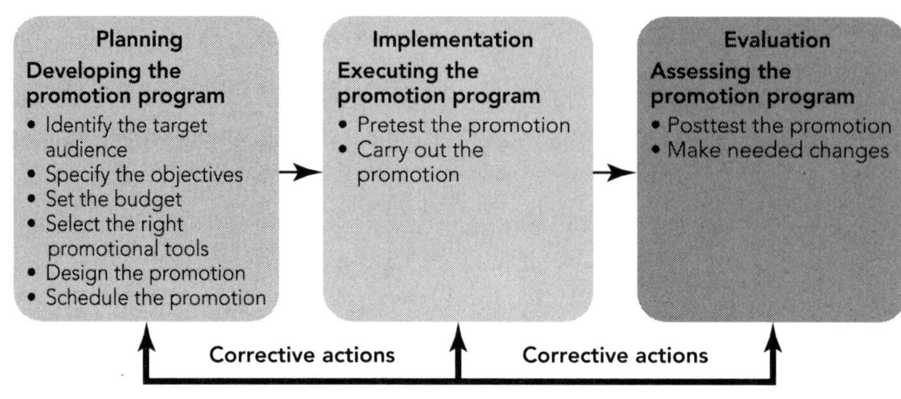

略营销过程（第 2 章）中讨论过的计划、执行与控制等步骤，促销决策过程也可以划分为（1）开发；（2）执行；（3）评估促销方案（图 13-6）。开发促销方案要关注 *4W*。

- 谁是目标受众？
- 促销目标、促销预算、促销方式是什么？
- 何地开展促销？
- 何时开展促销？

program (see Figure 13–6). Development of the promotion program focuses on the four *Ws*:

- *Who* is the target audience?
- *What* are (1) the promotion objectives, (2) the amounts of money that can be budgeted for the promotion program, and (3) the kinds of promotion to use?
- *Where* should the promotion be run?
- *When* should the promotion be run?

确定目标受众
Identifying the Target Audience

The first decision in developing the promotion program is identifying the *target audience*, the group of prospective buyers toward which a promotion program is directed. To the extent that time and money permit, the target audience for the promotion program is the target market for the firm's product, which is identified from marketing research and market segmentation studies. The more a firm knows about its target audiences—including their lifestyle, attitudes, and values—the easier it is to develop a promotion program. If a firm wanted to reach you with television and magazine ads, for example, it would need to know what TV shows you watch and what magazines you read.

明确促销目标
Specifying Promotion Objectives

After the target audience is identified, a decision must be reached on what the promotion should accomplish. Consumers can be said to respond in terms of a **hierarchy of effects**, which is the sequence of stages a prospective buyer goes through from initial awareness of a product to eventual action (either trial or adoption of the product). The five stages are:

- *Awareness*—the consumer's ability to recognize and remember the product or brand name.
- *Interest*—an increase in the consumer's desire to learn about some of the features of the product or brand.
- *Evaluation*—the consumer's appraisal of the product or brand on important attributes.
- *Trial*—the consumer's actual first purchase and use of the product or brand.
- *Adoption*—through a favorable experience on the first trial, the consumer's repeated purchase and use of the product or brand.

For a totally new product, the sequence applies to the entire product category, but for a new brand competing in an established product category it applies to the brand itself. These steps can serve as guidelines for developing promotion objectives.

hierarchy of effects 效果层级模式；awareness 认知；evaluation 评估。

Although sometimes an objective for a promotion program involves several steps in the hierarchy of effects, it often focuses on a single stage. Regardless of what the specific objective might be, from building awareness to increasing repeat purchases, promotion objectives should possess three important qualities. They should (1) be designed for a well-defined target audience, (2) be measurable, and (3) cover a specified time period.

建立促销预算
Setting the Promotion Budget

From Figure 13–7 it is clear that the promotion expenditures needed to reach U.S. households are enormous. Note that four companies—Procter & Gamble, AT&T, Verizon, and General Motors—each spend a total of more than $3 billion annually on promotion.

After setting the promotion objectives, a company must decide how much to spend. Determining the ideal amount for the budget is difficult because there is no precise way to measure the exact results of spending promotion dollars. However, several methods can be used to set the promotion budget.

在**销售百分比预算法**中，促销费用是根据过去或预期的销售额的一定百分比确定的。

Percentage of Sales In the **percentage of sales budgeting** approach, funds are allocated to promotion as a percentage of past or anticipated sales, in terms of either dollars or units sold. A common budgeting method, this approach is often stated in terms such as "Our promotion budget for this year is 3 percent of last year's gross sales." The advantage of this approach is obvious: It is simple and provides a financial safeguard by tying the promotion budget to sales. However, there is a major fallacy in this approach, which implies that sales cause promotion. Using this method, a company may reduce its promotion budget because of a downturn in past sales or an anticipated downturn in future sales—situations in which it may need promotion the most. See the Using Marketing Dashboards box on the next page for an application of the promotion-to-sales ratio to the automotive industry.

竞争对等预算法是根据竞争对手促销绝对费用或市场份额的每个百分点来确定自己的促销预算。它也被称为竞争者或市场份额匹配预算法。

Competitive Parity A second common approach, **competitive parity budgeting**, is matching the competitor's absolute level of spending or the proportion per point of market share. This approach has also been referred to as *matching competitors* or *share of market*. It is important to consider the competition in budgeting. Consumer responses to promotion are affected by competing promotional activities, so if a competitor runs 30 radio ads each week, it may be difficult for a firm to get its message across with only five messages. The competitor's budget level, however,

FIGURE 13–7
U.S. promotion expenditures of the top 10 companies

Rank	Company	Advertising (millions $)	+	All Other Promotion (millions $)	=	Total (millions $)
1	Procter & Gamble	$3,700		$1,530		$5,230
2	AT&T	$2,245		$962		$3,207
3	Verizon	$2,144		$872		$3,016
4	General Motors	$2,062		$948		$3,010
5	Time Warner	$1,738		$1,224		$2,962
6	Ford	$1,653		$872		$2,525
7	GlaxoSmithKline	$1,187		$1,270		$2,457
8	Johnson & Johnson	$1,421		$988		$2,409
9	Disney	$1,387		$906		$2,293
10	Unilever	$910		$1,336		$2,246

percentage of sales budgeting 销售百分比预算法；competitive parity budgeting 竞争对等预算法。

Using Marketing Dashboards

How Much Should You Spend on IMC?

Integrated marketing communications programs coordinate a variety of promotion alternatives to provide a consistent message across audiences. The amount spent on the various promotional elements, or on the total campaign, may vary depending on the target audience, the type of product, where the product is in the product life cycle, and the channel strategy selected. Managers often use the promotion-to-sales ratio on their marketing dashboard to assess how effective the IMC program expenditures are at generating sales.

Your Challenge As a manager at General Motors you've been asked to assess the effectiveness of all promotion expenditures during the past year. The promotion-to-sales ratio can be used by managers to make year-to-year comparisons of their programs, to compare the effectiveness of their program with competitor's programs, or to make comparisons with industry averages. You decide to calculate the promotion-to-sales ratio for General Motors. In addition, to allow a comparison, you decide to make the same calculation for one of your competitors, Ford, and for the entire automobile industry. The ratio is calculated as follows:

Promotion-to-sales ratio =
Total promotion expenditures/Total sales

Your Findings The information needed for these calculations is readily available from trade publications and annual reports. The following graph shows the promotion-to-sales ratio for General Motors and Ford (two companies featured in Figure 13–7) and the automotive industry. General Motors spent $3.01 billion on its IMC program to generate $182 billion in U.S. sales for a ratio of 1.65 (percent). Ford's ratio was 1.47, and the industry average was 1.56.

Your Action General Motors' promotion-to-sales ratio is higher than Ford's and higher than the industry average. This suggests that the current mix of promotional activities and the level of expenditures may not be creating an effective IMC program. In the future you will want to monitor the factors that may influence the ratio. The average ratio for the beverage industry has risen to 9 while the average for grocery stores is about 1.

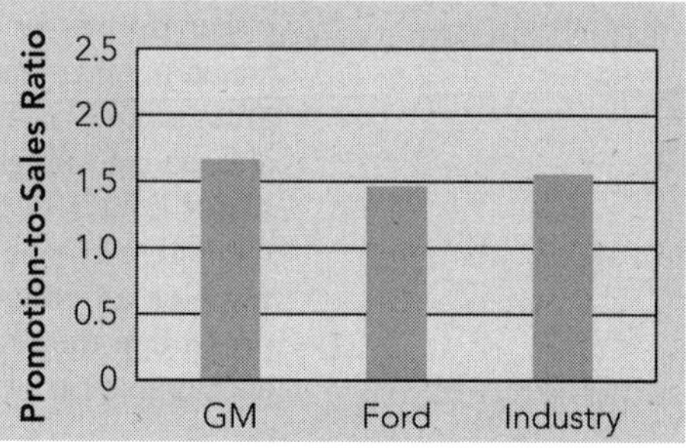

should not be the only determinant in setting a company's budget. The competition might have very different promotional objectives, which require a different level of promotion expenditures.

All You Can Afford Common to many small businesses is **all-you-can-afford budgeting**, in which money is allocated to promotion only after all other budget items are covered. As one company executive said in reference to this budgeting process, "Why, it's simple. First, I go upstairs to the controller and ask how much they can afford to give us this year. She says a million and a half. Later, the boss comes to me and asks how much we should spend, and I say 'Oh, about a million and a half.' Then we have our promotion appropriation."

Fiscally conservative, this approach has little else to offer. Using this budgeting philosophy, a company acts as though it doesn't know anything about a promotion-sales relationship or what its promotion objectives are.

最好的预算方法就是**目标任务预算法**，由此公司可以：(1) 确定促销目标；(2) 大体订出实现这些目标的任务；(3) 确定执行这些任务所需的促销费用。

Objective and Task The best approach to budgeting is **objective and task budgeting**, whereby the company (1) determines its promotion objectives, (2) outlines the tasks to accomplish these objectives, and (3) determines the promotion cost of performing these tasks. This method takes into account what the company wants to accomplish and requires that the objectives be specified. Strengths of the other budgeting methods are integrated into this approach because each previous

all-you-can-afford budgeting 量力而行预算法；objective and task budgeting 目标任务预算法。

method's strength is tied to the objectives. For example, if the costs are beyond what the company can afford, objectives are reworked and the tasks revised. The difficulty with this method is the judgment required to determine the tasks needed to accomplish objectives.

选择正确的促销工具
Selecting the Right Promotional Tools

Once a budget has been determined, the combination of the five basic IMC tools—advertising, personal selling, sales promotion, public relations, and direct marketing—can be specified. While many factors provide direction for selection of the appropriate mix, the large number of possible combinations of the promotional tools means that many combinations can achieve the same objective. Therefore, an analytical approach and experience are particularly important in this step of the promotion decision process. The specific mix can vary from a simple program using a single tool to a comprehensive program using all forms of promotion. The Olympics have become a very visible example of a comprehensive integrated communication program. Because the Games are repeated every two years, the promotion is continuous during "on" and "off" years. Included in the program are advertising campaigns, personal selling efforts by the Olympic committee and organizers, sales promotion activities such as product tie-ins and sponsorships, public relations programs managed by the host cities, online and digital communication, and direct marketing efforts targeted at a variety of audiences including governments, organizations, firms, athletes, and individuals. At this stage, it is also important to assess the relative importance of the various tools. While it may be desirable to utilize and integrate several forms of promotion, one may deserve emphasis. The Olympics, for example, place primary importance on public relations and publicity.

The Olympics use a comprehensive IMC program.

促销设计
Designing the Promotion

The central element of a promotion program is the promotion itself. Advertising consists of advertising copy and the artwork that the target audience is intended to see or hear. Personal selling efforts depend on the characteristics and skills of the salesperson. Sales promotion activities consist of the specific details of inducements such as coupons, samples, and sweepstakes. Public relations efforts are readily seen in tangible elements such as news releases, and direct marketing actions depend on written, verbal, and electronic forms of delivery. The design of the promotion will play a primary role in determining the message that is communicated to the audience. This design activity is frequently viewed as the step requiring the most creativity. In addition, successful designs are often the result of insight regarding consumer's interests and purchasing behavior. All of the promotion tools have many design alternatives. Advertising, for example, can utilize fear, humor, attractiveness, or other themes in its appeal. Similarly, direct marketing can be designed for varying levels of personal or customized appeals. One of the challenges of IMC is to design each promotional activity to communicate the same message.

确定促销进度
Scheduling the Promotion

Once the design of each of the promotional program elements is complete, it is important to determine the most effective timing of their use. The promotion schedule describes the order in which each promotional tool is introduced and the frequency of its use during the campaign.

Movie studio Columbia Pictures, for example, uses a schedule of several promotional tools for its movies. To generate interest in a movie such as *Angels and*

---

integrate 综合的；sweepstake 彩票。

What promotional tools did Columbia Pictures use to support the release of this movie?

Demons, a commercial was aired during the Super Bowl. The commercial generated more than 700,000 visits to the *Angels and Demons* Web site, which provided movie previews and clips, a Facebook link, and a contest with prizes related to movie scenes. In addition, Columbia held a press conference for science, religion, and entertainment journalists to initiate a public dialog that would appear in periodicals, blogs, and social networks. It also released a movie "trailer" that was shown on television and in theaters. Then movie-related partnerships such as Mastercard's promotion offering an opportunity to win tickets to a pre-screening of the film were announced. After the movie was released another contest and VIP parties encouraged fans to consider purchasing the DVD.

Overall, the scheduling of the various promotions was designed to generate interest, bring consumers into theaters, and then encourage additional purchases after seeing the movie. Several factors such as seasonality and competitive promotion activity can also influence the promotion schedule. Businesses such as ski resorts, airlines, and professional sports teams are likely to reduce their promotional activity during the "off" season. Similarly, restaurants, retail stores, and health clubs are likely to increase their promotional activity when new competitors enter the market.

执行和评估促销方案 EXECUTING AND ASSESSING THE PROMOTION PROGRAM

Carrying out the promotion program can be expensive and time consuming. One researcher estimates that "an organization with sales less than $10 million can successfully implement an IMC program in one year, one with sales between $200 million and $500 million will need about three years, and one with sales between $2 billion and $5 billion will need five years." In addition, firms with a market orientation are more likely to implement an IMC program. To facilitate the transition, approximately 200 integrated marketing communications agencies are in operation. In addition, some of the largest agencies are adopting approaches that embrace "total communications solutions."

Media agency Initiative, which recently won *Advertising Age* magazine's Media Agency of the Year award, for example, is part of an integrated network of 2,500 marketing professionals with 91 offices in 70 countries. The agency's services include planning, media buying, digital solutions, consumer research, ROI assessment, and sports and entertainment marketing. One of its integrated campaigns for Carl's Jr. restaurants included a partnership with the cable program *Family Guy*, a rap song for radio, bus bench advertising, video gaming, sports tie-ins, and free ring tones. The campaign resulted in a 47 percent increase in sales. Initiative has used this approach with other clients including Hyundai, MillerCoors, Dr Pepper, and Bayer. CEO Tim Spengler explains that one of the keys to the agency's success is an operations committee that encourages integration by including representatives that represent all forms of promotion. While many agencies may still be specialists, the trend today is clearly toward a long-term perspective in which all forms of promotion are integrated.

An important factor in developing successful IMC programs is to create a process that facilitates their design and use. A tool used to evaluate a company's current process is the IMC audit. The audit analyzes the internal communication network of the company; identifies key audiences; evaluates customer databases; assesses messages in recent advertising, public relations releases, packaging, Web sites, and e-mail communication, signage, sales promotions, and direct mail; and determines the IMC expertise of company and agency personnel. This process is becoming increasingly important as consumer-generated media such as blogs, RSS, podcasts,

entertainment 娱乐，消遣；journalist 记者。

and social networks become more popular and as the use of search engines increases. Now, in addition to ensuring that traditional forms of communication are integrated, companies must be able to monitor consumer content, respond to inconsistent messages, and even answer questions from individual customers.

As shown earlier in Figure 13–6, the ideal execution of a promotion program involves pretesting each design before it is actually used to allow for changes and modifications that improve its effectiveness. Similarly, posttests are recommended to evaluate the impact of each promotion and the contribution of the promotion toward achieving the program objectives. The most sophisticated pretest and posttest procedures have been developed for advertising and are discussed in Chapter 14. Testing procedures for sales promotion and direct marketing efforts currently focus on comparisons of different designs or responses of different segments. To fully benefit from IMC programs, companies must create and maintain a test-result database that allows comparisons of the relative impact of the promotional tools and their execution options in varying situations. Information from the database will allow informed design and execution decisions and provide support for IMC activities during internal reviews by financial or administrative personnel. The San Diego Padres baseball team, for example, developed a database of information relating attendance to its integrated campaign using a new logo, special events, merchandise sales, and a loyalty program.

Currently, about one-fourth of all businesses assess program effectiveness by measuring "most of their communication tactics." For most organizations, the assessment focuses on trying to determine which element of promotion works better. In an integrated program, however, media advertising might be used to build awareness, sales promotion to generate an inquiry, direct mail to provide additional information to individual prospects, and a personal sales call to complete the transaction. The tools are used for different reasons, and their combined use creates a synergy that should be the focus of the assessment. Another level of assessment is necessary when firms have international promotion programs.

learning review

10. What are the characteristics of good promotion objectives?
11. What is the weakness of the percentage of sales budgeting approach?
12. How have advertising agencies changed to facilitate the use of IMC programs?

直接营销
DIRECT MARKETING

Direct marketing has many forms and utilizes a variety of media. Several forms of direct marketing—direct mail and catalogs, television home shopping, telemarketing, and direct selling—were discussed as methods of nonstore retailing in Chapter 12. In addition, although advertising is discussed in Chapter 14, a form of advertising—direct response advertising—is an important form of direct marketing. In this section, the growth of direct marketing, its value for consumers and sellers, and key global, technological, and ethical issues are discussed.

对顾客关系管理的兴趣与日俱增充分体现了直接营销的显著增长。直接营销所具有的定制传播活动和创建一对一互动的能力受到大多数营销者，尤其是实施整合营销传播方案的营销者的欢迎。

直接营销的增长
The Growth of Direct Marketing

The increasing interest in customer relationship management is reflected in the dramatic growth of direct marketing. The ability to customize communication efforts and create one-to-one interactions is appealing to most marketers, particularly those with IMC programs. While many direct marketing methods are not new, the ability

modification 改良，改进；tactics 战术，策略。

FIGURE 13–8
Business usage and response rates of popular forms of direct marketing

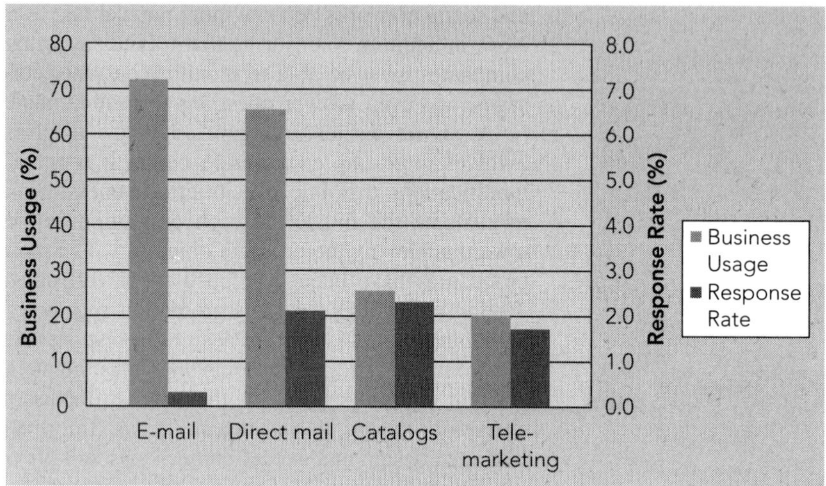

to design and use them has increased with the availability of customer information databases and new printing technologies. In recent years, direct marketing growth has outpaced total economic growth. Direct marketing expenditures of \$183 billion are expected to grow at a rate of 4 percent. Similarly, 2009 revenues of \$2.1 trillion are expected to grow to \$2.66 trillion by 2013. Direct marketing currently accounts for 10 percent of the total U.S. gross domestic product. Figure 13–8 shows some of the most popular forms of direct marketing and their typical response rates. For example, e-mail is the most popular method. It is used by 72 percent of marketers and generates less than a 1 percent response rate.

While e-mail is the most common form of direct marketing, most campaigns use several methods. JCPenney is one example of a company that has integrated its direct marketing activities. The company recently launched an interactive, virtual "runway show" by sending 15 million potential customers an e-mail inviting them to an online experience at www.jcp.com. Once consumers visit the Web site, JCPenney uses other forms of direct marketing, such as direct mail and catalogs, to follow up on the initial e-mail and online contacts. Many companies also integrate their direct marketing with other forms of promotion. Dannon, for example, uses television advertising and direct mail to promote its Activia brand yogurt products.

Another component of the growth in direct marketing is the increasing popularity of the Internet. Total online sales have risen from close to nothing in 1996 to projections of \$903 billion in 2013. Continued growth in the number of consumers with Internet access and the number of businesses with Web sites and electronic commerce offerings is likely to contribute to the future growth of direct marketing.

直接营销的价值
The Value of Direct Marketing

One of the most visible indicators of the value of direct marketing for consumers is the level of use of various forms of direct marketing. For example, 45 percent of the U.S. population has ordered merchandise or services by mail, phone, or Internet; 68 percent of households with Internet access shop online; consumers spent more than \$156 billion on products available through television offers; and more than 21 percent of all adults make three to five purchases from a catalog each year. Consumers report many benefits, including the following: They don't have to go to a store; they can usually shop 24 hours a day; buying direct saves time; they avoid hassles with salespeople; they can save money; it's fun and entertaining; and direct marketing offers more privacy than in-store shopping. Many consumers also believe that direct marketing provides excellent customer service. Toll-free telephone numbers, cus-

hassle 烦扰，纠缠；salespeople 销售人员。

Four Seasons uses direct mail to generate leads for its private residences.

tomer service representatives with access to information regarding purchasing preferences, overnight delivery services, and unconditional guarantees all help create value for direct marketing customers. At Landsend.com, when customers need assistance they can click the Live Help icon to receive help from a sales representative on the phone or online until the correct product is found. "It's like we were walking down the aisle in a store," says one Lands' End customer!

The value of direct marketing for sellers can be described in terms of the responses it generates. **Direct orders** are the result of offers that contain all the information necessary for a prospective buyer to make a decision to purchase and complete the transaction. Priceline.com, for example, will send *PriceBreaker* RSS alerts to people in its database. The messages offer discounted fares and rates to customers who can travel on very short notice. **Lead generation** is the result of an offer designed to generate interest in a product or service and a request for additional information. Four Seasons Hotels now sell private residences in several of their properties and send direct mail to prospective residents asking them to request additional information on the telephone or through a Web site. Finally, **traffic generation** is the outcome of an offer designed to motivate people to visit a business. Home Depot, for example, uses an opt-in e-mail alert to announce special sales that attract consumers to the store. Similarly, The Gap uses e-mails with coupons to increase store traffic.

直接营销中的技术、全球化以及道德问题
Technological, Global, and Ethical Issues in Direct Marketing

The information technology and databases described in Chapter 5 are key elements in any direct marketing program. Databases are the result of organizations' efforts to create profiles of customers so that direct marketing tools, such as e-mail and catalogs, can be directed at specific customers. While most companies try to keep records of their customer's past purchases, many other types of data are needed to use direct marketing to develop one-to-one relationships with customers. Some data, such as lifestyles, media use, and demographics, are best collected from the consumer. Other types of data, such as price, quantity, and brand, are best collected from the businesses where purchases are made. Increases in postage rates and the decline in the economy have also increased the importance of information related to the cost of direct marketing activities. Brookstone, for example, uses its database to mail more than 70 million catalogs to a specific profile of target customer each year. In addition, when the number of catalogs being sent to individual carrier routes is small, the database can add names to qualify for U.S. Postal Service discounts. This approach saves Brookstone $5,000 to $15,000 in postage each time it mails a catalog.

Direct marketing faces several challenges and opportunities in global markets today. Several countries such as Italy and Denmark, for example, have requirements for mandatory "opt-in"—that is, potential customers must give permission to include their name on a list for direct marketing solicitations. In addition the mail, telephone, and Internet systems in many countries are not as well developed as they are in the United States. The need for improved reliability and security in these countries has slowed the growth of direct mail, while the dramatic growth of mobile phone penetration has created an opportunity for direct mobile marketing campaigns. Another issue for global direct marketers is payment. The availability of credit and credit cards varies throughout the world, creating the need for alternatives such as C.O.D. (cash on delivery), bank deposits, and online payment accounts.

Global and domestic direct marketers both face challenging ethical and sustainability issues today. Concerns about privacy, for example, have led to various attempts to provide guidelines that balance consumer and business interests. The European Union passed a consumer privacy law, called the *Data Protection Directive*, after several years of discussion with the Federation of European Direct Marketing and the U.K.'s Direct Marketing Association. In the United States, the Federal Trade Commission and many state legislatures have also been concerned about privacy.

direct orders 直接订购；lead generation 潜在客户开发流程；traffic generation 客流量开发。

Making Responsible Decisions sustainability

Can Direct Marketing "Go Green"?

Each year consumers receive more than 100 billion pieces of direct mail. While this accounts for only 2.4 percent of the waste that ends up in landfills, it represents a huge opportunity for the direct marketing industry to adopt "green" business practices. A group of direct marketing companies and some of their corporate clients, called the Green Marketing Coalition, are developing best-practices guidelines. In addition, the United States Postal Service offers "green ideas for mailers" on its Web site. Some of the guidelines and ideas include:

- Use chlorine-free recycled paper.
- Create an "environMAIList" by removing names of people who are unlikely to respond.
- Let people easily opt out of mailings.
- Use paper from forests certified by The Sustainable Forest Initiative or the Forest Stewardship Council.
- Use printers with green certification.
- Encourage customers to recycle the mailing once they've read it.

These guidelines will have increasing importance as the direct marketing industry continues to grow. Experts have observed that there has been a 35 percent shift in spending from telemarketing to direct marketing since the Do Not Call Registry came into effect in the United States. To evaluate the environmental impact of a company, you can use the Direct Marketing Association's checklist called the Environmental Planning Tool (www.the-dma.org/envgen/envgen1.php). Can you think of other ideas that would help the direct marketing industry minimize its impact on the environment?

Several bills that call for a do-not-mail registry similar to the Do Not Call Registry are being discussed. Similarly, the proliferation of e-mail advertising, or "spam," has received increasing attention from consumers and marketers. Finally, in response to concerns raised by environmentalists, the industry is developing "green" best-practices guidelines for direct marketing companies. The Making Responsible Decisions box offers examples of some of the guidelines.

learning review

13. The ability to design and use direct marketing programs has increased with the availability of ________________ and ________________.
14. What are the three types of responses generated by direct marketing activities?

LEARNING OBJECTIVES REVIEW

LO1 *Discuss integrated marketing communication and the communication process.*

Integrated marketing communication is the concept of designing marketing communications programs that coordinate all promotional activities—advertising, personal selling, sales promotion, public relations, and direct marketing—to provide a consistent message across all audiences. The communication process conveys messages with six elements: a source, a message, a channel of communication, a receiver, and encoding and decoding. The communication process also includes a feedback loop and can be distorted by noise.

LO2 *Describe the promotional mix and the uniqueness of each component.*

There are five promotional alternatives. Advertising, sales promotion, and public relations are mass selling approaches, whereas personal selling and direct marketing use customized messages. Advertising can have high absolute costs but reaches large numbers of people. Personal selling has a high cost per contact but provides immediate feedback. Public relations is often difficult to obtain but is very credible. Sales promotion influences short-term consumer behavior. Direct marketing can help develop customer relationships although maintaining a database can be very expensive.

LO3 *Select the promotional approach appropriate to a product's target audience, life-cycle stage, and characteristics, as well as stages of the buying decision and channel strategies.*

The promotional mix depends on the target audience. Programs for consumers, business buyers, and intermediaries might emphasize advertising, personal selling, and sales promotion, respectively. The promotional mix also changes over the prod-

environmentalist 环境保护主义者，环境保护论者。

uct life-cycle stages. During the introduction stage, all promotional mix elements are used. During the growth stage advertising is emphasized, while the maturity stage utilizes sales promotion and direct marketing. Little promotion is used during the decline stage. Product characteristics also help determine the promotion mix. The level of complexity, risk, and ancillary services required will determine which element is needed. Knowing the customer's stage in the buying process can help select appropriate promotions. Advertising and public relations can create awareness in the prepurchase stage, personal selling and sales promotion can facilitate the purchase, and advertising can help reduce anxiety in the postpurchase stage. Finally, the promotional mix can depend on the channel strategy. Push strategies require personal selling and sales promotions directed at channel members, while pull strategies depend on advertising and sales promotion directed at consumers.

LO4 *Describe the elements of the promotion decision process.*
The promotional decision process consists of three steps: planning, implementation, and evaluation. The planning step consists of six elements: identify the target audience, specify the objectives, set the budget, select the right promotional elements, design the promotion, and schedule the promotion. The implementation step includes pretesting. The evaluation step includes posttesting.

LO5 *Explain the value of direct marketing for consumers and sellers.*
The value of direct marketing for consumers is indicated by its level of use. For example, 68 percent of them have made a purchase by phone or mail, and 12 million people have purchased items from a television offer. The value of direct marketing for sellers can be measured in terms of three types of responses: direct orders, lead generation, and traffic generation.

FOCUSING ON KEY TERMS

advertising
all-you-can-afford budgeting
channel of communication
communication
competitive parity budgeting
decoding
direct marketing
direct orders
encoding
feedback
field of experience
hierarchy of effects
integrated marketing communications (IMC)
lead generation
message
noise
objective and task budgeting
percentage of sales budgeting
personal selling
promotional mix
public relations
publicity
pull strategy
push strategy
receivers
response
sales promotion
source
traffic generation

APPLYING MARKETING KNOWLEDGE

1 After listening to a recent sales presentation, Mary Smith signed up for membership at the local health club. On arriving at the facility, she learned there was an additional fee for racquetball court rentals. "I don't remember that in the sales talk; I thought they said all facilities were included with the membership fee," complained Mary. Describe the problem in terms of the communication process.

2 Develop a matrix to compare the five elements of the promotional mix on three criteria—to *whom* you deliver the message, *what* you say, and *when* you say it.

3 Explain how the promotional tools used by an airline would differ if the target audience were (*a*) consumers who travel for pleasure and (*b*) corporate travel departments that select the airlines to be used by company employees.

4 Suppose you introduced a new consumer food product and invested heavily both in national advertising (pull strategy) and in training and motivating your field salesforce to sell the product to food stores (push strategy). What kinds of feedback would you receive from both the advertising and your salesforce? How could you increase both the quality and quantity of each?

5 Fisher-Price Company, long known as a manufacturer of children's toys, has introduced a line of clothing for children. Outline a promotional plan to get this product introduced in the marketplace.

6 Many insurance companies sell health insurance plans to companies. In these companies the employees pick the plan, but the set of offered plans is determined by the company. Recently Blue Cross–Blue Shield, a health insurance company, ran a television ad stating, "If your employer doesn't offer you Blue Cross–Blue Shield coverage, ask why." Explain the promotional strategy behind the advertisement.

7 Identify the sales promotion tools that might be useful for (*a*) Tastee Yogurt, a new brand introduction, (*b*) 3M self-sticking Post-it® Notes, and (*c*) Wrigley's Spearmint Gum.

8 Design an integrated marketing communications program—using each of the five promotional elements—for Rhapsody, the online music service.

9 BMW recently introduced its first sport activity vehicle, the X6, to compete with other popular crossover vehicles such as the Mercedes-Benz R-class and Buick's Enclave. Design a direct marketing program to generate (*a*) leads, (*b*) traffic in dealerships, and (*c*) direct orders.

10 Develop a privacy policy for database managers that provides a balance of consumer and seller perspectives. How would you encourage voluntary compliance with your policy? What methods of enforcement would you recommend?

building your marketing plan

To develop the promotion strategy for your marketing plan, follow the steps suggested in the planning phase of the promotion decision process described in Figure 13–6.

1 You should (*a*) identify the target audience, (*b*) specify the promotion objectives, (*c*) set the promotion budget, (*d*) select the right promotion tools, (*e*) design the promotion, and (*f*) schedule the promotion.

2 Also specify the pretesting and posttesting procedures needed in the implementation and control phases.

3 Finally, describe how each of your promotion tools are integrated to provide a consistent message.

video case 13 Under Armour: Using IMC to Create a Brand for this Generation's Athletes

"Under Armour sees itself as the athletic brand of this generation. Everything that we create, every message that we put out, that's what we want to be," observes Marcus Stevens, senior creative director for Under Armour. Stevens is responsible for the complete brand aesthetic across all media, including broadcast, print, Web, and point-of-sale. His responsibility is to attract new customers and increase sales of the brand. When the company introduced its first product, a form-fitting moisture-wicking t-shirt to be worn under sportswear, the branding efforts were limited by a very small budget. Today, Under Armour is undertaking the challenge of creating an integrated marketing campaign that utilizes a much larger pool of resources and still delivers a consistent message. As a result of Under Armour's communication activities, "We are poised for growth in the future," explains Stevens.

THE COMPANY

Under Armour was founded by Kevin Plank, a University of Maryland football player who didn't like changing out of the sweat-soaked t-shirts he wore under his jersey during practice and games. In 1996 he developed a moisture-wicking fabric and modeled his first product after a typical cotton t-shirt. After several trips to the patent office, and some input from his brother, Kevin decided on the name Under Armour and set up the business in his grandmother's basement. Early sales depended entirely on word-of-mouth advertising that was generated by events such as a *USA Today* photo of an Oakland Raider football player wearing an Under Armour shirt, and Georgia Tech ordering more than 300 shirts for its entire football team. The turning point for the company came when Under Armour products were used in the movie *Any Given Sunday*. Plank decided to build on the exposure provided by the movie and purchased a full-page ad in *ESPN The Magazine*. That ad generated $750,000 in sales and began the incredible growth of the company.

As the company grew, Plank developed four "Keys of Greatness" to guide him and the Under Armour employees. The keys are:

- Build a great product
- Tell a great story about the product
- Provide great service
- Build a great team

The success of Under Armour's first product soon led to a complete line of performance sports apparel including shirts, pants, shorts, outerwear, gloves, footwear, and accessories. Telling the story was the responsibility of the marketing department and emphasized the need for integrated marketing communications. Great service required support from sales and service representatives. Finally, building a great team meant that Plank always hired the best and brightest people possible. The focus on athletes led to many applications of sports concepts to the business—meetings are called "huddles," the huddle doesn't end until a "play is called," and rapid response to changes in the environment may require "calling an audible." The approach creates a team atmosphere where everyone works together to act on the play.

Today, Under Armour's mission is to make all athletes better through passion, science, and the relentless pursuit of innovation. It offers its product assortment to men, women, and youth online and through more than 15,000 retail locations including Dick's Sporting Goods, the Sports Authority, Hibbett Sporting Goods, and Modell's Sporting Goods. International distribution includes outlets in the United Kingdom, France, Germany, Italy, New Zealand, and Japan. Headquarters has moved from Plank's grandmother's basement to Baltimore, Maryland, and the number of employees has increased to 2,200. Under Armour sales now exceed $700 million!

THE IMC PROGRAM

Stevens first met Plank at an advertising agency where Stevens worked. Plank's idea for an athletic brand for this generation's athlete was very exciting and Stevens soon left the agency to work with Plank. With a limited budget, the challenge was getting the message out to consumers. According to Stevens, "We didn't come in with a polished business plan—and a calendar to execute against; we came in with an idea and a lot of passion." To compete with much larger apparel manufacturers Stevens knew that Under Armour's marketing activities would need to provide a consistent message through advertising, public relations, personal selling and all promotional efforts. Kevin Haley, senior vice president of sports marketing, agrees, "everything has to be integrated." Integrating all promotion activities allows Under Armour to increase the effectiveness of its budget as it strives to create and maintain its brand.

Advertising

Following the release of *Any Given Sunday* and their first print ad in *ESPN the Magazine*, Under Armour began work on a new television advertising campaign. The ad, featuring Eric Ogbogu as "Big E," introduced the tagline, "We must protect this house," and was released at the same time as ESPN's new series *Playmakers*, which featured football players wearing Under Armour apparel. According to Steven Battista, senior vice president of brand, the two coinciding events "propelled the brand into the national spotlight, and then soon after that you would see fans at games holding up signs saying, 'Protect this house.'" The phrase was used by sports fans, David Letterman, Oprah Winfrey, and many others and soon became part of American lexicon. Other campaigns also helped develop the Under Armour brand and image. For example, "Click, Clack" featured the familiar sound made by cleated shoes, and appealed to athletes in many sports such as golf, lacrosse, and baseball, in addition to football.

Under Armour decided to advertise on the Super Bowl to introduce a new performance training shoe. The message in the ad focused on the athlete of tomorrow and included the tagline, "The future is ours." The athletes in the ad included Carl Weathers, a NASCAR driver; Ray Lewis, a football linebacker; Kimmie Meissner, a figure skater; and many others. The ad made a statement that Under Armour could help all athletes train like champions. "The future is ours" was a huge success ranking in the top-five ads according to *USA Today*'s Ad Meter. In addition, Web site traffic tripled following the ad and orders for the product began pouring in! The Super Bowl ad also helped make a statement about the Under Armour brand—that the company, the CEO, the product, and the consumers all represented a new prototype for the future.

Public Relations and Promotion

According to Battista, "half the benefit of a 60-second ad in the Super Bowl is the PR leading up to it and the attention you get" from producing and running the advertisement. Marketing benefits also result from promotion activities such as athlete endorsements, sponsorships, and product placements. These activities play an important role in Under Armour's integrated marketing communications

strategy. Each potential athlete endorsement, for example, is evaluated in terms of the products they will be supporting, the media that would be used, and the potential for in-store and on-field visibility. Under Armour signed Alfonso Soriano, a Chicago Cubs baseball player, to support its baseball cleats and baseball apparel, the outdoor advertising at Wrigley Field, and the retail store in the Chicago market. Under Armour looks for athletes that are "all about performance," explains Haley. They "need to be a team player, who is doing everything they can to win on every single play."

Under Armour has also developed many sponsorship relationships with teams and organizations. For example, Under Armour is the official outfitter for the football programs at Auburn University, the University of Delaware, the University of Hawaii, the University of North Texas, the University of South Carolina, and many other schools. The company recently signed a 5-year agreement with the University of Maryland to outfit all of its 27 varsity sports. Similarly, Under Armour is the supplier for all 17 varsity athletic teams at Texas Tech University. Under Armour has also sponsored high school athletes, professional soccer teams, and the NFL.

Product placements in movies, television shows, and video games have reinforced Under Armour's branding efforts and provided exposure to new audiences. In addition to *Any Given Sunday* you may remember seeing Under Armour products in the movies *Gridiron Gang* and *The Replacements*. Television programs with Under Armour product placements include *Friday Night Lights*, *The Sopranos*, and *MTV Road Rules*. Under Armour even appears in video games such as *Tiger Woods Golf* and *Fight Night 3*!

Retail and Online

When Plank first started Under Armour, its Web site (www.underarmour.com) was its only means of sales and distribution. As the company grew it gained distribution in many retailers. The point-of-sale displays in the retailers, however, offered a unique opportunity to integrate Under Armour's branding. When Under Armour moved into large retailers it noticed that the mannequins in the stores didn't look like the athletes in the advertising because the mannequins did not have muscles. To create a consistent message Under Armour made its own mannequins for the stores so that the displays would look like the athletes in the commercials. Eventually, Under Armour also began opening its own stores. The first Under Armour store opened in Annapolis, Maryland in 2008 and many others soon followed.

The Under Armour Web site remains an important part of the integrated marketing program. Approximately 15 percent of all sales come through the Web site, and many Under Armour consumers use the Web site to learn about new products, study technical details, or view print or television ads. Consumers who register on the site can receive e-mail messages about new or seasonal products and new campaigns. Currently, the Under Armour Web site attracts an average of 35,000 visitors each day. The online program also includes several social networking elements. Under Armour, for example, is building a

presence on Facebook and on Xbox Live marketplace. All of these activities help ensure that consumers will be exposed to a consistent message regardless of the medium they utilize.

FUTURE STRATEGY

How can Under Armour continue its incredible record of growth? Experts observe that future growth will require the company to broaden its appeal without alienating the original segment of athletes interested in performance. There are opportunities to expand exposure in many sports such as the fast-growing lacrosse segment, to attract more men, women, and youth, and to introduce new products to the current line. Under Armour, for example, recently introduced a line of running shoes—a large category with broad appeal to many consumers. Integrating the growth activities will be critical to the company's success. As Battista observes, everything has to "look right and have the same message points and the same type of branding and look and feel!"

The future is likely to be very exciting for Under Armour as it continues to introduce new products and enter new markets. For example, the company recently introduced mouth guards and a body suit that helps athletes recover from a workout faster. To expand in international markets Under Armour is creating distribution networks in Europe and Asia and signing endorsement deals with rugby players, Olympians, and other international athletes. In addition, to change perceptions that Under Armour products are used primarily by football players, the company now sponsors 27 boys' and girls' high school basketball teams. Under Armour's branding and communication strategies have been extraordinarily successful as the company now is the fastest growing performance sports brand. In fact, the company has grown so quickly that it plans to add an additional 135,000 square feet of new space across the street from its headquarters to provide showrooms and new offices. According to one newspaper headline, the company is a "runaway success"!

Questions

1 What promotional opportunities gave Under Armour its initial success?

2 Which of the promotional elements described in Figure 13-2 are used by Under Armour in its IMC campaigns?

3 What are several new strategies Under Armour might pursue as it attempts to continue its extraordinary record of growth?

Alien Problem? Monster Solution.

DreamWorks

MONSTERS VS ALIENS

DREAMWORKS SKG PRESENTS "MONSTERS VS. ALIENS" MUSIC BY HENRY JACKMAN STORY BY ROB LETTERMAN & CONRAD VERNON SCREENPLAY BY MAYA FORBES & WALLY WOLODARSKY AND ROB LETTERMAN AND JONATHAN AIBEL & GLENN BERGER

PG PARENTAL GUIDANCE SUGGESTED MonstersVsAliens.com CO-PRODUCERS JILL HOPPER LATIFA OUAOU PRODUCED BY LISA STEWART DIRECTED BY ROB LETTERMAN CONRAD VERNON DreamWorks

A MONSTROUS 3D EVENT 

MARCH 2009

IN real D 3D AND IMAX 3D

14

广告、销售促进和公共关系
Advertising, Sales Promotion, and Public Relations

LEARNING OBJECTIVES

After reading this chapter you should be able to:

LO1 Explain the differences between product advertising and institutional advertising and the variations within each type.

LO2 Describe the steps used to develop, execute, and evaluate an advertising program.

LO3 Explain the advantages and disadvantages of alternative advertising media.

LO4 Discuss the strengths and weaknesses of consumer-oriented and trade-oriented sales promotions.

LO5 Recognize public relations as an important form of communication.

广告走向一个新的维度：第三维度
ADVERTISING MOVES TO A NEW DIMENSION: THE THIRD DIMENSION

If Jeffery Katzenberg, James Cameron, and Steven Spielberg have their way, most visual media, including advertising, could be presented in digital 3-D in the near future. Their movie studio, DreamWorks, is developing a technology to bring a true third dimension to movie theaters and television screens!

DreamWorks' first 3-D movie, *Monsters vs. Aliens*, was a huge step for the company. "This is really a revolution," explains CEO Katzenberg. In fact, he believes the change is so important that in the future all DreamWorks' movies will be made in 3-D. The technology is not just for movies and theaters, however; it will also change broadcasting, TV displays, gaming, videos, and all forms of advertising.

The first 3-D advertisements were 30-second spots on the Super Bowl for *Monsters vs. Aliens* and Sobe Life Water energy drinks. More than 125 million pairs of free 3-D glasses, using a new technology, were distributed in the United States for use during the Super Bowl. Other forms of 3-D are being developed also. For example, a Japanese company is developing a laser system that will project 3-D outdoor advertisements. Other applications will include digital billboards and signs. The combination of the two has the potential to allow consumers to experience advertising in a virtual 3-D environment.

Unlike traditional advertising, 3-D advertising is an opportunity to immerse consumers in an experience. Today's consumers are not passive; they want to be involved and engaged. The third dimension allows viewers to participate in the ad rather than just observe it. Advertisers can use 3-D to pull the audience into an ad to feel the message being communicated. Some observers believe that 3-D viewing is so close to a real experience that it will improve retention of the message. This new generation of 3-D technology is for both animation and live action. Comcast mixed animation and live action to create its recent 3-D ad campaign called "Comcast Town." The six TV spots create an imaginary 3-D world that illustrates connectivity and entertainment for live characters. Another ad, created by NBC, encoded a clip of its TV program *Chuck* in 3-D using only the live characters and setting.

Watch for a general trend toward 3-D. Katzenberg predicts that soon everyone will own a pair of 3-D glasses!

The 3-D explosion is just one of the many exciting changes occurring in the field of advertising today. They illustrate the importance of advertising as one of the five promotional mix elements in marketing communications programs. This chapter describes three of the promotional mix elements—advertising, sales promotion, and public relations. Direct marketing was covered in Chapter 13.

---

immerse 沉迷……中，陷入；explosion 激增，骤增。

广告的类型
TYPES OF ADVERTISEMENTS

Chapter 13 described **advertising** as any paid form of nonpersonal communication about an organization, a good, a service, or an idea by an identified sponsor. As you look through any magazine, watch television, listen to the radio, or browse the Internet, the variety of advertisements you see or hear may give you the impression that they have few similarities. Advertisements are prepared for different purposes, but they basically consist of two types: product advertisements and institutional advertisements.

产品广告
Product Advertisements

产品广告致力于销售商品或服务，它有三种类型：(1)开拓型广告（或称告知广告）；(2)竞争型广告（或称说服广告）；(3)提示型广告。

LO1

Focused on selling a good or service, **product advertisements** take three forms: (1) pioneering (or informational), (2) competitive (or persuasive), and (3) reminder. Look at the ads for Visa, Cadillac, and M&Ms to determine the type and objective of each ad.

Used in the introductory stage of the product life cycle, *pioneering* advertisements tell people what a product is, what it can do, and where it can be found. The key objective of a pioneering advertisement (such as the ad for Visa's new Black card) is to inform the target market. Informational ads, particularly those with specific information, have been found to be interesting, convincing, and effective.

Advertising that promotes a specific brand's features and benefits is *competitive*. The objective of these messages is to persuade the target market to select the firm's brand rather than that of a competitor. An increasingly common form of competitive advertising is *comparative* advertising, which shows one brand's strengths relative to those of competitors. The Cadillac ad, for example, highlights the competitive advantage of the Cadillac Escalade hybrid compared to other vehicles such as the BMW X3 and the Volvo XC90. Studies indicate that comparative ads attract more attention and increase the perceived quality of the advertiser's brand although their impact may vary by product type, message content, and audience gender. Firms that use comparative advertising need market research to provide legal support for their claims.

Reminder advertising is used to reinforce previous knowledge of a product. The M&Ms ad shown reminds consumers about a special event, in this case, Valentine's Day. Reminder advertising is good for products that have achieved a well-recognized position and are in the mature phase of their product life cycle. Another type of

Product advertisements serve varying purposes. Which ad would be considered a (1) pioneering, (2) competitive, and (3) reminder ad?

product advertisements 产品广告；pioneering 开拓型；comparative 竞争型；reminder 提示型。

Chevron uses an advocacy ad to communicate its position on the use of less energy. Amway uses a pioneering ad to inform readers about the company and its products.

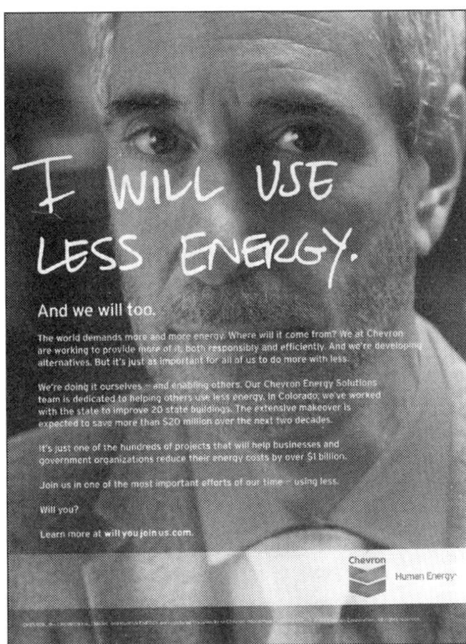

reminder ad, *reinforcement*, is used to assure current users they made the right choice. One example is used in Dial soap advertisements: "Aren't you glad you use Dial. Don't you wish everybody did?"

机构广告
Institutional Advertisements

The objective of **institutional advertisements** is to build goodwill or an image for an organization rather than promote a specific good or service. Institutional advertising has been used by companies such as Texaco, Pfizer, and IBM to build confidence in the company name. Often this form of advertising is used to support the public relations plan or counter adverse publicity. Four alternative forms of institutional advertisements are often used:

1. 倡议型广告用以表明公司在某一问题上的立场。

1. *Advocacy* advertisements state the position of a company on an issue. Chevron places ads encouraging consumers to use less energy. Another form of advocacy advertisement is used when organizations make a request related to a particular action or behavior, such as a request by American Red Cross for blood donations.

2. 开拓型机构广告，类似于前面所讨论过的开拓型产品广告，其目的主要是介绍这是一家什么样的公司，是做什么的，或公司位于什么地方。

2. *Pioneering institutional* advertisements, like the pioneering ads for products discussed earlier, are used for announcements about what a company is, what it can do, or where it is located. Recent Bayer ads stating, "We cure more headaches than you think," are intended to inform consumers that the company produces many products in addition to aspirin. Amway uses pioneering institutional ads in its "Know You Know" campaign to inform people about the company and its products.

3. 竞争型机构广告突出了某类产品优于其他替代品的优势，不同类型的产品在市场上争夺同一买主时会使用此类广告。

3. *Competitive institutional* advertisements promote the advantages of one product class over another and are used in markets where different product classes compete for the same buyers. America's milk processors and dairy farmers use their "Got Milk?" campaign to increase demand for milk as it competes against other beverages.

4. 提示型机构广告，类似于提示型产品广告，仅是为了再次引起目标市场对公司的关注。

4. *Reminder institutional* advertisements, like the product form, simply bring the company's name to the attention of the target market again. The Army branch of the U.S. military sponsors a campaign to remind potential recruits of the opportunities in the Army.

---

reinforcement 强化型；institutional advertisements 机构广告；advocacy 倡议型；pioneering institutional 开拓型机构；competitive institutional 竞争型机构；reminder institutional 提示型机构。

A competitive institutional ad by dairy farmers tries to increase demand for milk, and a reminder institutional ad by the U.S. Army tries to keep the attention of the target market.

learning review

1. What is the difference between pioneering and competitive ads?
2. What is the purpose of an institutional advertisement?

制定广告方案
DEVELOPING THE ADVERTISING PROGRAM

The promotion decision process described in Chapter 13 can be applied to each of the promotional elements. Advertising, for example, can be managed by following the three steps (developing, executing, and evaluating) of the process.

确定目标受众
Identifying the Target Audience

To develop an effective advertising program, advertisers must identify the target audience. All aspects of an advertising program are likely to be influenced by the characteristics of the prospective consumer. Understanding the lifestyles, attitudes, and demographics of the target market is essential. NBC, for example, promoted its medical/nurse drama "Mercy" to 18- to 34-year-old women, while Electronic Arts targeted 13- to 34-year-old men for The Beatles Rock Band video game. Both campaigns emphasized advertising techniques that matched the audience—program trailers for women and 30-second game demos for men. Similarly, the placement of ads depends on the audience. When Porsche began its 18-month-long "Can you afford a Porsche?" campaign, it used mobile phone ads to reach its target market—young tech-savvy, connected men. Even scheduling can depend on the audience. Nike schedules advertising, sponsorships, deals, and endorsements to correspond with the Olympics to appeal to "hard-core" athletes. To eliminate possible bias that might result from subjective judgments about some population segments, the Federal Communications Commission suggests that advertising program decisions be based on market research about the target audience.

emphasize 强调。

明确广告目标
Specifying Advertising Objectives

The guidelines for setting promotion objectives described in Chapter 13 also apply to setting advertising objectives. This step helps advertisers with other choices in the promotion decision process such as selecting media and evaluating a campaign. Advertising with an objective of creating awareness, for example, would be better matched with a magazine than a directory such as the Yellow Pages. The Magazine Publishers of America believe objectives are so important that they offer a $100,000 prize each year to the campaign that best meets its objectives. Recently, Pedigree food for dogs won with its "Adoption" campaign, which increased sales by 11 percent and raised $2.7 million for shelter dogs. Similarly, the Advertising Research Foundation sponsors an Advertising Effectiveness Council to investigate new techniques for measuring the impact of all forms of advertising. Experts believe that factors such as product category, brand, and consumer involvement in the purchase decision may change the importance—and, possibly, the sequence—of the stages of the hierarchy of effects. Snickers, for example, knew that its consumers were unlikely to engage in elaborate information processing when it designed a recent campaign. The result was ads with simple humorous messages rather than extensive factual information.

建立广告预算
Setting the Advertising Budget

During the 1990 Super Bowl, it cost companies $700,000 to place a 30-second ad. By 2009, the cost of placing a 30-second ad during Super Bowl XLIII was $3 million (see Figure 14–1). The reason for the escalating cost is the growing number of viewers: 100 million people, or about 50 percent of the viewing public, watch the game. In addition, the audience is attractive to advertisers because research indicates it is equally split between men and women and many viewers look forward to watching

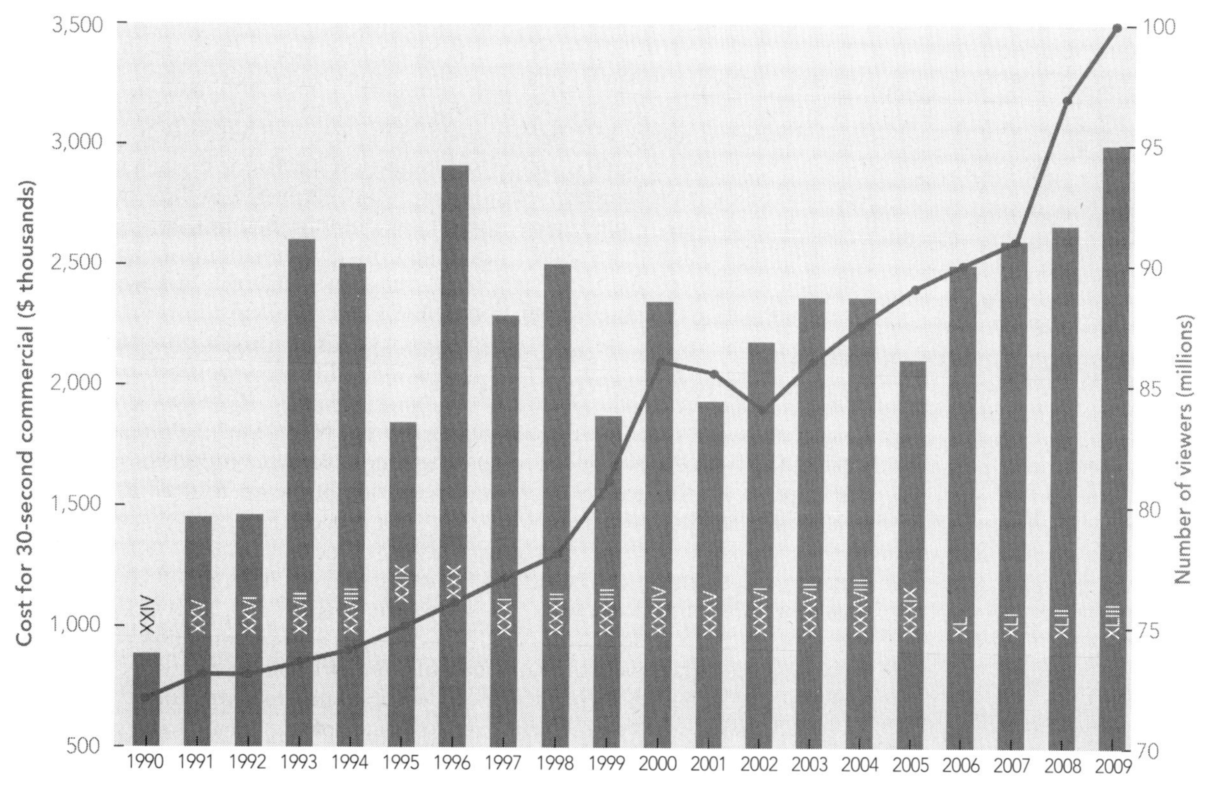

FIGURE 14–1
The Super Bowl delivers a huge audience, if you can afford the cost of placing an ad.

directory 通讯录；elaborate 繁复的，详尽的，过于复杂的。

Going Online

See Your Favorite Super Bowl Ads Again, and Again!

If you missed some of the ads during the last Super Bowl, or if you liked some of them so much you want to see them again, you can review the ads at www.superbowl-ads.com. All ads for the past 12 Super Bowls and classics like the "1984" Apple Computer ad are available to view.

Which ads are your favorites? Compare the ads from different years. For example, you might compare the 2009 Coke Zero ad to the 1980 Coke ad (click All-time). Do you notice any changes?

Do you remember this Doritos ad from the Super Bowl?

the 69 "spots." The ads are effective too: Movies promoted on the Super Bowl achieve 40 percent more revenue than movies not promoted on the Super Bowl; E*TRADE increased the number of new accounts by 32 percent in the week after the game; and Go Daddy estimates that it received $11.7 million in publicity as a result of its ads. As a result, the Super Bowl attracts relatively new advertisers such as Hulu and Denny's, and regular advertisers such as Anheuser-Busch, Doritos, and Coca-Cola. Coke Zero's remake of the 1980 "Mean Joe Green" ad and Monster.com were rated the highest. To learn how to see your favorite Super Bowl ad again, read the Going Online box.

While not all advertising options are as expensive as the Super Bowl, most alternatives still represent substantial financial commitments and require a formal budgeting process. In the beverage industry, for example, Coca-Cola and Pepsi have market shares of approximately 15.2 percent and 9.5 percent, and advertising and promotion budgets of $294.6 million and $162.1 million, respectively. Using a competitive parity budgeting approach, each company spends between $17 million and $19 million for each percent of market share. Using an objective and task approach, Honda allocated $50 million to introduce the Insight, its new, low-priced hybrid car. The campaign uses television, radio, magazine, newspaper, Internet, and movie theater advertising with the phrase "From Honda. For Everyone."

广告设计
Designing the Advertisement

An advertising message usually focuses on the key benefits of the product that are important to a prospective buyer in making trial and adoption decisions. The message depends on the general form or appeal used in the ad and the actual words included in the ad.

Message Content Most advertising messages are made up of both informational and persuasional elements. These two elements are so intertwined that it is sometimes difficult to tell them apart. For example, basic information contained in many ads such as the product name, benefits, features, and price are presented in a way that tries to attract attention and encourage purchase. On the other hand, even the most persuasive advertisements have to contain at least some basic information to be successful.

estimate 估计，预测；substantial 大量的，相当程度的。

Information and persuasive content can be combined in the form of an appeal to provide a basic reason for the consumer to act. Although the marketer can use many different types of appeals, common advertising appeals include fear, sex, and humor.

忧虑诉求意在让顾客认为通过购买和使用某产品（服务）、通过改变某一行为，或是减少使用某产品，他（她）就可以避免某些负面体验。

Fear appeals suggest to the consumer that he or she can avoid some negative experience through the purchase and use of a product or service, a change in behavior, or a reduction in the use of a product. Examples with which you may be familiar include: automobile safety ads that depict an accident or injury; political candidate endorsements that warn against the rise of other, unpopular ideologies; or social cause ads warning of the serious consequences of drug and alcohol use. Insurance companies often try to show the negative effects on the relatives of those who die prematurely without carrying enough life or mortgage insurance. Food producers encourage the purchase of low-carb, low-fat, and high-fiber products as a means of reducing weight, cholesterol levels, and the possibility of a heart attack. The Office of National Drug Control Policy previously ran an ad with a fear appeal: The headline read "Marijuana. Harmless?" and the statement "Didn't see merging truck." When using fear appeals, the advertiser must be sure that the appeal is strong enough to get the audience's attention and concern but not so strong that it will lead them to tune out the message. In fact, research on antismoking ads indicates that stressing the severity of long-term health risks may actually enhance smoking's allure among youth.

相反，性感诉求让观众认为该产品将会增加使用者的吸引力。

In contrast, *sex appeals* suggest to the audience that the product will increase the attractiveness of the user. Sex appeals can be found in almost any product category, from automobiles to toothpaste. The contemporary women's clothing store Bebe, for example, designs its advertising to "attract customers who are intrigued by the playfully sensual and evocative imagery of the Bebe lifestyle." Studies indicate that sex appeals increase attention by helping advertising stand out in today's cluttered media environment. Unfortunately, sexual content does not always lead to changes in recall, recognition, or purchase intent. Experts suggest that sexual content is most effective when there is a strong fit between the use of a sex appeal in the ad and the image and positioning of the brand.

幽默诉求无论是采用直接还是更微妙的形式，目的都是让观众认为其产品比竞争者的产品更具有趣味性或更激动人心。

Humorous appeals imply either directly or subtly that the product is more fun or exciting than competitors' offerings. As with fear and sex appeals, the use of humor is widespread in advertising and can be found in many product categories. You may have smiled at the popular Geico ads that use cavemen, a gecko, and a stack of money with eyes named Kash to use humor to differentiate the company from its

These ads are examples of fear appeal, sex appeal, and humor appeal, respectively.

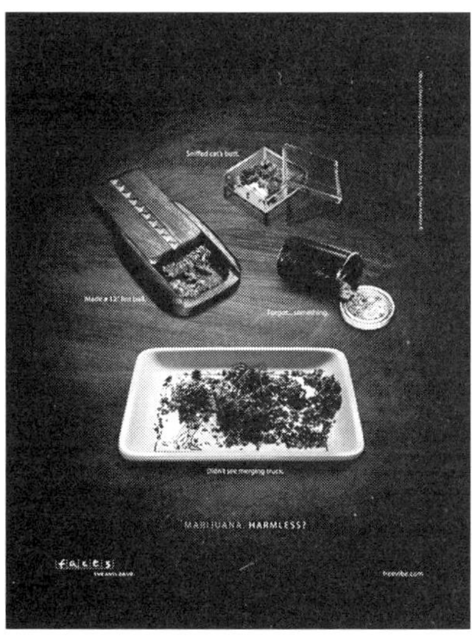

fear appeals 忧虑诉求；sex appeals 性感诉求；humorous appeals 幽默诉求。

competitors. The ads have been so popular that Geico has created an interactive Web site, www.cavemanscrib.com, to allow visitors to learn more about the cavemen. In addition, Geico has created viral videos featuring the gecko and posted them on video-sharing Web sites such as YouTube, Metacafe, and Slide, where millions of viewers watch them within days. You may have a favorite humorous ad character, such as the Energizer battery bunny, the AFLAC duck, or Travelocity's gnome. Advertisers believe that humor improves the effectiveness of their ads, although some studies suggest that humor wears out quickly, losing the interest of consumers. Another problem with humorous appeals is that their effectiveness may vary across cultures if used in a global campaign.

Creating the Actual Message Advertising agency Crispin, Porter & Bogusky was recently designated *Advertising Age* magazine's U.S. Agency of the Year for its unique ability to take "a simple proposition" and "somehow make it entertainment." Examples of the agency's approach include the "I'm a PC" campaign for Microsoft, the "Whopper Virgin" campaign for Burger King, and the "It's What the People Want" campaign for Volkswagen. Crispin was also recognized for adding product design to the services it offers clients. Some of its design ideas include a public bike-rental program, a pen version of WD-40, and an eco-friendly sponge!

Crispin, Porter & Bogusky and other agencies use many forms of advertising to create their messages. A very popular form of advertising today is the use of a celebrity spokesperson. Crispin's use of well-known personalities such as Brooke Shields, David Hasselhoff, and Heidi Klum in their Volkswagen ads is an example. Many companies use athletes, movie and television stars, musicians, and other celebrities to talk to consumers through their ads. Advertisers who use a celebrity spokesperson believe that the ads are more likely to influence sales. The popular "Got Milk?" campaign reversed a steady decline in milk consumption with celebrities such as musician Taylor Swift, model Christie Brinkley, NASCAR driver Jeff Gordon, fictional characters such as Batman and Ronald McDonald, and many others. You've probably seen ads with Nicole Kidman promoting Chanel No. 5 perfume or Tiger Woods endorsing American Express. The top five corporate celebrity spokespersons today are Tom Hanks, Will Smith, Michael Jordan, Morgan Freeman, and George Clooney. The top spokespersons for causes include Lance Armstrong for LiveStrong, Angelina

The Giro campaign is one example of creative advertising that helped agency Crispin, Porter & Bogusky win *Advertising Age*'s Agency of the Year award.

---

designated 指定的，选定的；consumption 消耗量，消费量。

Crispin, Porter & Bogusky uses a simple proposition to create a message for Microsoft.

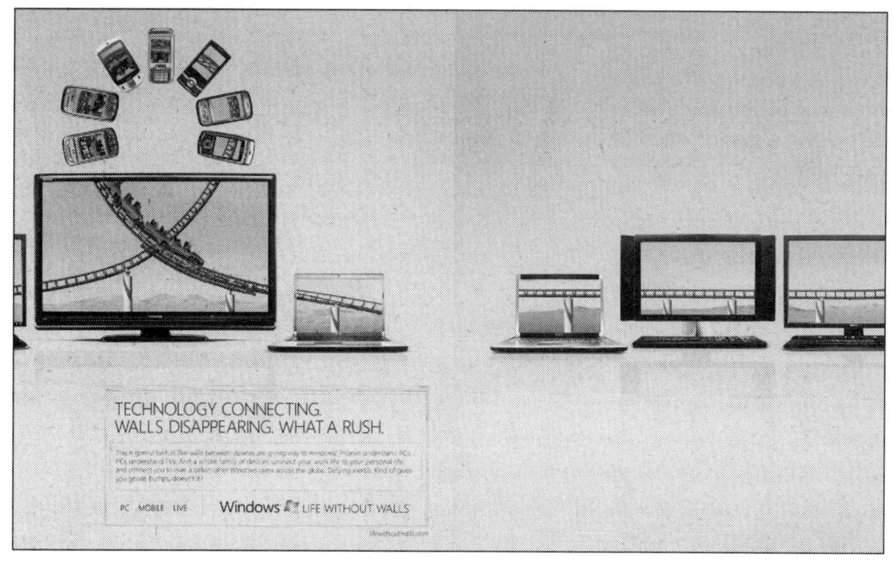

Jolie for UNICEF, and Bono for his work with RED. L'Oreal Paris recently signed actress Elizabeth Banks as its exclusive worldwide spokesperson for the company and its brands. Karen Fondu, president of L'Oreal Paris, explains that Elizabeth was selected because "she has a natural charm and an incredible ability to captivate an audience."

One potential shortcoming of this form of advertising is that the spokesperson's image may change to be inconsistent with the image of the company or brand. Olympic swimmer Michael Phelps lost an endorsement contract with Kellogg's after pictures of his activities at a party led to negative public attention. Many companies now probe the backgrounds of potential endorsers and consider retired athletes and legacy (deceased) athletes who are low risk and still have lasting appeal in the marketplace. Some companies are also using licensing agreements where the spokesperson's compensation is directly related to the success of the product they endorse.

Another issue involved in creating the message is the complex process of translating the copywriter's ideas into an actual advertisement. Designing quality artwork, layout, and production for advertisements is costly and time consuming. The American Association of Advertising Agencies reports that high-quality TV commercials typically cost about $361,000 to produce a 30-second ad. One reason for the high costs is that as companies have developed global campaigns, the need to shoot commercials in several locations has increased. Audi recently filmed commercials in Germany, Australia, and Morocco. Actors are also expensive: Compensation for a typical TV ad is $17,000.

learning review

3. What other decisions can advertising objectives influence?
4. What is a potential shortcoming of using a celebrity spokesperson?

选择合适的媒体
Selecting the Right Media

Every advertiser must decide where to place its advertisements. The alternatives are the *advertising media*, the means by which the message is communicated to the

shortcoming 短处，缺点；endorsement 赞同，支持；advertising media 广告媒体。

FIGURE 14–2
Television, direct mail, and newspapers account for more than 60 percent of all advertising expenditures (in millions).

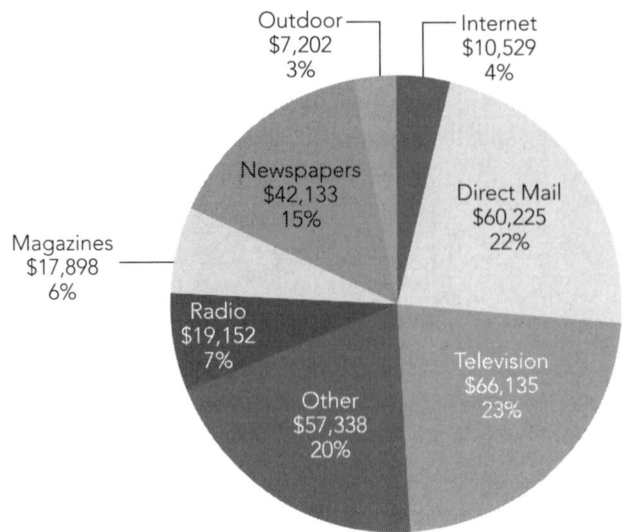

target audience. Newspapers, magazines, radio, and TV are examples of advertising media. This decision on media selection is related to the target audience, type of product, nature of the message, campaign objectives, available budget, and the costs of the alternative media. Figure 14–2 shows the distribution of the $279 billion spent on advertising among the many media alternatives.

Choosing a Medium and a Vehicle Within That Medium In deciding where to place advertisements, a company has several media to choose from and a number of alternatives, or vehicles, within each medium. Often advertisers use a mix of media forms and vehicles to maximize the exposure of the message to the target audience while at the same time minimizing costs. These two conflicting goals are of central importance to media planning.

Basic Terms Media buyers speak a language of their own, so every advertiser involved in selecting the right media for their campaigns must be familiar with some common terms used in the advertising industry.

Because advertisers try to maximize the number of individuals in the target market exposed to the message, they must be concerned with reach. **Reach** is the number of different people or households exposed to an advertisement. The exact definition of reach sometimes varies among alternative media. Newspapers often use reach to describe their total circulation or the number of different households that buy the paper. Television and radio stations, in contrast, describe their reach using the term **rating**—the percentage of households in a market that are tuned to a particular TV show or radio station. In general, advertisers try to maximize reach in their target market at the lowest cost.

Although reach is important, advertisers are also interested in exposing their target audience to a message more than once. This is because consumers often do not pay close attention to advertising messages, some of which contain large amounts of relatively complex information. When advertisers want to reach the same audience more than once, they are concerned with **frequency**, the average number of times a person in the target audience is exposed to a message or advertisement. Like reach, greater frequency is generally viewed as desirable. Studies indicate that with repeated exposure to advertisements consumers respond more favorably to brand extensions.

reach 覆盖面；rating 收视 / 收听率；frequency 频率。

Using Marketing Dashboards

What Is the Best Way to Reach 1,000 Customers?

Marketing managers must choose from many advertising options as they design a campaign to reach potential customers. Because there are so many media alternatives (television, radio, magazines, etc.) and multiple options within each of the media, it is important to monitor the efficiency of advertising expenditures on your marketing dashboard.

Your Challenge As the marketing manager for a company about to introduce a new soft drink into the U.S. market, you are preparing a presentation in which you must make recommendations for the advertising campaign. You have observed that competitors use magazine ads, newspaper ads, and even Super Bowl ads! To compare the cost of some of the alternatives you decide to use one of the most common measures in advertising: cost per thousand impressions (CPM). The CPM is calculated as follows:

Cost per thousand impressions =
Advertising cost ($)/Impressions generated (in 1000s)

Your challenge is to determine the most efficient use of your advertising budget.

Your Findings Your research department helps you collect cost and audience size information for three options: full-page color ads in *Sports Illustrated* magazine and *USA Today* newspaper, and a 30-second television ad during the Super Bowl. With this information you are able to calculate the cost per thousand impressions for each alternative.

Media Alternative	Cost of Ad	Audience Size	Cost per Thousand Impressions
Sports Illustrated (magazine)	$336,000	3,150,000	$107
USA Today (newspaper)	$197,720	2,109,628	$94
Super Bowl (television)	$3,000,000	100,000,000	$30

Your Action Based on the calculations for these options, you see that there is a large variation in the cost of reaching 1,000 potential customers (CPM) and also in the absolute cost of the advertising. Although advertising on the Super Bowl has the lowest CPM, $30 for each 1,000 impressions, it also has the largest absolute cost! Your next step will be to consider other factors such as your total available budget, the profiles of the audiences each alternative reaches, and whether the type of message you want to deliver is better communicated in print or on television.

When reach (expressed as a percentage of the total market) is multiplied by frequency, an advertiser will obtain a commonly used reference number called **gross rating points** (GRPs). To obtain the appropriate number of GRPs to achieve an advertising campaign's objectives, the media planner must balance reach and frequency. The balance will also be influenced by cost. **Cost per thousand** (CPM) refers to the cost of reaching 1,000 individuals or households with the advertising message in a given medium (*M* is the Roman numeral for 1,000). See the Using Marketing Dashboards box for an example of the use of CPM in media selection.

不同媒体选择
Different Media Alternatives

LO3

Figure 14–3 on the next page summarizes the advantages and disadvantages of the major advertising media, which are described in more detail below. Direct mail was discussed in Chapter 13.

Television Television is a valuable medium because it communicates with sight, sound, and motion. Print advertisements alone could never give you the sense of a sports car accelerating from a stop or cornering at high speed. In addition, network television reaches 98.9 percent of all households—114.5 million—more than any other advertising option. Unfortunately, the percentage of households watching network television has declined from 56 percent in 1973 to approximately 18 percent

gross rating points 毛评点；cost per thousand 每千人成本。

MEDIUM	ADVANTAGES	DISADVANTAGES
Television	Reaches extremely large audience; uses picture, print, sound, and motion for effect; can target specific audiences	High cost to prepare and run ads; short exposure time and perishable message; difficult to convey complex information
Radio	Low cost; can target specific local audiences; ads can be placed quickly; can use sound, humor, and intimacy effectively	No visual element; short exposure time and perishable message; difficult to convey complex information
Magazines	Can target specific audiences; high-quality color; long life of ad; ads can be clipped and saved; can convey complex information	Long time needed to place ad; relatively high cost; competes for attention with other magazine features
Newspapers	Excellent coverage of local markets; ads can be placed and changed quickly; ads can be saved; quick consumer response; low cost	Ads compete for attention with other newspaper features; short life span; poor color
Yellow Pages	Excellent coverage of geographic segments; long use period; available 24 hours/365 days	Proliferation of competitive directories in many markets; difficult to keep up-to-date
Internet	Video and audio capabilities; animation can capture attention; ads can be interactive and link to advertiser	Animation and interactivity require large files and more time to load; effectiveness is still uncertain
Outdoor	Low cost; local market focus; high visibility; opportunity for repeat exposures	Message must be short and simple; low selectivity of audience; criticized as a traffic hazard
Direct mail	High selectivity of audience; can contain complex information and personalized messages; high-quality graphics	High cost per contact; poor image (junk mail)

FIGURE 14–3
Advertisers must consider the advantages and disadvantages of the many media alternatives.

today. Out-of-home TV viewing, however, has been increasing as millions of viewers can now see televisions in bars, hotels, offices, airports, and college campuses.

Television's major disadvantage is cost: The price of a prime-time, 30-second ad run on *Sunday Night Football* is $339,700, and the average price for all prime-time programs is $125,283. Because of these high charges, many advertisers choose less expensive "spot" ads, which run between programs in 10-, 15-, 30-, or 60-second lengths. Shorter ads reduce costs but severely restrict the amount of information and emotion that can be conveyed. Miller, however, increased sales by 8 percent in the week after it ran one-second ads on the Super Bowl. In addition, there is some indication that advertisers are shifting their interest to live events rather than programs that might be watched on a DVR days later.

Another problem with television advertising is the likelihood of *wasted coverage*—having people outside the market for the product see the advertisement. The cost and wasted coverage problems of TV advertising can be reduced through the specialized cable and satellite channels. Advertising time is often less expensive on cable and satellite channels than on the broadcast networks. There are currently about 150 options, such as ESPN, MTV, Lifetime, Oxygen, the Speed Channel, the History Channel, the Science Channel, and the Food Network, that reach very nar-

likelihood 可能，可能性。

Oxygen is one of many specialized channels available to advertisers.

rowly defined audiences. Other forms of television viewing are changing advertising also. Many cable and satellite TV services offer DVRs and remotes with "skip" buttons for ad-zapping. Pay-per-view options and "download" services such as iTunes offer commercial-free viewing. In addition, Web sites such as Fancast, Hulu, Joost, and YouTube now provide access to cable and broadcast programming with limited advertising.

Another popular form of television advertising is the infomercial. **Infomercials** are program-length (30-minute) advertisements that take an educational approach to communication with potential customers. Each year *Response Magazine* and Infomercial Monitoring Service Inc. report on the growth and success of infomercials as a form of television advertising. More than 470 new infomercials are produced each year. Some of the most popular included Total Gym, Nutrisystem Advanced, Bowflex, and Sleep Number. Chrysler recently produced its first infomercial for the Dodge Ram, which ran on weekend mornings on CBS, Fox, Telemundo, and Univision. What was one of the most successful infomercials? During the 2008 presidential campaign, Barack Obama ran an infomercial that attracted 33.5 million viewers—more than the final game of the World Series!

Radio The United States has more than 14,000 radio stations—eight times as many as there are television stations. The major advantage of radio is that it is a segmented medium. For example, there are the Farm Radio Network, the Family Life Network, Business Talk Radio, and the Performance Racing Network, all listened to by different market segments. The large number of media options today has reduced the amount of time spent listening to radio also. The average 18- to 24-year-old, however, still listens to radio an average of 2.5 hours each day, making radio an important medium for businesses with college students as a target market.

A disadvantage of radio is that it has limited use for products that must be seen. Another problem is the ease with which consumers can tune out a commercial by switching stations. Satellite radio service Sirius XM offers more than 130 digital-quality, coast-to-coast channels to consumers for an annual subscription fee. Many of the channels are 100 percent commercial-free. Radio is also a medium that competes for people's attention as they do other activities such as driving, working, or relaxing. Radio listening time reaches its peak during the morning drive time (7 to 9 A.M.), remains high during the day, and then begins to decline in the afternoon (4 P.M.) as people return home and start evening activities.

Magazines such as *Sports Illustrated for Kids* appeal to narrowly defined segments.

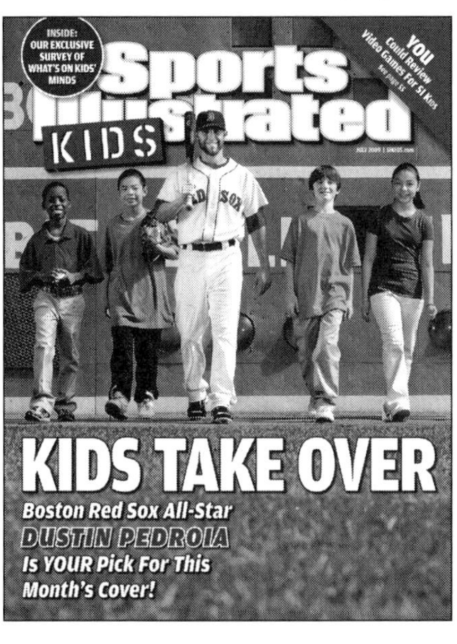

Magazines Magazines have become a very specialized medium, primarily because there are currently more than 19,532 magazines. Some 200 new magazines are introduced each year, such as *Disney Twenty-Three*, a quarterly magazine for Disney fans; *Bicycle Times*, a magazine about everyday bicycling experiences; and *Best You*, a magazine about health, diet, and exercise. A new form of existing magazines—issues containing reader-generated content—has also been introduced recently. *This Old House* and *BusinessWeek*, for example, asked readers to create substantial portions of special issues of the magazines.

The marketing advantage of this medium is the great number of special-interest publications that appeal to narrowly defined segments. Runners read *Runner's World*, sailors buy *Yachting*, gardeners subscribe to *Garden Design*, and children peruse *Sports Illustrated for Kids*. More than 645 publications focus on travel, 195 are dedicated to interior design and decoration, and 139 are related to golf. Each magazine's readers often represent a unique profile. Take the *Rolling Stone* reader, who tends to listen to music more than most people; Sirius XM satellite radio knows an ad in *Rolling Stone* is reaching the desired target audience. In addition, recent studies comparing advertising in different media suggest

infomercial 专题广告片；subscription 会员费，订阅费。

that magazine advertising is perceived to be more "trustworthy," "inspirational," and engaging than other media.

The cost of advertising in national magazines is a disadvantage, but many national publications publish regional and even metro editions, which reduces the absolute cost and wasted coverage. *Time* publishes well over 400 editions, including Latin American, Canadian, Asian, South Pacific, European, and U.S. editions. The U.S. editions include geographic and demographic options. In addition to cost, another limitation to magazines is their infrequency. At best, magazines are printed on a weekly basis, with many specialized publications appearing only monthly or less often. Although specialization can be an advantage of this medium, consumer interests can be difficult to translate into a magazine theme—a fact made clear by the hundreds of magazine failures during the past decade. *CosmoGirl*, *ElleGirl*, *Teen People*, *Virtual City*, *Business 2.0*, *PC Magazine*, *Men's Vogue*, and *Esquire Sportsman*, for example, all failed to attract and keep a substantial number of readers or advertisers. Which magazine has the highest circulation? It's *AARP The Magazine* with a circulation of 24 million!

Print ads help attract readers to *USA Today*.

www.usatoday.com

Newspapers Newspapers are an important local medium with excellent reach potential. Daily publication allows advertisements to focus on specific current events, such as a 24-hour sale. Local retailers often use newspapers as their sole advertising medium. Newspapers are rarely saved by the purchaser, however, so companies are generally limited to ads that call for an immediate customer response (although customers can clip and save ads they select). Companies also cannot depend on newspapers for color reproduction as good as that in most magazines.

National advertising campaigns rarely include this medium except in conjunction with local distributors of their products. In these instances, both parties often share the advertising costs using a cooperative advertising program, which is described later in this chapter. Another exception is the use of newspapers such as *The Wall Street Journal* and *USA Today*, both of which have national distribution of more than 2 million readers.

Several important trends are influencing newspapers today. First is the dramatic decline in circulation and advertising revenue. Of the 25 largest newspapers in 1990, 21 have declined. The result has been that many papers such as Denver's *Rocky Mountain News* and the Minneapolis *StarTribune* have closed or declared bankruptcy. Other newspapers, such as the *Christian Science Monitor*, have discontinued daily editions and moved to a once-each-week model. Only the *Arizona Republic* is growing, primarily due to population growth and a focus on its Sunday edition, which accounts for most of the advertising revenue. The second trend is the growth in online newspapers. Today, hundreds of newspapers including *The Wall Street Journal*, *The New York Times*, *Chicago Tribune*, and *Washington Post* offer online versions of the print newspaper. Research by the Newspaper Association of America indicates that 71 million people visit newspaper Web sites each month and they spend an average of 5.6 minutes on the sites each time they visit. A final trend is the growth in new types of news organizations such as the *Huffington Post*, covering entertainment, media, living, business, and politics, and *Politico*, designed exclusively for the 24-hour political news consumer. Both sites have more than 5 million visitors each month!

trustworthy 可信赖的，值得信赖的，可靠的；inspirational 给予灵感的，带有灵感的。

Yellow pages have many advantages including a long life span.

Yellow Pages Yellow pages represent an advertising media alternative comparable to radio and magazines in terms of expenditures—about $15 billion in the United States and $25 billion globally. According to the Yellow Pages Association, consumers turn to print yellow pages more than 13 billion times annually and online yellow pages an additional 3.8 billion times per year. One reason for this high level of use is that the 6,500 yellow pages directories reach almost all households with telephones. Yellow pages are a directional medium because they help consumers know where purchases can be made after other media have created awareness and demand.

The yellow pages face several disadvantages today. First is the proliferation of directories. AT&T (Real Yellow Pages), Idearc (Verizon Superpages), and R.H. Donnelley (DEX) now produce competing directories for many cities, neighborhoods, and ethnic groups. Second, relative to other advertising options, the yellow pages have limited accountability and ROI metrics. National advertisers, which represent $2.3 billion of the $15 billion industry, believe that yellow pages need to improve audience measurement research and circulation audition practices. Finally, many yellow pages customers are migrating to the Web. For many businesses, pay-per-click search ads on Google and Yahoo! are viewed as less expensive and more effective.

Internet The Internet represents a relatively new medium for advertisers although it has already attracted a wide variety of industries. Online advertising is similar to print advertising in that it offers a visual message. It has additional advantages, however, because it can also use the audio and video capabilities of the Internet. Sound and movement may simply attract more attention from viewers, or they may provide an element of entertainment to the message. Online advertising also has the unique feature of being interactive. Called *rich media*, these interactive ads have drop-down menus, built-in games, or search engines to engage viewers. Although online advertising is relatively small compared to other traditional media, it offers an opportunity to reach younger consumers who have developed a preference for online communication.

There are a variety of online advertising options. The most popular options are paid search, display (banner) ads, classified ads, and video. Paid search is one of the fastest-growing forms of Internet advertising, as approximately 80 percent of all Internet traffic begins at a search engine such as Google or Yahoo! (see Figure 14–4). *Advertising Age* magazine estimates that consumers conduct 11.8 billion

FIGURE 14–4
Google and Yahoo! have the largest shares of Internet searches and offer opportunities for online advertising.

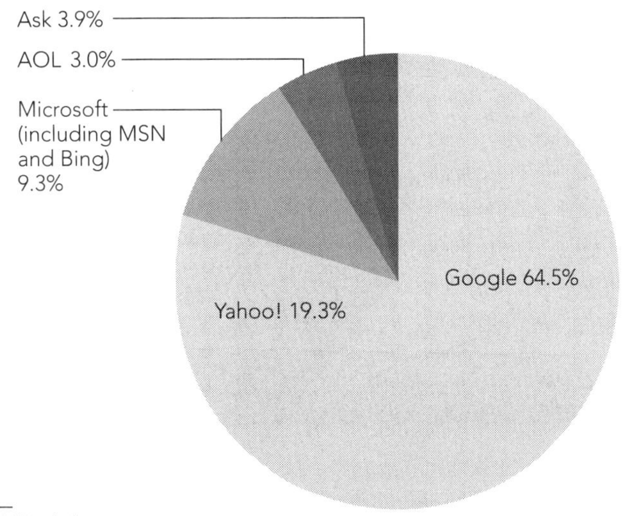

globally 全球的，全世界的；accountability 责任，义务。

DoubleClick's Dart Search service can provide an assessment of the effectiveness of a Web site.

searches each year. Now search engine agencies help firms add tags, wikis, and RSS to the content of a site to increase search rankings. Firms such as DoubleClick provide assessment of the effectiveness of a Web site. While the use of banner ads is growing also, there is some concern that consumers are developing "banner blindness" because the click-through rate has been declining to its current level of 0.1 percent. Classified ads, such as those on CraigsList, and video ads also contribute to the growth of online advertising by providing many of the advantages and characteristics of other media such as yellow pages, magazines, newspaper, and television.

One disadvantage of online advertising is that because the medium is relatively new, technical and administrative standards for the various formats are still evolving. This situation makes it difficult for advertisers to run national online campaigns across multiple sites. The Interactive Advertising Bureau provides "Standards, Guidelines & Best Practices" and creative guidelines to facilitate the use and growth of online advertising. Another disadvantage to online advertising is the difficulty of measuring impact. Several companies are testing methods of tracking where viewers go on their computer in the days and weeks after seeing an ad. Nielsen's online rating service, for example, measures actual Internet use through meters installed on the computers of 200,000 individuals in 10 countries. Measuring the relationship between online and offline behavior is also important. Recent research by ComScore, which studied 139 online ad campaigns, revealed that online ads didn't always result in a "click," but they increased the likelihood of a purchase by 17 percent and they increased visits to the advertiser's Web site by 40 percent. The Making Responsible Decisions box describes how click fraud is increasing the necessity of assessing online advertising effectiveness.

Outdoor A very effective medium for reminding consumers about your product is outdoor advertising, such as the scoreboard at San Diego's Qualcomm Stadium. The most common form of outdoor advertising, called *billboards*, often results in good reach and frequency and has been shown to increase purchase rates. The visibility of this medium is good supplemental reinforcement for well-known products, and it is a relatively low-cost, flexible alternative. A company can buy space just in the desired geographical market. A disadvantage to billboards, however, is that no opportunity exists for lengthy advertising copy. Also, a good billboard site depends on traffic patterns and sight lines.

Outdoor advertising can be an effective medium for reminding consumers about a product.

If you have ever lived in a metropolitan area, chances are you might have seen another form of outdoor advertising, *transit advertising*. This medium includes messages on the interior and exterior of buses, subway and light-rail cars, and taxis. As the use of mass transit grows, transit advertising may become increasingly important. Selectivity is available to advertisers, who can buy space by neighborhood or bus route. One disadvantage to this medium is that the heavy travel times, when the audiences are the largest, are not conducive to reading advertising copy. People are standing shoulder to shoulder on the subway, hoping not to miss their stop, and little attention is paid to the advertising.

The outdoor advertising industry has experienced a growth surge recently. According to the Outdoor Advertising Association of America, outdoor advertising expenditures have grown to $7 billion annually. Much of the growth is the result of creative forms of outdoor

---

administrative 管理的，行政的；metropolitan 大都会的，大都市的；transit advertising 交通广告。

Making Responsible Decisions ethics

Who Is Responsible for Click Fraud?

Spending on Internet advertising is expected to reach $36 billion in 2011 as many advertisers shift their budgets from print and TV to the Internet. For most advertisers one advantage of online advertising is that they pay only when someone clicks on their ad. Unfortunately, the growth of the medium has led to "click fraud," which is the deceptive clicking of ads solely to increase the amount advertisers must pay. There are several forms of click fraud. One method is the result of Paid-to-Read (PTR) Web sites that recruit and pay members to simply click on ads. Another method is the result of "clickbots," which are software programs that produce automatic clicks on ads. While the activity is difficult to detect and stop, experts estimate that up to 17 percent of clicks may be the result of fraud, and may be costing advertisers as much as $500 million each year!

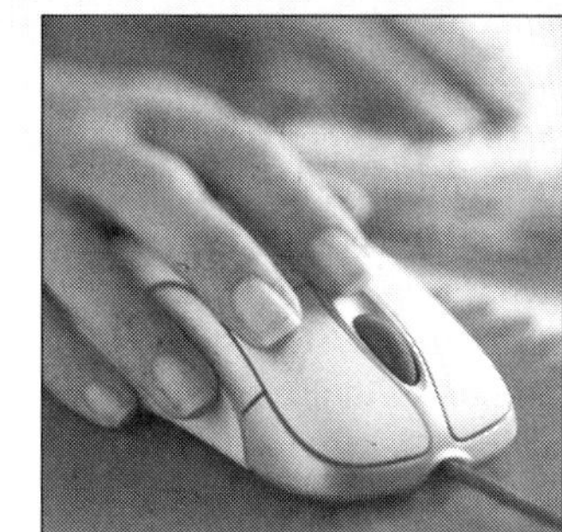

Two of the largest portals for Internet advertising are Google and Yahoo! Both firms try to filter out illegitimate clicks, although some advertisers claim that they are still being charged for PTR and clickbot traffic. Although the laws that may govern click fraud are not very clear, Google and Yahoo! have each settled class action lawsuits and agreed to provide rebates or credits to advertisers who were charged for fraudulent clicks.

Investigations of the online advertising industry have discovered a related form of click fraud that occurs when legitimate Web site visitors click on ads without any intention of looking at the site. As one consumer explains, "I always try and remember to click on the ad banners once in a while to try and keep the sites free." Stephen Dubner calls this "webtipping"!

As the Internet advertising industry grows it will become increasingly important to resolve the issue of click fraud. Consumers, advertisers, Web sites that carry paid advertising, and the large Web portals are all involved in a complicated technical, legal, and social situation. Who do you think is responsible for click fraud? Who should lead the way in the effort to find a solution?

---

advertising and the conversion to digital billboards that allow advertisers to change their ad messages quickly and efficiently. In Toledo, Ohio, for example, the newspaper used digital billboards to display the day's headlines. Similarly, television stations now use the technology to advertise the stories that will be covered on the evening news. Digital billboards can also provide a public service by displaying Amber alerts and weather reports. A recent study found that many commuters think that digital billboards are attractive and that they make the commute more interesting. While these trends have been positive, the outdoor advertising industry also faces important environmental concerns that must be addressed through self-regulation or be restricted by legislation. For example, several states have banned billboards, and the Los Angeles City Council is considering a comprehensive billboard policy that may restrict or ban building graphics and digital billboards.

Out-of-home advertising is also becoming interactive.

Other Media As traditional media have become more expensive and cluttered, advertisers have been attracted to a variety of nontraditional advertising options called out-of-home advertising, or *place-based media*. Messages are placed in locations that attract a specific target audience such as airports, doctors' offices, health clubs, theaters (where ads are played on the screen before the movies are shown), grocery stores, even bathrooms of bars, restaurants, and nightclubs. Soon there will be advertising on video screens on gas pumps, ATMs, and

---

placebased media 基于地点的媒体。

in elevators, and increasingly it will be interactive. The $2.5 billion industry has attracted advertisers such as AT&T and JCPenney, which use in-store campaigns, and Geico, Sprint, and FedEx, which use out-of-home advertising to reach mobile professionals in health clubs, airports, and hotels. Research suggests that creative use of out-of-home advertising, such as preshow theater ads, enhances consumer recall of the ads.

Selection Criteria Choosing between these alternative media is difficult and depends on several factors. First, knowing the media habits of the target audience is essential to deciding among the alternatives. Second, occasionally product attributes necessitate that certain media be used. For example, if color is a major aspect of product appeal, radio is excluded. Newspapers allow advertising for quick actions to confront competitors, and magazines are more appropriate for complicated messages because the reader can spend more time reading the message. The final factor in selecting a medium is cost. When possible, alternative media are compared using a common denominator that reflects both reach and cost—a measure such as CPM.

确定广告进度
Scheduling the Advertising

There is no correct schedule to advertise a product, but three factors must be considered. First is the issue of *buyer turnover*, which is how often new buyers enter the market to buy the product. The higher the buyer turnover, the greater is the amount of advertising required. A second issue in scheduling is the *purchase frequency*; the more frequently the product is purchased, the less repetition is required. Finally, companies must consider the *forgetting rate*, the speed with which buyers forget the brand if advertising is not seen.

确定广告进度表要求必须理解市场行为如何运作。大多数公司趋向于按照以下三个基本方法之一来确定：

1. 持续式（稳定式）进度。当季节因素影响不大时，广告可以在一年内按照一个持续的或稳定的进度来投放。
2. 跳跃式（间歇式）进度。根据季节性需求来安排广告进度，即存在广告期间和非广告期间。
3. 脉冲式（冲刺式）进度。在需求增长、密集促销或是新产品导入时，将时段式进度与持续式进度结合使用。

Setting schedules requires an understanding of how the market behaves. Most companies tend to follow one of three basic approaches:

1. *Continuous (steady) schedule.* When seasonal factors are unimportant, advertising is run at a continuous or steady schedule throughout the year.
2. *Flighting (intermittent) schedule.* Periods of advertising are scheduled between periods of no advertising to reflect seasonal demand.
3. *Pulse (burst) schedule.* A flighting schedule is combined with a continuous schedule because of increases in demand, heavy periods of promotion, or introduction of a new product.

For example, products such as breakfast cereals have a stable demand throughout the year and would typically use a continuous schedule of advertising. In contrast, products such as snow skis and suntan lotions have seasonal demands and receive flighting-schedule advertising during the seasonal demand period. Some products such as toys or automobiles require pulse-schedule advertising to facilitate sales throughout the year and during special periods of increased demand (such as holidays or new car introductions). Some evidence suggests that pulsing schedules are superior to other advertising strategies. In addition, research indicates the effectiveness of a particular ad wears out quickly and, therefore, many alternative forms of a commercial may be more effective.

learning review

5. You see the same ad in *Time* and *Fortune* magazines and on billboards and TV. Is this an example of reach or frequency?
6. Why has the Internet become a popular advertising medium?
7. What factors must be considered when choosing among alternative media?

continuous (steady) schedule 持续式（稳定式）进度；flighting (intermittent) schedule 跳跃式（间歇式）进度；pulse (burst) schedule 脉冲式（冲刺式）进度。

执行广告方案
EXECUTING THE ADVERTISING PROGRAM

Executing the advertising program involves pretesting the advertising copy and actually carrying out the advertising program. John Wanamaker, the founder of Wanamaker's Department Store in Philadelphia, remarked, "I know half my advertising is wasted, but I don't know what half." By evaluating advertising efforts, marketers can try to ensure that their advertising expenditures are not wasted. Evaluation is done usually at two separate times: before and after the advertisements are run in the actual campaign. Several methods used in the evaluation process at the stages of idea formulation and copy development are discussed below.

预先测试广告
Pretesting the Advertising

To determine whether the advertisement communicates the intended message or to select among alternative versions of the advertisement, **pretests** are conducted before the advertisements are placed in any medium.

Portfolio Tests Portfolio tests are used to test copy alternatives. The test ad is placed in a portfolio with several other ads and stories, and consumers are asked to read through the portfolio. Afterward, subjects are asked for their impressions of the ads on several evaluative scales, such as from "very informative" to "not very informative."

Jury Tesets Jury tests involve showing the ad copy to a panel of consumers and having them rate how they liked it, how much it drew their attention, and how attractive they thought it was. This approach is similar to the portfolio test in that consumer reactions are obtained. However, unlike the portfolio test, a test advertisement is not hidden within other ads.

Theater Tests Theater testing is the most sophisticated form of pretesting. Consumers are invited to view new television shows or movies in which test commercials are also shown. Viewers register their feelings about the advertisements either on handheld electronic recording devices used during the viewing or on questionnaires afterward.

执行广告方案
Carrying Out the Advertising Program

The responsibility for actually carrying out the advertising program can be handled in one of three ways, as shown in Figure 14–5. The **full-service agency** provides

FIGURE 14–5
Alternative structures of advertising agencies used to carry out the advertising program

TYPE OF AGENCY	SERVICES PROVIDED
Full-service agency	Does research, selects media, develops copy, and produces artwork; also coordinates integrated campaigns with all marketing efforts
Limited-service (specialty) agency	Specializes in one aspect of creative process; usually provides creative production work; buys previously unpurchased media space
In-house agency	Provides range of services, depending on company needs

pretest 事前测试；full-service agency 全面服务代理机构。

the most complete range of services, including market research, media selection, copy development, artwork, and production. In the past, agencies that assisted a client by both developing and placing advertisements often charged a commission of 15 percent of the media costs. As corporations introduced integrated marketing approaches, however, many advertisers switched from paying commissions to incentive plans based on performance. These plans typically pay for agency costs and a 5 to 10 percent profit, plus bonuses if specific performance goals are met. The Association of National Advertisers estimates that almost half of all agency clients currently use this approach. Anheuser-Busch recently introduced a new version of this approach when it announced it would begin to compensate agencies for their costs based on rigid scope-of-work agreements. Vice President of Marketing Keith Levy explains, "We want partner agencies really tied to the strategy of the brand." In the future, many clients may move to a value-based approach where compensation is dependent on sales of the advertised product or brand. This approach will add additional emphasis on agency contributions beyond advertising. In some instances, such as specialized direct-response agencies, compensation is already a percentage of revenue generated.

Limited-service agencies specialize in one aspect of the advertising process such as providing creative services to develop the advertising copy, buying previously unpurchased media (media agencies), or providing Internet services (Internet agencies). Limited-service agencies that deal in creative work are compensated by a contractual agreement for the services performed. Finally, **in-house agencies** made up of the company's own advertising staff may provide full services or a limited range of services.

评估广告方案
ASSESSING THE ADVERTISING PROGRAM

The advertising decision process does not stop with executing the advertising program. The advertisements must be evaluated to determine whether they are achieving their intended objectives, and results may indicate that changes must be made in the advertising program.

Starch scores an advertisement using aided recall.

GfK Custom Research, ® Starch Advertising Research
Cosmopolitan Magazine-November 2007
eStarch Readership Report

Garnier Fructis Advertisement

Noted	85%	Read Most	30%
Associated	84%	Brand Disposition	85% (top three score)
Read Some	69%		

事后测试广告
Posttesting the Advertising

An advertisement may go through **posttests** after it has been shown to the target audience to determine whether it accomplished its intended purpose. Five approaches common in posttesting are discussed here.

Aided Recall After being shown an ad, respondents are asked whether their previous exposure to it was through reading, viewing, or listening. The Starch test shown in the accompanying photo uses aided recall to determine the percentage of those (1) who remember seeing a specific magazine ad (*noted*), (2) who saw or read any part of the ad identifying the product or brand (*seen-associated*), (3) who read any part of the ad's copy (read some), and (4) who read at least half of the ad (*read most*). Elements of the ad are then tagged with the results, as shown in the picture.

limited-service agencies 有限服务代理机构；in-house agencies 专属代理机构；posttests 事后测试。

Unaided Recall A question such as "What ads do you remember seeing yesterday?" is asked of respondents without any prompting to determine whether they saw or heard advertising messages.

Attitude Tests Respondents are asked questions to measure changes in their attitudes after an advertising campaign, such as whether they have a more favorable attitude toward the product advertised.

Inquiry Tests Additional product information, product samples, or premiums are offered to an ad's readers or viewers. Ads generating the most inquiries are presumed to be the most effective.

Sales Tests Sales tests involve studies such as controlled experiments (e.g., using radio ads in one market and newspaper ads in another and comparing the results) and consumer purchase tests (measuring retail sales that result from a given advertising campaign). The most sophisticated experimental methods today allow a manufacturer, a distributor, or an advertising agency to manipulate an advertising variable (such as schedule or copy) through cable systems and observe subsequent sales effects by monitoring data collected from checkout scanners in supermarkets.

做必要的调整
Making Needed Changes

Results of posttesting the advertising copy are used to reach decisions about changes in the advertising program. If the posttest results show that an advertisement is doing poorly in terms of awareness, cost efficiency, or sales it may be dropped and other ads run in its place in the future. On the other hand, sometimes an advertisement may be so successful it is run repeatedly or used as the basis of a larger advertising program.

learning review

8. Explain the difference between pretesting and posttesting advertising copy.
9. What is the difference between aided and unaided recall posttests?

销售促进
SALES PROMOTION

Sales promotion has become a key element of the promotional mix, which now accounts for more than $45.8 billion in annual expenditures. In a recent survey by *Promo* magazine, marketing professionals reported that approximately 32 percent of their budgets were allocated to advertising, 37 percent to consumer promotion, 24 percent to trade promotion, and 7 percent to other marketing activities. The allocation of marketing expenditures reflects the trend toward integrated promotion programs, which include a variety of promotion elements. Selection and integration of the many promotion techniques require a good understanding of the advantages and disadvantages of each kind of promotion.

消费者导向销售促进
Consumer-Oriented Sales Promotions

消费者导向销售促进，或简称为消费者促销，是直接面向最终消费者，用以支持公司广告和人员推销的销售工具。

Directed to ultimate consumers, **consumer-oriented sales promotions**, or simply *consumer promotions*, are sales tools used to support a company's advertising and personal selling. The alternative consumer-oriented sales promotion tools include

unaided 独立的；inquiry 询问；consumer-oriented sales promotions 消费者导向的销售促进。

coupons, deals, premiums, contests, sweepstakes, samples, loyalty programs, point-of-purchase displays, rebates, and product placement (see Figure 14–6).

Coupons Coupons are sales promotions that usually offer a discounted price to the consumer, which encourages trial. Approximately 302 billion coupons worth $386 billion are distributed in the United States each year. Most coupons are distributed as freestanding inserts in newspapers and reach 60 million households each week. Research indicates that 89 percent of consumers use coupons. For the first time in 16 years, coupon redemptions did not decline in 2008, as the weak economy increased the attractiveness of coupons. Consumers redeemed $2.8 billion of the coupons, which was approximately $8.57 per person. Companies that have increased their use of coupons include Procter & Gamble, Nestlé, and Kraft, while the top retailers for coupon redemption were Wal-Mart and Kroger. The number of coupons generated at Internet sites (e.g., www.valpak.com and www.coupon.com) and cell

FIGURE 14–6
Sales promotions can be used to achieve many objectives.

KIND OF SALES PROMOTION	OBJECTIVES	ADVANTAGES	DISADVANTAGES
Coupons	Stimulate demand	Encourage retailer support	Consumers delay purchases
Deals	Increase trial; retaliate against competitor's actions	Reduce consumer risk	Consumers delay purchases; reduce perceived product value
Premiums	Build goodwill	Consumers like free or reduced-price merchandise	Consumers buy for premium, not product
Contests	Increase consumer purchases; build business inventory	Encourage consumer involvement with product	Require creative or analytical thinking
Sweepstakes	Encourage present customers to buy more; minimize brand switching	Get customer to use product and store more often	Sales drop after sweepstakes
Samples	Encourage new product trial	Low risk for consumer	High cost for company
Loyalty programs	Encourage repeat purchases	Help create loyalty	High cost for company
Point-of-purchase displays	Increase product trial; provide in-store support for other promotions	Provide good product visibility	Hard to get retailer to allocate high-traffic space
Rebates	Encourage customers to purchase; stop sales decline	Effective at stimulating demand	Easily copied; steal sales from future; reduce perceived product value
Product placements	Introduce new products; demonstrate product use	Positive message in a noncommercial setting	Little control over presentation of product

coupon 优惠券。

Coupons encourage trial by offering a discounted price.

phones has been increasing although they account for only 0.4 percent of all coupons. Coupons are often viewed as a key element of an integrated marketing program. Cream of Wheat recently ran banner ads on women's, parenting, food, and home and garden Web sites with the message "Free Cream of Wheat Is Just a Click Away." The link took people to a free sample order form. When the sample arrived in the mail, the package also contained a $1 coupon.

Do coupons help increase sales? Studies suggest that market share does increase during the period immediately after coupons are distributed. There are also indications, however, that couponing can reduce gross revenues by lowering the price paid by already-loyal consumers. Therefore, the 9,000 manufacturers that currently use coupons are particularly interested in coupon programs directed at potential first-time buyers. One means of focusing on these potential buyers is through electronic in-store coupon machines that match coupons to your most recent purchases.

Coupons are often far more expensive than the face value of the coupon; a 25-cent coupon can cost three times that after paying for the advertisement to deliver it, dealer handling, clearinghouse costs, and redemption. In addition, misredemption, or attempting to redeem a counterfeit coupon or a valid coupon when the product was not purchased, should be added to the cost of the coupon. The Coupon Information Corporation estimates that companies pay out refunds of more than $300 million each year as a result of coupon fraud. Recent growth in coupon fraud has marketers considering adding holograms and visual aids to coupons to help cashiers identify valid coupons.

产品优惠是一种短期减价，通常用于增加潜在顾客的试用或作为对竞争对手行动的一种报复。

Deals Deals are short-term price reductions, commonly used to increase trial among potential customers or to retaliate against a competitor's actions. For example, if a rival manufacturer introduces a new cake mix, the company responds with a "two packages for the price of one" deal. This short-term price reduction builds up the stock on the kitchen shelves of cake mix buyers and makes the competitor's introduction more difficult.

赠品是针对消费者的一种常用促销工具，它包括免费提供产品或以远低于零售价的价格出售产品。近来的一种赠品形式叫做自付优惠，因为消费者承担的价格中包含了优惠品的成本。

Premiums A promotional tool often used with consumers is the premium, which consists of merchandise offered free or at a significant savings over its retail price. This latter type of premium is called self-liquidating because the cost charged to the consumer covers the cost of the item. McDonald's, for example, used a free premium in a promotional partnership with DreamWorks during the release of the movie *Monsters vs. Aliens*. Collectible toys that portrayed movie characters were given away free with the purchase of a Happy Meal. What are the most popular premiums? According to the Promotional Products Association International, the top premiums are apparel, writing instruments, shopping bags, cups and mugs, and desk accessories. By offering a premium, companies encourage customers to return frequently or to use more of the product. Research suggests that deal-prone consumers and value seekers are attracted to premiums.

Contests A fourth sales promotion in Figure 14–6, the contest, is where consumers apply their skill or analytical or creative thinking to try to win a prize. This form of promotion has been growing as requests for videos, photos, and essays are a good match with the trend toward consumer-generated content. For example, Doritos sponsored the "Crash the Super Bowl" contest, asking people to create their own 30-second ad about Doritos. A panel of judges selected five finalists from the 2,000 entries, and the public voted online for its favorite. The winner aired on the Super Bowl, and when the ad hit No. 1 on *USA Today*'s Super Bowl Ad Meter, it was awarded a $1 million bonus! If you like contests, you can enter online now at Web sites such as www.contests.about.com.

premiums 赠品；contest 竞赛。

Sweepstakes Sweepstakes are sales promotions that require participants to submit some kind of entry but are purely games of chance requiring no analytical or creative effort by the consumer. Popular sweepstakes include the HGTV "Dream Home Giveaway," which receives more than 40 million entries each year, and McDonald's Monopoly, which offers a grand prize of $1 million.

Two variations of sweepstakes are popular now. First is the sweepstakes that offers products that consumers value as prizes. Mars Snackfood, for example, created a sweepstakes where consumers enter a UPC code from Mars products such as M&Ms, Milky Way, Snickers, Skittles, and 3 Musketeers for a chance to win a $1,000 Visa gift card. Coca-Cola has a similar sweepstakes called "My Coke Rewards" that allows consumers to use codes from bottle caps to enter to win prizes or to collect points to be redeemed for rewards. The second is the sweepstakes that offers an "experience" as the prize. For example, one of television's most popular series, *American Idol*, and AT&T sponsor a sweepstakes for a chance to win a trip for two to the season finale of *American Idol* in Los Angeles. Similarly, KFC created a sweepstakes where consumers enter for a chance to win a trip to the Super Bowl. Federal laws, the Federal Trade Commission, and state legislatures have issued rules covering sweepstakes, contests, and games to regulate fairness, ensure that the chance for winning is represented honestly, and guarantee that the prizes are actually awarded. Several well-known sweepstakes created by Publishers Clearing House and *Reader's Digest* have paid fines and agreed to new sweepstakes guidelines in response to regulatory scrutiny.

另一种常用的消费者销售促进工具是样品，即免费提供产品或以极低价格出售产品。

Samples Another common consumer sales promotion is sampling, which is offering the product free or at a greatly reduced price. Often used for new products, sampling puts the product in the consumer's hands. A trial size is generally offered that is smaller than the regular package size. If consumers like the sample, it is hoped they will remember and buy the product. When Mars changed its Milky Way Dark to Milky Way Midnight, it gave away more than 1 million samples to college students at nightclubs, several hundred campuses, and popular spring break locations. Awareness of the candy bar rose to 60 percent, trial rose 166 percent, and sales rose 25 percent. Recent research indicates that 63 percent of college students who receive a sample will also purchase the product. Overall, companies invest more than $2.3 billion in sampling programs each year.

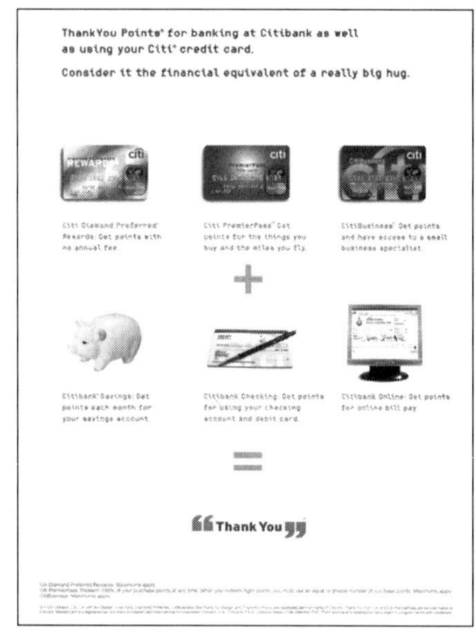

The Nestlé Crunch sweepstakes attract prospective customers while the Citi loyalty program rewards use of Citibank credit cards.

Nestlé
www.nestle.com

Citibank
www.citibank.com

legislatures 立法机关，立法团体；nightclub 夜总会。

Loyalty Programs Loyalty programs are a sales promotion tool used to encourage and reward repeat purchases by acknowledging each purchase made by a consumer and offering a premium as purchases accumulate. The most popular loyalty programs today are credit card reward programs. More than 75 percent of all cards offer incentives for use of their card. Citibank, for example, offers "Thank You" points for using Citi credit or debit cards. The points can be redeemed for books, music, gift cards, cash, travel, and special limited time rewards. Airlines, retailers, hotels, and grocery stores also offer popular loyalty programs. Some of the newest programs recently introduced have been by car rental and cruise line companies. There are now more than 1.8 billion loyalty program memberships, for an average of 14 for each household in the United States.

The trend in loyalty programs today is to customize the rewards and benefits for different segments of program members. This approach leads to promotions targeted at new members, members with unique purchase histories, or members who have self-selected into "elite" status groups. American Airlines, for example, has offered bonus points for new members, an additional 50 percent of award points for members who fly first class, and special benefits for members who join the American Airlines Admirals Club.

Point-of-Purchase Displays In a store aisle, you often encounter a sales promotion called a point-of-purchase display. These product displays take the form of advertising signs, which sometimes actually hold or display the product, and are often located in high-traffic areas near the cash register or the end of an aisle. The point-of-purchase display for Nabisco's annual back-to-school program is designed to maximize the consumer's attention to lunch box and after-school snacks, and to provide storage for the products. Annual expenditures on point-of-purchase promotions now exceed $20.3 billion and are expected to grow as point-of-purchase becomes integrated with all forms of promotion.

Point-of-purchase displays help increase consumers' attention in a store.

Some studies estimate that one-third of a consumer's buying decisions are made in the store. Grocery product manufacturers want to get their message to you at the instant you are next to their brand in your supermarket aisle, perhaps through a point-of-purchase display. At a growing number of supermarkets this may be done with digital signage. Walmart, for example, is replacing its satellite-based in-store TV network with an Internet protocol system called Walmart Smart Network, which allows eye-level screens that display short advertising clips. The advantage of these methods of promotion is that they do not rely on the consumers' ability to remember the message for long periods. Other in-store promotions such as interactive kiosks are also becoming popular.

Rebates Another consumer sales promotion in Figure 14–6, the cash rebate, offers the return of money based on proof of purchase. For example, Apple recently offered a $100 rebate to consumers who purchased an Apple computer and a printer during a three-month promotion period.

When a rebate is offered on lower-priced items, the time and trouble of mailing in a proof of purchase to get the rebate check often means that many buyers never take advantage of it. However, this "slippage" is less likely to occur with frequent users of rebate promotions. In addition, online consumers are more likely to take advantage of rebates.

最后一种消费者促销工具是**植入式广告**，是指将某一品牌产品安插在电影、电视节目、录像或其他产品的广告中。

Product Placements A final consumer promotion, **product placements**, involve the use of a brand-name product in a movie, television show, video game, or commercial for another product. It was Steven Spielberg's placement of Hershey's

point-of-purchase displays 销售点展示；product placement 植入式广告。

Can you identify these product placements?

Reese's Pieces in *E.T.* that first brought a lot of interest to the candy. Similarly, when Tom Cruise wore Bausch and Lomb's Ray-Ban sunglasses in *Risky Business* and its Aviator glasses in *Top Gun*, sales skyrocketed from 100,000 pairs to 7,000,000 pairs in five years. After *Toy Story*, Etch-A-Sketch sales increased 4,500 percent and Mr. Potato Head sales increased 800 percent.

More recently, you might remember seeing the American Express Black Card, Ray-Ban sunglasses, and Spalding basketballs in *17 Again*, Yamaha electronic equipment in *Monsters vs. Aliens*, or Sony televisions and Pepsi in *Watchmen*. Product placement has also grown in television programs. *The Biggest Loser* ranks No. 1 in product placements with Zip-Lock baggies, Extra gum, Macy's department store, *Prevention* magazine, and many other products making appearances. Companies are usually eager to gain exposure for their products, and studios believe that product placements add authenticity to the film or program. The producers usually receive fees in exchange for the exposure. Coca-Cola, for example, reportedly pays $26 million for its placement on the television hit *American Idol*. The Federal Communications Commission is currently writing guidelines for TV product placements and how they should be disclosed.

A variation of this form of promotion, called *reverse product placement*, brings fictional products to the marketplace. Bertie Bott's Every Flavor Beans, for example, began as an imaginary brand in Harry Potter books. Similarly, the movie *Forrest Gump* led to the Bubba Gump Shrimp Company restaurant chain. Finally, 7-Eleven converted 12 of its stores into Kwik-E-Marts, the imaginary convenience stores in the television cartoon series, *The Simpsons*, to coincide with the release of *The Simpsons Movie*.

贸易导向销售促进
Trade-Oriented Sales Promotions

贸易导向销售促进，或简称为贸易促销，是直接面向批发商、零售商或分销商的一种销售工具，用以支持公司的广告和人员推销。

Trade-oriented sales promotions, or simply *trade promotions*, are sales tools used to support a company's advertising and personal selling directed to wholesalers, retailers, or distributors. Some of the sales promotions just reviewed are used for this purpose, but three other common approaches are targeted uniquely to these intermediaries: (1) allowances and discounts, (2) cooperative advertising, and (3) training of distributors' salesforces.

Allowances and Discounts

Trade promotions often focus on maintaining or increasing inventory levels in the channel of distribution. An effective method for encouraging such increased purchases by intermediaries is the use of allowances and discounts. However, overuse of these price reductions can lead to retailers changing their ordering patterns in the expectation of such offerings. Although there are many variations that manufacturers can use with discounts and allowances, three common approaches are the merchandise allowance, the case allowance, and the finance allowance.

Reimbursing a retailer for extra in-store support or special featuring of the brand is a *merchandise allowance*. Performance contracts between the manufacturer and

reverse product placement 反植入；trade promotions 贸易促销；merchandise allowance 商品折让。

trade member usually specify the activity to be performed, such as a picture of the product in a newspaper with a coupon good at only one store. The merchandise allowance then consists of a percentage deduction from the list case price ordered during the promotional period. Allowances are not paid by the manufacturer until it sees proof of performance (such as a copy of the ad placed by the retailer in the local newspaper).

A second common trade promotion, a *case allowance*, is a discount on each case ordered during a specific time period. These allowances are usually deducted from the invoice. A variation of the case allowance is the "free goods" approach, whereby retailers receive some amount of the product free based on the amount ordered, such as 1 case free for every 10 cases ordered.

A final trade promotion, the *finance allowance*, involves paying retailers for financing costs or financial losses associated with consumer sales promotions. This trade promotion is regularly used and has several variations. One type is the floor stock protection program—manufacturers give retailers a case allowance price for products in their warehouse, which prevents shelf stock from running down during the promotional period. Also common are freight allowances, which compensate retailers that transport orders from the manufacturer's warehouse.

转销商通常在推动制造商产品在当地的销售水平发挥着重要作用。一种常用的销售促进活动是通过**联合广告**，鼓励转销商提高在当地广告宣传的质量和数量。

Cooperative Advertising Resellers often perform the important function of promoting the manufacturer's products at the local level. One common sales promotional activity is to encourage both better quality and greater quantity in the local advertising efforts of resellers through **cooperative advertising**. These are programs by which a manufacturer pays a percentage of the retailer's local advertising expense for advertising the manufacturer's products.

Usually, the manufacturer pays a percentage, often 50 percent, of the cost of advertising up to a certain dollar limit, which is based on the amount of the purchases the retailer makes of the manufacturer's products. In addition to paying for the advertising, the manufacturer often furnishes the retailer with a selection of different ad executions, sometimes suited for several different media. A manufacturer may provide, for example, several different print layouts as well as a few broadcast ads for the retailer to adapt and use.

Training of Distributors' Salesforces One of the many functions the intermediaries perform is customer contact and selling for the producers they represent. Both retailers and wholesalers employ and manage their own sales personnel. A manufacturer's success often rests on the ability of the reseller's salesforce to represent its products.

Thus, it is in the best interest of the manufacturer to help train the reseller's salesforce. Because the reseller's salesforce is often less sophisticated and knowledgeable about the products than the manufacturer might like, training can increase their sales performance. Training activities include producing manuals and brochures to educate the reseller's salesforce. The salesforce then uses these aids in selling situations. Other activities include national sales meetings sponsored by the manufacturer and field visits to the reseller's location to inform and motivate the salesperson to sell the products. Manufacturers also develop incentive and recognition programs to motivate reseller's salespeople to sell their products.

learning review

10. What's the difference between a coupon and a deal?
11. Which sales promotional tool is most common for new products?
12. Which trade promotion is used on an ongoing basis?

case allowance 项目折让；finance allowance 财务折让；cooperative advertising 联合广告。

公共关系
PUBLIC RELATIONS

LO5

As noted in Chapter 13, public relations is a form of communication management that seeks to influence the image of an organization and its products and services. Public relations efforts may utilize a variety of tools and may be directed at many distinct audiences. While public relations personnel usually focus on communicating positive aspects of the business, they may also be called on to minimize the negative impact of a problem or crisis. Nestlé, PepsiCo, and Coca-Cola, for example, have been facing substantial negative publicity about the environmental impact of the plastic bottles used for their Nestlé Waters, Aquafina, and Dasani brands. Newspapers, blogs, the general public, and even New York and San Francisco mayors have expressed concerns that the companies' public relations departments must address. The most frequently used public relations tool is publicity.

公共宣传工具
Publicity Tools

In developing a public relations campaign, several methods of obtaining nonpersonal presentation of an organization, good, or service without direct cost—**publicity tools**—are available to the public relations director. Many companies frequently use the *news release*, consisting of an announcement regarding changes in the company or the product line. The objective of a news release is to inform a newspaper, radio station, or other medium of an idea for a story.

A second common publicity tool is the *news conference*. Representatives of the media are all invited to an informational meeting, and advance materials regarding the content are sent. This tool is often used when new products are introduced or significant changes in corporate structure and leadership are being made.

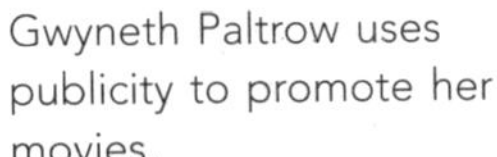
Gwyneth Paltrow uses publicity to promote her movies.

Nonprofit organizations rely heavily on *public service announcements* (PSAs), which are free space or time donated by the media. For example, the charter of the American Red Cross prohibits any local chapter from advertising, so to solicit blood donations local chapters often depend on PSAs on radio or television to announce their needs.

Finally, today many high-visibility individuals are used as publicity tools to create visibility for their companies, their products, and themselves. Richard Branson uses visibility to promote the Virgin Group, Gwyneth Paltrow uses it to promote her movies, and U.S. senators use it to promote themselves as political candidates. These publicity efforts are coordinated with news releases, conferences, advertising, donations to charities, volunteer activities, endorsements, and any other activities that may have an impact on public perceptions.

增加促销价值
INCREASING THE VALUE OF PROMOTION

Today's customers seek value from companies that provide leading-edge products, hassle-free transactions at competitive prices, and customer intimacy. Promotion practices have changed dramatically to improve transactions and increase customer intimacy by (1) emphasizing long-term relationships and (2) increasing self-regulation.

publicity tools 公共宣传工具；news release 新闻发布会；news conference 记者招待会；public service announcements 公益广告。

在促销中建立长期关系
Building Long-Term Relationships with Promotion

促销可以提高对目标市场个人偏好的掌握能力，可以推动与顾客进行有价值有趣味的沟通，进而有助于塑造品牌形象和顾客忠诚。

Many changes in promotional techniques have been driven by marketers' interest in developing long-term relationships with their customers. Promotion can contribute to brand and store loyalty by improving its ability to target individual preferences and by engaging customers in valuable and entertaining communication. New media such as the Internet and mobile telephones have provided immediate opportunities for personalized promotion activities such as e-mail advertising. In addition, technological developments have helped traditional media such as TV and radio focus on individual preferences through services such as TiVo and Sirius XM Satellite Radio. Although the future holds extraordinary promise for the personalization of promotion, the industry will need to manage and balance consumers' concerns about privacy as it proceeds.

Changes that help engage consumers have also been numerous. Marketers have attempted to utilize interactive technologies and to integrate new media and technologies into the overall creative process. Ad agencies are increasingly integrating public relations, direct marketing, advertising, and promotion into comprehensive campaigns. In fact, some experts predict that advertising agencies will soon become "communications consulting firms." Further, increasingly diverse and global audiences necessitate multimedia approaches and sensitivity communication techniques that engage the varied groups. Overall, companies hope that these changes will build customer relationships for the long term—emphasizing a lifetime of purchases rather than a single transaction.

自我调节
Self-Regulation

Unfortunately, over the years many consumers have been misled, or even deceived, by some promotions. Examples include sweepstakes in which the gifts were not awarded, rebate offers that were a terrible hassle, and advertisements whose promises were great, until the buyer read the small print. In one of the worst scandals in promotion history, McDonald's assisted an FBI investigation of the firm responsible for the fast-food chain's sweepstakes, because the promotion agency security director was suspected of stealing winning game pieces.

Promotions targeted at special groups such as children and the elderly also raise ethical concerns. For example, providing free samples to children in elementary schools or linking product lines to TV programs and movies have led to questions about the need for restrictions on promotions. Although the Federal Trade Commission does provide some guidelines to protect consumers and special groups from misleading promotions, some observers believe more government regulation is needed.

To rely on formal regulation by federal, state, and local governments of all promotional activities would be very expensive. As a result, there are increasing efforts by advertising agencies, trade associations, and marketing organizations at *self-regulation*. By imposing standards that reflect the values of society on their promotional activities, marketers can (1) facilitate the development of new promotional methods, (2) minimize regulatory constraints and restrictions, and (3) help consumers gain confidence in the communication efforts used to influence their purchases. As organizations strive for effective self-regulation, marketing executives will need to make sound ethical judgments about the use of existing and new promotional practices.

learning review

13. What is a news release?
14. What is the difference between government regulation and self-regulation?

self-regulation 自我调节；restrictions 限制，约束。

LEARNING OBJECTIVES REVIEW

LO1 *Explain the differences between product advertising and institutional advertising and the variations within each type.*
Product advertisements focus on selling a good or service and take three forms: Pioneering advertisements tell people what a product is, what it can do, and where it can be found; competitive advertisements persuade the target market to select the firm's brand rather than a competitor's; and reminder advertisements reinforce previous knowledge of a product. Institutional advertisements are used to build goodwill or an image for an organization. They include advocacy advertisements, which state the position of a company on an issue, and pioneering, competitive, and reminder advertisements, which are similar to the product ads but focused on the institution.

LO2 *Describe the steps used to develop, execute, and evaluate an advertising program.*
The promotion decision process can be applied to each of the promotional elements. The steps to develop an advertising program include identify the target audience, specify the advertising objectives, set the advertising budget, design the advertisement, create the message, select the media, and schedule the advertising. Executing the program requires pretesting, and evaluating the program requires posttesting.

LO3 *Explain the advantages and disadvantages of alternative advertising media.*
Television advertising reaches large audiences and uses picture, print, sound, and motion; its disadvantages, however, are that it is expensive and perishable. Radio advertising is inexpensive and can be placed quickly, but it has no visual element and is perishable. Magazine advertising can target specific audiences and can convey complex information, but it takes a long time to place the ad and is relatively expensive. Newspapers provide excellent coverage of local markets and can be changed quickly, but they have a short life span and poor color. Yellow pages advertising has a long use period and is available 24 hours per day; its disadvantages, however, are that there is a proliferation of directories and they cannot be updated frequently. Internet advertising can be interactive, but its effectiveness is difficult to measure. Outdoor advertising provides repeat exposures, but its message must be very short and simple. Direct mail can be targeted at very selective audiences, but its cost per contact is high.

LO4 *Discuss the strengths and weaknesses of consumer-oriented and trade-oriented sales promotions.*
Coupons encourage retailer support but may delay consumer purchases. Deals reduce consumer risk but reduce perceived value. Premiums offer consumers additional merchandise they want, but they may be purchasing only for the premium. Contests create involvement but require creative thinking. Sweepstakes encourage repeat purchases, but sales drop after the sweepstakes. Samples encourage product trial but are expensive. Loyalty programs help create loyalty but are expensive to run. Displays provide visibility but are difficult to place in retail space. Rebates stimulate demand but are easily copied. Product placement provides a positive message in a noncommercial setting but is difficult to control. Trade-oriented sales promotions include (*a*) allowances and discounts, which increase purchases but may change retailer ordering patterns, (*b*) cooperative advertising, which encourages local advertising, and (*c*) salesforce training, which helps increase sales by providing the salespeople with product information and selling skills.

LO5 *Recognize public relations as an important form of communication.*
Public relations activities usually focus on communicating positive aspects of the business. A frequently used public relations tool is publicity. Publicity tools include new releases and news conferences. Nonprofit organization often use public service announcements.

FOCUSING ON KEY TERMS

advertising
consumer-oriented sales promotions
cooperative advertising
cost per thousand
frequency
full-service agency
gross rating points
infomercials
in-house agencies
institutional advertisements
limited-service agencies
posttests
pretests
product advertisements
product placements
publicity tools
rating
reach
trade-oriented sales promotions

APPLYING MARKETING KNOWLEDGE

1 How does competitive product advertising differ from competitive institutional advertising?
2 Suppose you are the advertising manager for a new line of children's fragrances. Which form of media would you use for this new product?
3 You have recently been promoted to be director of advertising for the Timkin Tool Company. In your first meeting with Mr. Timkin, he says, "Advertising is a waste! We've been advertising for six months now and sales haven't increased. Tell me why we should continue." Give your answer to Mr. Timkin.
4 A large life insurance company has decided to switch from using a strong fear appeal to a humorous approach. What are the strengths and weaknesses of such a change in message strategy?
5 Which medium has the lowest cost per thousand?
6 Some national advertisers have found that they can have more impact with their advertising by running a

Medium	Cost	Audience
TV show	$5,000	25,000
Magazine	2,200	6,000
Newspaper	4,800	7,200
FM radio	420	1,600

large number of ads for a period and then running no ads at all for a period. Why might such a flighting schedule be more effective than a continuous schedule?

7 Each year managers at Bausch and Lomb evaluate the many advertising media alternatives available to them as they develop their advertising program for contact lenses. What advantages and disadvantages of each alternative should they consider? Which media would you recommend to them?

8 What are two advantages and two disadvantages of the advertising posttests described in the chapter?

9 Federated Banks is interested in consumer-oriented sales promotions that would encourage senior citizens to direct deposit their Social Security checks with the bank. Evaluate the sales promotion options, and recommend two of them to the bank.

10 How can public relations be used by Firestone and Ford following investigations into complaints about tire failures?

11 Describe a self-regulation guideline you believe would improve the value of (*a*) an existing form of promotion and (*b*) a new promotional practice.

building your marketing plan

To augment your promotion strategy from Chapter 13:

1 Use Figure 14–3 to select the advertising media you will include in your plan by analyzing how combinations of media (e.g., television and Internet advertising, radio and yellow pages advertising) can complement each other.

2 Use Figure 14–6 to select your consumer-oriented sales promotion activities.

3 Specify which trade-oriented sales promotions and public relations tools you will use.

video case 14 Google, Inc.: The Right Ads at the Right Time

"So what we did, in essence, is we said advertising should be useful to a consumer just as much as the organic search results, and we don't want people just to buy advertising and be able to show an ad if it's irrelevant to the consumer's need," says Richard Holden, director of product management at Google. To accomplish this, Google developed a "Quality Score" model to predict how effective an ad will be. The model uses many factors such as click-through rates, advertiser history, and keyword performance, to develop a score for each advertisement. "Essentially, what we're trying to do is predict ahead, before we actually show an ad, how a consumer will react to that ad, and our interest is in showing fewer ads, not more ads; just the right ads at the right time," Holden continues. The Google advertising model has revolutionized the advertising industry, and it continues to improve every day!

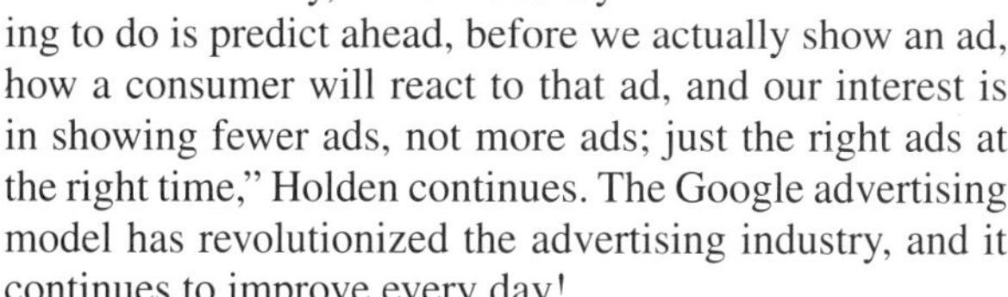

THE COMPANY

Google began in 1996 as a research project for Stanford computer science students, Larry Page and Sergey Brin. They started with a simple idea—that a search engine based on the relationships between Web sites would provide a better ranking than a search engine based only on the number of times a key term appeared on a Web site. The success of their model led to rapid growth and the founders moved the company from their dorm room, to a friend's garage, to offices in Palo Alto, California, and eventually to its current location, known as the Googleplex, in Mountain View, CA. In 2000, Google began selling advertising as a means of generating revenue. Their advertising model allowed advertisers to bid on search words and pay for each "click" by a search-engine user. The ads were required to be simple and text-based so that the search result pages remained uncluttered and the search time was as fast as possible.

Page and Brin's first search engine was called "BackRub" because their technique was based on relationships, or backlinks, between Web sites. The name quickly changed, however. The name "Google" is a misspelling of the word "googol" which is a mathematical term for a 1 followed by 100 zeros. Page and Brin used the name in the original domain, www.google.stanford.edu, to reflect their interest in organizing the immense amount of information available on the Web. The domain name, of course, became www.google.com and eventually Webster's dictionary added the verb "google" with the definition "to use the Google search engine to obtain information on the Internet." The name has become so familiar that *Advertising Age* recently reported that Google is "the world's most powerful brand"!

Today Google receives several hundred million inquiries each day as it pursues its mission: to organize the world's information and make it universally accessible and useful. The company generates more than $21 billion in annual revenue and has more than 20,000 employees. As Google has grown it has developed 10 guidelines that represent the corporate philosophy. They are:

1. Focus on the user and all else will follow.
2. It's best to do one thing really, really well.
3. Fast is better than slow.
4. Democracy on the Web works.
5. You don't need to be at your desk to need an answer.
6. You can make money without doing evil.
7. There's always more information out there.
8. The need for information crosses all borders.
9. You can be serious without a suit.
10. Great just isn't good enough.

Using these guidelines Google strives to continually improve its search engine. "The perfect search engine," explains Google co-founder Larry Page, "would understand exactly what you mean and give back exactly what you want."

ONLINE ADVERTISING

Google generates revenue by offering online advertising opportunities—next to search results or on specific Web pages. The company always distinguishes ads from the search results or the content of a Web page and it never sells placement in the search results. This approach ensures that Google Web site visitors always know when someone has paid to put a message in front of them. The advantage of online advertising is that it is measurable and allows immediate assessment of its effectiveness. As Gopi Kallayil, product marketing manager, explains: "There is a very high degree of measurability and trackability that you get through online advertising." In addition, he says, "With online advertising you can actually track the value of every single dollar that you spend, understand which particular customers the ad reached, and what they did after they received the advertising message."

The online advertising market has grown from its initial focus on simple text ads to a much larger set of options. There are five key categories of online advertising. They are:

- Search: 47%
- Display: 35%
- Classified: 10%
- Referral: 7%
- E-mail: 1%

Google is the dominant provider of online search requests and receives more than 60 percent of the search advertising revenue. The fastest-growing advertising category, however, is display advertising where Yahoo! and Microsoft are established providers. Google believes that there is an opportunity to grow its display advertising sales by making the ads useful information instead of visual clutter. According to Google co-founder Sergey Brin, "It's like search—matching people with information they want. It just happens to be promotional."

Several improvements in technology and business practice tools contributed to Google's success. First, Google developed its patented PageRank™ algorithm which evaluates the entire link structure of the Web and uses the link structure to determine which pages are most important. Then the process uses hypertext-matching analysis to determine which pages are relevant to a specific search. A combination of the importance and the relevance of Web pages provides the search results—in just a fraction of a second. Second, Google developed two business practice tools—AdWords and AdSense—to help (1) advertisers create ads, and (2) content providers generate advertising revenue. Both tools have become essential elements of Google's advertising model.

AdWords

To help advertisers place ads on their search-engine results, Google developed an online tool called AdWords. Advertisers can use AdWords to create ad text, select target keywords, and manage their account. The process allows advertisers to reach targeted audiences. Frederick Vallaeys, Adwords evangelist, explains: "One of my favorite things about AdWords is the fact that it really helps you find the right customer at the right time and show them the right message. With AdWords you can very specifically target your market because you're targeting them at a time when they do a search on Google. At that time they've told you a keyword, you know exactly what they're looking for, and here is your opportunity as a marketer to give them the exact answer to what they've just told you they wanted to find." Google has found that text ads that are relevant to the person reading them have much higher response ("clickthrough") rates than ads that are not targeted.

AdWords is also easy for any advertiser to use. Large or small businesses can simply open an account with a credit card and have ads appear within minutes. "When AdWords rolled out their self-service product, it really was one of the first times when it was very easy for a small business to put their ad up on the Internet on a search engine and compete on a level playing field alongside Fortune 1000 companies," says Vallaeys. Google has an experienced sales and service team available to help any advertiser select appropriate keywords, generate ad copy, and monitor campaign performance. The team is dedicated to helping its advertisers improve clickthrough rates because high clickthrough rates are an indication that ads are relevant to a user's interests. Methods of improving advertising performance include changing the keywords and rewriting copy. Because there is no limit to the number of keywords that an advertiser can select and each keyword can be matched with different ad copy, the potential for many very customer-specific options is high.

Another advantage of Google's AdWords program is that it allows advertisers to easily control costs. The ads appear as a "Sponsored Link" next to search results each time the Google search engine matches the search request with the ad's keywords and Quality Score, although the advertiser is not charged unless someone "clicks" on the link. In a traditional advertising model, advertisers were charged using a CPM (cost-per-thousand) approach, which charged for the impressions made by an ad. According to Holden, the Google model "transformed that to what we call a CPC, or a cost-per-click model, and this is a model that an advertiser, instead of paying for an impression, only pays when somebody actually clicks on that ad and is delivered to their Web site. So, in effect, they may be getting the benefit from impressions being shown, but we're not actually charging them anything unless there's a definite lead being delivered to their Web site." Google also offers advertisers real-time analytical services to allow assessment of and changes to any component of an advertising campaign.

AdSense

The AdSense program was designed for Web site owners as a tool for placing ads next to their Web page content rather than next to search results. Currently, thousands of Web site managers use AdSense to place ads on their sites and generate revenue. Google applies the same general philosophy to matching ads with Web sites as it does to matching ads to search requests. By delivering ads that precisely target the content on the site's pages, Google believes the advertising enhances the experience for visitors to the Web site. In this way advertisers, Web site publishers, and information seekers all benefit.

AdSense is one of the tools Google is using to pursue its goal of increasing its display advertising business. Yahoo! and Microsoft's MSN are leaders in display advertising because they can put ads on their own Web sites such as Yahoo! Finance and MSN Money. To provide additional outlets for display ads Google recently purchased YouTube. In addition, Google purchased DoubleClick, an advertising exchange where Web sites put space up for auction and ad agencies bid to place ads for their clients. Google is also trying to make it easy for anyone to create a display ad by introducing a new tool called Display Ad Builder. Some experts observe that because Google is so dominant at search advertising, its future growth will depend on success in display advertising.

GOOGLE'S FUTURE STRATEGY

How will Google continue its success? One possibility is that it will begin to try to win advertising away from the U.S. TV industry. While this is a new type of advertising requiring creative capabilities and relationships with large advertising agencies, Google has dedicated many of its resources to becoming competitive for television advertising expenditures. For example, Google recently helped Volvo develop a campaign that included a YouTube ad and Twitter updates. Google is also likely to develop new Web sites, establish blogs, and build relationships with existing sites.

Another opportunity for Google will be mobile telephone advertising. There are currently more than 3 billion mobile phones in use, and 600 million of those are Internet-capable. Just as Google's search engine provides a means to match relevant information with consumers, phones offer a chance to provide real-time and location-specific information. Some of the challenges in mobile advertising will be that the networks are not fast and that the ad formats are not standardized. Google believes its new phone and its Android operating system will also help.

Finally, as Google pursues its mission it will continue to expand throughout the world. Search results are already available in 35 languages and volunteers are helping with many others. It is obvious that Google is determined to "organize the world's information" and make it "accessible and useful."

Questions

1 Describe several unique characteristics about Google and its business practices.

2 What is Google's philosophy about advertising? How can less advertising be preferred to more advertising?

3 Describe the types of online advertising available today. Which type of advertising does Google currently dominate? Why?

4 How can Google be successful in the display advertising business? What other areas of growth are Google likely to pursue in the future?

Betty Crocker
Warm Delights
Hot Fudge Brownie

15

整合战略营销过程

Pulling It All Together: The Strategic Marketing Process

LEARNING OBJECTIVES

After reading this chapter you should be able to:

LO1 Explain how marketing managers allocate their limited resources.

LO2 Describe two marketing planning frameworks: Porter's generic business strategies and synergy analysis.

LO3 Explain what makes an effective marketing plan.

LO4 Use a Gantt chart to schedule a series of tasks.

LO5 Describe the alternatives for organizing a marketing department and the role of a product manager.

LO6 Explain how marketing ROI, metrics, and dashboards relate to evaluating marketing programs.

通用磨坊公司打破规则，抢夺今天的消费者

"BREAKING THE RULES" AT GENERAL MILLS TO REACH TODAY'S ON-THE-GO CONSUMER

"Sometimes you have to break the rules at every level," says Vivian Milroy Callaway about her challenges at General Mills.

Callaway is referring to the time a while back when you were growing up on Cheerios.® Then General Mills—or "Big G" from its logo—was known mainly for its breakfast cereals.

"Breaking the rules is what we did when we acquired Pillsbury in 2001," she explains. "After the acquisition, cereal went from being our No. 1 business to being one of a big three that includes meals like Hamburger Helper and Green Giant, as well as desserts like Pillsbury and Betty Crocker."

As vice president of the Center for Learning and Experimentation at Big G, Callaway is responsible for helping uncover new-product ideas for the company's product portfolio. Looking over her shoulder at General Mills reveals both how competitive today's cereal business is and a few of the company's creative initiatives outside the cereal industry.

Cereal Industry Facts of Life

A quick survey of the cereal industry shows:

- Only one out of four new brands "succeeds," defined as maintaining distribution for three to four years, in the $6 billion-a-year U.S. ready-to-eat (RTE) cereal market. But that RTE market has had flat or slightly declining sales in recent years.
- This decline in the ready-to-eat cereals market is caused by Americans following low-carbohydrate diets, munching breakfast bars, eating breakfast at fast-food restaurants, and buying lower-priced "bagged" or generic private-label brands.
- The launch of a new cereal typically costs up to $30 million and usually involves replacing one of more than 300 competing breakfast cereals already sitting somewhere on a supermarket shelf.

Callaway "broke the rules" in developing a new dessert concept: She looked at the concept *not alone* by itself—but in relation to *all* the other sweet treats people were eating. "One of my challenges," says Callaway, "is that consumers often say one thing in marketing research studies and then do something else when facing a supermarket shelf."

To overcome this problem, Callaway and her team did a lot of "iterative experimentation" in the marketplace. These marketing experiments involved putting a prototype dessert in a store, measuring

low-carbohydrate 低糖分；prototype 原型，样品，样本。

You've eaten healthy all day and want something quick for your sweet tooth? Try Warm Delights Minis microwavable desserts with only 150 calories—just add water and microwave in the container!

the results, improving the prototype, and repeating the process. The reward for Callaway and her team was a launch of its highly successful Warm Delights® microwavable desserts, followed quickly by Warm Delights Minis. Its special packaging is based on the team's research that showed extending the black microwavable bowl *outside* the edges of the Warm Delights package communicate its cooking convenience to prospective buyers.

Creative Initiatives Outside Cereals

General Mills annually introduces more than 300 new food products around the world that respond to what consumers are asking for: ability to eat the product on the go, single portions, healthier eating, and greater cooking convenience.

Sometimes it's possible to get all these features in the same new product and other times not. Examples of new noncereal products from General Mills include:

- Eat-on-the-go products—Fiber One® Fulfill™ nutrition bars with 35 percent of the daily value of fiber needed by adults.
- Single portions—Hamburger Helper Microwave Singles meals and Green Giant Just for One microwavable vegetables.
- Healthier eating—Progresso® light soups with only 60 calories and 0 Weight Watchers Points® per serving of vegetable soup and 1 point for its soups with meat.
- Greater cooking convenience—Betty Crocker® Warm Delights™ desserts (simply add water and microwave in the bowl), and Pillsbury® Ready to Bake!™ cookies (refrigerated cookie dough already formed into cookie shapes).

Introducing these new products may sound simple, but even technology can be a problem. For example, when Callaway's marketing researchers discovered that consumers actually like to *see* the chocolate chips *on top* of their chocolate chip cookies, General Mills invested in new manufacturing equipment to make this a reality. Putting the chocolate chips on top increased sales 50 percent.

This chapter discusses issues and techniques related to the planning, implementation, and evaluation phases of the strategic marketing process, which were introduced in Chapter 2. Throughout the chapter, you'll obtain insights into the marketing strategies now emerging at General Mills and other firms.

营销基础：做有用之事并配置资源
MARKETING BASICS: DOING WHAT WORKS AND ALLOCATING RESOURCES

As noted in Chapter 2, corporate and marketing executives search continuously to find a competitive advantage—a unique strength relative to what competitors are doing now and likely to do in the future. Having identified this competitive advantage, they must figure out how to exploit it. This involves (1) finding and using what works for their organization and industry and (2) allocating resources effectively.

---

microwavable 适合于微波炉烧煮的；implementation 履行，实施。

发现并利用真正起作用的东西
Finding and Using What Really Works

In a five-year study, researchers Nohria, Joyce, and Roberson conducted in-depth analysis of 160 companies and more than 200 management tools and techniques, such as supply chain management, customer relationship management (CRM), or use of an intranet. The result? Individual management tools and techniques had no direct relationship to superior business performance in the companies.

What *does* matter? The researchers concluded that four basic business and management practices are what matter—"what really works," to use their phrase. These are: (1) strategy, (2) execution, (3) culture, and (4) structure. Firms with excellence in all four of these areas are likely to achieve superior business performance. And in terms of individual tools and techniques, the researchers concluded that which of these the firm chooses to use is less important than flawless execution of the ones it does use.

Industry leaders such as Walmart, Home Depot, and Dell do all four of the basic practices extremely well, not just two or three, and are vigilant to keep doing them well when conditions change. Coca-Cola and Kodak, superstars a decade ago, are struggling today to get these basics right and regain past success. Let's look at companies that stand out today in each of the four basics:

These companies achieve excellence in what really matters—a clear focused strategy for Costco and a performance-oriented culture for Smucker's.

- 战略：设计并维持一个清晰集中的战略。
- 执行：开发并维持无缺陷的运营操作。
- 文化：开发并保持一种绩效导向的文化。
- 结构：构建并保持反应迅速、灵活、扁平化的组织。

- *Strategy: Devise and maintain a clearly stated, focused strategy.* While Walmart may be the unstoppable force in mass-merchandise retailing, in warehouse clubs its Sam's Club is not. The winner to date: Costco Wholesale, with 60 percent as many stores as Sam's Club but almost twice the sales revenue. A key reason is its focused strategy based on the knowledge that of all U.S. retail channels, warehouse clubs attract the largest proportion of affluent shoppers. Costco's strategy: Sell a limited selection of branded high-end merchandise at low prices. In the current recession its "$1.50 hot dog and soda combo" gets customers' attention.
- *Execution: Develop and maintain flawless operational execution.* Toyota is generally acknowledged as the best in the world in revolutionizing the design and manufacture of autos. Toyota managers created the doctrine of *kaizen*, or continuous improvement. For example, by speeding up decisions, Toyota reduced the time to get one model from the drawing board to the showroom to 19 months, about half the industry average.
- *Culture: Develop and maintain a performance-oriented culture.* Always near the top of *Fortune*'s list of the 100 Best Companies to Work For is Smucker's—yes, the "With a name like Smucker's" company. Its straightforward culture is based on four key elements in its code of conduct: "Listen with your full attention, look for the good in others, have a sense of humor, and say thank you for a job well done." The performance result? Low employee turnover and large appreciation in the value of its stock.
- *Structure: Build and maintain a fast, flexible, flat organization.* Successful small organizations often grow into bureaucratic large ones with layers of managers and red tape that slow decision making. An exception and the unquestioned all-time leader in delivering world-class aircraft with only about 50 engineers and designers and 100 expert machinists: Lockheed's Skunk Works. Discussed later in the chapter, its first director set guidelines for organizational structure and implementation. Attempts have been made to try to apply these Skunk Works guidelines to operations as far away as France and Russia. Key guidelines are (1) give the director the authority to make quick decisions and (2) use a small number of good people who can talk to anyone in the organization to solve a problem.

---

unstoppable 无法停止的，不可阻碍的；bureaucratic 官僚。

Of course, in practice a firm cannot allocate unlimited resources to achieving each of these business basics. It must make choices on where its resources can give the greatest return, the topic of the next section.

根据销售反应函数配置营销资源
Allocating Marketing Resources Using Sales Response Functions

销售反应函数表明的是营销活动费用与所获营销业绩之间的关系。

A **sales response function** relates the expense of marketing effort to the marketing results obtained. For simplicity in the examples that follow, only the effects of annual marketing effort on annual sales revenue will be analyzed, but the concept applies to other measures of marketing success—such as profit, units sold, or level of awareness.

Maximizing Incremental Revenue Minus Incremental Cost Economists give managers a specific guideline for optimal resource allocation: Allocate the firm's marketing, production, and financial resources to the markets and products where the excess of incremental revenues over incremental costs is greatest.

Figure 15–1 illustrates the resource allocation principle that is inherent in the sales response function. The firm's annual marketing effort, such as sales and advertising expenses, is plotted on the horizontal axis. As the annual marketing effort increases, so does the resulting annual sales revenue, which is plotted on the vertical axis. The relationship is assumed to be S-shaped, showing that an additional $1 million of marketing effort, from $3 million to $4 million, results in far greater increases of sales revenue in the midrange ($20 million) of the curve than at either end. An increase from $2 million to $3 million in spending yields an increase of $10 million in sales; an increase from $6 million to $7 million in spending leads to an increase of $5 million in sales.

A Numerical Example of Resource Allocation Suppose Figure 15–1 shows the situation for a new General Mills product such as Banana Nut Cheerios®, which is targeted at health-conscious consumers who want a great tasting cereal. Banana Nut Cheerios is an extension of the Cheerios name, the best selling ready-to-eat cereal brand in the United States.

Also assume that the sales response function in Figure 15–1 doesn't change through time as a result of changing consumer tastes and incomes. Point A shows the position of the firm in year 1, whereas Point B shows it three years later in year 4. Suppose General Mills decides to launch new advertising and sales promotions that,

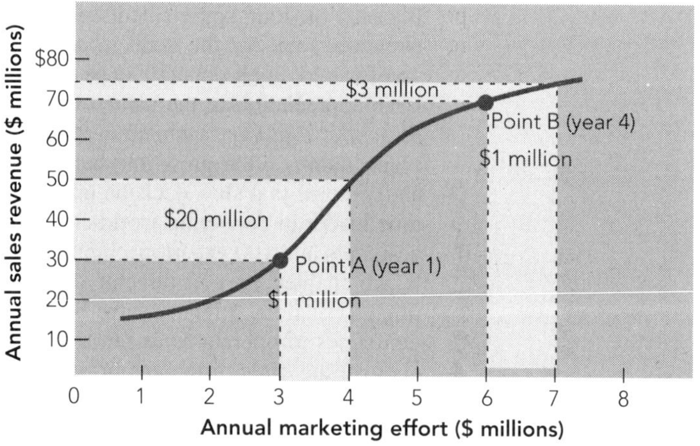

FIGURE 15–1
A sales response function shows the impact of various levels of marketing effort on annual sales revenue for two different years.

incremental 增加的；horizontal 水平的，横的。

These recently introduced products reflect General Mills' increased emphasis on healthy eating.

let's say, increase its marketing effort for the brand from $3 million to $6 million a year. If the relationship in Figure 15–1 holds true and is a good picture of consumer purchasing behavior, the sales revenues of Banana Nut Cheerios should increase from $30 million to $70 million a year.

Let's look at the major resource allocation question: What are the probable increases in sales revenue for Banana Nut Cheerios in year 1 and year 4 if General Mills were to spend an additional $1 million in marketing effort? As Figure 15–1 reveals,

Year 1

Increase in marketing effort from $3 million to $4 million = $1 million.

Increase in sales revenue from $30 million to $50 million = $20 million.

Ratio of incremental sales revenue to effort = $20,000,000:$1,000,000 20:1.

Year 4

Increase in marketing effort from $6 million to $7 million = $1 million.

Increase in sales revenue from $70 million to $73 million = $3 million.

Ratio of incremental sales revenue to effort = $3,000,000:$1,000,000 = 3:1.

Thus, in year 1 a dollar of extra marketing effort returned $20 in sales revenue, whereas in year 4 it returned only $3. If no other expenses are incurred, it might make sense to spend $1 million in year 4 to gain $3 million in incremental sales revenue. However, it may be far wiser for General Mills to invest the money in one of its other brands, such as its new line of Progresso Light soups.

The essence of resources allocation is simple: Put incremental resources where the incremental returns are greatest over the foreseeable future. For General Mills this means allocating its available resources efficiently among its broad portfolio of product lines and brands.

At General Mills extending a valuable brand name to new products provides it with important marketing synergies. For example, the Fiber One brand was used to introduce the cereal in 1985. Today the Fiber One brand name extends not only to other cereals but to snack bars, yogurt, and toaster pastries as well. Resource allocation decisions also must reflect changing consumer tastes and fluctuations in ingredient prices.

How can General Mills best allocate available resources among its portfolio of brands? Several frameworks within the strategic marketing process help answer this question.

Allocating Marketing Resources in Practice General Mills, like many firms in these businesses, does extensive analysis using **share points**, or percentage points of market share, as the common basis of comparison to allocate marketing resources effectively for different product lines within the same firm. This allows it to seek answers to the question, "How much is it worth to us to try to increase our market share by another 1 (or 2, or 5, or 10) percentage point?"

This analysis enables higher-level managers to make resource allocation trade-offs among different kinds of business units owned by the company. To make these resource allocation decisions, marketing managers must estimate: (1) the market share for the product, (2) the revenues associated with each point of market share (a share point in breakfast cereals may be five times what it is in cake mixes), (3) the contribution to overhead and profit (or gross margin) of each share point, and (4) possible cannibalization effects on other products in the line (for example, new Banana Nut Cheerios might reduce sales of regular Cheerios).

portfolio 投资组合；share points 市场份额点；cannibalization effects 蚕食效应。

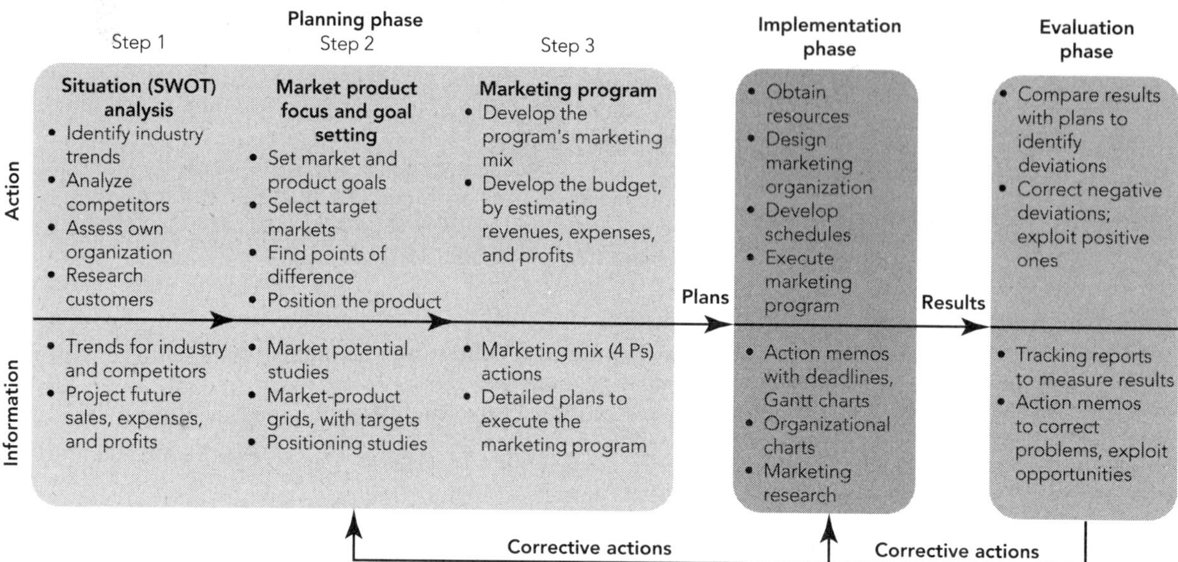

FIGURE 15–2
The actions in the strategic marketing process are supported and directed by detailed reports, studies, and memos.

Resource Allocation and the Strategic Marketing Process Company resources are allocated effectively in the strategic marketing process by converting marketing information into marketing actions. Figure 15–2 summarizes the strategic marketing process introduced in Chapter 2, along with some details of the marketing actions and information that comprise it. Figure 15–2 is really a simplification of the actual strategic marketing process: While the three phases of the strategic marketing process have distinct separations in the figure and the marketing actions are separated from the marketing information, in practice these blend and interact.

The upper half of each box in Figure 15–2 highlights the actions involved in that part of the strategic marketing process, and the lower half summarizes the information and reports used. Note that each phase has an output report:

Phase	Output Report
Planning	Marketing plans (or programs) that define goals (with pertinent marketing metrics) and the marketing mix strategies to achieve them
Implementation	Action memos that tell (1) *who* is (2) to do *what* (3) by *when*
Evaluation	Corrective action memos, triggered by comparing results with goals, often using the firm's marketing metrics and dashboards

The corrective action memos become feedback loops in Figure 15–2 that help improve decisions and actions in earlier phases of the strategic marketing process.

learning review

1. What are the four basic practices "that really work"—that are characteristics of industry-leading firms?
2. What is the significance of the S-shape of the sales response function in Figure 15–1?

simplification 简单化；corrective 改正的，纠正的，矫正的。

战略营销过程的计划阶段
THE PLANNING PHASE OF THE STRATEGIC MARKETING PROCESS

Four aspects of the strategic marketing process deserve special mention: (1) the vital importance of metrics in marketing planning, (2) the variety of marketing plans, (3) marketing planning frameworks that have proven useful, and (4) some key marketing planning and strategy lessons.

营销计划中衡量指标的重要意义
The Vital Importance of Metrics in Marketing Planning

In the past decade, measuring the effectiveness of marketing activities has become a central focus in many organizations. This boils down to defining "where the organization is going"—the goals—and "whether it is really getting there"—the marketing metrics used to measure actual performance.

Planners have a tongue-in-cheek truism: "If you don't know where you're going, any road will get you there." In making marketing plans, the "road" chosen is really the goal *plus* the metric used to measure whether the goal is achieved.

Even in today's economic turmoil, most firms stress innovation to help achieve growth. Marketing departments work closely with R&D operations departments to complete successful innovation projects. So what marketing metrics might they use to measure their innovation performance?

In a recent survey, responding firms reported that on average they used eight metrics to measure their innovation. Figure 15–3 shows that among firms that use more than three different innovation metrics, they use two different kinds—output metrics and input metrics. For example, 16 percent reported using revenue growth from new products or services, which is a measure of results—an *output metric*. In contrast, Figure 15–3 also shows that 10 percent used a metric of the number of ideas in the pipeline, which clearly is an *input metric* because there is no assurance the idea will actually convert into sales revenues.

FIGURE 15–3
Metric ranked No. 1 by respondents from organizations using more than three innovation metrics

Innovation Metric	Percentage of Respondents Ranking Innovation Metric No. 1*	Key
Revenue growth due to new products or services	16%	Output metric
Customer satisfaction with new products or services	13%	Output metric
Number of ideas or concepts in the pipeline	10%	Input metric
R&D spending as a percentage of sales	8%	Input metric
Percentage of sales from new products/services in given time period	8%	Output metric
Number of new products or services launched	8%	Output metric
Return on investment (ROI) in new products or services	6%	Output metric
Number of R&D projects	6%	Input metric

*Metrics ranked No. 1 by less than 6 percent of respondents are not shown; with these the percentages would total 100 percent.

---

framework 构架，框架；turmoil 混乱，焦虑。

A careful look at the innovation metrics shown in Figure 15–3 reveals that it is generally far easier to measure marketing inputs rather than marketing outputs. So measuring "the number of R&D projects" (an input) is far easier than measuring "customer satisfaction with new products or services" (an output). But as shown in Figure 15–2, the evaluation phase of the strategic marketing process involves comparing actual results—an output metric—with the goals set. So where possible, marketing managers prefer to use effective output metrics if they are available.

营销计划的多样性
The Variety of Marketing Plans

The planning phase of the strategic marketing process usually results in a marketing plan that sets the direction for the marketing activities of an organization. As noted earlier, a marketing plan is the heart of a business plan. Like business plans, marketing plans aren't all from the same mold; they vary with the length of the planning period, the purpose, and the audience. Let's look briefly at two kinds: long-range and annual marketing plans.

Long-Range Marketing Plans Typically, long-range marketing plans cover marketing activities from two to five years into the future. Except for firms in industries such as autos, steel, or forest products, marketing plans rarely go beyond five years into the future because the tremendous number of uncertainties makes the benefits of planning less than the effort expended. Such plans are often directed at top-level executives and the board of directors.

Annual Marketing Plans Usually developed by a marketing or product manager (discussed later in the chapter) in a consumer products firm such as General Mills, annual marketing plans deal with marketing goals and strategies for a product, product line, or entire firm for a single year. This annual planning cycle typically starts with a detailed marketing research study of current users and ends after 42 weeks with the approval of the plan by the division general manager, 10 weeks before the fiscal year starts. Between these points there are continuing efforts to uncover new ideas through key-issues sessions with specialists both inside and outside the firm. The plan is fine-tuned through a series of often excruciating reviews by several levels of management, which leaves few surprises and little to chance.

It is easier to talk about planning than to do it well. The next section describes some marketing planning frameworks to aid the process.

营销计划框架：寻求增长
Marketing Planning Frameworks: The Search for Growth

LO2

Marketing planning for a firm with many products competing in many markets is a complex process. Yet in a business firm all these planning efforts are directed at finding the means for increased growth in sales and profits. Two techniques that help corporate and marketing executives make important resource allocation decisions are: (1) Porter's generic business strategies and (2) synergy analysis. Both techniques relate to elements introduced in earlier chapters.

Porter's Generic Business Strategies As shown in Figure 15–4, Michael E. Porter has developed a framework in which he identifies four basic, or "generic," strategies. A **generic business strategy** is one that can be adopted by any firm, regardless of the product or industry involved, to achieve a competitive advantage.

通用经营战略是指没有产品或行业限制，任何公司都可以采用进而形成竞争优势的战略。

Although all the techniques discussed here involve generic strategies, the phrase is most often associated with Porter's framework. In this framework, the columns identify the two fundamental alternatives firms can use in seeking competitive advantage: becoming the low-cost producer within the markets in which it competes or differentiating itself from competitors by developing points of difference in its prod-

tremendous 极大的，巨大的；annual 年度的；generic business strategy 通用经营战略。

FIGURE 15–4
Porter's four generic business strategies involve combinations of (1) competitive scope or the breadth of the target markets and (2) a stress on costs versus product differentiation.

Competitive scope	SOURCE OF COMPETITIVE ADVANTAGE	
	Lower cost	Differentiation
Broad target	1. Cost leadership strategy	2. Differentiation strategy
Narrow target	3. Cost focus strategy	4. Differentiation focus strategy

uct offerings or marketing programs. In contrast, the rows identify the competitive scope: a broad target by competing in many market segments or a narrow target by competing in only a few segments or even a single segment. The columns and rows result in four generic business strategies, any one of which can provide a competitive advantage among similar business units in the same industry:

1. **成本领先战略**专注于降低成本，进而以低价占领广泛的目标细分市场。

1. A **cost leadership strategy** (cell 1) focuses on reducing expenses and, in turn, lowers product prices while targeting a broad array of market segments. One way is by securing raw materials from lower-cost suppliers. Also, significant investments in capital equipment may be necessary to improve the production or distribution process and achieve these lower unit costs. The cost leader still must have adequate quality levels. Campbell Soup's sophisticated product development and supply chain systems have led to huge cost savings. So its cost leadership strategy has resulted in lower prices for customers—causing its market share to increase in the current recession.

2. **差异化战略**要求产品具有显著特色，如卓越品牌形象、高质量、先进技术或出色服务，进而向广泛的细分市场索要高价。

2. A **differentiation strategy** (cell 2) requires products to have significant points of difference in product offerings, brand image, higher quality, advanced technology, or superior service to charge a higher price while targeting a broad array of market segments. This allows the firm to charge a price premium. General Mills uses this strategy in stressing its nutritious, high-quality brands in reaching a diverse array of customer segments.

3. **成本集聚战略**即控制成本支出，面向某个狭小目标细分市场低价销售产品。

3. A **cost focus strategy** (cell 3) involves controlling expenses and, in turn, lowering product prices targeted at a narrow range of market segments. Retail

Which of Porter's generic strategies are Campbell Soup and IKEA using? For the answers and a discussion of the strategies, see the text.

cost leadership strategy 成本领先战略；sophisticated 复杂的；differentiation strategy 差异化战略；nutritious 有营养的；cost focus strategy 成本聚焦战略。

chains targeting only a few market segments in a restricted group of products often use a cost focus strategy successfully. IKEA is now the world's largest furniture retailer by selling flat-pack, self-assembly furniture, accessories, and bathroom and kitchen items to cost-conscious consumers.

4. **差异集聚战略**要求产品针对一个或少数几个目标细分市场具有显著差异点。

4. Finally, a **differentiation focus strategy** (cell 4) requires products to have significant points of difference to target one or only a few market segments. The average age of today's Toyota owner is 47. So a concerned Toyota product planning group visited cities where young people are buying and renting loft apartments. The planners discovered these young city dwellers need smaller cars they can park in cramped spaces. This suggests offering a new Toyota model with an important point of difference for a narrow segment of buyers—a differentiation focus strategy.

These strategies also form the foundation for Michael Porter's theory about what makes a nation's industries successful.

Synergy Analysis **Synergy analysis** seeks opportunities by finding the optimum balance between marketing efficiencies versus R&D–manufacturing efficiencies. Using diversification analysis from Chapter 2 and the market–product grid framework from Chapter 6, we can see two kinds of synergy that are critical in developing corporate and marketing strategies: (1) marketing synergy and (2) R&D–manufacturing synergy. While the following example involves external synergies through mergers and acquisitions, the concepts apply equally well to internal synergies sought in adding new products or seeking new markets.

A critical step in the external analysis is to assess how these merger and acquisition strategies provide the organization with synergy, the increased customer value achieved through performing organizational functions more efficiently. The increased customer value can take many forms: more products, improved quality on existing products, lower prices, improved distribution, and so on. But the ultimate criterion is that customers should be better off as a result of the increased synergy. The firm, in turn, should be better off by gaining more satisfied customers resulting in increased sales and profits.

How might you segment the lawn mower market? What synergies might appear? For the answers, see the text.

As noted in the Marketing Matters box, assume you are vice president of marketing for Great States Corp.'s line of nonpowered lawn mowers and powered walking mowers sold to the consumer market. You are looking for new product and new market opportunities to increase your revenues and profits.

You conduct a market segmentation study and develop a market–product grid to analyze future opportunities. You identify three major segments in the consumer market based on geography: (1) city, (2) suburban, and (3) rural households. These market segments relate to the size of lawn a consumer must mow. The product clusters are: (1) nonpowered, (2) powered walking, and (3) powered riding mowers. Five alternative marketing strategies are shown in the market–product grids in Figure 15–5. As mentioned in Chapter 6, the important marketing synergies, or efficiencies, run horizontally across the rows in Figure 15–5. Conversely, the important R&D–manufacturing synergies, or efficiencies, run vertically down the columns. Let's look at the synergy effects for the five combinations in Figure 15–5.

A. *Market–product concentration.* The firm benefits from focus on a single product line and market segment, but it loses opportunities for significant synergies in both marketing and R&D–manufacturing.

B. *Market specialization.* The firm gains marketing synergy through providing a complete product line for the city market segment, but R&D–manufacturing has the difficulty of developing and producing three different products.

differentiation focus strategy 差异集聚战略；synergy analysis 多元化分析；market–product concentration 市场 - 产品集中型。

Marketing Matters >>>>>> customer value

A Test of Your Skills: Where Are the Synergies?

To try your hand in this multibillion-dollar synergy game, assume you are vice president of marketing for Great States Corp., which markets a line of nonpowered, powered walking, and powered riding lawn mowers throughout North America. A market–product grid for your business is shown. You distribute your nonpowered mowers in all three market segments shown and walking powered mowers only in suburban markets. However, you don't offer powered riding mowers for any of the three markets.

Here are your strategy dilemmas:

1. Where are the marketing synergies (efficiencies)?
2. Where are the R&D–manufacturing synergies (efficiencies)?
3. What would a market-product grid look like for an ideal company that Great States could merge with to achieve both marketing and R&D–manufacturing synergies (efficiencies)?

To consider these questions, read the text and study Figure 15–5 and the figure below.

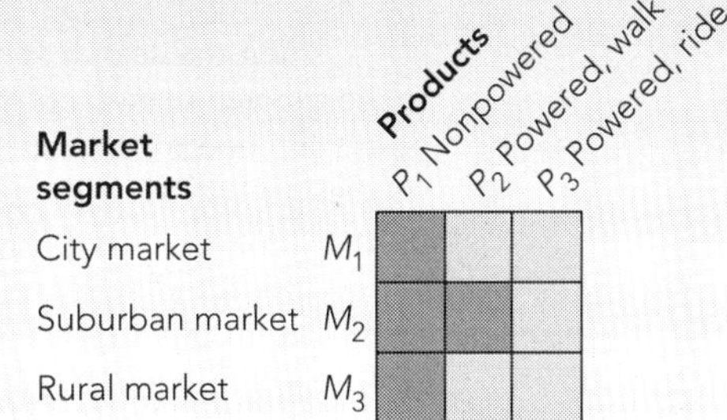

C. *Product specialization.* The firm gains R&D–manufacturing synergy through producing only a nonpowered lawn mower, but gaining market distribution in the three different geographic areas will be costly.

D. *Selective specialization.* The firm doesn't get either marketing or R&D–manufacturing synergies because of the uniqueness of the market–product combinations.

E. *Full coverage.* The firm has the maximum potential synergies in both marketing and R&D–manufacturing. The question: Is it spread too thin because of the resource requirements needed to reach all market–product combinations?

The Marketing Matters box poses the question of what the ideal partner for Great States would be if it merged with another firm, given the market–product combinations shown in the box. If, as vice president of marketing, you want to follow a full-coverage strategy, then the ideal merger partner is shown in Figure 15–6 on the next page. This would give the maximum potential synergies—if you are not spreading the resources of your merged companies too thin. Marketing gains by having a complete product line in all regions, and R&D–manufacturing gains by having access to new markets that can provide production economies of scale through producing larger volumes of its existing products.

FIGURE 15–5
Market–product grids show alternative strategies for a lawn mower manufacturer. Try to find synergies in each strategy—if any exist.

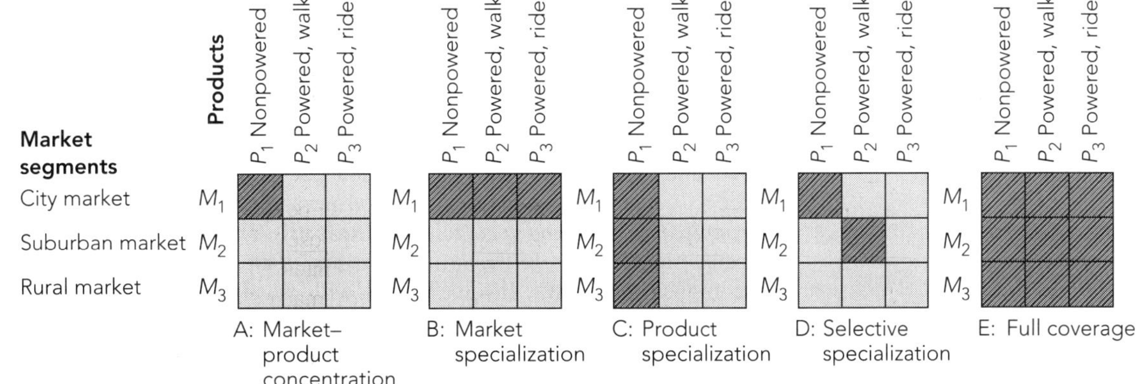

product specialization 产品专业化；selective specialization 选择性专业化；full coverage 专业覆盖。

FIGURE 15–6
This is the ideal merger for Great States to obtain full market–product coverage. The ideal partner offers lawn mower products to the exact segments of customers not now served by Great States.

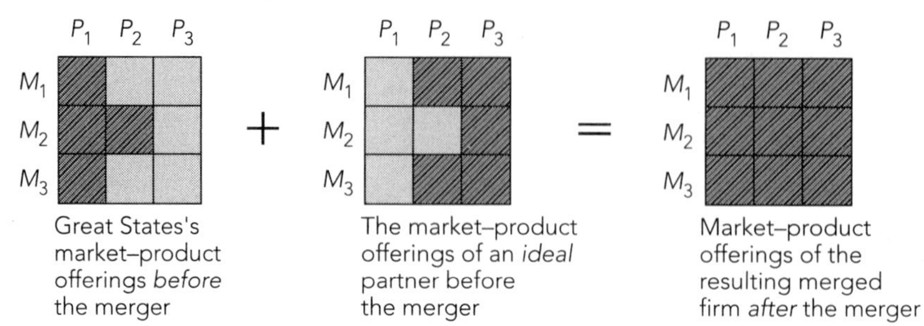

Often the search for synergies is within the company itself. The result often will be greater manufacturing synergies and efficiencies that in turn will lead to better quality control and happier customers. Procter & Gamble concluded the world didn't really need 31 varieties of its Head & Shoulders shampoo. Cutting the number in half, P&G also reduced its expenses and increased profits in the bargain.

learning review

3. What is the difference between an input metric and an output metric?
4. Describe Porter's four generic business strategies.
5. Where do (*a*) marketing synergies and (*b*) R&D–manufacturing synergies appear when using the synergy analysis framework?

一些营销计划和战略教训
Some Marketing Planning and Strategy Lessons

LO3

Applying these frameworks is not automatic but requires a great deal of managerial judgment. Commonsense requirements of an effective marketing plan are discussed next, followed by problems that can arise.

Guidelines for an Effective Marketing Plan President Dwight D. Eisenhower, when he commanded Allied armies in World War II, made his classic observation, "Plans are nothing; planning is everything." It is the process of careful planning that focuses an organization's efforts and leads to success. The plans themselves, which change with events, are often secondary. Effective planning and plans are inevitably characterized by identifiable objectives, specific strategies or courses of action, and the means to execute them. Here are some guidelines in developing effective marketing plans:

- *Set measurable, achievable goals.* Ideally, goals should be quantified and measurable in terms of what is to be accomplished and by when. So "Increase market share from 18 percent to 22 percent by December 31, 2011" is preferable to "Maximize market share given our available resources." Also, to motivate people the goals must be achievable.
- *Use a base of facts and valid assumptions.* The more a marketing plan is based on facts and valid assumptions, rather than guesses, the less uncertainty and risk are associated with executing it. Good marketing research helps.
- *Use simple, but clear and specific, plans.* Effective execution of plans requires that people at all levels in the firm understand what, when, and how they are to accomplish their tasks. Involve people with the right skills and experience in the planning.
- *Have complete and feasible plans.* Marketing plans must incorporate all the key marketing mix factors and be supported by adequate resources.

measurable 可衡量的；achievable 可实现的；assumption 假定。

- *Make plans controllable and flexible.* Marketing plans must enable results to be compared with planned targets, often using precise marketing metrics and dashboards. This allows replanning—the flexibility to alter the original plans based on recent results.
- *Find the right person to implement the plans.* But make sure that person is heavily involved in making the plans.
- *Work toward consensus-building.* "Ownership" of the plan by team members and stakeholders increases the chances for its success.

Problems in Marketing Planning and Strategy An all-too-frequent problem in marketing planning and strategy is that bad news is filtered out as information goes up the line to give top management a very rosy picture. J.D. Power III did marketing research at Ford four decades ago. "There was no interest in finding out what customers really thought," he says. "Instead, we were constantly asked to 'torture the data until it confessed,' giving us the answers the execs wanted." So he founded J.D. Power & Associates to do customer satisfaction studies. One of his first marketing research clients was Toyota, which listened and has used hundreds of J.D. Power studies over the years. Today J.D. Power & Associates is one of the world's best known marketing information companies and now serves not only the auto industry but also heath care, telecommunications, insurance, financial services, and more. Other key problems that emerge in a firm's strategic marketing process:

1. Plans may be based on very poor assumptions about environmental forces, especially changing economic conditions and competitors' actions. A Western Union plan failed because it didn't reflect the impact of deregulation and competitors' actions on business.
2. Planners and their plans may have lost sight of their customers' needs. But not at the Papa John's pizza chain. The "better ingredients, better pizza" slogan makes the hair stand up on the back of the necks of competing Pizza Hut executives. The reason is that this Papa John's slogan reflects the firm's obsessive attention to detail, which is stealing market share from much-bigger Pizza Hut. Sample detail: If the cheese on the pizza shows a single air bubble or the crust is not golden brown, the offending pizza is not served to the customer.
3. Too much time and effort may be spent on data collection and writing plans that are too complex to implement. One manufacturer cut its planning instructions "that looked like an auto repair manual" to five or six pages for operating units.
4. Line operating managers often feel no sense of ownership in implementing the plans. Andy Grove, when he was CEO of Intel, observed, "We had the very ridiculous system . . . of delegating strategic planning to strategic planners. The strategies these [planners] prepared had no bearing on anything we actually did." The solution is to assign more planning activities to line operating managers, the people who actually carry them out.

General Mills' successful introduction of French-developed Yoplait yogurt to U.S. consumers . . .

Big G: Global Strategies to Find Synergies, Segments, and Partners Competing in today's global marketplace, General Mills is concerned with *both* selling its products and brands in countries around the world *and* also obtaining ideas for new products from anyone, anywhere who has a great product or technology.

Easy to understand is the benefit for General Mills of moving its existing U.S. products into foreign markets. As mentioned in Chapter 10, the company's joint venture

controllable 可控的；flexible 灵活的。

. . . led the way to its global search for new products today, such as Wanchai Ferry dinner kits from Hong Kong.

with Swiss-based Nestlé in Cereal Partners Worldwide provides General Mills access to European, Latin American, and Asian consumers—offering everything from cereals to ice cream bars. This joint venture has achieved great success.

Less clear is the reason for Big G's current global search for new ideas, products, and technologies. The success of Yoplait yogurt ("The Yogurt of France") has led to bringing other products developed outside the United States to our shores. Wanchai Ferry™ brand dinner kits are coming to the United States through a collaboration managed by General Mills of scientists on three continents. The dinner kits, which do not require freezing or refrigeration, are an adaptation of frozen dumplings developed by Madame Kin Wo Chong, a Hong Kong entrepreneur who started by selling her dumplings in 1977 from a cart on the city's Wanchai Ferry pier.

Have a great idea for a new technology or product General Mills might use? Under its Worldwide Innovation Network, the company wants your idea to help accelerate its innovation efforts. You can contact General Mills online through an Internet portal at www.generalmills.com/win to submit your idea. But there's a wrinkle: The new product or technology must (1) have a patent or patent pending, (2) be fully developed and be on the market somewhere in the world, and (3) fit into Big G's product lines!

Balancing Value and Values in Strategic Marketing Plans Two important trends are likely to influence the strategic marketing process in the future. The first, *value-based planning*, combines marketing planning ideas and financial planning techniques to assess how much a division or strategic business unit (SBU) contributes to the price of a company's stock (or shareholder wealth). Value is created when the financial return of a strategic activity exceeds the cost of the resources allocated to the activity.

第一种趋势是基于价值制定计划，即将营销计划理念与财务计划技术联系起来，对每个部门或战略业务单位对公司股价（或股东财富）的贡献进行评估。

The second trend is the increasing interest in *value-driven strategies*, which incorporate concerns for ethics, integrity, employee health and safety, and environmental safeguards with more common corporate values such as growth, profitability, customer service, and quality. Some experts have observed that although many corporations cite broad corporate values in advertisements, press releases, and company newsletters, they have not yet changed their strategic plans to reflect the stated values. U.S. firms, like firms and governments around the world, are increasingly called on to be good global citizens and to support sustainable development.

第二种趋势就是日益受欢迎的价值导向战略，即把对商业道德、诚信、雇员的健康与安全以及环境保护的关注，与诸如增长、获利能力、顾客服务与质量等更为常见的公司价值观结合起来。

战略营销过程的执行阶段
THE IMPLEMENTATION PHASE OF THE STRATEGIC MARKETING PROCESS

The Monday morning diagnosis of a losing football coach often runs something like "We had an excellent game plan; we just didn't execute it."

是计划还是执行出了问题
Is Planning or Implementation the Problem?

The planning-versus-execution issue applies to the strategic marketing process as well: When a marketing plan fails, it's difficult to determine whether the failure is due to a poor plan or poor implementation.

Effective managers tracking progress on a struggling plan first try to identify whether the problems involve: (1) the plan and strategy, (2) its implementation, or (3) both, and then they try to correct the problems. But as discussed earlier in the chapter, research on what really works shows that successful firms have excellence on both the planning and strategy side and the implementation and execution side.

value-based planning 基于价值制定计划；value-driven strategies 价值导向战略。

Procter & Gamble's new Tide Stain Release launch shows how it has improved both planning and implementation by involving consumers earlier in its innovation activities.

For example, Procter & Gamble's consumer product success combines strong innovative products (planning and strategy) with excellent promotion and distribution (implementation and execution). Almost a decade ago P&G realized too many of its products were being pushed into the market before they were ready—really a planning glitch. P&G's mantra of "fearlessness when it comes to failure" stresses that failure isn't punished if those involved learn key lessons. So it reorganized itself around an innovation strategy to "involve some consumers in product design as soon as we have the concept," says P&G's chief executive officer, A.G. Lafley.

In the 2009 recession, consumers flocked to cheaper brands, causing Tide, P&G's biggest moneymaker, to lose market share. About half of Tide consumers already used some form of in-wash laundry additive, so P&G saw an opportunity it responded to quickly. In mid-2009 P&G launched Tide Stain Release, a new laundry additive to boost Tide's cleaning power. Its advertising tagline: "Stains Out. No Doubt."

At the other extreme, most of the hundreds of dot-com firms that failed in the late 1990s had both planning *and* implementation problems. Their bad planning often resulted from their focus on getting start-up money from investors and not providing real value to customers. Bad implementation by the dot-coms frequently led to their spending huge sums on wasteful ads to try to promote their failing Web sites. While some Internet firms may have had good ideas for delivering physical products such as toys and groceries to their customers' doors, they didn't understand key implementation issues that involved inventories, warehouses, and physical distribution.

日益重视营销计划的执行
Increasing Emphasis on Marketing Implementation

Today the implementation phase of the strategic marketing process often involves moving many planning activities away from the duties of planners to those of line managers and finding effective ways to convert new marketing opportunities to completed projects.

General Electric's Jack Welch became a legend in making GE more efficient and far better at implementation. When Welch became CEO in 1981 he faced an organization mired in red tape, turf battles, and slow decision making. Further, Welch saw GE bogged down with 25,000 managers and close to a dozen layers between him and the factory floor.

In his "delayering," he sought to cut GE's levels in half and to speed up decision making and implementation by building an atmosphere of trust and autonomy among his managers and employees. Where possible, Welch made the people planning the project responsible for carrying it out. In terms of implementation and meeting key goals, Welch also insisted General Electric's departments be "winners"—or No. 1 or No. 2 in their industry in terms of revenues and profits. Although there are debates on some Welch strategies, businesses around the world are using GE's focus on implementation as a benchmark.

改进营销方案的执行
Improving Implementation of Marketing Programs

No magic formula exists to guarantee effective implementation of marketing plans. In fact, the answer seems to be equal parts of good management skills and practices, from which have come some guidelines for improving program implementation.

计划执行者既要了解所追求的目标，又要掌握实现目标的手段。

Communicate Goals and the Means of Achieving Them Those called on to implement plans need to understand both the goals sought and how they are to be accomplished. Everyone in Papa John's—from founder John Schnatter to telephone order takers and make-line people—is clear on what the firm's goal

implementation 执行，实施；accomplish 完成，执行。

Core value #4—"PAPA"—makes very clear to all Papa John's Pizza employees what its priorities are!

is: to deliver better pizzas using better ingredients. The firm's orientation packet for employees lists its six core values that executives are expected to memorize. An example: Core value #4 is "PAPA," or "People Are Priority No. 1, Always."

Have a Responsible Program Champion Willing to Act Successful programs almost always have a **product or program champion** who is able and willing to cut red tape and move the program forward. Such a person often has the uncanny ability to move back and forth between big-picture strategy questions and specific details when the situation calls for it. Program champions are notoriously brash in overcoming organizational hurdles. The U.S. Navy's Admiral Grace Murray Hopper not only gave the world an early computer language but also the word *bug*, meaning any glitch in a computer or computer program. This program champion's famous advice for moving decisions to actions by cutting through an organization's red tape: "Better to ask forgiveness than permission."

Reward Successful Program Implementation When an individual or a team is rewarded for achieving the organization's goal, they have maximum incentive to see a program implemented successfully because they have personal ownership and a stake in that success.

Take Action and Avoid Paralysis by Analysis Management experts warn against "paralysis by analysis," the tendency to excessively analyze a problem instead of taking action. To overcome this pitfall, they call for a "bias for action" and recommend a "do it, fix it, try it" approach. Conclusion: Perfectionists finish last, so getting 90 percent perfection and letting the marketplace help in the fine-tuning makes good sense in implementation.

Lockheed Martin's Skunk Works got its name from the comic strip *L'il Abner* and its legendary reputation from achieving superhuman technical feats with a low budget and ridiculously short deadlines by stressing teamwork. Under the 35-year leadership of Kelly Johnson, the Skunk Works turned out a series of world-class aircraft from the world's fastest (the SR-71 Blackbird) to the nation's most untrackable aircraft (the F-117 Stealth fighter). Two of Kelly Johnson's basic tenets: (1) make decisions promptly and (2) avoid paralysis by analysis. In fact, one U.S. Air Force audit showed that Johnson's Skunk Works could carry out a program on schedule with 126 people, whereas a competitor in a comparable program was behind schedule with 3,750 people.

Open communications at the Skunk Works have led to state-of-the-art aircraft like this SR-71 Blackbird.

Foster Open Communication to Surface Problems Success often lies in fostering a work environment that is open enough so employees are willing to speak out when they see problems without fear of recrimination. The focus is placed on trying to solve the problem as a group rather than finding someone to blame. Solutions are solicited from anyone who has a creative idea to suggest—from the janitor to the president—without regard to status or rank in the organization.

Two more Kelly Johnson axioms from Lockheed Martin's Skunk Works apply here: (1) When trouble develops, surface the problem immediately, and (2) get help—don't keep the problem to yourself. This may even mean getting ideas from competitors, but more often it means combing

product or program champion 产品或方案拥护者；ridiculously 可笑地，荒谬地。

Marketing Matters > > > > > > > > > technology

Implementation Lessons from IBM: Converting Tough Global Problems into Results

In two decades IBM has reinvented itself twice—moving (1) from computer hardware into services and software and (2) from that into today's global "data analytics."

IBM's current "Smarter Planet" ad campaign stresses its new strategy: Find tough problems and "throw in billions of dollars in R&D," as *Fortune* magazine observes, and watch what happens. The breadth of the problems IBM is tackling is mind stretching—an *E. coli* outbreak in Norway, a hurricane in Texas causing huge power outages, a fungal disease in West Africa affecting cacao trees (and your future chocolate consumption), and bogged-down rush-hour traffic in Stockholm, Sweden.

The Stockholm traffic problem illustrates IBM's implementation know-how: Get ideas from all over the globe to solve technical problems, thereby avoiding the "NIH syndrome"—the aversion to accept ideas "not invented here," or not originated inside one's own firm. In 2003 Stockholm put out a request for the proposal to charge drivers a fee to reduce downtown traffic by 10 to 15 percent at peak hours. The cars wouldn't be required to carry transponders, so IBM was forced to use cameras with optical character recognition to identify 500,000 cars a day traveling 60 miles an hour.

Presto! Using 18 subcontractors—and an urgent request to its R&D facility in Israel—IBM installed the system. It reduced Stockholm peak-hours traffic 22 percent and emissions 14 percent. Stockholm hired 40 lawyers to handle expected complaints and appeals. Only six were received.

your own firm and key subcontractors to find talented people with solutions. The Marketing Matters box describes how IBM today seeks tough problems and then uses its global network of subcontractors and its own labs to find and implement solutions.

Schedule Precise Tasks, Responsibilities, and Deadlines Successful implementation requires that people know the tasks for which they are responsible and the deadline for completing them. To implement the thousands of tasks on a new aircraft design, Lockheed Martin typically holds weekly program meetings. The outcome of each of these meetings is an **action item list**, an aid to implementing a marketing plan consisting of four columns: (1) the task, (2) the person responsible for completing that task, (3) the date to finish the task, and (4) what is to be delivered. Within hours of completing a program meeting, the action item list is circulated to those attending. This then serves as the starting agenda for the next meeting. Meeting minutes are viewed as secondary and backward looking. Action item lists are forward looking, clarify the targets, and put strong pressure on people to achieve their designated tasks by the deadline.

LO4

与行动项目清单相联系的是正式的方案进度表，它表明了在一段时间内各种方案任务之间的关系。一项行动方案的进度安排包括：(1) 确定主要任务；(2) 决定完成每项任务所需的时间；(3) 设定每项活动的最后完成期限；(4) 安排完成每项任务的职责。

Related to the action item lists are formal *program schedules*, which show the relationships through time of the various program tasks. Scheduling an action program involves: (1) identifying the main tasks, (2) determining the time required to complete each task, (3) arranging the activities to meet the deadline, and (4) assigning people the responsibilities to complete each task.

action item list 行动项目清单。

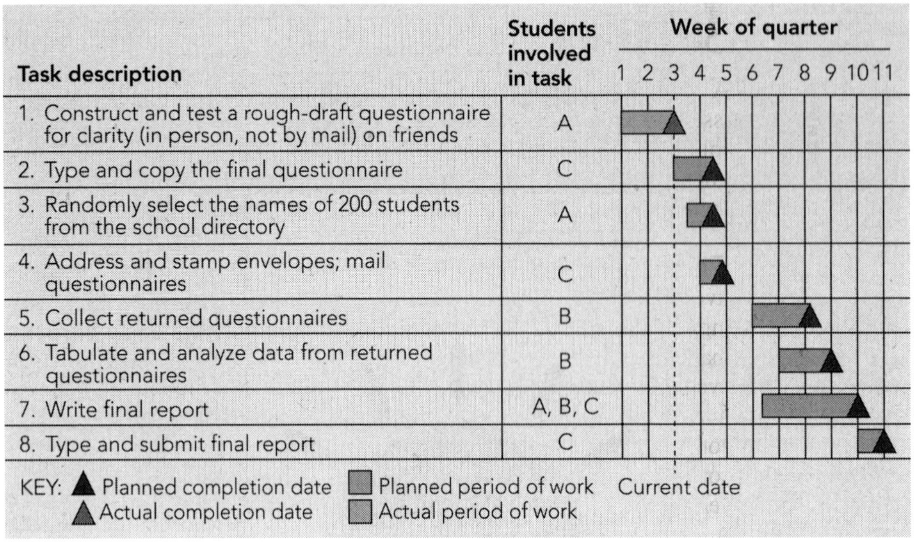

Task description	Students involved in task	Week of quarter 1 2 3 4 5 6 7 8 9 10 11
1. Construct and test a rough-draft questionnaire for clarity (in person, not by mail) on friends	A	
2. Type and copy the final questionnaire	C	
3. Randomly select the names of 200 students from the school directory	A	
4. Address and stamp envelopes; mail questionnaires	C	
5. Collect returned questionnaires	B	
6. Tabulate and analyze data from returned questionnaires	B	
7. Write final report	A, B, C	
8. Type and submit final report	C	

KEY: ▲ Planned completion date ▲ Actual completion date ■ Planned period of work ■ Actual period of work Current date

FIGURE 15–7
This Gantt chart for scheduling a student term project distinguishes the tasks that *must* be done sequentially from those that *can* be done concurrently.

Suppose, for example, that you and two friends are asked to do a term project on the problem, "How can the college increase attendance at its performing arts concerts?" And suppose further that the instructor limits the project in the following ways:

1. The project must involve a mail survey of the attitudes of a sample of students.
2. The term paper with the survey results must be submitted by the end of the 11-week quarter.

To begin the assignment, you need to identify all the project tasks and then estimate the time you can reasonably allocate to each one. To complete it in 11 weeks, your team must work on different parts at the same time, and some activities must be independent enough to overlap. This requires specialization and cooperation. Suppose that of the three of you (A, B, and C), only student C can type. Then you (student A) might assume the task of constructing the questionnaire and selecting samples, and student B might tabulate the data. You must also figure out which activities can be done concurrently to save time.

Scheduling production and marketing activities—from a term project to a new product rollout to a space shuttle launch—can be done efficiently with a *Gantt chart*, which is a graphical representation of a program schedule. Figure 15–7 shows one variation of a Gantt chart used to schedule the class project, demonstrating how the concurrent work on several tasks enables the students to finish the project on time. Developed by Henry L. Gantt, this method is the basis for the scheduling techniques used today, including elaborate computerized methods. The key to all scheduling techniques is to distinguish tasks that *must* be done sequentially from those that can be done concurrently. As in the case of the term project, scheduling tasks concurrently often reduces the total time required for a project. Software programs, such as Microsoft Project, simplify the task of developing a program schedule or Gantt chart.

learning review

6. What is the meaning and importance of a program champion?
7. What are one or two examples of lessons from Lockheed's Skunk Works that apply to implementing marketing programs?
8. Explain the difference between sequential and concurrent tasks in a Gantt chart.

Gantt chart 甘特图；demonstrate 证明，论证，表明，说明。

营销组织

Organizing for Marketing

A marketing organization is needed to implement the firm's marketing plans. Basic issues in today's marketing organizations include understanding (1) the evolving role of the chief marketing officer, (2) how line versus staff positions and divisional groupings interrelate to form a cohesive marketing organization, and (3) the role of the product manager.

The Evolving Role of the Chief Marketing Officer The senior executive responsible for a firm's marketing activities shown in Figure 15–8 is increasingly given the title of chief marketing officer (CMO), rather than vice president of marketing. This reflects the broadening of the CMO's role as the inside-the-company "voice of the consumer" in responding to dynamic marketplace changes. So today it is critical that CMOs understand (1) the changing characteristics of the global consumer segments served and (2) how to market to consumers who increasingly combine Internet online research with offline purchasing at a local store and vice versa. Along with these broadened responsibilities is higher turnover among CMOs. A recent sample of 100 large firms revealed the average CMO held the job for less than two years.

Line versus Staff and Divisional Groupings Although simplified, Figure 15–8 shows the organization of a typical business unit in a consumer packaged goods firm like Procter & Gamble, Kraft, or General Mills. This business unit consists of the Dinner Products, Baked Goods, and Desserts groups. It highlights the distinction between line and staff positions in marketing. Managers in **line positions**, such as the senior marketing manager for Biscuits, have the authority and responsibility to issue orders to the people who report to them, such as the two product managers shown in Figure 15–8. In this organizational chart, line positions are connected with solid lines. People in **staff positions** (connected by dotted lines) have the authority and responsibility to advise people in line positions but cannot issue direct orders to them.

直线部门的管理者，如负责饼干的高级营销经理，他有权且有责对向其报告的人员发号施令，如图 15-8 所示的两位产品经理。

FIGURE 15–8
This organization of a business unit in a typical consumer packaged goods firm shows two product or brand groups.

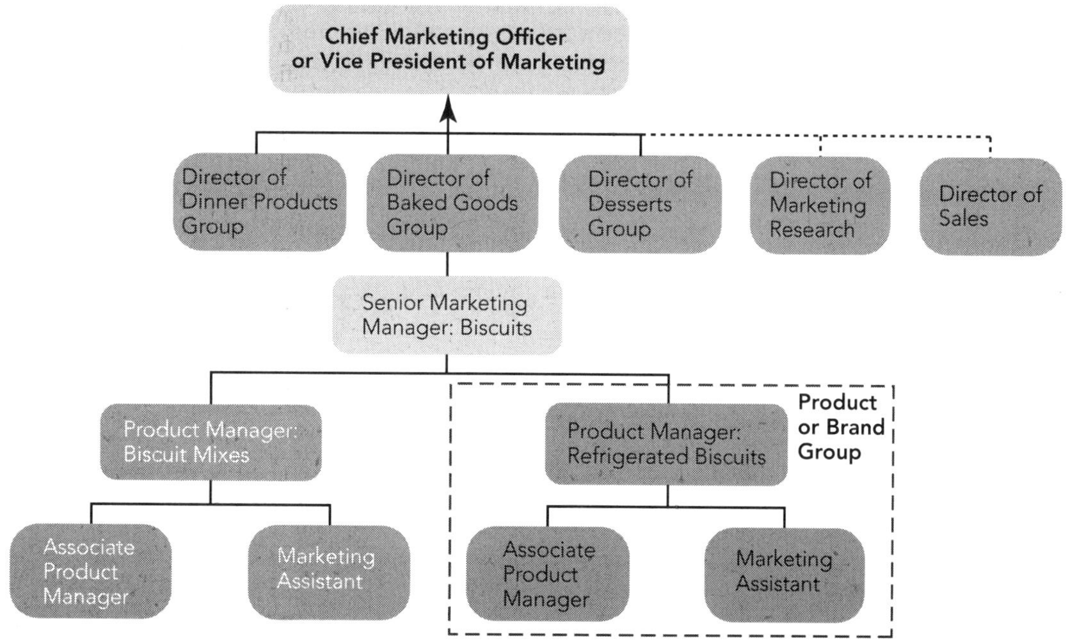

line positions 直线部门；staff positions 职能部门。

CHAPTER 15 PULLING IT ALL TOGETHER: THE STRATEGIC MARKETING PROCESS

Most marketing organizations use divisional groupings—such as product line, functional, geographical, and market-based—to implement plans and achieve objectives. Only the first of these appears in the organizational chart in Figure 15–8. The top of the chart shows organization by **product line groupings** in which a unit is responsible for specific product offerings, such as Dinner Products or Baked Goods.

At higher levels than shown in Figure 15–8, grocery products firms are organized by **functional groupings**—such as manufacturing, marketing, and finance—that represent the different departments or business activities within a firm.

Most grocery products firms use **geographical groupings** in which sales territories are subdivided according to geographical location. Each director of sales has several regional sales managers reporting to him or her, such as western, southern, and so on. These, in turn, have district managers reporting to them, with the field sales representatives at the lowest level.

A fourth method of organizing a company is to use **market-based groupings**, which utilize specific customer segments, such as the banking, health care, or manufacturing segments. When this method of organizing is combined with product groupings, the result is a *matrix organization*.

A relatively new position in consumer products firms is the *category manager* (senior marketing manager in Figure 15–8). Category managers have responsibility for an entire product line—all biscuit brands, for example. They attempt to reduce the possibility of one brand's actions hurting another brand in the same category. Procter & Gamble uses category managers to organize by "global business units" such as baby care and beauty care. Cutting across country boundaries, these global business units implement standardized worldwide pricing, marketing, and distribution.

Role of the Product Manager The key person in the product or brand group is the manager who heads it. As mentioned in Chapter 7, this person is often called the *product manager* or *brand manager*. This person and his or her assistants comprise the *product group* or *brand group*, enclosed by the dashed red line in Figure 15-8. These product or brand groups are the basic building blocks in the marketing department of most consumer and business product firms. The function of a product manager is to plan, implement, and evaluate the annual and long-range plans for the products for which he or she is responsible.

There are both benefits and dangers to the product manager system. On the positive side, product managers become strong advocates for the assigned products, cut red tape to work with people in various functions both inside and outside the organization, and assume profit-and-loss responsibility for the product line. On the negative side, even though product managers have major responsibilities, they have relatively little direct authority, so they must use persuasion rather than direct orders.

战略营销过程的评估阶段
THE EVALUATION PHASE OF THE STRATEGIC MARKETING PROCESS

To cover evaluation, the final phase of the strategic marketing process, we can describe (1) the elements of the marketing evaluation process; (2) the roles of marketing ROI, metric, and dashboards in evaluation; and (3) how General Mills uses marketing metrics and dashboards.

营销评估过程
The Marketing Evaluation Process

The essence of marketing evaluation is (1) comparing results with planned goals to identify deviations and (2) then taking corrective actions.

---

product line groupings 产品线分类制；functional groupings 职能分类制；geographical groupings 地区分类制；market-based groupings 以市场为基础的分类制。

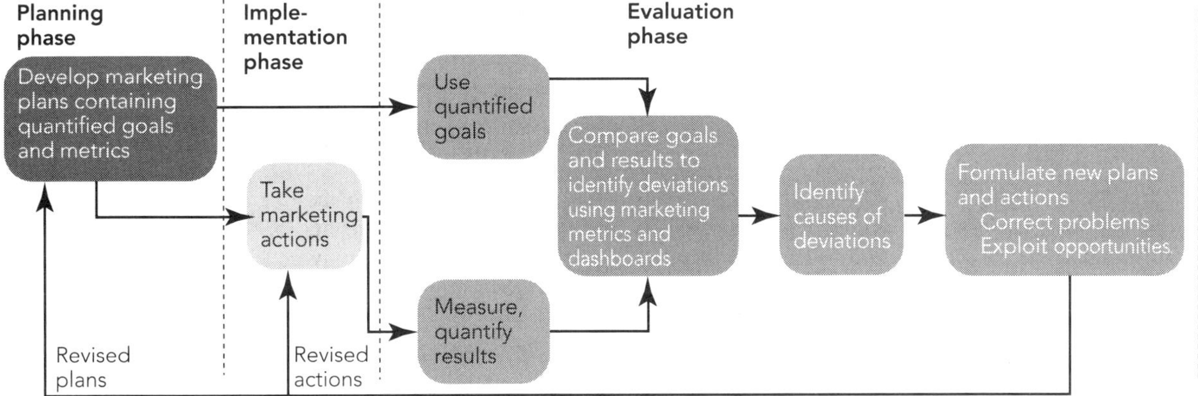

FIGURE 15–9
The evaluation phase of the strategic marketing process ties results and actions to goals, often using marketing metrics and dashboards.

Identifying Deviations from Goals Figure 15–9 shows that marketing plans made in the planning phase have both quantified goals and a specific marketing metric used to measure whether the goal is actually achieved. Marketing actions are taken in the implementation phase to attempt to achieve the goals set in the planning phase. In the evaluation phase, Figure 15–9 shows that the quantitative results are measured using the marketing metrics and compared with the actual results of the marketing actions. For speed and efficiency the results are compared with goals and often shown to marketing managers on marketing dashboards to enable them to take timely actions.

Acting on Deviations from Goals A marketing manager then interprets the marketing dashboard information using *management by exception*, which means identifying results that deviate from plans to diagnose their causes and take new actions. The marketing manager is looking for two kinds of deviations, each triggering a different kind of action:

- *Actual results fall short of goals.* This requires a corrective action. Beaten badly for years in the U.S. toothpaste market by P&G's Crest, Colgate used new technology in its labs to introduce its Total toothpaste, the first "oral pharmaceutical" ever approved by the U.S. Food and Drug Administration. Not only does Total clean teeth, but also its germ-fighting feature helps heal gingivitis, a bleeding-gum disease. Colgate marketed this feature aggressively, enabling Total to become No. 1 in the U.S. toothpaste market.
- *Actual results exceed goals.* Marketing must act quickly to identify the reasons and exploit the unforeseen opportunity. In recessions, most firms tighten their belts and watch sales revenues fall. Not McDonald's! Seeing hard-pressed consumers suddenly appearing at its counters in 2009, McDonald's aggressively marketed its new "Dollar Menu" and its quirky new "McCafe" mochas, hot cocoas, and lattes and watched 58 million customers a day appear—up 2 million from a year earlier.

What recession? McDonald's introduces new beverages quickly to reach hard-pressed consumers!

评估包括营销投资回报率、测量指标和仪表盘
Evaluation Involves Marketing ROI, Metrics, and Dashboards

In the past decade, measuring the performance of marketing activities has become a central focus in many organizations. This boils down to some form of the question, "What measure can I use to determine if my company's marketing is effective?"

No single measure exists to determine if a company's marketing is effective. In finance, the return on investment (ROI) metric relates the

management by exception 例外管理；aggressively 有闯劲地，积极进取地。

total investment made to the total return generated from the investment. The concept has been extended to trying to measure the effectiveness of marketing expenditures with **marketing ROI**, the application of modern measurement technologies to understand, quantify, and optimize marketing spending.

The strategic marketing process tries to improve marketing ROI through the effective use of marketing metrics and dashboards:

- 营销测量指标。根据特定目标选出一个或几个关键的营销测量指标，例如市场份额、单位成本、点击成本、每平方英尺销售额等等。
- 营销仪表盘。如果财务资源、技术齐全，上述的营销测量标准基本会每小时或每天出现在经理的电脑里，随着联合扫描数据、互联网点击数、电视收视率追踪等数据的获得，经理通常面临信息过多的问题。因此，有效的营销仪表盘会在实际结果与计划区别较大的地方用彩色加以强调，这有助于经理发现潜在问题。

- *Marketing metrics.* Depending on the specific goal or objective sought, one or a few key marketing metrics are chosen, such as market share, cost per sales lead, retention rate, cost per click, sales per square foot, and so on. This is setting market and product goals from step 2 of the planning phase shown in Figure 15–2.
- *Marketing dashboards.* If the financial resources and technology are available, the marketing metrics are displayed—often daily or weekly—on the marketing dashboard on the manager's computer. With today's syndicated scanner data, Internet clicks, and TV viewership tracking, the typical manager faces information overload. So an effective marketing dashboard displays actual results that vary significantly from plans. This alerts the manager to potential problems.

These highlighted exceptions, or deviations from plans shown in the evaluation phase in Figure 15–2, are the immediate focus of the marketing manager, who then tries to improve the firm's marketing ROI.

通用磨坊公司利用营销测量指标和营销仪表盘进行评估
Evaluation Using Marketing Metrics and Marketing Dashboards at General Mills

Let's assume it is mid-January and you are part of Vivian Callaway's Warm Delights team at General Mills. Your team is using the marketing data and metrics shown in the marketing dashboard in Figure 15-10. We can summarize the evaluation step of the strategic marketing process using this dashboard and the three-step challenge-findings-actions format used in the marketing dashboard boxes throughout the book.

The Distribution Challenge for Warm Delights Minis You've been asked to analyze the channel of distribution strategy of the Warm Delights Minis. This hypothetical example is based on the type of scanner data General Mills uses, but details have been modified to simplify the data and analysis.

The marketing dashboard in Figure 15-10 focuses on the distribution of the six existing Warm Delights Minis flavors and the impact of adding two new flavors introduced in the fall—Lemon Swirl cake and Cinnamon Swirl cake. As with all new grocery products, the challenge is to gain distribution on retailers' shelves. So the marketing metrics in Figure 15-10 focus on the distribution of Warm Delights Minis in the five main channels of distribution used by General Mills.

The Findings for Warm Delights Minis The three "buttons" in the left-hand column titled "Select Product Option" in Figure 15-10 show that this marketing dashboard can present the situation for any one of three levels in the Warm Delights product line. The three buttons show the analysis can be done for:

- *Warm Delights Total*—the entire Warm Delights product line
- *Warm Delights (Regular)*—only for the regular size packages of Warm Delights
- *Warm Delights Minis*—only for the single-serve size packages of the brand—the Warm Delights Minis

The red "active" button in the column shows the marketing dashboard figures apply only to Warm Delights Minis. The dashboard shows five marketing metrics

marketing ROI 营销投资回报率；marketing metrics 营销测量指标；marketing dashboards 营销仪表盘。

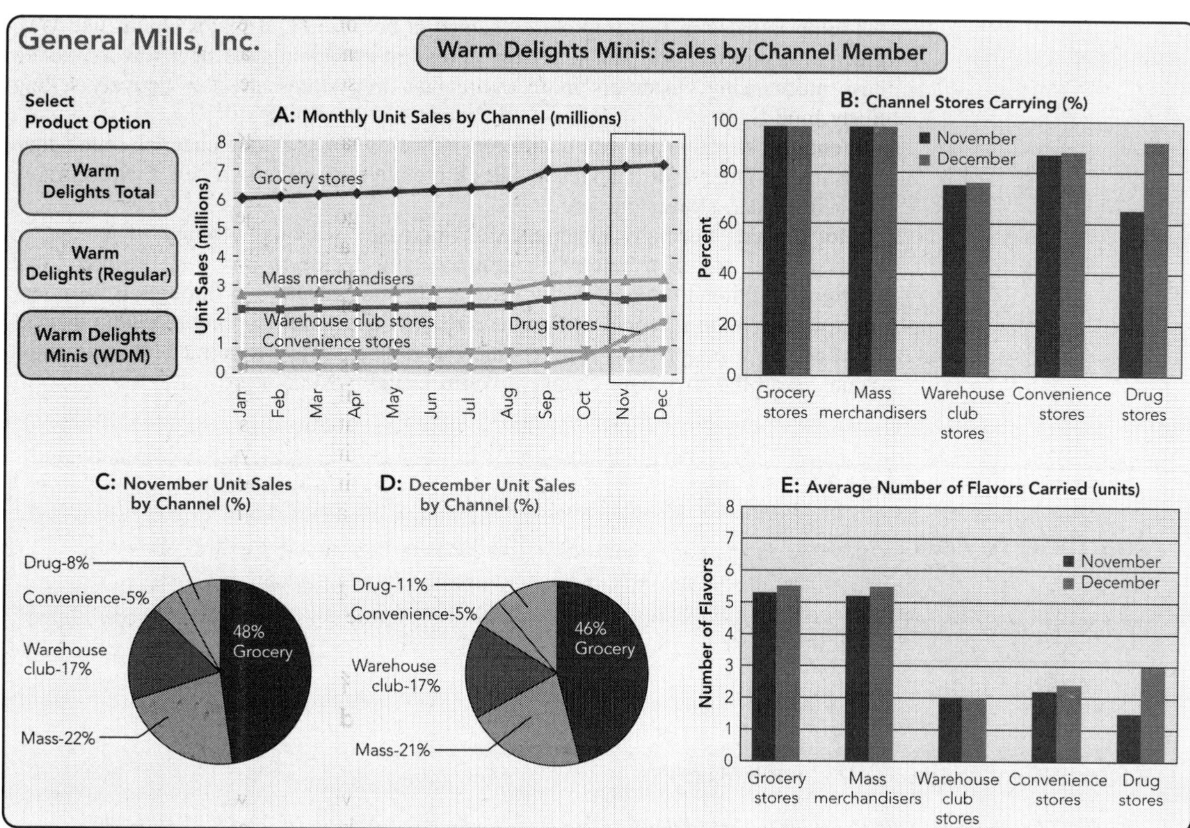

FIGURE 15–10
As a member of the Warm Delights team at General Mills, here is the marketing dashboard you can use to update the distribution channels strategy for the recently introduced line of Warm Delights Minis.

used in tracking how well Warm Delights Minis are doing in the five major channels they use:

- *Line chart A.* This shows monthly sales in millions of units for the five major channels. The grocery store channel is clearly the most important. With one exception, the sales in each channel have been increasing slightly throughout the year. The exception is the jump in sales in the drug store channel from September to December.
- *Bar chart B.* This shows the percentage of stores in each channel carrying one or more of the flavors of Warm Delights Minis in both November and December. The percentage of drug stores carrying at least one flavor jumped from 62 percent in November to 90 percent in December. Your team needs to understand better what happened.
- *Pie chart C.* This shows the percentage share of total unit sales of Warm Delights Minis going through each of the five channels in November.
- *Pie chart D.* This is similar to pie chart C, but applies to December. Comparing pie charts C and D reveals that the share of sales of Warm Delights Minis moving through the drug store channel grew from 8 percent in November to 11 percent in December—a 37.5 percent increase. Clearly your team must try to identify the reason for the increase.
- *Bar chart E.* This bar chart shows the average number of flavors of Warm Delights Minis carried by each store in the channel, the maximum possible being 8.0. But note that the Warm Delights Minis went from having only 1.4 flavors carried by the average drugstore in November to 3.0 in December, a trend worth investigating.

The Actions for Warm Delights Minis Further analysis of dashboards showing the sales by channel of individual flavors of Warm Delights Minis reveals

percentage 比例，百分率；drugstore 药店，药房。

the jump in sales in the drug store channel is because (1) a major chain (like Walgreen's) added the line and (2) drug stores are embracing the new flavors, which have made many customers more aware that drug stores are now actively selling many food lines.

Your investigation reveals a different situation for the four channels other than drug stores. The minor changes in sales there are due to the two new flavors simply replacing older, slower-moving ones.

Hot desserts normally experience an increased seasonal demand in winter. So because sales and distribution are growing, you decide to invest in the brand and schedule additional national TV advertising in late January and throughout February to exploit both the seasonal demand and recent sales trends. Seeing the jump in sales from adding a major drug store chain, you research ways to attract other potential chains in all the five main channels Warm Delights Minis uses.

learning review

9. What are four groupings used within a typical marketing organization?
10. How do marketing metrics tie the goal-setting element of the planning phase of the strategic marketing process to the evaluation phase?

LEARNING OBJECTIVES REVIEW

LO1 *Explain how marketing managers allocate their limited resources.*
Marketing managers use the strategic marketing process and marketing information, such as marketing plans, sales reports, and action memos, to effectively allocate their scarce resources to exploit the competitive advantages of their products. Marketers may use techniques like sales response functions or market share (share point) analysis to help them assess what the market's response will be to additional marketing efforts.

LO2 *Describe two marketing planning frameworks: Porter's generic business strategies and synergy analysis.*
Porter identifies four generic business strategies that firms can adopt: a cost leadership strategy, which focuses on reducing expenses to lower product prices while targeting many market segments; a differentiation strategy, which requires products to have significant points of difference to charge a premium price while targeting many market segments; a cost focus strategy, which involves controlling costs to lower prices of products targeting only a few market segments; and a differentiation focus strategy, which requires products to have significant points of difference to reach one or only a few market segments.

The synergy analysis framework focuses on two kinds of synergies: marketing synergies (efficiencies), which run horizontally across the row of the various products offered by the firm to a single market segment; and R&D–manufacturing synergies (efficiencies), which run vertically down a column of the various market segments targeted for a given product or product class. This results in five alternative combinations: market–product concentration, market specialization, product specialization, selective specialization, and full coverage.

LO3 *Explain what makes an effective marketing plan.*
An effective marketing plan has measurable, achievable goals; uses facts and valid assumptions; is simple, clear, and specific; is complete and feasible; and is controllable and flexible.

LO4 *Use a Gantt Chart to schedule a series of tasks.*
Successful implementation of a marketing plan requires that people know the tasks, responsibilities, and deadlines needed to complete it. Once the information for these three areas is generated, a program schedule can be developed. A Gantt chart is a graphical representation of this schedule. The key to this scheduling technique is to identify those tasks that must be done sequentially from those that can be done concurrently.

LO5 *Describe the alternatives for organizing a marketing department and the role of a product manager.*
First, marketing departments must distinguish between line positions, those individuals who have the authority and responsibility to issue orders to people that report to them and staff positions, those individuals who have the authority and responsibility to advise but not directly order people in line positions to do something.

Second, marketing organizations use one of four divisional groupings to implement marketing plans: product line groupings, responsible for specific product offerings; functional groupings that represent the different departments and business activities within a firm; geographical groupings, in which sales territories are subdivided on a geographical basis; and market-based groupings, which utilize specific customer segments.

Product managers interact with many people and groups both inside and outside the firm to coordinate the planning, implementation, and evaluation of the marketing plan and its budget

---

embrace 包括，接纳。

on an annual and long-term basis for the products for which they are responsible.

LO6 *Explain how marketing ROI, metrics, and dashboards relate to evaluating marketing programs.*
The evaluation phase of the strategic marketing process involves measuring the results of the actions from the implementation phase and comparing them with goals set in the planning phase. Marketing metrics, used to help quantify the goals in the planning stage, are of two kinds: input metrics and output metrics. The marketing manager then takes action to correct negative deviations from the plan and to exploit positive ones. Today, managers want an answer to the question "Are my marketing activities effective?" One answer is in using marketing ROI, which is the application of modern measurement technologies to understand, quantify, and optimize marketing spending. Quantifying a marketing goal with a carefully defined output metric and tracking this metric on a marketing dashboard can improve marketing ROI.

FOCUSING ON KEY TERMS

action item list
cost focus strategy
cost leadership strategy
differentiation focus strategy
differentiation strategy
functional groupings
generic business strategy
geographical groupings
line positions
market-based groupings
marketing ROI
product line groupings
product or program champion
sales response function
share points
staff positions
synergy analysis

APPLYING MARKETING KNOWLEDGE

1 Assume a firm faces an S-shaped sales response function. What happens to the ratio of incremental sales revenue to incremental marketing effort at the (*a*) bottom, (*b*) middle, and (*c*) top of this curve?
2 What happens to the ratio of incremental sales revenue to incremental marketing effort when the sales response function is an upward-sloping straight line?
3 Assume General Mills has to decide how to invest millions of dollars to try to expand its dessert and yogurt businesses. To allocate this money between these two businesses, what information would General Mills like to have?
4 Suppose your Great States lawn mower company has the market–product concentration situation shown in Figure 15–5A. What are both the synergies and potential pitfalls of following expansion strategies of (*a*) market specialization and (*b*) product specialization?
5 The first Domino's Pizza restaurant was near a college campus. What implementation problems are (*a*) similar and (*b*) different for restaurants near a college campus versus a military base?
6 A common theme among managers who succeed repeatedly in program implementation is fostering open communication. Why is this so important?
7 Parts of tasks 5 and 6 in Figure 15–7 are done both concurrently and sequentially. How can this be? How does it help the students meet the term paper deadline?
8 In the organizational chart for the consumer packaged goods firm in Figure 15–8, where do product line, functional, and geographical groupings occur?
9 Why are quantified goals in the planning phase of the strategic marketing process important for the evaluation phase?

building your marketing plan

Do the following activities to complete your marketing plan:

1 Draw a simple organization chart for your organization.
2 Develop a Gantt chart to schedule the key activities to implement your marketing plan.
3 In terms of the evaluation, list (*a*) the four or five critical factors (such as revenues, number of customers, variable costs) and (*b*) how frequently (monthly, quarterly) you will monitor them to determine if special actions are needed to exploit opportunities or correct deviations.

video case 15 General Mills Warm Delights™: Indulgent, Delicious, and Gooey!

Vivian Milroy Callaway, vice president for the Center for Learning and Experimentation at General Mills, retells the story for the "indulgent, delicious, and gooey" Warm Delights™. She summarizes, "When you want something that is truly innovative, you have to look at the rules you have been assuming in your category and break them all!"

When a new business achieves a breakthrough, it looks easy to outsiders. The creators of Betty Crocker Warm Delights stress that if the marketing decisions had been based on the traditions and history of the cake category, a smaller, struggling business would have resulted. The team chose to challenge the assumptions and expectations of accumulated cake category business experience. The team took personal and business risks and Warm Delights is a roaring success.

PLANNING PHASE: INNOVATION, BUT A SHRINKING MARKET

"In the typical grocery store, the baking mix aisle is a quiet place," says Callaway. Shelves sigh with flavors, types, and brands. Prices are low, but there is little consumer traffic. Cake continues to be a tradition for birthdays and social occasions. But, consumer demand declines. The percentage of U.S. households that bought at least one baking mix in 2000 was 80 percent. Four years later, the percentage of households was 77 percent, a very significant decline.

Today, a promoted price of 89 cents to make a 9×12 inch cake is common. Many choices, but little differentiation, gradually falling sales, and low uniform prices are the hallmarks of a mature category. But it's not that consumers don't buy cake-like treats. In fact, indulgent treats are growing. The premium prices for ice cream ($3.00 a pint) and chocolate ($3.00 a bar) are not slowing consumer purchases.

The Betty Crocker marketing team challenged the food scientists at General Mills to create a great tasting, easy to prepare, single-serve cake treat. The goal: Make it indulgent, delicious, and gooey. The team focused the scientists on a product that would have:

- Consistent great taste.
- Quick preparation.
- A single portion.
- No cleanup.

The food scientists delivered the prototype! Now, the marketing team began hammering out the four Ps. They started with a descriptive name "Betty Crocker Dessert Bowls" (see photo) and a plan to shelve it in the "quiet" cake aisle. This practical approach would meet the consumer need for a "small, fast, microwave cake" for dessert. Several marketing challenges emerged:

- *The comparison problem.* The easy shelf price comparison to 9×12 inch cakes selling for 89 cents would make it harder to price Dessert Bowls at $2.00.
- *The communication problem.* The product message "a small, faster-to-make cake" wasn't compelling. For example, after-school snacks should be fast and small, but "dessert" sounds too indulgent.
- *The quiet aisle problem.* The cake-aisle shopper is probably not browsing for a cake innovation.
- *The dessert problem.* Consumer's on-the-go, calorie conscious meal plans don't generally include a planned dessert.
- *The microwave problem.* Consumers might not believe it tastes good.

In sum, the small, fast-cake product didn't resonate with a compelling consumer need. But it would be a safe bet because the Dessert Bowl positioning fit nicely with the family-friendly Betty Crocker brand.

IMPLEMENTATION PHASE: LEAVING THE SECURITY OF FAMILY BEHIND

The consumer insights team really enjoyed the hot, gooey cake product. They feared that it would languish in the cake aisle under the Dessert Bowl name since this didn't capture the essence of what the food delivered. They explored who really are the indulgent treat customers. The data revealed that the heaviest buyers of premium treats are women without children. This focused the team on a target consumer: "What does she want?" They enlisted an ad agency and consultants to come up with a name that would appeal to "her." Several independently suggested the "Warm Delights" name, which became the brand name.

An interesting postscript to the team's brand name research: A competitor apparently liked not only the idea of a quick, gooey, microwavable dessert but also the "Dessert Bowls" name! You may now see its competitive product on your supermarket's shelves.

Targeting the on-the-go women who want a small, personal treat had marketing advantages:

- The $2.00 Warm Delights price compared favorably to the price of many single-serve indulgent treats.
- The product food message "warm, convenient, delightful" is compelling.
- On-the-go women's meal plans do include the occasional delicious treat.

One significant problem remained: the cake-aisle shopper is probably not browsing for an indulgent, single-serve treat.

The marketing team solved this shelving issue by using advertising and product displays outside the cake aisle. This would raise women's awareness of Warm Delights. Television advertising and in-store display programs are costly, so Warm Delights sales would have to be strong to pay back the investment.

Vivian Callaway and the team turned to market research to fine-tune the plan. The research put Warm Delights (and Dessert Bowls) on the shelf in real (different) stores. A few key findings emerged. First, the name "Warm Delights" beat "Dessert Bowls." Second, the Warm Delights with nuts simply wasn't easy to prepare, so nuts were removed. Third, the packaging with a disposable bowl beat the typical cake-mix packaging involving using your own bowl. Finally, by putting the actual product on supermarket shelves and in displays in the stores, sales volumes could be analyzed.

EVALUATION PHASE: TURNING THE PLAN INTO ACTION!

The marketing plan isn't action. Sales for "Warm Delights" required the marketing team to: (1) get the retailers to stock the product, preferably somewhere other than the cake aisle, and (2) appeal to consumers enough to have them purchase, like, and repurchase the product.

The initial acceptance of a product by retailers is important. But each store manager must experience good sales of Warm Delights to be motivated to keep its shelves restocked with the product. Also, the Warm Delights team must monitor the display activity in the store. Are the displays occurring as expected? Do the sales increase when a display is present? Watching distribution and display execution on a new product is very important so that sales shortfalls can be addressed proactively.

Did the customer buy one or two Warm Delights? Did the customer return for a second purchase a few weeks later? The syndicated services that sell household panel purchase data provide the answer. The Warm Delights team evaluates these reports to see if the number of people who tried the product matches with expectations and how the repeat purchases occur. Often, the "80/20 rule" applies. So, in the early months, is there a group of consumers that buys repeatedly and will fill this role?

For ongoing feedback, calls by Warm Delights consumers to the free consumer information line are monitored. This is a great source of real-time feedback. If a pattern emerges and these calls are mostly about the same problem, that is bad. However, when consumers call to say "thank you" or "it's great," that is good. This is an informal quick way to identify if the product is on track or further investigation is warranted.

GOOD MARKETING MAKES A DIFFERENCE

The team took personal and business risks by choosing a Warm Delights plan over the more conservative Dessert Bowl plan. Today, General Mills has loyal Warm Delights consumers who are open to trying new flavors, new sizes, and new forms. If you were a consultant to the Warm Delights team, what would you do to grow this brand?

Questions

1 What is the competitive set of desserts in which Warm Delights is located?

2 (*a*) Who is the target market? (*b*) What is the point of difference on the positioning for Warm Delights? (*c*) What are the potential opportunities and hindrances of the target market and positioning?

3 (*a*) What marketing research did Vivian Callaway execute? (*b*) What were the critical questions that she sought research and expert advice to get answers to? (*c*) How did this affect the product's marketing mix price, promotion, packaging, and distribution decisions?

4 (*a*) What initial promotional plan directed to consumers in the target market did Callaway use? (*b*) Why did this make sense to Callaway and her team when Warm Delights was launched?

5 If you were a consultant to Vivian Callaway, what product changes would you recommend to increase sales of Warm Delights?